Henry Barnard

Letters, Essays and Thoughts on Studies and Conduct

Henry Barnard

Letters, Essays and Thoughts on Studies and Conduct

ISBN/EAN: 9783742804860

Manufactured in Europe, USA, Canada, Australia, Japa

Cover: Foto ©Andreas Hilbeck / pixelio.de

Manufactured and distributed by brebook publishing software
(www.brebook.com)

Henry Barnard

Letters, Essays and Thoughts on Studies and Conduct

True Student Life.

LETTERS, ESSAYS, AND THOUGHTS

OF

STUDIES AND CONDUCT;

ADDRESSED TO YOUNG PERSONS
BY MEN EMINENT IN LITERATURE AND AFFAIRS.

EDITED BY

HENRY BARNARD, LL.D.

SECOND EDITION.

HARTFORD:
THE AMERICAN JOURNAL OF EDUCATION.
1873.

PREFACE.

The Letters, Essays, and Thoughts, embraced in this Volume, on the aims and methods of education, the relative value of sciences, and the right ordering of life, were actually addressed by men eminent in literature and affairs, to young persons in whose well-being and well-doing they were deeply interested. They were first issued in the chapter or article form in which they here appear, in successive numbers of the American Journal of Education, to give variety, and the personal application of principles, to the more elaborate expositions of national systems and institutions to which that periodical was devoted. Although these chapters do not cover the whole field of youthful culture, or all the aids, motives, and dangers of a scholarly and public career, and include a few sheaves only from the golden harvest of recent American didactic and pedagogical literature, they constitute a convenient and valuable manual of Student Life. The light which they shed, like that which Virtue cast on the diverging paths of Hercules, neither leads to bewilder or dazzle, to blind, and the advice which they drop is kindred to that which Wisdom of old uttereth in the street, APPLES OF GOLD—THE WORDS OF THE WISE.

HENRY BARNARD,
Editor of American Journal of Education.

HARTFORD, *Conn.*, Dec., 1872.

Note to Special Edition.

The Contents of the Volume on Studies and Conduct as announced, end with page 416. The pages which follow in this edition, devoted to selections from recent English publications on the relative value of classical and scientific studies in a liberal education, belong properly to the *Second Series* of Papers in English Pedagogy—*Education, the School and the Teacher in English Literature.*

CONTENTS.

PAGE.

PART I.

INTRODUCTION.

WHAT IS EDUCATION?

WHAT IS EDUCATION?

It has been held that *education*, according to its etymology, means a *drawing out* of the faculties of the mind, not a mere accumulation of things in the memory; and this is probably substantially true; but yet the etymology of *education* is not, directly at least, *educere*, but *educare*. Again, *education* has been distinguished from *information*; which may well be done, as the word *information* is now used; but yet the word *informare*, at first, implied as fundamental an operation on the mind as *educare*; the forming and giving a defined form and scheme to a mere rude susceptibility of thought in the human mind. Again, we use the term *learn*, both of the teacher and the scholar. (Thus we have, Psalm cxix. 66 and 71, *Learn me true understanding and knowledge; and I will learn thy laws.*) But the German distinguishes these two aspects of the same fundamental notion by different forms—*lehren* and *lernen*; and in a more exact stage of English, one of these is replaced by another word, *to teach*; which, though it is not the representative of a word used in this sense in German, is connected with the German verb *zeigen*, to show, and *zeichen*, a sign or mark; and thus directs us to the French and other daughters of the Latin language, in which the same notion is expressed by *enseigner*, *insegnare*, *enseñar*; which come from the Latin *insignire*, and are connected with *signum*. W. WHEWELL.

Education is the process of making individual men participators in the best attainments of the human mind in general: namely, in that which is most rational, true, beautiful, and good . . . the several steps by which man is admitted, from the sphere of his narrow individuality, into the great sphere of humanity; by which, from being merely a conscious animal, he becomes conscious of rationality; by which, from being merely a creature of sense, he becomes a creature of intellect; by which, from being merely a seeker of pleasurable sensations, he becomes an admirer of what is beautiful; by which, from being merely the slave of impulse, he becomes a reverencer of what is right and good. W. WHEWELL.

What is a man
If his chief good and market of his time
Be but to sleep and feed?—a beast, no more.
Sure, He that made us with such large discourse,
Looking before and after, gave us not
That capability and godlike reason
To rust in us unused. SHAKESPEARE.

In the bringing up of youth, there are three special points—truth of religion, honesty of living, and right order in learning. In which three ways, I pray God my poor children may walk.

ASCHAM. *Preface to Schoolmaster.*

Many examples may be put of the force of custom, both upon mind and body; therefore, since custom is the principal magistrate of man's life, let men by all means endeavor to obtain good customs. Certainly, custom is most perfect when it beginneth in young years; this we call education, which is, in effect, but an early custom. So we see in languages, the tone is more pliant to all expressions and sounds, the joints are more supple to all feats of activity and motions in youth than afterwards; for it is true, the late learners can not so well take up the ply, except it be in some minds that have not suffered themselves to fix, but have kept themselves open and prepared to receive continual amendment, which is exceeding rare: but the force of custom, copulate and conjoined, and collegiate, is far greater; for there example teacheth, company comforteth, emulation quickeneth, glory raiseth; so as in such places the force of custom is in his exaltation.

LORD BACON. *Essays. Custom and Education.*

I call a complete and generous education that which fits a man to perform justly, skillfully, and magnanimously all the offices, both private and public, of peace and war . . . inflamed with a study of learning, and the admiration of virtue; stirred up with high hopes of living to be brave men, and worthy patriots, dear to God, and famous to all ages.

JOHN MILTON.

The end of learning is to repair the ruins of our first parents, by regaining to know God aright, and out of that knowledge to love him, to imitate him, to be like him, as we may the nearest, by possessing our souls of true virtue, which being united to the heavenly grace of faith, makes up the highest perfection. JOHN MILTON.

First, there must precede a way how to discern the natural inclinations and capacities of children. Secondly, next must ensue the culture and furnishment of the mind. Thirdly, the molding of behavior and decent forms. Fourthly, the tempering of affections. Fifthly, the quickening and exciting of observations and practical judgment. Sixthly, and the last in order, but the principal in value, being that which must knit and consolidate all the rest, is the timely instilling of conscientious principles and seeds of religion. SIR HENRY WALTON.

How great soever a genius may be, and how much soever he may acquire new light and heat, as he proceeds in his rapid course, certain it is, that he will never shine in his full luster, nor shed the full influence he is capable of, unless to his own experience he adds of other men and other ages. BOLINGBROKE.

We are born under a law: it is our wisdom to find it out, and our safety to comply with it. DR. WHICHCOTE.

Since the time that God did first proclaim the edicts of his law upon the world, heaven and earth have hearkened unto his voice, and their labor hath been to do his will. "He made a law for the rain;" he gave his "decree unto the sea, that the waters should not pass his commandment." Now, if nature should intermit her course, and leave altogether, though it were for a while, the observation of her own laws, if these principal and mother elements of the world, whereof all things in this lower world are made, should lose the qualities which they now have; if the frame of that heavenly arch erected over our heads, should loosen and dissolve itself; if celestial spheres should forget their wonted motions, and by irregular volubility turn themselves any way as it may happen; if the prince of the lights of heaven, which now, as a giant, doth run his unwearied course, should, as it were, through a languishing faintness, begin to stand, and to rest himself; if the moon should wander from her beaten way, the times and seasons of the year blend themselves by disordered and confused mixture, the winds breathe out their last gasp, the clouds yield no rain, the earth be defeated of her heavenly influence, the fruits of the earth pine away, as children at the withered breasts of their mother no longer able to yield them relief; what would become of man himself, whom these things do now all serve? See we not plainly, that obedience of creatures unto the law of nature is the stay of the whole world.

Of law there can be no less acknowledged, than that her seat is the bosom of God, her voice the harmony of the world; all things in heaven and earth do her homage, the very least as feeling her care, and the greatest as not exempted from her power; both angels, and men, and creatures of what condition soever, though each in different sort and manner, yet all with uniform consent, admiring her as the mother of their peace and joy. RICHARD HOOKER.

The knowledge of Languages, Sciences, Histories, &c., is not innate to us; it doth not of itself spring in our minds; it is not any ways incident by chance, or infused by grace (except rarely by miracle); common observation doth not produce it; it can not be purchased at any rate, except by that for which, it was said of old, the gods sell all things, that is, for pains; without which the best wit and the greatest capacity may not render a man learned, as the best soil will not yield good fruit or grain, if they be not planted nor sown therein. DR. BARROW.

Powers act but weakly and irregularly till they are hightened and perfected by their habits. DR. SOUTH.

As this life is a preparation for eternity, so is education a preparation for this life; and that education alone is valuable which answers these great primary objects. BISHOP SHORT.

Forasmuch as all knowledge beginneth from experience, therefore also new experience is the beginning of new knowledge, and the increase of experience the beginning of the increase of knowledge. Whatsoever, therefore, happeneth new to a man, giveth him matter of hope of knowing somewhat that he knew not before. And this hope and expectation of future knowledge from any thing that happeneth new and strange, is that passion which we commonly call admiration; and the same considered as appetite, is called curiosity; which is appetite of knowledge. * * And from this beginning is derived all philosophy, as astronomy from the admiration of the course of heaven; natural philosophy from the strange effects of the elements and other bodies. And from the degrees of curiosity, proceed also the degrees of knowledge among men.

THOMAS HOBBES.

A sound mind in a sound body, is a short but full description of a happy state in this world.

Of all the men we meet with, nine parts often are what they are, good or evil, useful or not, by their education. It is that which makes the great difference in mankind. The little, or almost insensible, impressions on our tender infancies, have very important and lasting consequences: and there it is, as in the fountains of some rivers where a gentle application of the hand turns the flexible waters in channels, that make them take quite contrary courses; and by this little direction, given them at first, in the source, they receive different tendencies, and arrive at least at very remote and distant places.

That which every gentleman, that takes any care of his education, desires for his son, is contained in these four things: Virtue, Wisdom, Good-breeding and Learning. I place virtue as the first and most necessary of these endowments that belong to a man or a gentleman, as absolutely requisite to make him valued and beloved by others, acceptable or tolerable to himself. Without that, I think, he will be happy neither in this nor the other world.

It is virtue, direct virtue, which is the head and valuable part to be aimed at in education. All other considerations and accomplishments should give way, and be postponed, to this. This is the solid and substantial good, which tutors should not only read lectures, and talk of; but the labor and art of education should furnish the mind with, and fasten there, and never cease till the young man had a true relish of it, and placed his strength, his glory, and his pleasure in it.

As the strength of the body lies chiefly in being able to endure hardships, so also does that of the mind. And the great principle and foundation of all virtue and worth lies in this, that a man is able to deny himself his own desires, cross his own inclinations, and purely follow what reason directs as best, though the appetite lean the other way.

JOHN LOCKE. *Thoughts on Education.*

'Tis education forms the common mind,
Just as the twig is bent the tree is inclined. POPE.

Dr. Johnson and I [Boswell] took a sculler at the Temple Stairs, and set out for Greenwich. I asked him if he really thought a knowledge of the Greek and Latin languages an essential requisite to a good education. Johnson.—"Most certainly, sir; for those who know them have a very great advantage over those who do not. Nay, sir, it is wonderful what a difference learning makes upon people, even in the common intercourse of life, which does not appear to be much connected with it." And yet, said I, people go through the world very well, and carry on the business of life to good advantage without learning. Johnson.—"Why, sir, that may be true in cases where learning can not possibly be of any use; for instance, this boy rows us as well without learning as if he could sing the song of Orpheus to the Argonauts, who were the first sailors." He then called to the boy, "What would you give my lad to know about the Argonauts?" "Sir," said the boy, "I would give what I have." Johnson was much pleased with his answer, and we gave him a double fare. Dr. Johnson then turning to me, "Sir," said he "a desire of knowledge is the natural feeling of mankind; and every human being, whose mind is not debauched, will be willing to give all that he has to get knowledge."

Dr. Johnson. *Boswell's Life.*

If you love learning you will have learning. Greek Proverb.

Whether we provide for action or conversation, whether we wish to be useful or pleasing, the first requisite is the religious and moral knowledge of right and wrong; the next is an acquaintance with the history of mankind, and with these examples which may be said to embody truth, and prove by events the reasonableness of opinions.

Those authors, therefore, are to be read at school, that supply most axioms or prudence, most principles of moral truth and most materials for conversation; and these purposes are best served by poets, orators, and historians.

Dr. Johnson. *Life of Milton.*

Education in the most extensive sense of the word, may comprehend every preparation that is made in our youth for the sequel of our lives; and in this sense I use it. Some such preparation is necessary for all conditions, because without it they must be miserable, and probably will be vicious, when they grow up, either from the want of the means of subsistence, or from want of rational and inoffensive occupation. In civilized life, every thing is effected by art and skill. Whence, a person who is provided with neither (and neither can be acquired without exercise and instruction) will be useless; and he that is useless, will generally be at the same time mischievous to the community. So that to send an uneducated child into the world, is injurious to the rest of mankind; it is little better than to turn out a mad dog or a wild beast into the streets.

Paley.

The primary principle of education is the determination of the pupil to self-activity—the doing nothing for him which he is able to do for himself.

Sir William Hamilton. *Lecture on Metaphysics.*

I consider a human soul without education like marble in the quarry, which shows none of its inherent beauties, until the skill of the polisher fetches out the colors, makes the surface shine, and discovers every ornamental cloud, spot, and vein, that runs through the body of it.

Education, after the same manner, when it works upon a noble mind, draws out to view every latent virtue and perfection, which, without such helps, are never able to make their appearance.

If my reader will give me leave to change the allusion so soon upon him, I shall make use of the same instance to illustrate the force of education, which Aristotle has brought to explain his doctrine of substantial forms, when he tells us that a statue lies hid in a block of marble; and that the art of the statuary only clears away superfluous matter, and removes the rubbish. The figure is in the stone, and the sculptor only finds it. What sculpture is to the block of marble, education is to a human soul. The philosopher, the saint or the hero, the wise, the good or the great man, very often lie hid and concealed in a plebeian, which a proper education might have disinterred, and have brought to light. * * Those who have had the advantages of a more liberal education, rise above one another by several different degrees of perfection. For to return to our statue in the block of marble, we see it sometimes only begun to be chipped, sometimes rough hewn, and but just sketched into a human figure; sometimes we see the man appearing distinctly in all his limbs and features; sometimes we find the figure wrought up to great elegancy, but seldom meet with any to which the hand of a Phidias or a Praxiteles could not give several nice touches and finishings.

Joseph Addison.

Nothing is more absurd than the common notion of instruction; as if science were to be poured into the mind like water into a cistern, that passively waits to receive all that comes. The growth of knowledge resembles the growth of fruit; however external causes may in some degree coöperate, it is the internal vigor and virtue of the tree that must ripen the juices to their just maturity. James Harris. *Hermes*.

Human creatures, from the constitution of their nature, and the circumstances in which they are placed, can not but acquire habits during their childhood, by the impressions which are given them and their own customary actions; and long before they arrive at mature age these habits form a general settled character. And the observation of the text—"Train up a child in the way he should go; and when he is old he will not depart from it"—that the most early habits are generally the most lasting, is likewise every one's observation.

Bishop Butler.

Organic structure, temperament, things affecting the senses or bodily functions, are as closely linked with a right play of the faculties, as the material and condition of an instrument of music with that wonderful result called melody. W. B. Clulow.

The general principles of education are the same, or nearly the same in all ages, and at all times. They are fixed unalterably in the natural and moral constitution of man. They are to be found in our affections and passions, some of which must be controlled and some cherished in every state of manners, and under every form of society. From the right apprehensions of them, we discover "the way in which a child ought to go," and by the right use of them "when he is young," we shall qualify him, "when old," for not departing from it.

In promoting the happiness of our species, much is effected by authority of legal restraint, and much by public instruction from the pulpit. But education, in its large and proper sense, [of not merely the inculcation of moral precepts and religious doctrine, but a system of discipline applied to the hearts and lives of young persons,] may boast even of superior usefulness. It comes home directly to "the bosoms and business of" young persons, it rectifies every principle and controls every action; it prevents their attention from being relaxed by amusement, dissipated by levity, or overwhelmed by vice; it preserves them from falling a prey to the wicked examples of the world when they are in company, and from becoming slaves to their own turbulent appetites when they are in solitude. It is not occasional or desultory in its operation; on the contrary, it heaps "line upon line, and precept upon precept;" it binds the commands of religion, for a "sign upon the hands of young men, and frontlets between their eyes;" it is calculated to purify their desires and to regulate their conduct, when they "sit in the house, and when they walk in the way;" when they "lie down in peace to take their rest," and when they "rise up" to "go forth to their labor." DR. PARR.

What is the education of the generality of the world? Reading a parcel of books? No. Restraint of discipline, emulation, examples of virtue and justice, form the education of the world. EDMUND BURKE.

The heart of a nation comes by priests, by lawyers, by philosophers, by schools, by education, by the nurse's care, the mother's anxiety, the father's severe brow. It comes by letters, by silence, by every art, by sculpture, painting, and poetry; by the song on war, on peace, on domestic virtue, on a beloved and magnanimous king; by the Iliad, by the Odyssey, by tragedy, by comedy. It comes by sympathy, by love, by the marriage union, by friendship, generosity, meekness, temperance; by virtue and example of virtue. It comes by sentiments of chivalry, by romance, by music, by decorations and magnificence of buildings; by the culture of the body, by comfortable clothing, by fashions in dress, by luxury and commerce. It comes by the severity, the melancholy, the benignity of countenance; by rules of politeness, ceremonies, formalities, solemnities. It comes by rights attendant on law, by religion, by the oath of office, by the venerable assembly, by the judge's procession and trumpets, by the disgrace and punishment of crimes, by public fasts, public prayer, by meditation, by the Bible, by the consecration of churches, by the sacred festival, by the cathedral's gloom and choir.

PROF. RAMSDEN.

Education may be compared to the grafting of a tree. Every gardener knows that the younger the wilding-stock that is to be grafted is, the easier and the more effectual is the operation, because, then, one scion put on just above the root, will become the main stem of the tree, and all the branches it puts forth will be of the right sort. When, on the other hand, a tree is to be grafted at a considerable age, (which may be very successfully done,) you have to put on twenty or thirty grafts on the several branches; and afterwards you will have to be watching, from time to time, for the wilding shoots which the stock will be putting forth, and pruning them off. And even so, one whose character is to be reformed at mature age, will find it necessary not merely to implant a right principle once for all, but also to bestow a distinct attention on the correction of this, that, and the other bad habit.

But it must not be forgotten that education resembles the grafting of a tree in this point, also, that there must be some affinity between the stock and the graft, though a very important practical difference may exist; for example, between a worthless crab and a fine apple. Even so, the new nature, as it may be called, superinduced by education, must always retain some relation to the original one, though differing in most important points. You can not, by any kind of artificial training, make any thing of any one, and obliterate all trace of the natural character. Those who hold that this is possible, and attempt to effect it, resemble Virgil, who (whether in ignorance or, as some think, by way of poetical license) talks of grafting an oak on an elm: *glandesque sues fregere sub ulmis.*

ARCHBISHOP WHATELY. *Annotations on Bacon's Essays.*

What a man has learnt is of importance, but what he is, what he can do, what he will become, are more significant things. Finally, it may be remarked, that to make education a great work, we must have the educators great; that book learning is mainly good, as it gives us a chance of coming into the company of greater and better minds than the average of men around us; and that individual greatness and goodness are the things to be aimed at, rather than the successful cultivation of those talents which go to form some eminent membership of society. Each man is a drama in himself: has to play all the parts in it; is to be king and rebel, successful and vanquished, free and slave; and needs a bringing up fit for the universal creature that he is.

A. HELPS. *Friends in Council.*

Education is the placing of the growing human creature in such circumstances of direction and restraint, as shall make the most of him, or enable him to make the most of himself. JOHN GROTE.

A liberal education is an education in which the individual is cultivated, not as an instrument towards some ulterior end, but as an end unto himself alone; in other words, an education in which his absolute perfection as a man, and not merely his relative dexterity as a professional man, is the scope immediately in view. SIR WILLIAM HAMILTON.

Education does not commence with the alphabet; it begins with a mother's look, with a father's nod of approbation, or sign of reproof; with a sister's gentle pressure of the hand; a brother's noble act of forbearance; with handful of flowers in green dells, or hills, and daisy meadows; with birds-nest admired, but not touched; with creeping ants and almost imperceptible emmets; with humming bees, and glass bee hives; with pleasant walks in shady lanes, and with thoughts devoted, in sweet and kindly tones and words, to nature, to beauty, to acts of benevolence, to deeds of virtue, and to the source of all good—to God himself.

Dr. Ramsden.

He [man] would look round upon the world without, and the thought would arise in his mind—"*Where* am I?" He would contemplate himself, his form so curious, his feelings so strange and various; he would ask—"*What* am I?" Then reflection would begin to stir within him, and reviewing the world without and within, and pondering upon the mystery of existence, he would exclaim—"*Why* am I?" And the replies to these three questions compose the entire circle of human knowledge, developed in its natural order.

W. Cox. *The Advocate, his Training.*

I believe, that what it is most honorable to know, it is also most profitable to learn; and that the science which it is the highest power to possess, it is also the best exercise to acquire.

And if this be so, the question as to what should be the material of education, becomes singularly simplified. It might be matter of dispute what processes have the greatest effect in developing the intellect; but it can hardly be disputed what facts it is most advisable that a man entering into life should accurately know.

I believe, in brief, that he ought to know three things:

First. Where he is.

Secondly. Where he is going.

Thirdly. What he had best do under those circumstances.

First. Where he is.—That is to say, what sort of a world he has got into; how large it is; what kind of creatures live in it, and how; what it is made of, and what may be made of it.

Secondly. Where he is going.—That is to say, what chances or reports there are of any other world besides this; what seems to be the nature of that other world; and whether, for information respecting it, he had better consult the Bible, Koran, or Council of Trent.

Thirdly. What he had best do under those circumstances.—That is to say, what kind of faculties he possesses; what are the present state and wants of mankind; what is his place in society; and what are the readiest means in his power of attaining happiness and diffusing it. The man who knows these things, and who has had his will so subdued in the learning them, that he is ready to do what he knows he ought, I should call educated; and the man who knows them not, uneducated, though he could talk all the tongues of Babel. Ruskin.

Education does not mean merely reading and writing, nor any degree, however considerable, of mere intellectual instruction. It is, in its largest sense, a process which extends from the commencement to the termination of existence. A child comes into the world, and at once his education begins. Often at his birth the seeds of disease or deformity are sown in his constitution—and while he hangs at his mother's breast, he is imbibing impressions which will remain with him through life. During the first period of infancy, the physical frame expands and strengthens; but its delicate structure is influenced for good or evil by all surrounding circumstances—cleanliness, light, air, food, warmth. By and by, the young being within shows itself more. The senses become quicker. The desires and affections assume a more definite shape. Every object which gives a sensation; every desire gratified or denied; every act, word, or look of affection or of unkindness, has its effect, sometimes slight and imperceptible, sometimes obvious and permanent, in building up the human being; or, rather, in determining the direction in which it will shoot up and unfold itself. Through the different states of the infant, the child, the boy, the youth, the man, the development of his physical, intellectual, and moral nature goes on, the various circumstances of his condition incessantly acting upon him—the healthfulness or unhealthfulness of the air he breathes; the kind, and the sufficiency of his food and clothing; the degree in which his physical powers are exerted; the freedom with which his senses are allowed or encouraged to exercise themselves upon external objects; the extent to which his faculties of remembering, comparing, reasoning, are tasked; the sounds and sights of home; the moral example of parents; the discipline of school; the nature and degree of his studies, rewards and punishments; the personal qualities of his companions; the opinions and practices of the society, juvenile and advanced, in which he moves; and the character of the public institutions under which he lives. The successive operation of all these circumstances upon a human being from earliest childhood, constitutes his education;—an education which does not terminate with the arrival of manhood, but continues through life,—which is itself, upon the concurrent testimony of revelation and reason, a state of probation or education for a subsequent and more glorious existence.

John Lalor. *Prize Essay.*

The appropriate and attainable ends of a good education are the possession of gentle and kindly sympathies; the sense of self-respect and of the respect of fellow-men; the free exercise of the intellectual faculties; the gratification of a curiosity that "grows by what it feeds on," and yet finds food forever; the power of regulating the habits and the business of life, so as to extract the greatest possible portion of comfort out of small means; the refining and tranquilizing enjoyment of the beautiful in nature and art, and the kindred perception of the beauty and nobility of virtue; the strengthening consciousness of duty fulfilled, and, to crown all, "the peace which passeth all understanding."

Sarah Austin.

The most essential objects of education are the two following—first, to cultivate all the various principles of our nature, both speculative and active, in such a manner as to bring them to the greatest perfection of which they are susceptible; and, secondly, by watching over the impressions and associations which the mind receives in early life, to secure it against the influence of prevailing errors, and, as far as possible, engage its prepossessions on the side of truth.

To watch over the associations which they form in infancy; to give them early habits of mental activity; to rouse their curiosity, and direct it to proper objects; to exercise their ingenuity and invention; to cultivate in their minds a turn for speculation, and, at the same time, preserve their attention alive to the objects around them; to awaken their sensibilities to the beauties of nature, and to inspire them with a relish for intellectual enjoyment—these form but a part of the business of education.
DUGALD STEWART.

Education is that noble art which has the charge of training the ignorance and imbecility of infancy into all the virtue, and power, and wisdom of mature manhood—of forming, of a creature, the frailest and feeblest which heaven has made, the intelligent and fearless sovereign of the whole animated creation, the interpreter and adorer, and almost the representative of the Divinity.
THOMAS BROWN.

Education is a process calculated to qualify man to think, feel, and act in a manner most productive of happiness. It possesses three essentials—first, by early exercise to improve the powers and faculties, bodily and mental; secondly, to impart a knowledge of the nature and purposes of these powers and faculties; and, thirdly, to convey as extensive a knowledge as possible of the nature of external beings and things, and the relation of these to the human constitution.
J. SIMPSON.

The paramount end of liberal study is the development of the student's mind, and knowledge is principally useful as a means of determining the faculties to that exercise through which this development is accomplished. Self-activity is the indispensable condition of improvement; and education is only education—that is, accomplishes its purposes, only by affording objects and supplying incitements to this spontaneous exertion. Strictly speaking, every man must educate himself.
SIR WILLIAM HAMILTON. *Metaphysics.*

The great result of schooling is a mind with just vision to discern, with free force to do; the grand schoolmaster is Practice.

The first principle of human culture, the foundation-stone of all but false imaginary culture, is that men must before every other thing, be trained to do somewhat. Thus, and others only, the living Force of a new man can be awakened, enkindled, and purified into victorious clearness!
THOMAS CARLYLE. *Essays.*

The true end of education, is to unfold and direct aright our whole nature. Its office is to call forth power of every kind—power of thought, affection, will, and outward action; power to observe, to reason, to judge, to contrive; power to adopt good ends firmly, and to pursue them efficiently; power to govern ourselves, and to influence others; power to gain and to spread happiness. Reading is but an instrument; education is to teach its best use. The intellect was created, not to receive passively a few words, dates, facts, but to be active for the acquisition of truth. Accordingly, education should labor to inspire a profound love of truth, and to teach the processes of investigation. A sound logic, by which we mean the science or art which instructs us in the laws of reasoning and evidence, in the true methods of inquiry, and in the sources of false judgments, is an essential part of a good education. And yet, how little is done to teach the right use of the intellect, in the common modes of training either rich or poor. As a general rule, the young are to be made, as far as possible, their own teachers—the discoverers of truth—the interpreters of nature—the framers of science. They are to be helped to help themselves. They should be taught to observe and study the world in which they live, to trace the connections of events, to rise from particular facts to general principles, and then to apply these in explaining new phenomena. Such is a rapid outline of the intellectual education, which, as far as possible, should be given to all human beings; and with this, moral education should go hand in hand. In proportion as the child gains knowledge, he should be taught how to use it well—how to turn it to the good of mankind. He should study the world as God's world, and as the sphere in which he is to form interesting connections with his fellow-creatures. A spirit of humanity should be breathed into him from all his studies. In teaching geography, the physical and moral condition, the wants, advantages, and striking peculiarities of different nations, and the relations of climate, seas, rivers, mountains, to their characters and pursuits, should be pointed out, so as to awaken an interest in man wherever he dwells. History should be constantly used to exercise the moral judgment of the young, to call forth sympathy with the fortunes of the human race, and to expose to indignation and abhorrence that selfish ambition, that passion for dominion, which has so long deluged the earth with blood and woe. And not only should the excitement of just moral feeling be proposed in every study, the science of morals should form an important part of every child's instruction. One branch of ethics should be particularly insisted on by the government. Every school, established by law, should be specially bound to teach the duties of the citizen to the state, to unfold the principles of free institutions, and to train the young to an enlightened patriotism.

W. E. CHANNING. *Christian Examiner*, Nov., 1833.

The object of the science of education is to render the mind the fittest possible instrument for discovering, applying, or obeying the laws under which God has placed the universe. WAYLAND.

COLLEGE EDUCATION AND SELF EDUCATION.

A Lecture delivered in University College, London, introductory to the Session of the Faculty of Arts and Laws. By David Masson, Professor of Literature, University College, London.

Scope of Education.—The business of education, in its widest sense, is co-extensive with a man's life: that it begins with the first moment of life, and ends with the last; and, that it goes on not alone in buildings like that in which we are now assembled, but in every combination of place, company, and circumstance, in which a man may voluntarily station himself, or into which he may be casually thrust.

I will here understand education as a process extending only over that preparatory period of life which, with young men, may be supposed to close about the twentieth or twenty-fifth year. And, I will also understand the word as referring chiefly to those means, whether organized or casual, by which, during that period of life, knowledge is acquired and accumulated.

The School of the Family.—The first school in which a man is bound to learn, and in which every man does, in spite of himself, learn more or less, is the school of his own ancestry, parentage, and kindred. There is no man, however strong his character, and however migratory his life, in whose mature manner of thought there are not traces of impressions produced on him by the family faces amid which he first opened his eyes, the family joys or griefs with which his childhood laughed or sobbed, the family stories and traditions to which his childhood listened. Happy they to whom this has been a kindly school; the homes of whose infancy have been homes of peace, order, and courtesy; over whose early years just fatherly authority and careful motherly gentleness have watched; in whose experience there has been no contradiction between the sense of right and the ties of blood; and who can look back upon progenitors, remembered for probity, courage, and good citizenship, and round among living kinsmen well placed and well respected in the world. This is not the common notion of pedigree. That man were, indeed, little better than a liar who, counting high historic names among his ancestors, should pretend to be careless of the fact; but, the kind of pedigree of which we speak is to be found in the humblest lineage of the land; and, at this hour, over broad Britain, there are, as we all know, families neither rich nor noble, to have sprung from which, and to have been nursed on their unrecorded fireside legends, would, for the purposes of real outfit in life, be better than to have been born in a castle and had the blood of all the Plantagenets. And yet, on the other hand, even those,—and they are many,—to whom this school of family and kindred has been a hard school, may there, also, have received many a powerful and useful lesson. Men do learn very variously; and there is an education of revolt and reaction, as well as of acquiescence and imitation. The training received in the school of family and kindred may not have been a genial or promising one; it may not be from the past in his own lineage that one can derive any direct stimulus or inspiration; the house of the early education may have been one of penury, chill, and contention; a veritable picture of a household, with its household gods broken; and yet, even so, the culture may have been great and varied,—albeit, sometimes, a culture of strength at the expense of symmetry.

The School of Locality.—I have always felt disposed to attach a peculiar reverence and a peculiar sense of value to that arrangement, institution, or whatever you choose to call it, common to most societies, which we in Great Britain designate by the term neighborhood or parish. That every man should be related, and should feel himself related, in a particular manner, to that tract of earth which he is taught to regard as his parish, the assigned local scene of his habitation and activity on this side the grave, seems to me a natural and beautiful arrangement, which our political system would do well to respect, use, and consecrate. The limits of this smallest and most natural of territorial divisions may be variously defined. You may figure a parish as a tract of earth containing and supporting two thousand inhabitants, the ideal of a rural parish; or, you may figure it as a tract of earth underlying the sound of a particular church-bell. That this smallest of territorial divisions should merge and fit into larger and still larger divisions,—the district, the county, and so on,—is also necessary and natural; but, that a man's closest relations ought to be with his own parish and neighborhood, that it is with the natural and social phenomena lying around him on this piece of earth that he is bound primarily to make himself acquainted, and that all the elementary requirements of his life ought to be provided for by apparatus there set up, seems to me sound doctrine. For a man not to be so locally related during at least a portion of his life,—for a man to be shifting about in his youth from place to place, not remaining long enough in any to root his affections among its objects and details,—seems to me a misfortune. In point of fact, however, few are in this predicament. Removal from one's native place is common enough, and is becoming more common; but, almost all,—including even those exceptional persons who, having been born at sea, are reputed to belong to the parish of Stepney,—are located, during some part of their lives, in some one district, with the whole aspect and circumstance of which they become familiar, and which they learn to regard as native ground. Now, it is important to remark that there is no district, no patch of the habitable earth, in which a man can be placed and bred, but there are within that spot the materials and inducements toward a very considerable natural education. Nay, more, there is, to all ordinary intents and purposes, no one district in the natural and artificial circumstance of which there is not a tolerable representation and epitome of all that is general and fundamental in nature and life everywhere. Take Great Britain itself. Every British parish has its mineralogy; every British parish has its geology; every British parish has its botany; every British parish has its zoölogy; every British parish has its rains, its storms, its streams, and, consequently, its meteorology and hydrology; every British parish has its wonders of nature and art, impressive on the local imagination, and, in some cases, actually exerting a physical influence over the local nerve; and, though these objects and wonders vary immensely, though in one parish geological circumstance may predominate, in another botanical, and in a third hydrological or architectural; though in one the local wonder may be a marsh, in another a rocky cavern, and in a third an old fort or a bit of Roman wall; yet, in each there is a sufficient touch of what is generic in all. Over every British parish, at least when night comes, there hangs,—splendid image of our identity at the highest,—the same nocturnal glory, a sapphire concave of nearly the same stars. Descend to the life and living circumstance of the community, and it is still the same. There is no British parish in which all the essential processes, passions, and social ongoings of British humanity, from the chaffering of the market-place up to madness and murderous revenge, are not proportionately illustrated and epitomised. There is no British parish that has not its gossip, its humours, its customs, its oracular and remarkable individuals, its oddities and whimsicalities, all of which can be made objects of study. Finally, there is no British parish that has not its traditions, its legends, and histories, connecting the generation present upon it with the world of the antique. And, with some modification, it is the same, if, passing the limits of Britain, we extend our view to foreign lands and climes. The circumstance, physical, artificial, social and historical, of a district in Italy or in Spain, is largely different from the corresponding circumstance of a district in Britain; much more so the circumstance of a district in South America or Hindostan; and yet, generically, there is so much that is common, that, after all, a person educated in the midst of Italian or Spanish circumstance, has about the same stock of fundamental notions of things as an Englishman has, and that a Hindoo jest will pass current in Middlesex. Every man, then, learns a vast deal,—a large proportion of our surest knowledge is derived,—from this education which we all have, in spite of ourselves, in the school of native local circumstance. It appears to me that, in our educational theories, we do not sufficiently attend to this. It appears to me that, among all our schemes of educational reform, perhaps the most desirable would be one for the organization and systematic development of this education of local circumstance, which is, at any rate, everywhere going on. This, I conceive, is the true theory of the "teaching of common things." Every child born in a parish and resident in it, ought to have, as his intellectual outfit in life, a tolerably complete acquaintance with the concrete facts of nature and life presented by that parish; and, in every parish, there ought to be a systematic means for accomplishing this object. Every child ought to carry with him into life, as a little encyclopædia, a stock of facts and pictures collected from the scene of his earliest habitations and associations; ought to be familiar with that miscellany of natural and artificial circumstance which first solicited his observation in the locality where he was brought up; from its minerals, and wild plants, and birds, and molluscs, up to its manufactures, its economics, its privileges and by-laws, and its local mythology or legends. A reformed system of parochial education ought to take this in charge, and to secure to the young some instruction in local natural history, local antiquities, local manufactures and economics, and local institutions and customs. Meanwhile, in the absence of any systematic means of accomplishing the object, we see that everywhere healthy boys do, by their own locomotion and inquisitiveness, contrive to acquire a stock of concrete local fact and imagery. We see them roaming over the circle of their neighborhoods, singly and in bands, ascending hills, climbing trees and precipices, peeping into foundries, workshops, and police offices, peering, in short, into every thing open or forbidden to them, and, in the most literal sense of the phrase, pursuing knowledge under difficulties. And, here, accordingly, in addition to constitutional difference and the difference of family schooling, is another source of the intellectual diversity we find among grown-up men. The education of local circumstance, as we have said, is by no means necessarily a narrow education; all that is general and essential everywhere, whether as respects the main facts of nature or the habits and laws of the human mind, is repeated in miniature in every spot. Kant never slept out of Königsberg; and Socrates never wished to go beyond the walls of Athens. Yet, on the other hand, difference of local educating circumstance is one of the causes of difference of intellectual taste and style in mature life. No two districts or parishes are precisely alike in their suggestions and intellectual inducements. Some localities, as we have said, allure to geology, others to botany, others to fondness for landscape and color, others to mechanics and engineering, others to archæology and historical lore. Of those supposed three hundred youths, for example,—even omitting such of them as had been born and brought up abroad, amid scenes, and a vegetation, and costumes, and customs, aye, and under constellations different from our own,—hardly any two of the British-born would be found trading intellectually, so to speak, on the same stock of recollected facts and images. Some might have been born on the sea-coast, and the images most familiar to their memories would be those of rocks, and shingle, and a breaking surf, and brown fishing boats, and gulls dipping in the waves, and heavy clouds gathering for a storm.

> "I see a wretched isle, that ghost-like stands,
> Wrapt in its mist-shroud in the wintry main;
> And now a cheerless gleam of red-ploughed lands,
> O'er which a crow flies heavy in the rain."

Others might have been born and bred in sweet pastoral districts, and the images most kindly to their fancy would be those of still green valleys, and little streams flowing through them, and flocks, led by tinkling sheep-bells cropping the uplands. Others might be natives of rich English wheat flats; others of barren tracts of hill and torrent. Some might have been born in provincial towns, where the kinds of circumstance peculiar to street-life would preponderate over the purely agricultural or rural; others might be denizens of the great metropolis itself, with its endless extent of shops, warehouses, wharves, churches, and chimneys. In large towns, and, above all, in London, it is needless to say, the fact to be noted is the infinite preponderance of artificial and social circumstance over that of natural landscape, and its infinitely close intertexture. The spontaneous education there, accordingly, is chiefly in what is socially various, curious, highly developed, comic, and characteristic. So strong, however, is the instinct of local attachment, that natives of London do contract an affection for their own parishes and neighborhoods, and an acquaintance with their details and humors, over and above their general regard for those objects which claim the common worship of all. In short, however we turn the matter over, we still find that a large proportion of the most substantial education of every one consists of this unconscious and inevitable education of local circumstance; and that, in fact, much of the original capital on which we all trade intellectually during life is that mass of miscellaneous fact and imagery which our senses have taken in busily and imperceptibly amid the scenes of their first exercise. In the lives of most men who have become eminent, whether in speculative science or in imaginative literature, a tinge of characteristic local color may be traced to the last. Adam Smith meditated his "Wealth of Nations" on the sands of a strip of Fifeshire sea-coast, and drew the instances which suggested the doctrines of that work to his own mind, and by which he expounded them to others, from the petty circumstance of a small fishing and weaving community close by. And, in Shakspeare himself, widely as his imagination ranged, it will be found that, in his descriptions of natural scenery at least, large use is made of the native circumstance of his woody Warwickshire, with its elms, its willows, its crow-flowers, daisies, and long-purples. However migratory a man has been, and however thickly, by his migrations, he may have covered the tablets of his memory with successive coatings of imagery, there are times when, as he shuts his eyes, all these seem washed away, and the original photographs of his early years,—the hill, the moor, the village spire, the very turn of the road where he met the military horseman,—start out fresh as ever. Nay, more, it will be found, (and this is a fact of which Hartley and his laws of the association of ideas have never made any thing to the purpose,) that perpetually, underneath our formal processes of thinking, apparently independent of these processes, and yet somehow playing into them and qualifying them, there is passing through our minds a series of such unbidden reappearing photographs, a flow of such recollected imagery.

The School of Travel, Books and Friendship.—Under the head of the education of travel I include, as you may guess, all that comes of migration or change of residence; and my remarks under the former head will have enabled you to see that all this, important and varied as it may seem, consists simply in the extension of the field of observed fact and circumstance. All the celebrated effects of travel, purely as such, in enlarging the mind, breaking down prejudice, and what not, will be found to resolve themselves into this. If I pass now to the education of books, here also I find that the same phrase,—extension of the field of circumstance,—answers to a good deal of what this education accomplishes. Books are travel, so to speak, reversed; they bring supplies of otherwise inaccessible fact and imagery to the feet of the reader. Books, too, have this advantage over travel, that they convey information from remote times as well as from distant places. "If the invention of the ship," says Bacon, "was thought so noble, which carrieth riches and commodities from place to place, and consociateth the most remote regions in participation of their fruits, how much more are letters to be magnified, which, as ships, pass the vast seas of time, and make ages so distant to participate of the wisdom, illuminations, and inventions, the one of the other!" In these words, however, there is a suggestion that the education of books consists not alone in the mere extension of the field of the concrete. Books admit us to the accumulated past thought, as well as to the accumulated past fact and incident of the human race; and, though much of that thought,—as, for example, what comes to us in poetry,—consists but of a new form of concrete, (the concrete of the fantastic or ideal,) yet a large proportion of it consists of something totally different,—abstract or generalized science. It is in the school of books, more particularly, that that great step in education takes place,—the translation of the concrete into the abstract, the organization of mere fact and imagery into science. It is in conversation with books, more particularly, that one first sees unfolded, one by one, that splendid roll of the so-called sciences,—mathematics, astronomy, mechanics, chemistry, physiology, moral science, and politics, with all their attached sciences and subdivisions,—in which the aggregate thought of the human race on all subjects has been systematized; and that one first sees all knowledge laid out into certain great orders of ideas, any one of which will furnish occupation for a life. This great function, we say, peculiarly belongs to books. And what shall we say of the education of *friendship?* In what does this consist, and what does it peculiarly achieve? It consists, evidently, in all that can result, in the way of culture, from a closer relation than ordinary with certain selected individuals out of the throng through which one passes in the course of one's life. It is given to every one to form such close sentimental relations with perhaps six or seven individuals in the course of the early period of life; and these relationships,—far easier at this time of life than afterward,—are among the most powerful educating influences to which youth can be subjected. Friendship educates mainly in two ways. In the first place, it educates by disposing and enabling one to make certain individual specimens of human character, and all that is connected with them, objects of more serious and minute study than is bestowed on men at large; and, in the second place, it takes a man out of his own personality, and doubles, triples, or quintuples his natural powers of insight, by compelling him to look at nature and life through the eyes of others, each of whom is, for the time being, another self. This second function of friendship, as an influence of intellectual culture, is by far the most important. There are, of course, various degrees of friendship, and various exercises of it in the same degree. There is friendship with equals, friendship with inferiors, and friendship with superiors. Of all forms of friendship in youth, by far the most effective, as a means of education, is that species of enthusiastic veneration which young men of loyal and well-conditioned minds are apt to contract for men of intellectual eminence within their own circles. The educating effect of such an attachment is prodigious; and happy the youth who forms one. We all know the advice given to young men to "think for themselves;" and there is sense and soundness in that advice; but, if I were to select what I account perhaps the most fortunate thing that can befall a young man during the early period of his life,—the most fortunate, too, in the end, for his intellectual independence,—it would be his being voluntarily subjected, for a time, to some powerful intellectual tyranny.

Book Education.—All our schools, all our colleges, all our libraries, almost every thing, in fact, that we recognize as an educational institution, with the partial exception of recently founded industrial schools and schools of practical art, are but a machinery for forwarding what may be called book education. Here, however, we must make a distinction. This extensive machinery of book education, which is set up amongst us, consists of two portions. One portion has for its object simply the effective teaching of the art of reading, with its usual adjuncts; another has for its object the guidance of the community in the use of that art when it has been acquired. Let us say that the first function is performed by the *schools* of the country, and that the second is reserved for the *colleges* of the country. This does not exactly accord with the fact, many of our so-called schools going far beyond the mere teaching of reading and writing, and undertaking part of the duty we have assigned to colleges; and, many of our so-called colleges, alas! having devolved upon them too much of the proper drudgery of schools.

Teach a man to read and write perfectly, and the rest, generally speaking, is in his own power. He is no longer a Helot; you have put him in possession of the franchise of books. With this possession, and with such access as he may have to libraries, he may be any thing he pleases and has faculty for. By reading in one direction, he may make himself a mathematician; by reading in another, he may become an adept in political economy; by reading in many he may become a variously cultured man. The accomplishment of perfect and easy reading in one's own language is, after all, the grand distinction between the educated and the non-educated. There are, indeed, degrees and differences among those above this line; but, between those above it and those below it there is a great gulf.

Self Education.—Once in possession of the franchise of books, a man, as we have said, has, generally speaking, the rest in his own power. There is no limit to what, with talent and perseverance, he may attain. He may become a classical scholar and a linguist; or, he may grow eminent in speculation and the sciences. We have instances in abundance of such perseverance; and we have a name for those who so distinguish themselves. A person who, availing himself of the spontaneous means of education afforded by the other great schools, which we have enumerated,—the school of family, the school of native local circumstance, the school of travel, and the school of friendship, and having, also, somehow or other, been put in possession of the franchise of books,—conducts the rest of his book education himself, and conducts it so successfully as to become eminent, is called a self-educated man. Society often distinguishes between self-educated men and men who are college-bred,—that is, who have not only been taught to read and write in plain schools, but have had the benefit, for a certain period of their more advanced youth, of that higher pedagogic apparatus which directs and systematizes reading, and, to some extent, supersedes its use by imparting its results in an oral form. Now, the question has been raised, whether this higher pedagogic apparatus,—whether colleges, in fact,—are really of so much use as has been fancied; and, whether it would not be enough if, in these days, pedagogy were to stop at the first stage,—that of thoroughly teaching the mechanical art of reading,—and were then to turn the youth of a community so instructed loose upon the libraries and the miscellaneous teaching of life. This question is gaining ground, and not without apparent reason. Of the men of our own day who are eminent in station, influential in society, and distinguished in art, science, and letters, there are many who have not received what is generally called an academic education. I have only to glance round among those who are at present conspicuous in the various departments of British literature, and I find not a few who never studied in any university. And so, if I look back upon the past. The very king, the unapproachable monarch of our literature was a Warwickshire man, who had little Latin, less Greek, and, perhaps, no mathematics. True, the larger number of those examples of intellectual eminence attained without academic education, would be found to be not properly self-educated men, in the precise sense in which we are now using the term, but, to some extent, college-bred. Over Great Britain, and in England in particular, there are hundreds of public schools and private seminaries which do, though not to the same length as the great universities, perform the functions, as we have defined them, of colleges; and, it is in these that by far the largest proportion of young men, even of well-circumstanced families, are educated. Shakspeare was taught at the grammar-school of his native town, where the boys at this day wear square academic caps, whatever they did in his; so that the proper measure of Shakspeare's education, even scholastically, is that he was carried as far on by the pedagogy of his time as at least ninety-nine per cent. of his contemporaries. Perhaps the number of self-educated prodigies, in the present restricted sense of the term, is not so great as supposed. Still, there are examples of eminent men, self-educated even in this extreme sense of the term; that is, of men who, having received absolutely nothing from formal pedagogy but the plain faculty of reading and writing, if always that, have acquired all their subsequent book education privately for themselves.

Educational office of Colleges.—The question simply is whether, when a community has by one set of educational apparatus called schools, put its young men in possession of that faculty of reading and taste for the same, which are the key to all the knowledge contained in books, it may then leave them to their own private perseverance, according to their inclinations and opportunities or, whether finer results may not be attained by handing them over, at this point, to another and a higher kind of educational apparatus, called colleges, which will take charge of them a few years longer, assist them in their first inroads upon the vast mass of thought and knowledge accumulated in books, and, in part, supersede and supplement that method of acquiring knowledge by oral instruction.

In the first place, then, colleges fulfill this important function, that they guarantee to society a certain amount of competency in certain professions, in which previously guaranteed competency is necessary. The professions most ostensibly in this predicament are those of law, theology, and medicine; but, there are numberless other professions for the efficiency and respectability of which a certain amount of attested general acquirement, as well as of special professional training, in those who engage in them, is absolutely requisite. This function of insuring society against the intrusion of quacks and ignorant pretenders into important professions, is performed, as well as it admits of being performed, by colleges. Before a man can legally practice medicine, for example, it is required that he shall have attended courses of lectures, not only in what appertains to medical science but also in those general subjects which enter into a liberal education. And so, in various ways, and under various forms of regulation, with other professions.

It is not only with a view to professional qualification that persons are the better for being detained, whether they will or not, in places where knowledge is systematically administered. Indolence, love of amusement, preference for the pleasant, the trivial, and the immediate, over what is important, substantial and lasting, are besetting sins even in manhood, but in youth they are especially natural. If a body of young men, fresh from school, were turned loose upon the huge library of printed literature, to find their way into it and through it as they liked, many of them, doubtless, would prove insatiable readers; but, it is questionable whether many of them, of their own accord, would choose the right directions, or would pursue their reading beyond that point where toil and patience began to be requisite. But, what is clearly wanted is a kind of intellectual generalship, if we may so speak, that shall muster youth in front of the masses of literature which have to be pierced through and conquered; drill them; infuse a bold spirit into them; point out to them the proper points of attack, the redoubts where glory is to be won; and, while leaving them as much scope as possible for individual energy and inclination, lead them on, according to a plan, in regular order and column. This duty is undertaken by colleges. There young men are assembled in classes, the business of which has been arranged, however imperfectly, according to an idea of the best manner in which knowledge may be partitioned. They are obliged to be present so many hours a day in the selected classes, and there to hear lectures on various subjects deliberately read to them, whether they will or not; and thus, as well as by the discipline of examinations and the like, certain orders of ideas as well as certain intellectual tendencies are worked into them which they could not otherwise have acquired, and which place them at an advantage all the rest of their lives. That I have not exaggerated this use of colleges I believe observation will prove. I believe it will be found that many of our first speculative and scientific minds have derived the special tendencies which have made their lives famous from impulses communicated in colleges. I think, also, it will be found that strictly self-educated men,—of course I except the higher and more illustrious instances,—do not, as a body, exhibit the same tenacity and perseverance in pushing knowledge to its farthest limits as academic men of equal power. Their disposition, in most instances, is to be content with what I will call proximate knowledge,—that which lies about them and can be turned to immediate account. It is in current politics, in general literature, and in popular matter of thought, that they move and have their being; upon the laborious tracks of abstract science, or difficult and extreme speculation, they do not so often enter. Or if, occasionally, we do see a self-taught geologist, a self-taught botanist, or a self-taught mathematician, then, not unfrequently, there is an egotistic exultation over the labor gone through, and an exaggerated estimation of the particular science overtaken in its relations to the whole field of knowledge. There is too much, so to speak, of the spirit of the private soldier, whose idea of the field is but the recollection of his own movements. There are, I repeat, examples of self-educated men of so high an order as to be free from these faults. Still, I believe what I have said will be found, in the main, correct. Nay, abroad in society generally there is, I believe, too much of that spirit of contempt for the high, the profound, and the elaborate, in the way of speculation, which the worldly success of half taught men of good natural abilities is calculated to foster.

Even supposing that men could map out the field of knowledge for themselves, determine at a glance into what great orders of ideas the past thought of the human race could be best distributed for the purposes of study, and spontaneously go to work upon these in the right spirit, still, in the detailed prosecution of any study by means of books, assistance would be necessary. Accordingly, one use of colleges is that they direct and systematize reading. The art of recommending good books, and of leading on from one book to another, is one of the most useful qualifications of a teacher, and it may be carried to extraordinary perfection. Perhaps, indeed, we do not sufficiently attend to this function of colleges; perhaps we do not sufficiently attend to the fact that, since colleges were first instituted, their place in the general system of education has been greatly changed. When colleges were first instituted, books were scarce, and difficult of access; men were then their own encyclopædias; and, every Thomas Aquinas, Duns Scotus, or other ornament of a university, was bound to be a walking incarnation of the *totum scibile*. Hence, a course of lectures in those days was expected to be,—whatever might be its other merits,—a digest of all accessible information on the subject treated. Now, however, that there exist, on all subjects, books which it is impossible for even the best living thinker wholly to supersede, such lectures of a mere digest and detail are out of place; and, the business of teachers is rather to direct the reading of the pupils, and to reserve their original disquisitions for those points where they can hope to modify and extend what has been previously advanced.

Quite as much now as in those remote times when colleges were first set up in Europe they afford to youth that highest of all educational privileges, the chance of coming into personal contact with men either of original speculative power in their several departments, or of unusual fervor and enthusiasm, kindling into zeal all that come near them, and imparting life and fire to all that they touch. I have spoken of the wonderful efficacy of this influence casually encountered in society; but, it is the very nature of colleges to concentrate it and make it accessible.

Finally, I believe there is something in the oral method of conveying knowledge, whether after the tutorial or after the professorial fashion, but, perhaps, most effective in the latter, which fits it to perform certain offices of instruction far better than they could be performed by private communion with books. I will not enlarge on this topic. I will only say, that it appears to me that the forms and circumstantials of oral teaching are such that any thing in the shape of a general doctrine or principle is far more expeditiously and impressively inculcated, in this mode, through the ear, than it can usually be taken in through the eye; and that, consequently, any science, such as political economy, the proper teaching of which consists in the slow infiltration into the minds of the pupils of a series of such general doctrines, one by one, as well as those parts of all sciences which consist of massive single propositions, can be best taught by lectures and examinations. Curiously enough, this is precisely that function of colleges which, after the revolution in our educational system, caused by the increase of books, would still, at any rate, be reserved for them.

[The views of the efficiency of oral or professorial teaching, so felicitously expressed by Prof. Masson in the above extracts, are held by Prof. Vaughan, in his pamphlet entitled "*Oxford Reform and Oxford Professors.*"]

The type is a poor substitute for the human voice. It has no means of arousing, moderating, and adjusting the attention. It has no emphasis except italics, and this meagre notation can not finely graduate itself to the needs of the occasion. It can not in this way mark the heed which should be specially and chiefly given to peculiar passages and words. It has no variety of manner and intonation, to show, by their changes, how the words are to be accepted, or what comparative importance is to be attached to them. It has no natural music to take the ear, like the human voice; it carries with it no human eye to range, and to rivet the student, when on the verge of truancy, and to command his intellectual activity by an appeal to the common courtesies of life. Half the symbolism of a living language is thus lost when it is committed to paper; and, that symbolism is the very means by which the forces of the hearer's mind can be best economized, or most pleasantly excited. The lecture, on the other hand, as delivered, possesses all these instruments to win, and hold, and harmonize attention; and, above all, it imports into the whole teaching a human character, which the printed book can never supply. The Professor is the science or subject vitalized and humanized in the student's presence. He sees him kindle into his subject; he sees reflected and exhibited in him, his manner, and his earnestness, the general power of the science to engage, delight, and absorb a human intelligence. His natural sympathy and admiration attract or impel his tastes, and feelings, and wishes, for the moment, into the same current of feeling; and, his mind is naturally, and rapidly, and insensibly strung and attuned to the strain of truth which is offered to him.

One peculiarity and advantage, too, in this mode of communication, attends a comprehensive lecture, which is not shared by a book. All who hear it, must hear it at the same moment; it affects a large number of individuals at the same time; it, therefore, becomes straightway more or less a topic of conversation or conversational debate, in which the comparison and contribution of impressions tends to diffuse, and, in some degree, equalize, the benefit; especially in an academical city, where the dispersed audience quits the lecture-room to meet again in the halls and common-rooms of the university within a few hours.

NATURE AND VALUE OF EDUCATION.

BY JOHN LALOR.*

THE chief difficulty with which a writer, who urges a reform in education, has to struggle, is the general ignorance of its nature,—of what it can do for mankind. If correct notions of its power were once impressed upon the public mind, so that men should feel the extent of their own educational want, improvements, which are now year after year vainly urged upon their attention, would at once be carried into effect. The utmost that is hoped, or dreamed by theorists, would be outstripped in action and practice by the energies of society, working out education, as they have worked out the arts dependent on the physical sciences. In attempting, therefore, to prove the advantage of giving increased social importance to the educational profession, it will be requisite, in the first place, to point out how much more than is usually supposed is properly included in education, and to show something of its power over human happiness.

Education, then, does not mean merely reading and writing, nor any degree, however considerable, of mere intellectual instruction. It is, in its largest sense, a process which extends from the commencement to the termination of existence. A child comes into the world, and at once his education begins. Often at his birth the seeds of disease or deformity are sown in his constitution—and while he hangs at his mother's breast, he is imbibing impressions which will remain with him through life. During the first period of infancy, the physical frame expands and strengthens; but its delicate structure is influenced for good or evil by all surrounding circumstances,—cleanliness, light, air, food, warmth. By and by, the young being within shows itself more. The senses become quicker. The desires and affections assume a more definite shape. Every object which gives a sensation, every desire gratified or denied, every act, word, or look of affection or of unkindness, has its effect, sometimes slight and imperceptible, sometimes obvious and permanent, in building up the human being; or, rather, in determining the direction in which it will shoot up and unfold itself. Through the different states of the infant, the child, the boy, the youth, the man, the development of his physical, intellectual, and moral nature goes on, the various circumstances of his condition incessantly acting upon him—the healthfulness or unhealthfulness of the air he breathes; the kind, and the sufficiency of his food and clothing; the degree in which his physical powers are exerted; the freedom with which his senses are allowed or encouraged to exercise themselves upon external objects; the extent to which his faculties of remembering, comparing, reasoning, are tasked; the sounds and sights of home;

* Prize Essay on the Expediency and Means of Elevating the Profession of the Educator in Society. Published by the Central Society of Education. London.

the moral example of parents; the discipline of school; the nature and degree of his studies, rewards, and punishments; the personal qualities of his companions; the opinions and practices of the society, juvenile and advanced, in which he moves; and the character of the public institutions under which he lives. The successive operation of all these circumstances upon a human being from earliest childhood constitutes his education;—an education which does not terminate with the arrival of manhood, but continues through life,—which is itself, upon the concurrent testimony of revelation and reason, a state of probation or education for a subsequent and more glorious existence.

The first inquiries, then, which present themselves are, whether circumstances act upon the mind at random, or according to any fixed and discoverable laws?—and how far is it in our power to control their operation? To these it can be answered, that the growth of the human being, from infancy up, in mind as well as in body, takes place, at all events to *a great extent*, according to fixed laws. The assertion is qualified simply to avoid certain controversies which have no practical relation to the subject. No one can observe the movements of his own mind, or the mental operations of another, particularly a child, without discovering the frequent recurrence of the same combinations of thoughts, or of thoughts and acts. When two sensations, or a sensation and an idea, or two ideas, have been frequently experienced together, the recurrence of one calls up the other. The name "table" suggests the idea. The first word of a familiar poem brings the others after it. A sudden blow excites anger. Frequent pain makes fretfulness habitual. Here we see the operation of *laws*,—laws of mind discoverable by observation of nature, like the laws of mechanics or astronomy. These must form the basis of practical education,—the science on which the art is founded. The practical art of education has regard to a small part only of the long train of circumstances which operate upon a human being;—namely, that portion which belongs to his early life, and which is within the control of others. In this sense education means the body of practical rules, for the regulation of the circumstances about children, by which they may be trained up to the greatest perfection of their nature.

The nature of the laws of the human constitution, and of the power which a knowledge of them can give us, will appear more distinctly from a consideration of each of the three branches into which education is now, by common consent, divided—physical, intellectual, and moral. It is convenient to consider them separately, but each is intimately connected with the others. It will not be necessary to attempt, even in the most abridged form, a complete view of any one of these branches. A reference to a few principles in each will be sufficient to show that, by the general application of a system of education adapted to the wants and capacities of human nature, the condition of society, and particularly of its poorer classes, could be greatly elevated, and a host of evils which afflict mankind avoided.

PHYSICAL EDUCATION.

The influence of the physical frame upon the intellect, morals, and happiness of a human being, is now universally admitted. Perhaps the extent of this influence will be thought greater in proportion to the accuracy with which the subject is examined. The train of thought and feeling is perpetually affected by the recurrence of sensations arising from the state of our internal organs. The connection of high mental excitement with the physical system is obvious enough, when the latter is under the influence of stimulants, as wine or opium; but other mental states,—depression of spirits—irritability of temper—indolence, and the craving for sensual gratification, are, it is probable, no less intimately connected with the condition of the body. The selfish, exacting habits which so often attend ill health, and the mean artifices to which feebleness of body leads, are not, indeed, necessary results; but the physical weakness so often produces the moral evil, that no moral treatment can be successful which overlooks physical causes. Without reference to its moral effects, bodily pain forms a large proportion of the amount of human misery. It is, therefore, of the highest importance, that a child should grow up sound and healthful in body, and with the utmost degree of muscular strength that education can communicate.

There are a few common truths with respect to *food*, *air*, *cleanliness*, and *exercise*, which, if acted upon, would go far to accomplish as much for all children.

A regular and sufficient supply of nutritious food is essential to the healthful support of the body, and the proper development of its organs. If the food is insufficient, the whole system suffers,—the blood is impoverished, and produces general debility of the organs and bodily exhaustion. The moral effect is equally injurious. The almost perpetual craving caused by insufficiency of food absorbs the attention, and while such a state of mind continues, it is next to impossible that any strong moral feeling or regard for others can grow up. In most cases, where the natural appetites of children are unsatisfied, it unfortunately arises from the narrow circumstances of their parents; but there are multitudes of instances in which abundant means for the performance of this first duty of a father are squandered in ruinous excitement. It is to be feared, too, that the cheapness, with which some schools recommend themselves to the public, is accomplished at the expense of the children, by curtailing the quantity, or lowering the quality, of their food. An excessive quantity of food is equally fatal to the bodily and mental health. Children eat to excess when their food is of various kinds or of a highly stimulating nature. The digestive organs become oppressed, and a train of disorders follow. Tyrannical ill temper is the mental result, and parents and friends reap the natural harvest of pampering and sensual indulgence.

Pure air is as essential as food to the support of human existence. When the lungs are forced to breathe an impure atmosphere, the blood, deprived of its needful supply of oxygen, imperfectly depurated, and corrupted still further by contact with unwholesome gases, spreads weakness and disease through the system. The difference between city and country children, which strikes every eye, arises mainly from this cause. Amongst the wealthier class there is, generally, a strong sense of the importance of pure air, and a corresponding anxiety to obtain it for their children. Even among these classes, however, there is much neglect, as in the ventilation of bedrooms; and often an injurious excess of caution, which dreads the least exposure to a breeze, and by confining children to the house, not only prevents sufficient muscular exercise, but deprives the expanding frame of the delightful and invigorating stimulus of fresh air. But the children of the poorer classes in large towns are the great sufferers from impurity of atmosphere. Living in narrow lanes and courts, in which accumulated filth is perpetually loading the air with noxious ingredients, they are crowded in small rooms, which seldom receive even the wretched ventilation that such places admit of. The inmates of such habitations sleep together in a space the inclosed atmosphere of which, even with the best ventilation in the daytime, would supply but a small proportion of the requisite quantity of vital air. With its absolute impurities it is nothing less than slow poison to the sleepers. In these rooms it frequently happens that the children, particularly the younger ones, who need air most, are shut up for safety in the daytime, during the absence of working parents. And when they are let loose their sports take place in these same narrow lanes and alleys, where physical contaminations are the least evils that can befall them.

It is not easy to remedy these evils, but much may be done to diminish them. A good large play-ground should be considered an indispensable part of every school. Here, at least, the children might breathe as pure an atmosphere as large towns could supply, and, what is of not less consequence, feel practically its importance. Play-grounds would, indeed, frequently be expensive; but on what public object is expenditure justifiable if not on this, which so intimately concerns the health,—and through the health, as well as in a more direct manner, the morals of the people? It is not a good, but a mischief, to crowd children into rooms for the purpose of schooling, where there is no play-ground, and a supply of pure air is impossible. Yet, in all great towns, numbers of such schools may be found, in which, on entrance, the atmosphere is felt perfectly oppressive, and the children appear languid and restless, enlivened only by the casual opening of the door, to admit at the same moment a visitor and a stream of fresh air. The most open, airy, and healthful localities should invariably be selected for schools. School business should be frequently interrupted by a short run into the play-ground. A few minutes so used would infuse vigor into all proceedings. When the business of a class admitted of its being taken into the open air in fine weather, a master would often find the change sufficient to convert languor into alertness and attention.

Habits of cleanliness are both healthful and moralizing. The skin is an organ through which, by means of a constant but insensible perspiration, a great part of the waste matter of the human body is carried off. When it remains without washing for any length of time, the matter collected on its surface obstructs the minute vessels or apertures, of which it contains a greater number than an equal surface of the finest cambric, and prevents the waste matter from passing out. The consequence is, that some of the other excretory organs are stimulated to an unhealthy action,—and this gradually produces weakness and ill health, or some specific form of disease, as of the bowels or lungs. When we know that numbers pass through life, having scarcely ever given their entire persons a thorough ablution; that multitudes never dream of touching with water any part of their bodies but the face, the hands, and sometimes the feet, except during the extreme heat of summer, we can readily find in such habits the cause of a considerable portion of the disease which exists. The healthful action of the skin requires that its impurities should be removed by regular ablutions of the entire person. The delicious excitement of the first bath in summer, to those who discontinue bathing in winter, is chiefly caused by the stimulus given to the cutaneous vessels, and through them to the whole system, by the removal of the collected impurities of many months. Many, to whom entire ablution by bathing or sponging is a daily practice, can speak of its admirable efficacy in bracing and harmonizing the system, and guarding it against the varieties of colds, coughs, &c. Such habits appear extremely troublesome and difficult of acquirement to those who grow up to mature life with opposite ones; but it is in our power, by education, to make them an essential part of the nature of the young. Children might be trained to habits of strict and entire cleanliness which would never leave them, because they would make it far more painful to omit regular ablution than it now is to the most reluctant to practice it. If popular education did nothing more than create such habits in the children of the poor in towns, it would prevent a fearful amount of physical and moral disorder. Children habituated to cleanliness would make a change in the poorest abodes. The most wretched garrets or cellars might and would be made clean. Attention to cleanliness in the dwellings of the poor must co-exist with some degree of self-respect and moral feeling; and, where these are, there will be improvement. Habits of cleanliness, made general, would change bathing from a luxury for the few into a necessary for the many. Baths of all kinds would become cheap and accessible. If a working man, exhausted with toil, could have (as under such circumstances he might) a warm bath for the same or a less price than a glass of gin or spirits, he would learn to prefer it, as a more agreeable and effectual restorative.

Exercise, everybody admits, is essential to health. Exercise is the great law for securing the health and strength of every part of the constitution, physical and mental. In this place it is to be considered as promoting the action of the muscular system. The muscles of any portion of the body, when worked by exercise, draw additional nourishment from the blood, and by the repetition of the stimulus, if it is not excessive, increase in size, strength, and freedom of action. The regular action of the muscles promotes and preserves the uniform circulation of the blood, which is the prime condition of health. The strength of the body, or of a limb, depends upon the strength of the muscular system, or of the muscles of the limb; and as the constitutional muscular endowment of most people is tolerably good, the diversities of muscular power, observable amongst men, are chiefly attributable to exercise. The fleshy, or muscular part of a blacksmith's arm, is dense and powerful like the iron of his own anvil. Now and then individuals may be met with,—prize-fighters, gymnasticians, &c., who by careful training (which is simply judicious exercise) have communicated to every part of their bodies an extraordinary degree of strength and brought out the muscles in a corresponding development. The astonishing feats of strength and activity performed by tumblers, rope-dancers, and exhibitors of various kinds, show what can be done with the human body by the same means.

It should be an important object in education to give children a considerable degree of bodily strength. It is not merely of high utility for the laborious occupations in which most persons must pass their lives;—it is often a great support to moral dispositions. We should excite good impulses in children, and also give them the utmost strength of mind and body to carry them out. A child ought to be able to withstand injustice attempted by superior strength. Nothing demoralizes both parties more than the tyranny exercised over younger children by older ones at school. Many good impulses are crushed in a child's heart when he has not physical courage to support them. If we make a child as strong as his age and constitution permit, he will have courage to face greater strength. A boy of this kind, resisting firmly the first assumption of an elder tyrant, may receive some hard treatment in one encounter, but he will have achieved his deliverance. His courage will secure respect. The tyrant will not again excite the same troublesome and dangerous resistance. This is certainly not intended to encourage battles at school,—far from it. But, until a high degree of moral education is realized, the best security for general peace among children of different ages is to give each a strength and spirit which no one will like to provoke. It will further give each a confidence in his powers, and a self-respect, without which none of the hardy virtues can flourish.

The gymnastic exercises profess to be scientifically adapted to the development of the human frame; and many of them no doubt are so. They fail, or become injurious, by furnishing no contemporaneous mental excitement, or by being used without regard to the health or strength of the individual. The instruments for a few of the most approved and agreeable of these exercises ought to form a regular part of school machinery;—the circular swing, vaulting frame, climbing pole, and some others. But the great desideratum in physical education is, a series of games of an exciting character, arranged so as to develop the different muscles of the body. The mere exercise of the muscles, while the mind is inert or averse, is comparatively of little value. The efficacy of exercise requires the direction of the attention and the muscular effort to the same point at the same moment.* Most of the common sports of children secure this; but they seldom require the operation of more than a particular set of muscles. It would be desirable to have games which should at once interest, exercise various muscles, and keep all the players as active as possible. Football, perhaps, is one of the best in common use. It keeps a whole field in high excitement and action. Ball in a fives-court is excellent, but can occupy no more than four at the same time. Leap-frog exercises the muscles of the limbs and loins in running and jumping, and the muscles of the loins and back in supporting. The game of battle-door and shuttle-cock is excellent for the arms and chest, and should be played with both hands, not only for the development of the left muscles of the thorax, but also for the exercise of the left arm. Notwithstanding the unanswerable arguments of Franklin, the left arm labors under the grievance of entire neglect up to the present day. Cricket is a fine game; but there is little continuous exercise, except for the striker and the bowler. Prison-bass, hunt the hare, hoops, whipping-tops, are all good; but there is obviously required a set of games which, with an interesting purpose, would keep all engaged in them active, give full play to the voice, and call for the exercise of strength and activity in all the different muscles. Whoever shall supply this want will confer a service of no ordinary kind on education. The want exists to a still greater degree in female education, most of the best exercises for boys being unsuitable for girls; but there are some, such as battle-door and shuttle-cock, and hoops, which answer equally well for both, and an inventive mind, with a knowledge of the structure of the body, could no doubt multiply them.

Besides the communication of health and strength, physical education includes training in certain bodily accomplishments or arts. A few of these, which should be common to all classes, require notice. Children of both sexes may easily learn to swim, and when acquired early, the power may be increased to a great extent. There is, probably, no exercise which calls into play such a variety of organs. It purifies the skin, and stimulates its entire surface by a

* For a more full and interesting exposition of this and other laws of exercise, see Dr. A. Combe's "Principles of Physiology, applied to the preservation of Health, and the improvement of Education."

uniform and gentle friction. The muscles of the trunk, neck, and limbs are strongly called out. A facility in swimming would be an additional temptation to bathing, and therefore to cleanliness. The use of the accomplishment as a means of self-preservation, or of saving the lives of others, needs no remark.

Reciting and reading aloud are physical accomplishments, with important effects, both physical and mental. Clear enunciation is not unconnected with clearness of mind. By careful management from early childhood this habit may be established if the organs of speech are not defective. Speaking aloud is a powerful exercise of those all-important organs, the lungs, as well as of various muscles of the lower part of the trunk. Perhaps, if the physical power of distinct and composed utterance were general, it would tend, more than even a considerable increase of intelligence, to free men from the influence of demagogues. Persons who happen to possess this power, in conjunction with a certain superficial fluency, exercise in public meetings an influence almost marvelous over men vastly their superiors in intellect and information. A loud voice does wonders at a time of excitement. If every man who had thoughts had a power of uttering them before assemblies of his fellow-citizens, the despotism of demagogues would be at an end.

Singing is another branch of physical education, if that indeed can be called physical which ought also to be an exercise of the intellect and still more of the heart, and which may become a powerful instrument for the refinement and moral elevation of mankind. Its physical use is considerable. It gives as much healthful exercise to the lungs and chest as reading aloud or recitation. But, as a spring of cheerfulness,—a means of tranquillizing excited feelings,—a source of enjoyment when the exhaustion of bodily labor prevents the indulgence of more purely intellectual tastes,—and a mode of satisfying that desire of excitement which, in the intervals of business or study, is sure to present itself, and which, if it find no pure and legitimate gratifications, seeks those which are neither,—music is a blessing of which we can scarcely over-estimate the value. The faculty was not given to man to lie dormant. It is all but universal in the species. The kind may be rude where the taste is rude, but music, in some shape, everywhere gladdens man's existence. We can make the enjoyment more varied and intense by cultivation, and blend it with the purest and most exalted feelings, instead of allowing it to add force to temptation by its alliance with vicious pleasures. Wind and stringed instruments are expensive; but the most perfect of all instruments, the voice, is within reach of all. At least, there are few children who, being begun with at an early age, can not be trained to sing so as to derive and communicate pleasure. A fondness for music, even of the rudest kind, is a taste above the dominion of sense. It raises man above the level of brute appetite. A degree of cultivation, within reach of all, would make it a standard enjoyment. Love of music must bring innumerable gentle and kindly sympathies along with it. Whatever is greatest and most beautiful in thought, or nature, or in human deeds, finds fitting utterance in music, and through music finds a way to the general heart.

Music, thus appealing to the highest feelings, is a moral agent. It is also an organ of great power for the expression of religious feelings. The loftiest conceptions of the divinity—the profoundest adoration—the ideas struggling out of the depths of the soul, of the power and beauty and goodness of God and creation, to which language, made up by the senses, seems so weak and inadequate—

burst forth with the fullness of inspiration in the music of Handel; and who, with even the rudest power of appreciation, can listen to those immortal strains, without being raised into sympathy with the eternal aspirations of the highest minds for the spiritual and infinite?

In teaching children to sing, the simplest combinations, both of poetry and music, should be presented, but they should be beautiful as well as simple. The early associations are the most lasting. We ought to make them beautiful. The songs of childhood should be such as may be loved in after-life, and may contribute to form a pure taste. In the infant schools singing has received considerable attention, but has been much abused. Some of the rhymes in common use are miserable doggerel. It is an injury of no trifling kind to blend the enjoyment of singing with such wretched compositions. When the importance of presenting images of simplicity and beauty through the medium of singing, in early education, becomes generally understood, it will seem a worthy office for minds of a high order to compose songs for children.

It is unnecessary to pursue the subject of physical education farther. It opens a wide and important field for investigation. Enough has been said to show how large an amount of pain and suffering might be avoided by adapting education to the constitution of the human body, and how much a due cultivation of man's physical powers would contribute to his moral excellence and enjoyment

INTELLECTUAL EDUCATION.

Intellectual Education has a twofold object: first, the development of the intellectual powers; and second, the communication of knowledge. The mere communication of a certain amount of knowledge seems to be the object of a great deal of what passes for good education. But the matter of acquisition being ill selected, and the laws of the human intellect disregarded in the mode of presenting it to the mind, it happens that even this object is most imperfectly attained. *Words* instead of *things* form the staple of education; yet the merest smattering remains with most people, in after-life, of the languages at which so many of their early years are spent. Sometimes a certain amount of facts in history or natural philosophy is communicated in education; but being addressed to the memory, and taken in passively, it leads to nothing. When ideas are admitted without any working of the reflective faculties, they take no root, but lie in dead, useless masses on the surface of the mind. The communication of even real knowledge, for its own sake, is of secondary importance in early intellectual education. The main thing is the formation of habits of correct observation and clear reflection. The mind derives its knowledge, in the first place, from external objects acting upon the organs of sense. Sensations being once received, the corresponding ideas undergo various modifications, by the processes of comparison, abstraction, reasoning, &c. When the impressions of sense are indistinct, the subsequent operations share in the uncertainty and imperfection. Intellectual development, therefore, requires that the powers of accurate observation should be first unfolded. Clear ideas being furnished by them, the various intellectual habits of abstraction, classification, and reasoning, may be rendered quick and correct. The communication of knowledge in early education is primarily useful as the means of forming these habits. Education is a preparation for after-life. It should not attempt so much to communicate extensive knowledge as to excite the love of it. The results of the observations of the most eminent observers, received passively into the mind, are worthless compared with the habit of observing for one's self. In the one case, a man enters life with cumbrous stores which serve no purpose, because he knows not how to use them. In the other, he comes with a slender stock thoroughly at command, and with skill to increase it by daily fruits of original observation and reflection. Many children, the wonders of admiring circles, turn out common-place men, because their acquisitions are never converted by mental assimilation into part of their own nature. Others, pronounced idlers, while in fact they are developing their faculties after a fashion of their own, stand out as men, and take a lead in the business of life.

The development of the intellect begins in the infant. He is perpetually receiving sensations from the objects about him; and while awake, he is constantly seeking to get things within his grasp, to feel them, and see them. There is an impulse within him to find out the properties of every object he meets with, so fresh and vigorous that it may well seem enviable to students dulled by exclusive intercourse with books, and long abstraction from the actual world. This precious activity ought not to run to waste. It is in our power so to guide it, that instead of dim and imperfect impressions, speedily overlaid, confused and obliterated by other dim and imperfect impressions, the child shall constantly receive from without clear sensations, and by gradual steps attain full and correct ideas of the objects about him. We can present real objects to his senses in a certain order, and in such a manner as to attract his attention, until he becomes perfectly familiar with their sensible qualities. When he has got the idea of an object, or of one of its properties, and not before, we can give him the name. The name given when his interest is excited will be firmly associated with the idea. The child's attention is first drawn to the simplest sensations. The elements being clear, their combinations will be taken in clearly; and the perceptions of resemblances or differences must be also clear. Thus, by gradual steps, of which each is clear and certain, the development proceeds.

For the effective promulgation of this great principle of teaching by reality, which all philosophy of the mind supports, and which is destined to revolutionize education, the world is indebted to PESTALOZZI. It is practically exemplified in the well-known "Lessons on Objects" of Miss Mayo, in which the lessons are arranged so as to develop successively, by real objects, the faculties of observation, comparison, classification, abstraction, and to lead to composition.

The child's strong impulse to acquaint himself with things must not be blunted by a premature attempt at teaching him to read, or by that absurd and confusing process, as it is commonly practiced, of teaching him his letters. The child must know many things before reading or spelling. The principle of submitting objects in a certain progressive order to the examination of his senses must be the basis of his intellectual education; and the habits of correct observation so formed must be systematically exercised, so as to insure their continuance throughout his existence.

Upon this knowledge of things, as a basis, the child acquires his mother tongue, never learning any word until he has had the idea, and felt the want of the name. Names, however, are for the most part complex sounds, and a very considerable and careful training of the organs of speech is necessary, before they can be uttered correctly. Here also a progressive order must be observed. We should begin with the simplest words, and gradually lead the child to the pronunciation of them, by requiring him to repeat after us the simple sounds of which they are composed. The child teaches us so much himself when he begins with some such word as "ma," or its repetition, "mama." The syllable "ma" is composed of two simple sounds, a vowel and a consonant. A mother, without any knowledge of the principle, often exemplifies it when she pronounces this syllable for the child's imitation. She makes the two distinct sounds, *m* and *a*, (as in *bar*,) with a slight interval. She does not pronounce *em* and *a*, (as in *fate*,) the *names** of the letters, but she goes through the peculiar closing of the lips, by which *m* is produced in combination, and then sounds *a* as it is sounded in the word. The child imitates each motion, and at length utters the combination. In the same progressive manner in which a child learns to take in the most complex sensations, and to conceive the most complex ideas, his organs are brought to utter the most complex sounds correctly, and words become associated in an indissoluble union with the sensations and ideas they represent.

This is the basis, the only secure basis, on which to raise up a strong and clear intellect. When the first impressions are clear, and all the words that are known *represent* clear ideas, the processes of abstraction, classification, and reasoning may be made prompt, vigorous, and true.

At a very early period the child should be led, still from observation of real objects, to form ideas of number. And here also the progress must be by the most gradual steps. One finger, two fingers, three fingers. One finger and two fingers are three fingers. He must remain for a considerable time in the simplest and most obvious ideas. Here, if possible, more than anything else, is it necessary that each idea should be, as it were, worked into the texture of his mind before he proceeds to the next. The most complex combinations of number are made up of the simplest ideas; and, with many persons, ideas of number continue through life indistinct, because the simple elements of which they are composed were never clear in their minds. There should be none of the "senseless parroting" of the multiplication table, but a progressive attainment of real ideas of number from *real* objects,—addition and subtraction from real addition and subtraction; and from these that species of repeated addition which is called "multiplication," and that species of repeated subtraction which is called "division." Ideas of number, and of the elements of calculation, being obtained from real objects, and from different kinds of real objects, the mind may be led to clear *abstract* ideas of number. Clear ideas of number tend powerfully to general clearness of mind, and affect many subsequent acquirements. Confused ideas of number spread a haze and dimness over the whole field of knowledge.

Amongst the properties of external objects, of which the child obtains the knowledge by his senses, his attention may be early directed to their size and distances, and he will readily take in the simple ideas of measurement. He will have no difficulty in finding one thing to be longer than another, and, with the help of his clear ideas of number, one thing to be twice or three times as long as another; and two things, which can not be brought together, to be equal, by finding both equal to some third thing. His eye and hand should be exercised in measuring, and the engagement of both will interest him, and gratify

* We must be careful not to confound the *names* of the letters, as *bee*, *ess*, *aitch*, *double u*, with their *sounds* in combination.

the impulse to mental and bodily activity, which is almost incessant in childhood. Real measures of every kind, linear, superficial, solid and liquid, and weights,—as inches, yards, linear, square, and cubic feet, quarts, bushels, ounces, and pounds,—should be set before him, until his eye and touch are perfectly familiar with them. These should take the place of the tables of weights and measures, which, with so bold a defiance of common sense, as well as of the laws of mind, are given to children to be committed to memory, before they have a glimmering of their meaning.

From ideas of distance he will easily and naturally proceed to examine the position of external objects. Being presented with the simplest ideas of position, as straight lines, angles, &c., he delineates them on paper, or a slate, from the outlines of objects progressively set before him. He is gradually led on to many of the relations of triangles and circles,—the elements of geometry and of linear drawing.

When the eye has been in some degree trained to the observation of form, and the hand to the imitation of outline, the child may begin to read; not with letters, but sentences containing words of which the object is before his eyes. He will learn the letters of print by a species of analysis, and by attempting to form them with his pencil, and his formation of the writing character will be much more free and rapid by the accuracy and pliancy which drawing has given to his eye and hand.

When people attempt to teach children geography, by compelling them to commit to memory a number of proper names, it is almost needless to say, that they are following that wretched system of word-mongering which has so long reigned supreme in every department of education. When they set a globe or a map before his eyes, they do what is, indeed, much better, but they still begin at the wrong end. Here, as in every other branch of intellectual instruction, we ought to begin with the *existing experience* of the child, and evolve out of it, by the most gradual progression, what we want him to know. We must begin with the reality which is *in him and around him*, and make known to him what he can not see, by means of that which is before his senses. A map, or plan, of the school-room or the play-ground, which he should be led to draw for himself, ought to be his first lesson in geography. This should be followed by one of his own town or district, which he can verify by personal observation. When he thoroughly understands the relation which a map bears to the reality, he may be led to the map of his country, not crowded with names, but a simple outline, with the principal mountains and rivers and a few great towns marked. In conceiving the extent of a large country, or of the globe, his clear ideas of number, acting upon the real distances which he knows, will secure clearness in the combined ideas. The *natural* divisions of the earth should be the first learned, and the productions, tea, cotton, &c., and animals which are before his senses, referred to their several homes.

Naturally connected with ideas of the surface of the earth are those of remarkable events in different places, and of the past history of the earth's principal inhabitants. Although history, properly so-called, should be perhaps the latest of all studies, there are certain leading ideas of great events and characters, which may be advantageously made known at an early period. As a basis of this knowledge the child must be led to the measurement of time. And here, as before, he must begin with what is within reach of his senses, (or what may be popularly said to be so.) He must learn the comparative lengths of small portions of time,—as a minute, an hour, a day, a week. He should be led to think of the trifling events which he can recollect, in the order of time,—his getting up in the morning—his coming to school—his first lesson—his game in the play-ground. Having learned to conceive events of his own experience, in the order in which they occurred,—extending back over a continually increasing period,—his clear ideas of number, acting upon these clear ideas of his own little chronology, will lead him to a conception of the chronology of the human race. The chronological order will be found the most natural and easy way of presenting such interesting facts of past history as the child can comprehend.

Even if education were carried no farther than this, how great would be its effects! How superior a race of men might be produced by such a system thoroughly worked out! What power of observation, arrangement, and deduction,—what rapidity of eye and dexterity of hand, would be ready for application to any branch of the business of society. What independence of judgment would be generated in such men, by the sound and practical nature of their acquirements. Yet what modesty, from a just apprehension of the extent of knowledge above them; and what a tendency upward and onward, from the spirit of progression infused into all their labors.

It is plain, however, that if circumstances admitted of the education being carried farther, the same principles might be continued. The lessons on objects would flow on easily into complete courses of *Zoölogy*, Botany, Mineralogy, and Geology; the principle being strictly adhered to of examining real objects, when procurable, and when not, of using good pictures. Geometry, Algebra, Trigonometry, and the higher branches of mathematics, would easily follow, upon the thorough comprehension of the simple relations of number and position. The different branches in Natural Philosophy, exhibited by progressive experiments would be not so much a labor as a recreation.

There are two deeply important branches of study, which, as they are seldom considered proper to form a part of early education, deserve particular notice. They might be included under the single head of the study of the human constitution, but this at once presents two great divisions, which it is more convenient to consider apart. *Every child* then might be made to possess a considerable acquaintance with

1. The structure of his own body.
2. The structure or constitution of his mind.

It ought to require little reasoning to prove the utility of making these studies a part of general education. Indeed, if education were not beyond all other things governed by mere prejudice and custom, this kind of knowledge would seem the most fitting for universal acquisition, as concerning all men alike and affecting all pursuits. A knowledge of the structure of a man's own body, acquired in early life, would prevent many injurious practices, which, in most cases, are persevered in through ignorance,—such as want of cleanliness, deficient ventilation, excessive or insufficient exercise,—over-action of diseased organs. People may be told forever that they should have a regular supply of fresh air; they assent in words, and forget it because it does not get into their thoughts. A single exposition of the use of the blood, and of the part performed by the lungs, in fitting it for its purposes, would stamp the idea deeply, and arouse the mind to act upon it. A thousand precepts against the hideous distortion caused by tight stays would not be half so effective as an exhibition of the organs in the cavity of the thorax,—or a discovery of the facility with which the lower ribs may be bent by pressure. Knowledge of this kind would be an effective aid to physical education. It would remove a host of popular prejudices. It would destroy the trust in confident empirics, and the distrust of regular practitioners. It would enable a patient, and those about him, to afford to a medical attendant that hearty coöperation which in nine cases out of ten facilitates—if it is not requisite to—recovery. To females the study is peculiarly needful. "The theory of society," in the words of Dr. Southwood Smith, "according to its present institutions, supposes that this knowledge is possessed by the mother." She is intrusted with the first and most important part of the physical and moral education of the child. Mothers, in fact, make society what it is; for the physical and moral tendencies which make up character, are generally communicated or excited before the child passes from the sphere of his mother's influence. There is thus a twofold necessity for making this study a part of female education,—to enable women, as individuals, to protect their own health and coöperate in their own physical education, and to enable them as mothers to do all that enlightened reflectiveness can for the happiness of the beings intrusted to them. In addition to these great and obvious utilities, the study of man's physical structure deserves a first place in education as matter of science. No object in external nature presents combinations so varied and beautiful, or instances of adjustment so likely to fill a young mind with wonder and veneration, as the exquisite mechanism of life.

Nor can it be doubted that a knowledge of the human structure, not vague and general, but with considerable minuteness of detail, can be conveyed in an agreeable manner to children. The well-known publication of Dr. Southwood Smith, on the "Philosophy of Health," contains an account of the structure and functions of the human body, which is not only a model of beautiful exposition, but has been found in practice an admirable manual for imparting this kind of knowledge. The whole, or in any case, the fifth, sixth, and seventh chapters, of the first volume, might be acquired in no very long period; and there is no existing school study which it would not with great advantage displace. Upon the principle of teaching by reality, the objects themselves should, as far as possible, be presented. A collection of human bones ought to form a part of the apparatus of every school. An idea might be formed of several organs from an exhibition of those of animals. A sheep's heart, for instance, which might always be procured, would give a vivid conception of the human organ, and so of others. The deficiency of real objects might be supplied by colored anatomical plates, which, like many other expensive articles, would become cheap, if a general sense of their utility in education led to an extended demand for them.

A knowledge, not quite so accurate, but still sufficiently so to serve many important purposes, of the powers of his own mind, might also be communicated to the child. Much of the misery with which the world abounds is the result of acts performed from impulse without reflection. To those whose attention from childhood has been absorbed by external objects so as never to have been directed to the operations of their own minds, it seems the most natural thing in the word to give way to a strong impulse. To pause upon the trains of their ideas and feelings, and subject their impulses to examination, are to some persons impossible, and to most extremely difficult. The unpleasantness of the effort accompanying these states of mind hurries men for relief to any decision. There are few persons unsuccessful in life who can not trace their misfortunes to some inconsiderate impulse,—some course determined upon hastily to escape the painful balancing of reflection. Habits of reflectiveness are essential to steadiness of conduct; and they may, by early training, be made easy and familiar as the series of complicated muscular motions by which the hand goes through the process of writing.

A child, whose faculties have been properly called out by previous intellectual training, will have little difficulty in receiving correct notions of the use of his organs of sense—(he will be familiar with their material structure from the previous study)—in giving him a knowledge of the sensible qualities of external objects. He will readily discover that what he has once seen, felt, heard, tasted, or smelt, may be remembered; and thus, that of all sensations there are corresponding ideas. The synchronous and successive associations—the combination of several into one, and the separation of one into several—the mental grouping of like objects together, under one name, and the mental separation of unlike ones—the detection of the different relations of position, proportion, resemblance, difference, and comprehension, and of the composition of the trains called processes of reasoning—in short, the whole phenomena of intellect will easily follow. Nor will it be difficult to make the child discover, that there are certain motives or desires which lead him to act as he does; that he eats in obedience to the impulse of appetite; that he strikes from anger, or desire to do others injury; that he is pleased when others approve of his conduct, and pained by their disapprobation; that he loves certain individuals, and would give up his pleasures for theirs; that it is pleasant to make others happy; that some of these desires require to be controlled, and that all are to be regulated by the reasoning faculties. In the acquirement of this knowledge the young mind would be led to turn its attention upon itself, and so to form habits of self-examination. A great insight into human motives would thus be gained, and an extraordinary correctness of moral judgment both on self and others. Reflectiveness, the true soil for the growth of whatever is best in character, would be made general; and the public opinion of a school would acquire such a justness and force, as to become a powerful engine of moral education. It would be difficult to point out a book perfectly adapted to give this knowledge to children. The purpose might be answered by a judicious abridgment of Brown's Lectures, or, still better, by a small compilation from the works of Berkeley, Hartley, Adam Smith, Stewart, Brown, and Mill, and the phrenological writings of Mr. Combe and some others; avoiding all great disputed questions, and confined to those expositions of the human faculties which may be considered as established. As matter of science, and as affording perpetual illustrations of the Divine wisdom and goodness, the philosophy of the mind is even more deserving of a place in education than the study of man's physical structure. The double necessity of making it a part of female education holds likewise; for in addition to its use for moral guidance and self-government, it is especially needful for the mother, to whom nature and society intrust the early rearing of the child.

Other sciences, as Political Economy, the elements of which ought to enter into general education, need not be particularly remarked upon.

There is one subject which requires a short consideration before passing to the third branch of education, or that which relates to the formation of moral character.

It may be thought extravagant to propose the cultivation of a taste for poetry as a regular part of education, especially for the poorer classes. Yet education, which seeks to develop the faculties of a human being, must be very inadequate if it neglects the culture of the imagination. The power of poetic creation is, indeed, the rarest of endowments, but the power of enjoyment is general. The highest human mind differs not in kind, but in degree, from the humblest. The deepest principles of science discovered by the slow toil of the greatest men, the loftiest imaginings of the poet, having once been revealed in the form of human conceptions, and embodied in language, become the common property of the race, and all who go out of life without a share in these treasures, which no extent of participation diminishes, have lost the richest portion of their birthright. Man rarely feels the dignity of his nature in the small circle of his common cares. It is when brought into communion with the great spirits of the present and the past,—when he beholds the two worlds of imagination and reality in the light of Shakspeare's genius,—or is filled with the sacred sublimities of Milton,—or from Wordsworth learns the beauty of common things, and catches a glimpse of those "clouds of glory" out of which his childhood came,—that he feels the elevating sense of what he is and may become. In this high atmosphere, so bracing to the moral nerves, no selfish or sordid thoughts can live.

But assuredly there is no class in society to whom the sustainment of such communion is more requisite than to the largest and poorest. The harshness of the realities about them requires its softening and soothing influence. It is a good which they may have with no evil attendant. Its purifying excitement may displace stimulants which brutalize and degrade them. Let it not be said that a poetic taste would turn their thoughts from their occupations, or fill them with discontent. Their thoughts will and must fly at times from their occupations, and find forgetfulness in snatches of drunken revelry, from which they return to labor with double distaste, in mental and bodily exhaustion. A power of enjoying the beauty of poetic creations would afford an easier and far more delicious oblivion of their sorrows. It would send them back tranquilized and refreshed—reanimated with hope and faith for the continued struggle of existence. While poetry continues a rare enjoyment, a taste for it may sometimes suggest vain ambition and discontent, but let it be made a universal possession, and it will no more puff up than the common capability of mechanical or manual labor. But it is sufficient for the argument that poetry appeals to faculties common to all. That is our warrant for their educational development. Who shall pronounce that capacities given by God ought to lie idle? Who shall put out the love of beauty which he has kindled? Who shall exclude the bulk of mankind from that rich heritage of noble thoughts, which has been bequeathed, with no restrictions, to the whole human family?

The practical working of this part of education will have many difficulties; but none which enlightened observation must not ultimately overcome. A taste for poetry, of course, can only be awakened in a child by a mature mind which possesses it. Simple and progressive pieces, chiefly narrative, containing natural sentiments, should be presented as a pleasure and a reward. Selections might be made from Goldsmith, Cowper, Scott, Mary Howitt, and others. With constant care to avoid disgust by too long continuance, by unintelligibility, or by exciting the associations of a task, the child would feel poetry an enjoyment, and his powers of appreciation would gradually unfold themselves. The use of tales about fairies, genii, and other supernaturalisms, or of juvenile novels in childhood,—their applicability to individual characters—the means of cherishing a love of the beautiful in art and in nature—in a word, the culture of the imagination is a deeply interesting and almost untrodden field of investigation; but the present purpose does not require the further prosecution of the topic.

MORAL EDUCATION.

The human body may attain its noblest perfection of health and strength—the observation may be acute—the intellect profound—the imagination rich; and yet these varied and glorious powers be turned to evil. Strength may support tyranny, acuteness and depth raise up obstacles to truth, and imagination spend its gorgeous eloquence in the service of the basest vices. The work is incomplete if the moral nature remains uncultivated. Physical and intellectual education aim at the perfection of the instruments, which may become splendid implements of evil if moral education does not succeed in regulating the power which is to use them.

When the child is hanging at his mother's breast his moral education is going on. His impulses are growing into those habits of action which will constitute his moral character. His pleasures come from his mother, and his pains are relieved by her. His little heart is drawn towards her with the first movements of affection. By her, and at this early period, the foundation of moral education ought to be laid. His dawning feelings should be watched over by a patient and thinking love. His affection for his mother should be gently led to embrace other beings, and raised reverently to God, as the cause of all his happiness, and the living Father of all.

It would be idle to expect, however, in the present state of society, that the mother's precious opportunities should be generally made use of. Many minds must bestow their energies upon education before mothers can be brought to feel their most important duties, or become capable of discharging them. Meanwhile, the practical course is to consider what can be done for moral education by the professional educator.

In the first place, he must seek to supply the omissions of the mother. Having obtained as much power as possible over the pains and pleasures of the child, he must use it to obtain the child's affection. Nothing but real fondness will do this. The teacher should struggle to have a mother's sympathy with the pains and pleasures of the child, and aim at its utmost present happiness consistent with its future good. Real affection, which will manifest itself not merely in action, but in every look and tone, will not fail to meet a return. The human heart, and particularly the child's heart, "leaps kindly back to kindness." By the love thus excited the moral character must be unfolded.

The affection of the child soon shows itself in little acts of kindness to those whom it loves. Every such act should be acknowledged, not with praise, but with affection in return, showing itself in its natural language of looks and caresses. Nothing is too trifling to deserve notice. The first buddings of the infant feelings must be feeble, and a slight chill may wither or destroy them.

Only by the most delicate and assiduous cultivation can they be reared up to their full vigor and beauty. When a child offers some little gift, great to him, and which he thinks must be equally pleasurable to us, if we slight or neglect it, he is hurt and confused. The good impulse is disappointed, and therefore weakened. If we cause him to feel that he can not make us happy, he will cease to make the attempt; and so love perishes in his heart. We should attend to every act of kindness, think of it as it is in his thoughts, and respond to the feelings which prompted it. We must, if possible, not let one of these precious impulses be wasted, but so treat them as to encourage a repetition, until they acquire the strength and permanence of habit.

If we select the moments when a child is enjoying some particular pleasure, to point out to him how others may be made to enjoy pleasure also, his sympathy will be excited, and his efforts prompted to communicate happiness. His attention may easily be drawn to the symptoms of suffering in others, and his natural impulse will be to relieve it. We must be careful, however, not to excite his feelings of compassion, except where he can do something to alleviate the pain which calls them forth. When his good impulses are watched, and his little acts of kindness receive the sympathy which is their due, the kind dispositions will be strengthened into habits. He will find it a delight of a very exquisite kind to communicate happiness to others. He will find additional satisfaction in the increased kindness and esteem of those about him, and he will find his own little pleasures made doubly sweet by being enjoyed along with companions.

But RELIGION ought to be the basis of education, according to often repeated writings and declamations. The assertion is true. Christianity furnishes the true basis for raising up character; but the foundation must be laid in a very different manner from that which is commonly practiced.

In nothing is more ignorance of the nature of the human constitution shown, than in the modes by which it is attempted to implant religion in the young mind. In no other part of education (where almost all has been empiricism and practical denial of the existence of mental laws) has there been so resolute a disregard of the dictates of common sense; and the general cowardice of opinion on such matters has tended to perpetuate absurdities in defiance of repeated exposure. It must be admitted that to love God and our fellow-men is the great law of Christianity. It is not enough that these principles should be mere conclusions of the intellect, still less that they should dwell only in external profession. They should have possession of the innermost stronghold of man's heart. They should enter into his home of familiar and cherished feelings, and be blended with his ruling motives, that they may have power to inspire him with allegiance to the law of duty in the most trying contingencies, and to uphold him in the shipwreck of earth's hopes and happiness.

Now if the love of God, including, as it must, the steadfast faith in the tendency of his works to good, is to be the great central reality of human existence, how may we lay the foundation for it in the mind of the child? By the constitution of his nature he loves those things which excite agreeable feelings, and dislikes their opposites. Things kind, beautiful, and harmonious, are loveable; things cruel, severe, discordant, tedious, are fearful and hateful. If, therefore, we begin to lead a child to God, by teaching creeds or catechisms beyond his comprehension, or by causing him to read and repeat Scripture, before it can excite ideas, we do indeed manifold mischief, but we do nothing to excite affection. We present no images of beauty and love to fill his heart with delight, and we leave no impression but one of tedium from listening to or repeating unintelligible sounds. If, however, we do not content ourselves with such mindless repetition, but succeed in communicating distinct impressions, not of the merciful and loving Father, the Author of the infinite variety of our happy feeling, and of the wondrous beauty with which creation teems, but of the Avenger and terrible Judge, who will inflict everlasting torture on transgressors,—then we not merely fail to excite love to God, but lay a lasting foundation for feelings which, as long as they exist, render that love impossible. If "perfect love casteth out fear," it is because these feelings are mutually destructive. Terror is opposed to love. It is allied to hate, and wants only courage to show abhorrence. If we make the idea of God terrible on the impressible and retentive mind of childhood, religion will become a painful weight, which ordinary minds will escape from when they can—which the more feeble (often, like Cowper, the most finely organized of our race) will sink under—but which the vigorous few will, at maturity, fling boldly off, incurring, as the cost of their mental freedom, whatever injury to their moral nature may follow from the loss of their early faith.

Infinite, therefore, is the mischief of disregarding the operation of the laws, according to which the Author of nature has made our feelings to grow up; and incalculable would be the good of humbly following these laws, in rearing up the religious being of the child. By the delight which he has in loving human beings, his mind may be raised in affection to God. The reality of human love is the germ of that deeper, purer love, or rather loving veneration, with which it is the highest characteristic of the human mind to regard the Deity. The moments of enjoyment, in which the little heart is full of gratitude,—of vague, indistinct, but loving impulses,—should be seized to give the idea of the great cause from which its happiness springs. The idea should be associated with every thing that is pleasant and beautiful, and invested with the parental character, to which the love of human parents can be extended. We shall thus make the love of God a reality. If we continue to link it more and more closely with whatever is dearest, by systematically calling it forth, in conjunction with the operation of all faculties, and by making it enter into all enjoyments, it would acquire that mastery over the character which our present ignorant and neglectful treatment of children insures to the lower passions.

Whatever is beautiful or noble in conduct requires only to be presented to the young mind to excite its sympathy and admiration. The New Testament, properly used, is the best of all books for a child, as well as for a man. Its stories, so simple and beautiful, are exactly fitted to attract his attention, and supply his imagination and moral feelings with the food proper for each. Used with a constant regard to its effect upon his thoughts, so as to stimulate his mental activity and give it a right direction, it must be a grand instrument of moral and religious education, even in their very early stages. The deeds of great men—of those who have acted and suffered in all ages for the benefit of their fellow-creatures—will likewise have immense power. The histories of the Oberlins, the Pestalozzis, the Howards, and the Clarksons, the true heroes of our race, are the best commentaries on the Christian Scriptures. These chosen missionaries of God have left no richer heritage behind them than the unconquerable and self-sacrificing zeal for human improvement, which their example will inspire in generation after generation.

But, while we should commence the child's moral education by surrounding him with all influences of love and happiness, and lay the foundation of religion deep in his nature, by associating its primary ideas with what is most loved, it does not follow that we should withhold all knowledge of God's severer dispensations. The great law of education, as of all science, is Truth. We must lead the child to know things as they are, and, therefore, he must know what is terrible in appearance, as well as what is kind in God's dealings with mankind. But if there be some aspects of the providential dispensations so awful that the firmest faith can not look upon them with a steady eye, of how much consequence is it that the feeble and susceptible mind of childhood should be preoccupied with ideas which give it strength while they excite its love, before it is acquainted with those that are fearful. The first feelings color the after-life. When a child's first impressions of the Divine Being represent him as a loving father, and when these have been confirmed by repetition, we may gradually show to the opening reason that it is sometimes the part of a father to chasten those whom he loves. As the child's faculties ripen, we may lead him more and more to understand the wholesomeness to the moral being of many of the miseries and misfortunes of life, until he is left at maturity in the best plight that the care and culture of others can leave him, to combat the temptations of the world, and struggle with the awful mystery of evil. Thus by acting on the mind according to the laws of its moral development, we might insure that whatever peculiar doctrines the individual afterwards took up, the great moral principles of Christianity would have taken root in the depths of his nature, and would be interwoven with his earliest prejudices. The spirit of love and hope, and faith in good, would remain unshaken by calamities, shedding perpetual light on the dark and thorny path of life, revealing in the present evil the future good, and clothing the changeful incidents of this shifting scene with the hues and harmonies of a better existence. We can, indeed, scarcely conceive the purity, the self-denial, and the power, that might be given to the human character by systematic development. Recollecting how the finest minds have had to struggle with bad passions strengthened before the maturity of reason, and how much power has been expended in those internal strivings, who shall set limits to the moral force which might be attained by one trained from the first to combat and keep down its selfish impulses? What mighty object for the regeneration of mankind might not be accomplished by a mind impelled from the outset in one direction, and instead of working with what energy remains after its self-conflicts and dubious wanderings in speculations darkened by passion, directing its full unwasted endowment of WILL against external obstacles?

Veracity—truthfulness in thought, word, and deed—is a first principle of morals. It would almost seem as if we need not teach children truthfulness, provided only we could avoid teaching them falsehood. The child's impulse is unreservedly to believe and to speak the truth. We teach him doubt and falsehood. We teach him doubt by repeatedly deceiving him. We teach him falsehood by our own example, and by making it easier for him to say what is false than what is true. That truth is the natural impulse of the mind, is manifest from the slightest consideration of the laws of its development. The ideas of the objects or events which have had words associated with them (*i. e.*, which the child has learned to speak of) invariably call up in his mind those words and no other. If the child is questioned about any particular occurrence, the words which describe what he thinks to have taken place are precisely those which present themselves. The ideas in his mind call up the words which have been associated with them, and it requires an effort to reject these, and call up others expressing something which did not take place. This effort the child makes only from a motive, and after he has seen it made by others. We use words to him expressing what he discovers to be contrary to the fact. We parry some inconvenient query by an invention; or we attempt to quiet him by threatening something frightful, which does not come. He witnesses falsehood in many of the daily transactions of life. Thus the natural association between words and the things they represent is broken. He soon learns the convenience of falsehood. He is questioned as to some little mischief, which he, without suspicion or hesitation, confesses; and he is punished. He sees a servant or a play-fellow escape by denial. He associates punishment with confession, and impunity with falsehood.

We must take care of this. Our intercourse with children, and, if only for their sakes, with others, should be marked by perfect truthfulness. It will preserve the confidence of the child, which is one of the most powerful, nay, indispensable, instruments for his improvement. His own veracity we must preserve at all events. Full, frank confession should always obtain its reward of approbation, even if it does not wholly remove the displeasure at what has been done wrong. This fearless spirit of truth, so beautiful in childhood, and the companion of all noble virtues in mature life, requires only not to be withered in its first shoots by severe rebuke, or cold displeasure. Severity is one of the chief causes of falsehood. It excites terror, and terror seeks refuge in deceit. Fear will oppose falsehood and cunning to the force with which it can not openly contend. The acuteness of the mind is tasked to devise the means of successful duplicity, and its beautiful structure runs out into a distorted development, which future training can do but little to alter. We must preserve, therefore, in our own affairs, a supreme regard to truth. We should hold it up as a glorious principle worth suffering for, and show our warm admiration for those men who in various ages have chosen neglect and poverty and death for truth's sake.

It would, perhaps, be generally admitted that, upon these great principles of love to God and to man, and perfect truthfulness, (if the two former do not include the latter,) we ought to shape the moral being. This would seem less difficult if the mind were, as Locke supposed, like a sheet of white paper on which we might inscribe what characters we pleased. Our task is very different when we know that it is a germ with distinct tendencies folded up within it, and that, although we may make it flourish or decay, the form which it will take is not what we might arbitrarily determine, but one mainly depending on its own internal forces, and which can be only modified by the treatment it receives from us. We are not, then, to expect that by mere appeals to the child's capacity for loving, and his impulse to truth, he can be made loving and truthful; these feelings are obstructed and modified by other powerful impulses, which show themselves at the earliest period of his being. Such are the animal appetites; irascibility, or the impulse to anger; fear; love of distinction or attention;—these impulses are perpetually crossing the more elevated ones;

and by one or other the character is borne along. The main difficulty in moral education is the subjection of these impulses (their suppression being neither possible nor desirable) to the higher feelings. And here, as elsewhere, we must be guided by the laws according to which these passions are strengthened in the mind.

The appetites necessary for the preservation of our physical frame are felt at the earliest period of life—hunger and thirst are among the first sensations of the infant. They are, for a long time, the strongest and most constantly recurring of all impulses. This arises, necessarily, from the constitution of the human being, which requires that its physical powers should be the earliest developed, afterwards its observational and intellectual, and lastly its moral faculties. Hence it happens that the impulses for the satisfaction of those wants, which we have in common with animals, are confirmed by repetition into *habits* long before the higher principles of our nature. We can not alter this; and our business is, first, to avoid any more excitement of these appetites than is necessary for the fulfillment of their functions; secondly, to prevent them, as far as possible, from coming into collision with the higher impulses of justice, kindness, generosity; and lastly, when such collisions can not be prevented, to strengthen the child's better nature to deny the appetite.

In the first place, we must avoid all undue excitement of the appetites. Children are often treated as if eating and drinking were their only pleasures. They are made the great rewards,—the motives of action. "Learn your lesson and I will give you a sugar-plum." "Be good boys, tell the truth, and you shall have a peach after dinner." Sugar-plums and peaches are made to sweeten the bitters of intellectual exertion and moral conduct. By exciting the imagination to work upon the appetites, we open an indefinite field for their extension, and we subject to them the intellectual and moral being. The pleasures of eating and drinking fill the thoughts, and ingenuity is tasked to obtain them. The character is borne onward by one impulse, acquiring intensity by daily gratification, until it settles into that most debasing form of selfishness in which the appetite is made a god; all affections, charities, human feelings, are sacrificed at its shrine, and whatever power of intellect or graces of imagination linger serve only to decorate its altar.

The appetites of children are unnaturally excited when they see us make the gratification of our own subjects of conversation and anxiety. To save *them* from the mischiefs of inordinate appetite, we must be simple and moderate ourselves. We must show that we regard eating for its use; that it occupies little of our attention, and forms no part of our favorite enjoyments. Undue excitement may also be avoided by giving children their meals with perfect regularity, so that the appetites may be habituated to arise at fixed times, and at no others. Nor should meals ever be made use of for the purposes of reward or punishment. Either will give them a mischievous importance, and we should avoid whatever makes them a subject of attention until they arrive. Eating and drinking will, under any circumstances, be positive and very vivid pleasures, and therefore must be made subservient to moral education. Meals should, wherever it is possible, be taken by several children together, and without allowing discussion as to rights or quantity, the strictest justice of distribution should be observed. Each child should have his attention called to the gratification of his companions, and he should be encouraged to contribute to their enjoyment. Many beautiful impulses of generosity, and of that sympathy which is the foundation of politeness, would be observed in such a group, where nature had not been corrupted by unnatural stimulants. The pleasure of society, and of communicating enjoyment, would soon be felt more vividly than the mere gratification of appetite. Dinners would come to be regarded as dull and cheerless without the circle of happy faces; and thoughts of pleasures of the palate would be clustered round and interwoven with ideas of similar gratification in others. Many a warm and benevolent heart has been first moved to its good work by feelings which, if analyzed, would present, simply, a deep and strong conception of the physical wants of others.

We may thus do much to prevent the clashing of appetites with higher impulses. If a child is debarred from the gratification of his natural appetite, he will use any means in his power to obtain the requisite satisfaction. His appetite is a powerful impulse growing continually more urgent. If he can set it at rest by falsehood or theft, he is certain, after more or less hesitation, to do so. The principles of truth and justice, in a child of the best organization, are feebler than the principle of appetite; and where we compel a collision in which these forces are left to their own unaided strength, the appetite must prevail. Whatever the Spartan discipline might have been able to effect in more advanced youth, such self-command as would maintain truth and justice against cravings of a growing appetite is not possible in childhood.

The general rule, therefore, should be to avoid such collisions. But it is necessary that the man should be able to control his appetites, and, therefore, the child must attempt it. The early strength of these impulses is probably not more necessary for the preservation of our physical frame, than for our moral probation and advancement. We must begin with the slightest trials. If the child's attention has been awakened to the pleasure or pain of others, he will often be disposed to give up a pleasure in order to relieve pain, or to make another happy. All such impulses and acts should receive their due reward of affectionate encouragement. He should be made to feel that such things, above all others, win for him our esteem; and his own feeling will teach him that self-denial has its reward. His imagination should be excited by brief and vivid anecdotes of those who have given up their pleasure to benefit mankind; but particularly of Him so humble and so gentle, the friend of little children, and so like one that little children would love; who gave up all for the good of men; and rejecting the bright road of ambition and of royal power, took up the bitter and humiliating cross. But we must guard against any unnatural forcing. We must beware of exciting a false and calculating benevolence. Every act of kindness in the child should be followed by its precise natural consequences, both painful and pleasant. All education ought to lead the mind to a more perfect acquaintance with the realities of nature and society—the real properties of things, the real consequences of actions. If a child has willingly sacrificed his own enjoyment for another, he must suffer the loss, and find his reward in the pleasure of doing the kindness and of seeing the happiness he produces. But if we, as a reward for his benevolence, pamper the appetite which he has denied—if we restore the apple or orange which he has given up that he might bestow a penny in charity, we do much to destroy the good of his action and to teach him the trick of hypocrisy. On the next occasion he will expect his loss to be made good, and he will readily please his teacher, or his mama, by benevolence which costs him nothing. If we would avoid this, we must be content to see the power of self-control at first very feeble. By apportioning its trials to its strength, it will grow until the enlightenment of the intellect and the increased appreciation of enjoyments other than sensual confirm it into a ruling principle of action.

Passing over appetites, such as that for intoxicating liquors, which may be called artificial, since they are acquired, and which spring only from that general desire of excitement which a good education would otherwise satisfy, it seems not unsuitable, in this place, to refer to another powerful animal impulse, more properly a characteristic of mature life, but which requires much care in the management of the ideas connected with it at an earlier period than is commonly supposed. The impulse and ideas of sex form so essential part of human nature, which, whether it be attended to or neglected, will be sure to develop itself. There is a miserably false delicacy in parents and teachers which prevents them from communicating with children on this subject. Natural inquiries are parried and baffled, or answered with falsehood, by those who might state the truth with perfect purity and safety; and in consequence, the ideas which can not be excluded, are obtained through channels which convey corruption along with the information. The mischiefs of this course are fearful. The matters which are so carefully avoided by instructors and parents, are freely talked over and joked about by servants and elder playfellows. Unspeakable evils to mind and body are the consequence. The instructor, or the parent, must often know what is going forward; but he willfully shuts his eyes to what seems irremediable; yet, when the son, or pupil, becomes openly profligate, the guardian of his youth thinks himself only unfortunate, as if it was not the natural and necessary consequence of his own criminal neglect. There is no part of education which has been not merely so much neglected, but so resolutely avoided, as this; and hence, there is no one source from which a deeper and broader current of vice and misery flows through society. The destructive effects of that perpetual movement under the surface, which the decent hypocrisies of society keep out of view, exceed infinitely in amount its more public and glaring consequences. But even these latter—embodied, as it were, in one wretched class, living examples of physical and mental ruin—are so appalling, that society could receive no greater blessing, than some purer and more enlightened educational management which would stop them at the source.

This wants simply that the difficulty shall be fairly grappled with, and that instructors shall not willfully surrender any part of the confidence of their pupils, by want of frankness upon matters which others, with different feelings, will be found ready to discuss. They must speak unreservedly, seriously, and with perfect purity of thought, so as to keep away the piquant and attractive associations of secrecy and jocularity. The physical and moral bearings of the subject should be fully explained: and thus, by ideas addressed to the reason, while the feelings and imagination are at rest, we may plant the only real safeguard of purity in the breast. Minds, whose natural curiosity is thus satisfied, without any prurient excitement of imagination, and who have received through the intellect just notions of the moral and physical evils of unlawful indulgence, would, from reason and taste alike, repel the communications of profligate companions.

In the management of children at the earliest period of life, we have to contend with an irritability which is then the necessary and useful attendant of their fragile structure and helpless condition; but which, with a little neglect in childhood, will grow into an uncontrollable bad temper in mature life. The cries of an infant are the language of nature, given to supply the place of the yet impossible words, in communicating its wants to its protectors. Its first cries are from pain of some kind. The moment it is relieved they cease. When the cries for assistance are disregarded or rudely repressed, the first feeling of anger arises at the disappointment of the expected relief. The cries are increased with more bitterness and intensity, until they are perhaps hushed by terror or physical exhaustion. If the first attendant of an infant be herself ill-tempered, she can hardly fail to make the child so. Her changeful moods, her fondling and harshness, will perpetually disappoint his expectations. The occasions of ill-humor will be frequent; and his ill-humor, being troublesome, is likely to excite hers. Thus his outbreaks will continually call down the very treatment most likely to confirm them into habits. The proper management of the temper requires that the child should be surrounded from the first by a steady and enlightened affection. The first movements of its irritable nature require all the softness and patience of a mother. The occasions of irritability should, as far as possible, be foreseen and avoided. Clothes too tight, or not sufficiently warm; unnecessary dressings and undressings—these, and a hundred apparent trifles, which might be prevented, are to the child pain, and nothing more. When pain does exist from any cause, it should be at once attended to, promptly relieved, and the irritation set at rest, by affectionate soothing. Every instant that irritation, arising *from a real cause*, is suffered to continue, tends to fix it in the character. This, however, is never likely where there is affection acting upon principle. The first gleams of thought in the child will check his disposition to be angry with those who love him. As he grows, the operation of a uniform system of treatment will teach him to regulate his expectations of the future. Indulgence, however, has its peculiar danger. When the cries of the infant procure relief from pain, crying becomes associated with the satisfaction of its wants, and is resorted to when there is no pain, for the gratification of some whim, such as to ill-managed children are occurring incessantly. If this be given way to, the association is confirmed, and crying becomes the regular mode of obtaining what is desired. It is found to be an instrument of power, and it is used tyrannically. The mother and the household are subjected to no easy yoke. In this manner, unwise affection is as likely to spoil the temper as capricious severity. We must avoid both. A practised eye can distinguish between the cry which springs from real pain, and the mechanical imitation of it which is used for the gratification of a whim. Pain should be affectionately attended to; but a fit of crying for a plaything or a sweetmeat should never obtain the least satisfaction. If it is found useless, it will soon be discontinued, and cheerfulness and good humor, as more effectual means of gratification, will become the habits. Before we reach this point, we may have to witness some bursts of temper, and no little violent sobbing; but these will rapidly disappear. We need not fear the growth of unkind feelings in the child's mind from such treatment. He will soon feel the real affection which dictates it, and which he feels in so many other ways. His sagacity, so acute in all that relates to himself, will discover that there is a real anxiety to make him happy. This will be certain to call forth the best feelings of his nature; and the fixed system by which he finds himself governed, assuming the character of indispensable necessity, will prevent those innumerable contests and uncertainties which try the temper of children beyond their power of control.

Closely connected with the foregoing is the working of another principle, which shows itself at a very early period. Almost as early as we can examine, we trace a remarkable difference between children in respect to firmness or flexibility of character. Some are soft and impressible as wax; others evince a stubborn tenacity of their ideas and purposes, which the whole force of authority often contends with in vain. Ordinary people, disliking trouble, think the former are exactly what children ought to be, and augur the happiest results from their pliancy and docility. The others, who are often the choice spirits of the earth, the men of original character, with force of will to think and do, are set down as unmanageable, wayward, good for no useful purpose, and they labor under the stigma, until circumstances bring them to the work they are destined for, when the guardians of their infancy tardily and with difficulty recognize their powers. Many a defect and infirmity do such men carry to their high functions, which might have been prevented by a little more knowledge of human character in their instructors. Many a distortion of thought or feeling remains through life, from the injudicious opposition, reproof, or contempt, to which their misunderstood peculiarities exposed them.

The child, however, must learn obedience. The mature man, in the vigor of body and intellect, must know how to obey; for the feeble frame and imperfect intelligence of the child, it is absolutely indispensable. We must begin from the first. Real affection, working through an enlightened judgment, will secure implicit obedience, and nothing else will. A child soon learns to submit to inevitable necessity. He may quarrel with the stone or the tree which impedes his progress, but soon gives over when he finds that his cries or his struggles make no change. Our resistance to him when he is wrong should bear the appearance of the same inevitable necessity. It, and indeed our whole conduct, should be as uniform and consistent as the laws of nature, or as near to this as our imperfect natures can carry it. No tears, or cries, or struggles, should move us. Without the slightest variation of temper, we must gently but inflexibly refuse to do anything for the gratification of a wrong impulse. Yielding to urgency in a single instance may overthrow the labor of months in the formation of the habit. Authority exercised in this manner will soon be submitted to without a murmur. The kind caress upon his submission, and the good consequences of obedience to the child's own happiness, which he can often perceive, will soon make ready submission a pleasanter course than obstinate entreaty, or sullenness at refusal.

Besides learning to submit quietly to our refusal of improper gratifications, he must acquire the habit of obedience to positive commands. With many children obedience will be a matter of course, or will become so with little trouble; with one of firmer texture we must proceed cautiously. We should begin, as Miss Edgeworth recommends,* with making him absolutely do what we desire, which must, therefore, be something that we can make him do, such as taking him to bed at a particular hour. When this has become, by frequent repetition, fixed on his mind as a thing which must be done, we may ingraft upon the habit so formed the additional one of obedience to command. In all this, the look and

* See Practical Education, Vol. I., p. 150 8vo. 1811.

tone of true affection will have infinite power. Obedience will seem to the child a necessary result of his affection for his teacher; and so it will be a joyful, eager obedience, springing from the heart and a blessing to both.

To make the obedience most complete and most healthful for the moral nature of the child, our commands, our whole system of conduct, should, if possible, present, as before stated, the uniformity and consistency of the laws of nature. There should be no bursts of extravagant kindness and fondling, to be followed by fits of cold neglect; no overweening attention to the little prattler to-day, and ill-tempered rejection of his playfulness to-morrow; no promises made incautiously at night, to be laughed away or reluctantly performed in the morning; no menaces uttered in passion and forgotten when the gust has blown over. Promises should be performed in the spirit and to the letter; threats, if we use them, executed with absolute exactness. There should be a total absence of caprice or variableness. The child should know what he has to expect—what consequences will be sure to follow certain acts. This smooth, fixed, harmonious revolution of the machinery about him, will prevent the thought of disobedience, and, at the same time, the obedience which it will tend to form will not break his spirit, or impair his energy. Capricious, varying commands, unexpected thwartings, bring about those unhappy contests with positive children, by which they are either fixed in a sullen, incurable doggedness, or forcibly reduced to submission, at the cost of that invaluable tenacity of purpose, which is the prime element of success, either in action or speculation. It is a miserable mistake that we must "break a child's will," as the first step in education. On the contrary, we should, by all means, strengthen it, but habituate it to the control of the reason and the higher feelings. If, by a severe and capricious treatment, we could succeed in crushing that original tendency in the mind to abide by its purposes, to encounter opposition for their sake, and to cling to them in proportion to the force brought against them, what would remain? Of what avail would it be that a mind thus emasculated was molded into the form of virtue—that it had a knowledge of science—a love of justice—a sense of harmony and beauty? What would be the security for the continuance of such qualities, rooted in mere obedience and perhaps imitation, where the center of nourishment and self-support was gone? Why should not external influence, like that which gave them life, destroy them? What likelihood of their withstanding the gusts of opinion sweeping hither and thither over the face of society? What possible destiny, beyond mere passive contemplation, could they fulfill in a world of earnest and vigorous action? No. We can not spare a jot of that self-sustaining, self-impelling power from the mind. In the great benefactors of our race it has shone most conspicuously, and even in ordinary life it is an essential condition of a steady and prosperous career.

We must endeavor, then, to secure obedience through the affections, and by a treatment from the first so uniform, that it will enter into and modify the child's ideas and expectations, as they are modified by the regular succession of cause and effect in the natural world. Further, by giving perfect freedom when it is possible, and by encouraging children to work out and act upon their own conclusions, we must cultivate self-reliance and decision of character. This, like all superior qualities, is not to be, as it were, stuck into the mind from without, but unfolded from the working of its own faculties. The noble plant must acquire its beauty and its strength from those internal forces which God has given. The skillful cultivator takes for his guidance the hints of Nature herself—now aiding her efforts by a sprinkling of encouragement, and now by the removal of some external obstacle which impedes her development.

Another original impulse necessary for the preservation of the human being, but without careful management a fruitful source of unhappiness, is fear or terror. What has once given a child pain is dreaded; the idea of the pain is called up by the sight of the object. New and unusual objects are frequently causes of pain to children; and any new or unusual object becomes invested with associations of pain, and produces terror. This feeling is so easily excited in children, and it so conveniently puts to flight previous feelings of petulance, or of anxiety to have something inconvenient, that it is almost constantly abused. It is the regular resource of laziness, ignorance, and ill-temper, in attendants. The child is terrified into doing, or terrified from doing, whatever his nurse, or instructor, feel inconvenient or otherwise. According to the general law, the feeling thus frequently exercised is strengthened, and the mind, of course, permanently enfeebled. A thousand false and fantastic terrors are thus implanted in the minds of children,—dark clouds that hover continually in view through life, and darken the sunshine of many otherwise happy hours. The energy of the mind is seriously impaired. The imagination, exercised by frequent fears, is perpetually suggesting dangers in any deviation from the beaten track of habit, and even in the most ordinary circumstances. The free, courageous spirit of investigation, the great spring of intellectual advancement, is weakened, if not altogether destroyed.

The education of this impulse is mismanaged in various ways—by an absolutely reckless and wanton excitement of the feeling in children—by a capricious severity, which, by its uncertainty, keeps terror almost constantly alive, and uses it as an instrument to affect its purposes—by an extreme and morbid caution, which fears to let children do any thing for themselves, lest they may receive some trifling hurt or damage; clothes the commonest acts and objects with terrors; and, by stopping examination, hinders the acquirement of the knowledge and habits which are a better safeguard against danger than a thousand anxious parents or instructors.

With respect to the first—the excitement of children's fears without a distinct purpose, or for amusement—it scarcely deserves remark. It is so gratuitously mischievous, such a wicked sporting with the lifelong happiness of human beings, that no mind of the least sense or good feeling can hesitate to condemn it. With respect to the second—the management of children by their terrors, whether by the nurse with her threats of monsters and ghosts, or the instructor with his corporeal and other punishments—it has already been seen how obedience may be attained in a better way. It is enough here to remark, that an education of terror, although it may partially succeed in causing intellectual acquirement, must be morally destructive. It will instill cunning and falsehood, the vices of the slave. Its most favorable results will be the production of men, clever, smooth, obedient instruments, capable, when the pressure of authority is removed, of good or evil, but with a considerable bias towards the latter. In an atmosphere of terror the nobler impulses wither and die, or if by unusual strength they survive, their growth will catch some distortion from the blighting process they have gone through.

The remaining cause by which children are made feeble and cowardly, is the feverish anxiety about their safety in those who have them in charge. When extreme affection, as it frequently happens, takes this form, it is scarcely less fatal to the best interests of its objects than injudicious severity. The little beings, full of joyous activity, moved by the healthful impulses of nature, with their senses all awake, surrounded by objects which are to them full of wonder and delight, are perpetually carrying on processes of education beyond the reach of human art to equal. Observation, abstraction, reasoning, invention, are doing their rapid work, while the young investigators are running in the way of innumerable dangers. The anxious parent is not content with this education of Nature's choosing, but must interpose her protection between the child and the knowledge, which, by the ordinance of Nature, every one must learn from his own experience. He must not go here, for fear of knocking his head against the table,—nor there, lest he may tumble over the footstool,—nor play with a glass, lest it may break and cut him,—nor approach the hot water, lest it may scald his fingers;—he must beware of the dog, because it may bite—of the cat, because it can scratch—and of fifty other things, frogs, mice, beetles, &c., for no reason but because his mother has an aversion to them. All these things the mother does her best to plant as objects of dread, and too often with success. Her incessant alarms are caught up by the child, and his terrors are perpetually excited. The feeling of fear acquires the rapidity and certainty of habit; the child becomes helpless, his active power almost paralyzed, and his powers of observation enfeebled by the spectres raised up in the way of their exercise. In his intercourse with others, his cowardice tempts to low tricks and base compliances, and he lives under the most wretched and agonizing slavery to his fears.

It is of immense importance that a child's physical courage should be strengthened, and that he should be trained to habits of steady circumspection and decision, in new or dangerous circumstances. We must preserve him from the contamination of groundless fears, as we would from a pestilence. Instead of perpetual injunction to avoid this or that, he should be allowed, as far as it can be done without serious danger, to obtain his knowledge of what things are safe, and what are hurtful for himself. His proceedings should be carefully superintended, but (for various reasons) his attention should be as little as possible drawn to the fact that he is watched. If he get a fall, or a wetting, or burn his finger, or draw a little blood, the pain will be worth innumerable injunctions to avoid similar dangers. The memory of it will be a sentinel which no accident will call away from his post. We should do nothing for the child which we can lead him to do for himself. We should lead him to examine new objects with his own senses. If any symptoms of fear present themselves, we should remove them by showing him the harmlessness of what he dreads. A little management will set groundless fears at rest. While the root is yet loose in the soil, it may be easily, and without injury, pulled up. The child's free course of experience will give him the blended habit of caution and confidence. No slavish apprehensions will mar his natural frankness. He will be guarded against real perils by habits of self-possession. Our explanations of the precise nature of danger, when there is any, will be thoughtfully attended to. Our warnings, when they are absolutely necessary, will have tenfold force, by not being wasted on frequent and frivolous occasions.

One other impulse of great importance in childhood, and of almost universal influence in mature life, deserves notice,—the desire of the favorable opinion of others, or of being the subject of attention. There is no question that this feeling shows itself in infancy. The power of praise and attention over a child is soon perceived, and it is, in most cases, made the mainspring of scholastic education. If we let other feelings grow up by neglect, we often deliberately encourage this, and make it the principal motive of action,—the basis of the moral character. We stimulate to intellectual labor, not by the purifying and ennobling pleasure of knowledge, but by adventitious rewards and distinctions. We hold up to youth wealth and high place as the chief goods, because they will secure the regard and respect of society. We show by our actions—always more effective than our precepts—that our master-feeling is the worship of respectability. It is worth considering whether this principle deserves the supremacy which is practically accorded to it, and if not, how it ought to be regulated by education.

A child is early plied with stimulants to its vanity. Its pretty face—its beautiful eyes—its agreeable prattle—its nice dress—its clever feats—are all loaded with encomiums. Schools take up the growing feeling, and strengthen it with prizes, honors, public declamations, and exhibitions, by which the young heart is swelled with vanity, and the craving for attention and praise made more voracious. The tendencies of home and society are, for the most part, to the aggravation of this sensitiveness to opinion. The plans of life are formed under its influence. It insinuates itself into every fibre of the moral being; and all faculties and feelings become subservient to its gratification. In public life it may communicate an immense energy, but such power can not be trusted. It will play courtier in the monarchy and demagogue in the republic. Its veering will be precisely regulated by the shifting winds of passion in the holders of power. Whatever be the existing evils of society, from a man whose master-passion this is, they are more likely to receive aggravation than check. The enlightenment of its ignorance, the destruction of popular fallacies, the upholding despised truths for a brighter day, must be accomplished by men who can bear neglect or unpopularity, from a deep conviction of truth, and a steadfast adherence to the lasting interests of mankind.

The effects of a slavish deference to opinion, upon individual happiness, are perhaps of more consequence, as they are more intimately felt, than those which society experiences from the influence of its leading minds. In private life, one whose education has made this feeling all-powerful has no peace. The free play of his affections, the sole sources of happiness, is controlled by incidents fixing his attention perpetually on himself. The grace of unconsciousness, the delight of self-abandonment, he can not know. Society has a thousand stings for his trembling sensitiveness;—fancied neglects, imagined contempts, possible absurdities, the success of rivals. Now and then an hour of triumph sets him ablaze, and whatever is best in his nature seems to flow out freely under the excitement; but when the temporary incentives are withdrawn, the return of daily life and its common duties contracts the expansion into the hard, cold selfishness, which is the basis of vanity.

Those who admit that the morality of Christ ought to form the basis of character, must feel bound, in education, to make this principle subject to others. Christianity requires that a far higher motive than the good opinion of men should be the mainspring of our actions. It was itself an insurrection against ancient and cherished prejudices. It admitted of no compromise; it imperatively demanded that the opinion of men should be set at nought; that contempt, calumny, injustice,—all the penalties of rebellion against established usages,—should be met and borne without repining, by the strength of that love for the erring children of the same common Father, which triumphed on the cross. The model of this high morality remains and will remain—ages may pass before society shall answer its lofty requirements; but unless we fling it aside and convert its shrine to some meaner worship, we can not deliberately disobey the ordinance to bring "little children" within the sanctuary.

We must, however, use the stimulus of praise in education, and obtain the command of the instrument, or others will seize it to thwart our purposes. We must praise, but praise sparingly, that it may be of value. A very little from those who give with judgment and exact justice will have great power. We should praise affectionately, that the gratification which it gives may be associated with the kind feelings. Our praise should be regulated by the nature of the action that calls it forth, and be always most warm for moral excellence. Here, as in all other treatment, the peculiarities of individual character must guide us; a touch is enough for the quick mettle of one child—much spurring will be required to remove the sluggishness of another. Prizes and distinctions—matters which provoke competition, and set in antagonism those between whom Christianity requires love—are mischievous. The winners and the losers are equally liable to injury. The pride of success may be as unchristian and as unfavorable to happiness, as the burning of envious disappointment.

The working of these various conflicting impulses, which seldom present themselves but in combination, makes soon apparent the presence of feelings to which we give the name of conscience, or the moral sense. Without entering into the controversy respecting their origin, whether they are instinctive impulses, or whether their gradual formation from simpler elements may be traced, it is enough for the present purpose that their existence, at a very early period of life, is admitted. They are real feelings; and, like other feelings, may be greatly modified by education. The contradictory forms in which they appear among different nations and different individuals has led to the denial of the reality of moral distinctions; but if the discrepancies do not warrant this conclusion, they at least establish the power of circumstances over the development of the feelings. We may enlist them in support of empty ceremonies and unintelligible creeds, or give their sanction to the hatreds of sect and party. No animosity—individual, sectarian, or national—should, either by direct precept or casual remark, receive such sanction. The great Christian principle of the brotherhood of men will tolerate no exception. Our aim should be to give depth and clearness to the moral emotions. The mind should be led to regard the moral qualities of actions, and to reason upon them. It should be taught to look back on what it has done; and, for the sake of methodizing its ideas, to record the results of its self-examination. The exercise of the moral sense will give it strength, and will constantly tend to harmonize the impulses with the moral judgments. The blending of the two would give the rectitude and steadiness of moral calculation to impulse; the passionate energy and beauty of impulse to morality. Instead of the unhappy conflict between liking and duty, which, when the passions are matured before the sense of right is awakened, often continues through life, wasting the internal force and producing vacillation, despondency, and innumerable failures, the mind would move in a direct line with the impetus of its utmost power,—its highest delight and its highest duty being one and the same.

These notices will be sufficient to indicate what is meant by moral education. It must be unnecessary to repeat, that the foregoing remarks are not meant to present any thing like a complete view or outline of education. If there were no other reasons against making such an attempt in this place, it would, in fact, be impossible from the state in which education at present exists. As an art, or body of rules founded on science, it is too imperfectly developed to admit of an outline being given. There are systems in actual operation distinguished by partial excellencies; valuable hints of physical, intellectual, and moral management, in various books; and the works of Hartley, Stewart, Brown, and Mill, contain expositions of the laws of mind very suggestive of the art that ought to be built upon them; but nowhere has this scattered knowledge been reduced to a system. Nor perhaps is the time come,—until the ground is more accurately marked by continued observation, and the materials collected by additional and better directed industry,—to set about raising the structure.

It is too true that education now realizes but little of the good which an examination of the principles on which it ought to proceed would lead us to hope for. Except the mechanical processes of reading and writing, the mass of society derives little from its *designed* education. The ignorance of the poorer classes is scarcely touched by the feeble educational machinery brought to bear against it. The children of the middle ranks acquire some small knowledge which is useful in their worldly callings; and the "educated classes" obtain a smattering of the dead languages, though most of them lose it within a few years by neglect. In every class there are individuals who, by their own energy, make considerable acquirements; but the effect of education is to be estimated by the condition of the majority subject to its influence. Tried by this test, existing education is all but universally inefficient. Real knowledge is not derived from schools or instructors, but from unaided observation both by boys and men; and their morals are as little affected by the dry precepts and empty routine which make up their religious education. Men's governing principles spring from their *undesigned* education; not from what has been *said to* them, but from what has been often unconsciously *done before* them, and from the workings of their own minds unsympathized with, and therefore unguided by their instructors. Hence, learned and studious men send forth pupils confirmed in vicious dispositions, because they do not see the powerful education received by boys from each other, which goes on under their own eyes. Innumerable are the abortive results of the most anxious efforts in education. Men, distinguished by every virtue, not seldom have the evening of their days imbittered by the ingratitude and profligacy of their offspring. It would seem, indeed, in most cases, a matter of chance whether children grow up dull or clear-headed; with good, or with evil dispositions; or, as if there were no fixed principles by which slow intellect might be unfolded, or man be led to love virtue rather than vice.

But the intellectual and moral nature of man is not an anomaly in a world of harmony and order. It is no shapeless and unintelligible chaos, where good and evil are in perpetual commotion, without object or law. It is a creation surpassing all others in the nicety of its adaptation to the circumstances in which it is placed; and possessing seeds which, under a right culture, would burst forth into forms of yet unimagined power and beauty. But education fails, miserably fails—it brings no germ of intellectual or moral greatness to maturity; and for this all-sufficient reason, that those to whom its business is intrusted are incompetent to the task; to the most arduous duties they bring the least qualifications. The highest interests are intrusted to the meanest hands. Society tolerates an unfitness in those who profess to form its young minds, which it would not endure in the lowest menial offices that minister to its material interests or enjoyments. For, if there be any act which, more than another, requires in those who practice it a high union of skill and character, that art, beyond a question, is education. In no department of exertion does success so absolutely depend on the personal qualifications of the workman. "As is the master, so is the school," says the Prussian maxim: a few words mineraled, as it were, with truth. The system is indeed truly important; but the main part of a system is, what is in the master's mind. The form—the external material adjuncts—of a system are of themselves nothing; its living spirit, that part of it which has got into the thoughts and feelings of him who is to work it, is everything.

The process of education, whether at home or in school, is perpetually going on; the instructor may guide but can not stop it. Whether he is attentive or neglectful, observation is at work, intellect is developing, character is forming, and all under the most powerful influences from him, whether for good or evil. What he says earnestly, and, above all, what he does, is graving itself on the tenacious memory of childhood. His inconsistencies, partialities, ill-temper, tyranny, selfishness, leave lasting traces. If his dispositions are unfavorable, no check from without can remedy the evil. Parents can control him little. They are managed through their prejudices at the expense of their children. A superior authority, with the most perfect machinery of inspection, will fail to get the work of good men performed by bad ones. Its laws will be no restraint on him to whom their execution is intrusted; its best systems fruitless, where they can not insure states of mind according with their spirit. The government of children must be a despotism, and it must have all the vices of a despotism, if we can not purify the depositaries of supreme power. But, if the instructor be one who is filled with a consciousness of his high duties, how mighty is his influence! He is the fountain of instruction, and the prime source of enjoyment to his pupils. Their little difficulties are brought to him, and in his solution rest. His casual remarks sink into their minds. His opinions on men and things make their way by the double force of authority and affection. His companionship, his sympathy, are above all things delightful. The imitative principle, so powerful in early life, is incessantly in action. The children are daily assimilating parts of his nature—making it one with their own. What an influence is his over their future destiny!

Education is, in truth, the first concern of society, and it ought to have the energies of society's best minds. The Athenians, who had glimpses of whatever was most glorious, did in this matter leave mankind a great example. Teaching was the honorable occupation of their greatest men. The brightest minds of Athenian Philosophy were the instructors of Athenian youth; so keenly was the truth felt, that the mature intelligence and moral power, acquired in the struggles of a distinguished life, could perform no higher function than that of rearing up the same precious fruits in the rising minds of the community.

PART II.

STUDIES AND CONDUCT.

STUDIES AND CONDUCT.

SUGGESTIONS BY MEN EMINENT IN LETTERS AND AFFAIRS.

SIR THOMAS WYATT TO HIS SON.

INASMUCH as now you are come to some years of understanding, and that you gather within yourself some fame of honesty, I thought that I should not lose my labour wholly, if now I did something advertise you to take the sure foundations and stablished opinions that leadeth to honesty.

And here, I call not honesty that men commonly call honesty, as reputation for riches, for authority, or some like thing; but that honesty, that I dare well say your grandfather had rather left to me than all the lands he did leave me,—that was, wisdom, gentleness, soberness, desire to do good, friendship to get the love of many, and truth above all the rest. A great part to have all these things, is to desire to have them. And although glory and honest name are not the very ends wherefore these things are to be followed, yet surely they must needs follow them, as light followeth the fire, though it were kindled for warmth. Out of these things the chiefest and infallible ground is the dread and reverence of God, whereupon shall ensue the eschewing of the contraries of these said virtues; that is to say, ignorance, unkindness, rashness, desire of harm, unquiet enmity, hatred, many and crafty falsehoods, the very root of all shame and dishonesty. I say, the only dread and reverence of God, that seeth all things, is the defence of the creeping in of all these mischiefs into you. And for my part, although I do well say there is no man that would wish his son better than I; yet, on my faith, I had rather have you lifeless, than subject to these vices. Think and imagine always that you are in presence of some honest men that you know; as Sir John Russell, your father-in-law, your uncle Parson, or some other such; and ye shall, if at any time ye find a pleasure in naughty touches, remember what shame it were before these men to do naughtily. And sure this imagination shall cause you to remember that the pleasure of a naughty deed is soon past, and the rebuke, shame, and the note thereof shall remain ever. Then, if these things ye take for vain imaginations, yet remember that it is certain, and no imagination, that ye are always in the presence and sight of God; and though you see Him not, so much is the reverence the more to be had, for that He seeth, and is not seen.

Men punish with shame as greatest punishment on earth—yea, greater than death; but His punishment is, first, the withdrawing of His favour and grace, and, in leaving His hand to rule the stern, to let the ship run without guide to its own destruction; and suffereth so the man that He forsaketh to run headlong, as subject to all mishaps, and at last, with shameful end, to everlasting shame and death. You may see continual examples both of one sort and of the other; and the better, if ye mark them well that yourself are come of; and consider well your good grandfather, what things there were in him, and his end. And they that knew him, noted him thus: first and chiefly, to have a great reverence of God, and good opinion of godly things. Next, that there was no man more pitiful; no man more true of his word; no man faster to his friends; no man diligenter or more circumspect, which thing, both the kings his masters noted in him greatly. And if these things, and especially the grace of God, that the fear of God always kept with him, had not been, the chances of this troublesome world that he was in had long ago overwhelmed him. This preserved him in prison from the hands of the tyrant,* that could find in his heart to see him racked; from two years' or more imprisonment in Scotland, in irons and stocks; from the danger of sudden changes and commotions divers, till that well-beloved of many, hated of none, in his fair age and good reputation, godly and christianly he went to Him that loved him, for that he always had Him in reverence. And of myself, I must be a near example unto you of my folly and nothingness, that hath, as I well observed, brought me into a thousand dangers and hazards, enmities, hatreds, prisonments, despites, and indignations; but that God hath of His goodness chastised me, and not cast me clean out of His favour; which thing I can impute to nothing but the goodness of my good father, that, I dare well say, purchased with continual request of God His grace towards me, more than I regarded or considered myself; and a little part to the small fear I had of God in the most of my rage, and the little delight that I had in mischief. You, therefore, if ye be sure and have God in your sleeve to call you to His grace at last, venture hardly by mine example upon naughty unthriftiness in trust of His goodness; and, besides the shame, I dare lay ten to one ye shall perish

* Richard the Third.

in the adventure; for trust me that my wish or desire of God for you shall not stand you in as much effect as I think my father's did for me. We are not all accepted of Him. Begin, therefore, betimes. Make God and goodness your foundations. Make your examples of wise and honest men; shoot at that mark; be no mocker—mocks follow them that delight therein. He shall be sure of shame that feeleth no grief in other men's shames. Have your friends in a reverence, and think unkindness to be the greatest offence, and least punished among men; but so much the more to be dreaded, for God is justiser upon that alone. Love well and agree with your wife; for where is noise and debate in the house, there is unquiet dwelling; and much more when it is in one bed. Frame well yourself to love and rule well and honestly your wife as your fellow, and she shall love and reverence you as her head. Such as you are to her, such shall she be unto you. Obey and reverence your father-in-law, as you would me; and remember that long life followeth them that reverence their fathers and elders; and the blessing of God, for good agreement between the wife and husband, is fruit of many children.

Read oft this my letter, and it shall be as though I had often written to you; and think that I have herein printed a fatherly affection to you. If I may see that I have not lost my pain, mine shall be the contentation, and youre the profit; and, upon condition that you follow my advertisement, I send you God's blessing and mine, and as well to come to honesty as to increase of years.

SIR HENRY SIDNEY TO HIS SON, PHILIP SIDNEY.*

I have received two letters from you, one written in Latin, the other in French, which I take in good part, and will you to exercise that practice of learning often; for that will stand you in most stead in that profession of life that you are born to live in. And since this is my first letter that ever I did write to you, I will not that it be all empty of some advices, which my natural care for you provoketh me to wish you to follow, as documents to you in this your tender age.

Let your first action be the lifting up of your mind to Almighty God, by hearty prayer; and feelingly digest the words you speak in prayer, with continual meditation, and thinking of Him to whom you pray, and of the matter for which you pray. And use this as an ordinary act, and at an ordinary hour; whereby the time itself

* Sir Philip Sidney, to whom this letter was addressed, was then twelve years of age, at school at Shrewsbury.

will put you in remembrance to do that which you are accustomed to do. In that time apply your study to such hours as your discreet master doth assign you, earnestly; and the time (I know) he will so limit, as shall be both sufficient for your learning, and safe for your health. And mark the sense and matter of all that you read, as well as the words. So shall you both enrich your tongue with words, and your wit with matter; and judgment will grow as years groweth in you. Be humble and obedient to your master; for unless you frame yourself to obey others, yea, and feel in yourself what obedience is, you shall never be able to teach others how to obey you. Be courteous of gesture, and affable to all men, with diversity of reverence, according to the dignity of the person. There is nothing that winneth so much, with so little cost. Use moderate diet, so as, after your meat, you may find your wit fresher, and not duller, and your body more lively, and not more heavy. Seldom drink wine, and yet sometimes do, lest being enforced to drink upon the sudden, you should find yourself inflamed. Use exercise of body, but such as is without peril of your joints or bones. It will increase your force, and enlarge your breath. Delight to be cleanly as well in all parts of your body as in your garments. It shall make you grateful in each company; and, otherwise, loathsome. Give yourself to be merry; for you degenerate from your father, if you find not yourself most able in will and body to do any thing when you be most merry; but let your mirth be ever void of all scurrility, and biting words to any man; for a wound given by a word is oftentimes harder to be cured, than that which is given with the sword. Be you rather a hearer and bearer away of other men's talk, than a beginner or procurer of speech; otherwise you shall be counted to delight to hear yourself speak. If you hear a wise sentence or an apt phrase, commit it to your memory, with respect of the circumstance when you shall speak it. Let never oath be heard to come out of your mouth, nor words of ribaldry; detest it in others, so shall custom make to yourself a law against it in yourself. Be modest in each assembly; and rather be rebuked of light fellows for a maiden-like shamefacedness, than of your sad friends for pert boldness. Think upon every word before you utter it; and remember how nature hath rampired up (as it were) the tongue with teeth, lips, yea, and hair without the lips, and all betokening reins, or bridles, for the loose use of that member. Above all things, tell no untruth—no, not in trifles. The custom of it is naughty; and let it not satisfy you, that for a time the hearers take it for a truth; for after it will be known as it is, to your shame;

for there can not be a greater reproach to a gentleman than to be accounted a liar. Study and endeavour yourself to be virtuously occupied. So shall you make such an habit of well-doing in you, that you shall not know how to do evil, though you would. Remember, my son, the noble blood you are descended of, by your mother's side; and think, that only by virtuous life and good action you may be an ornament to that illustrious family; and otherwise, through vice and sloth, you shall be counted *labes generis*, one of the greatest curses that can happen to man. Well, my little Philip, this is enough for me, and too much, I fear, for you. But if I shall find that this light meal of digestion nourish any thing the weak stomach of your young capacity, I will, as I find the same grow stronger, feed it with tougher food. Your loving father, so long as you live in the fear of God.

SIR THOMAS BODLEIGH TO FRANCIS BACON.

My Good Cousin,—According to your request in your letter (dated the 19th of Oct. at Orleans) I received here the 18th of Dec., I have sent you by your marchant 30*l.* sterling, for your present supply; and had sent you a greater sum, but that my extraordinary charge this year hath utterly unfurnished me. And now, cousin, though I will be no severe exacter of accounts, either of your money or of time, yet, for the love I bear you, I am very desirous both to satisfy myself and your friends, how you prosper in your travels, and how you find yourself bettered thereby, either in knowledge of God or of the world; the rather, because the days you have already spent abroad are now both sufficient to give you light how to fix yourself and end with counsel, and accordingly to shape your course constantly upon it. Besides, it is a vulgar scandal to travellers, that few return more religious than they went forth; wherein both my hope and request is to you, that your principal care be to hold your foundation, and to make no other use of informing yourself in the corruptions and superstitions of other nations, than only thereby to engage your own heart more firmly to the truth. You live, indeed, in a country of two several professions; and you shall return a novice, if you be not able to give an account of the ordinances, strength, and progress of each, in reputation and party, and how both are supported, balanced, and managed by the state, as being the contrary humours in the temper of predominacy, whereof the health or disease of that body doth consist. These things you will observe, not only as an Englishman, whom it may concern to know what interest his country may expect in the consciences of their neighbours;

but also as a Christian, to consider both the beauties and blemishes, the hopes and dangers, of the Church in all places. Now for the world, I know it too well to persuade you to dive into the practices thereof; rather stand upon your own guard against all that attempts you thereunto, or may practise upon you in your conscience, reputation, or your purse. Resolve no man is wise or safe but he that is honest; and let this persuasion turn your studies and observations from the compliment and impostures of the debased age, to more real grounds of wisdom, gathered out of the story of times past, and out of the government of the present state. Your guide to this is, the knowledge of the country and the people among whom you live; for the country, though you can not see all places, yet if, as you pass along, you inquire carefully, and further help yourself with books that are written of the cosmography of those parts, you shall sufficiently gather the strength, riches, traffic, havens, shipping, commodities, vent, and the wants and disadvantages of all places. Wherein, also, for your own good hereafter, and for your friends, it will be fit to note their buildings, furnitures, their entertainments; all their husbandry, and ingenious inventions in whatsoever concerneth either pleasure or profit.

For the people, your traffic among them, while you learn their language, will sufficiently instruct you in their habilities, dispositions, and humours, if you a little enlarge the privacy of your own nature, to seek acquaintance with the best sort of strangers, and restrain your affections and participation for your own countrymen of whatsoever condition. In the story of France, you have a large and pleasant field in three lines of their kings,—to observe their alliances and successions, their conquests, their wars, especially with us; their councils, their treaties; and all rules and examples of experience and wisdom, which may be lights and remembrances to you hereafter, to judge of all occurrents both at home and abroad.

Lastly, for the government: your end must not be, like an intelligencer, to spend all your time in fishing after the present news, humours, graces, or disgraces of court, which happily may change before you come home; but your better and more constant ground will be, to know the consanguinities, alliances, and estates of their princes; the proportion between the nobility and magistracy; the constitutions of their courts of justice; the state of their laws, as well for the making as the execution thereof; how the sovereignty of the king infuseth itself into all acts and ordinances; how many ways they lay impositions and taxations, and gather revenues to the crown; what be the liberties and servitudes of all degrees; what discipline and preparation for wars; what inventions for increase of traffic at home, for multiplying their commodities, encouraging arts, manufactures, or of worth in any kind; also what good establishment, to prevent the necessities and discontentment of people, to cut off suits at law, and duels, to suppress thieves, and all disorders.

To be short,—because my purpose is not to bring all your observations to heads, but only by these few to let you know what manner of return your friends expect from you,—let me, for all these and all the rest, give you this one note, which I desire you to observe as the counsel of a friend: not to spend your spirits, and the precious time of your travel, in a captious prejudice and censuring of all things, nor in an infectious collection of base vices and fashions of men and women, or general corruption of these times, which will be of use only among humorists, for jests and table-talk; but rather strain your wits and industry soundly to instruct yourself in all things between heaven and earth which may tend to virtue, wisdom, and honour, and which may make your life more profitable to your country, and yourself more comfortable to your friends, and acceptable to God. And, to conclude, let all these riches be treasured up, not only in your memory, where time may lessen your stock; but rather in good writings, and books of account, which will keep them safe for your use hereafter. And if in this time of your liberal traffic, you will give me an advertisement of your commodities in these kinds, I will make you as liberal a return from myself and your friends here as I shall be able. And so commending all your endeavours to Him that must either wither or prosper them, I very kindly bid you farewell.

LORD STRAFFORD TO HIS SON. (*Extracts.*)

My dearest Will,—Be careful to take the advice of those friends which are by me desired to advise you for your education. Serve God diligently morning and evening; and recommend yourself unto Him and have Him before your eyes in all your ways. Lose not the time of your quiet, but gather those seeds of virtue and knowledge which may be of use to yourself and comfort to your friends, for the rest of your life. Attend thereto with patience and refrain yourself from anger. Suffer not sorrow to cast you down, but with cheerfulness and good courage go on the race you are to run, in all sobriety and truth. In all your duties and devotions towards God, rather perform them joyfully than pensively, for God loves a cheerful giver. And God Almighty of His infinite goodness bless you and your children's children.—[*Written shortly before his execution.*]

SIR WILLIAM CECIL.—ADVICE TO HIS SON, ROBERT CECIL.

Sir William Cecil, for forty years Secretary of State under Queen Elizabeth, and raised to the peerage by the title of Baron of Burleigh, in 1571, was born at Bourn, in Lincolnshire, September 13, 1520,—educated at the grammar school of Grantham and Stamford, at St. John's College, Cambridge, and at Gray's Inn, London,—was married to a sister of Sir John Cheke, in 1541, and on her death in 1543, to a daughter of Sir Anthony Cook in 1545, and was largely concerned in the public affairs of his country and age. He was a hard student in early life, a thoughtful reader of books, as well as observer of men, wise and moderate in his political measures, and never unmindful of his family and social duties in his anxious labors for the state. Much light is thrown on the domestic habits of Lord Burleigh, in the "Diary of a Domestic"—or "*The Complete Statesman*," as it is entitled by the writer, who describes himself as having "lived with him during the last twenty-five years of his life."

"His kindness, as nature ever leads all men, was most expressed to his children; if he could get his table set round with his young little children, he was then in his kingdom; and it was an exceeding pleasure to hear what sport he would make with them, and how aptly and merrily he would talk with them,—with such pretty questions and witty allurements, as much delighted himself, the children, and the hearers. * * He had his own children, grand children, and great grand children, ordinarily at his table, sitting about him like olive branches. * * He was of spare and temperate diet, * * and above all things, what business soever was in his head, it was never perceived at his table, where he would be so merry, as one would imagine he had nothing else to do; directing his speech to all men according to their qualities and capacities, so as he raised mirth out of all men's speeches, augmenting it with his own, whereby he was never in want of company, so long as he was able to keep company. * * His recreation was chiefly in his books, wherewith if he had time, he was more delighted than others with play at cards. * Books were so pleasing to him, as when he got liberty from the queen to go unto his country house to take air, if he found but a book worth the opening, he would rather lose his riding than his reading. And yet riding in his garden and walks, upon his little mule, was his greatest disport. But, so soon as he came in, he fell to his reading again, or else to dispatching of business. * * * His favorite book was Cicero's Offices. His kindness of nature was seen in his declaration that he entertained malice toward no individual, and thanked God that he never retired to rest out of charity with any man."

While appreciating the advantages of the best education, and striving to secure them at any price for his own children, Lord Burleigh deemed "human learning, without the fear of God, of great hurt to all youth." With the most profound reverence for "divine and moral documents," his "Advices to his son, Robert Cecil," are characterized by the shrewdest worldly wisdom.

Son Robert,

The virtuous inclinations of thy matchless mother,* by whose tender and godly care thy infancy was governed, together with thy education under so zealous and excellent a tutor, puts me in rather assurance than hope that thou art not ignorant of that summum bonum which is only able to make thee happy as well in thy death as in thy life: I

* Lady Burleigh, was one of five daughters of Sir Anthony Cook, preceptor of Edward VI., all of whom were distinguished for their mental accomplishments, and for their exemplary deportment as mothers of families. Her death, after sharing his fortunes for forty-three years, Lord Burleigh regarded as the great calamity of his life.

mean the true knowledge and worship of thy Creator and Redeemer; without which all other things are vain and miserable. So that thy youth being guided by so sufficient a teacher, I make no doubt that he will furnish thy life with divine and moral documents. Yet, that I may not cast off the care beseeming a parent toward his child, or that thou shouldest have cause to derive thy whole felicity and welfare rather from others than from whence thou receivedst thy breath and being, I think it fit and agreeable to the affection I bare thee, to help thee with such rules and advertisements for the squaring of thy life as are rather gained by experience than by much reading. To the end that, entering into this exorbitant age, thou mayest be the better prepared to shun those scandalous courses whereunto the world, and the lack of experience, may easily draw thee. And because I will not confound thy memory, I have reduced them into ten precepts; and, next unto Moses' Tables, if thou imprint them in thy mind, thou shalt reap the benefit, and I the content. And they are these following:—

I. When it shall please God to bring thee to man's estate, use great providence and circumspection in choosing thy wife; for from thence will spring all thy future good or evil. And it is an action of thy life like unto a stratagem of war, wherein a man can err but once. If thy estate be good, match near home and at leisure; if weak, far off and quickly. Inquire diligently of her disposition, and how her parents have been inclined in their youth. Let her not be poor, how generous* soever; for a man can buy nothing in the market with gentility. Nor choose a base and uncomely creature altogether for wealth; for it will cause contempt in others and loathing in thee. Neither make a choice of a dwarf or a fool; for by the one thou shalt beget a race of pigmies; the other will be thy continual disgrace; and it will yirke† thee to hear her talk. For thou shalt find it to thy great grief, that there is nothing more fulsome‡ than a she-fool.

And touching the guiding of thy house, let thy hospitality be moderate, and, according to the means of thy estate, rather plentiful than sparing, but not costly; for I never knew any man grow poor by keeping an orderly table. But some consume themselves through secret vices, and their hospitality bears the blame. But banish swinish drunkards out of thine house, which is a vice impairing health, consuming much, and makes no show. I never heard praise ascribed to the drunkard but the well-bearing his drink, which is a better commendation for a brewer's horse or a drayman than for either a gentleman or a serving man. Beware thou spend not above three or four parts of thy revenues, nor above a third part of that in thy house; for the other two parts will do no more than defray thy extraordinaries, which always surmount the ordinary by much; otherwise thou shalt live, like a rich beggar, in continual want. And the needy man can never live happily nor contentedly; for every disaster makes him ready to mortgage or sell. And that gentleman who sells an acre of land sells an ounce of credit; for gentility is nothing else but ancient riches. So that, if the foundation shall at any time sink, the building must needs follow. So much for the first precept.

II. Bring thy children up in learning and obedience, yet without outward austerity. Praise them openly, reprehend them secretly. Give them good countenance, and convenient maintenance, according to thy ability; otherwise thy life will seem their bondage, and what portion thou shalt leave them at thy death they will thank death for it, and not thee. And I am persuaded that the foolish cockering§ of some parents, and the over-stern carriage of others, causeth more men and women to take ill courses than their own vicious inclinations. Marry thy daughters in time lest they marry themselves. And suffer not thy sons to pass the Alps; for they shall learn nothing but pride, blasphemy, and atheism.‖ And if by travel they get a few broken languages, that shall profit them nothing more than to have one meat served in divers dishes. Neither, by my consent, shalt thou train them up in wars; for he that sets up his rest to live by that profession can hardly be an honest man or a good christian. Besides, it is a science no longer in request than use. For soldiers in peace are like chimneys in summer.

III. Live not in the country without corn and cattle about thee; for he that putteth

* Well-born. † Irk. ‡ Disgusting. § Over-indulgence.
‖ In this strong aversion to foreign travel, Ascham sympathized.

his hand to the purse for every expense of household, is like him that keepeth water in a sieve. And what provision thou shalt want, learn to buy it at the best hand; for there is one penny saved in four betwixt buying in thy need and when the markets and seasons serve fittest for it. Be not served with kinsmen, or friends, or men intreated to stay; for they expect much, and do little; nor with such as are amorous, for their heads are intoxicated. And keep rather two too few, than one too many. Feed them well, and pay them with the most; and then thou mayest boldly require service at their hands.

IV. Let thy kindred and allies be welcome to thy house and table. Grace them with thy countenance, and further them in all honest actions; for, by this means, thou shalt so double the band of nature, as thou shalt find them so many advocates to plead an apology for thee behind thy back. But shake off those glow-worms, I mean parasites and sycophants, who will feed and fawn upon thee in the summer of prosperity; but, in an adverse storm, they will shelter thee no more than an arbor in winter.

V. Beware of suretyship for thy best friends. He that payeth another man's debt seeketh his own decay. But if thou canst not otherwise choose, rather lend thy money thyself upon good bonds, although thou borrow it. So shalt thou secure thyself, and pleasure thy friend. Neither borrow money of a neighbor or a friend, but of a stranger; where paying for it, thou shalt hear no more of it. Otherwise thou shalt eclipse thy credit, lose thy freedom, and yet pay as dear as to another. But in borrowing of money be precious of thy word; for he that hath care of keeping days of payment is lord of another man's purse.

VI. Undertake no suit against a poor man with receiving* much wrong; for besides that thou makest him thy compeer, it is a base conquest to triumph where there is small resistance. Neither attempt law against any man before thou be fully resolved that thou hast right on thy side; and then spare not for either money or pains; for a cause or two so followed and obtained will free thee from suits a great part of thy life.

VII. Be sure to keep some great man thy friend, but trouble him not for trifles. Compliment him often with many, yet small gifts, and of little charge. And if thou hast cause to bestow any great gratuity, let it be something which may be daily in sight: otherwise, in this ambitious age, thou shalt remain like a hop without a pole, live in obscurity, and be made a foot-ball for every insulting companion to spurn at.

VIII. Toward thy superiors be humble, yet generous.† With thine equals familiar yet respective. Toward thine inferiors show much humanity, and some familiarity: as to bow the body, stretch forth the hand, and to uncover the head; with such like popular compliments. The first prepares thy way to advancement,—the second makes thee known for a man well bred,—the third gains a good report; which, once got, is easily kept. For right humanity takes such deep root in the minds of the multitude, as they are more easily gained by unprofitable curtesies than by churlish benefits. Yet I advise thee not to affect, or neglect, popularity too much. Seek not to be Essex: shun to be Raleigh.§

IX. Trust not any man with thy life, credit or estate. For it is mere folly for a man to enthral himself to his friend, as though, occasion being offered, he should not dare to become an enemy.

X. Be not scurrilous in conversation, nor satirical in thy jests. The one will make thee unwelcome to all company; the other pull on quarrels, and get the hatred of thy best friends. For suspicious jests, when any of them savor of truth, leave a bitterness of mind of those which are touched. And, albeit I have already pointed at this inclusively, yet I think it necessary to leave it to thee as a special caution; because I have seen many so prone to quip and gird,‡ as they would rather lose their friend than their jest. And if perchance their boiling brain yield a quaint scoff, they will travel to be delivered of it as a woman with child. These nimble fancies are but the froth of wit."

* Though you receive. † Not mean. ‡ Mock and jibe.

§ Essex was the idol of the people; his rival, Raleigh, their aversion, till his undeserved misfortunes attracted their compassion, and his heroism their applause.

SIR MATTHEW HALE.

PLAN OF EDUCATION FOR HIS GRANDCHILDREN.

Written in 1673.

In a "*Letter of Advice to his Grandchildren,*" written when he was "threescore and four years," and published after his death, Sir Matthew Hale—one of the most resplendent names in the annals of jurisprudence, for mental ability, general learning, purity of life, and impartiality as judge—gives the following plan for their education, in which he differs "upon great reason and observation" "from the ordinary method of tutors," not only in his day, but for two centuries afterwards in England:—

PLAN OF EDUCATION FOR BOYS BETWEEN THE AGES OF EIGHT AND TWENTY

As to you, my grandsons, you must know, that till you come to be about eighteen or twenty years old, you are but in preparation to a settled estate of life; as there is no certain conjecture to be made before that age what you will be fit for, so till that age you are under the hammer and the file, to fit, dispose, and prepare you for your future condition of life, if God be pleased to lend it you; and about that time it will probably appear, both what you will be fit for, and whether you are like to make a prosperous voyage in the world or not.

1. Until you come to eight years old, I expect no more of you than to be good English scholars, to read perfectly and distinctly any part of the Bible, or any other English book, and to carry yourselves respectfully and dutifully to those that are set over you.

2. About eight years old, you are to be put or sent to a grammar school, where I expect you should make a good progress in the Latin tongue, in oratory and poetry; but above all to be good proficients in the Latin tongue, that you may be able to read, understand and construe any Latin author, and to make true and handsome Latin; and though I would have you learn somewhat of Greek, yet the Latin tongue is that which I most value, because almost all learning is now under that language. And the time for your abode at the grammar school is till you are about sixteen years old.

3. After that age, I shall either remove you to some university, or to some tutor that may instruct you in university learning, there to be educated till you are about twenty years old; and herein I shall alter the ordinary method of tutors, upon great reason and observation.

I therefore will have you employed from sixteen to seventeen in reading some Latin authors to keep your Latin tongue; but principally and chiefly in arithmetic and geometry, and geodesy or measuring of heights, distances, and superficies and solids, for this will habituate and enlarge your understanding.

and will furnish you with a knowledge which will be both delightful and useful all the days of your life; and will give you a pleasant and innocent diversion and entertainment when you are weary and tired with any other business.

From seventeen years old till nineteen or twenty, you may principally intend logic, natural philosophy, and metaphysics, according to the ordinary discipline of the university; but after you have read some systems or late topical or philosophical tracts that may give you some taste of the nature of those sciences, I shall advise your tutor to exercise you in Aristotle, for there is more sound learning of this kind to be found in him, touching these sciences, than in a cart-load of modern authors; only tutors scarce take the pains to understand him themselves, much less to instruct their scholars and pupils in them, insomuch, that there are few that have read his books.

And under the title of philosophy, I do not only intend his eight books of physics, but his books de Natura et Generatione Animalium, his books de Incessu Animalium, de Anima, de Meteoris, de Somno et Vigilia, de Morte, de Plantis, de Mundo, and his Mechanics; if you join thereunto Archimedes'.

These are part of real philosophy, and excellently handled by him, and have more of use and improvement of the mind than other notional speculations in logic or philosophy delivered by others; and the rather, because bare speculations and notions have little experience and external observation to confirm them, and they rarely fix the minds, especially of young men. But that part of philosophy that is real, may be improved and confirmed by daily observation; and is more stable, and yet more certain and delightful, and goes along with a man all his life, whatever employments or profession he undertakes.

4. When you come to above twenty years old, you are come to the critical age of your life; you are in that state of choice that the ancients tell us was offered to Hercules; on the left hand, a way of pleasure, of luxury, of idleness, intemperance, wantonness, which though it first be tempting and flattering, yet it ends in dishonor, in shame, in infamy, in poverty; such a way as the wise man spoke of, "There is a way that is pleasant and delightful, but the end of that way is death;" and that which the same wise man speaks of, (Eccles. xi. 9,) "Rejoice, O young man, in thy youth, and let thy heart cheer thee in the days of thy youth, and walk in the ways of thine heart. But know for all these things, God will bring thee into judgment." Again, on the right hand, there is a way of honesty and sobriety, of piety and the fear of God, of virtue and industry; and though this way may seem at first painful and rugged, yet it ends in peace and favor with God, and commonly in honor and reputation, in wealth and contentation even in this life. For although Almighty God hath reserved greater rewards for virtue and goodness than this life affords, yet he loves and delights to behold good and comely order among the children of men; and therefore a wise father will draw on his children to goodness, and learning, and obedience to him, with handsome rewards and encouragements, suitable to the age and disposition of his children. So the great Master and Father of the children of men, and of the great family of heaven and earth, doth commonly invite and draw men to ways of piety, virtue and goodness, by the encouragements of reputation, honor, esteem, wealth and other outward advantages, and thereby in great measure governs the children of men, and maintains that order that is necessary and convenient for the world of mankind.

And although this is neither the only nor chief reward of goodness and virtue yet till men are grown to that ripeness of understanding to look after re-

wards of a higher nature, namely, the happiness of the life to come, he is pleased
most wisely to make use of these inferior encouragements and invitations, like
so many little pulleys and cords, to draw men to the ways of virtue, piety and
goodness, wherein, when they are once led and confirmed, they are established
in higher and nobler expectations, namely, the love of God and the beauty of
goodness and virtue. And on the right-hand way, there are not only pro-
pounded certain general virtues of sobriety, temperance and industry, but there
are also certain particular walks of industry and virtue, and the exercise thereof
in certain special callings and employments, some more liberal and eminent, as
divines, physicians, lawyers, &c. Some more laborious, yet generous enough,
as husbandry, the primitive and most innocent employment, is such as becomes
noblemen and gentlemen. Some of other kinds, as merchants and handicrafts.
And to all these employments, justly and industriously followed, Almighty God
hath annexed a blessing; for they conduce to the good of mankind, and the
maintenance of human societies, and the convenient support of persons and
families.

And when you come to about this age, unless you are corrupted by idleness,
evil company or debauchery, your minds will begin to settle, and your inclinations will begin to bend themselves towards some of these employments, and
to a steady course of life. And although it may please God to order things so
that you may not be put upon the necessity to take any of these professions
upon you for your subsistence, because I may leave you a competent provision
otherways, yet assure yourselves a calling is so far from being a burthen or
dishonor to any of you, that it will be a great advantage to you every way to
be of some profession; and therefore I commend some of them to your choice,
especially for such of you whose fortunes may not be so plentiful.

But if you should not fix to any of these more regular professions, as divinity,
law, or physic, yet I would have you so far acquainted with them, as that you
may be able to understand, and maintain, and hold fast, the religion in which
you have by me been educated; and so much of the laws of the kingdom, as
may instruct you how to defend the estate that shall be left you, and to order
your lives conformable to those laws under which you live, and to give at least
common advice to your neighbors in matters of ordinary or common concernment; and so much of physic, especially of anatomy, as may make you know
your own frame, and maintain and preserve your health by good diet, and those
ordinary helps, a good herbal or garden may afford.

And although you should not addict yourselves professedly to any of these
three callings, yet I would have you all acquainted with husbandry, planting
and ordering of a country farm, which is the most innocent, and yet most necessary employment, and such as becomes the best gentlemen in England; for it
is a miserable thing to see a man master of an estate in lands, and yet not know
how to manage it, but must either be at the mercy of tenants or servants, or
otherwise he knows not how to live, being utterly a stranger to husbandry; and
therefore must be beholden to a tenant or a servant for his subsistence, who
many times knowing their own advantage, by the ignorance, carelessness or idleness of a master or landlord, set the dice upon him, and use him as they please.
I have always observed, a country gentleman that hath a competent estate of
lands in his hands, and lives upon it, stocks it himself, and understands it, and
manages it in his own hands, lives more plentifully, breeds up his children more
handsomely, and in a way of industry, is better loved in his country, and doth

more good to it, than he that hath twice the revenue and lives upon his rents, or it may be in the city, whereby both himself, and family, and children, learn a life of idleness and expense, and many times of debauchery. And therefore if you can not settle your minds to any other profession, yet I would have you be acquainted with the course of husbandry, and manage at least some considerable part of your estate in your own hands. And this you may do without any disparagement, for the life of a husbandman is not unseemly for any of the children of Adam or Noah, who began it; and although that employment requires attendance and industry, as well as knowledge and experience, yet it will afford a man competent time for such other studies and employments as may become a scholar or a gentleman, a good patriot or justice in his country.

Though all callings and employments carry with them a gratefulness and contenting variety much more than idleness and intemperance, or debauchery, yet in whatsoever calling you are settled, though that calling must be your principal business, and such as you must principally apply yourselves unto, yet I thought it always necessary to have some innocent diversions for leisure times; because it takes off the tediousness of business, and prevents a worse misspending of the time. I therefore commend to those gentlemen, of what profession soever, that they spend their spare and leisure hours in reading of history or mathematics, in experimental philosophy, in searching out the kinds and natures of trees and plants, herbs, flowers, and other vegetables; nay, in observing of insects, in mathematical observations, in measuring land; nay, in the more cleanly exercise of smithery, watch-making, carpentry, joinery works of all sorts. These and the like innocent diversions give these advantages:— 1. They improve a man's knowledge and understanding; 2. They render him fit for many employments of use; 3. They take off the tediousness of one employment; 4. They prevent diversions of worse kinds, as going to taverns, or games, and the like; 5. They rob no time from your constant calling, but only spend with usefulness and delight that time that can be well spared.

STUDIES AND CONDUCT.

SUGGESTIONS BY EMINENT DIVINES

BISHOP HALL TO LORD DENNY ON THE ORDERING OF A DAY.*

Every day is a little life: and our whole life is but a day repeated; whence it is that old Jacob numbers his life by days; and Moses desires to be taught this point of holy arithmetic, to number not his years, but his days. Those, therefore, that dare lose a day, are dangerously prodigal; those that dare mis-spend it, desperate. We can best teach others by ourselves; let me tell your lordship, how I would pass my days, whether common or sacred, that you (or whosoever others, overhearing me), may either approve my thriftiness, or correct my errors: to whom is the account of my hours either more due, or more known. All days are His, who gave time a beginning and continuance; yet some he hath made ours, not to command, but to use.

In none may we forget Him; in some we must forget all, besides Him. First, therefore, I desire to awake at those hours, not when I will, but when I must; pleasure is not a fit rule for rest, but health; neither do I consult so much with the sun, as mine own necessity, whether of body or in that of the mind. If this vassal could well serve me waking, it should never sleep; but now it must be pleased, that it may be serviceable. Now when sleep is rather driven away than leaves me, I would ever awake with God; my first thoughts are for Him, who hath made the night for rest, and the day for travel; and as He gives, so blesses both. If my heart be early seasoned with His presence, it will savor of Him all day after. While my body is dressing, not with an effeminate curiosity, nor yet with rude neglect, my mind addresses itself to her ensuing task, bethinking what is to be done, and in what order,

---

* Joseph Hall, Bishop of Norwich, was born at Ashby-de-la-Zouch, in Leicestershire, July 1, 1574; was educated at Emmanuel College, Cambridge; in 1597 published a volume of Satires; was Dean of Worcester in 1617; Bishop of Exeter in 1627, and translated to Norwich in 1641. The revenues of his bishopric were sequestered in 1643, and he died in great poverty at Higham, in 1656.

and marshaling (as it may) my hours with my work; that done, after some whiles meditation, I walk up to my masters and companions, my books, and, sitting down amongst them with the best contentment, I dare not reach forth my hand to salute any of them, till I have first looked up to heaven, and craved favor of him to whom all my studies are duly referred: without whom, I can neither profit nor labor. After this, out of no over great variety, I call forth those which may best fit my occasions, wherein I am not too scrupulous of age; sometimes I put myself to school to one of those ancients whom the Church hath honored with the name of Fathers; whose volumes I confess not to open without a secret reverence of their holiness and gravity; sometimes to those later doctors, which want nothing but age to make them classical; always to God's Book. That day is lost, whereof some hours are not improved in those divine monuments: others I turn over out of choice; these out of duty. Ere I can have sat unto weariness, my family, having now overcome all household distractions, invites me to our common devotions; not without some short preparation. These, heartily performed, send me up with a more strong and cheerful appetite to my former work, which I find made easy to me by intermission and variety; now, therefore, can I deceive the hours with change of pleasures, that is, of labors. One while mine eyes are busied, another while my hand, and sometimes my mind takes the burthen from them both; wherein I would imitate the skillfulest cooks, which make the best dishes with manifold mixtures; one hour is spent in textual divinity, another in controversy; histories relieve them both. Now, when the mind is weary of others' labors, it begins to undertake her own; sometimes, it meditates and winds up for future use; sometimes it lays forth her conceits into present discourse; sometimes for itself, after for others. Neither know I whether it works or plays in these thoughts; I am sure no sport hath more pleasure, no work more use; only the decay of a weak body makes me think these delights insensibly laborious. Thus could I all day (as ringers use) make myself music with changes, and complain sooner of the day for shortness than of the business for toil, were it not that this faint monitor interrupts me still in the midst of my busy pleasures, and enforces me both to respite and repast; I must yield to both; while my body and mind are joined together in these unequal couples, the better must follow the weaker. Before my meals, therefore, and after, I let myself loose from all thoughts, and now would forget that I ever studied; a full mind takes away the body's appetite no less than a full body makes a dull and unwieldy mind; company, discourse, recreations, are now seasonable and welcome: these prepare me for a diet, not gluttonous, but medicinal; the palate may not be pleased, but the stomach, nor that for its own sake; neither would I think any of these comforts worth respect in themselves but in their use, in their end, so far as they may enable me to better things. If I see any dish to tempt my palate, I fear a serpent in that apple, and would please myself in a willful denial; I rise capable of more, not desirous; not now immediately from my trencher to my book, but after some intermission. Moderate speed is a sure help to all proceedings; where those things which are prosecuted with violence of endeavor or desire, either succeed not, or continue not.

After my later meal, my thoughts are slight; only my memory may be charged with her task, of recalling what was committed to her custody in the day; and my heart is busy in examining my hands and mouth, and all other senses, of that day's behavior. And now the evening is come, no tradesman doth more carefully take in his wares, clear his shopboard, and shut his window, than I would shut up my thoughts, and clear my mind. That student shall live miserably, which like a camel lies down under his burden. All this done, calling together my family, we end the day with God. Thus do we rather drive the time away before us, than follow it. I grant neither is my practice worthy to be exemplary, neither are our callings proportionable. The lives of a nobleman, of a courtier, of a scholar, of a citizen, of a countryman, differ no less than their dispositions; yet must all conspire in honest labor.

Sweet is the destiny of all trades, whether of the brows or of the mind. God never allowed any man to do nothing. How miserable is the condition of those men, which spend the time as if it were given them, and not lent; as if hours were waste creatures, and such as should never be accounted for; as if God would take this for a good bill of reckoning: *Item*, spent upon my pleasures forty years! These men shall once find that no blood can privilege idleness, and that nothing is more precious to God, than that which they desire to cast away—time. Such are my common days; but God's day calls for another respect. The same sun arises on this day and enlightens it; yet because that sun of Righteousness arose upon it, and gave a new life unto the world in it, and drew the strength of God's moral precept unto it, therefore, justly do we sing with the psalmist; This is the day which the Lord hath made. Now I forget the world and in a sort myself;

and deal with my wonted thoughts, as great men use, who, at sometimes of their privacy, forbid the access of all suitors. Prayer, meditation, reading, hearing, preaching, singing, good conference, are the businesses of this day, which I dare not bestow on any work, or pleasure, but heavenly.

I hate superstition on the one side, and looseness on the other; but I find it hard to offend in too much devotion, easy in profaneness. The whole week is sanctified by this day; and according to my care of this, is my blessing on the rest. I show your lordship what I would do, and what I ought; I commit my desires to the imitation of the weak, my actions to the censures of the wise and holy, my weaknesses to the pardon and redress of my merciful God.

LETTER TO MR. MILWARD ON THE PLEASURES OF STUDY AND CONTEMPLATION.

I can wonder at nothing more than how a man can be idle; but of all others, a scholar; in so many improvements of reason, in such sweetness of knowledge, in such varieties of studies, in such importunity of thoughts: other artisans do but practice, we still learn; others run still in the same gyre to weariness, to satiety; our choice is infinite; other labors require recreations; our very labor recreates our sports; we can never want either somewhat to do, or somewhat that we would do. How numberless are the volumes which men have written of arts, of tongues! How endless is that volume which God hath written of the world! wherein every creature is a letter; every day a new page. Who can be weary of either of these? To find wit in poetry; in philosophy, profoundness; in mathematics, acuteness; in history, wonder of events; in oratory, sweet eloquence; in divinity, supernatural light, and holy devotion; as so many rich metals in their proper mines; whom would it not ravish with delight! After all these, let us but open our eyes, we can not look beside a lesson, in this universal book of our Maker, worth our study, worth taking out. What creature hath not his miracle? what event doth not challenge his observation? And if, weary of foreign employment, we list to look home into ourselves, there we find a more private world of thoughts which set us on to work anew, more busily and not less profitably: now our silence is vocal, our solitariness popular; and we are shut up, to do good unto many; if once we be cloyed with our own company, the door of conference is open; here interchange of discourse (besides pleasure) benefits us; and he is a weak companion from whom we return not wiser. I could envy, if I could believe that anchoret, who, secluded from the world, and pent up in his voluntary prison walls, denied that he thought the day long, whiles yet he wanted learning to vary his thoughts. Not to be cloyed with the same conceit is difficult, above human strength; but to a man so furnished with all sorts of knowledge, that according to his dispositions he can change his studies, I should wonder that ever the sun should seem to pass slowly. How many busy tongues chase away good hours in pleasant chat, and complain of the haste of night! What ingenious mind can be sooner weary of talking with learned authors, the most harmless and sweetest companions? What a heaven lives a scholar in, that at once in one close room can daily converse with all the glorious martyrs and fathers? that can single out at pleasure, either sententious Tertullian, or grave Cyprian, or resolute Hierome, or flowing Chrysostome, or divine Ambrose, or devout Bernard, or (who alone is all these) heavenly Augustine, and talk with them and hear their wise and holy counsels, verdicts, resolutions; yea (to rise higher) with learned Paul, with all their fellow-prophets, apostles; yet more, like another Moses, with God himself, in them both! Let the world contemn us; while we have these delights we can not envy them; we can not wish ourselves other than we are. Besides, the way to all other contentments is troublesome; the only recompense is in the end. To delve in the mines, to scorch in the fire for the getting, for the fining of gold is a slavish toil; the comfort is in the wedge to the owner, not the laborers: where our very search of knowledge is delightsome. Study itself is our life; from which we would not be barred for a world. How much sweeter then is the fruit of study, the conscience of knowledge! In comparison whereof the soul that hath once tasted it, easily contemns all human comforts. Go now, ye worldlings, and insult over our paleness, our neediness, our neglect. Ye could not be so jocund if you were not ignorant; if you did not want knowledge, you could not overlook him that hath it; for me, I am so far from emulating you, that I profess I had as lieve be a brute beast, as an ignorant rich man. How is it then, that those gallants, which have privilege of blood and birth, and better education, do so scornfully turn off these most manly, reasonable, noble exercises of scholarship? a hawk becomes their fist better than a book; no dog but is a better company: any thing or nothing, rather than what we ought. O minds brutishly sensual! Do they think that God made them for disport, who even in his paradise would not allow pleasure without work! And if for business, either of body or mind: those of the body are commonly servile, like itself. The mind therefore, the mind only, that honorable and divine part, is fittest to be employed of those which would reach to the highest perfection of men, and would be more than the most. And what work is there of the mind but the trade of a scholar, study? Let me therefore fasten this problem on our school gates, and challenge all comers, in the defense of it; that no scholar can not but be truly noble. And if I make it not good, let me never be admitted further then to the subject of our question. Thus we do well to congratulate to ourselves our own happiness; if others will come to us, it shall be our comfort, but more theirs; if not, it is enough that we can joy in ourselves, and in Him in whom we are that we are.

ADVICE FOR MEN OF ALL DEGREES AND OCCUPATIONS.

Let us begin with him who is the first and last; inform yourself aright concerning God; without whom, in vain do we know all things; be acquainted with that Saviour of yours, which paid so much for you on earth, and now sues for you in heaven. Think all God's outward favors and provisions the best for you: your own ability and actions the meanest. Suffer not your mind to be either a drudge or a wanton; exercise it ever, but overlay it not: in all your businesses, look, through the world, at God; whatsoever is your level, let him be your scope; every day take a view of your last; and think either it is this or may be: offer not yourself either to honor or labor, let them both seek you: care you only to be worthy, and you can not hide you from God. So frame yourself to the time and company, that you may neither serve it nor sullenly neglect it; and yield so far as you may neither betray goodness nor countenance evil. Let your words be few and digested. There are but two things which a Christian is charged to buy, and not to sell, Time and Truth; both so precious that we must purchase them at any rate. So use your friends as those which should be perpetual, may be changeable. While you are within yourself, there is no danger; but thoughts once uttered must stand to hazard. Do not hear from yourself what you would be loth to hear from others. In all good things, give the eye and ear the full scope, for they let into the mind; restrain the tongue, for it is a spender. Few men have repented them of silence. In all serious matters take counsel of days, and nights, and friends: and let leisure ripen your purposes; neither hope to gain aught by suddenness. The first thoughts may be confident, the second are wiser. Serve honesty ever, though without apparent wages; she will pay sure, if slow. As in apparel, so in actions, know not what is good, but what becomes you. Excuse not your own ill, aggravate not others: and if you love peace, avoid censures, comparisons, contradictions. Out of good men choose acquaintance; of acquaintance, friends; of friends, familiars; after probation admit them; and after admittance, change them not. Age commendeth friendship. Do not always your best; it is neither wise nor safe for a man ever to stand upon the top of his strength. If you would be above the expectation of others, be ever below yourself. Expend after your purse, not after your mind; take not where you may deny, except upon conscience of desert, or hope to requite. Either frequent suits or complaints are wearisome to a friend. Rather smother your griefs and wants as you may, than be either querulous or importunate. Let not your face belie your heart, nor always tell tales out of it; he is fit to live amongst friends or enemies that can ingenuously close. Give freely, sell thriftily; change seldom your place, never your state; either amend inconveniences or swallow them, rather than you should run from yourself to avoid them.

JEREMY TAYLOR, D.D.—1613-1667.*

THE MANLY ELEMENT IN CHILDREN'S TRAINING.

Otherwise do fathers, and otherwise do mothers handle their children. These soften them with kisses and imperfect noises, with the pap and breast-milk of soft endearments; they rescue them from tutors, and snatch them from discipline: they desire to keep them fat and warm, and their feet dry, and their bellies full; and then the children govern, and cry, and prove fools and troublesome, so long as the feminine republic does endure. But fathers, because they design to have their children wise and valiant, apt for counsel or for arms, send them to severe governments, and tie them to study, to hard labor, and afflictive contingencies. They rejoice when the bold boy strikes a lion with his hunting spear, and shrinks not when the beast comes to affright his early courage. Softness is for slaves and beasts, for minstrels and useless persons, for such who can not ascend higher than the state of a fair ox, or a servant entertained for vainer offices; but the man that designs his son for nobler employments,—to honors and to triumphs, to consular dignities, and presidencies of councils, loves to see him pale with study, or panting with labor, hardened with sufferings, or eminent by dangers. (*Holy Dying, ch. iii.*)

THE AGE OF REASON AND DISCRETION IN YOUTH.

We must not think that the life of a man begins when he can feed himself or walk alone, when he can fight or beget his like, for so he is contemporary with a camel or a cow; but he is first a man when he comes to a certain steady use of reason, according to his proportion; and when that is, all the world of men can not tell precisely. Some are called at age at fourteen, some at one-and-twenty, some never; but all men late enough; for the life of a man comes upon him slowly and insensibly. But as when the sun approaching towards the gates of the morning, he first opens a little eye of heaven, and sends away the spirits of darkness, and gives light to a cock, and calls up the lark to matins, and by and by gilds the fringes of a cloud, and peeps over the eastern hills, thrusting out his golden horns like those which decked the brows of Moses when he was forced to wear a veil because himself had seen the face of God; and still, while a man tells the story, the sun gets up higher, till he shows a fair face and a full light, and then he shines

* Jeremy Taylor was born in Cambridge in 1613—the son of a barber, who secured for him admission to Emmanuel College—was made fellow of All-Soul's College in Oxford in 1636; rector of Uppingham in 1638; Bishop of Down and Connor, and Vice-Chancellor of the University of Dublin in 1660; and died, August 13, 1667.

one whole day, under a cloud often, and sometimes weeping great and little showers, and sets quickly. So is a man's reason and his life. He first begins to perceive himself, to see or taste, making little reflections upon his actions of sense, and can discourse of flies and dogs, shells and play, horses and liberty: but when be is strong enough to enter into arts and little institutions, he is at first entertained with trifles and impertinent things, not because he needs them, but because his understanding is no bigger, and little images of things are laid before him, like a cock-boat to a whale, only to play withal: but before a man comes to be wise, he is half dead with gouts and consumption, with catarrhs and aches, with sore eyes and a worn-out body. So that, if we must not reckon the life of a man but by the accounts of his reason, he is long before his soul be dressed; and he is not to be called a man without a wise and an adorned soul, a soul at least furnished with what is necessary towards his well-being.

And now let us consider what that thing is which we call years of discretion. The young man is passed his tutors, and arrived at the bondage of a caitiff spirit; he is run from discipline, and is let loose to passion. The man by this time hath wit enough to choose his vice, to act his lust, to court his mistress, to talk confidently, and ignorantly, and perpetually: to despise his betters, to deny nothing to his appetite, to do things that when he is indeed a man he must for ever be ashamed of: for this is all the discretion that most men show in the first stage of their manhood. They can discern good from evil; and they prove their skill by leaving all that is good, and wallowing in the evils of folly and an unbridled appetite. And by this time the young man hath contracted vicious habits, and is a beast in manners, and therefore it will not be fitting to reckon the beginning of his life: he is a fool in his understanding, and that is a sad death, &c. (*Holy Dying*, *ch. i.*)

CONVERSATION.

The following is the Analysis of Bishop Taylor's sermon on "*The Good and Evil Tongue.*"

I. General Observations.

II. The vices of Conversation.

- 1. Talking too much.
  - 1. Talking foolishly.
  - 2. Scurrility.
  - 3. Revealing Secrets.
  - 4. Common swearing.
  - 5. Contentious wrangling.
- 2. Slander.
- 3. Flattery.

III. The virtues of Conversation.

- 1. Instruction.
- 2. Comfort.
- 3. Reproof.

THOMAS FULLER, D.D.—1608-1661.

MEMORY.

It is the treasure-house of the mind, wherein the monuments thereof are kept and preserved. Plato makes it the mother of the Muses. Aristotle sets it in one degree further, making experience the mother of arts, memory the parent of experience. Philosophers place it in the rear of the head; and it seems the mine of memory lies there, because there men naturally dig for it, scratching it when they are at a loss. This again is twofold; one, the simple retention of things; the other, a regaining them when forgotten.

Brute creatures equal if not exceed men in a bare retentive memory. Through how many labyrinths of woods, without other clue of thread than natural instinct, doth the hunted hare return to her meuse! How doth the little bee, flying into several meadows and gardens, sipping of many cups, yet never intoxicated, through an ocean (as I may say) of air, steadily steer herself home, without help of card or compass. But these can not play an aftergame, and recover what they have forgotten, which is done by the meditation of discourse.

Artificial memory is rather a trick than an art, and more for the gain of the teacher than profit of the learners. Like the tossing of a pike, which is no part of the postures and motions thereof, and is rather for ostentation than use, to show the strength and nimbleness of the arm, and is often used by wandering soldiers, as an introduction to beg. Understand it of the artificial rules which at this day are delivered by memory mountebanks; for sure an art thereof may be made (wherein as yet the world is defective) and that no more destructive to natural memory than spectacles are to eyes, which girls in Holland wear from twelve years of age. But till this be found out, let us observe these plain rules.

First, soundly infix in thy mind what thou desirest to remember. What wonder is it if agitation of business jog that out of thy head, which was there rather tacked than fastened! whereas those notions which get in by "violenta possessio," will abide there till "ejectio firma," sickness, or extreme age dispossess them. It is best knocking in the nail over night, and clinching it the next morning.

Overburthen not thy memory to make so faithful a servant a slave. Remember, Atlas was weary. Have as much reason as a camel, to rise when thou hast thy full load. Memory, like a purse, if it be over full that it can not shut, all will drop out of it; take heed of a gluttonous curiosity to feed on many things, lest the greediness of the appetite of thy memory spoil the digestion thereof. Beza's case was peculiar and memorable; being above fourscore years of age, he perfectly could say by heart any Greek chapter in St. Paul's epistles, or any thing else which he had learnt long before, but forgot whatsoever was newly told him; his memory, like an inn, retaining old guests, but having no room to entertain new.

Spoil not thy memory by thine own jealousy, nor make it bad by suspecting it. How canst thou find that true which thou wilt not trust? St. Augustine tells us of his friend Simplicius, who being asked, could tell all Virgil's verses backward and forward, and yet the same party avowed to God, that he knew not that he could do it till they did try him. Sure there is concealed strength in men's memories, which they take no notice of.

Marshal thy notions into a handsome method. One will carry twice more weight trussed and packed up in bundles, than when it lies untoward flapping and hanging about his shoulders. Things orderly fardled up under heads are most portable.

Adventure not all thy learning in one bottom, but divide it betwixt thy memory and thy note-books. He that with Bias carries all his learning about him in his head, will utterly be beggared and bankrupt, if a violent disease, a merciless thief, should rob and strip him. I know some have a commonplace against commonplace books, and yet perchance will privately make use of what they publicly declaim against. A commonplace book contains many notions in garrison, whence the owner may draw out an army into the field on competent warning.

Moderate diet and good air preserve good memory; but what air is best I dare not define, when such great ones differ. Some say a pure and subtle air is best, another commends a thick and foggy air. For the Pisans sited in the fens and marshes of Arnus have excellent memories, as if the foggy air were a cap for their heads.

Thankfulness to God for it continues the memory; whereas some proud people have been visited with such oblivion, that they have forgotten their own names. Staupitius, tutor to Luther, and a godly man, in a vain ostentation of his memory, repeated Christ's genealogy by heart in his sermon, but being out about the captivity of Babylon, I see, saith he, God resisteth the proud, and so betook himself to his book.

Abuse not thy memory to be sin's register, nor make advantage thereof for wickedness. Excellently Augustine, "Quidam vero pessimi memoria sunt mirabili, qui tanto pejores sunt, quanto minus possunt, quæ male cogitant, oblivisci."

FOREIGN TRAVEL.

Travel not early before thy judgment be risen; lest thou observest rather shows than substance.

Get the language (in part) without which key thou shalt unlock little of moment.

Know most of the rooms of thy native country before thou goest over the threshold thereof.

To travel from the sun is uncomfortable. Yet the northern parts with much ice have some crystal.

If thou wilt see much in a little, travel the Low Countries. Holland is all Europe in an Amsterdam print.

Be wise in choosing objects, diligent in marking, careful in remembering of them. Yet herein men much follow their own humors. One asked a barber who never before had been at the court, what he saw there? "Oh," said he, "the king was excellently well trimmed!"

Labor to distil and unite into thyself the scattered perfections of several nations. Many weed foreign countries, bringing home Dutch drunkenness, Spanish pride, French wantonness, and Italian Atheism; as for the good herbs, Dutch industry, Spanish loyalty, French courtesy, and Italian frugality, these they leave behind them; others bring home just nothing; and, because they singled not themselves from their countrymen, though some years beyond sea, were never out of England.

SMALL BOOKS.

We shall generally find, that the most excellent books in any art or science, have been still the smallest and most compendious; and this not without ground; for it is an argument that the author was a master of what he wrote, and had a clear notion, and a full comprehension of the subject before him. For the reason of things lies in a little compass, if the mind could at any time be so happy as to light upon it: most of the writings and discourses in the world are but illustration and rhetoric, which signifies as much as nothing to a mind eager in pursuit after the causes and philosophical truth of things.

KNOWLEDGE OF GOOD AND EVIL.—HOW ATTAINED.

The natural inability of most men to judge exactly of things, makes it very difficult for them to discern the real good and evil of what comes before them, to consider and weigh circumstances, to scatter and look through the mists of error, and so separate appearances from reality. For the greater part of mankind is but slow and dull of apprehension; and therefore in many cases under a necessity of seeing with other men's eyes, and judging with other men's understandings. To which their want of judging or discerning abilities, we may add also their want of leisure and opportunity, to apply their minds to such a serious and intent consideration, as may let them into a full discovery of the true goodness and evil of things, which are qualities which seldom display themselves to the first view. There must be leisure and retirement, solitude and a sequestration of man's self from the noise and toil of the world; for truth scorns to be seen by eyes too much fixed upon inferior objects. It lies too deep to be fetched up with the plough, and too close to be beaten out with the hammer. It dwells not in shops or workhouses; nor till the late age was it ever known, that any one served seven years to a smith or a tailor, that he might at the end thereof, proceed master of any other arts, but such as those trades taught him: and much less that he should commence doctor or divine from the shop-board, or the anvil; or from whistling to a team, come to preach to a congregation. These were the peculiar, extraordinary privileges of the late blessed times of light and inspiration: otherwise nature will still hold on its old course, never doing any thing which is considerable without the assistance of its two great helps—art and industry. But above all, the knowledge of what is good and what is evil, what ought and what ought not to be done in the several offices and relations of life, is a thing too large to be compassed, and too hard to be mastered, without brains and study, parts, and contemplation.

Shakspeare, in Troilus and Cressida says:

> ——"Pleasure and revenge
> Have ears more deaf than adders to the voice
> Of any true decision."

Lord Bacon claims: "It is not a pure and primitive knowledge of nature, by the light whereof man did give names to other creatures in paradise, but the aspiring of overmuch knowledge of good and evil, with an intent to shake off God and to give law unto himself, which was the original temptation and sin." "The excellent books and discourses of antiquity are of little effect towards honesty of life and the reformation of corrupt manners, because they are read, not by men mature in years and judgment, but are left and confined only to boys and beginners."

ISAAC BARROW, D.D.—1630-1677.

WISDOM.

WISDOM of itself is delectable and satisfactory, as it implies a revelation of truth and a detection of error to us. 'Tis like light, pleasant to behold, casting a sprightly lustre, and diffusing a benign influence all about; presenting a goodly prospect of things to the eyes of our minds; displaying objects in their due shapes, postures, magnitudes, and colors; quickening our spirits with a comfortable warmth, and disposing our minds to a cheerful activity; dispelling the darkness of ignorance, scattering the mists of doubt, driving away the spectres of delusive fancy; mitigating the cold of sullen melancholy; discovering obstacles, securing progress, and making the passages of life clear, open, and pleasant. We are all naturally endowed with a strong appetite to know, to see, to pursue truth; and with a bashful abhorrency from being deceived and entangled in mistake. And as success in inquiry after truth affords matter of joy and triumph; so being conscious of error and miscarriage therein, is attended with shame and sorrow. These desires wisdom in the most perfect manner satisfies, not by entertaining us with dry, empty, fruitless theories upon mean and vulgar subjects; but by enriching our minds with excellent and useful knowledge, directed to the noblest objects, and serviceable to the highest ends.

Wisdom is exceedingly pleasant and peaceable; in general, by disposing us to acquire and to enjoy all the good delight and happiness we are capable of; and by freeing us from all the inconvenience, mischiefs, and infelicities our condition is subject to. For whatever good from clear understanding, deliberate advice, sagacious foresight, stable resolution, dexterous address, right intention, and orderly proceeding doth naturally result, wisdom confers: whatever evil blind ignorance, false presumption, unwary credulity, precipitate rashness, unsteady purpose, ill contrivance, backwardness, inability, unwieldiness and confusion of thought beget, wisdom prevents. From a thousand snares and treacherous allurements, from innumerable rocks and dangerous surprises, from exceedingly many needless incumbrances and vexatious toils of fruitless endeavors, she redeems and secures us.

Wisdom instructs us to examine, compare, and rightly to value the objects that court our affections and challenge our care? and thereby regulates our passions and moderates our endeavors, which begets a pleasant serenity and peaceable tranquillity of mind. For when being deluded with false shows, and relying upon ill-grounded presumptions, we highly esteem, passionately affect, and eagerly pursue things of little worth in themselves or concernment to us; as we unhandsomely prostitute our affections, and prodigally misspend our time, and vainly lose our labor, so the event not answering our expectation, our minds thereby are confounded, disturbed, and distempered. But, when guided by right reason, we conceive great esteem of, and zealously are enamored with, and vigorously strive to attain things of excellent worth and weighty consequence, the conscience of having well placed our affections and well employed our pains, and the experience of fruits corresponding to our hopes, ravishes our minds with unexpressible content. And so it is: present appearance and vulgar conceit ordinarily impose upon our fancies, disguising things with a deceitful varnish, and representing those that are vainest with the greatest advantage; whilst the noblest objects, being of a more subtle and spiritual nature, like fairest jewels inclosed in a homely box, avoid the notice of gross sense, and pass undiscerned by us. But the light of wisdom, as it unmasks specious imposture and bereaves it of its false colors, so it penetrates into the retirements of true excellency, and reveals its genuine lustre.

Wisdom makes all the troubles, griefs, and pains incident to life, whether casual adversities, or natural afflictions, easy and supportable, by rightly valuing the importance and moderating the influence of them. It suffers not busy fancy to alter the nature, amplify the degree, or extend the duration of them, by representing them more sad, heavy, and remediless than they truly are. It allows them no force beyond what naturally and necessarily they have, nor contributes nourishment to their increase. It keeps them at a due distance, not permitting them to encroach upon the soul, or to propagate their influence beyond their proper sphere.

Charity.

How like a paradise the world would be, flourishing in joy and rest, if men would cheerfully conspire in affection, and helpfully contribute to each other's content: and how like a savage wilderness now it is, when like wild beasts, they vex and persecute, worry and devour each other. How not only philosophy hath placed the supreme pitch of happiness in a calmness of mind, and tranquillity of life, void of care and trouble, of irregular passions and perturbations; but that holy scripture itself in that one term of peace most usually comprehends all joy and content, all felicity and prosperity: so that the heavenly consort of angels, when they agree most highly to bless, and to wish the greatest happiness to mankind, could not better express their sense, than by saying, "Be on earth peace, and good will among men."

Books.

He that loveth a book will never want a faithful friend, a wholesome counselor, a cheerful companion, an effectual comforter. By study, by reading, by thinking, one may innocently entertain himself, as in all matters, so in all fortunes.

ROBERT BURNS.

EPISTLE TO A YOUNG FRIEND.

I lang hae thought, my youthfu' friend,
  A something to have sent you,
Though it should serve nae other end
  Than just a kind *memento*;
But how the subject-theme may gang
  Let time and chance determine;
Perhaps it may turn out a sang,
  Perhaps turn out a sermon.

Ye'll try the world soon, my lad,
  And, *Andrew* dear, believe me,
Ye'll find mankind an unco squad,
  And muckle they may grieve ye.
For care and trouble set your thought,
  Ev'n when your end's attained;
And a' your views may come to nought,
  Where ev'ry nerve is strained.

I'll no say, men are villains a';
  The real, harden'd, wicked,
Who hae nae check but human law,
  Are to a few restricked:
But och! mankind are unco weak,
  An' little to be trusted;
If *self* the wavering balance shake
  It's rarely right adjusted!

Yet they wha fa' in fortune's strife,
  Their fate we should na censure,
For still th' *important end* of life,
  They equally may answer;
A man may hae an honest heart,
  Tho' poortith hourly stare him;
A man may tak a neebor's part,
  Yet hae nae cash to spare him.

Ay free, aff han' your story tell,
  When wi' a bosom crony;
But still keep something to yoursel
  Ye scarcely tell to ony.
Conceal yoursel as weel's ye can
  Frae critical dissection;
But keek thro' ev'ry other man,
  Wi' sharpen'd, slee inspection.

The sacred lowe o' weel-plac'd love,
  Luxuriantly indulge it;
But never tempt th' *illicit rove*,
  Tho' naething should divulge it.
I wave the quantum o' the sin,
  The hazard of concealing;
But och! it hardens a' within,
  And petrifies the feeling!

To catch dame Fortune's golden smile,
  Assiduous wait upon her;
And gather gear by ev'ry wile
  That's justified by honour;
Not for to hide it in a hedge,
  Not for a train-attendant;
But for the glorious privilege
  Of being *independent*.

ROBERT BURNS.

The fear o' hell's a hangman's whip,
  To haud the wretch in order;
But where ye feel your *honour* grip,
  Let that ay be your border;
Its slightest touches, instant pause—
  Debar a' side pretences;
And resolutely keep its laws
  Uncaring consequences.

The great *Creator* to revere,
  Must sure become the *creature;*
But still the preaching cant forbear,
  And ev'n the rigid feature:
Yet ne'er with wits profane to range,
  Be complaisance extended;
An Atheist's laugh's a poor exchange
  For Deity offended!

When ranting round in pleasure's ring,
  Religion may be blinded;
Or if she gie a *random sting,*
  It may be little minded;
But when on life we're tempest-driv'n,
  A conscience but a canker—
A correspondence fix'd wi' Heav'n,
  Is sure a noble *anchor!*

Adieu, dear, amiable youth!
  Your heart can ne'er be wanting:
May prudence, fortitude, and truth,
  Erect your brow undaunting!
In ploughman's phrase, "God send you speed,"
  Still daily to grow wiser:
And may you better reck the *rede*,
  Than ever did th' adviser!

A BARD'S EPITAPH.

Is there a man, whose judgment clear
Can others teach the course to steer,
Yet runs, himself, life's mad career,
    Wild as the wave;
Here pause—and thro' the starting tear,
    Survey this grave.

The poor inhabitant below
Was quick to learn, and wise to know,
And keenly felt the friendly glow,
    And softer flame,
And thoughtless follies laid him low,
    And stained his name.

Reader, attend—whether thy soul
Soars fancy's flights beyond the pole,
Or darkly grubs this earthly hole,
    In low pursuit,
Know, prudent, cautious, self-control
    Is wisdom's root.

O wad some pow'r the giftie gie us
To see oursels as others see us!
It wad frae monie a blunder free us
    And foolish notion.

PRODICUS—THE CHOICE OF HERCULES.

Prodicus, the author of the allegory which Xenophon has preserved for the guidance of the young of all countries, in his *Memorabilia*, where Socrates, in his conversation with Aristippus, to enforce his arguments for temperance, piety and labor, cites the language addressed by Virtue to Hercules against the specious promises of Sensuality which lead to bewilder, and dazzle to blind—was a native of Iulis in the island of Ceos, and flourished about B. C. 450.

THE CHOICE OF HERCULES.

Hercules having attained to that stage of life when man being left to the government of himself, seldom fails to give certain indications whether he will walk in the paths of virtue or wander through all the intricacies of vice, perplexed and undetermined what course to pursue, retired into a place where silence and solitude might bestow on him that tranquillity and leisure so necessary for deliberation, when two women, of more than ordinary stature, came on towards him. The countenance of the one, open and amiable, and elevated with an air of conscious dignity. Her person was adorned with native elegance, her look with modesty, every gesture with decency, and her garments were altogether of the purest white. The other was comely, but bloated, as from too high living. Affecting softness and delicacy, every look, every action, was studied and constrained; while art contributed all its powers to give those charms to her complexion and shape which nature had denied her. Her look was bold, the blush of modesty she was a stranger to, and her dress was contrived, not to conceal, but display those beauties she supposed herself possessed of. She would look round to see if any observed her; and not only so, but she would frequently stand still to admire her own shadow. Drawing near to the place where the hero sat musing, eager and anxious for the advantage of first accosting him, she hastily ran forward; while the person who accompanied her moved on with her usual pace, composed and majestic. Joining him, she said, 'I know, my Hercules! you have long been deliberating on the course of life you should pursue; engage with me in friendship, and I will lead you through those paths which are smooth and flowery, where every delight shall court your enjoyment, and pain and sorrow shall not once appear. Absolved from all the fatigue of business and the hardships of war, your employment shall be to share in the social pleasures of the table, or repose on beds of down; no sense shall remain without its gratification; beauty shall delight the eye and melody the ear, and perfumes shall breathe their odors around you. Nor shall your care be once wanted for the procuring of these things: neither be afraid lest time should exhaust your stock of joys, and reduce you to the necessity of purchasing new, either by the labor of body or mind: it is to the toil of others that you alone shall owe them! Scruple not, therefore, to seize whatever seemeth most desirable; for this privilege I bestow on all who are my votaries.'

Hercules, having heard so flattering an invitation, demanded her name.—'My friends,' said she, 'call me Happiness; but they who do not love me endeavor to make me odious, and therefore brand me with the name of Sensuality.'

By this time the other person being arrived, thus addressed him in her turn: 'I also, O Hercules! am come to offer you my friendship, for I am no stranger to your high descent: neither was I wanting to remark the goodness of your disposition in all the exercises of your childhood; from whence I gather hopes, if you choose to follow where I lead the way, it will not be long ere you have an opportunity of performing many actions glorious to yourself and honorable to me. But I mean not to allure you with specious promises of pleasure, I will plainly set before you things as they really are, and show you in what manner the gods think proper to dispose them. Know therefore, young man, these wise governors of the universe have decreed, that nothing great, nothing excellent, shall be obtained without care and labor. They give no real good, no true happiness, on other terms. If, therefore, you would secure the favor of these gods, adore them. If you would conciliate to yourself the affection of your friends, be of use to them. If to be honored and respected of the republic be your aim, show your fellow-citizens how effectually you can serve them. But if it is your ambition that all Greece shall esteem you, let all Greece share the benefits arising from your labors. If you wish for the fruits of the earth, cultivate it. If for the increase of your flocks or your herds, let your flocks and your herds have your attendance and your care. And if your design is to advance yourself by arms, if you wish for the power of defending your friends, and subduing your enemies, learn the art of war under those who are acquainted with it; and, when learnt, employ it to the best advantage. And if to have a body ready and well able to perform what you wish from it be your desire, subject yours to your reason, and let exercise and hard labor give to it strength and agility.'

At these words, as Prodicus informs us, the other interrupted her:—'You see,' said she, 'my Hercules, the long, the laborious road she means to lead you; but I can conduct you to happiness by a path more short and easy.'

'Miserable wretch!' replied Virtue, 'what happiness canst thou boast of? Thou, who wilt not take the least pains to procure it! Doth not satiety always anticipate desire? Wilt thou wait till hunger invites thee to eat, or stay till thou art thirsty before thou drinkest? Or, rather, to give some relish to thy repast, must not art be called in to supply the want of appetite? while thy wines, though costly, can yield no delight, but the ice in summer is sought for to cool and make them grateful to thy palate! Beds of down, or the softest couch, can procure no sleep for thee, whom idleness inclines to seek for repose; not labor and fatigue, which alone prepare for it. Nor dost thou leave it to nature to direct thee in thy pleasures, but all is art and shameless impurity. The night is polluted with riot and crimes, while the day is given up to sloth and inactivity: and, though immortal, thou art become an outcast from the gods, and the contempt and scorn of all good men. Thou boastest of happiness, but what happiness canst thou boast of? Where was it that the sweetest of all sounds, the music of just self-praise, ever reached thine ear? Or when couldst thou view, with complacency and satisfaction, one worthy deed of thy own performing? Is there any one who will trust thy word, or depend upon thy promise; or, if sound in judgment, be of thy society? For, among thy followers, which of them, in youth, are not altogether effeminate and infirm of body? Which of them, in age, not stupid and debilitated in every faculty of the mind? While wasting their time in thoughtless indulgence, they prepare for themselves all that pain and remorse so sure to attend the close of such a life! Ashamed of the past, afflicted with the present, they weary themselves in bewailing that folly which lavished on youth all the joys of life, and left nothing to old age but pain and imbecility!'

'As for me, my dwelling is alone with the gods and good men; and, without me, nothing great, nothing excellent, can be performed, whether on earth or in the heavens; so that my praise, my esteem, is with all who know me! I make the labor of the artist pleasant, and bring to the father of his family security and joy; while the slave, as his lord, is alike my care. In peace I direct to the most useful councils, in war approve myself a faithful ally; and I only can tie the bond of indissoluble friendship. Nor do my votaries even fail to find pleasure in their repasts, though small cost is wanted to furnish out their table: for hunger, not art, prepares it for them; while their sleep, which follows the labor of the day, is far more sweet than whatever expense can procure for idleness: yet, sweet as it is, they quit it unreluctant when called by their duty, whether to the gods or men. The young enjoy the applause of the aged, the aged are reverenced and respected by the young. Equally delighted with reflecting on the past, or contemplating the present, their attachment to me renders them favored of the gods, dear to their friends, and honored by their country. And when the fatal hour is arrived, they sink not, like others, into an inglorious oblivion, but, immortalized by fame, flourish for ever in the grateful remembrance of admiring posterity! Thus, O Hercules! thou great descendant of a glorious race of heroes! thus mayest thou attain that supreme felicity wherewith I have been empowered to reward all those who willingly yield themselves up to my direction.'—FIELDING'S *Version*.

ROBERT SOUTHEY—A FIRESIDE LESSON ON CONDUCT AND WISDOM.

[The readers of that most remarkable production of Robert Southey—"The Doctor, &c."—will recall in the following conversation the principal characters which figure in the volume, so full of rare learning, quaint humor, and practical wisdom, viz., Daniel, the veritable Doctor Daniel Dove, and Dinah, his wife, and Daniel, their only son, born to them after fifteen years of wedlock, a healthy, apt, and docile child, who was growing up under the wholesome teaching of outward nature, of a quiet, pious, industrious, and reading household, and of the more formal but simple teaching of a country schoolmaster by the name of William Guy, and of a loving but half-witted uncle, William Dove:—

"Father," said the boy Daniel one day, after listening to a conversation upon this subject, [of Alchemy,] "I should like to learn to make gold."

"And what wouldst thou do, Daniel, if thou couldst make it?" was the reply.

"Why, I would build a great house, and fill it with books, and have as much money as the king, and be as great a man as the squire."

"Mayhap, Daniel, in that case thou wouldst care for books as little as the squire, and have as little time for them as the king. Learning is better than house or land. As for money, enough is enough; no man can enjoy more; and the less he can be contented with, the wiser and better he is likely to be. What, Daniel, does our good poet tell us in the great verse book?

> Nature's with little pleased; enough's a feast;
> A sober life but a small charge requires;
> But man, the author of his own unrest,
> The more he hath, the more he still desires.

No, boy, thou canst never be so rich as the king, nor so great as the squire; but thou mayst be a philosopher, and that is being as happy as either."

"A great deal happier," said Guy. "The squire is as far from being the happiest man in the neighborhood as he is from being the wisest or the best. And the king, God bless him! has care enough upon his head to bring on early gray hairs."

Uneasy lies the head that wears a crown.

"But what does a philosopher do?" rejoined the boy. "The squire hunts, and shoots, and smokes, and drinks punch, and goes to justice meetings. And the king goes to fight for us against the French, and governs the parliament, and makes laws. But I can not tell what a philosopher's business is. Do they do any thing else besides making almanacs and gold?"

"Yes," said William, "they read the stars."

"And what do they read there?"

"What neither thou nor I can understand, Daniel," replied the father, "however nearly it may concern us."

That grave reply produced a short pause. It was broken by the boy, who said, returning to the subject, "I have been thinking, father, that it is not a good thing to be a philosopher."

"And what, my son, has led thee to that thought?"

"What I have read at the end of the dictionary, father. There was one philosopher that was pounded in a mortar."

"That, Daniel," said the father, "could neither have been the philosopher's fault nor his choice."

"But it was because he was a philosopher, my lad," said Guy, "that he bore it so bravely, and said, 'Beat on; you can only bruise the shell of Anaxarchus!' If he had not been a philosopher they might have pounded him just the same, but they would never have put him in the dictionary. Epictetus in like manner bore the torments which his wicked master inflicted upon him without a groan, only saying, 'Take care, or you will break my leg;' and when the leg was broken, he looked the wretch in the face, and said, 'I told you you would break it.'"

"But," said the youngster, "there was one philosopher who chose to live in a tub; and another, who, that he might never again see any thing to withdraw his mind from meditation, put out his eyes by looking upon a bright brass basin, such as I cured my warts in."

"He might have been a wise man," said William Dove, "but not wondrous wise; for if he had, he would not have used the basin to put his eyes out. He would have jumped into a quickset hedge, and scratched them out, like the man of our town; because, when he saw his eyes were out, he might then have jumped into another hedge and scratched them in again. The man of our town was the greatest philosopher of the two."

"And there was one," continued the boy, "who had better have blinded himself at once, for he did nothing else but cry at every thing he saw. Was not this being very foolish?"

"I am sure," says William, "it was not being merry and wise."

"There was another who said that hunger was his daily food."

"He must have kept such a table as Duke Humphrey," quoth William; "I should not have liked to dine with him."

"Then there was Crates," said the persevering boy; "he had a good estate, and sold it, and threw the money into the sea, saying, 'Away, ye paltry cares! I will drown you, that ye may not drown me.'"

"I should like to know," said William, "what the overseer said to that chap, when he applied to the parish for support."

"They sent him off to bedlam, I suppose," said the mother;" "it was the fit place for him, poor creature."

"And when Aristippus set out upon a journey, he bade his servants throw away all their money, that they might travel the better. Why, they must have begged their way, and it can not be right to beg if people are not brought to it by misfortune. And there were some who thought there was no God. I am sure they were fools, for the Bible says so."

"Well, Daniel," said Guy, "thou hast studied the end of the dictionary to some purpose!"

"And the Bible, too, Master Guy!" said Dinah, her countenance brightening with joy at her son's concluding remark.

"It's the best part of the book," said the boy, replying to the schoolmaster; "there are more entertaining and surprising things there than I ever read in any other place, except in my father's book about Pantagruel."

The elder Daniel had listened to this dialogue in his usual quiet way, smiling sometimes at his brother William's observations. He now stroked his forehead, and looking mildly but seriously at the boy, addressed him thus:—

"My son, many things appear strange or silly in themselves if they are presented to us simply, without any notice when and where they were done, and upon what occasion. The things which the old philosophers said and did, would appear, I dare say, as wise to us as they did to the people of their own times, if we knew why and in what circumstances they were done and said.

Daniel, there are two sorts of men in all ranks and ways of life, the wise and the foolish; and there are a great many degrees between them. That some foolish people have called themselves philosophers, and some wicked ones, and some who were out of their wits, is just as certain as that persons of all these descriptions are to be found among all conditions of men.

Philosophy, Daniel, is of two kinds: that which relates to conduct, and that which relates to knowledge. The first teaches us to value all things at their real worth, to be contented with little, modest in prosperity, patient in trouble, equal-minded at all times. It teaches us our duty to our neighbor and ourselves. It is that wisdom of which King Solomon speaks in our rhyme book. Reach me the volume." Then turning to the passage in his favorite Du Bartas, he read these lines:—

> She's God's own mirror; she's a light whose glance
> Springs from the lightning of his countenance.
> She's mildest heaven's most sacred influence;
> Never decays her beauties' excellence.
> Aye like herself; and she doth always trace
> Not only the same path but the same pace.
> Without her honor, health, and wealth would prove
> Three poisons to me. Wisdom from above
> Is the only moderatrix, spring and guide,
> Organ and honor, of all gifts beside.

"But let us look in the Bible: aye, this is the place:"—

For in her is an understanding spirit, holy, one only, manifold, subtile, lively, clear, undefiled, plain, not subject to hurt, loving the thing that is good, quick, which can not be letted, ready to do good;

Kind to man, steadfast, sure, free from care, having all power, overseeing all things, and going through all understanding, pure and most subtile spirits.

For wisdom is more moving than any motion: she passeth and goeth through all things by reason of her pureness.

For she is the breath of the power of God, and a pure influence, flowing from the glory of the Almighty; therefore can no defiled thing fall into her.

For she is the brightness of the everlasting light, the unspotted mirror of the power of God, and the image of his goodness.

And being but one she can do all things; and remaining in herself she maketh all things new: and in all ages entering into holy souls she maketh them friends of God and prophets.

For God loveth none but him that dwelleth with wisdom.

For she is more beautiful than the sun, and above all the order of stars: being compared with the light she is found before it.

For after this cometh night: but vice shall not prevail against wisdom.

He read this with a solemnity that gave weight to every word. Then closing the book, after a short pause, he proceeded in a lower tone:—

"The philosophers of whom you have read in the dictionary possessed this wisdom only in part, because they were heathens, and therefore could see no further than the light of mere reason could show the way. The fear of the Lord is the beginning of wisdom, and they had not that to begin with. So the thoughts which ought to have made them humble produced pride, and so far their wisdom proved but folly. The humblest Christian who learns his duty, and performs it, as well as he can, is wiser than they. He does nothing to be seen of men; and that was their motive for most of their actions.

Now for the philosophy which relates to knowledge. Knowledge is a brave thing. I am a plain, ignorant, untaught man, and know my ignorance. But it is a brave thing when we look around us in this wonderful world to understand something of what we see; to know something of the earth on which we move, the air which we breathe, and the elements whereof we are made; to comprehend the motions of the moon and stars, and measure the distances between them, and compute times and seasons; to observe the laws which sustain the universe by keeping all things in their courses; to search into the mysteries of nature, and discover the hidden virtue of plants and stones, and read the signs and tokens which are shown us, and make out the meaning of hidden things, and apply all this to the benefit of our fellow-creatures.

Wisdom and knowledge, Daniel, make the difference between man and man, and that between man and beast is hardly greater.

These things do not always go together. There may be wisdom without knowledge, and there may be knowledge without wisdom. A man without knowledge, if he walk humbly with his God, and live in charity with his neighbors, may be wise unto salvation. A man without wisdom may not find his knowledge avail him quite so well. But it is he who possesses both that is the true philosopher. The more he knows, the more he is desirous of knowing; and yet the further he advances in knowledge the better he understands how little he can attain, and the more deeply he feels that God alone can satisfy the infinite desires of an immortal soul. To understand this is the perfection of philosophy."

Then opening the Bible which lay before him, he read these verses:—

My son, if thou wilt receive my words,—
So that thou incline thine ear unto wisdom, and apply thine heart to understanding;
Yea, if thou criest after knowledge, and liftest up thy voice for understanding;
If thou seekest after her as silver, and searchest for her as for hid treasures;
Then shalt thou understand the fear of the Lord, and find the knowledge of God.
For the Lord giveth wisdom: out of his mouth cometh knowledge and understanding.
He layeth up sound wisdom for the righteous: he is a buckler to them that walk uprightly.
He keepeth the paths of judgment, and preserveth the way of his saints.
Then shalt thou understand righteousness, and judgment, and equity; yea, every good path.
When wisdom entereth into thine heart, and knowledge is pleasant unto thy soul;
Discretion shall preserve thee, understanding shall keep thee,
To deliver thee from the way of evil.

"Daniel, my son," after a pause he pursued, "thou art a diligent and good lad. God hath given thee a tender and dutiful heart; keep it so, and it will be a wise one, for thou hast the beginning of wisdom. I wish thee to pursue knowledge, because in pursuing it, happiness will be found by the way. If I have said any thing now which is above thy years, it will come to mind in after time, when I am gone, perhaps, but when thou mayst profit by it. God bless thee, my child!"

He stretched out his right hand at these words, and laid it gently upon the boy's head. What he said was not forgotten, and throughout life the son never thought of that blessing without feeling that it had taken effect.

LORD BACON AND ARCHBISHOP WHATELY ON STUDIES.

BACON'S ESSAY L. OF STUDIES.

Studies serve for delight, for ornament, and for ability. Their chief use for delight is in privateness,[1] and retiring; for ornament, is in discourse; and for ability, is in the judgment and disposition of business; for, expert men can execute, and perhaps judge of particulars, one by one; but the general counsels, and the plots and marshaling of affairs, come best from those that are learned. To spend too much time in studies, is sloth; to use them too much for ornament, is affectation; to make[2] judgment wholly by their rules, is the humor of a scholar; they perfect nature, and are perfected by experience—for natural abilities are like natural plants, that need pruning by study; and studies themselves do give forth directions too much at large, except they be bounded in by experience. Crafty men contemn studies, simple men admire them, and wise men use them, for they teach not their own use; but that is a wisdom without them, and above them, won by observation. Read not to contradict and confute, nor to believe and take for granted, nor to find talk and discourse, but to weigh and consider. Some books are to be tasted, others to be swallowed, and some few to be chewed and digested; that is, some books are to be read only in parts; others to be read, but not curiously;[3] and some few to be read wholly, and with diligence and attention. Some books also may be read by deputy, and extracts made of them by others; but that would[4] be only in the less important arguments, and the meaner sort of books; else distilled books are, like common distilled waters, flashy things. Reading maketh a full man, conference a ready man, and writing an exact man; and, therefore, if a man write little, he had need have a great memory; if he confer little, he had need have a present wit; and if he read little, he had need have much cunning, to seem to know that[5] he doth not. Histories make men wise; poets, witty; the mathematics, subtle; natural philosophy, deep; moral, grave; logic and rhetoric, able to contend: "Abeunt studia in mores"[6]—nay, there is no stond[7] or impediment in the wit, but may be wrought[8]

---

1 Privateness. *Privacy.*

2 Make. *Give.*

3 Curiously. *Attentively.* "At first I thought there had been no light reflected from the water; but observing it more curiously, I saw within it several spots which appeared darker than the rest."—*Sir Isaac Newton.*

4 Would. *Should.*

5 That. *What.*

6 "Manners are influenced by studies."

7 Stond. *Hindrance.*

8 Wrought. *Worked.* "Who, through faith, wrought righteousness."—*Heb.* xi. 33. "How great is Thy goodness, which Thou hast *wrought* for them that trust in Thee!"—*Psalm* xxxi. 19.

out by fit studies, like as diseases of the body may have appropriate exercises—bowling is good for the stone and reins,[1] shooting for the lungs and breast, gentle walking for the stomach, riding for the head, and the like; so, if a man's wits be wandering, let him study the mathematics, for in demonstrations, if his wit be called away never so little, he must begin again; if his wit be not apt to distinguish or find differences,[2] let him study the schoolmen, for they are "cymini sectores;"[3] if he be not apt to beat over matters, and to call upon one thing to prove and illustrate another, let him study the lawyers' cases—so every defect of the mind may have a special receipt.

ANTITHETA ON STUDIES.

PRO.

"Lectio est conversatio cum prudentibus; actio fere cum stultis."

"*In reading, we hold converse with the wise; in the business of life, generally with the foolish.*"

"Non inutiles scientiæ existimandæ sunt, quarum in se nullus est usus, si ingenia acuant, et ordinent."

"*We should not consider even those sciences which have no actual practical application in themselves, as without value, if they sharpen and train the intellect.*"

CONTRA.

"Quæ unquam ars docuit tempestivum artis usum?"

"*What art has ever taught us the suitable use of an art?*"

"Artis sæpenumero ineptus usus est, ne sit nullus."

"*A branch of knowledge is often put to an improper use, for fear of its being idle.*"

ANNOTATIONS BY ARCHBISHOP WHATELY.

"*Crafty men contemn studies.*"

This contempt, whether of crafty men or narrow-minded men, often finds its expression in the word "smattering;" and the couplet is become almost a proverb—

> "A little learning is a dangerous thing;
> Drink deep, or taste not the Pierian spring."

But the poet's remedies for the dangers of a little learning are both of them impossible. None can "drink deep" enough to be, in truth, anything more than very superficial; and every human being, that is not a downright idiot, must *taste*.

It is plainly impossible that any man should acquire a knowledge of all that is to be known, on *all* subjects. But is it then meant that, on each particular subject on which he does learn anything at all, he should be perfectly well informed? Here it may fairly be asked, what is the "well?"—how much knowledge is to be called "little" or "much?" For, in many departments, the very utmost that had been acquired by the greatest proficients, a century and a half back, falls short of what is familiar to many a boarding-school miss now. And it is likely that our posterity, a century and a half hence, will in many things be just as much

---

1 Reins. *Kidneys; inward parts.* "Whom I shall see for myself, though my *reins* be consumed within me."—*Job* xix. 27.

2 Differences. *Distinctions.*

3 "Splitters of cummin." Vid. *A. L.* i. vii 2.

in advance of us. And in most subjects, the utmost knowledge that any man can attain to, is but "a little learning" in comparison of what he remains ignorant of. The view resembles that of an American forest, in which, the more trees a man cuts down, the greater is the expanse of wood he sees around him.

But supposing you define the "much" and the "little" with reference to the existing state of knowledge in the present age and country, would any one seriously advise that those who are not proficients in astronomy should remain ignorant whether the earth moves or the sun?—that unless you are complete master of agriculture, as far as it is at present understood, there is no good in your knowing wheat from barley?—that unless you are such a Grecian as Porson, you had better not learn to construe the Greek Testament?

The other recommendation of the poet, "taste not"—that is to say, have no learning—is equally impossible. The truth is, every body has, and every body ought to have, a slight and superficial knowledge—a "smattering," if you will—of more subjects than it is possible for the most diligent student to acquire thoroughly. It is very possible, and also very useful, to have that slight smattering of chemistry which will enable one to distinguish from the salts used in medicine, the oxalic acid, with which, through mistake, several persons have been poisoned. Again, without being an eminent botanist, a person may know—what it is most important to know—the difference between cherries and the berries of the deadly nightshade; the want of which knowledge has cost many lives.

Again, there is no one, even of those who are not profound politicians, who is not aware that we have Rulers; and is it not proper that he should understand that government is necessary to preserve our lives and property? Is he likely to be a worse subject for knowing that? That depends very much on the kind of government you wish to establish. If you wish to establish an unjust and despotic government—or, if you wish to set up a false religion—then it would be advisable to avoid the danger of enlightening the people. But if you wish to maintain a good government, the more the people understand the advantages of such a government, the more they will respect it; and the more they know of true religion, the more they will value it.

There is nothing more general among uneducated people than a disposition to socialism, and yet nothing more injurious to their own welfare. An equalization of wages would be most injurious to themselves, for it would, at once, destroy all emulation. All motives for the acquisition of skill, and for superior industry, would be removed. Now, it is but a *little* knowledge of political economy that is needed for the removal of this error; but that little is highly useful.

Again, every one knows, no matter how ignorant of medicine, that there is such a thing as disease. But as an instance of the impossibility of the "taste not" recommendation of the poet, a fact may be mentioned, which perhaps is known to most. When the cholera broke out in Poland, the peasantry of that country took it into their heads that the nobles were poisoning them in order to clear the country of them; they believed the rich to be the authors of that terrible disease; and the consequence was that the peasantry rose in masses, broke into the houses of the nobility, and finding some chloride of lime, which had been used for the purpose of disinfecting, they took it for the poison which had caused the disease; and they murdered them. Now, that was the sort of "little learning" which was very dangerous.

Again we can not prevent people from believing that there is some superhuman

Being who has regard to human affairs. Some clowns in the Weald of Kent, who had been kept as much as possible on the "taste not" system,—left in a state of gross ignorance,—yet believed that the Deity did impart special powers to certain men; and that belief, coupled with excessive stupidity, led them to take an insane fanatic for a prophet. In this case, this "little learning" actually caused an insurrection in his favor, in order to make him king, priest and prophet of the British empire; and many lives were sacrificed before this insane insurrection was put down. If a "little learning" is a "dangerous thing," you will have to keep people in a perfect state of idiotcy in order to avoid that danger. I would, therefore, say that both the recommendations of the poet are impracticable.

The question arises, what are we to do? Simply to impress upon ourselves and upon all people the importance of laboring in that much neglected branch of human knowledge—the knowledge of our own ignorance;—and of remembering that it is by a confession of real ignorance that real knowledge must be gained. But even when that further knowledge is not attained, still even the knowledge of the ignorance is a great thing in itself; so great, it seems, as to constitute Socrates the wisest of his time.

Some of the chief sources of unknown ignorance may be worth noticing here. They are to be found in our not being aware: 1. How inadequate a medium language is for conveying thought. 2. How inadequate our very minds are for the comprehension of many things. 3. How little we need understand a word which may yet be familiar to us, and which we may use in reasoning. This piece of ignorance is closely connected with the two foregoing. (Hence, frequently, men will accept as an explanation of a phenomenon, a mere statement of the difficulty in other words.) 4. How utterly ignorant we are of efficient causes; and how the philosopher who refers to the law of gravitation the falling of a stone to the earth, no further explains the phenomenon than the peasant, who would say it is the nature of it. The philosopher knows that the stone obeys the same law to which all *other* bodies are subject, and to which, for convenience, he gives the name of gravitation. His knowledge is only more *general* than the peasant's; which, however, is a vast advantage. 5. How many words there are that express, not the nature of the thing they are applied to, but the manner in which they *affect us;* and which, therefore, give about as correct a notion of those things, as the word "crooked" would, if applied to a stick half immersed in water. (Such is the word *Chance*, with all its family.) 6. How many causes may, and usually do, conduce to the same effect. 7. How liable the faculties, even of the ablest, are to occasional failure; so that they shall overlook mistakes (and those often the most at variance with their own established notions) which, *when once exposed*, seem quite gross even to inferior men. 8. How much all are biassed, in all their moral reasonings, by self-love, or perhaps, rather, partiality to *human nature*, and other passions. 9. Dugald Stewart would add very justly, How little we know of *matter;* no more indeed than of mind; though all are prone to attempt explaining the phenomena of mind by those of matter: for, what is *familiar* men generally consider as *well known*, though the fact is oftener otherwise.

The errors arising from these causes, and from not calculating on them,—that is, in short, from ignorance of our own ignorance, have probably impeded philosophy more than all other obstacles put together.

Certain it is, that only by this ignorance of our ignorance can "a little learning" become "a dangerous thing." The dangers of knowledge are not to be compared with the dangers of ignorance. A man is more likely to miss his way in darkness than in *twilight;* in twilight than in full sun. And those contemners of studies who say (with Mandeville, in his *Treatise against Charity-schools*) "If a horse knew as much as a man, I should not like to be his rider," ought to add, "If a man knew as little as a horse, I should not like to trust him to ride." It is indeed possible to educate the children of the poor so as to disqualify them for an humble and laborious station in life; but this mistake does not so much consist in the *amount* of the knowledge imparted, as in the *kind* and the *manner* of education. Habits early engrafted on children, of regular attention,—of steady application to what they are about,—of prompt obedience to the directions they receive,—of cleanliness, order, and decent and modest behavior, can not but be of advantage to them in after life, whatever their station may be. And certainly, their familiar acquaintance with the precepts and example of Him who, when all stations of life were at his command, chose to be the reputed son of a poor mechanic, and to live with peasants and fishermen; or, again, of his apostle Paul, whose own hands "ministered to his necessities," and to those of his companions:—such studies, I say, can surely never tend to unfit any one for a life of humble and contented industry.

What, then, is the "smattering"—the imperfect and superficial knowledge—that really does deserve contempt? A slight and superficial knowledge is justly condemned, when it is put in the place of more full and exact knowledge. Such an acquaintance with chemistry and anatomy, *e. g.* as would be creditable, and not useless, to a lawyer, would be contemptible for a physician; and such an acquaintance with law as would be desirable for him, would be a most discreditable smattering for a lawyer.

It is to be observed that the word smattering is applied to two different kinds of scanty knowledge—the *rudimentary* and the *superficial;* though it seems the more strictly to belong to the latter. Now, as it is evident that no one can learn all things perfectly, it seems best for a man to make some pursuit his main object, according to, first, his *calling;* secondly, his *natural bent;* or thirdly, his *opportunities:* then, let him get a slight knowledge of what else is worth it, regulated in his choice by the same three circumstances; which should also determine, in great measure, where an elementary and where a superficial knowledge is desirable. Such as are of the most dignified and philosophical nature are most proper for elementary study; and such as we are the most likely to be called upon to practice for ourselves, the most proper for superficial; *e. g.*, it would be to most men of no practical use, and, consequently, not worth while, to learn by heart the meaning of some of the Chinese characters; but it might be very well worth while to study the principles on which that most singular language is constructed; *contra*, there is nothing very curious or interesting in the structure of the Portuguese language; but if one were going to travel in Portugal, it would be worth while to pick up some words and phrases. If both circumstances conspire, then, both kinds of information are to be sought for; and such things should be learned a little at *both ends;* that is, to understand the elementary and fundamental *principles*, and also to know some of the most remarkable *results*—a little of the rudiments, and a little of what is most called for in practice. *E. g.*, a man who has not made any of the physical or mathematical sciences his favorite pursuit, ought yet to know the principles of geometrical reasoning, and the elements of mechanics; and also to know, by rote, something of the magnitude, distances, and motions of the heavenly bodies, though without having gone over the intermediate course of scientific demonstration.

Grammar, logic, rhetoric, and metaphysics, [or the philosophy of mind,] are manifestly studies of an *elementary* nature, being concerned about the instruments which we employ in effecting our purposes; and ethics, which is, in fact, a branch of metaphysics, may be called the elements of conduct. Such knowledge is far from showy. Elements do not much come into sight; they are like that part of a bridge which is under water, and is therefore least admired, though it is not the work of least art and difficulty. On this ground it is suitable to females, as least leading to that pedantry which learned ladies must ever be peculiarly liable to, as well as least exciting that jealousy to which they must ever be exposed, while learning in them continues to be a *distinction*. A woman might, in this way, be very learned without any one's finding it out.

"*Read not to contradict and confute, nor to believe and take for granted, nor to find talk and discourse, but to weigh and consider. Some books are to be tasted, others to be swallowed, and some few to be chewed and digested.*"

It would have been well if Bacon had added some hints as to the *mode* of study: *how* books are to be chewed, and swallowed, and digested. For, besides inattentive readers, who measure their proficiency by the pages they have gone over, it is quite possible, and not uncommon, to read most laboriously, even so as to get by heart the words of a book, without really *studying* it at all; that is, without employing the *thoughts* on the *subject*.

In particular, there is, in reference to Scripture,[1] "a habit cherished by some persons, of reading—assiduously, indeed—but without any attentive reflection and studious endeavor to ascertain the real sense of what they read—concluding that whatever impression is found to be left on the mind after a bare perusal of the words, must be what the sacred writers designed. They use, in short, little or none of that care which is employed on any other subject in which we are much interested, to read through each treatise consecutively as a whole,—to compare one passage with others that may throw light on it, and to consider what was the general drift of the author, and what were the occasions, and the persons he had in view.

"In fact, the real *students* of Scripture, properly so called, are, I fear, *fewer* than is commonly supposed. The theological student is often a student chiefly of some human system of divinity, fortified by *references* to Scripture, introduced from time to time as there is occasion. He proceeds—often unconsciously—by setting himself to ascertain, not what is the information or instruction to be derived from a certain narrative or discourse of one of the sacred writers, but what aid can be derived from them towards establishing or refuting this or that point of dogmatic theology. Such a mode of study surely ought at least not to be exclusively pursued. At any rate, it can not properly be called a *study of Scripture*.

"There is, in fact, a danger of its proving a great *hindrance* to the profitable study of Scripture; for so strong an association is apt to be established in the mind between certain expressions, and the *technical* sense to which they have been confined in some theological system, that when the student meets with them

1 See *Essays on the Difficulties of St Paul's Epistles.* Essay X. page 122.

in Scripture, he at once understands them in that sense, in passages where perhaps an unbiassed examination of the context would plainly show that such was not the author's meaning. And such a student one may often find expressing the most unfeigned wonder at the blindness of those who can not find in Scripture such and such doctrines, which appear to him to be as clearly set forth there as words can express; which perhaps they are, on the (often gratuitous) supposition that those words are everywhere to be understood exactly in the sense which he has previously derived from some human system,—a system through which, as through a discolored medium, he views Scripture. But this is not to take Scripture for one's guide, but rather to make one's self a *guide* to Scripture.

"Others, again, there are, who are habitual readers of the Bible, and perhaps of little else, but who yet can not properly be said to *study* anything at all on the subject of religion, because, as was observed just above, they do not even attempt to exercise their mind on the subject, but trust to be sufficiently enlightened and guided by the mere act of perusal, while their minds remain in a passive state. And some, I believe, proceed thus on principle, considering that they are the better recipients of revealed truth the less they exercise their own reason.

"But this is to proceed on a totally mistaken view of the real province of reason. It would, indeed, be a great error to attempt *substituting* for revelation conjectures framed in our own mind, or to speculate on matters concerning which we have an imperfect knowledge imparted to us by revelation, and could have had, without it, none at all. But this would be, not to use, but to abuse, our rational faculties. By the use of our senses, which are as much the gift of the Creator as anything else we enjoy,—and by employing our reason on the objects around us, we can obtain a certain amount of valuable knowledge. And beyond this, there are certain other points of knowledge unattainable by these faculties, and which God has thought fit to impart to us by his inspired messengers. But *both* the volumes—that of Nature and that of Revelation—which He has thought good to lay before us, are to be carefully studied. On both of them we must diligently employ the faculties with which He, the Author of both, has endued us, if we would derive full benefit from his gifts.

"The telescope, we know, brings within the sphere of our own vision much that would be undiscernible by the naked eye; but we must not the less employ our eyes in making use of it; and we must watch and calculate the motions, and reason on the appearances, of the heavenly bodies, which are visible only through the telescope, with the same care we employ in respect of those seen by the naked eye.

"And an analogous procedure is requisite if we would derive the intended benefit from the pages of inspiration, which were designed not to save us the trouble of inquiring and reflecting, but to enable us, on some points, to inquire and reflect to better purpose,—not to supersede the use of our reason, but to supply its deficiencies."

Although, however, it is quite right, and most important, that the *thoughts* should be exercised on the subject of what you are reading, there is one mode of exercising the thoughts that is very hurtful; which is, that of *substituting conjectures* for attention to what the author says. *Preliminary* reflection on the subject is, as has been above said, very useful in many cases; though, by the way, it is unsafe as a preparation for the study of *Scripture*; and, in all studies, care should be taken to guard against allowing the judgment to be biased by notions hastily and prematurely adopted. And again, *after* you have studied an author, it will be very advisable (supposing it is an uninspired and consequently fallible one) to reflect on what he says, and consider whether he is right, and how far.

But while *actually engaged* in perusal, attend to what the writer actually says, and endeavour fairly to arrive at *his* meaning, *before* you proceed to speculate upon it for yourself.

The study of a book, in short, should be conducted nearly according to the same rule that Bacon lays down for the study of nature.' He warns philosophers, earnestly and often, against substituting for what he calls the "interrogatio naturæ," the "anticipatio naturæ;" that is, instead of attentive observation and experiment, forming conjectures as to what seems to us *likely*, or *fitting*, according to some hypothesis devised by ourselves. In like manner, in studying an author, you should *keep apart* interpretation and conjecture.

A good teacher warns a student of some book in a foreign language that he is learning, not to guess what the author is likely to have meant, and then twist the words into that sense, against the idiom of the language; but to be *led by* the words in the first instance; and then, if a difficulty as to the sense remains, to guess which of the possible meanings of the words is the most likely to be the right.

E. g. The words in the original of John xviii. 15, ὁ ἄλλος μαθητής, plainly signify "*the* other disciple;" and one of the commentators, perceiving that this is inconsistent with the opinion he had taken up, that this disciple was John himself, (since John had not been mentioned before, and the article, therefore, would make it refer to Judas, who alone had been just above named,) boldly suggests that the *reading must be wrong*, (though all the MSS. agree in it,) and that the article ought to be omitted, because it *spoils the sense*; that is, the sense which agrees with a *conjecture* adopted in defiance of the words of the passage.

This one instance may serve as a specimen of the way in which some, instead of interpreting an author, undertake to re-write what he has said.

The like rule holds good in other studies, quite as much as in that of a language. We should be ever on our guard against the tendency to read through *colored spectacles*.

Educational habits of thought, analogies, antecedent reasonings, feelings, and wishes, &c., will be always leading us to form some conjectural hypothesis, which is not necessarily hurtful, and may sometimes furnish a useful hint, but which must be most carefully watched, lest it produce an unfair bias, and lead you to strain into a conformity with it the words or the phenomena before you.

A man sets out with a conjecture as to what the Apostles are *likely* to have said, or *ought* to have said, in conformity with the the theological system he has learnt; or what the Most High may have done or designed; or what is or is not agreeable to the "analogy of faith," (see Campbell *on the Gospels*;) *i. e.*, of a piece with the christian system—namely, that which *he* has been taught, by fallible men, to regard as the christian system; and then he proceeds to examine Scripture, as he would examine with *leading questions* a witness whom he had summoned in his cause.

"As the fool thinketh,
So the bell clinketh."

Perhaps he "*goes through*" all the Bible; not with a candid and teachable mind, seeking instruction, but unconsciously praying that he may *find himself in the right*. And he will seldom fail.

> "Hic liber est in quo quærit sua dogmata quisque;
> Invenit et pariter dogmata quisque sua."
>
> "In this book many students seek each one to find
> The doctrine or precept that's most to his mind:
> And each of them finds what they earnestly seek;
> For as the fool thinks, even so the bells speak."

It is the same with philosophy. If you have a strong wish to find phenomena such as to confirm the conjectures you have formed, and allow that wish to bias your examination, you are ill-fitted for interrogating nature. Both that, and *the other volume of* the records of what God does,—Revelation,—are to be interrogated, not as *witnesses*, but as *instructors*. You must let all your conjectures *hang loose* upon you; and be prepared to learn *from* what is written in each of those volumes, with the aid of the conjectures of reason; not *from* reason, (nor, by the by, from feelings and fancies, and wishes, and human authority,) with Scripture for your *aid*.

This latter procedure, which is a very common one with theological students, may be called making an *anagram* of Scripture,—taking it to pieces and reconstructing it in the model of some human system of "Institutes:" building a temple of one's own, consisting of the stones of the true one pulled down and put together in a new fashion.

Yet divines of this description are *often* considered by others as well as by themselves, pre-eminently scriptural, from their continual employment of the *very words* of Scripture, and their readiness in citing a profusion of texts. But, in reality, instead of using a human *commentary* on Scripture, they use Scripture itself as a kind of commentary on some human system. They make the warp human, and interweave an abundance of Scripture as a *woof;* which is just the reverse of the right procedure. But this may be called, truly, in a certain sense, "*taking* a text *from* Scripture," "preaching such and such a doctrine *out of* Scripture," and "*improving* Scripture."

Thus it is that men, when comparing their opinions with the standard of God's Word, *suffer* those opinions to *bend the rule* by which they are to be measured. But he who studies the Scriptures should remember that he is consulting the Spirit of Truth, and if he would hope for his aid, through whose enlightening and supporting grace alone those Scriptures can be read with advantage, he must search honestly and earnestly for the truth.

"*Read not to contradict and confute; nor to believe and take for granted.*"

With respect to the deference due to the opinions (written or spoken) of intelligent and well-informed men, it may be remarked, that *before* a question has been fully argued, there is a presumption that they are in the right; but *afterwards*, if objections have been brought which they have failed to answer, the presumption is the other way. The wiser, and the more learned, and the more numerous, are those opposed to you, and the more strenuous and persevering their opposition, the greater is the probability that if there were any flaw in your argument they would have refuted you. And therefore your adhering to an opposite opinion from theirs, so far from being a mark of arrogant contempt, is, in reality, the strongest proof of a high respect for them. For example—The strongest confirmation of the fidelity of the translations of Scripture published by the Irish School Commissioners, is to be found in the many futile attempts, made by many able and learned men, to detect errors in them.

This important distinction is often overlooked.

"*Reading maketh a full man, conference a ready man, and writing an exact man.*"

Writing an Analysis, table of Contents, Index, or Notes to any book, is very important for the study, properly so called, of any subject. And so, also, is the practice of *previously* conversing or writing on the subject you are about to study.

I have elsewhere alluded to this kind of practice,[1] and suggested to the teacher "to put before his pupils, *previously* to their reading each lesson, some questions pertaining to the matter of it, requiring of them answers, oral or written, the best they can think of *without* consulting the book. Next, let them read the lesson, having other questions, such as may lead to any needful explanations, put before them as they proceed. And afterwards let them be examined (introducing numerous examples framed by themselves and by the teacher) as to the portion they have learned, in order to judge how far they remember it.

"Of the three kinds of questions,—which may be called, 1, *preliminary* questions; 2, questions of *instruction;* and 3, questions of *examination,*—the last alone are, by a considerable portion of instructors, commonly employed. And the elementary books commonly known as 'catechisms,' or 'books in question and answer,' consist, in reality, of questions of this description.

"But the second kind—what is properly to be called instructive questioning—is employed by all who deserve to be reckoned good teachers.

"The first kind—the preliminary questioning—is employed (systematically and constantly) but by few. And, at first sight, it might be supposed by those who have not had experience of it, that it would be likely to increase the learner's difficulties. But if any well-qualified instructor will but carefully and judiciously try the experiment (in teaching any kind of science,) he will be surprised to find to how great a degree this exercise of the student's mind on the subject will contribute to his advancement. He will find that what has been taught in the mode above suggested, will have been learnt in a shorter time, will have been far the more thoroughly understood, and will be fixed incomparably the better in the memory."

Curiosity is as much the parent of attention, as attention is of memory; therefore the first business of a teacher—first, not only in point of time, but of importance—should be to excite, not merely a general curiosity on the subject of the study, but a particular curiosity on particular points in that subject. To teach one who has no curiosity to learn, is to sow a field without ploughing it.

And this process saves a student from being (as many are) intellectually damaged by having a very good memory. For an unskillful teacher is content to put before his pupils what they have to learn, and ascertaining that they remember it. And thus those of them whose memory is ready and attentive, have their mind left in a merely passive state, and are like a person always carried about in a sedan chair, till he has almost lost the use of his limbs. And then it is made a wonder that a person who has been so well taught, and who was so quick in

---

[1] See Preface to *Easy Lessons on Reasoning.* Page v.

learning and remembering, should not prove an able man; which is about as reasonable as to expect that a capacious cistern, if filled, should be converted into a perennial fountain. Many are saved, by the deficiency of their memory, from being spoiled by their education; for those who have no extraordinary memory, are driven to supply its defects by *thinking*. If they do not remember a mathematical demonstration, they are driven to devise one. If they do not exactly retain what Aristotle or Smith have said, they are driven to consider what they were *likely* to have said, or ought to have said. And thus their faculties are invigorated by exercise.

Now, this kind of exercise a skillful teacher will afford to *all*; so that no one shall be spoiled by the goodness of his memory.

A very common practice may be here noticed, which should be avoided, if we would create a habit of studying with profit—that of making children *learn by rote* what they do not *understand*. "It is done on this plea—that they will hereafter learn the meaning of what they have been thus taught, and will be able to make a practical use of it."[1] But no attempt at economy of time can be more injudicious. Let any child whose capacity is so far matured as to enable him to comprehend an explanation,—*e. g.*, of the Lord's Prayer,—have it *then* put before him for the first time, and when he is made acquainted with the meaning of it, set to learn it by heart; and can any one doubt that, in less than a half a day's application, he would be able to repeat it fluently? And the same would be the case with other forms. All that is learned by rote by a child before he is competent to attach a meaning to the words he utters, would not, if all put together, amount to so much as would cost him, when able to understand it, a week's labor to learn perfectly. Whereas, it may cost the toil, often the vain toil, of many years, to unlearn the habit of *formalism*—of repeating words by rote without attending to their meaning; a habit which every one conversant with education knows to be in all subjects most readily acquired by children, and with difficulty avoided even with the utmost care of the teacher; but which such a plan must inevitably tend to generate. It is often said, and very truly, that it is important to form early habits of piety; but to train a child in one kind of habit, is not the most likely way of forming the opposite one; and nothing can be more contrary to true piety, than the Romish superstition (for such in fact it is) of attaching efficacy to the repetition of a certain form of words as a charm, independent of the understanding and of the heart.

"It is also said, with equal truth, that we ought to take advantage of the facility which children possess of learning; but to infer from thence, that Providence designs us to make such a use (or rather abuse) of this gift as we have been censuring, is as if we were to take advantage of the readiness with which a new-born babe swallows whatever is put into its mouth, to dose it with ardent spirits, instead of wholesome food and necessary medicine. The readiness with which children learn and remember words, is in truth a most important advantage if rightly employed; viz., if applied to the acquiring that mass of what may be called *arbitrary* knowledge of insulated facts, which can *only* be learned by rote, and which is necessary in after life; when the acquisition of it would both be more troublesome, and would encroach on time that might otherwise be better employed. Chronology, names of countries, weights and measures, and indeed all the words of any language, are of this description. If a child had even ten times the ordi-

[1] *London Review*. No. ii., pages 412, 413.

nary degree of the faculty in question, a judicious teacher would find abundance of useful employment for it, without resorting to any that could possibly be detrimental to his future habits, moral, religious, or intellectual."

One very useful precept for students, is never to *remain long* puzzling out any difficulty; but lay the book and the subject aside, and return to it some hours after, or next day; after having turned the attention to something else. Sometimes a person will weary his mind for several hours in some efforts (which might have been spared) to make out some difficulty; and next day, when he returns to the subject, will find it quite easy.

The like takes place in the effort to recollect some *name*. You may fatigue yourself in vain for hours together; and if you turn to something else (which you might as well have done at once) the name will, as it were, flash across you without an effort.

There is something analogous to this, in reference to the scent of dogs. When a wounded bird, for instance, has been lost in the the thicket, and the dogs fail, after some search, to find it, a skillful sportsman always draws them off, and hunts them elsewhere for an hour, and then brings them back to the spot to try afresh; and they will often, then, find their game readily: though, if they had been hunting for it all the time, they would have failed.

It seems as if the dog—and the mind—having got into a kind of *wrong track*, continued in the same error, till drawn completely away elsewhere.

Always trust, therefore, for the overcoming of a difficulty, not to *long continued* study after you have once got bewildered, but to *repeated* trials, at intervals

It may be here observed, that the student of any science or art should not only distinctly understand all the technical language, and all the rules of the art, but also learn them by heart, so that they may be remembered as familiarly as the alphabet, and employed *constantly* and with scrupulous exactness. Otherwise, technical language will prove an encumbrance instead of an advantage, just as a suit of clothes would be, if instead of putting them on and wearing them, one should carry them about in his hand.

"*There is no stond or impediment in the wit, but may be wrought out by fit studies.*"

It is a pity that Bacon did not more fully explain the mode in which different kinds of studies act on the mind. As an exercise of the reasoning faculty, pure mathematics is an admirable exercise, because it consists of *reasoning* alone, and does not encumber the student with any exercise of *judgment*: and it is well always to begin with learning one thing at a time, and to defer a combination of mental exercises to a later period. But then it is important to remember that mathematics does *not* exercise the *judgment*; and consequently, if too exclusively pursued, may leave the student very ill qualified for moral reasonings.

"The definitions, which are the principles of our reasoning, are very *few*, and the axioms still fewer; and both are, for the most part, *laid down* and *placed before the student in the outset;* the introduction of a new definition or axiom being of comparatively rare occurrence, at wide intervals, and with a *formal* statement, besides which, there is no room for *doubt* concerning either. On the other hand, in all reasonings which regard matters of fact, we introduce, almost at *every step*, fresh and fresh propositions (to a very great number) which had not been elicited in the course of our reasoning, but are taken for granted; viz., facts, and laws of nature, which are here the principles of our reasoning, and *maxims*, or 'elements of belief,' which answer to the axioms in mathematics. *If*, at the opening of a treatise, for example, on chemistry, on agriculture, on political economy, &c., the author should make, as in mathematics, a formal statement of all the propositions he intended to assume as granted, throughout the whole work, both he and his readers would be astonished at the number; and, of these, many would be only probable, and there would be much room for doubt as to the *degree* of probability, and for judgment in ascertaining that degree.

"Moreover, mathematical axioms are always employed precisely in *the same simple form*: *e. g.*, the axiom that 'the things equal to the same are equal to one another,' is cited, whenever there is need, in those very words; whereas the maxims employed in the other class of subjects, admit of, and require, continual modifications in the application of them. *E. g.*, 'the stability of the laws of nature,' which is our constant assumption in inquiries relating to natural philosophy, appears in many different shapes, and in some of them does not possess the same complete certainty as in others; *e. g.*, when, from having always observed a certain sheep ruminating, we infer, that this individual sheep will continue to ruminate, we assume that 'the property which has hitherto belonged to this sheep will remain unchanged;' when we infer the same property of all sheep, we assume that 'the property which belongs to this individual belongs to the whole species;' if, on comparing sheep with some other kinds of horned animals,[1] and finding that all agree in ruminating, we infer that 'all horned animals ruminate,' we assume that 'the whole of a genus or class are likely to agree in any point wherein many species of that genus agree:' or in other words, 'that if one of two properties, &c., has *often* been found accompanied by another, and never without it, the former will be *universally* accompanied by the latter;' now all these are merely different forms of the maxim, that 'nature is uniform in her operations,' which, it is evident, varies in expression in almost every different case where it is applied, and the application of which admits of every degree of evidence, from perfect moral certainty, to mere conjecture.

"The same may be said of an infinite number of principles and maxims appropriated to, and employed in, each particular branch of study. Hence, all such reasonings are, in comparison of mathematics, very complex; requiring so much more than that does, beyond the process of merely deducing the conclusion logically from the premises: so that it is no wonder that the longest mathematical demonstration should be so much more easily constructed and understood than a much shorter train of just reasoning concerning real facts. The former has been aptly compared to a long and steep, but even and regular, flight of steps, which tries the breath, and the strength, and the perseverance only; while the latter resembles a short, but rugged and uneven, ascent up a precipice, which requires a quick eye, agile limbs, and a firm step; and in which we have to tread now on this side, now on that—ever considering, as we proceed, whether this or that projection will afford room for our foot, or whether some loose stone may not slide from under us. There are probably as many steps of pure reasoning in one of the longer of Euclid's demonstrations, as in the whole of an argumentative treatise on some other subject, occupying perhaps a considerable volume.

[1] Viz., having horns on *the skull*. What are called the horns of the rhinoceros are quite different in origin, and in structure, as well as in situation, from what are properly called horns.

"It may be observed here that mathematical reasoning, as it calls for no exercise of judgment respecting probabilities, is the best kind of introductory exercise; and from the same cause, is apt, when too exclusively pursued, to make men incorrect moral reasoners.

"As for those ethical and legal reasonings which were lately mentioned as in some respects resembling those of mathematics, (viz., such as keep clear of all assertions respecting facts,) they have this difference; that not only men are not so completely *agreed* respecting the maxims and principles of ethics and law, but the meaning also of each term can not be absolutely, and for ever, fixed by an arbitrary definition; on the contrary, a great part of our labor consists in distinguishing accurately the various senses in which men employ each term,—ascertaining which is the most proper,—and taking care to avoid confounding them together.

"It may be worth while to add in this place, that as a candid disposition,—a hearty desire to judge fairly, and to attain truth,—are evidently necessary with a view to give fair play to the reasoning powers, in subjects where we are liable to a bias from interest or feelings, so, a fallacious perversion of this maxim finds a place in the minds of some persons; who accordingly speak disparagingly of *all* exercise of the reasoning faculty in moral and religious subjects; declaiming on the insufficiency of *mere* intellectual power for the attainment of truth in such matters,—on the necessity of appealing to the heart rather than to the head, &c., and then leading their readers or themselves to the conclusion that the less we *reason* on such subjects the safer we are.

"But the proper office of candor is to *prepare* the mind not for the *rejection* of all evidence, but for the right *reception* of evidence;—not to be a *substitute* for reasons, but to enable us *fairly to weigh* the reasons on both sides. Such persons as I am alluding to are in fact saying that since just weights *alone*, without a just balance, will avail nothing, therefore we have only to take care of the scales, and let the weights take care of themselves.

"This kind of tone is of course most especially to be found in such writers as consider it expedient to inculcate on the mass of mankind what—there is reason to suspect—they do not themselves fully believe, and which they apprehend is the more likely to be rejected the more it is investigated."

A curious anecdote (which I had heard, in substance, some years before) was told me by the late Sir Alexander Johnstone. When he was acting as temporary governor of Ceylon, (soon after its cession,) he sat once as Judge in a trial of a prisoner for a robbery and murder; and the evidence seemed to him so conclusive, that he was about to charge the jury (who were native Cingalese) to find a verdict of guilty. But one of the jury asked and obtained permission to examine the witnesses himself. He had them brought in one by one, and cross-examined them so ably as to elicit the fact that they were *themselves* the perpetrators of the crime, which they afterwards had conspired to impute to the prisoner. And they were accordingly put on their trial and convicted.

Sir A. J. was greatly struck by the intelligence displayed by this juror; the more, as he was only a small farmer, who was not known to have had any remarkable advantages of education. He sent for him, and after commending the wonderful sagacity he had shown, inquired eagerly what his studies had been. The man replied that he had never read but one book, the only one he possessed, which had long been in his family, and which he delighted to study in his leisure hours. This book he was prevailed on to show to Sir A. J., who put it into the hands of one who knew the Cingalese language. It turned out to be a translation into that language of a large portion of Aristotle's *Organon*. It appears that the Portuguese, when they first settled in Ceylon and other parts of the East, translated into the native languages several of the works then studied in the European Universities; among which were the Latin versions of Aristotle.

The Cingalese in question said that if his understanding had been in any degree cultivated and improved, it was to that book he owed it.

It is very important to warn all readers of the influence likely to be exercised in the formation of their opinions, *indirectly*, and by works not professedly argumentative, such as Poems and Tales. Fletcher of Saltoun said, he would let any one have the making of the laws of a country, if he might have the making of their ballads.

An observation in the *Lectures on Political Economy* on one cause which has contributed to foster an erroneous opinion of the superior moral purity of poor and half-civilized countries, is equally applicable to a multitude of other cases, on various subjects. "One powerful, but little suspected cause, I take to be, an early familiarity with poetical descriptions of pure, unsophisticated, rustic life, in remote, sequestered, and unenlightened districts;—of the manly virtue and practical wisdom of our simple forefathers, before the refinements of luxury had been introduced;—of the adventurous wildness, so stimulating to the imagination, of savage or pastoral life, in the midst of primeval forests, lofty mountains, and all the grand scenery of uncultivated nature. Such subjects and scenes are much better adapted for poets, than thronged cities, workshops, coalpits, and iron-founderies. And poets, whose object is to please, of course keep out of sight all the odious or disgusting circumstances pertaining to the life of the savage or the untutored clown, and dwell exclusively on all the amiable and admirable parts of that simplicity of character which they feign or fancy. Early associations are thus formed, whose influence is often the stronger and the more lasting, from the very circumstance that they are formed unconsciously, and do not come in the form of propositions demanding a deliberate assent. Poetry does not *profess* to aim at conviction; but it often leaves impressions which affect the reasoning and the judgment. And a false impression is perhaps oftener conveyed in other ways than by sophistical argument; because *that* rouses the mind to exert its powers, and to assume, as it were, a reasoning mood."[1]

The influence exercised by such works is overlooked by those who suppose that a child's character, moral and intellectual, is formed by those books only which are put into his hands with that *design*. As hardly anything can accidentally touch the soft clay without stamping its mark on it, so, hardly any reading can interest a child without contributing in some degree, though the book itself be afterwards totally forgotten, to form the character; and the parents, therefore, who, merely requiring from him a certain course of *study*, pay little or no attention to story-books, are educating him they know not how.

And here, I would observe that in books designed for children there are two extremes that should be avoided. The one, that reference to religious principles

---

1 In an article in a Review I have seen mention made of a person who discovered the fallacy of a certain doctrine (which, by the way, is nevertheless a true one, that of Malthus,) *instinctively*. This kind of instinct, *i. e.* the habit of forming opinions at the suggestion rather of feeling than of reason, is very common.

in connection with matters too trifling and undignified, arising from a well-intentioned zeal, causing a forgetfulness of the maxim whose notorious truth has made it proverbial, "Too much familiarity breeds contempt." And the other is the contrary, and still more prevailing extreme, arising from a desire to preserve a due *reverence* for religion, at the expense of its useful application in conduct. But a line may be drawn which will keep clear of both extremes. We should not exclude the association of things sacred with whatever are to *ourselves* trifling matters, (for "these little things are great" to children,) but, with whatever is viewed by *them* as trifling. Every thing is great or small in reference to the parties concerned. The private concerns of any obscure individual are very insignificant to the world at large, but they are of great importance to himself. And all worldly affairs must be small in the sight of the Most High; but irreverent familiarity is engendered in the mind of any one, then, and then only, when things sacred are associated with such as are, to him, insignificant things.

And here I would add that those works of fiction are worse than unprofitable that inculcate morality, with an exclusion of all reference to religious principle. This is obviously and notoriously the character of Miss Edgeworth's moral tales. And so entire and resolute is this exclusion, that it is maintained at the expense of what *may* be called poetical truth; it destroys, in many instances, the probability of the tale, and the naturalness of the characters. That Christianity does exist, every one must believe as an incontrovertible truth; nor can any one deny that, whether true or false, it does exercise,—at least is supposed to exercise,—an influence on the feelings and conduct of some of the believers in it. To represent, therefore, persons of various ages, sex, country, and station in life, as practising, on the most trying occasions, every kind of duty, and encountering every kind of danger, difficulty, and hardship, while none of them ever makes the least reference to a religious motive, is as decidedly at variance with reality,—what is called in works of fiction *unnatural*,—as it would be to represent Mahomet's enthusiastic followers as rushing into battle without any thought of his promised paradise. This, therefore, is a blemish in *point of art*, which every reader possessing taste must perceive, whatever may be his religious or non-religious persuasion. But a far higher, and more important, question than that of taste is involved. For though Miss Edgeworth may entertain opinions which would not permit her, with consistency, to attribute more to the influence of religion than she has done, and in that case may stand acquitted, *in foro conscientiæ*, of wilfully suppressing anything which she acknowledges to be true and important; yet, as, a *writer*, it must still be considered as a great blemish, in the eyes at least of those who think differently, that virtue should be studiously inculcated, with scarcely any reference to what they regard as the mainspring of it,—that vice should be traced to every other source except the want of religious principle,—that the most radical change from worthlessness to excellence should be represented as wholly independent of that Agent which they consider as the only one that can accomplish it,—and that consolation under affliction should be represented as derived from every source, except the one which they look to as the only true and sure one. "Is it not because there is no God in Israel, that ye have sent to inquire of Baalzebub, the God of Ekron?" This vital defect in such works should be constantly pointed out to the young reader; and he should be warned that, to realise the picture of noble, disinterested, thorough-going virtue, presented in such and such an instance, it is absolutely necessary to resort to those principles which in these fictions are sanctioned. He should, in short, be reminded that all those "things that are lovely and of good report," which have been placed before him, are the genuine fruits of the Holy Land; though the spies who have brought them bring also an evil report of that land, and would persuade us to remain wandering in the wilderness.

The student of history, also, should be on his guard against the indirect influence likely to be exercised on his opinions. On this point I take the liberty of quoting a passage from my *Lectures on Political Economy*:—

"An injudicious reader of history is liable to be misled by the circumstance, that historians and travelers occupy themselves principally (as is natural) with the relation of whatever is *remarkable*, and different from what commonly takes place in their own time or country. They do not dwell on the ordinary transactions of human life, (which are precisely what furnish the data on which political economy proceeds,) but on every thing that appears an exception to general rules, and in any way such as could not have been anticipated. The sort of information which the political economist wants is introduced, for the most part, only incidentally and obliquely; and is to be collected, imperfectly, from scattered allusions. So that if you will give a rapid glance, for instance, at the history of these islands, from the time of the Norman conquest to the present day, you will find that the differences between the two states of the country, in most of the points with which our science is conversant, are but very imperfectly accounted for in the main outline of the narrative.

"If it were possible that we could have a full report of the common business and common conversation, in the markets, the shops, and the wharfs of Athens and Piræus, for a single day, it would probably throw more light on the state of things in Greece at that time, in all that political economy is most concerned with, than all the histories that are extant put together.

"There is a danger, therefore, that the mind of the student, who proceeds in the manner I have described, may have been even drawn off from the class of facts which are, for the purpose in question, most important to be attended to.

"For, it should be observed that in all studies there is a danger to be guarded against, which Bacon, with his usual acuteness, has pointed out; that most men are so anxious to make or seek for some application of what they have been learning, as not unfrequently to apply it improperly, by endeavoring, lest their knowledge should lie by them idle, to bring it to bear on some question to which it is irrelevant; like Horace's painter, who, being skillful in drawing a cypress, was for introducing one into the picture of a shipwreck. Bacon complains of this tendency among the logicians and metaphysicians of his day, who introduced an absurd and pernicious application of the studies in which they had been conversant, into natural philosophy: 'Artis sæpe ignarus fit usus, ne sit nullus.' But the same danger besets those conversant in every other study likewise, (political economy of course not excepted,) that may from time to time have occupied a large share of such man's attention. He is tempted to seek for a solution of every question on every subject, by a reference to his own favorite science or branch of knowledge; like a schoolboy when first intrusted with a knife, who is for trying its edge on every thing that comes in his way.

"Now in reference to the point immediately before us, he who is well read in history and in travels should be warned of the danger (the more on account of the real high importance of such knowledge) of misapplying it,—of supposing that because political economy is conversant with *human transactions*, and he is acquainted with so much greater an amount of *human transactions* than the generality of men, he must have an advantage over them in precisely the same degree, in discussing questions of political economy. Undoubtedly he *has* a great advantage, if he is careful to keep in view the true principles of the science; but otherwise he may even labor under a *dis*-advantage, by forgetting that (as I just now observed) the kind of transactions which are made most prominent and occupy the chief space, in the works of historians and travelers, are usually not those of every-day life, with which political economy is conversant. It is in the same way that an accurate *military survey* of any district, or a series of sketches accompanying a *picturesque* tour through it, may even serve to mislead one who is seeking for a knowledge of its *agricultural* condition, if he does not keep in mind the different objects which different kinds of survey have in view.

"Geologists, when commissioning their friends to procure them from any foreign country such specimens as may convey an idea of its geological character, are accustomed to warn them against sending over collections of *curiosities*—i. e. specimens of spars, stalactites, &c., which are accounted, in that country, curious, from being *rarities*, and which consequently convey no correct notion of its general features. What they want is, specimens of the *commonest* strata,—the stones with which the roads are mended, and the houses built, &c. And some fragments of these, which in that country are accounted mere rubbish, they sometimes, with much satisfaction, find *casually adhering* to the specimens sent them as curiosities, and constituting, for their object, the most important part of the collection. Histories are in general, to the political economist, what such collections are to the geologist. The casual allusions to common, and what are considered insignificant matters, conveying to him the most valuable information.

"An injudicious study of history, then, may even prove a hindrance instead of a help to the forming of right views of political economy. For not only are many of the transactions which are, in the historian's view, the most important, such as are the least important to the political economist, but also a great proportion of them consists of what are in reality the greatest *impediments* to the progress of a society in wealth: viz., wars, revolutions, and disturbances of every kind. It is not in consequence of these, but in spite of them, that society has made the progress which in fact it has made. So that in taking such a survey as history furnishes of the course of events, for instance, for the last eight hundred years, (the period I just now alluded to,) not only do we find little mention of the causes which have so greatly increased national wealth during that period, but what we chiefly do read of is, the *counteracting* causes; especially the wars which have been raging from time to time, to the destruction of capital, and the hindrance of improvement. Now, if a ship had performed a voyage of eight hundred leagues, and the register of it contained an account chiefly of the contrary winds and currents, and made little mention of favorable gales, we might well be at a loss to understand how she reached her destination; and might even be led into the mistake of supposing that the contrary winds had forwarded her in her course. Yet such is history!"

In reference to the study of history, I have elsewhere remarked upon the importance, among the intellectual qualifications for such a study, of a vivid imagination,—a faculty which, consequently, a skillful narrator must himself possess, and to which he must be able to furnish excitement in others. Some may, per haps, be startled at this remark, who have been accustomed to consider imagination as having no other office than to *feign* and to falsify. Every faculty is liable to abuse and misdirection, and imagination among the rest; but it is a mistake to suppose that it necessarily tends to pervert the truth of history, and to mislead the judgment. On the contrary, our view of any transaction, especially one that is remote in time or place, will necessarily be imperfect, generally incorrect, unless it embrace something more than the bare outline of the occurrences,—unless we have before the mind a lively idea of the scenes in which the events took place, the habits of thought and of feeling of the actors, and all the circumstances connected with the transaction; unless, in short, we can in a considerable degree transport ourselves out of our own age, and country, and persons, and imagine ourselves the agents or spectators. It is from consideration of all these circumstances that we are enabled to form a right judgment as to the facts which history records, and to derive instruction from it. What we imagine may indeed be merely *imaginary*, that is, unreal; but it may again be what actually does or did exist. To say that imagination, if not regulated by sound judgment and sufficient knowledge, may chance to convey to us false impressions of past events, is only to say that man is fallible. But such false impressions are even much *the more* likely to take possession of those whose imagination is feeble or uncultivated. They are apt to imagine the things, persons, times, countries, &c., which they read of, as much less different from what they see around them than is really the case.

The practical importance of such an exercise of imagination to a full, and clear, and consequently profitable view of the transactions related in history, can hardly be over-estimated. In respect of the very earliest of all human transactions, it is matter of common remark how prone many are to regard with mingled wonder, contempt, and indignation, the transgression of our first parents; as if they were not a fair sample of the human race; as if any of us would not, if he had been placed in precisely the same circumstances, have acted as they did. The Corinthians, probably, had perused with the same barren wonder the history of the backslidings of the Israelites; and needed that Paul should remind them, that these things were written for their example and admonition. And all, in almost every portion of history they read, have need of a corresponding warning, to endeavor to fancy themselves the persons they read of, that they may recognise in the accounts of past times the portraiture of our own. From not putting ourselves in the place of the persons living in past times, and entering fully into all their feelings, we are apt to forget how probable many things might appear, which we know did not take place; and to regard as perfectly chimerical, expectations which we know were not realized, but which, had we lived in those times, we should doubtless have entertained; and to imagine that there was no *danger* of those evils which, were, in fact, escaped. We are apt also to make too little allowances for prejudices and associations of ideas, which no longer exist precisely in the same form among ourselves, but which, perhaps, are not more at variance with right reason than others with which ourselves are infected.

"*Studies serve for delight, for ornament, and for ability.*"

We should, then, cultivate, not only the cornfields of our minds, but the pleasure-grounds also. Every faculty and every study, however worthless they may be, when not employed in the service of God,—however debased and polluted when devoted to the service of sin,—become ennobled and sanctified when directed, by one whose constraining motive is the love of Christ, towards a good object. Let not the Christian, then, think "scorn of the pleasant land." That land is the field of ancient and modern literature—of philosophy, in almost all its departments—of the arts of reasoning and persuasion. Every part of it may be cultivated with advantage, as the Land of Canaan when bestowed upon God's peculiar people. They were not commanded to let it lie waste, as incurably polluted by the abominations of its first inhabitants; but to cultivate it, and dwell in it, living in obedience to the divine laws, and dedicating its choicest fruits to the Lord their God.

DIFFERENT ASPECTS OF A LIBERAL EDUCATION.

LORD CHESTERFIELD'S LETTERS TO HIS SON.

PHILIP DORMER STANHOPE, fourth Earl of Chesterfield, was born in London, September 22, 1694. Having graduated at Cambridge, he made the tour of Europe in 1714. In 1715 he was appointed a gentleman of the bed-chamber of the Prince of Wales, and was elected to Parliament, where he signalized his entrance by his graceful elocution. On the death of his father, in 1726, he passed into the House of Lords. In 1728 he was made Special Ambassador to Holland; and, on his return, George II. appointed him Lord Steward of the Household; and, in 1745, he was made Lord Lieutenant of Ireland, where he inaugurated a policy of conciliation which made his administration very popular. He accepted the office of Principal Secretary of State in April. 1746, which he resigned in 1748.

Lord Chesterfield was intimate with Pope, Swift, Voltaire, Montesquieu, and other literary men of his time. His intercourse with Dr. Johnson, which was at no time intimate, was abruptly closed by the well-known indignant letter from the lexicographer, on the appearance of a patronizing notice of his great work in the world, of November 22, 1754, and which has outlived much of the literature of that day.

"Seven years, my lord, have now passed since I waited in your outward room, or was repulsed from your door; during which time I have been pushing on my work through difficulties, of which it is useless to complain, and have brought it at last to the verge of publication, without one act of assistance, one word of encouragement, or one smile of favor. . . . The notice which you have been pleased to take of my labors, had it been early, had been kind; but it has been delayed till I am indifferent, and cannot enjoy it till I am solitary, and cannot impart it; till I am known, and do not want it. . . . Having carried on my work thus far with so little obligation to any favorer of learning, I shall not be disappointed, though I should conclude it, if less be possible with life."

Chesterfield's reputation as an author is founded chiefly on his *Letters to his Son*, which appeared in 1774, after his death; and, although written for a special purpose, and without reference to publication, and published without reference to his ultimate judgment as to special suggestions, they have been widely read, and have exerted a wide and deep influence on the aims and details of liberal culture.

HIS OWN EDUCATION AND TRAINING.

His mother, daughter of George Savile, Marquis of Halifax, died while this son was quite young, and his education, through a neglect of the father, devolved, mainly, upon his grandmother, Lady Halifax, a woman of much sense and sensibility. Her house was the resort of the leading politicians and best company of the city, whose conversation decided the tastes of the youth, who was a nice observer of men and manners. And he owed much to a casual remark of Lord Galway, who, observing in him a strong inclination to political life, but at the same time an unconquerable taste for pleasure, with some tincture of laziness, remarked: "If you intend to be a man of business, you must be an early riser. In the distinguished posts your parts, rank, and fortune will entitle you to fill, you will be liable to have visitors at every hour of the day, and unless you will rise early, you will never have any leisure to yourself." He took the hint, and acted upon it through life.

His early instruction, till he was eighteen, was by private tutors, and his desire to excel was the spur of youthful exertion both in books and plays. In a letter to his son (then eleven), he says: 'I should have been ashamed if any boy of that age had learned his book better, or played at any game better than I did; I should not have rested a moment till I had got before him.' In 1712 (then in his eighteenth year) he entered Trinity Hall, Cambridge. In a letter to his French teacher in London he writes: 'I have passed the last week at the Bishop of Ely's, who lives fifteen miles off, and have seen more of the country than I had seen in all my life, and which is very agreeable in this neighborhood. I continue constant at my studies, which as yet are but Latin and Greek, but I shall soon commence civil law, philosophy, and mathematics. I find this college infinitely the best in the whole university, for it is the smallest, and is filled with lawyers, who have been in the world and understand life. We have but one clergyman, who is the only man in the college who gets drunk.' While at the university he paid particular attention to the great masters of oratory. In a letter to his son, he refers to this subject: 'Whenever I read pieces of eloquence, whether ancient or modern, I used to write down the shining passages, and then translate them as well and elegantly as I could; if in Latin or French, into English; if English, into French. This, which I practiced for some years, not only improved and formed my style, but imprinted in my mind and memory the best thoughts of the best authors.'

In 1714 he sets out on the grand tour of Holland, France, and Italy—and as he was without a tutor, he was left to his own judgment, which proved in some respects excellent, and in others perilous. His love of shining, and his avowed principle of observing and copying the habits and manners of polite society, led him into gambling, 'which,' he remarks in a letter to his son: 'far from adorning my character, has, I am conscious, been a great blemish to it.' His introduction to the world of men and women is thus described:

At nineteen I left the University of Cambridge, where I was an absolute pedant: when I talked my best, I quoted Horace; when I aimed at being facetious, I quoted Martial; and when I had a mind to be a fine gentleman, I talked Ovid. I was convinced that none but the ancients had common sense; that the classics contained everything that was either necessary, useful, or ornamental to men; and I was not without thought of wearing the *toga virilis* of the Romans, instead of the vulgar and illiberal dress of the moderns. With these excellent notions, I went first to the Hague, where, by the help of several letters of recommendation, I was soon introduced into all the best company; and where I very soon discovered that I was totally mistaken in almost every one notion I had entertained. Fortunately, I had a strong desire to please (the mixed result of good-nature, and a vanity by no means blamable), and was sensible that I had nothing but the desire. I therefore resolved, if possible, to acquire the means too. I studied attentively and minutely the dress, the air, the manner, the address, and the turn of conversation, of all those whom I found to be the people in fashion and most generally allowed to please. I imitated them as well as I could; if I heard that one man was reckoned remarkably genteel, I carefully watched his dress, motions, and attitudes, and formed my own upon them. When I heard of another, whose conversation was agreeable and engaging, I listened and attended to the turn of it. I addressed myself, though '*de très mauvaise grace*,' to all the most fashionable fine ladies; confessed and laughed with them at my own awkwardness and rawness, recommending myself as an object for them to try their skill in forming. By these means and with a passionate desire for pleasing everybody, I came by degrees to please some; and I can assure you, that whatever little figure I have made in the world has been much more owing to that passionate desire I had of pleasing universally, than to any intrinsic merit, or sound knowledge, I might ever have been master of. My passion for pleasing was so strong (and I am very glad it was so), that I own to you fairly, I wished to make every woman I saw in love with me, and every man I met with admire me. Without this passion for the object, I should never have been so attentive to the means; and I own I cannot conceive how it is possible for any man of good nature and good sense to be without this passion. Does not good-nature incline us to please all those we converse with, of whatever rank or station they may be? And does not good-sense and common observation show of what infinite use it is to please? 'Oh, but one may please by the good qualities of the heart and the knowledge of the head, without the fashionable air, address, and manner, which is mere tinsel.' I deny it. A man may be esteemed and respected, but I defy him to please without them. Moreover, at your age, I would not have contented myself with barely pleasing; I wanted to shine, and to distinguish myself in the world, as a man of fashion and gallantry, as well as business. And that ambition, or vanity, call it what you please, was a right one; it hurt nobody, and made me exert whatever talents I had. It is the spring of a thousand right and good things.

To these extracts from Lord Chesterfield's own letters, written to encourage the efforts of his son to acquire the art of pleasing in society, we add passages from the graceful and, in the main, just criticisms of the eminent French essayist, C. A. Sainte-Beuve: *

In 1744, when he was only fifty years of age, his political ambition seemed, in part, to have died out, and the indifferent state of his health left him to choose a private life. And then the object of his secret ideal and his real ambition we know now. Before his marriage, he had, about the year 1732, by a French lady (Mdme. du Bouchet), whom he met in Holland, a natural son, to whom he was tenderly attached. He wrote to this son, in all sincerity, "From the first day of your life, the dearest object of mine has been to make you as perfect as the weakness of human nature will allow." Towards the education of this son all his wishes, all his affectionate and worldly predilections tended. And whether Viceroy of Ireland, or Secretary of State in London, he found time to write long letters, full of minute details, to him, to instruct him in small matters, and to perfect him in mind and manner

The Chesterfield, then, that we love especially to study, is the man of wit and experience, who knew all the affairs, and passed through all the phases of political and public life only to find out its smallest resources, and to tell us the last mot; he who, from his youth, was the friend of Pope and Bolingbroke, the introducer into England of Montesquieu and Voltaire, the correspondent of Fontenelle and Mdme. de Tencin; he whom the Academy of Inscriptions placed among its members, who united the wit of the two nations, and who, in more than one intellectual essay, but particularly in his letters to his son, shows himself to us as a moralist, as amiable as he is consummate, and one of the masters of life. It is the Rochefoucauld of England of whom

* Prefixed to a late London edition of Lord Chesterfield's *Letters, Sentences, and Maxims*, in the *Bayard Series of Pleasure Books of Literature*, by Sampson Low, Son & Marston. We can most heartily commend this beautifully printed volume as containing all there is truly valuable in the four volumes of letters.

we speak. Montesquieu, after the publication of "*L'Esprit des Lois*," wrote to the Abbé de Guasco, who was then in England, "Tell my Lord Chesterfield that nothing is so flattering to me as his approbation; but that, though he is reading my work for the third time, he will only be in a better position to point out to me what wants correcting and rectifying in it; nothing could be more instructive to me than his observations and his *critique*." It was Chesterfield who, speaking to Montesquieu, one day, of the readiness of the French for revolutions, and their impatience at slow reforms, spoke this sentence, which is a *résumé* of our whole history: "You French know how to make barricades, but you never raise barriers."

The letters begin with the A B C of education and instruction. Chesterfield teaches his son, in French, the rudiments of mythology and history. I do not regret the publication of these first letters. He lets slip some very excellent advice in those early pages. The little Stanhope is no more than eight years old when his father suits a little rhetoric to his juvenile understanding, and tries to show him how to use good language, and to express himself well. He especially recommends to him *attention* in all that he does, and he gives the word its full value. "It is attention alone," he says, "which fixes objects in the memory. There is no surer mark of a mean and meagre intellect in the world than inattention. All that is worth the trouble of doing at all, deserves to be done well, and nothing can be well done without attention." This precept he incessantly repeats, and varies the application of it as his pupil grows, and is in a condition to comprehend it to its fullest extent. Whether pleasure or study, everything one does must be well done, done entirely, and at its proper time, without allowing any distraction to intervene. "When you read Horace, pay attention to the accuracy of his thoughts, to the elegance of his diction, and to the beauty of his poetry, and do not think of the '*De Homine et Cive*' of Puffendorf; and when you read Puffendorf, do not think of Mdme. de St. Germain; nor of Puffendorf when you speak to Mdme. de St. Germain." But this strong and easy subjugation of the order of thought to the will only belongs to great or very good intellects. M. Royer-Collard used to say that "what was most wanting in our day, was *respect* in the moral disposition, and *attention* in the intellectual." Lord Chesterfield, in a less grave manner, might have said the same thing. He was not long in finding out what was wanting in this child whom he wished to bring up; whose bringing up was, indeed, the end and aim of his life. "On sounding your character to its very depths," he said to him, "I have not, thank God, discovered any vice of heart or weakness of head, so far; but I have discovered idleness, inattention, and indifference, which are only pardonable in the aged, who, in the decline of life, when health and spirits give way, have a sort of right to that kind of tranquillity. But a young man ought to be ambitious to shine and excel." And it is precisely this sacred fire, this lightning, that makes Achilles, the Alexanders, and the Caesars *to be the first in every undertaking*, this motto of noble hearts and of eminent men of all kinds, that nature had primarily neglected to place in the honest but thoroughly mediocre soul of the younger Stanhope: "You appear to want," said his father, "that *vivida vis animi* which excites the majority of young men to please, to strive, and to outdo others." "When I was your age," he says again, "I should have been ashamed for another to know his lesson better or to have been before me in a game, and I should have had no rest till I had regained the advantage." All this little course of education by letters, offers a sort of continuous dramatic interest; we follow the efforts of a fine, distinguished, energetic nature as Lord Chesterfield's was, engaged in a contest with a disposition honest but indolent, with an easy and dilatory temperament, from which it would, at any expense, form a masterpiece accomplished, amiable and original, and with which it only succeeded in making a sort of estimable copy. What sustains and almost touches the reader in this strife, where so much art is used, and where the inevitable counsel is the same beneath all metamorphoses, is the true fatherly affection which animates and inspires the delicate and excellent master, as patient as he is full of vigor, lavish in resources and skill, never discouraged, untiring in sowing elegances and graces on this infertile soil. The young man is placed at the Academy, with M. de la Guérinière (not till 1751, when he was nineteen, too old to profit by such instruction); the morning he devotes to study, and the rest of the time is to be consecrated to the world. "Pleasure is now the last branch of your education," this indulgent father writes; "it will soften and polish your manners, it will incite you to seek, and finally to acquire *graces*." Upon this last point he is exacting, and shows no quarter. *Graces*, he returns continually to them, for without them all effort is vain. "If they are not natural to you, cultivate them," he cries. He indeed speaks confidently; as if, to cultivate graces, it is not necessary to have them already!

The gentle and the frivolous are perpetually mingling in these letters. Marcel, the dancing-master, is very often recommended, Montesquieu no less. The Abbé de Guasco, a sort of toady to Montesquieu, is a useful personage for introductions. "Between you and me," writes Chesterfield, "he has more knowledge than genius; but *a clever man knows how to make use of everything*, and every man is good for something. As to the President de Montesquieu, he is in all respects a precious acquaintance; *he has genius, with the most extensive reading in the world. Drink of this fountain as much as possible.*"

Of authors, those whom Chesterfield particularly recommends at this time, and those whose names occur most frequently in his counsels, are La Rochefoucald and La Bruyère. "If you read some of La Rochefoucald's maxims in the morning, consider them, examine them well, and compare them with the originals you meet in the evening. Read La Bruyère in the morning, and see in the evening if his portraits are correct." But these guides, excellent as they are, have no other use by themselves than that of a map. Without personal observation and experience, they would be useless, and would even be conducive to error, as a map might be if one thought to get from it a complete knowledge of towns and provinces. Better read one man than ten books. "The world is a country that no one has ever known by means of descriptions; each must traverse it in person to be thoroughly initiated into its ways."

Lord Chesterfield intended this beloved son for a diplomatic life; he at first found some difficulties in the way on account of his illegitimacy. To cut short these objections, he sent his son to Parliament; it was the surest method of conquering the scruples of the court. Mr. Stanhope, in his maiden speech, hesitated a moment, and was obliged to have recourse to notes. He did not make a second attempt at speaking in public. It appears that he succeeded better in diplomacy, in those second-rate places where solid merit is sufficient. He filled the post of ambassador extraordinary to the court of Dresden. But his health, always delicate, failed, and his father had the misfortune to see him die before him, when he was scarcely thirty-six years old (1768).

HINTS ON CONVERSATION.

Talk often, but never long; in that case, if you do not please, at least you are sure not to tire your hearers. Pay your own reckoning, but do not treat the whole company; this being one of the very few cases in which people do not care to be treated, every one being fully convinced that he has wherewithal to pay.

Tell stories very seldom, and absolutely never but when they are very apt, and very short. Omit every circumstance that is not material, and beware of digressions. To have frequent recourse to narrative, betrays great want of imagination.

Never hold anybody by the button, or the hand, in order to be heard out; for, if people are not willing to hear you, you had much better hold your tongue than them.

Take, rather than give, the tone of the company you are in. If you have parts, you will show them, more or less, upon every subject; and if you have not, you had better talk sillily upon a subject of other people's, than of your own choosing.

Avoid, as much as you can, in mixed companies, argumentative, polemical conversations; which, though they should not, yet certainly do, indispose, for a time, the contending parties towards each other; and if the controversy grows warm and noisy, endeavor to put an end to it by some genteel levity or joke. I quieted such a conversation hubbub once, by representing to them that, though I was persuaded none there present would repeat, out of company, what passed in it, yet I could not answer for the discretion of the passengers on the street, who must necessarily hear all that was said.

Above all things, and upon all occasions, avoid speaking of yourself, if it be possible. Such is the natural pride and vanity of our hearts, that it perpetually breaks out, even in people of the best parts, in all the various modes and figures of the egotism.

This principle of vanity and pride is so strong in human nature, that it descends even to the lowest objects; and one often sees people angling for praise, when, admitting all they say to be true (which, by the way, it seldom is), no just praise is to be sought. One man affirms that he has rode post an hundred miles in six hours. Probably it is a lie; but supposing it to be true, what then? Why, he is a very good post-boy, that is all. Another asserts, and probably not without oaths, that he has drank six or eight bottles of wine at a sitting. Out of charity, I will believe him a liar; for if I do not, I must think him a beast.

Always look people in the face when you speak to them; the not doing it is thought to imply conscious guilt; besides that, you lose the advantage of observing, by their countenances, what impression your discourse makes upon them. In order to know people's real sentiments, I trust much more to my eyes than to my ears; for they can say whatever they have a mind I should hear; but they can seldom help looking what they have no intention I should know.

Neither retail nor receive scandal, willingly; for though the defamation of others may for the present gratify the malignity or pride of our hearts, cool reflection will draw very disadvantageous conclusions from such a disposition; and in the case of scandal, as in that of robbery, the receiver is always thought as bad as the thief.

SELF-KNOWLEDGE AND JUDGMENT OF OTHERS.

In order to judge of the inside of others, study your own; but men in general are very much alike; and though one has one prevailing passion, and another has another, yet their operations are much the same; and whatever engages or disgusts, pleases or offends you in others, will, *mutatis mutandis*, engage, disgust, please, or offend others in you. Observe, with the utmost attention, all the operations of your own mind, the nature of your passions, and the various motives that determine your will, and you may, in a great degree, know all mankind. For instance, do you find yourself hurt and mortified when another makes you feel his superiority, and your own inferiority, in knowledge, parts, rank, or fortune? You will certainly take great care not to make a person, whose good will, good word, interest, esteem, or friendship you would gain, feel that superiority in you, in case you have it. If disagreeable insinuations, sly sneers, or repeated contradictions tease and irritate you, would you use them where you wished to engage and please? Surely not; and I hope you wish to engage and please almost universally. The temptation of saying a smart or witty thing, or *bon mot*, and the malicious applause with which it is commonly received, has made people who can say them, and, still oftener, people who think they can, but yet cannot, and yet try, more enemies, and implacable ones, too, than any one thing that I know of. When such things, then, shall happen to be said at your expense (as sometimes they certainly will), reflect seriously upon the sentiments, uneasiness, anger, and resentment which they excite in you; and consider whether it can be prudent by the same means to excite the same sentiments in others against you. It is a decided folly to lose a friend for a jest; but, in my mind, it is not a much less degree of folly to make an enemy of an indifferent and neutral person for the sake of a bon mot.

STUDIES AND CONDUCT.

SUGGESTIONS BY MEN EMINENT IN LETTERS AND AFFAIRS.

LETTERS OF WILLIAM PITT (EARL OF CHATHAM) TO HIS NEPHEW, THOMAS PITT (LORD CAMELFORD), WRITTEN 1751–71

WILLIAM PITT, the Great Commoner of England, as he was generally spoken of until this honorably won designation was lost in the less characteristic title of Earl of Chatham (conferred, 1766), was born at Boconnoc, November 15, 1708. He was educated at Eton, whence he went, as a gentleman commoner, to Trinity College, Oxford. From ill health, he left the university without taking a degree, and made a tour through France and Italy. On his return he obtained a cornetcy in the Blues, and entered Parliament in January, 1735, as one of the representatives of the borough of Old Sarum, which was the property of his family. On this field he won the reputation as an orator and statesman, which, to the American as well as the English mind, is the goal and stimulus of the highest talents, properly trained, worthily directed, and successfully rewarded. His death (May 11, 1778, its fatal stroke April 7) in the House of Lords, after one of his outbursts of patriotic eloquence, has passed into the keeping of painting as well as of history.

The following series of letters were addressed by their author to his nephew, Thomas Pitt, the only son of Thomas Pitt (the Earl of Chatham's eldest brother), of Boconnoc, in the county of Cornwall. He was born in March, 1737, and died in Florence in 1793. He sat in several parliaments, for the borough of Old Sarum, was a lord of the Admiralty in 1763, and created Lord Camelford in 1783. He was married to Anne, daughter of Pinkney Wilkinson. Their only son was killed in a duel in 1804, and their only daughter was married, in 1792, to William Lord Grenville. The letters coming, by this marriage, into the possession of Lord Grenville, were first published by him in 1804, with a Dedication to the Rt. Hon. William Pitt, 'whose career teaches how great talents may be most successfully cultivated, and to what objects they may most honorably be directed.'

On their first publication, the Edinburgh Review (vol. iv.) justly observed: 'In every line of these interesting relics, we discover proof that Lord Chatham was as amiable in private life as the annals of the Old and New World proclaim him to have been transcendently great in the management of affairs.'

The original edition (1804) was introduced by Lord Grenville with the following

Preface.

The following letters were addressed by the late Lord Chatham to his nephew, Mr. Pitt (afterwards Lord Camelford), then at Cambridge. They are few in number, written for the private use of an individual during a short period of time, and containing only such detached observations on the extensive subjects to which they relate, as occasion might happen to suggest, in the course of familiar correspondence. Yet even these imperfect remains will, undoubtedly, be received by the public with no common interest, as well from their own intrinsic value, as from the picture which they display of the character of their author. The editor's wish to do honor to the memory, both of the person by whom they were written and of him to whom they were addressed, would alone have rendered him desirous of making these papers public. But he feels a much higher motive, in the hope of promoting by such a publication the inseparable interests of learning, virtue, and religion. By the writers of that school whose philosophy consists in the degradation of virtue, it has often been triumphantly declared, that no excellence of character can stand the test of close observation: that no man is a hero to his domestic servants, or to his familiar friends. How much more just, as well as more amiable and dignified, is the opposite sentiment, delivered to us in the words of Plutarch, and illustrated throughout all his writings! "Real virtue," says that inimitable moralist, in his Life of Pericles, "is most loved where it is most nearly seen; and no respect which it commands from strangers, can equal the never ceasing admiration it excites in the daily intercourse of domestic life."

The following correspondence, imperfect as it is (and who will not lament that many more such letters are not preserved?), exhibits a great orator, statesman and patriot, in one of the most interesting relations of private society. Not as in the cabinet or the senate, enforcing, by a vigorous and commanding eloquence, those councils to which his country owed her preeminence and glory; but implanting with parental kindness, into the mind of an ingenious youth, seeds of wisdom and virtue, which ripened into full maturity in the character of a most accomplished man; directing him to the acquisition of knowledge, as the best instrument of action; teaching him, by the cultivation of his reason, to strengthen and establish in his heart those principles of moral rectitude which were congenial to it; and, above all, exhorting him to regulate the whole conduct of his life by the predominant influence of gratitude and obedience to God, as the only sure groundwork of every human duty.

What parent, anxious for the character and success of a son, born to any liberal station in this great and free country, would not, in all that related to his education, gladly have resorted to the advice of such a man? What youthful spirit, animated by any desire of future excellence, and looking for the gratification of that desire in the pursuits of honorable ambition, or in the consciousness of an upright, active, and useful life, would not embrace with transport any opportunity of listening on such a subject to the lessons of Lord Chatham? They are here before him. Not delivered with the authority of a preceptor or a parent, but tempered by the affection of a friend towards a disposition and character well entitled to such regard.

On that disposition and character the editor forbears to enlarge. Their best panegyric will be found in the following pages. Lord Camelford is there described such as Lord Chatham judged him in the first dawn of his youth, and such as he continued to his latest hour. The same suavity of manners and steadiness of principle, the same correctness of judgment and integrity of heart, distinguished him through life; and the same affectionate attachment from those who knew him best, has followed him beyond the grave.

It will be obvious to every reader, on the slightest perusal of the following letters, that they were never intended to comprise a perfect system of education, even for the short portion of time to which they relate. Many points in which they will be found deficient, were undoubtedly supplied by frequent opportunities of personal intercourse, and much was left to the general rules of study established at an English university. Still less, therefore, should the temporary advice addressed to an individual, whose previous education had labored under some disadvantage, be understood as a general dissuasive from the cultivation of Grecian literature. The sentiments of Lord Chatham were in direct opposition to any such opinion. The manner in which, even in these letters, he speaks of the first of poets, and the greatest of orators: and the stress which he lays on the benefits to be derived from their immortal works, could leave no doubt of his judgment on this important point. That judgment was afterwards most unequivocally manifested, when he was called upon to consider the question with a still higher interest, not only as a friend and guardian, but also as a father.

"I call that," says Milton, "a complete and generous education, which fits a man to perform justly, skilfully, and magnanimously, all the offices, both public and private, of peace and war." This is the purpose to which all knowledge is subordinate; the test of all intellectual and moral excellence. It is the end to which the lessons of Lord Chatham are uniformly directed. May they contribute to promote and encourage its pursuit! Recommended, as they must be, to the heart of every reader, by their warmth of sentiment and eloquence of language; deriving additional weight from the affectionate interest by which they were dictated; and most of all, enforced by the influence of his great example, and the authority of his venerable name.

LETTER I.

September, 1751.

My Dear Child,—I am extremely pleased with your translation, now it is written over fair. It is very close to the sense of the original, and done, in many places, with much spirit, as well as the numbers not lame or rough. However, an attention to Mr. Pope's numbers will make you avoid some ill sounds, and hobbling of the verse, by only transposing a word or two, in many instances. I have, upon reading the Eclogue over again, altered the third, fourth, and fifth lines, in order to bring them nearer to the Latin, as well as to render some beauty which is contained in the repetition of words in tender passages. You give me great pleasure, my dear child, in the progress you have made. I will recommend to Mr. Leech to carry you quite through Virgil's Æneid, from beginning to ending. Pray show him this letter, with my service to him, and thanks for his care of you. For English poetry, I recommend Pope's translation of Homer, and Dryden's Fables in particular. I am not sure if they are not called Tales instead of Fables. Your cousin, whom, I am sure, you can overtake if you will, has read Virgil's Æneid quite through, and much of Horace's Epistles. Terence's plays I would also desire Mr. Leech to make you perfect master of. Your cousin has read them all. Go on, my dear, and you will at least equal him. You are so good that I have nothing to wish but that you may be directed to proper books; and I trust to your spirit, and desire to be praised for things that deserve praise, for the figure you will hereafter make. God bless you, my dear child.

Your most affectionate Uncle,

William Pitt.

LETTER II.

Bath, *Oct.* 12, 1751.

My Dear Nephew,—As I have been moving about from place to place, your letter reached me here, at Bath, but very lately, after making a considerable circuit to find me. I should have otherwise, my dear child, returned you thanks for the very great pleasure you have given me, long before now. The very good account you give me of your studies, and that delivered in very good Latin, for your time, has filled me with the highest expectation of your future improvements. I see the foundations so well laid, that I do not make the least doubt but you will become a perfect good scholar; and have the pleasure and applause that will attend the several advantages hereafter, in the future course of your life, that you can only acquire now by your emulation and noble labors in the pursuit of learning, and of every acquirement that is to make you superior to other gentlemen. I rejoice to hear that you have begun Homer's Iliad, and have made so great a progress in Virgil. I hope you taste and love those authors particularly. You cannot read them too much: they are not only the two greatest poets, but they contain the finest lessons for your age to imbibe: lessons of honor, courage, disinterestedness, love of truth, command of temper, gentleness of behavior, humanity, and, in one word, virtue in its true signification. Go on, my dear nephew, and drink as deep as you can of these divine springs: the pleasure of the draught is equal, at least, to the prodigious advantages of it to the heart and morals. I hope you will drink them, as somebody does in Virgil of another sort of cup: 'Ille impiger hausit spumantem pateram' (Quickly he drained the flowing bowl.) I shall be highly pleased to hear from you, and to know what authors give you most pleasure. I desire my service to Mr. Leech; pray tell him I will write to him soon about your studies.

LETTER III.

BATH, *Jan.* 12, 1754.

MY DEAR NEPHEW,—Your letter from Cambridge affords me many very sensible pleasures: first, that you are at last in a proper place for study and improvement, instead of losing any more of that most precious thing, time, in London; in the next place, that you seem pleased with the particular society you are placed in, and with the gentleman to whose care and instructions you are committed; and, above all, I applaud the sound, right sense and love of virtue which appears through your whole letter. You are already possessed of the true clue to guide you through this dangerous and perplexing part of life's journey, the years of education; and upon which the complexion of all the rest of your days will infallibly depend. I say you have the true clue to guide you in the maxim you lay down in your letter to me, namely, that the use of learning is to render a man more wise and virtuous, not merely to make him more learned. *Macte tua virtute;* "Go on and prosper." Go on, my dear boy, by this golden rule, and you cannot fail to become everything your generous heart prompts you to wish to be, and that mine most affectionately wishes for you. There is but one danger in your way, and that is, perhaps, natural enough to your age—the love of pleasure, or the fear of close application and laborious diligence. With the last, there is nothing you may not conquer; and the first is sure to conquer and enslave whoever does not strenuously and generously resist the first allurements of it, lest, by small indulgences, he fall under the yoke of irresistible habit. Vitanda est improba siren, desidia; ("*Avoid that ugly syren, idleness*"), I desire may be affixed to the curtains of your bed, and to the walls of your chambers.' If you do not rise early, you never can make any progress worth talking of. Another rule is, if you do not set apart your hours of reading, and never suffer yourself or any one else to break in upon them, your days will slip through your hands unprofitably and frivolously; unpraised by all you wish to please, and really unenjoyable to yourself. Be assured, whatever you take from pleasure, amusements, or indolence, for these first few years of your life, will repay you a hundred-fold in the pleasures, honors, and advantages of all the remainder of your days. My heart is so full of the most earnest desire that you should do well, that I find my letter has run into some length, which you will, I know, be so good as to excuse. There remains now nothing to trouble you with, but a little plan for the beginning of your studies, which I desire, in a particular manner, may be exactly followed in every tittle. You are to qualify yourself for the part in society to which your birth and estate call you. You are to be a gentleman of such learning and qualifications as may distinguish you in the service of your country hereafter; not a pedant, who reads only to be called learned, instead of considering learning only as an instrument for action. Give me leave, therefore, my dear nephew, who have gone before you, to point out to you the dangers in your road; to guard you against such things as I experience my own defects to arise from; and, at the same time, if I have had any little successes in the world, to guide you to what I have drawn many helps from. I have not the pleasure of knowing the gentleman who is your tutor, but I dare say he is every way equal to such a charge, which I think no small one. You will communicate this letter to him, and I hope he will be so good as to concur with me, as to the course of study I desire you may begin with; and that such books, and such only, as I have pointed out, may be read. They are as follows: Euclid; a course of Logic; a course of Experimental Philosophy; Locke's Conduct of the Understanding; his Treatise also on the Understanding; his Treatise on Government, and Letters on Toleration. I desire, for the present, no books of poetry but Horace and Virgil; of Horace, the Odes, but above all, the Epistles, and Ars Poetica. These parts, *Nocturna versate manu, versate diurna.* Tully de Officiis, de Amicitia, de Senectute; his Catilinarian Oration and Philippics. Sallust. At leisure hours, an abridgement of the history of England to be run through, in order to settle in the mind a general chronological order and series of principal events and succession of kings; proper books of English history, on the true principles of our happy constitution, shall be pointed out afterwards. Burnett's History of the Reformation, abridged by himself, to be read with great care. Father Paul (Sarpi's History, with Notes and Observations by Amelot de la Houssaie, London, 17[illegible]) on beneficiary matters, in English. A French master, and only Molière's Plays to be read with him, or by yourself, till you have gone through them all. Spectators, especially Mr. Addison's papers, to be read very frequently at broken times in your room. I make it my request that you will forbear* drawing totally, while you are at Cambridge; and not meddle with Greek, otherwise than to know a little the etymology of words in Latin, or English, or French; nor to meddle with Italian. I hope this little course will soon be run through. I intend it as a general foundation for many things, of infinite utility, to come as soon as this is finished.

LETTER IV.

BATH, JAN. 14, 1754.

MY DEAR NEPHEW,—You will hardly have read over one very long letter from me before you are troubled with a second. I intended to have written soon, but I do it the sooner on account of your letter to your aunt, which she transmitted to me here. If anything, my dear boy, could have happened to raise you higher in my esteem, and to endear you more to me, it is the amiable abhorrence you feel for the scene of vice and folly (and of real misery and perdition, under the false notion of pleasure and spirit), which has opened to you at your college, and, at the same time, the manly, brave, generous, and wise resolution and true spirit with which you resisted and repulsed the first attempts upon a mind and heart, I thank God, infinitely too firm and noble, as well as too elegant and enlightened, to be in any danger of yielding to such contemptible and wretched corruptions. You charm me with the

---

* Lord Grenville, in a note to the first edition of 1804, remarks

This plan, drawn up for one whose previous education had not been systematic, does not claim to be complete. Lord Chatham had a high appreciation of Grecian literature, and Earl Stanhope, in his life of William Pitt, quotes Bishop Tomline: "It was by Lord Chatham's particular desire that Thucydides was the first Greek book which Mr. Pitt read after he came to college. The only other wish ever expressed by his lordship, relative to Mr. Pitt's studies, was, that I would read Polybius with him."

description of Mr. Wheeler, and while you say you could adore him, I could adore you for the natural, genuine love of virtue which speaks in all you feel, say, or do. As to your companions, let this be your rule: Cultivate the acquaintance with Mr. Wheeler which you have so fortunately begun; and, in general, be sure to associate with men much older than yourself; scholars, whenever you can; but always with men of decent and honorable lives. As their age and learning, superior both to your own, must necessarily, in good sense, and in the view of acquiring knowledge from them, entitle them to all deference, and submission of your lights to theirs, you will particularly practice that first and greatest rule for pleasing in conversation, as well as for drawing instruction and improvement from the company of one's superior in age and knowledge, namely, to be a patient, attentive, and well-bred hearer, and to answer with modesty; to deliver your own opinions sparingly and with proper diffidence; and if you are forced to desire farther information or explanation on a point, to do it with proper apologies for the trouble you give; or, if obliged to differ, to do it with all possible candor, and an unprejudiced desire to find and ascertain truth, with an entire indifference to the side on which that truth is to be found. There is, likewise, a particular attention required to contradict with good manners; such as, begging pardon, begging leave to doubt, and such like phrases. Pythagoras enjoined his scholars an absolute silence for a long novitiate. I am far from approving such a taciturnity, but I highly recommend the end and intent of Pythagoras' injunction; which is to dedicate the first parts of life more to hear and learn, in order to collect materials out of which to form opinions founded on proper lights, and well examined sound principles, than to be presuming, prompt, and flippant in hazarding one's own slight crude notions of things, and thereby exposing the nakedness and emptiness of the mind, like a house opened to company before it is fitted either with necessaries, or ornaments for their reception and entertainment. And not only will this disgrace follow from such temerity and presumption, but a more serious danger is sure to ensue, that is, the embracing errors for truth, prejudices for principles; and when that is once done (no matter how vainly and weakly), the adhering, perhaps, to false and dangerous notions, only because one has declared for them, and submitting, for life, the understanding and conscience to a yoke of base and servile prejudices, vainly taken up and obstinately retained. This will never be your danger; but I thought it not amiss to offer these reflections to your thoughts. As to your manner of behaving toward these unhappy young gentlemen you describe, let it be manly and easy; decline their parties with civility; retort raillery with raillery, always tempered with good breeding; if they banter your regularity, order, decency, and love of study, banter, in return, their neglect of them; and venture to own frankly, that you came to learn what you can, not to follow what they are pleased to call pleasure. In short, let your external behavior to them be as full of politeness and ease as your inward estimation of them is full of pity, mixed with contempt. I come now to the part of the advice I have to offer you, which most nearly concerns your welfare, and upon which every good and honorable purpose of your life will assuredly turn; I mean the keeping up in your heart the true sentiments of religion. If you are not right towards God, you can never be so towards man; the noblest sentiment of the human breast is here brought to the test. Is gratitude in the number of a man's virtues? If it be, the highest benefactor demands the warmest returns of gratitude, love, and praise: Ingratum qui dixerit, omnia dixit (*"When you have spoken ingratitude, you have spoken everything"*). If a man wants this virtue, where there are infinite obligations to excite and quicken it, he will be likely to want all others toward his fellow creatures, whose utmost gifts are poor compared to those he daily receives at the hands of his never-failing Almighty friend. 'Remember thy Creator in the days of thy youth,' is big with the deepest wisdom; 'the fear of the Lord is the beginning of wisdom; and, an upright heart, that is understanding.' This is eternally true, whether the wits and rakes of Cambridge allow it or not; nay, I must add of this religious wisdom, 'Her ways are ways of pleasantness and all her paths are peace,' whatever your young gentlemen of pleasure may think of a tainted health and battered constitution. Hold fast, therefore, by this sheet-anchor of happiness, religion; you will often want it in the times of most danger, the storms and tempests of life. Cherish true religion as preciously as you will fly with abhorrence and contempt superstition and enthusiasm.* The first is the perfection and glory of the human nature; the two last, the depravation and disgrace of it. Remember, the essence of religion is a heart void of offence towards God and man; not subtle, speculative opinions, but an active vital principle of faith. The words of a heathen were so fine that I must give them to you:

> Compositum Jus, fasque animi; sanctosque recessus
> Mentis, et incoctum generoso pectus honesto.†

Go on, my dear child, in the admirable dispositions you have toward all that is right and good, and make yourself the love and admiration of the world! I have neither paper nor words to tell you how tenderly I am yours.

LETTER V.

BATH, *Jan.* 24, 1754.

I will lose not a moment before I return my most tender and warm thanks to the most amiable, valuable, and noble-minded of youths, for the infinite pleasure his letter gives me. My dear nephew, what a beautiful thing is genuine goodness, and how lovely does the human mind appear in its native purity (in a nature as happy as yours), before the taints of a corrupted world have touched it! To guard you from the fatal effects of all the dangers that surround and beset youth (and many there are), I thank God, is become my pleasing and very important charge; your own choice, and our nearness in blood, and, still more, a nearer and dearer relation of hearts, which I feel between us all concur to make it so. I shall seek, then, every occasion, my dear young friend, of being useful to you, by offering you those lights which one must have lived some years in the world to see the full force and extent of, and which the best mind and clearest understanding will suggest imper-

---

* Lord Grenville remarks, in a note (1804):

Plutarch, in his Life of Pericles, notices the benefit which that great statesman derived from the study of natural philosophy, as taught by Anaxagoras. "The lessons of Anaxagoras gave elevation to his soul and sublimity to his eloquence; they diffused over the whole tenor of his life a temperate and majestic grandeur; taught him to raise his thoughts from the works of Nature to the contemplation of that Perfect and Pure Intelligence from which they originate, and instilled into his mind, instead of the dark and fearful superstition of his times, that piety which is confirmed by Reason, and animated by Hope."

† Persius, Sat. II., thus translated by Dryden:

> A soul where laws both human and divine,
> In practice more than speculation shine;
> A genuine virtue of a vigorous kind,
> Pure in the last recesses of the mind.

Gifford, in his translation of these lines, appends the remark: "These two lines are not only the quintessence of morality, but of language. Circumlocution cramps, and paraphrase enfeebles their nature."

fectly, in any case, and in the most difficult, delicate, and essential points, perhaps not at all, till experience, that dear-bought instructor, comes to our assistance. What I shall, therefore, make my task (a happy, delightful task, if I prove a safeguard to so much opening virtue), is to be, for some years, what you cannot be to yourself, your experience; experience anticipated, and ready digested for your use. Thus we will endeavor, my dear child, to join the two best seasons of life, to establish your virtue and your happiness upon solid foundations. So much in general. I will now, my dear nephew, say a few things to you upon a matter where you have surprisingly little to learn, considering you have seen nothing but Boconnoc; I mean behavior.

Behavior is of infinite advantage or prejudice to a man, as he happens to have formed it to a graceful, noble, engaging and proper manner, or to a vulgar, coarse, ill-bred, or awkward and ungenteel one. Behavior, though an external thing, which seems rather to belong to the body than to the mind, is certainly founded in considerable virtues; though I have known instances of good men with something very revolting and offensive in their manner of behavior, especially when they have the misfortune to be naturally very awkward and ungenteel; and which their mistaken friends have helped to confirm them in, by telling them they were above such trifles as being genteel, dancing, fencing, riding, and doing all manly exercises, with grace and vigor. As if the body, because inferior, were not a part of the composition of man; and the proper, easy, ready, and graceful use of himself, both in mind and limb, did not go to make up the character of an accomplished man. You are in no danger of falling into this preposterous error; and I had a great pleasure in finding you, when I first saw you in London, so well disposed by nature, and so properly attentive to make yourself genteel in person, and well bred in behavior. I am very glad you have taken a fencing master; that exercise will give you some manly, firm, and graceful attitudes; open your chest, place your head upright, and plant you well upon your legs. As to the use of the sword, it is well to know it; but remember, my dearest nephew, it is a science of defence, and that a sword can never be employed, by the hand of a man of virtue, in any other cause. As to the carriage of your person, be particularly careful, as you are tall and thin, not to get a habit of stooping; nothing has so poor a look; above all things, avoid contracting any peculiar gesticulations of the body, or movements of the muscles of the face. It is rare to see in any one a graceful laughter; it is generally better to smile than to laugh out, especially to contract a habit of laughing at small or no jokes. Sometimes it would be affectation, or worse, mere moroseness, not to laugh heartily, when the truly ridiculous circumstances of an incident, or the true pleasantry and wit of a thing, call for and justify it; but the trick of laughing frivolously is, by all means, to be avoided: Risu inepto, res ineptior nulla est (Nothing is so silly as a silly laugh.)

Now, as to politeness: many have attempted definitions; I believe it is best to be known by description, definition not being able to comprise it. I would, however, venture to call it *benevolence in trifles*, or the preference of others to ourselves in little daily, hourly occurrences in the commerce of life. A better place, a more commodious seat, priority in being helped at table, etc., what is it but sacrificing ourselves in such trifles to the convenience and pleasure of others? And this constitutes true politeness. It is a perpetual attention (by habit it grows easy and natural to us) to the little wants of those we are with, by which we either prevent or remove them. Bowing, ceremonious, formal compliments, stiff civilities, will never be politeness; that must be easy, natural, unstudied, manly, noble. And what will give this but a mind benevolent and perpetually attentive to exert that amiable disposition in trifles toward all you converse and live with? Benevolence in greater matters takes a higher name, and is the queen of virtues. Nothing is so incompatible with politeness as any trick of absence of mind. I would trouble you with a word or two more upon some branches of behavior, which have a more serious moral obligation in them than those of mere politeness, which are equally important in the eye of the world. I mean a proper behavior, adapted to the respective relations we stand in toward the different ranks of superiors, equals, and inferiors. Let your behavior towards superiors in dignity, age, learning, or any distinguished excellence, be full of respect, deference, and modesty. Toward equals, nothing becomes a man so well as well-bred ease, polite freedom, generous frankness, manly spirit, always tempered with gentleness and sweetness of manner, noble sincerity, candor, and openness of heart, qualified and restrained within the bounds of prudence, and ever limited by a grateful regard to secrecy in all things entrusted to it, and an inviolable attachment to your word. To inferiors, gentleness, condescension, and affability is the only dignity. Towards servants, never accustom yourself to rough and passionate language. When they are good, we should consider them as *humbler friends*, as fellow Christians, *ut conservi*; and when they are bad, pity, admonish, and part with them, if incorrigible. On all occasions beware, my dear child, of anger, that demon, that destroyer of our peace.

Ira furor brevis est, animum rege, qui nisi paret
Imperat; hunc frenis, hunc tu compesce catena.—*

LETTER VI.

BATH, *Feb.* 3, 1754.

Nothing can or ought to give me a higher satisfaction, than the obliging manner in which my dear nephew receives my most sincere and affectionate endeavors to be of use to him. You much overrate the obligation, whatever it be, which youth has to those who have trod the paths of the world before them, for their friendly advice how to avoid the inconveniences, dangers, and evils which they themselves may have run upon for want of such timely warnings, and to seize, cultivate, and carry forward toward perfection, those advantages, graces, virtues, and felicities, which they may have totally missed, or stopped short in the generous pursuit. To lend this helping hand to those who are beginning to tread the slippery way, seems, at best, but an office of common humanity to all; but to withhold it from one we truly love, and whose heart and mind bear every genuine mark of the very soil proper for all the amiable, manly, and generous virtues to take root, and bear their heavenly fruit; inward, conscious peace, fame amongst men, public love, temporal and eternal happiness; to withhold it, I say, in such an instance, would deserve the worst of names. I am greatly pleased, my dear young friend, that you do me the justice to believe I do not mean to impose any yoke of authority upon your understanding and conviction. I wish to warn, admonish, instruct, enlighten, and convince your reason; and so determine your judgment to right things, when you shall be made to see that they are right; not to overbear and impel you to adopt anything before you perceive it to be right or wrong, by the force of authority. I hear, with great pleasure, that Locke lay before you when you last wrote to me; and I like the observation you make from him, that we must use our own reason, not that of another, if we would deal fairly by ourselves, and hope to enjoy a peaceful

---

* Horace, thus rendered by Francis:

'Anger's a shorter madness of the mind;
Subdue the tyrant, and in fetters bind.'

and contented conscience. This precept is truly worthy of the dignity of rational natures. But here, my dear child, let me offer one distinction to you, and it is of much moment. It is this: Mr. Locke's precept is applicable only to such opinions as regard moral or religious obligations, and which, as such, our own consciences alone can judge and determine for ourselves: matters of mere expediency, that affect neither honor, morality, or religion, were not in that great and wise man's view: such are the usages, forms, manners, modes, proprieties, decorums, and all those numberless ornamental little acquirements, and genteel, well-bred attentions, which constitute a proper, graceful, amiable, and noble behavior. In matters of this kind, I am sure, your own reason, to which I shall always refer you, will at once tell you that you must, at first, make use of the experience of others; in effect, see with their eyes, or not be able to see at all; for the ways of the world, as to its usages and exterior manners, as well as to all things of expediency and prudential considerations, a moment's reflection will convince a mind as right as yours, must necessarily be, to inexperienced youth, with ever so fine natural parts, a *terra incognita*. As you would not, therefore, attempt to form notions of China or Persia but from those who have travelled those countries, and the fidelity and sagacity of whose relations you can trust; so will you as little, I trust, prematurely form notions of your own concerning that usage of the world (as it is called) into which you have not yet travelled, and which must be long studied and practised before it can be tolerably well known. I can repeat nothing to you of so infinite consequence to your future welfare, as to conjure you not to be hasty in taking up notions and opinions; guard your honest and ingenious mind against this main danger of youth. With regard to all things that appear not to your reason, after due examination, evident duties of honor, morality, or religion (and in all such as do, let your conscience and reason determine your notions and conduct), in all other matters, I say, be slow to form opinions, keep your mind in a candid state of suspense, and open to full conviction when you shall procure it; using, in the meantime, the experience of a friend you can trust, the sincerity of whose advice you will try and prove by your own experience hereafter, when more years will have given it to you. I have been longer upon this head than I hope there was any occasion for; but the great importance of the matter, and my warm wishes for your welfare, figure, and happiness, have drawn it from me. I wish to know, if you have a good French master: I must recommend the study of the French language, to speak and write it correctly, as to grammar and orthography, as a matter of the utmost and indispensable use to you, if you would make any figure in the great world. I need say no more to enforce this recommendation: when I get to London, I will send you the best French dictionary. Have you been taught geography and the use of the globes by Mr. Leech? If not, pray take a geography master and learn the use of the globes; it is soon known. I recommend to you to acquire a clear and thorough notion of what is called the solar system, together with the doctrine of comets. I wanted as much, or more, to hear of your private reading at home, as of public lectures, which, I hope, however, you will frequent for example's sake. Pardon this long letter, and keep it by you if you do not hate it.

LETTER VII.

BATH, *March* 30, 1754.

MY DEAR NEPHEW,—I am much obliged to you for your kind remembrance and wishes for my health. It is much recovered by the regular fit of gout, of which I am still lame in both feet, and I may hope for better health hereafter in consequence. I have thought it long since we conversed: I waited to be able to give you a better account of my health, and, in part, to leave you time to make advances in your plan of study, of which I am very desirous to hear an account. I desire you will be so good as to let me know particularly, if you have gone through the abridgement of Burnet's History of the Reformation, and the treatise of Father Paul on Benefices; also, how much of Locke you have read. I beg you not to mix any other English reading with what I recommended to you. I propose to save you much time and trouble by pointing out to you such books, in succession, as will carry you the shortest way to the things you must know to fit yourself for the business of the world, and give you the clearer knowledge of them, by keeping them unmixed with superfluous, vain, empty trash. Let me hear, my dear child, of your French also, as well as of those studies which are more properly university studies. I cannot tell you better how truly and tenderly I love you, than by telling you I am most solicitously bent on your doing everything that is right, and laying the foundations of your future happiness and figure in the world, in such a course of improvement as will not fail to make you a better man, while it makes you a more knowing one. Do you rise early? I hope you have already made to yourself the habit of doing it; if not, let me conjure you to acquire it. Remember your friend Horace:

> 'Et ni
> Posces ante diem librum cum lumine; si non
> Intendes animum studiis, et rebus honestis,
> Invidiâ vel amore vigil torquebere.' *

LETTER VIII.

BATH, *May* 4, 1754.

DEAR NEPHEW,—I use a pen with some difficulty, being still lame in my hand, with the gout. I cannot, however, delay writing this line to you, on the course of English history I propose for you. If you have finished the abridgement of English History and of Burnet's History of the Reformation, I recommend to you next (before any other reading of history) Oldcastle's Remarks on the History of England, by Lord Bolingbroke.† Let me apprise

---

* Horace, thus rendered by Francis:

> 'Unless you light your early lamp, to find
> A moral book; unless you form your mind
> To nobler studies, you shall forfeit rest,
> And love or envy shall disturb your breast.'

† Lord Grenville, in a note on this recommendation, remarks:

"Some early impressions had prepossessed Lord Chatham's mind with a much more favorable opinion of the political writings of Lord Bolingbroke, than he might himself have retained on a more impartial consideration. To a reader of the present day, the 'Remarks on the History of England' would probably appear but ill entitled to the praises which are, in these letters, so liberally bestowed upon them. For himself, at least, the editor may be allowed to say, that their style is, in his judgment, declamatory, diffused, and involved; deficient both in elegance and in precision, and little calculated to satisfy a taste formed, as Lord Chatham's was, on the purest models of classic simplicity. Their matter he thinks more substantially defective; the observations which they contain display no depth of thought or extent of knowledge; their reasoning is, for the most part, trite and superficial; while on the accuracy with which the facts themselves are represented, no reliance can safely be placed. The principles and character of their author Lord Chatham himself condemns, with just reprobation. And when, in addition to this general censure, he admits that in these writings the truth of history is occasionally warped, and its application distorted for party purposes, what farther notice can be wanted of the caution with which such a book must always be regarded?"

you of one thing before you read them, and that is, that the author has bent some passages to make them invidious parallels to the times he wrote in; therefore, be aware of that, and depend, in general, on finding the truest constitutional doctrines, and that the facts of history, though warped, are nowhere falsified. I also recommend Nathaniel Bacon's Historical and Political Observations;* it is, without exception, the best and most instructive book we have on matters of that kind. They are both to be read with much attention, and twice over; Oldcastle's Remarks to be studied and almost got by heart, for the inimitable beauty of the style, as well as the matter; Bacon for the matter chiefly; the style being uncouth, but the expression forcible and striking. I can write no more, and you will hardly read what is writ.

LETTER IX.

ASTROP WELLS, *Sept.* 5, 1754.

MY DEAR NEPHEW,—I have been a long time without conversing with you, and thanking you for the pleasure of your last letter. You may possibly be about to return to the seat of learning on the banks of the Cam; but I will not defer discoursing to you on literary matters till you leave Cornwall, not doubting but you are mindful of the muses amidst the very savage rocks and moors, and yet more savage natives, of the ancient and respectable duchy. First: With regard to the opinion you desire concerning a common-place book: in general, I much disapprove the use of it; it is chiefly intended for persons who mean to be authors, and tends to impair the memory, and to deprive you of a ready, extempore use of your reading, by accustoming the mind to discharge itself of its reading on paper, instead of relying on its natural power of retention, aided and fortified by frequent revisions of its ideas and materials. Some things must be common-placed in order to be of any use; dates, chronological order, and the like; for instance, Nathaniel Bacon (author of a work on the History of England) ought to be extracted in the best method you can; but, in general, my advice to you is, not to put common-place upon paper, but, as an equivalent to it, to endeavor to range and methodize in your head what you read, and, by so doing frequently and habitually, to fix matter in the memory. I desired you, some time since, to read Lord Clarendon's History of the Civil Wars. I have lately read a much honester and more instructive book of the same period of history, by Thomas May, which I will send to you. If you have not read Burnet's History of His Own Times, I beg you will. I hope your father is well. My love to the girls.

---

* On this book Lord Grenville remarks:

"This book, though at present little known, formerly enjoyed a very high reputation. It is written with a very evident bias to the principles of the parliamentary party to which Bacon adhered, but contains a great deal of very useful and valuable matter. It was published in two parts, the first in 1647, the second in 1651, and was secretly reprinted in 1672, and again in 1682; after which edition, the publisher was indicted and outlawed. After the Revolution, a fourth edition was printed, with an advertisement asserting, on the authority of Lord Chief Justice Vaughan, one of Selden's executors, that the groundwork of this book was laid by that great and learned man. And it is probable, on the ground of this assertion, that in the folio edition of Bacon's book, printed in 1739, it is said, in the title-page, to have been 'collected from some manuscript notes of John Selden, Esq.' But it does not appear that this notion rests on any sufficient evidence. It is, however, manifest from some expressions in the very unjust and disparaging account given of this work in Nicholson's Historical Library (part i. p. 180), that Nathaniel Bacon was generally considered as an imitator and follower of Selden."

LETTER X.

PAY OFFICE, *April* 9, 1755.

MY DEAR NEPHEW,—I rejoice extremely to hear that your father and the girls are not unentertained on their travels. In the meantime, your travels through the paths of literature, arts, and sciences (a road sometimes set with flowers, and sometimes difficult, laborious, and arduous), are not only infinitely more profitable in future, but at present, upon the whole, infinitely more delightful. My own travels at present are none of the pleasantest. I am going through a fit of the gout, with much proper pain and what proper patience I may. *Avis au lecteur*, my sweet boy; remember thy Creator in the days of thy youth. Let no excesses lay the foundations of gout and the rest of Pandora's box; nor any immoralities or vicious courses sow the seeds of a too late and painful repentance. Here ends my sermon, which, I trust, you are not fine gentleman enough, or, in plain English, silly fellow enough, to laugh at. Lady Hester is much yours. Let me hear some account of your intercourse with the muses.

LETTER XI.

PAY OFFICE, *April* 15, 1755.

A thousand thanks to my dear boy for a very pretty letter. I like extremely the account you give of your literary life; the reflections you make upon some West Saxon actors in the times you are reading are natural, manly, and sensible, and flow from a heart that will make you far superior to any of them. I am content you should be interrupted (provided the interruption be not long) in the course of your reading, by declaiming in defence of the thesis you have so wisely chosen to maintain. It is true, indeed, that the affirmative maxim, "Omne solum forti patria est (Every soil is his country to the brave)" has supported some great and good men under the persecutions of faction and party injustice, and taught them to prefer an hospitable retreat in a foreign land to an unnatural mother country. Some few such may be found in ancient times: in our own country also some. Such was Algernon Sidney, Ludlow, and others. But how dangerous it is to trust frail, corrupt man, with such an aphorism! What fatal casuistry is it big with! How many a villain might and has masked himself in the sayings of ancient illustrious exiles, while he was, in fact, dissolving all the nearest and dearest ties that hold societies together, and spurning at all laws, divine and human! How easy the transition from this political to some impious ecclesiastical aphorisms! If all soils are alike to the brave and virtuous, so may all Churches and modes of worship; that is, all will be equally neglected and violated. Instead of every soil being his country, he will have no one for his country; he will be the forlorn outcast of mankind. Such was the late Bolingbroke of impious memory. Let me know when your declamation is over. Pardon an observation on style. "I received yours," is vulgar and mercantile; "your letter," is the way of writing.

LETTER XII.

PAY OFFICE, *May* 20, 1755.

MY DEAR NEPHEW,—I am extremely concerned to hear that you have been ill, especially as your account of an illness you speak of as past, implies such remains of disorder as I beg you will give all proper attention to. By the medicine your physician has ordered, I conceive he considers your case in some degree nervous. If that be so, advise with him whether a little change of air and of the scene, together with some weeks' course of steel waters, would not be highly proper for you. I am to go, the day after to-morrow, to

Sunning Hill, in Windsor Forest, where I propose to drink those waters for about a month. Lady Hester and I will be happy in your company, if your doctor shall be of opinion that such waters may be of service to you; which, I hope, will be his opinion. Besides health recovered, the muses shall not be quite forgot; we will ride, read, walk, and philosophize, extremely at our ease, and you may return to Cambridge with new ardor, or, at least, with strength repaired, when we leave Sunning Hill. If you come, the sooner the better on all accounts. We propose to go into Buckinghamshire in about a month. I rejoice that your declamation is over, and that you have begun, my dearest nephew, to open your mouth in public. I wish I had heard you perform; the only way I ever shall hear your praises from your own mouth. My gout prevented my so much intended and wished for journey to Cambridge, and now my plan of drinking waters renders it impossible. Come, then, my dear boy, to us; and so Mahomet and the mountain may meet, no matter which moves to the other.

LETTER XIII.

July 13, 1755.

My dear Nephew,—I have delayed writing to you in expectation of hearing farther from you upon the subject of your stay at college. No news is the best news, and I will hope now that all your difficulties upon that head are at an end. I represent you to myself deep in study, and drinking large draughts of intellectual nectar; a very delicious state to a mind happy enough, and elevated enough, to thirst after knowledge, and true, honest fame, even as the hart panteth after the water brooks. When I name knowledge, I ever intend learning as the weapon and instrument only of manly, honorable, and virtuous action upon the stage of the world, both in private and public life; as a gentleman, and as a member of the commonwealth, who is to answer for all he does to the laws of his country, to his own breast and conscience, and at the tribunal of honor and good fame. You, my dear boy, will not only be acquitted, but applauded and dignified at all those respectable and awful bars. So, go on and prosper in your glorious and happy career; not forgetting to walk an hour briskly, every morning and evening, to fortify the nerves. I wish to hear, in some little time, of the progress you shall have made in the course of reading chalked out. Adieu.

LETTER XIV.

Stowe, *July* 24, 1755.

My dear Nephew,—I am just leaving this place to go to Wotton; but I will not lose the post, though I have time but for one line. I am extremely happy that you can stay at your college, and pursue the prudent and glorious resolution of employing your present moments with a view to the future. May your noble and generous love of virtue pay you with the sweet rewards of a self-approving heart and an applauding country! and may I enjoy the true satisfaction of seeing your fame and happiness, and of thinking that I may have been fortunate enough to have contributed, in any small degree, to do common justice to kind nature by a suitable education. I am no very good judge of the question concerning the books; I believe they are your own in the same sense that your wearing apparel is. I would retain them, and leave the candid and equitable Mr. —— to plan, with the honest Mr. ——, schemes of perpetual vexation. As to the persons just mentioned, I trust that you bear about you a mind and heart much superior to such malice; and that you are as little capable of resenting it, with any sensations but those of cool, decent contempt, as you are of fearing the consequences of such low efforts. As to the caution money, I think you have done well. The case of the chambers, I conceive, you likewise apprehend rightly. Let me know in your next what these two articles require you to pay down, and how far your present cash is exhausted, and I will direct Mr. Campbell to give you credit accordingly. Believe me, my dear nephew, truly happy to be of use to you.

LETTER XV.

BATH, *Sept.* 28, 1755.

I have not conversed with my dear nephew a long time: I have been much in a post-chaise, living a wandering Scythian life, and he has been more usefully employed than in reading or writing letters; travelling through the various, instructing, and entertaining road of history. I have a particular pleasure in hearing, now and then, a word from you in your journey, just while you are changing horses, if I may so call it, and getting from one author to another. I suppose you are going through the biographers, from Edward the Fourth downwards, not intending to stop till you reach to the continuator of honest Rapin. . . . I have met with a scheme of chronology by Blair, showing all contemporary historical characters, through all ages: it is of great use to consult frequently, in order to fix periods and throw collateral light upon any particular branch you are reading. Let me know, when I have the pleasure of a letter from you, how far you are advanced in English history. You may probably not have heard authentically of Governor Lyttleton's captivity and release. He is safe and well in England, after being taken and detained in France some days. Sir Richard and he met, unexpectedly enough, at Brussels, and came together to England. I propose to return to London in about a week, where I hope to find Lady Hester as well as I left her. We are both much indebted for your kind and affectionate wishes. "In publica commoda peccem, si longo sermone morer (I would sin against the public weal were I to detain with a long discourse)," one bent on so honorable and virtuous a journey as you are.

LETTER XVI.

PAY OFFICE, *Dec.* 6, 1755.

Of all the various satisfactions of mind I have felt upon some late events, none has affected me with more sensibility and delight than the reading my dear nephew's letter. The matter of it is worthy of a better age than that we live in; worthy of your own noble, untainted mind; and the manner and expression of it is such as, I trust, will one day make you a powerful instrument toward mending the present degeneracy. Examples are unnecessary to happy natures; and it is well for your future glory and happiness that this is the case; for to copy any now existing, might cramp genius and check the native spirit of the piece, rather than contribute to the perfection of it. I learn, from Sir Richard Lyttleton, that we may have the pleasure of meeting soon, as he has already, or intends to offer you a bed at his house. It is on this, as on all occasions, little necessary to preach prudence, or to intimate a wish that your studies at Cambridge might not be broken by a long interruption of them. I know the rightness of your own mind, and leave you to all the generous and animating motives you find there, for pursuing improvements in literature and useful knowledge, as much better counsellors than your ever most affectionate uncle.

LETTER XVII.

HORSE GUARDS, *Jan.* 18, 1756.

MY DEAR NEPHEW,—Let me thank you a thousand times for your remembering me; and giving me the pleasure of hearing that you was well, and had laid by the ideas of London and its dissipations, to resume the sober train of thoughts that gowns, square caps, quadrangles, and matin-bells naturally draw after them. I hope the air of Cambridge has brought no disorder upon you, and that you will compound with the muses so as to dedicate some hours, not less than two, of the day to exercise. The earlier you rise, the better your nerves will bear study. When you next do me the pleasure to write to me, I beg a copy of your elegy on your mother's picture: it is such admirable poetry, that I beg you to plunge deep into prose and severer studies, and not indulge your genius with verse for the present. Substitute Tully and Demosthenes in the place of Homer and Virgil; and arm yourself with all the variety of manner, copiousness, and beauty of diction, nobleness and magnificence of ideas, of the Roman consul; and render the powers of eloquence complete by the irresistible torrent of vehement argumentation, the close and forcible reasoning, and the depth and fortitude of mind of the Grecian statesman. This I mean at leisure intervals, and to relieve the course of those studies which you intend to make your principal object. The book relating to the empire of Germany, which I could not recollect, is Vitriarius's Institutiones Juris Publici, an admirable book in its kind, and esteemed of the best authority in matters much controverted. We are all well.

Your affectionate uncle,

William Pitt.

In the 'Correspondence of the Earl of Chatham,' edited by the executors of his son, John, Earl of Chatham, and published from the original manuscripts in their possession, '1838,' there are three more letters addressed to Mr. Thomas Pitt, during his studies at Cambridge, but they are without significance, beyond inquiries after the health of his nephew, who was admitted to the degree of A.M. in 1759. In February, 1760, he visited Portugal, attached to the British Legation to the Court of Lisbon, and, accompanied by the Earl of Strathmore, made a tour through Spain, and into Italy. On his return, he soon entered Parliament, and, until his death, was connected with the public service.

JOHN LOCKE.—ON STUDY.

ITS LIMITATIONS, OBJECTS, AND METHODS.

LIMITATIONS OF THE FIELD.

The end of study is knowledge, and the end of knowledge is practice or communication—for delight is so commonly joined with all improvements in knowledge, that it need not be proposed as an end. The extent of knowledge, or things knowable, is so vast, our duration here so short, the entrance by which the knowledge of things gets into our understanding so narrow, with the necessary allowances for childhood and old age in which so little can be acquired beyond the range of the senses, and the refreshments of our bodies and unavoidable avocations, that it much behooves us to improve, the best we can, our time and talent on things most worthy of being known, and take the most direct road we can to our objects. To this purpose, it may not, perhaps, be amiss to decline some things that are likely to bewilder us, or at least lie out of our way—

1. As all that maze of words and phrases which have been invented and employed only to instruct and amuse people in the art of disputing, and will be found, perhaps, when looked into, to have little or no meaning; and with this kind of stuff the logics, physics, ethics, metaphysics, and divinity of the schools are thought by some to be too much filled. This I am sure, that where we leave distinctions without finding a difference in things; where we make variety of phrases, or think we furnish ourselves with arguments without a progress in the real knowledge of things, we only fill our heads with empty sounds, which however thought to belong to learning and knowledge, will no more improve our understandings and strengthen our reason, than the noise of a jack will fill our bellies or strengthen our bodies; and the art to fence with those which are called subtleties, is of no more use than it would be to be dexterous in tying and untying knots in cobwebs.

2. An aim and desire to know what hath been other men's opinions. Truth needs no recommendation, and error is not mended by it; and in our inquiry after knowledge, it as little concerns us what other men have thought, as it does one who is to go from Oxford to London, to know what scholars walk quietly on foot, inquiring the way and surveying the country as they went, who rode post after their guide without minding the way he went, who were carried along muffled up in a coach with their company, or where one doctor lost or went out of his way, or where another stuck in the mire. I do not say this to

* Abridged. This essay is not contained in Locke's collected works, but was first published in Lord King's Life of the author.

undervalue the light we receive from others, or to think there are not those who assist us mightily in our endeavors after knowledge; perhaps without books we should be as ignorant as the Indians, whose minds are as ill clad as their bodies; but I think it is an idle and useless thing to make it one's business to study what have been other men's sentiments in things where reason is only to be judge, on purpose to be furnished with them, and to be able to cite them on all occasions. However it be esteemed a great part of learning, yet to a man that considers how little time he has, and how much work to do, how many things he is to learn, how many doubts to clear in religion, how many rules to establish to himself in morality, how much pains to be taken with himself to master his unruly desires and passions, how to provide himself against a thousand cases and accidents that will happen, and an infinite deal more, both in his general and particular calling; I say, to a man that considers this well, it will not seem much his business to acquaint himself designedly with the various conceits of men that are to be found in books even upon subjects of moment.

3. Purity of language, a polished style, or exact criticism in foreign languages—thus I think Greek and Latin may be called, as well as French and Italian,—and to spend much time in these may perhaps serve to set one off in the world, and give one the reputation of a scholar. But if that be all, methinks it is laboring for an outside; it is at best but a handsome dress of truth or falsehood that one busks one's self about, and makes most of those who lay out their time this way rather as fashionable gentlemen, than as wise or useful men.

There are so many advantages of speaking one's own language well, and being a master in it, that let a man's calling be what it will, it can not but be worth our taking some pains in it, but men's style is by no means to have the first place in our studies: but he that makes good language subservient to a good life, and an instrument of virtue, is doubly enabled to do good to others.

4. Antiquity and history as far as they are designed only to furnish us with story and talk. For the stories of Alexander and Cæsar, no farther than they instruct us in the art of living well, and furnish us with observations of wisdom and prudence, are not one jot to be preferred to the history of Robin Hood, or the Seven Wise Masters. I do not deny but history is very useful, and very instructive of human life; but if it be studied only for the reputation of being an historian, it is a very empty thing; and he that can tell all the particulars of Herodotus and Plutarch, Curtius and Livy, without making any other use of them, may be an ignorant man with a good memory, and with all his pains hath only filled his head with Christmas tales. And which is worse, the greatest part of history being made up of wars and conquests, and their style, especially the Romans, speaking of valor as the chief, if not the only virtue, we are in danger to be misled by the general current and business of history, and looking on Alexander and Cæsar, and such like heroes, as the highest instances of human greatness, because they each of them caused the death of several hundred thousand men, and the ruin of a much greater number, overrun a great part of the earth, and killed the inhabitants to possess themselves of their countries—we are apt to make butchery, and rapine the chief marks and very essence of human greatness.

5. Nice questions and remote useless speculations, as where the earthly

paradise was—or what fruit it was that was forbidden—where Lazarus's soul was whilst his body lay dead—and what kind of bodies we shall have at the resurrection? &c., &c.

These things, well regulated, will cut off at once a great deal of business from one who is setting out into a course of study; not that all these are to be counted utterly useless, and lost time cast away on them. The four last may be each of them the full and laudable employment of several persons who may with great advantage make languages, history, or antiquity, their study.

OBJECTS IN LIFE TO BE REGARDED.

1. Heaven being our great business and interest, the knowledge which may direct us thither is certainly so too, so that this is without peradventure, the study that ought to take the first, and chiefest place in our thoughts; but wherein it consists, its parts, method, and application, will deserve a chapter.

2. The next thing to happiness in the other world, is a quiet prosperous passage through this, which requires a discreet conduct and management of ourselves, in the several occurrences of our lives. The study of prudence then seems to me to deserve the second place in our thoughts and studies. A man may be, perhaps, a good man (which lives in truth and sincerity of heart towards God), with a small portion of prudence, but he will never be very happy in himself, nor useful to others without. These two are every man's business.

3. If those who are left by their predecessors with a plentiful fortune are excused from having a particular calling, in order to their subsistence in this life, it is yet certain that, by the law of God, they are under an obligation of doing something; which, having been judiciously treated by an able pen, I shall not meddle with, but pass to those who have made letters their business; and in these I think it is incumbent to make the proper business of their calling the third place in their study.

This order being laid, it will be easy for every one to determine with himself what tongues and histories are to be studied by him, and how far in subserviency to his general or particular calling.

HEALTH OF BODY AND MIND TO BE WATCHED.

Our bodies and our minds are neither of them capable of continual study, and we must therefore take a just measure of both in our endeavors. He that sinks his vessel by overloading it, though it be with gold and silver, and precious stones, will give his owner but an ill account of his voyage. General rules must be adapted to the constitution and strength of each individual, and the mode of study may be varied, from books to conversation, according to the condition of mind or body.

Great care is to be taken that our studies encroach not upon our sleep: this I am sure, sleep is the great balsam of life and restorative of nature, and studious sedentary men have more need of it than the active and laborious. We are to lay by our books and meditations when we find either our heads or stomachs indisposed upon any occasion; study at such time doing great harm to the body and very little good to the mind.

I. As the body, so the mind also, gives laws to our studies; I mean to the duration and continuance of them: let it be never so capacious, never so active, it is not capable of constant labor nor total rest. The labor of the mind is study, or intention of thought, and when we find it is weary, either in pursuing other men's thoughts, as in reading, or tumbling or tossing its own as in meditation, it is time to give off and let it recover itself. Sometimes meditation gives a refreshment to the weariness of reading, and *vice versa*, sometimes the change of ground, *i. e.*, going from one subject or science to another, rouses the mind, and fills it with fresh vigor; oftentimes discourse enlivens it when it flags, and puts an end to the weariness without stopping it one jot, but rather forwarding it in its journey; and sometimes it is so tired, that nothing but a perfect relaxation will serve the turn. All these are to be made use of according as every one finds most successful in himself to the best husbandry of his time and thought.

2. The mind has sympathies and antipathies as well as the body; it has a natural preference often of one study before another. It would be well if one had a perfect command of them, and sometimes one is to try for the mastery, to bring the mind into order and a pliant obedience; but generally it is better to follow the bent and tendency of the mind itself, so long as it keeps within the bounds of our proper business, wherein there is generally latitude enough. By this means, we shall go not only a great deal faster, and hold out a great deal longer, but the discovery we shall make will be a great deal clearer, and make deeper impressions in our minds. The inclination of the mind is as the palate of the stomach; that seldom digests well in the stomach, or adds much strength to the body that nauseates the palate, and is not recommended by it.

There is a kind of restiveness in almost every one's mind; sometimes without perceiving the cause, it will boggle and stand still, and one can not get it a step forward; and at another time it will press forward and there is no holding it in. It is always good to take it when it is willing, and keep on whilst it goes at ease.

TRUTH—THE MAIN OBJECT OF STUDY—METHOD.

1. It is a duty we owe to God as the fountain and author of all truth, who is truth itself; and it is a duty also we owe our own selves, if we will deal candidly and sincerely with our own souls, to have our minds constantly disposed to entertain and receive truth wheresoever we meet with it, or under whatsoever appearance of plain or ordinary, strange, new, or perhaps displeasing, it may come in our way. Truth is the proper object, the proper riches and furniture of the mind, and according as his stock of this is, so is the difference and value of one man above another. He that fills his head with vain notions and false opinions, may have his mind perhaps puffed up and seemingly much enlarged, but in truth it is narrow and empty; for all that it comprehends, all that it contains, amounts to nothing, or less than nothing; for falsehood is below ignorance, and a lie worse than nothing.

Our first and great duty, then, is to bring to our studies and to our inquiries after knowledge, a mind covetous of truth; that seeks after nothing else, and after that impartially, and embraces it, how poor, how contemptible, how unfashionable soever it may seem. This is that which all studious men profess to do, and yet it is that where I think very many miscarry. Who is there almost that has not opinions planted in him by education time out of mind; which by that means come to be as the municipal laws of the country, which must not be questioned, but are then looked on with reverence as the standards of right and wrong, truth and falsehood; when perhaps these so sacred opinions were but the oracles of the nursery, or the traditional grave talk of those who pretend to inform our childhood; who received them from hand to hand without ever examining them. This is the fate of our tender age, which being thus seasoned early, it grows by continuation of time, as it were into the very constitution of the mind, which afterwards very difficultly receives a different tincture. When we are grown up, we find the world divided into bands and companies; not only as congregated under several polities and governments, but united only upon account of opinions, and in that respect, combined strictly one with another, and distinguished from others, especially in matters of religion. If birth or chance have not thrown a man young into any of these, which yet seldom fails to happen, choice, when he is grown up, certainly puts him into some or other of them; often out of an opinion that that party is in the right, and sometimes because he finds it is not safe to stand alone, and therefore thinks it convenient to herd somewhere. Now, in every one of these parties of men there are a certain number of opinions which are received and owned as the doctrines and tenets of that society, with the profession and practice whereof all who are of their communion ought to give up themselves, or else they will be scarce looked on as of that society, or at best, be thought but lukewarm brothers, or in danger to apostatize.

It is plain in the great difference and contrariety of opinions that are amongst these several parties, that there is much falsehood and abundance of mistakes in most of them. Cunning in some, and ignorance in others, first made them keep them up; and yet how seldom is it that implicit faith, fear of losing credit with the party or interest (for all these operate in their turns), suffers any one to question the tenet of his party; but altogether in a bundle he receives, embraces, and without examining, professes, and sticks to them, and measures all other opinions by them. Worldly interest also insinuates into several men's minds divers opinions, which suiting with their temporal advantage, are kindly received, and in time so riveted there, that it is not easy to remove them. By these, and perhaps other means, opinions come to be settled and fixed in men's minds, which, whether true or false, there they remain in reputation as substantial material truths, and so are seldom questioned or examined by those who entertain them; and if they happen to be false, as in most men the greatest part must necessarily be, they put a man quite out of the way in the whole course of his studies; and though in his reading and inquiries, he flatters himself that his design is to inform his understanding in the real knowledge of truth, yet in effect it tends and reaches to nothing but the confirming of his already received opinions, the things he meets with in other men's writings and discoveries being received or neglected as they hold proportion with those anticipations which before had taken possession of his mind. . . . These ancient pre-occupations of our minds, these several and almost sacred opinions, are to be examined, if we will make way for truth, and put our minds in that freedom which belongs and is necessary to them. A mistake is not the less so, and will never grow into a truth, because we have believed it a long time, though perhaps it be the harder to part with; and an error is not the less dangerous, nor the less contrary to truth, because it is cried up and had in veneration by any party, though it is likely that we shall be the less disposed to think it so. Here, therefore, we have need of all our force and all our sincerity; and here it is we have use of the assistance of a serious and sober friend, who may help us sedately to examine these our received and beloved opinions; for the mind by itself being prepossessed with them can not so easily question, look round, and argue against them.

2. This grand miscarriage in our study draws after it another of less consequence, which yet is very natural for bookish men to run into, and that is the reading of authors very intently and diligently to mind the arguments pro and con they use, and endeavor to lodge them safe in their memory, to serve them upon occasion.

He that desires to be knowing indeed, that covets rather the possession of truth than the show of learning, that designs to improve himself in the solid substantial knowledge of things, ought, I think, to take another course; *i. e.* to endeavor to get a clear and true notion of things as they are in themselves. This being fixed in the mind well (without trusting to or troubling the memory, which often fails us), always naturally suggests arguments upon all occasions, either to defend the truth or confound error. This seems to me to be that which makes some men's discourses to be so clear, evident, and demonstrative, even in a few words; for it is but laying before us the true nature of any thing we would discourse of, and our faculty of reason is so natural to us, that the clear inferences do, as it were, make themselves: we have, as it were, an instinctive knowledge of the truth, which is always most acceptable to the mind, and the mind embraces it in its native and naked beauty.

3. Another thing, which is of great use for the clear conception of truth, is, if we can bring ourselves to it, to think upon things, abstracted and separate from words. Words, without doubt, are the great and almost only way of conveyance of one man's thoughts to another man's understanding; but when a man thinks, reasons, and discourses within himself, I see not what need he has of them.

4. It is of great use in the pursuit of knowledge not to be too confident, nor too distrustful of our own judgment, nor to believe we can comprehend all things nor nothing. He that distrusts his own judgment in every thing, and

thinks his understanding not to be relied on in the search of truth, cuts off his own legs that he may be carried up and down by others, and makes himself a ridiculous dependant upon the knowledge of others, which can possibly be of no use to him; for I can no more know any thing by another man's understanding, than I can see by another man's eyes.

5. It would, therefore, be of great service to us to know how far our faculties can reach, that so we might not go about to fathom where our line is too short; to know what things are the proper objects of our inquiries and understanding, and where it is we ought to stop, and launch out no farther for fear of losing ourselves or our labor. . . . That which seems to me to be suited to the end of man, and lie level to his understanding, is the improvement of natural experiments for the conveniences of this life, and the way of ordering himself so as to attain happiness in the other—i. e. moral philosophy, which, in my sense, comprehends religion too, or a man's whole duty.

6. For the shortening of our pains, and keeping us from incurable doubt and perplexity of mind, and an endless inquiry after greater certainty than is to be had, it would be very convenient in the several points that are to be known and studied, to consider what proofs the matter in hand is capable of, and not to expect other kind of evidence than the nature of the thing will bear.

7. A great help to the memory, and means to avoid confusion in our thoughts, is to draw out and have frequently before us a scheme of those sciences we employ our studies in, a map, as it were, of the *mundus intelligibilis*. This, perhaps, will be best done by every one himself for his own use, as best agreeable to his own notion, though the nearer it comes to the nature and order of things, it is still the better.

8. It will be no hinderance at all to our study if we sometimes study ourselves, i. e. our own abilities and defects. There are peculiar endowments and natural fitnesses, as well as defects and weaknesses, almost in every man's mind; when we have considered and made ourselves acquainted with them, we shall not only be the better enabled to find out remedies for the infirmities, but we shall know the better how to turn ourselves to those things which we are best fitted to deal with, and so to apply ourselves in the course of our studies, as we may be able to make the greatest advantage.

READING—MEDITATION—DISCOURSE.

Converse with books, even good books (and all others are a loss of time and even worse), is not, in my opinion, the principal part of study; there are two others that ought to be joined with it, each whereof contributes their share to our improvement in knowledge; and those are meditation and discourse. Reading, methinks, is but collecting the rough materials, amongst which a great deal must be laid aside as useless. Meditation is, as it were, choosing and fitting the materials, framing the timbers, squaring and laying the stones, and raising the building; and discourse with a friend (for wrangling in a dispute is of little use), is, as it were, surveying the structure, walking in the rooms, and observing the symmetry and agreement of the parts, taking notice of the solidity or defects of the works, and the best way to find out and correct what is amiss; besides that, it helps often to discover truths, and fix them in our minds, as much as either of the other two.

THE TIME AND ADVANTAGES OF READING HISTORY.

Whereas in the beginning I cut off history, when read for its tales, so, after the principles of morality are settled, and the capacity of forming a judgment on the actions of men is formed, then the study of history is one of the most useful a young man can apply himself to. There he shall see a picture of the world and the nature of mankind, and so learn to think of men as they are. There he shall see the rise of opinions, and find from what slight, and sometimes shameful occasions, some of them have taken their rise, which yet afterwards have had great authority, and passed almost for sacred in the world, and borne down all before them. There also one may learn great and useful instructions of prudence, and be warned against the cheats and rogueries of the world, with many more advantages, which I shall not here enumerate.

TRACTATE ON EDUCATION

A LETTER TO MASTER SAMUEL HARTLIB.[1]

BY JOHN MILTON.

MASTER HARTLIB:—I am long since persuaded, that to say and do aught worth memory and imitation, no purpose or respect should sooner move us than simply the love of God and of mankind. Nevertheless, to write now the reforming of education, though it be one of the greatest and noblest designs that can be thought on, and for the want whereof this nation perishes, I had not yet at this time been induced but by your earnest entreaties and serious conjurements; as having my mind half diverted for the present in the pursuance of some other assertions, the knowledge and the use of which, can not but be a great furtherance both to the enlargement of truth and honest living with much more peace. Nor should the laws of any private friendship have prevailed with me to divide thus, or transpose my former thoughts; but that I see those aims, those actions which have won you with me the esteem of a person sent hither by some good providence from a far country to be the occasion and incitement of great good to this island. And as I hear you have obtained the same repute with men of most approved wisdom and some of the highest authority among us, not to mention the learned correspondence which you hold in foreign parts, and the extraordinary pains and diligence which you have used in this matter both here and beyond the seas, either by the definite will of God so ruling, or the peculiar sway of nature, which also is God's working. Neither can I think, that so reputed and so valued as you are, you would, to the forfeit of your own discerning ability, impose upon me an unfit and over-ponderous argument; but that the satisfaction which you profess to have received from those incidental discourses which we have wandered into, hath pressed and almost constrained you into a persuasion, that what you require from me in this point, I neither ought nor can in conscience defer beyond this time both of so much need at once, and so much opportunity to try what God hath determined. I will not resist, therefore, whatever it is, either of divine or human obligement, that you lay upon me; but will forthwith set down in writing, as you request me, that voluntary idea, which hath long in silence presented itself to me, of a better education, in extent and comprehension far more large, and yet of time far shorter and of attainment far more certain, than hath been yet in practice. Brief[3] I shall endeavor to be; for that which I have to say, assuredly this nation hath extreme need should be done sooner than spoken. To tell you, therefore, what I have benefited herein among old renowned authors I shall spare; and to search what many modern *Januas*[4] and *Didactics*, more than ever I shall read, have projected, my inclination leads me not. But if you can accept of these few observations which have flowered off, and are, as it were, the burnishing of many studious and contemplative years altogether spent in the search of religious and civil knowledge, and such as pleased you so well in the relating, I here give you them to dispose of.

The end then of learning is, to repair the ruins of our first parents by regaining to know God aright, and out of that knowledge to love him, to imitate him, to be like him, as we may the nearest by possessing our souls of true virtue, which being united to the heavenly grace of faith, makes up the highest perfection. But because our understanding cannot in this body found itself but on sensible things, nor arrive so clearly to the knowledge of God and things invisible, as by orderly coning over the visible and inferior creature, the same method is necessarily to be followed in all discreet teaching.[5] And seeing every nation affords not experience and tradition enough for all kind of learning, therefore we are chiefly taught the languages of those people who have at any time been most industrious after wisdom; so that language is but the instrument conveying to us things useful to be known. And though a linguist should pride himself to have all the tongues that Babel cleft the world into,[6] yet if he have not studied the solid things in them, as well as the words and lexicons, he were nothing so much to be esteemed a learned man, as any yeoman or tradesman competently wise in his mother-dialect only. Hence appear the many mistakes which have made learning generally so unpleasing and so unsuccessful. First, we do amiss to spend seven or eight years merely in scraping together so much miserable Latin and Greek as might be learned otherwise easily and delightfully in one year.[7] And that which casts our proficiency therein so much behind, is our time lost partly in too oft idle vacancies given both to schools and universities; partly in a preposterous exaction, forcing the empty wits of children to compose themes, verses and orations, which are the acts of ripest judgment, and the final work of a head filled by long reading and observing with elegant maxims and copious invention.[7] These are not matters to be wrung from poor striplings, like blood out of the nose, or the plucking of untimely fruit; besides all the ill habit which they get of wretched barbarizing against the Latin and Greek idiom, with their untutored Anglicisms, odious to be read, yet not to be avoided without a well-continued and judicious conversing among pure authors, digested, which they scarce taste.[8] Whereas, if after some preparatory grounds of speech by their certain forms got into memory, they were led to the praxis hereof in some chosen short book lessoned thoroughly to them, they might then forthwith proceed to learn the substance of good things and arts in due order, which would bring the whole language quickly into their power. This I take to be the most rational and most profitable way of learning languages, and whereby we may best hope to give account to God of our youth spent herein. And for the usual method of teaching arts, I deem it to be an old error of universities,[9] not yet well recovered from the scholastic grossness of barbarous ages, that instead of beginning with arts most easy, (and those be such as are most obvious to the sense,) they present their young, unmatriculated novices, at first coming with the most intellective abstractions of logic and metaphysics; so that they having but newly left those grammatic flats and shallows, where they stuck unreasonably to learn a few words with lamentable construction, and now on the sudden transported under another climate, to be tossed and turmoiled with their unballasted wits in fathomless and unquiet deeps of controversy, do for the most part grow into hatred and contempt of learning, mocked and deluded all this while with ragged notions and babblements, while they expected worthy and delightful knowledge; till poverty or youthful years call them importunely their several ways, and hasten them,[10] with the sway of friends, either to an ambitious and mercenary, or ignorantly zealous divinity: some allured to the trade of law,[11] grounding their purposes not on the prudent and heavenly contemplation of justice and equity,[12] which was never taught them, but on the promising and pleasing thoughts of litigious terms, fat contentions, and flowing fees: others betake them to state affairs with souls so unprincipled in virtue and true generous breeding, that flattery, and court-shifts, and tyrannous aphorisms, appear to them the highest points of wisdom;[13] instilling their barren hearts with a conscientious slavery, if, as I rather think, it be not feigned: others, lastly, of a more delicious and airy spirit, retire themselves, knowing no better, to the enjoyments of ease and luxury,[14] living out their days in feast and jollity, which indeed is the wisest and safest course of all these, unless they were with more integrity undertaken. And these are the errors, and these are the fruits of mis-spending our prime youth at the schools and universities, as we do, either in learning mere words, or such things chiefly as were better unlearnt.

I shall detain you no longer in the demonstration of what we should not do, but straight conduct you to a hillside, where I will point you out the right path of a virtuous and noble education; laborious indeed at the first ascent, but else so smooth, so green, so full of goodly prospect and melodious sounds on every side, that the harp of Orpheus was not more charming.[15] I doubt not but ye shall have more ado to drive our dullest and laziest youth, our stocks and stubs, from the infinite desire of such a happy nurture, than we have now to haul and drag our choicest and hopefullest wits to that asinine feast of sow-thistles and brambles which is commonly set before them as all the food and entertainment of their tenderest and most docible age.[9] I call, therefore, a complete and generous education, that which fits a man to perform justly, skilfully, and magnanimously, all the offices both private and public, of peace and war.[16] And how all this may be done between twelve and one-and-twenty, less time than is now bestowed in pure trifling at grammar and sophistry, is to be thus ordered.

First, to find out a spacious house and ground about it fit for an ACADEMY,[17] and big enough to lodge one hundred and fifty persons, whereof twenty or thereabout may be attendants, all under the government of one who shall be thought of desert sufficient, and ability either to do all, or wisely to direct and oversee it done. This place should be at once both school and university,[18] not needing a remove to any other house of scholarship, except it be some peculiar college of law or physic where they mean to be practitioners; but as for those general studies which take up all our time from *Lilly*[19] to the commencing,[20] as they term it, master of art, it should be absolute. After this pattern as many edifices may be converted to this use as shall be needful in every city[21] throughout this land, which would tend much to the increase of learning and civility everywhere. This number, less or more, thus collected, to the convenience of a foot-company or interchangeably two troops of cavalry, should divide their day's work into three parts as it lies orderly,—their studies, their exercise, and their diet.

I. For their studies: first, they should begin with the chief and necessary rules of some good grammar, either that now used or any better;[22] and while this is doing, their speech is to be fashioned to a distinct and clear pronunciation,[23] as near as may be to the Italian, especially in the vowels. For we Englishmen being far northerly, do not open our mouths in the cold air wide enough to grace a southern tongue, but are observed by all other nations to speak exceeding close and inward; so that to smatter Latin with an English mouth, is as ill a hearing as law French. Next, to make them expert in the usefullest points of grammar, and withal to season them and win them early to the love of virtue and true labor, ere any flattering seducement or vain principle seize them wandering, some easy and delightful book[21] of education should be read to them, whereof the Greeks have store, as *Cebes*, *Plutarch*, and other Socratic discourses;[22] but in Latin we have none of classic authority extant, except the two or three first books of Quintilian,[23] and some select pieces elsewhere. But here the main skill and groundwork will be, to temper them such lectures and explanations, upon every opportunity, as may lead and draw them in willing obedience, inflamed with the study of learning and the admiration of virtue, stirred up with high hopes of living to be brave men and worthy patriots, dear to God and famous to all ages. That they may despise and scorn all their childish and ill-taught qualities, to delight in manly and liberal exercises; which he who hath the art and proper eloquence to catch them with, what with mild and effectual persuasions, and what with the intimation of some fear, if need be, but chiefly by his own example, might in a short space gain them to an incredible diligence and courage, infusing into their young breasts such an ingenuous and noble ardor as would not fail to make many of them renowned and matchless men. At the same time, some other hour of the day, might be taught them the rules of arithmetic, and, soon after, the elements of geometry, even playing, as the old manner was. After evening repast, till bed-time, their thoughts would be best taken up in the easy grounds of religion, and the story of scripture.[27] The next step would be to the authors of agriculture, *Cato*, *Varro*, and *Columella*, for the matter is most easy; and if the language be difficult, so much the better; it is not a difficulty above their years. And here will be an occasion of inciting and enabling them hereafter to improve the tillage of their country, to recover the bad soil, and to remedy the waste that is made of good; for this was one of Hercules' praises.[28] Ere half these authors be read, (which will soon be with plying hard and daily,) they can not choose but be masters of any ordinary prose: so that it will be then seasonable for them to learn in any modern author the use of the globes and all the maps, first with the old names, and then with the new;[29] or they might then be capable to read any compendious method of natural philosophy. And at the same time might be entering into the Greek tongue, after the same manner as was before prescribed for the Latin; whereby the difficulties of grammar being soon overcome, all the historical physiology[30] of *Aristotle* and *Theophrastus*, are open before them, and as I may say, under contribution.

The like access will be to Vitruvius, to Seneca's Natural Questions, to Mela, Celsus, Pliny, or Solinus.[31] And having thus past the principles of arithmetic, geometry, astronomy, and geography, with a general compact of physics, they may descend in mathematics to the instrumental science of trigonometry, and from thence to fortification, architecture, enginery, or navigation.[32] And in natural philosophy they may proceed leisurely from the history of meteors, minerals, plants, and living creatures, as far as anatomy.[33] Then also in course might be read to them out of some not tedious writer the institution of physic; that they may know the tempers, the humors, the seasons and how to manage a crudity; which he who can wisely and timely do is not only a great physician to himself and to his friends, but also may at some time or other save an army by this frugal and expenseless means only, and not let the healthy and stout bodies of young men rot away under him for want of this discipline, which is a great pity, and no less a shame to the commander.[34] To set forward all these proceedings in nature and mathematics, what hinders but that they may procure, as oft as shall be needful, the helpful experiences of hunters, fowlers, fishermen, shepherds, gardeners, apothecaries; and in other sciences, architects, engineers, mariners, anatomists, who doubtless would be ready, some for reward, and some to favor such a hopeful seminary.[35] And this will give them such a real tincture of natural knowledge as they shall never forget, but daily argument with delight. Then also those poets which are now counted most hard, will be both facile and pleasant, *Orpheus*, *Hesiod*, *Theocritus*, *Aratus*, *Nicander*, *Oppian*, *Dionysius*; and, in Latin, *Lucretius*, *Manilius*, and the rural part of Virgil.[36]

By this time years and good general precepts will have furnished them more distinctly with that act of reason which in ethics is called *proairesis*, that they may with some judgment contemplate upon moral good and evil.[37] Then will be required a special reinforcement of constant and sound endoctrinating, to set them right and firm, instructing them more amply in the knowledge of virtue and hatred of vice; while their young and pliant affections are led through all the moral works of *Plato*, *Xenophon*, *Cicero*, *Plutarch*, *Laertius*, and those *Locrian* remnants; but still to be reduced in their nightward studies wherewith they close the day's work under the determinate sentence of David or Solomon, or the evangelist and apostolic Scriptures.[38] Being perfect in the knowledge of personal duty, they may then begin the study of economics.[39] And either now or before this, they may have easily learned at any odd hour the Italian tongue.[40] And soon after, but with wariness and good antidote, it would be wholesome enough to let them taste some choice comedies, Greek, Latin or Italian; those tragedies also that treat of household matters, as *Trachiniæ*, *Alcestis*, and the like." The next remove must be to the study of Politics;" to know the beginning, end, and reasons of political societies, that they may not, in a dangerous fit of the commonwealth, be such poor shaken uncertain reeds, of such a tottering conscience as many of our great councilors have lately shown themselves, but steadfast pillars of the state. After this they are to dive into the grounds of law and legal justice, delivered first and with the best warrant by Moses, and, as far as human prudence can be trusted, in those extolled remains of Grecian lawgivers, *Lycurgus*, *Solon*, *Zaleucus*, *Charondas*; and thence to all the Roman edicts and tables, with their Justinian; and so down to the Saxon and common laws of England, and the statutes." Sundays, also, and every evening may now be understandingly spent in the highest matters of theology and church history, ancient and modern: and ere this time at a set hour the Hebrew tongue might have been gained, that the Scriptures may now be read in their own original; whereto it would be no impossibility to add the Chaldee and the Syrian dialect." When all these employments are well conquered, then will the choice histories, heroic poems, and attic tragedies of stateliest and most regal argument, with all the famous political orations, offer themselves; which, if they were not only read, but some of them got by memory, and solemnly pronounced with right accent and grace, as might be taught, would endure them even with the spirit and vigor of Demosthenes or Cicero, Euripides or Sophocles." And now, lastly, will be the time to read with them those organic arts which enable men to discourse, and write perspicuously, elegantly, and according to the fitted style of lofty, mean or lowly." Logic, therefore, so much as is useful, is to be referred to this due place, with all her well couched heads and topics, until it be time to open her contracted palm into a graceful and ornate rhetoric taught out of the rule of Plato, Aristotle, Phalereus, Cicero, Hermogenes, Longinus." To which poetry would be made subsequent, or indeed rather precedent, as being less subtile and fine, but more simple, sensuous and passionate. I mean not here the prosody of a verse, which they could not but have hit on before among the rudiments of grammar, but that sublime art which in Aristotle's Poetics, in Horace, and the Italian commentaries of Castlevetro, Tasso, Mazzoni, and others, teaches what the laws are of a true epic poem, what of a dramatic, what of a lyric, what decorum is, which is the grand master-piece to observe." This would make them soon perceive what despicable creatures our common rhymers and play-writers be; and show them what religious, what glorious and magnificent use might be made of poetry, both in divine and human things."[9] From hence, and not till now, will be the right season of forming them to be able writers and composers in every excellent matter, when they shall be thus fraught with an universal insight into things: or whether they be to speak in parliament or council, honor and attention would be waiting on their lips."[9] There would then appear in pulpits other visages, other gestures, and stuff otherwise wrought, than we now sit under, oft-times to as great a trial of our patience as any other that they preach to us."[1] These are studies wherein our noble and our gentle youth ought to bestow their time in a disciplinary way from twelve to one-and-twenty, unless they rely more upon their ancestors dead, than upon themselves living."[1] In which methodical course it is so supposed they must proceed by the steady pace of learning onward, as at convenient times for memory's sake to retire back into the middle ward, and sometimes into the rear of what they have been taught, until they have confirmed and solidly united the whole body of their perfected knowledge, like the last embattling of a Roman legion."[9] Now will be worth the seeing what exercises and recreations may best agree and become these studies.

II. The course of study hitherto briefly described is, what I can guess by reading, likest to those ancient and famous schools of Pythagoras, Plato, Isocrates, Aristotle, and such others, out of which were bred such a number of renowned philosophers, orators, historians, poets, and princes, all over Greece, Italy, and Asia, besides the flourishing studies of Cyrene and Alexandria."[1] But herein it shall exceed them, and supply a defect as great as that which Plato noted in the commonwealth of Sparta; whereas that city trained up their youth most for war, and these in their academies and Lycæum all for the gown, this institution of breeding which I here delineate, shall be equally good both for peace and war."[9] Therefore, about an hour and a half ere they eat at noon should be allowed them for exercise, and due rest afterwards; but the time for this may be enlarged at pleasure, according as their rising in the morning shall be early."[1] The exercise which I commend first is the exact use of their weapon, to guard, and to strike safely with edge or point. This will keep them healthy, nimble, strong, and well in breath; is also the likeliest means to make them grow large and tall, and to inspire them with a gallant and fearless courage, which being tempered with seasonable lectures and precepts to make them of true fortitude and patience, will turn into a native and heroic valor, and make them hate the cowardice of doing wrong."[7] They must be also practiced in all the locks and gripes of wrestling, wherein Englishmen are wont to excel, as need may often be in fight to tug, to grapple, and to close.[59] And this perhaps will be enough wherein to prove and heat their single strength. The interim of unsweating themselves regularly, and convenient rest before meat, may both with profit and delight be taken up in recreating and composing their travailed spirits with the solemn and divine harmonies of music[60] heard or learned, either whilst the skillful organist plies his grave and fancied descant in lofty fugues,[61] or the whole symphony with artful and unimaginable touches adorn and grace the well studied chords of some choice composer;[62] sometimes the lute or soft organ-stop waiting on elegant voices either to religious, martial, or civil ditties, which, if wise men and prophets be not extremely out, have a great power over dispositions and manners to smooth and make them gentle from rustic harshness and distempered passions.[63] The like also would not be inexpedient after meat, to assist and cherish nature in her first concoction, and send their minds back to study in good tune and satisfaction. Where having followed it under vigilant eyes until about two hours before supper, they are, by a sudden alarum or watchword, to be called out to their military motions, under sky or covert according to the season, as was the Roman wont; first on foot, then, as their age permits, on horseback to all the art of cavalry;[64] that having in sport, but with much exactness and daily muster, served out the rudiments of their soldiership in all the skill of embattling, marching, encamping, fortifying, besieging, and battering, with all the helps of ancient and modern stratagems, tactics, and warlike maxims, they may, as it were out of a long war, come forth renowned and perfect commanders in the service of their country.[65] They would not then, if they were trusted with fair and hopeful armies, suffer them for want of just and wise discipline to shed away from about them like sick feathers, though they be never so oft supplied; they would not suffer their empty and unrecruitable colonels of twenty men in a company to quaff out or convey into secret hoards the wages of a delusive list and miserable remnant;[66] yet in the meanwhile to be overmastered with a score or two of drunkards, the only soldiery left about them, or else to comply with all rapines and violences. No, certainly, if they knew ought of that knowledge which belongs to good men or good governors, they would not suffer these things. But to return to our own institute. Besides these constant exercises at home, there is another opportunity of gaining experience to be won from pleasure itself abroad: In those vernal seasons of the year, when the air is calm and pleasant, it were an injury and sullenness against nature not to go out and see her riches, and partake in her rejoicing with heaven and earth."[6] I should not, therefore, be a persuader to them of studying much then, after two or three years that they have well laid their grounds, but to ride out in companies with prudent and staid guides to all the quarters of the land, learning and observing all places of strength, all commodities of building, and of soil for towns and tillage, harbors, and ports for trade."[7] Sometimes taking sea as far as to our navy, to learn there also what they can in the practical knowledge of sailing and sea-fight. These ways would try all their peculiar gifts of nature, and if there were any secret excellence among them, would fetch it out and give it fair opportunities to advance itself by, which could not but mightily redound to the good of this nation, and bring into fashion again those old admired virtues and excellencies with far more advantage now in this purity of Christian knowledge."[8] Nor shall we then need the monsieurs of Paris to take our hopeful youth into their slight and prodigal custodies, and send them over back again transformed into mimics, apes, and kikshoes. But if they desire to see other countries at three or four and twenty years of age, not to learn principles but to enlarge experience and make wise observation, they will by that time be such as shall deserve the regard and honor of all men where they pass, and the society and friendship of those in all places who are best and most eminent."[9] And perhaps then other nations will be glad to visit us for their breeding, or else to imitate us in their own country.

III. Now, lastly, for their diet there can not be much to say, save only that it would be best in the same house; for much time else would be lost abroad, and many ill habits got; and that it should be plain, healthful, and moderate, I suppose is out of controversy."[1]

Thus, Mr. Hartlib, you have a general view in writing, as your desire was, of that which at several times I had discoursed with you concerning the best and noblest way of education; not beginning, as some have done, from the cradle, which yet might be worth many considerations, if brevity had not been my scope."[1] Many other circumstances also I could have mentioned, but this, to such as have the worth in them to make trial, for light and direction may be enough. Only I believe that this is not a bow for every man to shoot in that counts himself a teacher, but will require sinews almost equal to those which Homer gave Ulysses;"[2] yet I am withal persuaded that it may prove much more easy in the essay than it now seems at distance, and much more illustrious; howbeit not more difficult than I imagine, and that imagination presents me with nothing but very happy, and very possible, according to best wishes, if God have so decreed, and this age have spirit and capacity enough to apprehend.

STUDIES AND CONDUCT.

SUGGESTIONS BY MEN EMINENT IN LETTERS AND AFFAIRS.

Second Article.

LETTER FROM LORD BROUGHAM TO ZACHARY MACAULEY, ESQ., ON THE TRAINING OF HIS SON, (THE LATE LORD MACAULEY,) AS AN ORATOR.

NEWCASTLE, *March* 10, 1823.

MY DEAR FRIEND:—My principal object in writing to you to-day is to offer you some suggestions, in consequence of some conversation I have just had with Lord Grey, who has spoken of your son (at Cambridge) in terms of the greatest praise. He takes his account from his son; but from all I know, and have learnt in other quarters, I doubt not that his judgment is well formed. Now you, of course, destine him for the bar, and, assuming that this, and the public objects incidental to it, are in his views, I would fain impress upon you, (and through you, upon him,) a truth or two which experience has made me aware of, and which I would have given a great deal to have been acquainted with earlier in life from the experience of others.

First, that the foundation of all excellence is to be laid in early application to general knowledge, is clear; that he is already aware of; and equally so it is, (of which he may not be so well aware,) that professional eminence can only be attained by entering betimes into the lowest drudgery—the most repulsive labors of the profession—even a year in an attorney's office, as the law is now practiced, I should not hold too severe a task, or too high a price to pay, for the benefit it must surely lead to; but, at all events, the life of a special pleader, I am quite convinced, is the thing before being called to the bar. A young man whose mind has once been well imbued with general learning, and has acquired classical propensities, will never sink into a mere drudge. He will always save himself harmless from the dull atmosphere he must live and work in, and the sooner he will emerge from it, and arrive at eminence. But what I wish to inculcate especially, with a view to the great talent for public speaking which your son happily possess, is that he should cultivate that talent in the only way in which it can reach the height of the art, and I wish to turn his attention to two points. I speak on this subject with the authority both of experience and observation;

I have made it very much my study in theory; have written a great deal upon it which may never see the light, and something which has been published; have meditated much and conversed much on it with famous men; have had some little practical experience in it, but have prepared for much more than I ever tried, by a variety of laborious methods, reading, writing, much translation, composing in foreign languages, &c., and I have lived in times when there were great orators among us; therefore I reckon my opinion worth listening to, and the rather, because I have the utmost confidence in it myself, and should have saved a world of trouble and much time had I started with a conviction of its truth.

1. The first point is this,—the beginning of the art is to acquire a habit of easy speaking; and, in whatever way this can be had (which individual inclination or accident will generally direct, and may safely be allowed to do so,) it must be had. Now, I differ from all other doctors of rhetoric in this,—I say, let him first of all learn to speak easily and fluently, as well as sensibly as he can no doubt, but at any rate let him learn to speak. This is to eloquence, or good public speaking, what the being able to talk in a child is to correct grammatical speech. It is the requisite foundation, and on it you must build. Moreover, it can only be acquired young, therefore let it by all means, and at any sacrifice, be gotten hold of forthwith. But in acquiring it every sort of slovenly error will also be acquired. It must be got by a habit of easy writing (which, as Wyndham said, proved hard reading) by a custom of talking much in company; by speaking in debating societies, with little attention to rule, and more love of saying something at any rate than of saying any thing well. I can even suppose that more attention is paid to the matter in such discussions than in the manner of saying it; yet still to say it easily, *ad libitum*, to be able to say what you choose, and what you have to say,—this is the first requisite, to acquire which every thing else must for the present be sacrificed.

2. The next step is the grand one—to convert this style of easy speaking into chaste eloquence. And here there is but one rule. I do earnestly entreat your son to set daily and nightly before him the Greek models. First of all he may look to the best modern speeches (as he probably has already); Burke's best compositions, as the "Thoughts on the Cause of the Present Discontents;" speech "On the American Conciliation," and "On the Nabob of Arcot's Debt;" Fox's "Speech on the Westminster Scrutiny," (the first part of which he should pore over till he has it by heart); "On the Russian Armament," and "On the War," 1803, with one or two of

Wyndham's best, and very few, or rather none, of Sheridan's; but he must by no means stop here. If he would be a great orator, he must go at once to the fountain head, and be familiar with every one of the great orations of Demosthenes. I take for granted that he knows those of Cicero by heart; they are very beautiful, but not very useful, except perhaps the *Milo*, *pro Ligario*, and one or two more; but the Greek must positively be the model; and merely reading it, as boys do, to know the language, won't do at all; he must enter into the spirit of each speech, thoroughly know the positions of the parties, follow each turn of the argument, and make the absolutely perfect and most chaste and severe composition familiar to his mind. His taste will improve every time he reads and repeats to himself (for he should have the fine passages by heart,) and he will learn how much may be done by a skillful use of a few words and a rigorous rejection of all superfluities. In this view I hold a familiar knowledge of Dante to be next to Demosthenes. It is in vain to say that imitations of these models will not do for our times. First, I do not counsel any imitation, but only an imbibing of the same spirit. Secondly, I know from experience that nothing is half so successful in these times (bad though they be) as what has been formed on the Greek models. I use a very poor instance in giving my own experience, but I do assure you that both in courts of law and Parliament, and even to mobs, I have never made so much play (to use a very modern phrase) as when I was almost translating from the Greek.

I commenced the peroration of my speech for the Queen, in the Lords, after reading and repeating Demosthenes for three or four weeks, and I composed it twenty times over at least, and it certainly succeeded in a very extraordinary degree, and far above any merits of its own. This leads me to remark, that though speaking, with writing beforehand, is very well until the habit of easy speech is acquired, yet after that he can never write too much; this is quite clear. It is laborious, no doubt, and it is more difficult beyond comparison than speaking off-hand; but it is necessary to perfect oratory, and at any rate it is necessary to acquire the habit of correct diction. But I go further, and say, even to the end of a man's life he must prepare word for word most of his finer passages. Now, would he be a great orator or no? In other words, would he have almost absolute power of doing good to mankind, in a free country or no? So he wills this, he must follow these rules.

Believe me truly yours,

H. Brougham.

It is but reciting the ordinary praises of the art of persuasion, to remind you how sacred truths may be most ardently promulgated at the altar—the cause of oppressed innocence be most powerfully defended—the march of wicked rulers be most triumphantly resisted—defiance the most terrible be hurled at the oppressor's head. In great convulsions of public affairs, or in bringing about salutary changes, every one confesses how important an ally eloquence must be. But in peaceful times, when the progress of events is slow and even as the silent and unheeded pace of time, and the jars of a mighty tumult in foreign and domestic concerns can no longer be heard, then too she flourishes,—protectress of liberty,—patroness of improvement,—guardian of all the blessings that can be showered upon the mass of human kind; nor is her form ever seen but on ground consecrated to free institutions. "Pacis comes, otiique socia, et jam bene constitutæ reipublicæ alumna eloquentia." To me, calmly revolving these things, such pursuits seem far more noble objects of ambition than any upon which the vulgar herd of busy men lavish prodigal their restless exertions. To diffuse useful information,—to further intellectual refinement, sure forerunner of moral improvement,—to hasten the coming of the bright day when the dawn of general knowledge shall chase away the lazy, lingering mists, even from the base of the great social pyramid;—this indeed is a high calling, in which the most splendid talents and consummate virtue may well press onward, eager to bear a part.

Let me, therefore, indulge in the hope, that, among the illustrious youths whom this ancient kingdom famed alike for its nobility and its learning, has produced, to continue her fame through after ages, possibly among those I now address, there may be found some one—I ask no more—willing to give a bright example to other nations in a path yet untrodden, by taking the lead of his fellow-citizens,—not in frivolous amusements, nor in the degrading pursuits of the ambitious vulgar,—but in the truly noble task of enlightening the mass of his countrymen, and of leaving his own name no longer encircled, as heretofore, with barbaric splendor, or attached to courtly gewgaws, but illustrated by the honors most worthy of our rational nature—coupled with the diffusion of knowledge—and gratefully pronounced through all ages by millions whom his wise beneficence has rescued from ignorance and vice. This is the true mark for the aim of all who either prize the enjoyment of pure happiness, or set a right value upon a high and unsullied renown.—And if the benefactors of mankind, when they rest from their pious labors, shall be permitted to enjoy hereafter, as an appropriate reward of their virtue, the privilege of looking down upon the blessings with which their toils and sufferings have clothed the scene of their former existence; do not vainly imagine that, in a state of exalted purity and wisdom, the founders of mighty dynasties, the conquerors of new empires, or the more vulgar crowd of evil-doers, who have sacrificed to their own aggrandizement the good of their fellow-creatures, will be gratified by contemplating the monuments of their inglorious fame:—theirs will be the delight—theirs the triumph—who can trace the remote effects of their enlightened benevolence in the improved condition of their species, and exult in the reflection, that the prodigious change they now survey, with eyes that age and sorrow can make dim no more—of knowledge become power—virtue sharing in the dominion—superstition trampled under foot—tyranny driven from the world—are the fruits, precious, though costly, and though late reaped, yet long enduring, of all the hardships and all the hazards they encountered here below!—LORD BROUGHAM—*Inaugural Discourse at Glasgow as Lord Rector*, 1825.

THE TEACHERS OF MANKIND.

Such men—men deserving the glorious title of Teachers of Mankind, I have found laboring conscientiously, though perhaps obscurely, in their blessed vocation, wherever I have gone. God be thanked, their numbers every where abound, and are every day increasing. Their calling is high and holy; their fame is the property of nations; their renown will fill the earth in after ages, in proportion as it sounds not far off in their own times. Each one of these great teachers of the world, possessing his soul in peace—performs his appointed course—awaiting in patience the fulfillment of the promises—resting from his labors, bequeathes his memory to the generations whom his works have blessed—and sleeps under the humble but not inglorious epitaph, commemorating one in whom mankind had a friend, and no man got rid of an enemy.—*Address at Corner Stone of Mechanics' Institute, Liverpool*, 1825.

WILLIAM PITT.—TRAINING FOR PUBLIC SPEAKING.

THE Letters addressed by Lord Chatham to his son, William Pitt, have not been preserved, or, at least, are not published in the Correspondence of the former, or in the Life of the latter, by Earl Stanhope. In this Life, and in an address to the University of Glasgow on the training of an orator, Earl Stanhope remarks:

In 1803 my father, then Lord Mahon, had the high privilege, as a relative, of being for several weeks an inmate of Mr. Pitt's house, at Walmer Castle. Presuming on that familiar intercourse, he told me that he ventured on one occasion to ask Mr. Pitt by what means he had acquired his admirable readiness of speech—his aptness of finding the right word without pause or hesitation. Mr. Pitt replied, that whatever readiness he might be thought to possess in that respect, was, he believed, greatly owing to a practice which his father had impressed upon him. Lord Chatham had bid him take up any book in some foreign language with which he was well acquainted, in Latin or Greek especially. Lord Chatham then enjoined him to read out of this work a passage in English, stopping when he was not sure of the word to be used in English, until the right word came to his mind, and then proceed. Mr. Pitt said that he had assiduously followed this practice. We may conclude that, at first, he had often to stop for awhile before he could recollect the proper word, but that he found the difficulties gradually disappear, until what was a toil to him at first became at last an easy and familiar task.

To an orator, the charm of voice is of very far more importance than mere readers of speeches would find it easy to believe. I have known several speakers in whom that one advantage seemed almost to supply the place of every other. The tones of William Pitt were by nature sonorous and clear; and the farther art, how to manage and modulate his voice to the best advantage, was instilled into him by his father with exquisite skill. Lord Chatham himself was preëminent in that art, as also in the graces of action, insomuch that these accomplishments have been sometimes imputed to him as a fault. In a passage of Horace Walpole, written with the manifest desire to disparage him, we find him compared to Garrick.

To train his son in sonorous elocution, Lord Chatham caused him to recite, day by day in his presence, passages from the best English poets. The two poets most commonly selected for this purpose were Shakspeare and Milton, and Mr. Pitt continued through life familiar with both. There is another fact which Lord Macaulay has recorded from tradition, and which I also remember to have heard: "The debate in Pandemonium was, as it well deserved to be, one of his favorite passages; and his early friends used to talk, long after his death, of the just emphasis and melodious cadence with which they had heard him recite the incomparable speech of Belial."

But whatever the studies of Pitt, whether in the ancient languages or in his own, the aim of public speaking was kept steadily in view. He continued with Mr. Pretyman the same practice of extemporaneous translation which, with his father, he had commenced. We further learn from his preceptor that "when alone he dwelt for hours upon striking passages of an orator or historian, in noticing their turn of expression, and marking their manner of arranging a narrative. A few pages sometimes occupied a whole morning. It was a favorite employment with him to compare opposite speeches upon the same subject, and to observe how each speaker managed his own side of the question. The authors whom he preferred for this purpose were Livy,

Thucydides, and Sallust. Upon these occasions, his observations were not unfrequently committed to paper, and furnished a topic of conversation with me at our next meeting. He was also in the habit of copying any eloquent sentence, or beautiful or forcible expression which occurred in his reading."

According to the unanimous assurance of those who knew him well, Mr. Pitt (the son) did not prepare the structure or the wording of his sentences, far less write them down beforehand. His own manuscript notes were very brief, and mainly confined to figures, to aid him in his financial statements.

CICERO.—PROFESSIONAL AND ORATORICAL TRAINING.

The following autobiographical account of Cicero's training for eloquence, both forensic and deliberative, is taken from his Treatise de Claris Oratoribus, entitled 'Brutus:'

When I became acquainted with the Roman Forum, Hortensius was at the height of his reputation, Crassus was dead, Cotta had been banished, and judicial proceedings were suspended in consequence of the war. Hortensius was in the army, performing his term of service, according to the Roman discipline, one year as a common soldier, another as a military tribune. Sulpicius was absent, as was also M. Antony. Trials were conducted under the Varian law alone, as there was occasion for no other, by reason of the war. L. Memmius and Q. Pompey were habitually present, and spoke as their manner was. They were not distinguished in their profession; but still they are honored with the title of orators by the eloquent Philip, according to whose testimony their speaking had the vehemence and fluency which belongs to the style of accusation.

The other most celebrated orators of the time were in office, and I had almost daily opportunities of hearing them speak in public. For C. Curio was then tribune of the people,—he, however, was not in the habit of speaking, since he had, on one occasion, been deserted by the whole assembly,—Q. Metellus Celer was not distinguished, but spoke occasionally. Q. Varius, C. Carbo, and Cn. Pomponius were distinguished orators, and may almost be said to have lived in the Forum. C. Julius, also, Curule Ædile, almost daily delivered speeches in a very accurate style. As I had been extremely desirous to hear Cotta, I regretted his banishment; still I attended on the speaking of the other orators with great zeal. In the meantime, I was not satisfied with hearing oratorical performances only, but passed no day without reading, writing, and meditation. The next year, Q. Varius was condemned to banishment under his own law. Moreover, I attended diligently to the study of the civil law under Q. Scævola, who, though he did not give formal instruction on the subject, yet permitted such as were desirous of learning to attend his consultations, and learn what they could in that way. The year succeeding, Sylla and Pompey were elected consuls, and P. Sulpicius tribune. With the oratorical style of the latter, I became intimately acquainted, as he spoke daily in some cause or other.

About the same time, Philo, the head of the Academy, and some of the principal men of Athens, left that city and came to Rome, being driven away by the Mithridatic war. To his instructions I devoted myself with the greatest ardor, not only because I was enthusiastically fond of philosophy itself, and delighted with the variety and importance of the subjects with which it made me acquainted, but because I was impressed with the belief that the whole judicial system was abolished forever. During this year, Sulpicius died. The next, three of the most distinguished orators, Q. Catulus, M. Antony, and C. Julius, were most cruelly put to death. This same year I also took lessons at Rome, of Molo, the Rhodian, who was both an eminent pleader at the bar and skilful teacher of rhetoric. Although this account of my studies may seem irrelevant to the object of this treatise, yet I have given it that you, Brutus (as it is already known to Atticus), might have your wish gratified, of being made perfectly acquainted with the course I have pursued, and that you might likewise see how closely I have followed the footsteps of Hortensius throughout the whole of it. For almost three years after this, the city was free from any disturbance; but by reason either of the death, or departure, or banishment of the public speakers (for even M. Crassus and the two Lentuli were not at Rome), Hortensius took the lead in pleading causes; the reputation, however, of Antistius daily increased; Piso spoke frequently; Pomponius not so often; Carbo seldom; Philip once or twice only.

During this whole period, I was engaged, night and day, in the assiduous study of every branch of knowledge. I used to be with Diodotus, the Stoic, who died lately at my house, where he had long resided. From him I learned, among other things, the principles of dialectics, which deserves to be considered as a more contracted and circumscribed eloquence, and without which you, too, Brutus, have judged it impossible to attain to that higher kind of eloquence which is regarded as only a diffusive or expanded dialectics. To this teacher, and to the various branches of knowledge he professed, I devoted myself; but not so exclusively as not to continue my oratorical exercises regularly every day. I studied and declaimed together, often with M. Piso and Q. Pompey, or with somebody else, sometimes in Latin, but more frequently in Greek, both because the Greek being richer in oratorical embellishments, naturally led to the same perfection in the use of the Latin language, and because I could not be instructed, nor have my errors corrected by Greek masters, unless I spoke Greek. In the meantime came the tumult about re-establishing the commonwealth, and the cruel deaths of Scaevola, Carbo, Antistius; the return of Cotta, Curio, Crassus, the Lentuli, Pompey; law and judicature restored; the republic recovered; out of the number of orators, however, three perished—Pomponius, Censorinus, Murena. Then, for the first time, we began to be concerned in causes, both private and public; not to learn our business in the Forum, as many do, but that, as far as possible, we might go into it ready prepared. At the same time, we studied once more under Molo, who had come as ambassador to the Senate, touching the rewards of the Rhodians. Thus it was that our first speech in a public (or criminal) cause, that, namely, for Sextus Roscius, was so highly commended, that no undertaking of the kind was thought beyond our talents; and from that time forward we appeared in many others, in which we prepared ourselves elaborately, and even by midnight studies.

And since it is your wish to know me, not by a few prominent marks, but by a full-length portrait, I shall include some things in this account of myself which may, perhaps, seem to be of minor importance. I was, at that time, remarkably spare and feeble of body; with a long, attenuated neck, and, altogether, such a frame and constitution as is thought to make any extraordinary exertion of the lungs imminently dangerous. The concern of those to whom I was dear was so much the more increased, that I spoke always, without the least remission or variety, with my voice stretched to the utmost pitch, and my whole body laboring and agitated. So that my friends and the physicians advised me to abandon all idea of the Forum; but I thought it better to encounter any peril, than renounce the pursuit of that glory which I believed to be within my reach. And thinking that, by altering my manner of speaking, and modulating my voice with greater skill, I should at once avoid all danger, and improve my elocution,—with a view of effecting such a change, I determined to go to Asia. So, after having been engaged in practice as an advocate for two years, and when my name was now become celebrated in the Forum, I left Rome. At Athens, I staid six months, attending the prelections of Antiochus, the most renowned and able philosopher of the old Academy, and thus renewed, under the directions of a great master, the study of philosophy, which I had cultivated from my earliest youth, and progressively improved myself in ever since. At the same time, I used sedulously to practice speaking under Demetrius, the Syrian, an old and not undistinguished professor of the art. Afterwards, I traveled all over Asia, taking lessons of the greatest orators, with whom I exercised myself in the same way, by their own invitation. Of these, the most distinguished was Menippus of Stratonice; in my opinion, the best speaker of that day in all Asia; and, if to be entirely free from affectation and impertinences of all sorts (nihil habere molestiarum nec ineptiarum) is to be Attic, none was more so than this orator. Dionysius, also, was continually with me; as were Aeschylus, the Cnidian, and Xenocles, of Adramyttium. These were then reckoned the principal speakers of Asia. But, not satisfied with their assistance, I went to Rhodes, and applied myself to the same Molo whom I had heard at Rome; who, whilst he was himself distinguished in the management of causes, and a writer of eminence, was the severest of critics in detecting and censuring any fault, and very able in the business of elementary instruction. He took particular pains (I will not say with what success) to prune away my style, which was redundant, and rioted in a sort of youthful luxuriance and licentiousness, and to keep it, so to express myself, within its banks. So that I returned, at the end of two years, not only better disciplined and practiced, but quite changed; for I had acquired a proper control of my voice, and what may be called the effervescence of my oratory had passed off, my lungs had gathered strength, and my whole constitution some small degree of vigor and consistency.

There were two orators, at that time preëminent, to excite my emulation,—Cotta and Hortensius: the former, pleasant and equable, expressing himself with great propriety, and with a careless ease and freedom; the other, ornate, animated, and not as you knew him, Brutus, when he was on the wane, but much more vehement, both in style and delivery. I, therefore, supposed that Hortensius was to be my principal rival, both as I resembled him more by the animation of my manner, and was nearer to him in age; and, besides that, in the most important causes the leading part was always conceded to him by Cotta himself; for a concourse of people, and the tumult of the Forum, require an impassioned and ardent speaker, with a musical voice, and an impressive and rather dramatic manner. In the course of the first year after my return from Asia, I pleaded several important causes whilst I was suing for the Quæstorship, Cotta for the Consulship, and Hortensius for the place of Ædile. The next year I passed in Sicily; Cotta, after his Consulship, went to Gaul; Hortensius was, and was reputed to be, first at the bar. When I came back from Sicily, my talent (whatever it was) seemed to have attained to its full maturity and perfection. I fear I am dwelling too long upon these things, especially as they concern myself; but my object in all that I have said, is not to make a boast of any genius and eloquence, which I am far from pretending to, but to show you what my labor and industry have been. After having been employed, then, for five years, in the most important causes, and among the leading advocates, I was fairly matched with Hortensius in the impeachment of Verres, just after he had been elected Consul, and I Ædile. But, as this conversation, besides a bare recital of facts, calls for some ideas upon the art, I will briefly state what I think was most remarkable in Hortensius. After his consulship (probably because he had no competitor among the Consulars, and he did not care about those who had not been Consuls), he relaxed from that application and study which had been so intense in him from his childhood, and, surrounded with the good things of life, he determined to live more happily, as he reckoned it, more at his ease, certainly. The first, and second, and third year, the coloring of his eloquence, like that of an old picture, began gradually to fade, so gradually, however, that an unpracticed eye could not detect the change, although connoisseurs might. As he grew older, he seemed to fall off every day, as in other respects, so particularly in the command of language. While, on the other hand, I did not for a moment neglect, by every sort of exercise, but, especially, by writing a great deal, to increase the talent, whatever it was, that I possessed in that way. Meanwhile (to omit other things), in the election of Prætors, I stood at the head of the college by a very large majority; for, not only by my industry and assiduity in the management of causes, but also by a more exquisite and an uncommon style of speaking, I had forcibly drawn the attention of men toward me. I will say nothing of myself. I shall confine myself to the rest of our public speakers, among whom there was none who seemed to have cultivated more thoroughly than other people, those literary studies in which the fountains of eloquence are contained; none who had made himself master of philosophy, mother both of good words and actions; none who was sufficiently versed in the civil law, a knowledge of which is so essential to an orator, especially in private causes; none who was so familiar with the Roman history, as to be able to call witnesses of high authority from the dead whenever need were; none who, when he had fairly caught his adversary in his toils, could relax the minds of the judges, and divert them for awhile from the severity of their character and situation, to mirth and laughter; none who could expatiate at large, and introduce into the discussion of a particular case, general views and universal principles; none who, to amuse an audience, could digress from the subject in hand, who could inflame their minds with anger, or melt them to tears,—none, in short, who possessed that control over the human soul, which is the peculiar privilege of the orator.

Eloquence Defined.

True eloquence I find to be none but the serious and hearty love of truth, and that whose mind soever is fully possessed with a fervent desire to know good things, and with the dearest charity to infuse the knowledge of them into others. When such a man would speak, his words, by what I can express, like so many nimble and airy servitors, trip about him at command, and in well-ordered files, as he would wish, fall aptly into their own places.—MILTON.

True eloquence, indeed, does not consist in speech. It must exist in the man, in the subject, and in the occasion.—WEBSTER.

ADVICE ON STUDIES AND CONDUCT,

BY MEN EMINENT IN LETTERS AND AFFAIRS.

GEORGE BERTHOLD NIEBUHR.

George Berthold Niebuhr, the Philologist, Diplomatist, and Historian, was born in Copenhagen, August 27, 1776, but his early years were spent in South Ditmarsh, where his father, Carsten Niebuhr, the celebrated traveler in the East, held an appointment from the Prussian government, and by whom he was principally instructed until he joined the university at Kiel in 1773. In 1795 he went to Edinburgh and pursued his studies for two years, including his visits to different parts of England. His professional studies were jurisprudence and finance, and for several years he was secretary of the Minister of Finance (Count Bernstorff) at Copenhagen, and one of the directors of the Bank. In 1806 he entered the Prussian service, was appointed one of the counselors of public affairs under Prince Hardenberg, in 1808 was sent as embassador to Holland and again in 1812, and 1816 as minister plenipotentiary to Rome. This last appointment was given in furtherance of his historical studies, to which he had devoted himself with great zeal, having given his first course of lectures on Roman History in the University of Berlin in 1810, and published the first and second volumes of his History of Rome in 1811 and 1812. While at Rome he prosecuted his historical studies, examining ancient manuscripts, edited some unpublished manuscripts of Cicero and Livy, and made his house the resort of learned men and artists of all countries who congregate at Rome. In 1823 he retired to Bonn, and in the following years until his death, on the 2d of January, 1831, he continued to read lectures in the university on Roman History and Antiquities, Greek History, Ancient Geography and Statistics, and kindred subjects, and commenced rewriting his History of Rome, and a new edition of the Byzantine Historians. In his domestic and social relations, he was simple, affectionate, and influential. He loved to have students consult him in reference to their reading, and "I have found him," says Lieber in his Reminiscences, "repeatedly rolling on the ground with his children."

LETTER FROM BARTHOLD GEORGE NIEBUHR TO HIS NEPHEW, ON PHILOLOGICAL STUDIES.

[NIEBUHR, the historian, diplomatist, and philologist, addressed the following letter, while residing at Rome as Prussian Minister, to his nephew, then nineteen years of age. It is a precious manual of advice from a ripe scholar and an eminent statesman, not only on the intellectual processes of education, but on the true ideal of conduct—simplicity, energy, truthfulness—in every walk of life.]

When your dear mother wrote to me, that you showed a decided inclination for philological studies, I expressed my pleasure to her at the tidings; and begged her and your father not to cross this inclination by any plans they might form for your future life. I believe I said to her, that, as philology is the introduction to all other studies, he who pursues it in his school-years with eagerness, as if it were the main business of his life, prepares himself by so doing for whatever study he may choose at the university. And besides, philology is so dear to me, that there is no other calling I would rather wish for a young man for whom I have so great an affection as for you. No pursuit is more peaceful or cheering; none gives a better security for tranquillity of heart and of conscience, by the nature of its duties, and the manner of exercising them: and how often have I lamented with sorrow that I forsook it, and entered into a more bustling life, which perhaps will not allow me to attain to any lasting quiet, even when old age is coming on! The office of a schoolmaster especially is a thoroughly honorable one; and, notwithstanding all the evils which disturb its ideal beauty, truly for a noble heart one of the happiest ways of life. It was once the course I had chosen for myself; and it might have been better had I been allowed to follow it. I know very well, that, spoilt as I now am by the great sphere in which I have spent my active life, I should no longer be fitted for it; but for one whose welfare I have so truly at heart, I should wish that he might not be spoilt in the same manner, nor desire to quit the quietness and the secure narrow circle in which I, like you, passed my youth.

Your mother told me that you wanted to show me something of your writing, as a mark of your diligence, and in order that I might perceive what progress you have already made. I begged she would bid you do so, not only that I might give you and your friends a proof of the sincere interest I take in you; but also because in philology I have a tolerably clear knowledge of the end to be aimed at, and of the paths which lead to it, as well as of those which tempt us astray: so that I can encourage any one who has had the good fortune to enter on one of the former, while I feel the fullest confidence in warning such as are in danger of losing their way, and can tell them whither they will get unless they turn back. I myself had to make my way through a thorny thicket, mostly without a guide; and, alas, at times in opposition to the cautions given me but too forbearingly by those who might have been my guides. Happily—I thank God for it—I never lost sight of the end, and found the road to it again; but I should have got much nearer that end, and with less trouble, had the road been pointed out to me.

I tell you with pleasure, and can do so with truth, that your composition is a creditable proof of your industry; and that I am very glad to see how much you have studied and learnt in the six years since I last saw you. I perceive you have read much, and with attention and a desire of knowledge. In the first place however, I must frankly beg you to examine your Latin, and to convince yourself that in this respect much is wanting. I will not lay a stress on certain grammatical blunders: on this point I agree entirely with my dear friend Spalding, whom such blunders in his scholars did not provoke, provided his pointing them out availed by degrees to get rid of them. A worse fault is, that you have more than once broken down in a sentence; that you employ words in an incorrect sense; that your style is turgid and without uniformity; that you use your metaphors illogically. You do not write simply enough to express a thought unpretendingly, when it stands clearly before your mind. That your style is not rich and polished is no ground for blame; for although there have been some, especially in former times, who by a peculiarly happy management of a peculiar talent have gained such a style at your age, yet in ordinary cases such perfection is quite unattainable. Copiousness and nicety of expression imply a maturity of intellect, which can only be the result of a progressive development. But what every one can and ought to do, is, not to aim at an appearance of more than he really understands; but to think and express himself simply and correctly. Here, therefore, take a useful rule. When you are writing a Latin essay, think what you mean to say with the utmost distinctness you are capable of, and put it into the plainest words. Study the structure of the sentences in great writers; and exercise yourself frequently in imitating some of them: translate passages so as to break up the sentences; and when you translate them back again, try to restore the sentences. In this exercise you will not need the superintendence of your teacher; do it, however, as a preparation for the practice of riper years. When you are writing, examine carefully whether your language be of one color. It matters not to my mind, whether you attach yourself to that of Cicero and Livy, or to that of Tacitus and Quintilian: but one period you must choose: else the result is a motley style, which is as offensive to a sound philologer, as if one were to mix up German of 1650 and of 1800.

You were very right not to send the two projected essays which you mention; because you can not possibly say any thing sound on such questions. Dissertations on particular points can not be written, until we have a distinct view of the whole region wherein they are comprised, until we can feel at home there, and moreover have a sufficient acquaintance with all their bearings upon other provinces of knowledge. It is quite another matter, that we must advance from the special to the general, in order to gain a true understanding of a complex whole. And here we need not follow any systematic order, but may give way to our accidental inclinations, provided we proceed cautiously, and do not overlook the gaps which remain between the several parts.

You have undertaken to write about the Roman colonies, and their influence on the state. Now it is quite impossible that you can have so much as a half-correct conception of the Roman colonies; and to write about their influence on the state, you should not only accurately understand the constitution of Rome and its history, but should be acquainted with the principles and history of politics; all of which as yet is impossible. When I say this, I will add, that none of us, who are entitled to the name of philologers, could have treated this subject at your age; not even Grotius, or Scaliger, or Salmasius, who were excellent grammarians so much earlier than any of us. Still less suited to you is your second subject. You must know enough of antiquity to be aware that the philosophy of young men, down to a much riper age than yours, consisted in silent listening, in endeavoring to understand and to learn. You can not even have an acquaintance with the facts, much less carry on general reflections,—to let pass the word *philosophical*,—on questions of minute detail, mostly problematical. To learn, my dear friend, to learn conscientiously,—to go on sifting and increasing our knowledge,—this is our speculative calling through life: and it is so most especially to youth, which has the happiness that it may give itself up without hinderance to the charms of the new intellectual world opened to it by books. He who writes a dissertation,—let him say what he will,—pretends to teach: and one can not teach without some degree of wisdom; which is the amends that, if we strive after it, God will give us for the departing bliss of youth.

What I wish above all things to impress on you, my young friend, is, that you should purify your mind to entertain a sincere reverence for every thing excellent. This is the best dower of a youthful spirit, its surest guide.

I must now say something more to you about your style of writing. It is too verbose; and you often use false metaphors. Do not suppose that I am unreasonable enough to require a finished style. I expect not such from you, nor from any one at your age; but I would warn you against a false mannerism. All writing should merely be the expression of thought and speech. A man should either write just as he actually delivers a continuous discourse, expressing his genuine thoughts accurately and fully; or, as he would speak, if placed in circumstances, in which in real life he is not placed, where he might be called upon to do so. Every thing should spring from thought; and the thoughts should fashion the structure of the words. To be able to do this, we must study language, must enrich our memory with an abundant supply of words and phrases, whether in our mother tongue, or in foreign tongues, living or dead, must learn to define words precisely, and to determine the idiomatic meaning of phrases, and their limits. The written exercises of a boy or lad should have no other object than to develop his power of thinking, and to enrich and purify his language. If we are not content with our thoughts,—if we twist and turn about under a feeling of our emptiness, writing becomes terribly up-hill work, and we have hardly courage to persevere in it. This was my case at your age, and long after. There was no one who would enter into my distress and assist me; which in my youth would have been easy.

Above all things, however, in every branch of literature and science, must we preserve our truth so pure, as utterly to shun all false show,—so as never to assert any thing, however slight, for certain, of which we are not thoroughly convinced,—so as to take the utmost pains, when we are expressing a conjecture, to make the degree of our belief apparent. If we do not, where is it possible, ourselves point out defects which we perceive, and which others are not likely to discover,—if, when we lay down our pen, we can not say, in the presence of God, *I have written nothing knowingly, which, after a severe examination, I do not believe to be true; in nothing have I deceived my reader, either with regard to myself or others; nor have I set my most odious adversary in any other light than I would answer for at my last hour,*—if we can not do this, learning and literature make us unprincipled and depraved.

Here I am conscious that I demand nothing from others, of which a higher spirit, reading my soul, could reproach me with ever having done the reverse. This scrupulousness, combined with my conception of what a philologer can and ought to be, if he comes before the world, and with my reverence for great scholars, made me so reluctant, long after I had attained to manhood, to appear with any work. Though often urged to do so, not without reproaches, by my friends, I felt that my hour was not yet come; which, had my life taken another course, might have come several years earlier.

From a young man, were it merely as an exercise of honesty, I demand the most scrupulous truth in literature, as in all other things, absolutely and without exception; so that it may become an integral part of his nature; or rather, that the truth, which God planted in his nature, may abide there. By it alone can we fight our way through the world. The hour when my Marcus should say an untruth, or give himself the show of a merit which he had not, would make me very unhappy.

I come now to another part of my task of giving you advice. I wish you were not so fond of satires, even of Horace's. Turn to those works which elevate the heart, in which you see great men and great events, and live in a higher world: turn away from those which represent the mean and contemptible side of ordinary relations and degenerate ages. They are not fitted for the young; and the ancients would not have let them fall into your hands. Homer, Æschylus, Sophocles, Pindar,—these are the poets for youth, the poets with whom the great men of antiquity nourished themselves; and as long as literature shall give light to the world, they will ennoble the youthful souls, that are filled with them, for life. Horace's Odes, as copies of Greek models, are also good reading for the young; and I regret that it is become the practice to depreciate them, which only a few masters are entitled to do, or can do without arrogance. In his Epistles, Horace is original, and more genial; but he who reads them intelligently, reads them with sorrow; they can not do good to any one. We see a man of noble disposition, but who, from inclination and reflection, tries to adapt himself to an evil age, and who has given himself up to a vile philosophy, which does not prevent his continuing noble, but lowers all his views. His morality rests on the principle of suitableness, decorum, reasonableness: he declares expediency (to take the most favorable expression) to be the source of the idea of right (Sat. I. iii. 98.) Baseness discomposes him, and excites him, not to anger, but to a slight chastisement. That admiration for virtue, which constrains ns to scourge vice, and which we see not only in Tacitus, but also in Juvenal,—in the latter disgustingly,—is not found in Horace. Juvenal, however, you must not read yet, with the exception of a few pieces: nor is this any loss; for even if you might be allowed to read him, it would not be wholesome at your age, to dwell on the contemplation of vice, instead of enriching your mind with great thoughts.

To these poets, and among prose writers to Herodotus, Thucydides, Demosthenes, Plutarch, Cicero, Livy, Cæsar, Sallust, Tacitus, I earnestly entreat you to turn, and to keep exclusively to them. Do not read them to make esthetical remarks on them, but to read yourself into them, and to fill your soul with their thoughts, that you may gain by their reading, as you would gain by listening reverently to the discourses of great men. This is the philology which does one's soul good: learned investigations, when one has attained to the capacity of carrying them on, still are only of secondary value. We must be accurately acquainted with grammar, according to the ancient, wide acceptation of that term: we must acquire all branches of archæology, so far as lies in our power. But even though we were to make the most brilliant emendations, and could explain the most difficult passages off hand, this is nothing but mere trickery, unless we imbibe the wisdom and the magnanimity of the great ancients, feel like them, and think like them.

For the study of language, I recommend you, above all, Demosthenes and Cicero. Take the speech of the former *for the Crown*, that of the latter *pro Cluentio*, and read them with all the attention you are master of. Then go through them, giving account to yourself of every word, of every phrase. Draw up an argument: try to get a clear view of all the historical circumstances, and to arrange them in order. This will give you an endless work; and hence you will learn how little you can, and consequently do yet know. Then go to your teacher,—not to surprise him with some unexpectedly difficult questions (for in the speech for Cluentius there are difficulties with regard to the facts, which, even after the longest familiarity with it, can only be solved by conjectures, such as will not occur to the best scholar at the moment) but that he may have the kindness to consider the passages, and to consult the commentators for you, where your powers and means are at fault. Construct a sketch of the procedure in the accusation against Cluentius. Make a list of the expressions, especially epithets and the nouns they are applied to, and mark the key of the metaphors. Translate passages; and a few weeks after, turn your translation back into the original tongue.

Along with this grammatical exercise, read those great writers, one after the other, with more freedom. But after finishing a book, or a section, recall what you have been reading in your memory, and note down the substance as briefly as you can. Note also the phrases and expressions which recur to you the most forcibly; and you should always write down every new word you meet with immediately, and read over the list in the evening.

Leave the commentators and emendators for the present unread. The time will come, when you may study them to advantage. A painter must first learn to draw, before he begins to use colors: and he must know how to handle the ordinary colors, before he decides for or against the use of ultramarines. Of writing I have already spoken to you. Keep clear of miscellaneous reading, even of the ancient authors: among them too there are many bad ones. Æolus only let the one wind blow, which was to bear Ulysses to his goal: the others he tied up: when let loose, and crossing each other, they occasioned him endless wanderings.

Study history in two ways, according to persons, and according to states. Often make synchronistical surveys.

The advice which I give you, I would give to any one in your place. The blame I should have to give to very many. Do not fancy that I don't know this, or that I do not willingly take account of your industry according to its deserts.

The study which I require of you will make no show, will advance slowly: and it will perhaps discourage you to find that many years of studentship are still before you. But, my friend, true learning and true gain are the real blessings of speculative life; and our lifetime is not so short. Still, however long it may be, we shall always have more to learn: God be praised that it is so!

And now, may God bless your labors, and give you a right mind, that you may carry them on to your own welfare and happiness, to the joy of your parents and of us all, who have your virtue and respectability at heart.

"A bad handwriting ought never to be forgiven. Sending a badly written letter to a fellow-creature is as impudent an act as I know of. Can there be any thing more unpleasant, than to open a letter which at once shows that it will require long deciphering? Besides, the effect of the letter is gone, if we must spell it. Many applications for aid, positions, and coöperation are prejudiced and even thrown aside, merely because they are written so badly."

"Writing seems to me just like dressing: we ought to dress well and neat; but as we may dress too well, so may a pedantically fine hand show that the writer has thought more of the letters than the sense."—*Conversation—in Lieber's Reminiscences of Niebuhr.*

STUDIES AND CONDUCT.

CONVERSATION—AS A PART OF EDUCATION.

LORD BACON. ESSAY.—ON DISCOURSE.

Some in their discourse desire rather commendation of wit, in being able to hold all arguments, than of judgment, in discerning what is true, as if it were a praise to know what might be said, and not what should be thought. Some have certain common places and themes wherein they are good, and want variety; which kind of poverty is for the most part tedious, and when it is once perceived—ridiculous. The honorablest part of the talk is to give the occasion, and again to moderate and pass to somewhat else, for then a man leads the dance. It is good in discourse and speech of conversation to vary and intermingle speech of the present occasion with arguments, tales with reasons, asking of questions with telling of opinions, and jest with earnest, for it is a dull thing to tire, and as we say now, to jade (*over-ride or drive*) anything too far. As for jest, there be certain things which ought to be privileged from it—namely: religion, matters of state, great persons, any man's present business of importance, and any case that deserveth pity; yet there be some that think their wits have been asleep except they dart out somewhat that is piquant, and to the quick—that is a vein which would be bridled—

"Parce puer stimulus, et fortius utere loris."
(Boy, spare the spur, and more tighly hold the reins.—Ovid Met. ii. 127).

And, generally, men ought to find the difference between saltness and bitterness. Certainly, he that hath a satirical vein as he maketh others afraid of his wit, so he had need be afraid of other's memory. He that questioneth much shall learn much, and content much, but especially if he apply his questions to the skill of the persons whom he asketh, for he shall give them occasion to please themselves in speaking, and himself shall continually gather knowledge; but let his questions not be troublesome, for that is fit for a poser (*over nice examiner*), and let him be sure to leave other men their turns to speak; nay, if there be any that would reign, and take up all the time, let him find means to take them off, and bring others on, as musicians used to do with those that dance too long galliards (*merry measures*). If you dissemble, sometimes your knowledge of that (*that which*) you are thought to know, you shall be thought another time to know that you know not. Speech of man's self ought to be seldom, and well-chosen. I knew one was wont to say in scorn, "He must needs be a wise man, he speaks so much of himself," and there is but one case wherein a man may commend himself with a good grace, and that is in commending virtue in another, especially if it be a virtue whereunto himself pretendeth (*lay claim to*). Speech of touch (*particular application*) towards others should be sparingly used, for discourse ought to be as a field, without coming home to any man. I knew two noblemen of the west part of England, whereof the one was given to scoff, but kept ever royal cheer in his house; the other would ask of those that had been at the other's table, "Tell truly was there never a flout (*jeer*) or dry blow given?" To which the guest would answer "Such and such a thing passed." The lord would say, "I thought he would mar a good dinner." Discretion of speech is more than eloquence, and to speak agreeably (*in a manner suited*) to him with whom we deal, is more than to speak in good words and in good order. A good continued speech, without a good speech of interlocution, shows slowness, and a good reply, or second speech, without a good settled speech, showeth shallowness and weakness. As we see in beasts, that those that are weakest in the course are yet nimblest in the turn, as it is betwixt the greyhound and the hare. To use too many circumstances (*non-essential particulars*) ere one come to the matter is wearisome; to use none at all is blunt.

Archbishop Whately in his annotations to the above Essay remarks:—

Among the many just and admirable remarks in this essay on "Discourse," Bacon does not notice the distinction—which is an important one—between those who speak because they wish to say something, and those who speak because they have something to say: that is, between those who are aiming at displaying their own knowledge or ability, and those who speak from fulness of matter, and are thinking only of the matter, and not of themselves and the opinion that will be formed of them. This latter Bishop Butler calls (in reference to writings) "a man's writing with simplicity and in earnest." It is curious to observe how much more agreeable is even inferior conversation of this latter description, and how it is preferred by many—they know not why—who are not accustomed to analyse their own feelings, or to enquire why they like or dislike.

Something nearly coinciding with the above distinction, is that which some draw between an "unconscious" and a "conscious" manner, only that the latter extends to persons who are not courting applause, but anxiously guarding against censure. By a "conscious" manner is meant, in short, a continued thought about oneself, and about what the company will think of us. The continued effort and watchful care on the part of the speaker, either to obtain approbation, or at least to avoid disapprobation, always communicates itself in a certain degree to the hearers.

Some draw a distinction again, akin to the above, between the desire to please and the desire to give pleasure; meaning by the former an anxiety to obtain for yourself the good opinion of those you converse with, and by the other, the wish to gratify them.

Aristotle, again draws the distinction between the Eiron and the Bomolochus —that the former seems to throw out his wit for his own amusement, and the other for that of the company. It is this latter, however, that is really the "conscious" speaker, because he is evidently seeking to obtain credit as a wit by his diversion of the company. The word seems nearly to answer to what we call a "wag." The other is letting out of his good things merely from his own fulness.

When that which has been called "consciousness" is combined with great timidity, it constitutes what we call "shyness," a thing disagreeable to others, and a most intense torture to the subject of it.

There are many (otherwise) sensible people who seek to cure a young person of that very common complaint by *exhorting* him not to be shy,—telling him what an awkward appearance it has,—and that it prevents his doing himself justice, &c. All which is manifestly pouring oil on the fire to quench it. For, the very cause of shyness is an over-anxiety as to what people are thinking of you; a morbid attention to your own appearance. The course, therefore, that ought to be pursued is exactly the reverse. The sufferer should be exhorted to think as little as possible about himself, and the opinion formed of him—to be assured that most of the company do not trouble their heads about him—and to harden him against any impertinent criticisms that may be supposed to be going on—taking care only to do what is right, leaving others to think and say what they will.

And the more intensely occupied any one is with the subject matter of what he is saying, the business itself that he is engaged in, the less will his thoughts be turned on himself, and what others think of him.

DEAN SWIFT. HINTS TOWARD AN ESSAY ON CONVERSATION.

I HAVE observed few obvious subjects to have been so seldom, or at least so slightly, handled as this; and indeed I know few so difficult to be treated as it ought, nor yet upon which there seems so much to be said.

Most things pursued by men for the happiness of public or private life, our wit or folly have so refined, that they seldom subsist but in idea; a true friend, a good marriage, a perfect form of government, with some others, require so many ingredients, so good in their several kinds, and so much niceness in mixing them, that for some thousands of years men have despaired of reducing their schemes to perfection: but in conversation it is, or might be, otherwise; for here we are only to avoid a multitude of errors, which, although a matter of some difficulty, may be in every man's power, for want of which it remains as mere an idea as the other. Therefore it seems to me, that the truest way to understand conversation, is to know the faults and errors to which it is subject, and from thence every man to form maxims to himself whereby it may be regulated, because it requires few talents to which most men are not born, or at least may not acquire, without any great genius or study. For nature has left every man a capacity of being agreeable, though not of shining in company; and there are a hundred men sufficiently qualified for both, who, by a very few faults that they might correct in half an hour, are not so much as tolerable.

I was prompted to write my thoughts upon this subject by mere indignation, to reflect that so useful and innocent a pleasure, so fitted for every period and condition of life, and so much in all men's power, should be so much neglected and abused.

And in this discourse it will be necessary to note those errors that are obvious, as well as others which are seldomer observed, since there are few so obvious, or acknowledged, into which most men, some time or other, are not apt to run.

For instance: nothing is more generally exploded than the folly of talking too much; yet I rarely remember to have seen five people together, where some one among them has not been predominant in that kind, to the great constraint and disgust of all the rest. But among such as deal in multitudes of words, none are comparable to the sober deliberate talker, who proceeds with much thought and caution, makes his preface, branches out into several digressions, finds a hint that puts him in mind of another story, which he promises to tell you when this is done; comes back regularly to his subject, cannot readily call to mind some person's name, holding his head, complains of his memory; the whole company all this while in suspense; at length says, it is no matter, and so goes on. And, to crown the business, it perhaps proves at last a story the company has heard fifty times before; or, at best, some insipid adventure of the relater.

Another general fault in conversation is that of those who affect to talk of themselves: some, without any ceremony, will run over the history of their lives; will relate the annals of their diseases, with the several symptoms and circumstances of them; will enumerate the hardships and injustice they have suffered in court, in parliament, in love, or in law. Others are more dexterous, and with great art will lie on the watch to hook in their own praise: they will call a witness to remember they always foretold what would happen in such a case, but none would believe them; they advised such a man from the beginning, and told him the consequences, just as they happened; but he would have his own way. Others make a vanity of telling their faults; they are the strangest men in the world, they cannot dissemble; they own it is a folly; they have lost abundance of advantages by it, but if you would give them the world, they cannot help it; there is something in their nature that abhors insincerity and constraint; with many other insufferable topics of the same altitude.

Of such mighty importance every man is to himself, and ready to think he is so to others; without once making this easy and obvious reflection, that his affairs can have no more weight with other men, than theirs have with him; and how little that is, he is sensible enough.

Where a company has met, I often have observed two persons discover, by some accident, that they were bred together at the same school or university; after which the rest are condemned to silence, and to listen while these two are refreshing each other's memory, with the arch tricks and passages of themselves and their comrades.

I know a great officer of the army who will sit for some time with a supercillous and impatient silence, full of anger and contempt for those who are talking; at length of a sudden, demanding audience, decide the matter in a short dogmatical way; then withdraw within himself again, and vouchsafe to talk no more, until his spirits circulate again to the same point.

There are some faults in conversation which none are so subject to as the men of wit, nor ever so much as when they are with each other. If they have opened their mouths without endeavoring to say a witty thing, they think it is so many words lost: it is a torment to their hearers, as much as to themselves, to see them upon the rack for invention, and in perpetual constraint, with so little success. They must do something extraordinary in order to acquit themselves, and answer their character, else the standers-by may be disappointed, and be apt to think them only like the rest of mortals. I have known two men of wit industriously brought together in order to entertain the company, where they have made a very ridiculous figure, and provided all the mirth at their own expense.

I know a man of wit who is never easy but where he can be allowed to dictate and preside: he neither expects to be informed or entertained, but to display his own talents. His business is to be good company, and not good conversation; and therefore he chooses to frequent those who are content to listen, and to profess themselves his admirers. And indeed the worst conversation I ever remember to have heard in my life was that at Will's coffee-house, where the wits (as they were called) used formerly to assemble; that is to say, five or six men who had writ plays, or at least prologues, or had share in a miscellany, came thither, and entertained one another with their trifling composures, in so important an air as if they had been the noblest efforts of human nature, or that the fate of kingdoms depended on them; and they were usually attended with an humble audience of young students from the inns of court, or the universities; who, at due distance, listened to these oracles, and returned home with great contempt for their law and philosophy, their heads filled with trash, under the name of politeness, criticism, and belles lettres.

By these means the poets, for many years past, were all overrun with pedantry. For, as I take it, the word is not properly used; because pedantry is the too frequent or unseasonable obtruding our own knowledge in common discourse, and placing too great a value upon it; by which definition, men of the court, or the army, may be as guilty of pedantry as a philosopher or a divine; and it is the same vice in women, when they are over-copious upon the subject of their petticoats, or their fans, or their china. For which reason, although it be a piece of prudence, as well as good manners, to put men upon talking on subjects they are best versed in, yet that is a liberty a wise man could hardly take; because, beside the imputation of pedantry, it is what he would never improve by.

The great town is usually provided with some player, mimic, or buffoon, who has a general reception at the good tables; familiar and domestic with persons of the first quality, and usually sent for at every meeting to divert the company; against which I have no objection. You go there as to a farce or a puppet-show; your business is only to laugh in season, either out of inclination or civility, while this merry companion is acting his part. It is a business he has undertaken, and we are to suppose he is paid for his day's work. I only quarrel, when, in select and private meetings, where men of wit and learning are invited to pass an evening, this jester should be admitted to run over his circle of tricks, and make the whole company unfit for any other conversation, beside the indignity of confounding men's talents at so shameful a rate.

Raillery is the finest part of conversation; but, as it is our usual custom to counterfeit and adulterate whatever is too dear for us, so we have done with this, and turned it all into what is generally called repartee, or being smart; just as when an expensive fashion comes up, those who are not able to reach it, content themselves with some paltry imitation. It now passes for raillery to run a man down in discourse, to put him out of countenance and make him ridiculous; sometimes to expose the defects of his person or understanding; on all which occasions, he is obliged not to be angry, to avoid the imputation of not being able to take a jest. It is admirable to observe one who is dexterous at this art, singling out a weak adversary, getting the laugh on his side, and then carrying all before him. The French, from whence we borrow the word, have a quite different idea of the thing, and so had we in the politer age of our fathers. Raillery was to say something that at first appeared a reproach or reflection, but, by some turn of wit, unexpected and surprising, ended always in a compliment, and to the advantage of the person it was addressed to. And surely one of the best rules in conversation is, never to say a thing which any of the company can reasonably wish we had rather left unsaid: nor can there anything be well more contrary to the ends for which people meet together, than to part unsatisfied with each other or themselves.

There are two faults in conversation, which appear very different, yet arise from the same root, and are equally blamable; I mean an impatience to interrupt others; and the uneasiness of being interrupted themselves. The two chief ends of conversation are to entertain and improve those we are among, or to receive those benefits ourselves; which, whoever will consider, cannot easily run into either of these two errors; because, when any man speaks in company, it is to be supposed he does it for his hearers' sake, and not his own; so that common discretion will teach us not to force their attention, if they are not willing to lend it; nor, on the other side, to interrupt him who is in possession, because that is in the grossest manner to give the preference to our own good sense.

There are some people whose good manners will not suffer them to interrupt you, but, what is almost as bad, will discover abundance of impatience, and lie upon the watch until you have done, because they have started something in their own thoughts, which they long to be delivered of. Meantime, they are so far from regarding what passes, that their imaginations are wholly turned upon what they have in reserve, for fear it should slip out of their memory; and thus they confine their invention, which might otherwise range over a hundred things full as good, and that might be much more naturally introduced.

There is a sort of rude familiarity, which some people, by practising among their intimates, have introduced into their general conversation, and would have it pass for innocent freedom of humor; which is a dangerous experiment in our northern climate, where all the little decorum and politeness we have are purely forced by art, and are so ready to lapse into barbarity. This, among the Romans, was the raillery of slaves, of which we have many instances in Plautus. It seems to have been introduced among us by Cromwell, who, by preferring the scum of the people, made it a court entertainment, of which I have heard many particulars; and considering all things were turned upside-down, it was reasonable and judicious: although it was a piece of policy found out to ridicule a point of honor in the other extreme, when the smallest word misplaced among gentlemen ended in a duel.

There are some men excellent at telling a story, and provided with a plentiful stock of them, which they can draw out upon occasion in all companies; and, considering how low conversation runs now among us, it is not altogether a contemptible talent; however, it is subject to two unavoidable defects, frequent repetition, and being soon exhausted; so that, whoever values this gift in himself, has need of a good memory, and ought frequently to shift his company, that he may not discover the weakness of his fund; for those who are thus endued have seldom any other revenue, but live upon the main stock.

Great speakers in public are seldom agreeable in private conversation, whether their faculty be natural, or acquired by practice, and often venturing. Natural elocution, although it may seem a paradox, usually springs from a barrenness of invention, and of words; by which men who have only one stock of notions upon every subject, and one set of phrases to express them in, they swim upon the superficies, and offer themselves on every occasion; therefore men of much learning, and who know the compass of a language, are generally the worst talkers on a sudden, until much practice has inured and emboldened them; because they are confounded with plenty of matter, variety of notions and of words, which they cannot readily choose, but are perplexed and entangled by too great a choice; which is no disadvantage in private conversation; where, on the other side, the talent of haranguing is, of all others, most unsupportable.

Nothing has spoiled men more for conversation than the character of being wits, to support which they never fail of encouraging a number of followers and admirers, who list themselves in their service, wherein they find their accounts on both sides by pleasing their mutual vanity. This has given the former such an air of superiority, and made the latter so pragmatical, that neither of them are well to be endured. I say nothing here of the itch of dispute and contradiction, telling of lies, or of those who are troubled with the disease called the wandering of the thoughts, so that they are never present in mind at what passes in discourse; for whoever labors under any of these possessions, is as unfit for conversation as a madman in Bedlam.

I think I have gone over most of the errors in conversation that have fallen under my notice or memory, except some that are merely personal, and others too gross to need exploding; such as lewd or profane talk; but I pretend only to treat the errors of conversation in general, and not the several subjects of discourse, which would be infinite. Thus we see how human nature is most debased, by the abuse of that faculty which is held the great distinction between men and brutes: and how little advantage we make of that, which might be the greatest, the most lasting, and the most innocent, as well as useful pleasure of life: in default of which we are forced to take up with those poor amusements of dress and visiting, or the more pernicious ones of play, drink, and vicious amours; whereby the nobility and gentry of both sexes are entirely corrupted, both in body and mind, and have lost all notions of love, honor, friendship, generosity: which, under the name of fopperies, have been for some time laughed out of doors.

This degeneracy of conversation, with the pernicious consequences thereof upon our humors and dispositions, has been owing, among other causes, to the custom arisen, for some time past, of excluding women from any share in our society, farther than in parties at play or dancing, or in the pursuit of an amour.

I take the highest period of politeness in England (and it is of the same date in France) to have been the peaceable part of king Charles I.'s reign, and from what we read of those times, as well as from the accounts I have formerly met with from some who lived in that court, the methods then used for raising and cultivating conversation were altogether different from ours: several ladies, whom we find celebrated by the poets of that age, had assemblies at their houses, where persons of the best understanding, and of both sexes, met to pass the evenings in discoursing upon whatever agreeable subjects were occasionally started; and although we are apt to ridicule the sublime Platonic notions they had, or personated, in love and friendship, I conceive their refinements were grounded upon reason, and that a little grain of the romance is no ill ingredient to preserve and exalt the dignity of human nature, without which it is apt to degenerate into everything that is sordid, vicious, and low. If there were no other use in the conversation of ladies, it is sufficient that it would lay a restraint upon those odious topics of immodesty and indecencies, into which the rudeness of our northern genius is apt to fall. And, therefore, it is observable in those sprightly gentlemen about the town, who are so very dexterous at entertaining a vizard mask in the park or the playhouse, that in the company of ladies of virtue and honor, they are silent and disconcerted, and out of their element.

There are some people who think they sufficiently acquit themselves, and entertain their company, with relating facts of no consequence, nor at all out of the road of such common incidents as happen every day; and this I have observed more frequently among the Scots than any other nation, who are very careful not to omit the minutest circumstances of time or place; which kind of discourse, if it were not a little relieved by the uncouth terms and phrases, as well as accent and gesture peculiar to that country, would be hardly tolerable. It is not a fault in company to talk much; but to continue it long is certainly one; for, if the majority of those who are got together be naturally silent or cautious, the conversation will flag, unless it be often renewed by one among them, who can start new subjects, provided he does not dwell upon them, that leave room for answers and replies.

The first thing to consider in falling into conversation with any one is, whether he has a greater inclination to hear you, or that you should hear him.—*Steele.*

In conversation, humor is more than wit, easiness more than knowledge; few desire to learn, or think they need it; all desire to be pleased, or if not, to be easy.—*Sir William Temple.*

He who sedulously attends, pointedly asks, coolly answers, calmly speaks, and ceases when he has nothing to say, is in possession of the best requisites of a good converser.—*Lavater.*

The listening well and answering well is one of the perfections to be attained in conversation.—*La Rochefoucauld.*

We should bring into society our proportion of good will or good humor, and not trouble our friends with our real or imaginary afflictions. Cares, distresses, diseases, animosities, and dislikes should not be obtruded on others who have little sorrows enough of their own; and valetudinarians should be sworn before they enter into company not to say a word of themselves until the meeting breaks up.—*Addison.*

Self is a subject on which all are fluent and few interesting.—*Byron.*

CONVERSATION—AN ART.

LETTER OF THOMAS DeQUINCEY TO A YOUNG FRIEND.—*Abridged.*

Amongst the arts connected with the *elegances* of social life, in a degree which nobody denies, is the art of Conversation; but in a degree which almost everybody denies, if one may judge by their neglect of its simplest rules, this same art is not less connected with the *uses* of social life. Neither the luxury of conversation, nor the possible benefit of conversation, is to be found under that rude administration of it which generally prevails. Without an art, without some simple system of rules, gathered from experience of such contingencies as are most likely to mislead the practice, when left to its own guidance, no act of man nor effort accomplishes its purposes in perfection. Yet for conversation, the great paramount purpose of social meetings, no art exists or has been attempted.

That seems strange, but is not entirely so. A limited process submits readily to the limits of technical system; but a process so unlimited as the interchange of thought, seems to reject them. And even if an art of conversation were less unlimited, the means of carrying such an art into practical effect, amongst so vast a variety of minds, seem wanting. Yet again, perhaps, after all, this may rest on a mistake. What we begin by misjudging is the particular phasis of conversation which brings it under the control of art and discipline. It is not in its relation to the intellect that conversation has been improved or *will* be improved primarily, but in its relation to manners. Has a man ever mixed with what in technical phrase is called "good company," meaning company in the highest degree polished, company which (being or not being aristocratic as respects its composition) is aristocratic as respects the standard of its manners and usages? If he really *has*, and does not deceive himself from vanity or from pure acquaintance with the world, in that case he must have remarked the large effect impressed upon the grace and upon the freedom of conversation by a few simple instincts of real good breeding. Good breeding—what is it? There is no need in this place to answer that question comprehensively; it is sufficient to say, that it is made up chiefly of *negative* elements; that it shows itself far less in what it prescribes, than in what it forbids. Now, even under this limitation of the idea, the truth is, that more will be done for the benefit of conversation by the simple magic of good manners (that is, chiefly by a system of forbearances), applied to the besetting vices of social intercourse, than ever was or can be done by all varieties of intellectual power assembled upon the same arena. Intellectual graces of the highest order may perish and confound each other when exercised in a spirit of ill temper, or under the license of bad manners; whereas, very humble powers, when allowed to expand themselves colloquially in that genial freedom which is possible only under the most absolute confidence in the self-restraint of your collocutors, accomplish their purpose to a certainty, if it be the ordinary purpose of liberal amusement, and have a chance of accomplishing it even when this purpose is the more ambitious one of communicating knowledge or exchanging new views upon truth.

In my own early years, having been formed by nature too exclusively and morbidly for solitary thinking, I observed nothing. Seeming to have eyes, in reality I saw nothing. But it is a matter of no uncommon experience, that, whilst the mere observers never become meditators, the mere meditators, on the other hand, may finally ripen into close observers. Strength of thinking, through long years, upon innumerable themes, will have the effect of disclosing a vast variety of questions, to which it soon becomes apparent that answers are lurking up and down the whole field of daily experience; and thus an external experience which was slighted in youth, because it was a dark cipher that could be read into no meaning, a key that answered to no lock, gradually becomes interesting as it is found to yield one solution after another to problems that have independently matured in the mind. Thus, for instance, upon the special functions of conversation, upon its powers, its laws, its ordinary diseases, and their appropriate remedies, in youth I never bestowed a thought or a care. I viewed it, not as one amongst the gay ornamental arts of the intellect, but as one amongst the dull necessities of business. Loving solitude too much, I understood too little the capacities of colloquial intercourse. And thus it is, though not for my reason, that most people estimate the intellectual relations of conversation. Let these, however, be what they may, one thing seemed undeniable—that this world talked a great deal too much. Lord Bacon had been led to remark the capacities of conversation as an organ for sharpening one particular mode of intellectual power. Circumstances, on the other hand, led me into remarking the special capacities of conversation, as an organ for absolutely creating another mode of power. Let a man have read, thought, studied, as much as he may, rarely will he reach his possible advantages as a *ready* man, unless he has exercised his powers much in conversation—that was Lord Bacon's idea. Now, this wise and useful remark points in a direction not objective, but subjective—that is, it does not promise any absolute extension to truth itself, but only some greater facilities to the man who expounds or diffuses the truth. Nothing will be done for truth objectively that would not at any rate be done, but subjectively it will be done with more fluency, and at less cost of exertion to the doer. On the contrary, my own growing reveries on the latent powers of conversation (which, though a thing that then I hated, yet challenged at times unavoidably my attention), pointed to an absolute birth of new insight into the truth itself, as inseparable from the free and more scientific exercise of the talking art. It would not be the brilliancy, the ease, or the adroitness of the expounder, that would benefit, but the absolute interests of the thing expounded. A feeling dawned on me of a secret magic lurking in the peculiar life, velocities, and contagious ardor of conversation, quite separable from any which belonged to books; arming a man with new forces, and not merely with a new dexterity in wielding the old ones. I felt, and in this I could not be mistaken, as too certainly it was a fact of my own experience, that in the electric kindling of life between two minds, and far less from the kindling natural to conflict (though *that* also is something) than from the kindling through sympathy with the object discussed, in its momentary coruscations of shifting phases, there sometimes arise glimpses and shy revelations of affinity, suggestion, relation, analogy, that could not have been approached through any avenues of methodical study. Great organists find the same effect of inspiration, the same result of power creating and revealing, in the mere movement and velocity of their own voluntaries, like the heavenly wheels of Milton, throwing off fiery flakes and bickering flames; *impromptu* torrents of music create rapturous *fioriture*, beyond all capacity in the artist to register, or afterwards to imitate. One remarkable evidence of a *specific* power lying in conversation, may be seen in such writings as have moved by impulses most nearly resembling those of conversation; for instance, into those of Edmund

Burke. For one moment, reader, pause upon the spectacle of two contrasted intellects, Burke's and Johnson's: one an intellect essentially going forward, governed by the very necessity of growth—by the law of motion in advance; the latter, essentially an intellect retrogressive, retrospective, and throwing itself back on its own steps. This original difference was aided accidentally in Burke by the tendencies of political partisanship, which, both from moving amongst moving things and uncertainties, as compared with the more stationary aspects of moral philosophy, and also from its more fluctuating and fiery passions, must unavoidably reflect in greater life the tumultuary character of conversation. The result from these original differences of intellectual constitution, aided by these secondary differences of pursuit, is, that Dr. Johnson never, in any instance, grows a truth before your eyes, whilst in the act of delivering it or moving towards it. All that he offers up to the end of the chapter he had when he began. But to Burke, such was the prodigious elasticity of his thinking, equally in his conversation and his writings, the mere act of movement became the principle or cause of movement. Motion propagated motion, and life threw off life. The very violence of a projectile, as thrown by *him*, caused it to rebound in fresh forms, fresh angles, splintering, coruscating, which gave out thoughts as new (and that would at the beginning be as startling) to himself as they are to his reader. In this power, which might be illustrated largely from the writings of Burke, is seen something allied to the powers of a prophetic seer, who is compelled oftentimes into seeing things, as unexpected by himself as by others. Now, in conversation, considered as to its *tendencies* and capacities, there sleeps an intermitting spring of such sudden revelation, showing much of the same general character; a power putting on a character *essentially* differing from the character worn by the power of books.

Many people think Dr. Johnson the *exemplar* of conversational power. I think otherwise, for reasons I shall soon explain, and far sooner should I look for such an *exemplar* in Burke. But neither Johnson nor Burke, however they might rank as *powers*, was the *artist* that I demand. Burke valued not at all the reputation of a great performer in conversation; he scarcely contemplated the skill as having a real existence; and a man will never be an artist who does not value his art, or even recognise it as an object distinctly defined. Johnson, again, relied sturdily upon his natural powers for carrying him aggressively through all conversational occasions or difficulties that English society, from its known character and composition, could be supposed likely to bring forward, without caring for any art or system of rules that might give further effect to that power. If a man is strong enough to knock down ninety-nine in a hundred of all antagonists, in spite of any advantages as to pugilistic science which they may possess over himself, he is not likely to care for the improbable case of a hundredth man appearing with strength equal to his own, superadded to the utmost excess of that artificial skill which is wanting in himself. Against such a contingency it is not worth while going to the cost of a regular pugilistic training. Half a century might not bring up a case of actual call for its application. Or, if it did, for a single *extra* case of that nature, there would always be a resource in the *extra* (and, strictly speaking, foul) arts of kicking, scratching, pinching, and tearing hair.

The conversational powers of Johnson were narrow in compass, however strong within their own essential limits. As a *conditione sine quâ non*, he did not absolutely demand a *personal* contradiction by way of "stoker" to supply fuel and keep up his stream, but he demanded at least a *subject* teeming with elements of known contradictory opinion, whether linked to partisanship or not. His views of all things tended to negation, never to the positive and the creative. Hence may be explained a fact, which cannot have escaped any keen observer of those huge Johnsonian memorabilia which we possess, namely, the gyration of his flight upon any one question that ever came before him was so exceedingly brief. There was no process, no evolution, no movements of self-conflict or preparation; a word, a distinction, a pointed antithesis, and, above all, a new abstraction of the logic involved in some popular fallacy, or doubt, or prejudice, or problem, formed the utmost of his efforts. He dissipated some casual perplexity that had gathered in the eddies of conversation, but he contributed nothing to any weightier interest; he unchoked a strangulated sewer in some blind alley, but what river is there that felt his cleansing power? There is no man that can cite any single error which Dr. Johnson unmasked, or any important truth which he expanded.

But there was a greater defect in Dr. Johnson, for purposes of conversation, than merely want of eye for the social phenomena rising around him. He had no eye for such phenomena, because he had a somnolent want of interest in them; and why? because he had little interest in man. Having no sympathy with human nature in its struggles, or faith in the progress of man, he could not be supposed to regard with much interest any forerunning symptoms of changes that to him were themselves indifferent. And the reason he felt thus careless was the desponding taint in his blood. It is good to be of a melancholic temperament, as all the ancient physiologists held, but only if the melancholy is balanced by fiery aspiring qualities, not when it gravitates essentially to the earth. Hence the drooping, desponding character, and the monotony of the estimate which Dr. Johnson applied to life. We were all, in *his* view, miserable, scrofulous wretches; the "strumous diathesis" was developed in our flesh, or soon would be, and, but for his piety, which was the best indication of some greatness latent within him, he would have suggested to all mankind a nobler use for garters than any which regarded knees. In fact, I believe that but for his piety, he would not only have counseled hanging in general, but hanged himself in particular. Now, this gloomy temperament, not as an occasional, but as a permanent state, is fatal to the power of brilliant conversation, in so far as that power rests upon raising a continual succession of topics, and not merely of using with lifeless talent the topics offered by others. Man is the central interest about which revolve all the fleeting phenomena of life; these secondary interests demand the first; and with the little knowledge about them which must follow from little care about them, there can be no salient fountain of conversational themes. *Pectus—id est quod disertum facit.* From the heart, from an interest of love or hatred, of hope or care, springs all permanent eloquence; and the elastic spring of conversation is gone, if the talker is a mere showy man of talent, pulling at an oar which he detests.

In speaking above of conversation, we have fixed our view on those uses of conversation which are ministerial to intellectual culture; but, in relation to the majority of men, conversation is far less valuable as an organ of intellectual culture than of social enjoyment. For one man interested in conversation as a means of advancing his studies, there are fifty men whose interest in conversation points exclusively to convivial pleasure. This, as being a more extensive function of conversation, is so far the more dignified function; whilst, on the other hand, such a purpose as direct mental improvement seems by its superior gravity to challenge the higher rank. Yet, in fact, even here the more general purpose of conversation takes precedency; for, when dedicated to the objects of festal delight, conversation rises by its tendency to the rank of a fine art. It is true that not one man in a million rises to any distinction in this art; nor, whatever France may conceit of herself, has any one nation, amongst other nations, a real precedency in this art. The artists are rare indeed; but still the art, as distinguished from the artist, may, by its difficulties, by the quality of its graces, and by the range of its possible brilliancies, take as a *fine* art; or at all events, according to its powers of execution, it tends to that rank; whereas the best order of conversation that is simply ministerial to a purpose of use, cannot pretend to a higher name than that of a *mechanic* art.

In the course of our life we have heard much of what was reputed to be the select conversation of the day, and we have heard many of those who figured at the moment as effective talkers; yet in mere sincerity, and without a vestige of misanthropic retrospect, we must say, that never once has it happened to us to come away from any display of that nature without intense disappointment; and it always appeared to us that this failure (which soon ceased to be a *disappointment*) was inevitable by a necessity of the case. For here lay the *stress* of the difficulty; almost all depends, in most trials of skill, upon the parity of those who are matched against each other. An ignorant person supposes that, to an able disputer, it must be an advantage to have a feeble opponent; whereas, on the contrary, it is ruin to him; for he cannot display his own powers but through something of a corresponding power in the resistance of his antagonist. A brilliant fencer is lost and confounded in playing with a novice; and the same thing takes place in playing at ball, or battledore, or in dancing, where a powerless partner does not enable you to shine the more, but reduces you to mere helplessness, and takes the wind altogether out of your sails. Now, if by some rare good luck the great talker—the protagonist—of the evening has been provided with a commensurate second, it is just possible that something like a brilliant "passage of arms" may be the result, though much, even in that case, will depend on the chances of the moment for furnishing a fortunate theme; and even then, amongst the superior part of the company, a feeling of deep vulgarity and of mountebank display is inseparable from such an ostentatious duel of wit. On the other hand, suppose your great talker to be received like any other visitor, and turned loose upon the company, then he must do one of two things; either he will talk upon *outré* subjects specially tabooed to his own private use, in which case the great man has the air of a quack-doctor addressing a mob from a street stage; or else he will talk like ordinary people upon popular topics; in which case the company, out of natural politeness, that they may not seem to be staring at him as a lion, will hasten to meet him in the same style; the conversation will become general; the great man will seem reasonable and well-bred; but at the same time, we grieve to say it, the great man will have been extinguished by being drawn off from his exclusive ground.

Yet surely Coleridge *had* such a reputation (for brilliant talking), and without needing any collusion at all; for Coleridge, unless he could have all the talk, would have none. But then this was not conversation; it was not *colloquium*, or talking *with* the company, but *alloquium*, or talking *to* the company. As Madame de Staël observed, Coleridge talked, and *could* talk, only by monologue. Such a mode of systematic trespass upon the conversational rights of a whole party, gathered together under pretence of amusement, is fatal to every purpose of social intercourse, whether that purpose be connected with direct use and the service of the intellect, or with the general graces and amenities of life.

We see the same temper illustrated at times in traveling; a brutal person, as we are disposed at first to pronounce him, but more frequently one who yields unconsciously to a lethargy of selfishness, plants himself at the public fireplace, so as to exclude his fellow-travelers from all but a fraction of the warmth. Yet he does not do this in a spirit of willful aggression upon others; he has but a glimmering suspicion of the odious shape which his own act assumes to others, for the luxurious torpor of self-indulgence has extended its mists to the energy and clearness of his perceptions. Meantime, Coleridge's habit of soliloquizing through a whole evening of four or five hours had its origin neither in arrogance nor in absolute selfishness. The fact was that he *could* not talk unless he were uninterrupted, and unless he were able to count upon this concession from the company. It was a silent contract between him and his hearers, that nobody should speak but himself. If any man objected to this arrangement, why did he come? For the custom of the place, the *lex loci*, being notorious, by coming at all he was understood to profess his allegiance to the autocrat who presided. It was not, therefore, by an insolent usurpation that Coleridge persisted in monology through his whole life, but in virtue of a concession from the kindness and respect of his friends. You could not be angry with him for using his privilege, for it was a privilege conferred by others, and a privilege which he was ready to resign as soon as any man demurred to it. But though reconciled to it by these considerations, and by the ability with which he used it, you could not but feel that it worked ill for all parties. Himself it tempted oftentimes into pure garrulity of egotism, and the listeners it reduced to a state of debilitated sympathy or of absolute torpor. Prevented by the custom from putting questions, from proposing doubts, from asking for explanations, reacting by no mode of mental activity, and condemned also to the mental distress of hearing opinions or doctrines stream past them by flights which they must not arrest for a moment, so as even to take a note of them, and which yet they could not often understand, or, seeming to understand, could not always approve, the audience sank at times into a listless condition of inanimate vacuity. To be acted upon forever, but never to react, is fatal to the very powers by which sympathy must grow, or by which intelligent admiration can be evoked. For his own sake, it was Coleridge's interest to have forced his hearers into the active commerce of question and answer, of objection and demur. Not otherwise was it possible that even the attention could be kept from drooping, or the coherency and dependency of the arguments be forced into light.

The French rarely make a mistake of this nature. The graceful levity of the nation could not easily err in this direction, nor tolerate such defiration in the greatest of men. Not the gay temperament only of the French people, but the particular qualities of the French language, (which however poor for the higher purposes of passion) is rich beyond all others for purposes of social intercourse, prompt them to rapid and vivacious exchange of thought. It is not strange, therefore, that Madame de Staël noticed little as extraordinary in Coleridge beyond this one capital monstrosity of unlimited soliloquy, that being a peculiarity which she never could have witnessed in France; and, considering the burnish of her French tastes in all that concerned colloquial characteristics, it is creditable to her forbearance that she noticed even this rather as a memorable fact than as the inhuman fault which it was. On the other hand, Coleridge was not so forbearing as regarded the brilliant French lady. He spoke of her to ourselves as a very frivolous person, and in short summary terms that disdained to linger upon a subject so inconsiderable. It is remarkable that Goethe and Schiller both conversed with Madame de Staël, like Coleridge, and both spoke of her afterwards in the same disparaging terms as Coleridge. But it is equally remarkable that Baron *William* Humboldt, who was personally acquainted with all the four parties,—Madame de Staël, Goethe, Schiller, and Coleridge,—gave it as his opinion (in letters subsequently published) that the lady had been calumniated through a very ignoble cause, namely, mere ignorance of the French language, or, at least, non-familiarity with the fluency of *oral* French. Neither Goethe nor Schiller, though well acquainted with written French, had any command of it for purposes of *rapid* conversation; and Humboldt supposes that mere spite at the trouble which they found in limping after the lady so as to catch one thought that she uttered, had been the true cause of their unfavorable sentence upon her. Not malice aforethought, so much as vindictive fury for the sufferings they had endured, accounted for their severity in the opinion of the diplomatic baron. He did not extend the same explanation to Coleridge's case, because, though even then in habits of intercourse with Coleridge, he had not heard of *his* interview with the lady, nor of the results from that interview; else what was true of the two German wits was true *à fortiori* of Coleridge; the Germans at least *read* French and talked it slowly, and occasionally understood it when talked by others. But Coleridge did none of these things.

It will come to be considered an infringement of the general rights for any man to detain the conversation, or arrest its movement, for more than a short space of time, which gradually will be more and more defined. This one curtailment of arrogant pretensions will lead to others. Egotism will no longer frame the openings to intellectual discussions; and conversation will then become, what it never *has* been before, a powerful ally of education, and generally of self-culture. The main diseases that besiege conversation at present are—

1st. The want of *timing*. Those who are not recalled, by a sense of courtesy and equity, to the continual remembrance that, in appropriating too large a share of the conversation, they are committing a fraud upon their companions, are beyond all control of monitory hints or of *reproof*, which dare not take a direct and open shape of personal remonstrance; but this, where the purpose of the assembly is festive and convivial, bears too harsh an expression for most people's feelings. That objection, however, would not apply to any mode of admonition that was universally established. A public memento carries with it no personality. For instance, in the Roman law-courts, no advocate complained of the *clepsydra*, or water timepiece, which regulated the duration of his pleadings. Now, such a contrivance would not be impracticable at an after-dinner talk. To invert the clepsydra, when all the water had run out, would be an act open to any one of the guests, and liable to no misconstruction, when this check was generally applied, and understood to be a simple expression of public defence, not of private rudeness or personality. The clepsydra ought to be filled with some brilliantly colored fluid, to be placed in the centre of the table, and with the capacity, at the very most, of the little minute glasses used for regulating the boiling of eggs. It would obviously be insupportably tedious to turn the glass every two or three minutes; but to do so occasionally would avail as a sufficient memento to the company.

2d. Conversation suffers from the want of some discretional power lodged in an individual for controlling its movements. Very often it sinks into flats of insipidity through mere accident. Some trifle has turned its current upon ground where few of the company have anything to say—the commerce of thought languishes; and the consciousness that it *is* languishing about a narrow circle, "unde pedem proferre pudor vetat," operates for the general refrigeration of the company. Now, the ancient Greeks had an officer appointed over every convivial meeting, whose functions applied to all cases of doubt or interruption that could threaten the genial harmony of the company. We also have such officers—presidents, vice-presidents, &c.; and we need only to extend their powers, so that they may exercise over the movement of the conversation the beneficial influence of the Athenian *symposiarch*. At present the evil is, that conversation has no authorized originator; it is servile to the accidents of the moment; and generally these accidents are merely verbal. Some word or some name is dropped casually in the course of an illustration; and *that* is allowed to suggest a topic, though neither interesting to the majority of the persons present, nor leading naturally into other collateral topics that are more so. Now, in such cases it will be the business of the symposiarch to restore the interest of the conversation, and to rekindle its animation, by recalling it from any tracks of dullness or sterility into which it may have rambled. The natural *discursiveness* of colloquial intercourse, its tendency to advance by subtle links of association, is one of its advantages; but mere vagrancy from passive acquiescence in the direction given to it by chance or by any verbal accident, is amongst its worst diseases. The business of the symposiarch will be, to watch these morbid tendencies, which are not the deviations of graceful freedom, but the distortions of imbecility and collapse. His business it will also be to derive occasions of discussion bearing a general and permanent interest from the fleeting events of the casual disputes of the day. His business again it will be to bring back a subject that has been imperfectly discussed, and has yielded but half of the interest which it promises, under the interruption of any accident which may have carried the thoughts of the party into less attractive channels. Lastly, it should be an express office of education to form a particular style, cleansed from verbiage, from elaborate parenthesis, and from circumlocution, as the only style fitted for a purpose which is one of pure enjoyment.

Many other suggestions for the improvement of conversation might be brought forward with ampler limits; and especially for that class of conversation which moves by discussion, a whole code of regulations might be proposed, that would equally promote the interests of the individual speakers and the public interests of the truth involved in the question discussed. Meantime nobody is more aware than we are, that no style of conversation is more essentially vulgar than that which moves by disputation. This is the vice of the young and the inexperienced, but especially of those amongst them who are fresh from academic life. But discussion is not necessarily disputation; and the two orders of conversation—*that*, on the one hand, which contemplates an interest of knowledge, and of the self-developing intellect; *that*, on the other hand, which forms one and the widest amongst the gay embellishments of life—will always advance together. Whatever may remain of illiberal in the first, will correct itself, or will tend to correct itself, by the model held up in the second; and thus the great organ of social intercourse, by means of speech, which hitherto has done little for man, except through the channel of its ministrations to the direct *business* of daily necessities, will at length rise into a rivalship with books, and become fixed amongst the alliances of intellectual progress, not less than amongst the ornamental accomplishments of convivial life.

EDUCATION, STUDIES, AND CONDUCT.

SUGGESTIONS AND ENCOURAGEMENTS FOR SELF-EDUCATION.

LETTERS OF THOMAS DE QUINCEY TO A YOUNG MAN WHOSE EDUCATION HAD BEEN NEGLECTED.

THE following suggestions are taken from a series of Letters addressed by the author to a young man, whose early education had been neglected, but who, coming to the possession of abundant means, and to the consciousness of his own intellectual deficiencies, applied to Mr. De Quincey for a plan of study and reading by which he might supply them. The entire series, if completed, we have not seen in print, and must confine our extracts to the preliminary suggestions, leaving out much which is valuable:

MY DEAR SIR,

Your cousin L—— has explained to me all that your own letter had left imperfect; in particular, how it was that you came to be defrauded of the education to which even your earliest and humblest prospects had entitled you; by what heroic efforts, but how vainly, you laboured to repair that greatest of losses; what remarkable events concurred to raise you to your present state of prosperity; and all other circumstances which appeared necessary to put me fully in possession of your present wishes and intentions.

The two questions which you addressed to me through him I have answered below: these were questions which I could answer easily and without meditation; but for the main subject of our future correspondence, it is so weighty, and demands such close attention (as even *I* find, who have revolved the principal points almost daily for many years), that I would willingly keep it wholly distinct from the hasty letter which I am now obliged to write: on which account it is that I shall forbear to enter at present upon the series of letters which I have promised, even if I should find that my time were not exhausted by the answers to your *two questions below*. . . .

To your first question,—whether to you, with your purposes and at your age of thirty-two, a residence at either of our English universities, or at any foreign university, can be of much service?—my answer is, firmly and unhesitatingly, no. The majority of the undergraduates of your own standing, in an academic sense, will be your juniors by twelve or fourteen years; a disparity of age which could not but make your society mutually burthensome. What, then, is it that you would seek in a university? Lectures? These, whether public or private, are surely the very worst modes of acquiring any sort of accurate knowledge; and are just as much inferior to a good book on the same subject, as that book, hastily read aloud and then immediately withdrawn, would be inferior to the same book, left in your possession, and open at any hour, to be consulted, retraced, collated, and, in the fullest sense, studied. But, besides this, university lectures are naturally adapted, not so much to the general purpose of communicating knowledge, as to the specific purpose of meeting a particular form of examination for degrees, and a particular profession to which the whole course of the education is known to be directed. The two single advantages which lectures can ever acquire, to balance those which they forego, are either, *first*, the obvious one of a better apparatus for displaying illustrative experiments than most students can command; and the cases where this becomes of importance it cannot be necessary to mention; *second*, the advantage of a rhetorical delivery, when *that* is of any use (as in lectures on poetry, etc.). These, however, are advantages more easily commanded in a great capital than in the most splendid university. What, then, remains to a university, except its libraries? And, with regard to those, the answer is short: to the greatest of them undergraduates have not free access; to the inferior ones (of their own college, etc.) the libraries of the great capitals are often equal or superior: and, for mere purposes of study, your own private library is far preferable to the Bodleian or the Vatican. To you, therefore, a university can offer no attraction, except on the assumption that you see cause to adopt a profession; and, as a degree from some university would, in that case, be useful (and indispensable, except for the bar), your determination on this first question must still be dependent on that which you form upon the second.

In this second question you call for my opinion upon the eleventh chapter of Mr. Coleridge's Biographia Literaria, as applied to the circumstances in which you yourself are placed. This chapter, to express its substance in the most general terms, is a dissuasion from what Herder, in a passage there quoted, calls "*Die Autorschaft*;" or, as Mr. Coleridge expresses it, "the trade of authorship;" and the amount of the advice is,—that, for the sake of his own happiness and respectability, every man should adopt some trade or profession, and should make literature a subordinate pursuit. On this advice, I understand you to ask, *first*, whether it is naturally to be interpreted as extending to cases such as yours; and, *second*, if so, what is my judgment on such advice so extended? As to my judgment upon this advice, supposing it addressed to men of your age and situation, you will easily collect, from all which I shall say, that I think it as bad as can well be given.

What Mr. Coleridge really has in his view are two most different objections to literature, as the principal pursuit of life; which, as I have said, continually alternate with each other as the objects of his arguments, and sometimes become perplexed together, though incapable of blending into any real coalition. The objections urged are: *First*. To literature considered as a means of livelihood,—as any part of the resources which a man should allow himself to rely on for his current income, or worldly credit and respectability; here the evils anticipated by Mr. Coleridge are of a high and positive character, and such as tend directly to degrade the character, and indirectly to aggravate some heavy domestic evils. *Second*. To literature considered as the means of sufficiently occupying the intellect. Here the evil apprehended is an evil of defect; it is alleged that literature is not adequate to the main end of giving due and regular excitement to the mind and the spirits, unless combined with some other summons to mental exercise of periodical recurrence,—determined by an overruling cause, acting from without,—and not dependent, therefore, on the accidents of individual will, or the caprices of momentary feeling springing out of temper or bodily health. Upon the last objection, as by far the most important in any case, and the only one at all applicable to yours, I would wish to say a word; because my thoughts on that matter are from the abundance of my heart, and drawn up from the very depths of my own experience. If there has ever lived a man who might claim the privilege of speaking with emphasis and authority on this great question,—By what means shall a man best support the activity of his own mind in solitude?—I, probably, am that man; and upon this ground, that I have passed more of my life in absolute and unmitigated solitude, voluntarily, and for intellectual purposes, than any person of my age whom I have ever met with, heard of, or read of. With such pretensions, what is it that I offer as the result of my experience, and how far does it coincide with the doctrine of Mr. Coleridge?

Briefly this: I wholly agree with him that literature, in the proper acceptation of the term, as denoting what is otherwise called *Belles Lettres*, etc.,—that is, the most eminent of the fine arts, and so understood, therefore, as to exclude *all science* whatsoever, is not, to use a Greek word, αὐτάρκης,—not self-sufficing; no, not even when the mind is so far advanced that it can bring what have hitherto passed for merely literary or *æsthetic* questions, under the light of philosophic principles; when problems of "taste" have expanded to problems of human nature. And why? Simply for this reason,—that our power to exercise the faculties on such subjects is not, as it is on others, in defiance of our own spirits; the difficulties and resistances to our progress in these investigations are not susceptible of minute and equable partition (as in mathematics); and, therefore, the movements of the mind cannot be continuous, but are either, of necessity, tumultuary and *per saltum*, or none at all. When, on the contrary, the difficulty is pretty equally dispersed and broken up into a series of steps, no one of which demands any exertion sensibly more intense than the rest, nothing is required of the student beyond that sort of application and coherent attention which, in a sincere student of any standing, may be presumed as a habit already and inveterately established. The dilemma, therefore, to which a student of pure literature is continually reduced—such a student, suppose, as the Schlegels, or any other man who has cultivated no acquaintance with the severer sciences—is this: either he studies literature as a mere man of taste, and, perhaps, also as a philologer,—and, in that case, his understanding must find a daily want of some masculine exercise to call it out and give it play,—or (which is the rarest thing in the world), having begun to study literature as a philosopher, he seeks to renew that elevated walk of study at all opportunities; but this is often as hopeless an effort as to a great poet it would be to sit down upon any predetermination to compose in his character of poet. Hence, therefore,—if (as too often it happens) he has not cultivated those studies (mathematics, *e. g.*) which present such difficulties as will bend to a resolute effort of the mind, and which have the additional recommendation that they are apt to stimulate and irritate the mind to make that effort,—he is often thrown, by the very cravings of an unsatisfied intellect, and not by passion or inclination, upon some vulgar excitement of business or pleasure, which becomes constantly more necessary.

GENERAL MEANS OF STUDY.

According to my view, they are three,—first, Logic; secondly, Languages; thirdly, Arts of Memory. With respect to these, it is not necessary that any special end should be previously given. Be his end what it may, every student must have thoughts to arrange, knowledge to transplant, and facts to record. Means which are thus universally requisite may safely have precedency of the end; and it will not be a preposterous order if I dedicate my first three letters to the several subjects of Logic, Languages, and Arts of Memory, which will compose one half of my scheme, leaving to the other half the task of unfolding the course of study for which these instruments will be available. Having thus settled the arrangement, and implicitly, therefore, settled in part the idea or *ratio* of my scheme, I shall go on to add what may be necessary to confine your expectations to the right track, and prevent them from going above or below the true character of the mark I aim at. I profess, then, to attempt something much higher than merely directions for a course of reading. Not that such a work might not be of eminent service; and in particular at this time, and with a constant adaptation to the case of rich men, not literary, I am of opinion that no more useful book could be executed than a series of letters (addressed, for example, to country gentlemen, merchants, etc.) on the formation of a library. The uses of such a treatise, however, are not those which I contemplate; for, either it would presume and refer to a plan of study already settled,—and in that light it is a mere complement of the plan I propose to execute,—or else it would attempt to *involve* a plan of study in the course of reading suggested; and *that* would be neither more nor less than to do *in concreto*, what it is far more convenient, as well as more philosophical, to do (as I am now going to do) directly and *in abstracto*. A mere course of reading, therefore, is much below what I propose; on the other hand, an organon of the human understanding is as much above it. Such a work is a labor for a life; that is to say, though it may take up but a small part of every day, yet could it in no other way accumulate its materials than by keeping the mind everlastingly on the watch to seize upon such notices as may arise daily throughout a life under the favor of accident or occasion. Forty years are not too large a period for such a work; and my present work, however maturely meditated, must be executed with rapidity. Here, in fact, I do but sketch or trace in outline (ὡς ἐν τύπῳ [illegible]) what there it would become my duty to develop, to fill up in detail, to apply, and to illustrate on the most extensive scale.

After having attempted, in my first part, to put you in possession of the best method for acquiring the *instruments* of study; and, with respect to logic in particular, having directed a philosophic light upon its true meaning and purpose, with the hope of extinguishing that anarchy of errors which have possessed this ground from the time of Lord Bacon to the moment at which I write; I then, in the second division, address myself to the question of *ends*. Upon which word let me distinguish: upon ends, in an absolute sense, as ultimate ends, it is presumption in any man to offer counsel to another of mature age. Advice of that sort, given under whatever hollow pretences of kindness, is to be looked upon as arrogance in the most repulsive shape; and to be rejected with that sort of summary disdain, which any man not of servile nature would testify towards him who should attempt to influence his choice of a wife. A student of mature age must be presumed to be best acquainted with his own talents and his own intellectual infirmities, with his "forte" and his "foible," with his own former experience of failure or success, and with the direction in which his inclinations point. Far be it from me to violate, by the spirit of my counsels, a pride so reasonable, which, in truth, I hold sacred. My scheme takes an humbler ground. *Ends*, indeed, in a secondary sense, the latter half professes to deal with; but such ends as, though bearing that character in relation to what is purely and merely instrumental, yet again become *means* in relation to ends absolutely so called. The *final* application of your powers and knowledge, it is for yourself only to determine; my pretensions, in regard to that election, are limited to this,—that I profess to place you on a vantage ground from which you may determine more wisely, by determining from a higher point of survey. My purpose is not to map the whole course of your journey, but to serve as your guide to that station at which you may be able to lay down your future route for yourself. The former half of my work I have already described to you; the latter half endeavors to construct such a system of study as shall combine these two advantages: I. Systematic unity; that is, such a principle of *internal* connection, so that the several parts of the plan shall furnish assistance interchangeably. 2. The largest possible compass of *external* relations. Some empires, you know, are built for growth; others are essentially unprogressive, but are built for duration, on some principle of strong internal cohesion. Systems of knowledge, however, and schemes of study, should propose both ends; they should take their foundations broad and deep,

"And lay great bases for eternity,"

which is the surest key to internal and systematic connection; and, secondly, they should provide for future growth and accretion, regarding all knowledge as a nucleus and centre of accumulation for other knowledge. It is on this latter principle, by the way, that the system of education in our public schools, however otherwise defective, is justly held superior to the specious novelties of our suburban academies; for it is more radical, and adapted to a larger superstructure. Such, I say, is the character of my scheme; and, by the very act of claiming for it, as one of its benefits, that it leaves you in the *centre* of large and comprehensive relations to other parts of knowledge, it is pretty apparent that I do not presume to suggest in what direction of these manifold relations you should afterwards advance; *that*, as I have now sufficiently explained, will be left to your own self-knowledge; but to your self-knowledge illumined at the point where I leave you by that other knowledge which my scheme of study professes to communicate.

When I spoke above of the student's taking his foundations broad and deep, I had my eye chiefly on the corner-stones of strong-built knowledge, namely, on logic; on a proper choice of languages; on a particular part of what is called metaphysics; and on mathematics. Now, you allege (I suppose upon occasion of my references to mathematics in my last letter) that you have no "genius" for mathematics; and you speak with the usual awe (*pavor attonitorum*) of the supposed "profundity" of intellect necessary to a great progress in this direction. Be assured that you are in utter error; though it be an error all but universal. In mathematics, upon two irresistible arguments which I shall set in a clear light, when I come to explain the procedure of the mind with regard to that sort of evidence and that sort of investigation, there can be no subtlety; all minds are levelled except as to the rapidity of the course, and, from the entire absence of all those acts of mind which do really imply profundity of intellect, it is a question whether an idiot might not be made an excellent mathematician. Listen not to the romantic notions of the world on this subject; above all, listen not to mathematicians. Mathematicians, *as mathematicians*, have no business with the question. It is one thing to understand mathematics, another, and far different, to understand the philosophy of mathematics. With respect to this, it is memorable that, in no one of the great philosophical questions which the ascent of mathematics has, from time to time, brought up above the horizon of our speculative view, has any mathematician who was merely such (however eminent) had depth of intellect adequate to its solution, without insisting on the absurdities published by mathematicians, on the philosophy of the *infinite*, since that notion was introduced into mathematics, or on the fruitless attempts of all but a metaphysician to settle the strife between the conflicting modes of valuing *living forces*,—I need only ask what English or French mathematician has been able to exhibit the notion of *negative quantities*, in a theory endurable even to a popular philosophy, or which has commanded any assent? Or, again, what Algebra is there existing which does not contain a false and ludicrous account of the procedure in that science, as contrasted with the procedure in geometry? But, not to trouble you with more of these cases so opprobrious to mathematicians, lay this to heart, that mathematics are very easy and very important; they are, in fact, the organ of one large division of human knowledge. And, as it is of consequence that you should lose no time by waiting for my letter on that subject, let me forestall so much of it as to advise that you would immediately commence with Euclid; reading those eight books of the Elements which are usually read, and the Data. If you should go no farther, so much geometry will be useful and delightful; and so much, by reading for two hours a day, you will easily accomplish in about thirteen weeks, that is, one quarter of a year.

LANGUAGES.

On this Babel of an earth which you and I inhabit, there are said to be about three thousand languages and jargons. Of nearly five hundred, you will find a specimen in the Mithridates of Adelung, and in some other German works of more moderate bulk. . . .

To a professed linguist, therefore, the natural advice would be—examine the structure of as many languages as possible; gather as many thousand specimens as possible into your *hortus siccus*, beginning with the eldest forms of the Teutonic, namely, the Visigothic and the Icelandic, for which the aids rendered by modern learning are immense. To a professed philologist, I say, the natural advice would be this. But to you, who have no such purposes, and whom I suppose to wish for languages simply as avenues to literature, not otherwise accessible, I will frankly say—start from this principle—that the act of learning a language is in itself an evil; and so frame your selection of languages, that the largest possible body of literature *available for your purposes* shall be laid open to you at the least possible price of time and mental energy squandered in this direction. I say this with some earnestness. For I will not conceal from you that one of the habits most unfavorable to the growth and sincere culture of the intellect in our day, is the facility with which men surrender themselves to the barren and ungenial labor of language-learning. Unless balanced by studies that give more exercise, more excitement, and more aliment to the faculties, I am convinced, by all I have observed, that this practice is the dry-rot of the human mind. How should it be otherwise? The act of learning a science is good, not only for the knowledge which results, but for the exercise which attends it; the energies which the learner is obliged to put forth are true intellectual energies, and his very errors are full of instruction. He fails to construct some leading idea, or he even misconstructs it; he places himself in a false position with respect to certain propositions; views them from a false centre; makes a false or an imperfect antithesis; apprehends a definition with insufficient rigor; or fails in his use of it to keep it self-consistent. These and a thousand other errors are met by a thousand appropriate resources—all of a true intellectual character—comparing, combining, distinguishing, generalizing, subdividing, acts of abstraction and evolution, of synthesis and analysis, until the most torpid minds are ventilated, and healthily excited by this introversion of the faculties upon themselves.

But, in the study of language (with an exception, however, to a certain extent, in favor of Latin and Greek, which I shall notice hereafter), nothing of all this can take place, and for one simple reason,—that all is arbitrary. Wherever there is a law and system, wherever there is relation and correspondence of parts, the intellect will make its way,—will interfuse amongst the dry bones the blood and pulses of life, and create "a soul under the ribs of death." But whatsoever is arbitrary and conventional,—which yields no reason why it should be this way rather than that, obeying no theory or law,

—must, by its lifeless forms, kill and mortify the action of the intellect. If this be true, it becomes every student to keep watch upon himself, that he does not, upon any light temptation, allow himself an overbalance of study in this direction; for the temptations to such an excess, which in our days are more powerful than formerly, are at all times too powerful. Of all the weapons in the armory of the scholar, none is so showy or so captivating to commonplace minds as skill in languages. *Vanity* is, therefore, one cause of the undue application to languages. A second is the national *fashion*. What nation but ourselves ever made the language of its eternal enemy an essential part of even a decent education? What should we think of Roman policy if, during the second Punic War, the Carthaginian language had been taught, as a matter of course, to the children of every Roman citizen? But a third cause, which, I believe, has more efficacy than either of the former, is mere *levity*,—the simple fact of being unballasted by any sufficient weight of plan or settled purpose to present a counterpoise to the slightest momentum this way or that, arising from any impulse of accident or personal caprice. When there is no resistance, a breath of air will be sufficient to determine the motion. I remember once, that, happening to spend an autumn in Ilfracombe, on the west coast of Devonshire, I found all the young ladies whom I knew busily employed in the study of marine botany. On the opposite shore of the channel, in all the South Welsh ports of Tenby, etc., they were no less busy upon conchology. In neither case, from any previous love of the science, but simply availing themselves of their local advantages. . . .

In a celebrated satire (*The Pursuits of Literature*), much read in my youth, and which I myself read about twenty-five years ago, I remember one counsel —there addressed to young men, but, in fact, of universal application. "I call upon them," said the author, "to *dare* to be ignorant of many things:" a wise counsel, and justly expressed; for it requires much courage to forsake popular paths of knowledge, merely upon a conviction that they are not favorable to the ultimate ends of knowledge. In you, however, *that* sort of courage may be presumed; but how will you "dare to be ignorant" of many things in opposition to the cravings of your own mind? Simply thus: destroy these false cravings by introducing a healthier state of the organ. A good scheme of study will soon show itself to be such by this one test—that it will exclude as powerfully as it will appropriate; it will be a system of repulsion no less than of attraction; once thoroughly possessed and occupied by the deep and genial pleasures of one truly intellectual pursuit, you will be easy and indifferent to all others that had previously teased you with transient excitement. . . . If your intentions, as I suppose, lean most to literature, let me establish one necessary distinction, because the word literature is used in two senses; the philosophical, in which it is the direct and adequate antithesis of books of knowledge, and the popular, in which it is a mere term of convenience for expressing inclusively the total books in a language. In the former sense, it will exclude all books in which the matter is paramount to the manner or form, in which literature is a fine art. The true antithesis of literature to books of knowledge (books written to instruct) is power. Henceforth I should use the antitheses power and knowledge as the most philosophical expression for literature (that is, *literæ humaniores*), and anti-literature (that is, *literæ didacticæ*), [meaning by literature of power, books written not simply to amuse or instruct, but, like *Paradise Lost* or *King Lear*, to call forth the deepest emotions, and inspire new conceptions of ideal beauty and grandeur].

CLASSICAL LANGUAGES.

Now, then, prepared with this distinction, let us inquire whether—weighing the difficulties against the benefits—there is an overbalance of motive for you, with your purposes, to study what are inaccurately termed* the "classical" languages. And, first, with respect to Greek, we have often had the question debated, and, in our own days, solemn challenges thrown out and solemn adjudications given on the question, whether any benefit corresponding to the time and the labor can be derived from the study of the ancient classics. Hitherto, however, the question could not be rightly shaped; for, as no man chose to plead "amusement" as a sufficient motive for so great an undertaking, it was always debated with a single reference to the *knowledge* involved in those literatures. But this is a ground wholly untenable. For, let the knowledge be what it might, all knowledge is translatable, and translatable without one atom of loss. If this were all, therefore, common sense would prescribe that faithful translations should be executed of all the classics, and all men in future depend upon these vicarious labors. With respect to the Greek, this would soon be accomplished; for what is the knowledge which lurks in that language? All knowledge may be commodiously distributed into science and erudition; of the latter (antiquities, geography, philology, theology, etc.), there is a very considerable body; of the former, but little, namely, the mathematical and musical works,—and the medical works—what else? Nothing that can deserve the name of science, except the single organon of Aristotle. With Greek medicine, I suppose that you have no concern. As to mathematics, a man must be an idiot if he were to study Greek for the sake of Archimedes, Apollonius, or Diophantus. In Latin or in French you may find them all regularly translated, and parts of them embodied in the works of English mathematicians. Besides, if it were otherwise, where the notions and all the relations are so few, elementary, and determinate, and the vocabulary, therefore, so scanty, as in mathematics, it could not be necessary to learn Greek, even if you were disposed to read them.

It is not for knowledge that Greek is worth learning, but for power. Here arises the question—Of what value is this power? that is, how is the Grecian literature to be rated in relation to other literatures? . . . The question is limited wholly, as you see, to the value of the literature in the proper sense of that word. Now, it is my private theory, to which you will allow what degree of weight you please, that the antique or pagan literature is a polar antagonist to the modern or Christian literature; that each is an evolution from a distinct principle, having nothing in common but what is necessarily common to all modes of thought, namely, good sense and logic; and that they are to be criticised from different stations and points of view. . . .

So much for the Greek. Now, as to the Latin, the case is wholly reversed. Here the literature is of far less value; and, on the whole, with your views, it might be doubted whether it would recompense your pains. But the anti-literature (as, for want of a strict antithesis, I must call it) is inestimable,

* A late writer has announced it as a matter of discovery, that the term "classics" is applicable also to the modern languages. But, surely, this was never doubted by any man who considered the meaning and origin of the term. It is drawn, as the reader must be reminded, from the political economy of Rome. Such a man was rated as to his income in the third class, such another in the fourth, and so on; but he who was in the highest, was said emphatically to be of *the* class, "classicus," a class-man, without adding the number, as in that case superfluous. Hence, by an obvious analogy, the best authors were rated as classici, or men of the highest class; just as, in English, we say, "men of rank," absolutely, for men who are in the highest ranks of the state. The particular error by which this mere formal term of relation was *materiated* (if I may so say) in one of its accidents (namely, the application to Greek and Roman writers), is one of the commonest and most natural.

Latin having been the universal language of Christendom for so long a period. The Latin works since the restoration of letters are alone of immense value for knowledge of every kind; much science, inexhaustible erudition; and, to this day, in Germany, and elsewhere on the Continent, the best part of the latter is communicated in Latin. Now, though all knowledge *is* (which power is not) adequately communicable by translation, yet as there is no hope that the immense bibliothecs of Latin accumulated in the last three centuries ever will be translated, you cannot possibly dispense with this language. . . .

MODERN LANGUAGES.

Reserving to my conclusion anything I have to say upon these *languages*, as depositories of *literature* properly so called, I shall first speak of them as depositories of *knowledge*. Among the four great races of men in Europe, namely, 1. The Celtic, occupying a few of the western extremities of Europe; 2. The Teutonic, occupying the northern and midland parts; 3. The Latin (blended with Teutonic tribes), occupying the south; and, 4. The Sclavonic, occupying the east, it is evident that of the first and the last it is unnecessary to say anything in this place, because their pretensions to literature do not extend to our present sense of the word. No Celt even, however extravagant, pretends to the possession of a body of Celtic philosophy and Celtic science of independent growth. The Celtic and Sclavonic languages, therefore, dismissed, our business at present is with those of the Latin and the Teutonic families. Now, three of the Latin family, namely, the Italian, Spanish, and Portuguese, are at once excluded for the purpose before us; because it is notorious that, from political and religious causes, these three nations have but feebly participated in the general scientific and philosophic labors of the age. Italy, indeed, has cultivated natural philosophy with an exclusive zeal; a direction probably impressed upon the national mind by patriotic reverence for her great names in that department. But, merely for the sake of such knowledge (supposing no other motive), it would be idle to pay the price of learning a language,—all the current contributions to science being regularly gathered into the general garner of Europe by the scientific journals, both at home and abroad. Of the Latin languages, therefore, which are wholly the languages of Catholic nations, but one—that is, the French—can present any sufficient attractions to a student in search of general knowledge. Of the Teutonic literatures, on the other hand, which are the adequate representatives of the Protestant intellectual interest in Europe (no Catholic nations speaking a Teutonic language except the southern states of Germany and part of the Netherlands), all give way at once to the paramount pretensions of the English and the German. I do not say this with the levity of ignorance, as if presuming, as a matter of course, that in a small territory, such as Denmark, *e. g.*, the literature must, of necessity, bear a value proportioned to its political rank. On the contrary, I have some acquaintance with the Danish literature; and though, in the proper sense of the word literature as a body of creative art, I cannot esteem it highly, yet, as a depository of knowledge in one particular direction,—namely, the direction of historical and antiquarian research,—it has, undoubtedly, high claims upon the student's attention. . . .

Waiving all mere presumptive arguments, the bare amount of books annually published in the several countries of Europe puts the matter out of all doubt, that the great commerce of thought and knowledge in the civilized world is, at this day, conducted in three languages—the English, the German, and the French. You, therefore, having the good fortune to be an Englishman, are to make your choice between the two last; and, this being so, I conceive that there is no room for hesitation,—the "detur pulchriori" being, in this case (that is, remember, with an exclusive reference to *knowledge*), a direction easily followed.

Dr. Johnson was accustomed to say of the French literature, as the kindest thing he had to say about it, that he valued it chiefly for this reason: that it had a book upon every subject. How far this might be a reasonable opinion fifty years ago, and understood, as Dr. Johnson must have meant it, of the French literature as compared with the English of the same period, I will not pretend to say. It has certainly ceased to be true, even under these restrictions, and is in flagrant opposition to the truth if extended to the French in its relation to the German. Undoubtedly, the French literature holds out to the student some peculiar advantages, as what literature does not?—some, even, which we should not have anticipated; for, though we justly value ourselves, as a nation, upon our classical education, yet no literature is poorer than the English in the learning of classical antiquities,—our Bentleys, even, and our Porsons, having thrown all their learning into the channel of philology; whilst a single volume of the Memoirs of the French Academy of Inscriptions contains more useful antiquarian research than a whole English library. In digests of history, again, the French language is richer than ours, and in their dictionaries of miscellaneous knowledge (*not* in their encyclopedias). But all these are advantages of the French only in relation to the English, and not to the German literature, which, for vast compass, variety, and extent, far exceeds all others as a depository for the current accumulations of knowledge. The mere number of books published annually in Germany, compared with the annual product of France and England, is alone a satisfactory evidence of this assertion. With relation to France, it is a second argument in its favor that the intellectual activity of Germany is not intensely accumulated in one great capital, as it is in Paris; but, whilst it is here and there converged intensely enough for all useful purposes (as at Berlin, Königsberg, Leipsic, Dresden, Vienna, Munich, etc.), it is also healthily diffused over the whole territory. There is not a sixth-rate town in Protestant Germany which does not annually contribute its quota of books: intellectual culture has manured the whole soil; not a district but it has penetrated,

——"like Spring,
Which leaves no corner of the land untouched."

A third advantage on the side of Germany (an advantage for this purpose), is its division into a great number of independent states. From this circumstance it derives the benefit of an internal rivalship amongst its several members, over and above that general external rivalship which it maintains with other nations. An advantage of the same kind we enjoy in England. The British nation is fortunately split into three great divisions, and thus a national feeling of emulation and contest is excited,—slight, indeed, or none at all, on the part of the English (not from any merit, but from mere decay of patriotic feeling), stronger on the part of the Irish, and sometimes illiberally and odiously strong on the part of the Scotch (especially as you descend below the rank of gentlemen). But, disgusting as it sometimes is in its expression, this nationality is of great service to our efforts in all directions. A triple power is gained for internal excitement of the national energies; whilst, in regard to any external enemy, or any external rival, the three nations act with the unity of a single force. But the most conspicuous advantage of the German literature is its great originality and boldness of speculation, and the character of masculine austerity and precision impressed upon their scientific labors by the philosophy of Leibnitz and Wolff heretofore, and by the severer philosophy of modern days.

LETTER FROM THOMAS CARLYLE TO A STUDENT, ASKING ADVICE AS TO READING AND A PROFESSION.

Dear Sir:—Some time ago your letter was delivered to me; I take literally the first half-hour I have had since to write you a word of answer. It would give me true satisfaction could any advice of mine contribute to forward you in your honorable course of self-improvement, but a long experience has taught me that advice can profit but little; that there is a good reason why advice is so seldom followed; this reason, namely, that it so seldom, and can almost never be, rightly given. No man knows the state of another; it is always to some more or less imaginary man that the wisest and most honest adviser is speaking.

As to the books which you—whom I know so little of—should read, there is hardly any thing definite that can be said. For one thing, you may be strenuously advised to keep reading. Any good book, any book that is wiser than yourself, will teach you something—a great many things, indirectly and directly, if your mind be open to learn. This old counsel of Johnson's is also good, and universally applicable: "Read the book you do honestly feel a wish and curiosity to read." The very wish and curiosity indicates that you, then and there, are the person likely to get good of it. "Our wishes are presentiments of our capabilities;" that is a noble saying, of deep encouragement to our wishes and efforts in regard to reading, as to other things. Among all the objects that look wonderful or beautiful to you, follow with fresh hope that one which looks wonderfulest, beautifulest. You may gradually find by various trials (which trials see that you make honest, manful ones, not silly, short, fitful ones,) what *is* for the wonderfulest, beautifulest—what is your *true* element and province, and be able to profit by that. True desire, the monition of nature, is much to be attended to. But here also, you are to discriminate carefully between *true* desire and false. The medical men tell us that we should eat what we *truly* have an appetite for; but what we only *falsely* have an appetite for we should resolutely avoid. It is very true: and flimsy desultory readers, who fly from foolish book to foolish book, and get good of none, and mischief of all—are not those as foolish, unhealthy eaters, who mistake their superficial false desire after spiceries and confectioneries for their real appetite, of which even they are not destitute, though it lies far deeper, far quieter, after solid nutritive food? With these illustrations I will recommend Johnson's advice to you.

Another thing, and only one other I will say. All books are

properly the record of the history of past men—what thoughts past men had in them, what actions past men did: the summary of all books whatsoever lies *there*. It is on this ground that the class of books specifically named History can be safely recommended as the basis of all study of books. Past history, and especially the past history of one's own native country, everybody may be advised to begin with that. Let him study that faithfully; innumerable inquiries will branch out from it; he has a broad beaten highway, from which all the country is more or less visible; there traveling, let him choose where he will dwell. Neither let mistakes and wrong directions—of which every man in his studies and elsewhere, falls into many—discourage you. There is precious instruction to be got by finding we are wrong. Let a man try faithfully, manfully to be right, he will grow daily more and more right. It is at bottom the condition on which all men have to cultivate themselves. Our very walking is an incessant falling and catching of ourselves before we come actually to the pavement! It is emblematic of all things a man does.

In conclusion, I will remind you, it is not books alone, or by books chiefly, that a man becomes in all points a man. Study to do faithfully whatsoever thing in your actual situation, there and now, you find either expressly or tacitly laid to your charge; that is your post; stand in it like a true soldier. Silently devour the many chagrins of it, as all human situations have many; and see you aim not to quit it without being all that it at least required of you. A man perfects himself by work much more than by reading. They are a growing kind of men that can wisely combine the two things—wisely, valiantly, can do what is laid to their hand in their present sphere, and prepare themselves for doing other wider things, if such lie before them.

With many good wishes and encouragements, I remain, yours sincerely, THOMAS CARLYLE.

Chelsea, 13th March, 1843

A loving heart is the beginning of all knowledge. This it is that opens the whole mind, quickens every faculty of the intellect to do its fit work, that of *knowing*; and therefore, by sure consequence of wisely *uttering* forth.

The courage we desire and prize is not the courage to die decently, but to live manfully. This, when by God's grace it has been given, lies deep in the soul; like genial heat, fosters all other virtues and gifts; without it they could not live.

Clearly connected with this quality of valor, partly as springing from it, partly as protected by it, are the more recognizable qualities of truthfulness and honesty in action.

That mercy can dwell only with valor is an old sentiment.

CARLYLE—*Review of Boswell's Life of Johnson.*

EDUCATION, STUDIES, AND CONDUCT.

WHAT TO READ, AND HOW TO READ.

VALUE OF GOOD BOOKS.

LORD BACON thus summarizes the advantages of knowledge, of which good books are the treasure-house:

We see then how far the monuments of wit and learning are more durable than the monuments of power or of the hands. For have not the verses of Homer continued twenty-five hundred years or more; during which time infinite palaces, temples, castles, cities, have been decayed and demolished, and the pictures and statues of kings and great personages have perished. But the images of man's wits and knowledges remain in books, exempted from the wrong of time, and capable of perpetual renovation. Neither are they fitly to be called images, because they generate still, and cast their seeds in the minds of others, provoking and causing infinite actions and opinions in succeeding ages, so that, if the invention of the ship was thought so noble, which carrieth riches and commodities from place to place, and consociateth the most remote regions in participations of their fruits, how much more are letters to be magnified, which, as ships, pass through the vast seas of time, and make ages so distant to participate of the wisdom, illuminations, and inventions, the one of the other.

MILTON in his eloquent plea for the Liberty of the Press, thus characterizes a good book:

Books are not absolutely dead things, but do contain a progeny of life in them, to be as active as that soul was whose progeny they are; nay, they do preserve, as in a vial, the purest efficacy and extraction of that living intellect that bred them. I know they are as lively, and as vigorously productive as those fabulous dragon's teeth; and being sown up and down, may chance to bring up armed men. And yet, on the other hand, unless wariness be used, as good almost kill a man as kill a book. Who kills a man, kills a reasonable creature—God's image, but he who destroys a good book, destroys reason itself, kills the image of God, as it were, in the eye. Many a man lives a burden to the earth: but a good book is the precious life-blood of a master spirit, embalmed and treasured up on purpose to a life beyond life.

SIR JOHN HERSCHEL in an address to men whose education had been neglected or necessarily limited says:

Of all amusements that can possibly be imagined for a hard-working man after his toil, or in its intervals, there is nothing like reading an interesting newspaper or book. It calls for no bodily exertion, of which he has already had enough, or perhaps too much. It relieves his home of its dullness and sameness. It transports him into a livelier and gayer, and more diversified and interesting scene; and while he enjoys himself there, he may forget the evil of the present moment fully as much as if he were ever so drunk,—with the great advantage of finding himself next day with the money in his pocket, or at least laid out in real necessaries and comforts for himself and family,—and without a headache. Nay, it accompanies him to his next day's work; and if what he has been reading be any thing above the idlest and lightest, gives him something to think of, besides the mere mechanical drudgery of his every-day occupation,—something he can enjoy while absent, and look forward to with pleasure. If I were to pray for a taste which should stand me in stead, under every variety of circumstances, and be a source of happiness and cheerfulness to me through life, and a shield against its ills, however things might go amiss, and the world frown upon me, it would be a taste for reading. I speak of it of course only as a worldly advantage, and not in the slightest degree as superseding or derogating from the higher office and surer and stronger panoply of religious principles—but as a taste, an instrument, and a mode of pleasurable gratification. Give a man this taste, and the means of gratifying it, and you can hardly fail of making a happy man, unless, indeed, you put into his hands a most perverse selection of books. You place him in contact with the best society in every period of history—with the wisest, the wittiest—with the tenderest, the bravest, and the purest characters that have adorned humanity. You make him a denizen of all nations—a contemporary of all ages. The world has been created for him. It is hardly possible but the character should take a higher and better tone from the constant habit of associating in thought with a class of thinkers, to say the least of it, above the average of humanity. It is morally impossible but that the manners should take a tinge of good breeding and civilization from having constantly before one's eyes the way in which the best bred and the best informed men have talked and conducted themselves in their intercourse with each other. There is a genial, but perfectly irresistible coercion in a habit of reading, well directed, over the whole tenor of a man's character and conduct, which is not the less effectual because it works insensibly, and because it is really the last thing he dreams of. It can not, in short, be better summed up than in the words of the Latin poet[1]—*It civilizes the conduct of men—and suffers them not to remain barbarous.*

[1] *Emollit mores, nec sinit esse feros.*

T. B. MACAULAY, M. P. [since called Lord Macaulay], in an address before a Mechanics' Institute, remarked:

There is, I may well say, no wealth, there is no power, there is no rank, which I would accept, if in exchange I were to be deprived of my books, of the privilege of conversing with the greatest minds of all past ages, of searching after the truth, of contemplating the beautiful, of living with the distant, the unreal, the past, and the future. Knowing, as I do, what it is to enjoy these pleasures myself, I do not grudge them to the laboring men, who, by their honorable, independent, and gallant efforts, have advanced themselves within their reach; and owing all that I owe to the soothing influences of literature, I should be ashamed of myself if I grudged the same advantages to them.

HON. RUFUS CHOATE in a speech in the Senate of the United States, pleading for the establishing of a great National Library out of the annual income of the Smithsonian Bequest, says:

Nobody can doubt that such a library comes within the terms and spirit of the trust. That directs us 'to increase and diffuse knowledge among men.' And does not the judgment of all the wise; does not the experience of all enlightened states; does not the whole history of civilization concur to declare that a various and ample library is one of the surest, most constant, most permanent, and most economical instrumentalities to increase and diffuse knowledge? There it would be,—durable as liberty, durable as the union; a vast storehouse, a vast treasury, of all the facts which make up the history of man and of nature, so far as that history has been written; of all the truths which the inquiries and experiences of all the races and ages have found out; of all the opinions that have been promulgated; of all the emotions, images, sentiments, examples, of all the richest and most instructive literatures; the whole past speaking to the present and the future; a silent, yet wise and eloquent teacher; dead yet speaking—not dead! for Milton has told us that a 'good book is not absolutely a dead thing—the precious life-blood rather of a master spirit; a seasoned life of man embalmed and treasured up on purpose to a life beyond life.' Is not that an admirable instrumentality to increase and diffuse knowledge among men? It would place within the reach of our minds, of our thinkers, and investigators, and scholars, all, or the chief, intellectual and literary materials, and tools and instruments, now within the reach of the cultivated foreign mind, and the effect would be to increase the amount of individual acquisition, and multiply the number of the learned. It would raise the standard of our scholarship, improve our style of investigation, and communicate an impulse to our educated and to the general mind. * * *

By such a library as you can collect here, something will be done, much will be done, to help every college, every school, every studious man, every writer and thinker in the country, to just what is wanted most. Inquirers after truth may come here and search for it. It will do them no harm at all to pass a few studious weeks among these scenes. Having pushed their investigations as far as they may at home, and ascertained just what, and how much more, of helps they require, let them come hither and find it. Let them replenish themselves, and then go back and make distribution among their pupils; ay, through the thousand channels, and by the thousand voices of the press, let them make distribution among the people! Let it be so, that—

> "Hither as to their fountain other stars
> Repairing, in their golden urns draw light."

* * * Think of the large absolute numbers of those who, in the succession of years, will come and partake directly of these stores of truth and knowledge! Think of the numbers without number, who, through them, who, by them directly, will partake of the same stores! Studious men will come to learn to speak and write to and for the growing millions of a generally educated community. They will learn that they may communicate. They can not hoard if they would, and they would not if they could. They take in trust to distribute; and every motive of ambition, of interest, of duty, will compel them to distribute. They buy in gross, to sell by retail. The lights which they kindle here will not be set under a bushel, but will burn on a thousand hills. No, sir; a rich and public library is no anti-republican monopoly. Who was the old Egyptian king that inscribed on his library the words, the dispensary of the soul? You might quite as well inscribe on it, armory, and light, and fountain of liberty!

Dr. Channing in his Address to Young Men generally, and to Workingmen in particular, thus speaks of books as the powerful means of Self-Culture:

In the best books, great men talk to us, give us their most precious thoughts, and pour their souls into ours. God be thanked for books. They are the voices of the distant and the dead, and make us heirs of the spiritual life of past ages. Books are the true levelers. They give to all, who will faithfully use them, the society, the spiritual presence, of the best and greatest of our race. No matter how poor I am. No matter though the prosperous of my own time will not enter my obscure dwelling. If the Sacred Writers will enter and take up their abode under my roof, if Milton will cross my threshold to sing to me of Paradise, and Shakspeare to open to me the worlds of imagination and the workings of the human heart, and Franklin to enrich me with his practical wisdom, I shall not pine for want of intellectual companionship, and I may become a cultivated man though excluded from what is called the best society in the place where I live.

To make this means of culture effectual, a man must select good books, such as have been written by right-minded and strong-minded men, real thinkers, who instead of diluting by repetition, what others say, have something to say for themselves, write to give relief to full, earnest souls; and these works must not be skimmered over for amusement, but read with fixed attention and a reverential love of truth. In selecting books, we may be aided much by those who have studied more than ourselves. But, after all, it is best to be determined in this particular a good deal by our own tastes. The best books for a man are not always those which the wise recommend, but often those which meet the peculiar wants, the natural thirst of his mind, and therefore awaken interest and rivet thought.

Nothing can supply the place of books. They are cheering or soothing companions in solitude, illness, affliction. The wealth of both continents would not compensate for the good they impart. Let every man, if possible, gather some good books under his roof, and obtain access for himself and family to some social library. Almost any luxury should be sacrificed to this.

CHANNING.—*On Self Culture.*

A GREAT LIBRARY—THE TREASURE-HOUSE OF LITERATURE.

There, is collected the accumulated experience of ages—the volume of the historian, like lamps, to guide our feet:—there stands the heroic patterns of courage, magnanimity, and self-denying virtue:—there are embodied the gentler attributes, which soften and purify, while they charm, the heart:—there lie the charts of those who have explored the deeps and shallows of the soul:—there the dear-bought testimony, which reveals to us the ends of the earth, and shows that the girdle of the waters is nothing but their Maker's will:—there stands the Poet's harp, of mighty compass, and many strings:—there hang the deep-toned instruments through which patriotic eloquence has poured its inspiring echoes over oppressed nations:—there, in the sanctity of their own self-emitted light, repose the Heavenly oracles. This glorious fane, vast, and full of wonders, has been reared and stored by the labors of Lettered Man; and could it be destroyed, mankind might relapse to the state of savages.

JAMES A. HILLHOUSE.—*Relations of Literature to a Republican Government.*

Hail, Learning's Pantheon! Hail, the sacred ark,
Where all the world of science doth embark,
Which ever shall withstand, as it hath long withstood,
Insatiate Time's devouring flood!
Hail, Bank of all past ages, where they lie
T' enrich with interest all posterity!
Where thousand lights into one brightness spread,
Hail, Living university of the Dead!

COWLEY.—*University Library of Oxford*, 1652.

TEMPLE OF THE ENGLISH LANGUAGE.

I can believe that the English language is destined to be that in which shall arise, as in one universal temple, the utterance of the worship of all hearts. Broad and deep have the foundations been laid; and so vast is the area which they cover, that it is co-extensive with the great globe itself. For centuries past, proud intellectual giants have labored at this mighty fabric; and still it rises, and will rise for generations to come: and on its massive stones will be inscribed the names of the profoundest thinkers, and on its springing arches the records of the most daring flights of the master minds of genius, whose fame was made enduring by their love of the Beautiful and their adoration of the All Good. In this temple the Anglo-Saxon mosaic of the sacred words of truth will be the solid and enduring pavement; the dreams of poets will fill the rich tracery of its windows with the many-colored hues of thought; and the works of lofty philosophic minds will be the stately columns supporting its fretted roof, whence shall hang, sculptured, the rich fruits of the tree of knowledge, precious as "apples of gold,"—"the words of the wise."

G. W. MOON.—*Dean's English.*

EXTRACTS *from the Addresses delivered on the occasion of the Dedication of the Public Library of the City of Boston, on the 1st of January,* 1858.

HON. ROBERT C. WINTHROP, President of the Board of Commissioners, charged with the erection of the building, on delivering the keys to the mayor, spoke as follows:—

Welcome, fathers and mothers of our city; welcome, young ladies and children of the schools; welcome, lovers and patrons of literature and learning, of science and the arts; welcome, friends to good manners and good morals, and to those innocent recreations and ennobling pursuits by which alone vulgarity and vice can be supplanted; welcome, pastors and teachers of our churches and colleges; welcome, rulers and magistrates of our city, of our commonwealth, and of our whole country; welcome, citizens and residents of Boston, one and all, to an edifice which is destined, we trust, to furnish a resort, in many an hour of leisure and in many an hour of study, not for yourselves alone, but for those who shall come after you, through countless generations; and where shall constantly be spread, and constantly be served, without money and without price, an entertainment ever fresh, ever abundant, and ever worthy of intelligent and enlightened freemen. * * *

This substantial and spacious building owes its existence exclusively to the enlightened liberality of the municipal government. And I avail myself of the earliest opportunity to acknowledge most gratefully, in behalf of the Board of Commissioners as now composed, and of all who have been associated with us during its existence, the unhesitating promptness and unanimity with which every appropriation which has been asked, or even intimated as desirable, has been granted by successive City Councils. * * *

When a celebrated ruler and orator of Greece was arraigned for the costliness of some one of the many magnificent structures which are associated with his administration, and whose very ruins are now the admiration of the world, he is said to have replied, that he would willingly bear all the odium and all the onus of the outlay, if the edifice in question might henceforth bear his own name, instead of being inscribed with that of the people of Athens. But the people of ancient Athens indignantly rejected the idea, and refused to relinquish, even to the illustrious and princely Pericles, the glory of such a work.

Nor will the people of Boston, I am persuaded, be less unwilling to disown or abandon the credit which is legitimately theirs, for the noble hall in which we are assembled;—and while the munificence of benefactors, abroad and at home, and the diligence and devotion of Trustees or of Commissioners, may be remembered with gratitude by us all, the city herself—"our illustrious parent," as she was well entitled by our venerable benefactor, Mr. Jonathan Phillips—will never fail to claim the distinction as exclusively her own, that with no niggardly or reluctant hand, but promptly, liberally, and even profusely, if you will, she supplied the entire means for its erection.

These empty shelves will soon be filled. Gems and jewels more precious than any which the mines of either continent can ever yield, will soon find their places in the caskets and cabinets which have here been prepared for them; and living jewels, like those of the Roman matron of old—even the sons and daughters of our city—will soon be seen clustered around them.

It was a poetical and beautiful conceit of the great philosopher of our motherland—of Bacon, I mean, the contemporary and fellow-countryman of our Pilgrim Fathers—that "libraries are as the shrines where all the relics of the ancient saints, full of true virtue, and that without delusion or imposture, are preserved and reposed." But Cicero, methinks, did better justice to the theme. We are told that, when that illustrious orator and statesman saw the books, which composed his precious private library, fairly arranged in the apartment which he had provided for them, in his villa at Antium, he wrote to his friend Atticus, "*Postea vero quam Tyrannio mihi libros disposuit, mens addita videtur meis aedibus.*"

"Now that my books have been put in their places by your learned Greek, Tyrannio, a soul seems to have been added to my dwelling."

Yes, my friends; within these walls shall soon be gathered, not merely the mighty masters of philosophy and rhetoric, of history and poetry, whom the Roman Cicero recognized and reverenced as introducing a soul into his dwelling, but the great lights of all ages, the wise and learned of all climes—and those, especially, who have adorned a civilization, and vindicated a liberty, and illustrated a Christianity which that Cicero never conceived of, shall be congregated around them. Here soon shall many a waiting heart be kindled into something of the exultation of that good old Bishop of Norwich, when he exclaimed, at the sight of a great library, "What a happiness is it, that, without all offence of necromancy, I may here call up any of the ancient worthies of learning, whether human or divine, and confer with them of all my doubts!—that I can at pleasure summon up whole synods of reverend fathers and acute doctors, from all the coasts of the earth, to give their well-studied judgments on all points and questions which I may propose!"

And not the reverend fathers and acute doctors only shall answer to our call;—but here also the poets of all ages shall be ever ready to sing to us their choicest strains;—the dramatists of all ages to rehearse to us their richest scenes of weal or of woe;—the orators of all ages to recite to us the triumphant argument, or the thrilling appeal, which may have shaken empires from their base, or changed the current of the world's affairs. Here, too, the practical inventor and ingenious mechanic shall exhibit to us his specifications, his plans, and his drawings. Here the great interpreters of Nature shall unfold to us the mechanism of the heavens, the testimony of the rocks, and the marvels and mysteries of animal and vegetable life. Here the glowing pictures of fiction and fancy shall pass and repass before our vision, beneath the magic wand of a Scott, a Dickens, or a Cooper;—the living portraits of sages and patriots, of other lands and of our own land, be displayed to us by a Guizot or a Brougham, a Carlyle or a Campbell, a Sparks or an Irving;—and the grander panorama of history be unrolled for us by a Gibbon or a Grote, a Hume or a Macaulay, a Bancroft, a Prescott, or a Motley.

May God, in his goodness, grant that increased supplies of wisdom, and knowledge, and virtue, for us and our posterity, may be its rich and abundant fruits;—that it may be so sanctified by His grace to the highest interests of the whole community, that here, at least, the tree of knowledge may never be disunited from the tree of life;—and that, constituting, as it will, the complement and the crown of our great republican system of popular education, it may do its full part in bearing up and sustaining, for a thousand generations, a well-compacted and imperishable fabric of freedom;—of that freedom which rests upon intelligence, which must be regulated by law, and which can only be maintained by piety, philanthropy, and patriotism.

At the close of Mr. Winthrop's address, His Honor, Alexander H. Rice, mayor of the city, on receiving the keys of the building, made a very appropriate address, from which we give the closing paragraphs:—

Our city has sometimes been called the Athens of America; sometimes in compliment; let it never be in derision. The real claim to that shining title must rest upon the culture which is bestowed upon the institutions and the arts, which suggest a resemblance to the charming "Eye of Greece." In the rising greatness of that peerless city, we are told that the enlightened and patriotic arbiter of its fortunes, the patron of literature and learning, not only reclaimed the works of Homer from threatened oblivion, but established a public library at Athens, open to the free use of its citizens, and by these acts established there the home of the Muses. The golden age of Cimon and Pericles followed—the age of the Gymnasium, of the Academy, of the Agora, of the Temple of Eleusis, of the Parthenon, and of the Propylæa, and of all the culture which produced and surrounded them—that age of dazzling splendor which has not yet ceased to excite the wonder and admiration of mankind. I may not pause to compare the civilization of that age with ours, in all that is useful and beneficent to man; but if, in our contemplations of the glory of that era, there come to us impressions of enhanced in wealth, vast extent, and resources unapproachable to us of the present, let it be remembered that the wonderful Athens of history contained a population less than that of Boston to-day, and that the number of those who might exercise the rights of citizenship therein was less than our number of voters. How far the free library of Pisistratus affected the character and fortunes of the Grecian city, neither history nor tradition discloses; but we know that it preceded its power and splendor, and that these all came from the brain and the hand of man. Whether the noble institution, whose flattering auspices we here hail to-day, shall be the harbinger of a more illustrious future to our Athens, may depend, in some degree, upon the patronage which shall await upon these halls; for the power of knowledge is essentially the same in every period of time, though the fruits of its cultivation may be changed by the altered conditions of the race and the age.

But time forbids that I should pursue the theme; a single word more, and I have done. While here, gathered in joyous assemblage to-day, there are those—some of whom are before me, others are absent and distant—all of whom should have a place in our memories. It was the custom at certain Athenian festivals for the knights to make the circuit of the Agora, beginning at the statue of Hermes and paying their homage to the statues and temples around it. On this new year's festival, now first celebrated within these walls, since we have not yet their statues about us, let us summon to our thoughts, in living personality, the images of all the noble benefactors of our Public Library, the contributors of funds, of books, and of valued service; and let us pay to each the homage of our hearts' best gratitude, as they pass through the courts of our memories. Length of days and happiness to the living—fresh laurels for the memory of the departed—praises to Heaven for their gifts and their example.

Hon. Edward Everett, President of the Board of Trustees, on receiving the keys from the mayor, delivered an address, from which the following passages are taken:—

The City of Boston, owing to peculiar circumstances in its growth and history, has been, at all times, as I think, beyond most cities in the world, the object of an affectionate attachment on the part of its inhabitants—a feeling entitled to respect, and productive of good, even if it may sometimes seem to strangers overpartial in its manifestations. It is not merely its commanding natural situation, the triple hills on which it is enthroned, its magnificent bay and harbor, and the group of islands and islets that sparkle like emeralds on their surface—not merely this most admirable Common, which opens before our windows, delightful even at this season of the year, and affording us in summer, in its noble malls and shady walks, all that the country can boast of cool, and beautiful, and salubrious, transported to the heart of the city; "the poor man's pleasure-ground," as it has been well called, though a king might envy it;—nor the environs of our city, of surpassing loveliness, which incline it on every side in kindly embrace; it is not solely nor principally these natural attractions which endear Boston to its citizens. Nor is it exclusively the proud and grateful memories of the past—of the high-souled fathers and mothers of the land, venerable in their self-denying virtues, majestic in the austere simplicity of their manners, conscientious in their errors, who, with amazing sacrifices, and hardships never to be described, sought out new homes in the wilderness, and transmitted to us delights and blessings which it was not given to themselves to enjoy—of those who in succeeding generations deserved well of their country—the pioneers of the Revolution, the men of the stamp-act age, whose own words and acts are stamped on the pages of history, in characters never to be effaced—of those who, when the decisive hour came, stood forth in that immortal hall, the champions of their country's rights, while it scarcely yet deserved the name of a country; it is not exclusively these proud and grateful associations, which attach the dutiful Bostonian to the city of his birth or adoption.

No, Mr. Mayor, it is not exclusively these, much as they contribute to strengthen the sentiment. It has its origin, in no small degree, in the personal relation in which Boston places herself to her children; in the parental interest which she cherishes in their welfare, which leads her to take them by the hand almost from the cradle—to train them up in the ascending series of her excellent free schools;

watching over them as a fond father watches over the objects of his love and hope; in a word, to confer upon them a first-rate school education at the public expense. Often have I attempted, but with very partial success, both in this country and in Europe, to persuade inquiring friends from countries and places where no such well-organized system of public education prevails, that our free schools do really afford to the entire population means of elementary education, of which the wealthiest citizen is glad to avail himself.

And now, Mr. Mayor, the enlightened counsels of the City Government are about to give new strength to these ties of gratitude and affection, which bind the hearts of the children of Boston to their beloved city. Hitherto the system of public education, excellent as it is, and wisely supported by a princely expenditure, does but commence the work of instruction and carry it to a certain point; well advanced, indeed, but far short of the goal. It prepares our young men for college, for the counting-room, for the office of the engineer, the *studio* of the artist, the shop of the artisan, the laboratory of the chemist, or whatever field of employment they may be destined to enter; but there it leaves them, without further provision for the culture of the mind. It disciplines the faculties, and forms a taste for the acquisition of knowledge, on the part of our young men and women; but it provides no means for their exercise and gratification. It gives them the elementary education requisite for their future callings, but withholds all facilities of access to those boundless stores of recorded knowledge, in every department, by which alone that elementary education can be completed and made effectual for the active duties of life.

But to-day our honored city carries on and perfects her work. The Trustees, from their first annual report to the present time, have never failed to recommend a first-class public library, such as that, sir, for whose accommodation you dedicate this noble building, as the completion of the great system of public education. Its object is to give to the entire population, not merely to the curious student, but to the inquisitive member of either of the professions, to the intelligent merchant, mechanic, machinist, engineer, artist, or artisan, in short, to all of every age and of either sex, who desire to investigate any subject, either of utility or taste, those advantages which, without such an ample public collection, must necessarily be monopolized by the proprietors of large private libraries, or those who by courtesy have the use of them; nay, to put within the reach of the entire community advantages of this kind, far beyond those which can be afforded by the largest and best provided private libraries. * * *

I am aware that there is still floating about in the community a vague prejudice against what is called book-learning. One sometimes hears doubts expressed of the utility of public libraries; opinions that they are rather ornamental than necessary or useful; and the fact that our time-honored city, never indifferent to the mental improvement of her children, has subsisted more than two centuries without one, is a sufficient proof that, until within a very few years, their importance has not been particularly felt. There is perhaps, even now a disposition to claim some superiority for what is called practical knowledge—knowledge gained by observation and experience, (which most certainly the Trustees would not disparage,) and a kind of satisfaction felt in holding up the example of self-taught men, in supposed contradistinction from those who have got their knowledge from books; and no name, perhaps, is so frequently mentioned in this connection as that of Franklin, who, because he had scarce any school education, and never went to college, has been hastily set down as a brilliant example to show the inutility of book-learning. It has been quoted to me in this way, and to show that libraries are of no use, within three days.

Now, Mr. Mayor, I need not tell you that there never was a greater mistake in point of fact. A thirst for books, which he spared no pains to allay, is the first marked trait disclosed in the character of Franklin; his success throughout the early period of his life can be directly traced to the use he made of them; and his very first important movement for the benefit of his fellow-men, was to found a public library, which still flourishes;—one of the most considerable in the country. Franklin not a book-man! whoever labors under that delusion, shows that somebody else is not much of a book-man, at least so far as concerns the biography of our illustrious townsman. We happen to have a little information on that subject in a book written by Franklin himself.

Hear his words: "From my *infancy* I was passionately fond of reading, and all the money that came into my hands was laid out in purchasing books. I was very fond of voyages. My first acquisition was Bunyan's Works, in separate little volumes. I afterward sold them, to enable me to buy R. Burton's '*Historical Collections*.' They were small Chapman's books, and cheap; forty volumes in all. My father's little library consisted chiefly of books in polemic divinity, most of which I read. I have often regretted, [and this is a sentence that might be inscribed on the lofty cornice of this noble hall,] that, at a time when I had such a thirst for knowledge, more proper books had not fallen in my way. . . . There was among them Plutarch's Lives, which I read abundantly, and I still think that time spent to great advantage. There was also a book of Defoe's, called an '*Essay on Projects*,'* and another of Dr. Mather's, called an '*Essay to do Good*,' which" did what, sir?—for I am now going to give you, in Franklin's own words (they carry with them the justification of every dollar expended in raising these walls,) the original secret of his illustrious career—what was the effect produced by reading these two little books of Defoe and Cotton Mather? "They perhaps gave me a turn of thinking, which had an influence on some of the principal future events of my life."

Yes, sir, in the reading of these books was the acorn, that sprouted into that magnificent oak; there was the fountain-drop, which a fairy might sip from a buttercup, from which has flowed the Missouri and the Mississippi—the broad, deep river of Franklin's fame, winding its way through the lapse of ages, and destined to flow on, till it shall be ingulfed in the ocean of eternity. From his "infancy," sir, "passionately fond of reading;" nay, with the appetite of a vulture, with the digestion of an ostrich, attacking the great folios of polemic divinity in his father's library. Not a dull boy, either, sir; not a precocious little book-worm; fond of play; doesn't dislike a little mischief; sometimes, as he tells us, "led the other boys into scrapes;" but in his intervals of play, in his leisure moments, up in the lonely garret, when the rest of the family were asleep, holding converse in his childhood with the grave old non-conformists, Howe, and Owen, and Baxter—communing with the mastered lords of thought; the demigods of puritanism—

Nec sine dis animosus infans.

Franklin not a book-man! Why, he goes on to tell us that it was "this bookish inclination which at length determined his father to make him a printer," against his own inclination, which was for the sea; and when he had thus by constraint become a printer, his great consolation was, as he says, that "I now had access to better books. An acquaintance with the apprentices of booksellers enabled me sometimes to borrow a small one, which I was careful to return soon and clean. Often I sat up in my chamber reading the greatest part of the night, when the book was borrowed in the evening and to be returned in the morning, lest it should be found missing."

Then he made the acquaintance of Mr. Matthew Adams, an ingenious, sensible man, "who had a pretty collection of books." He frequented the printing office, took notice of the bright little apprentice, and "very kindly proposed to lend me such books as I chose to read." Having taken to a vegetable diet at the age of sixteen, he persuaded his brother to allow him in cash half the price of his board, lived upon potatoes and hasty pudding, soon found that he could save half even of that little allowance, (which could not have exceeded two-and-sixpence a week, lawful money,) and this poor little economy "was an additional fund for buying books." What would the poor, under-fed boy, who was glad to buy books on the savings of his potato diet, have said, could he have had free access to a hall like this, stored as it soon will be with its priceless treasures? Further, sir, while working as a journeyman in England, he says, "I made the acquaintance of one William Wilcox, a bookseller, whose shop was next door. He had an immense collection of second-hand books;"—(somewhat, I suppose, like our friend Burnham, in Cornhill;)—"circulating libraries were not then in use, but we agreed that, upon certain reasonable terms, which I have now forgotten, I might take, read, and return any of his works. This I esteemed a great advantage, and I made as much use of it as I could."

* We have never seen Defoe's "*Essay on Projects*," or the man or woman who had. The Essay is not contained in our edition of Defoe's Works, in twenty volumes.

Finally, sir, as I have already said, Franklin's first important movement for the good of his fellow-men was the foundation of the public library in Philadelphia. At his instance, the members of a little club, to which he belonged, tradesmen and mechanics of narrow means, threw into common stock the few books which belonged to them. A subscription was obtained from fifty young men, principally tradesmen, of two pounds each, and ten shillings per annum, and with this little fund they began. "The books were imported, the library was opened one day in the week for lending them to the subscribers, on their promissory notes to pay double the value if not duly returned." "This was the mother," says Franklin, "of all the North American subscription libraries, now so numerous. It has become a great thing itself, and continually goes on increasing. These libraries have improved the general conversation of the Americans, made the common tradesmen and farmers as intelligent as most gentlemen from other countries, and, perhaps, have contributed in some degree to the stand so generally made throughout the colonies in defense of their privileges."

No, sir; if there is one lesson more than another directly deducible from the life of Franklin, it is the close connection of a thoroughly practical and useful life and career with books, libraries, and reading. If there is a thing on earth which would have gladdened his heart, could he have anticipated it, it would be the knowledge that his native city, in two generations after his death, would found a library like this, to give to the rising generation, and to the lovers of knowledge of every age, that access to books of which he so much felt the want. And could it be granted to him, even now, to return to his native city, which dwelt in his affections to the close of his life, his first visit would be to the center of the ancient burial-ground, where, in after life, he dutifully placed a marble slab on the graves of his parents; his second visit would be to the spot in Milk street where he was born; his third to the corner of Union and Hanover street, where he passed his childhood, in a house still standing; his fourth visit would be to the site of the free, grammar school-house, where, as he says in his will, he received "his first instruction in literature," and which is now adorned with the statue which a grateful posterity has dedicated to his memory; and his last and longest would be to this noble hall, where you are making provision for an ample supply of that reading of which, "from his infancy, he was passionately fond."

The shades of evening are falling around us; these crescets, which lend us their mild and tasteful illumination, will soon be extinguished; and the first day of the new year, rich in the happy prospects we now inaugurate, will come to a close. May the blessing of Heaven give effect to its largest anticipations! A few more days—a few more years—will follow their appointed round, and we, who now exchange our congratulations on this magnificent new year's gift of our City Fathers, will have passed from the scene; but firm in the faith that the growth of knowledge is the growth of sound principles and pure morals, let us not doubt, that, by the liberality of the City Government and of our generous benefactors at home and abroad, a light will be kindled and go forth from these walls, now dedicated to the use of the FREE BOSTON PUBLIC LIBRARY, which will guide our children and our children's children in the path of intelligence and virtue, till the sun himself shall fall from the heavens.

After reading the extracts from Franklin's "*Autobiography*," Mr. Everett added:—

In your presence, Mr. Mayor, and that of this vast assembly, on this first of January, 1858, I offer this copy of Franklin's "*Autobiography*," in Spark's edition, as a new year's gift to the Boston Public Library. Nay, sir, I am going to do more, and make the first, and perhaps the last, motion ever made in this hall; and that is, that every person present, of his own accord, if of age—with the consent of parent or guardian, if a minor—man, woman, boy, or girl, be requested, on going home, to select one good book, and, in memory of the poor boy, who half-fed himself to gratify his taste for reading, present it as a new year's gift to the Boston Public Library.

In consequence of this motion, many books (over 1400 in one month,) were received in the library, as donations.

HINTS ON READING.

SELECTED BY REV. T. H. VAIL.

"I no sooner come into the Library, but I bolt the door to me, excluding Lust, Ambition, Avarice, and all such vices, whose nurse is Idleness, the mother of Ignorance and Melancholy. In the very lap of eternity, among so many divine souls, I take my seat with so lofty a spirit, and sweet content, that I pity all that know not this happiness."

[HEINSIUS, of Leyden, in D'Israeli's Curiosities of Literature.]

"Read not to contradict and confute, nor to believe and take for granted, nor find talk and discourse, but to weigh and consider."

[BACON'S Essays—On Studies. Harpers' ed. p. 179.]

1. DEFINITION OF READING.

Reading, in its true sense and use, is *study*—sometimes a laborious sometimes an entertaining perusal of books—but always *the study of books.*—"Reading," says Dr. Watts, "is that *means or method of knowledge*, whereby we acquaint ourselves with what other men have published to the world, in their writings."—*Watts on the Improvement of the Mind*, p. 39.

2. OBJECTS OF READING.

"The question recurs, What is the proper object of Reading? what the end to be kept in view, in the choice and perusal of books? One great end, doubtless, is *Knowledge*. . . . . One object of reading, then, is to acquire knowledge. But we must bear in mind that knowledge, in itself, is not so much an end as a means, and that we are always to keep in view its ulterior uses and applications. . . . . Knowledge brings with it *duties* which are not to be neglected. It is a *talent or trust*; and to enable us to employ it aright, we should understand well the end for which God has given us capacities for acquiring it. On no subject are men more likely to err; and how grievous the error is, and in what ways it manifests itself let Lord Bacon teach. 'But the greatest error,' says that great writer, 'of all the rest, is the mistaking or misplacing of the last or farthest end of knowledge; for men have entered into a desire of learning and knowledge, sometimes upon, &c., ... seldom sincerely to give a true account of their gift of reason to the benefit and use of men, as if there were sought in knowledge a couch, &c., &c., and not *a rich store-house for the glory of the Creator and the relief of man's estate.*' Such, then, is the use of knowledge. It constitutes a rich store-house, whence we should draw materials for glorifying God, and improving man's estate. In other words knowledge is to be employed by us in doing good. . . . . . This remark leads us to notice another of the benefits to be derived from books, when judiciously selected and properly read. This is *the improvement of our intellectual powers and moral sentiments*. . . . . . So, again, *in regard to taste*. . . . . What is true of intellect and taste, is not less true of our *moral sentiments*. . . . . (Recapitulation.) *Why should we read?* Partly to procure immediate gratification, but principally,—1st, to acquire knowledge, both for its own sake, and for its uses; 2ndly, to improve the intellectual powers; 3dly, to refine taste; and 4thly, to strengthen the moral and religious sentiments."—*Professor Alonzo Potter, D. D. Advantages of Science, Harpers' Ed.*, pp. 14, 19, 20, 21, 23, 24, 31.

"In all our studies and pursuits of knowledge, let us remember that virtue and vice, sin and holiness, and the conformation of our hearts and lives to the duties of true religion and morality, are things of far more consequence than all the furniture of our understandings, and the richest treasures of mere speculative knowledge."—*Watts on the Mind*, p. 60.

3. General Advantages of Reading.

"These arts of reading and writing are of infinite advantage; for by them we are made partakers of the sentiments, observations, reasonings and improvements of all the learned world, in the most remote nations, and in former ages, almost from the beginning of mankind. . . . . . The advantages (of reading) are such as these: 1. By reading, we acquaint ourselves, in a very extensive manner, with the affairs, actions, and thoughts of the living and the dead, in the most remote nations, and in most distant ages; and that with as much ease, as though they lived in our own age and nation. By reading we may learn something from all parts of mankind. . . . . . 2. By reading, we learn not only the actions and the sentiments of distant nations and ages, but we transfer to ourselves the knowledge and improvements of the most learned men, the wisest and the best of mankind, when or wheresoever they lived. For though many books have been written by weak and injudicious persons, yet the most of those books, which have obtained great reputation in the world, are the products of great and wise men in their several ages and nations. . . 3. When we read good authors, we learn the *best* sentiments, even of those wise and learned men. For they studied hard, and committed to writing their maturest thoughts, and the result of their long study and experience. . . 4. It is another advantage of reading that we may review what we read, we may consult the page again and again, and meditate on it, at successive seasons, in our serenest and retired hours, having the book always at hand."—*Watts*, pp. 38, 41, 42.

"Written records constitute the only authentic memorials of the past; and, since those records have been multiplied by printing, and spread over the world, they are truly imperishable. Nor only so; they are now the property of the whole race. . . . . Now almost all minds experience their enlightening and quickening influence. There is hardly an individual whose knowledge is not enlarged by the use of books; while, at the same time, multitudes are incited by them to add, by their own labors and discoveries, to the great sum of human attainments. Another advantage of the knowledge gained from books is, that . . . . . it is much of it arranged and systematized. Thus we are enabled to see the dependence and connection of different truths; and, what is more important, we learn to study *principles and laws*, instead of losing ourselves amid a multitude of incongruous facts. . . . How important, then, that every one, who would cultivate in his own mind the true spirit of investigation, or who would acquire that power which results from knowledge, how important that he should become familiar *with such books* as illustrate the nature, and imbody the fruits of this system of inquiry."—*Potter: Advantages of Science*, pp. 16, 17.

4. Importance of Reading, to the Business Man, the Mechanic and the Manufacturer.

"Let me invite your attention to the consideration of the probable beneficial effect of the diffusion of scientific knowledge, among those practically and habitually employed in the mechanic and manufacturing arts, and it is likely to operate upon the improvement and advancement of the arts and sciences themselves. . . . . Perhaps there is no better definition of science, than that it is knowledge acquired by the thoughts and the experience of many, and so methodically arranged, as to be comprehended by any one. .... The theory of science, then, is the exposition of known facts, arranged in classes, and expressed in words. ..... The advantages of experience and observation on a large scale, are by no means peculiar to mechanical ingenuity. .... It is peculiarly true with regard to the chemistry of the arts. ..... In fact, the very foundation of modern chemistry, or, at least, of that branch of it termed pneumatic chemistry, was laid in a brewery. There had been no lack of ingenuity, no sparing of labor or expense, no flagging of zeal or curiosity among the old chemists. But the larger and more striking field of observation and combination afforded to Dr. Priestley, by the vats and gases of his neighbor, the brewer, opened a new world to inquiry. From the thick vapors of the brew-house, like one of the gigantic genii of oriental romance, arose that mighty science which has given to enlightened art a more than magical sway. ... It is wonderful how the elements of the most precious knowledge are spread around us; how to the curious and instructed observer every thing is full and rich with the means of benefiting the human race. The slightest accession to our knowledge of nature, or our command over it, is sure, ultimately, to connect itself with some other truth, or to unfold its own powers or relations, and thus to lead on to some practical benefit, which the boldest conjecture could never have anticipated. The ignorant and the idle, suffer all such opportunities to pass by them as the vagrant breeze. But such will surely not be the case with industrious men, prepared by general science to turn those occasions to the best account. ..... I argue from experience. ... Take, for instance, the history of one of the most recent and precious gifts which chemistry has made to medicine. A few years ago, a soap manufacturer of Paris, M. Courtois, remarked that the residuum of his lye, when exhausted of the alkali, produced a corrosion of his copper boilers, which struck him as deserving special inquiry. 'He put it,' says Mr. Herschel, 'into the hands of a scientific chemist for analysis, and the result was, the discovery of one of the most singular and important chemical elements, *iodine*. .... Curiosity was excited; the origin of the new substance was traced to the sea-plants, from whose ashes the principal ingredient of soap is obtained, and ultimately to the sea-water itself. It was thence hunted through nature, discovered in salt mines and springs, and pursued into all bodies which have a marine origin; *among the rest into sponge*. A medical practitioner, (Dr. Coindet, a Swiss physician,) then called to mind a reputed remedy for the cure of one of the most grievous and unsightly disorders to which the human species is subject—the *goitre*. .... and which was said to have been originally cured by the ashes of burned sponge. Led by this indication, he tried the effect of iodine on that complaint, and the result established the extraordinary fact, that this substance, taken as a medicine, acts with the utmost promptitude and energy on goitre, dissipating the largest and most inveterate in a short time, and acting (of course with occasional failures, like all other medicines,) as a specific or natural antagonist against that odious deformity.' Now consider what a mass of human misery, for a long series of generations to come, has been relieved or removed by this discovery, arising from *the single circumstance of a Parisian soap manufacturer being an observing man, who understood the uses and nature of chemical analysis*. ...... Let us cross the channel to Great Britain, for some further examples. .... *The Telescope*, in its earliest stages of invention had received all the improvement that could then be furnished by the genius of the great Galileo, the father of modern science, and by the superhuman philosophical sagacity of Sir Isaac Newton, as well as of their disciples and followers, the most learned and ingenious men of Europe, such as the English Hooke, the Dutch Huygens, and the German Euler.—The product of these labors was admirable proof of the power of human invention; yet it was accompanied *with imperfections, especially in the refracting telescope*, that seemed insuperable. ...... The removal of this defect was reserved for *John Dollond*, originally a silk weaver, and afterward an optician and instrument-maker, of London. Half a century after Newton's experments, Dollond conceived the idea, that the refractive powers of different kinds of glass might be made to correct each other. In this he completely succeeded. Had he not *been familiar with the science* of Newton, Dollond would never have attempted this discovery; had he not also been *a practical mechanic*, it is hardly probable that he would have *succeeded*. The incidental mention of the ultimate advantages derived by the art of navigation from the labors of Dollond, suggests to my mind another illustration, and recalls the name of *John Smeaton*. He was by regular trade, a philosophical instrument-maker, but his active mind had taken a broad range of rational curiosity and employment, embracing almost every thing in science or art, that could throw light on mechanical contrivance. His inventions of this sort were very numerous and ingenious, but his solid fame rests chiefly upon the erection of the Eddystone lighthouse. .... There are few narratives of more intense interest or varied instruction than his own account of this great work....... The names and lives of our own distinguished benefactors of mankind—Franklin, and Rittenhouse, and Whitney, and Fulton, and Perkins—press upon my memory...... The history of Printing offers another tempting field of collateral illustration....... I might tell of the Italian Aldus and his sons, of Henry Stephens, of Paris, and his learned family, of the Dutch Elzevirs, the English Bowyer, the Scotch Foulis and Duncan, and surely could not forget the noblest name of them all, our own Franklin...... I must also reluctantly refrain from detailing the studies, inventions and improvements of the potter, *Josiah Wedgewood*. .... But from among the names which thus crowd upon me, let me adduce one more bright example........ It was about this season of the year, just seventy years ago, that the instrument-maker employed by the University of Glasgow, received from the professor of natural philosophy in that ancient seminary of learning, a broken model of the steam-engine, as then used, to be put in order for his lectures. ...... An ordinary workman, after admiring the ingenuity of this imperfect machine, would have made the necessary repairs, sent it back to the lecture-room, and the world would have gone on as usual. But it had fallen into the hands of *James Watt*, a young mechanic, of singular and various inventive sagacity, and of most patient and persevering ingenuity, who, *in addition to much miscellaneous information, and some mathematical acquirement, had been led by a liberal curiosity to master all that was then known of chemistry, and theoretical natural philosophy in its broadest sense*......... Look around for yourselves—on our rivers and lakes—on the manufactures of Europe and America, piled up in our shops—on the railroads which traverse, or are just about to traverse, our continent—on the wealth, the power, the rapid interchange of commerce and intelligence produced by the modern steam-engine, and then let me remind you, that all this is the fruit of the solitary labors and studies of a Glasgow work-shop; directed by an active, vigorous, daring, but most patient and persevering *mind, which knew how to use well the knowledge that other wise or ingenious men had previously reasoned out or discovered*....... I have not yet touched upon the influence of knowledge, upon the operative and producing classes themselves, in improving the character, raising the thoughts, awakening sleeping talent, and thus qualifying this great and valuable body, for the able, just, right, wise and honorable discharge of all the duties of men, of citizens, of freemen, of patriots. This is alone, and in itself, a theme full of interest—full of excitement... Such were Saratoga's victors, such the brave men whose blood earned our liberties. Foremost among them was *the blacksmith* of Rhode Island, *Nathaniel Greene*; he whom Hamilton, while he honored Washington as 'the first man of the country,' did not hesitate to style 'the first *soldier* of the Revolution....... There also was the *book-binder*, *Knox*, and from among *the mechanics* of New York, came forth our *Willet*, 'the bravest of the brave.' ..... Abroad, our interests were watched over, and our national dignity represented, by the *printer*, *Franklin*........ Foremost in our councils at home, and enrolled among the immortal names of the committee of five, who prepared and reported the Declaration of Independence, was the *shoemaker*, *Roger Sherman*, a man self-educated and self-raised. . . . . . . Here were other names like these which I cannot now pause to recapitulate. . . . . Still I cannot forbear from paying a passing tribute to the memory of a townsman and a friend. . . . . . . The courage, seamanship, and ability of *Commodore Chauncey*, would have been exerted in vain, had they not been seconded by the skill, the enterprise, the science, the power of combination, and the ready and inexhaustible resources of his *ship-builder*, *Henry Eckford*. . . . . . . The ardor for improvement, the thirst for knowledge, manifested by the mechanics of this and others of our cities, are gratifying indeed. . . . . . . But they derive a tenfold interest and value from the greater results which they foretell, and the more glorious future they appear to usher in." *Gulian C. Verplanck's Discourse before the Mechanics' Institute of New York*, *Nov.* 27, 1833—passim.

5. Choice of Books.

"The world is full of books; but there are multitudes which are so ill-written, that they were never worthy any man's reading; and there are thousands more which may be good in their kind, but are worth nothing, when the month, or year, or occasion is past, for which they were written. Others may be valuable in themselves for some special purpose, or in some peculiar science, but are not fit to be perused by any but those who are engaged in that particular science or business. . . . . . It is of vast advantage or improvement of knowledge and saving time, for a young man to have the most proper books for his reading recommended by a judicious friend. . . . . . . There is yet another sort of books, (in addition to *books of science and complete treatises* on subjects, which are first recommended,) of which it is proper I should say something while I am treating on this subject; and these are *history, poesy, travels, books of diversion or amusement*; among which we may reckon also, little common *pamphlets, newspapers, or such like*. For many of these, I confess, *once reading may be sufficient*, where there is a tolerably good memory. . . . . . . Still let it be remembered, that where the historical narrative is of considerable moment, where the poesy, oratory, &c., shine with some degrees of perfection and glory, a single reading is neither sufficient to satisfy a mind, that has a true taste for this sort of writing; nor can we make the fullest and best improvement of them, without proper reviews, and that in our retirement as well as in company. . . . . . . Among these writings of the latter kind, we may justly reckon *short miscellaneous essays* on all manner of subjects; such as the Occasional Papers, the Tattlers, the Spectators, and some other books, that have been compiled out of the weekly or daily products of the press. . . . . . Among other books, which are proper and requisite, in order to improve our knowledge in general, or our acquaintance with any particular science, it is necessary that we should be furnished with *vocabularies and dictionaries of several sorts*, namely, of *common words, idioms, and phrases*, in order to explain their sense; of *technical words, or the terms of art*, to show their use in arts and sciences; of *names of men, countries, towns, rivers, &c.*, which are called *historical and geographical dictionaries*, &c. *These are to be consulted and used upon every occasion*. . . . . If such books are not at hand, you must supply the want of them, as well as you can, by consulting such as can inform you." *Watts on the Mind*, pp. 59, 69, 71, 72.

"A wise and good man was accustomed, in his devotion, to thank God for books. He did well; *good books, rightly used*, are among our greatest blessings. . . . . . . Books introduce us to the noblest minds of our race, and permit us to commune intimately with them, even at those privileged hours, when they obtain their brightest visions of truth, and pour forth their loftiest or most touching eloquence. It must be remembered, however, that *all books are not good books*, and that *even good books may be so read, as to fail of their appropriate ends*. Milton has said, that 'a wise man can sooner gather gold out of the drossiest volume, than a fool, wisdom out of Scripture.' It is certain that the effect of reading depends nearly as much on the disposition and taste of the reader, as on the character of the writer. Hence the great importance of considering not only *what* we read, but also in what way, and for what *ends*. . . . . A love of books can be acquired only by those who find pleasure in using them; and hence, whoever would cultivate in himself or others this most desirable taste, *should select, especially at first*, such works as can be read with sustained and quickened attention. But let it not be forgotten, that *such* books, if read *only to amuse* and entertain, must, if *good*, *fail* of much of their effect, while, *if bad, their influence will be deplorable*. . . . . . . By degrading them into instruments of momentary pleasure, we shall lose sight of their true worth, and learn to confound them with that herd of books, usually known as 'light reading;' books which seem to have been written in order to be *once read*, and then *forever forgotten*. Soon, too, we shall disrelish all books that contain any serious matter, and be content only with those of the most frivolous and exciting kind. These last will claim every hour that can be allotted to *reading*; and happy shall we be, if they do not *steal hours that ought to have been given to study*. . . . . . To this danger we are peculiarly exposed in our own day. . . . . . . We should choose books that will exercise the faculty of close and continuous *attention*, and as we advance, we should subject it to the necessity of more strenuous and protracted effort. They should be books, too, which require us to *think*; which sometimes incline us to close our volume, that we may review the arguments and statements of the writer, and test them by the rules of sound reasoning; books, which call us to analyze what is complicated, to arrest what is fugitive, and trace out what is subtle; which suggest new subjects for reflection and inquiry, and gradually lead us to appreciate and enjoy the pleasure that results from the mere exercise of our intellectual powers. . . . . So, again, in regard to *taste*. All men have been endowed, though in different degrees, with a relish for what is beautiful or perfect of its kind. . . . . . . Hence, books, as well as companions, should be *selected with reference to the cultivation*, not only of the understanding, but also of the taste. And in this respect we are exposed to much danger. Not a few of the works of our day (especially those of a fictitious and periodical character—works, too, which command enthusiastic applause,) are directly calculated to encourage a false taste in literature, as well as a vicious tone in manners and morals. . . . . . What is true of intellect and taste is not less true of our *moral sentiments*. . . . . And, as our moral judgments, moreover, are insensibly but powerfully affected by companions, so are they by books—companions, against whom we are apt to be least on our guard, whose instructions we are disposed to receive with a too implicit faith, and whose society we enjoy at those seasons of relaxation, when the heart is most open to influence. It is nearly an axiom, that people will not be better than the books they read. . . . . It is important that all books be proscribed, which inculcate indifference to moral distinctions; which tend, however indirectly, or insidiously, to excite our evil passions; which exhibit the guilty and profligate as objects of sympathy and admiration; or which serve to lessen, in the least, our reverence for principle, or our hatred of a mean and time-serving policy. . . . . . In thus explaining the objects which ought to be kept in view in reading, I have, in effect, furnished rules for judging of books, of their character and value. If *one great end of reading* be to enlarge our knowledge, then we should, for the most part, read no books which do not *furnish useful information*. I say, *for the most part*, because we *sometimes* read rather to improve taste, quicken and cultivate imagination, or discipline reason, rather than to gain knowledge. Hence *another rule*, by which we may try a book, is *the effect it has upon the understanding*. Does it require thought, and excite to reflection? Does it deal in *sound reasoning* only, avoiding all specious fallacies, and making no appeals to mere prejudice or passion? Does it cultivate in our minds a disinterested *love of truth*? . . . . If, on the other hand, it be a *work of imagination* or *taste*, it should be tried by *its influence on the sensitive part of our nature*. If it pro-sent us with images of beauty and simplicity, enable us to view the works of nature and art, with a keener and more discriminating relish, inspire us with a love for the perfect, and, above all, if it strengthen and animate our noble sentiments of virtue, it merits frequent and careful perusal. But, *if otherwise*, &c., I need not add, that it is a book to be reprobated and avoided. . . . . WHAT SHOULD WE READ? Only good books; which Milton describes as 'the precious life-blood of master-spirits, embalmed and treasured up on purpose to a life beyond life.' To know whether a book be good, consider, 1st, whether it adds to our sum of knowledge: 2ndly, whether it induces thought, and exercises reason: 3dly, whether it improves taste: and 4thly, whether it strengthens conscience.'—*Dr. Potter: Advantages of Science*, pp. 9—12, 22—27, 31.

"Read *always the best and most recent book on the subject which you wish to investigate.* 'You are to remember,' says Pliny the younger, 'that the most approved authors of each sort are to be carefully chosen, for, as it has been well observed, though we should *read much*, we should not *read many* authors.'"—*Dr. Potter: Hand-book for Readers*, p. 18.

6. SYSTEMATIC READING; OR READING IN COURSES, OR BY SUBJECTS.

"Some prejudice, against what are called courses of study, has been justly provoked by the great number and variety of those which have been proposed from time to time. . . . . . At the outset, *almost any course of reading* is better than the desultory and irregular habits which prevail so extensively. When once the student has acquired a taste for good books, and some just ideas of the object and uses of reading, he may be safely left to glean for himself, from the counsels of others, such hints and directions as are best adapted to his own case. . . . . . . Do not become so far enslaved by any system or course of study, as to think it may not be altered when alteration would contribute to the healthy and improving action of the mind. . . . . Beware, on the other hand, of *frequent changes* in your *plan* of study. This is the besetting sin of young persons. 'No, take your course wisely, but firmly,' says Wirt, 'and having taken it, hold upon it with heroic resolution, and the Alps and Pyrenees will sink before you. The whole empire of learning will be at your feet, while those who set out with you, *but stopped to change their plans*, are yet employed in the very profitable business of changing their plans. Let your motto be, *Perseverando vinces.* (*by perseverance thou shalt conquer.*) Practice upon it, and you will be convinced of its value, by the distinguished eminence to which it will conduct you.' . . . . . Study *subjects*, rather than books; therefore, compare *different authors* on the *same subjects*; the *statements* of authors, with information collected from *other sources*; and the conclusions drawn by a writer with the rules of sound logic. 'Learning,' says Feltham, 'falls far short of wisdom; nay, so far that you scarcely find a greater fool than is sometimes a mere scholar.' . . . . 'I take care,' says one of the profoundest and most versatile scholars in England, as quoted by Mr. Warren, in his Law Studies, 'always to ascertain the value of what I look at, and if satisfied on that score, I most carefully stow it away. I pay, besides, frequent visits to my 'magazine,' and keep an inventory of at least every thing important, which I frequently compare with my stores. It is, however, the *systematic disposition and arrangement* I adopt, which lightens the labors of memory. I was by no means remarkable for memory, when young; on the contrary, I was considered rather defective on that score.' . . . . . . *Dare to be ignorant of many things.* 'In a celebrated satire, (*the Pursuits of Literature*) much read in my youth,' says De Quincy, 'and which I myself read about twenty-five years ago, I remember one counsel there addressed to young men, but, in fact, of universal application. I call upon *them*, said the author, to *dare* to be ignorant of many things; a wise counsel and justly expressed. . . . . . . *A good scheme of study will soon show itself to be such by this one test*, that it will exclude as powerfully as it will appropriate; it will be a *system* of repulsion no less than of attraction; once thoroughly possessed and occupied by the deep and genial pleasures of one truly intellectual pursuit, you will be easy and indifferent to all others that had previously teased you with transient excitement."—*Dr. Potter: Handbook for Readers*, pp. 15—18, 20, 21.

"In learning any new thing, there should be as little as possible first proposed to the mind at once. That being understood, and *fully mastered*, proceed to the *next* adjoining part, yet unknown. This is a slow, but safe and sure way to arrive at knowledge. The mind will be able, in this manner, to cope with great difficulties, and prevail over them, with amazing and happy success. . . . . . Engage not the mind in the intense pursuit of too many things at once; especially, such as have no relation to one another. This will be ready to distract the understanding, and hinder it from attaining *perfection in any one subject of study*. . . . . . In the pursuit of every valuable subject of knowledge, keep the end always in your eye, and be not diverted from it by every petty trifle you meet with in the way. . . . . . Be not satisfied with a mere knowledge of the best *authors*, that treat of any subject, instead of acquainting yourselves *thoroughly with the subject itself*."—*Dr. Watts on the Mind*, pp. 131—133, 72.

7. Reading conjoined with Thinking.

"Deal freely with every author you read; and yield up your assent only to evidence and just reasoning on the subject. . . . . In the compositions of men, remember, you are a man as well as they; and it is not their reason, but your own, that is given to guide you, when you arrive at years of discretion. . . . Enter into the sense and argument of the authors you read; examine all their proofs, and then judge of the truth or falsehood of their opinion. . . You will acquire by degrees a habit of judging justly, and of reasoning well, in imitation of the good writer, whose works you peruse. . . . Never apply yourself to read any human author, with a determination beforehand either for or against him; nor with a settled resolution to believe or disbelieve, to confirm or to oppose whatsoever he says; but always read with design to lay your mind open to truth, and to embrace it, as well as to reject every falsehood, though it appears under ever so fair a disguise. . . . . . Never *let an unknown word pass in your reading*, without seeking for its meaning. . . . And, indeed, how many volumes soever of learning a man possesses, he is still deplorably poor in his understanding, till *he has made these several parts of learning his own property*, by reasoning, by judging for himself, and remembering what he has read.—*Dr. Watts on the Mind*, pp. 61, 63, 66, 67, 72 73.

"Says Locke, 'Reading furnishes the mind only with *materials* of knowledge; it is *thinking* that makes what we read *ours*.' . . . Says Dugald Stewart, 'nothing, in truth, has such a tendency *to weaken*, not only the powers of invention, but the intellectual powers in general, as a habit of *extensive and various reading without reflection*.' . . . Accustom yourself to refer whatever you read to the general head to which it belongs, and trace it, *if a fact*, to the *principle* it involves or illustrates; *if a principle*, to the *facts* which it produces or explains."—*Dr. Potter: Handbook for Readers*, pp. 16, 17, 19.

"*Reading, to be useful*, should *be combined with reflection*. Books can afford but little improvement to those who do not *think as well as read*. . . . . Thus we see the great necessity of reading with deliberation; and may I not add, that in this respect, *laboring people*, and those whose pursuits give to them almost constant engagement, *have advantages which they are not apt to appreciate*. By reading at intervals, some portion of a good book, and then carrying the matter with them to their places of business, as a subject for thought and conversation, they will soon discover that the subject grows upon them in interest, that their views insensibly become clearer and more enlarged, and that useful reflections, not suggested by the author, rise before their minds. And thus it is, *that men of active pursuits are more apt, as all expe rience testifies, to accumulate useful knowledge, than those whose lives are passed in leisure and in the midst of books.* . . . . . . Let me advise, then, that *books be read deliberately.* The old maxim, that 'if a thing be worth doing at all, it is worth doing well,' is peculiarly applicable to reading. A book run over hastily, is rarely understood; if not understood, it is not remembered; and if not remembered, the time spent in reading it is lost. . . . By deep and diligent meditation, we (should) acquire something which may truly be called our own; for, as Milton says:—who reads

> 'Incessantly, and to his reading brings not
> A spirit and judgment equal or superior,
> Uncertain and unsettled still remains,
> Deep versed in books, but shallow in himself.'"

Dr. Potter: Advantages of Science, pp. 17, 18, 27, 30.

8. Social or Class Reading.

"If three or four persons agree *to read the same book, and each brings his own remarks upon it*, at some set hours appointed for conversation, and they communicate, mutually, their sentiments on the subjects, and debate about it in a friendly manner, the practice will render the reading of any author more abundantly beneficial to every one of them. . . . . If several persons engaged in the same study, take *into their hands distinct treatises on one subject*, and appoint a season of communication once a week, they may inform each other in a brief manner, concerning the sense, sentiments and method of those several authors, and thereby promote each other's improvement, &c. . . . . Talking over the things which you have read to your companions, on the first proper opportunity, is a most useful manner of review or repetition, in order to fix them upon the mind. Teach them to your younger friends, in order to establish your own knowledge, while you communicate it to them."—*Dr. Watts on the Mind*, pp. 60, 61, 178.

"'Company and conversation,' says Feltham, 'are the best instructors for a noble nature.' 'An engagement and combating of wits,' says Erasmus, 'does, in an extraordinary manner, both show the strength of geniuses, rouses them and augments them. If you are in doubt of any thing, do not be ashamed to ask, or, if you have committed an error, be corrected."—*Dr. Potter: Hand-book for Readers*, p. 19.

"*Some books should be read in company with others, especially with our family.* We never relish a good book so highly as when we read it with a friend of congenial tastes. . . . . . . And in this plan of social reading, what friends so proper as those of our household! What employment more appropriate *for the domestic circle*, than one which causes the minds of all to move in unison, thus strengthening the ties of mutual affection, and causing us to *associate with home, the remembrance of our intellectual pleasures!* . . . . It will not be easy to preserve *the good old practice* of collecting our families around the cheerful fire, and teaching them to relish early the home-bred delights of affection, and of a common intercourse with those *best and most improving visiters, good books.*" *Dr. Potter: Advantages of Science*, pp. 27, 29.

9. Re-reading or Reviewing.

"A *frequent review* and careful repetition of the things we would learn, and an abridgment of them in a narrow compass, has a great influence to fix them in the memory. . . . . *Repetition* is so very useful a practice, that Winemon, even from his youth to his old age, never read a book without making some small points, dashes, or hooks in the margin, to mark what parts of the discourse were *proper for review*; and when he came to the end of a section or chapter, he always shut his book, and recollected all the sentiments or expressions he had marked, so that he could give a tolerable analysis and abstract of every treatise he had read, just after he had finished it. Hence he became so well furnished with a rich variety of knowledge."—*Dr. Watts on the Mind*, p. 177.

"Strive, *by frequent reviews*, to keep your knowledge *always at command*. 'What booteth,' says an old writer, 'to read much, which is a weariness to the flesh; to meditate often, which is a burden to the mind; to learn daily, with increase of knowledge, when he is *to seek* for what he *hath* learned, and perhaps *then*, especially, when he hath most need thereof? Without this, (reviewing) our studies are but lost labor.'"—*Dr. Porter: Handbook for Readers*, p. 20.

"I would recommend, that when we become acquainted with a truly good book, we *read it often*. Cecil tells us that he had a '*shelf for tried books*; books, which he could never open without being incited to reflection, and enriched by some new hint or principle. It should be so with all of us. *A few books properly selected and faithfully read*, would suffice to yield us more, both of pleasure and profit, than any number, however great, taken at random, and read, as they usually are, in a hurried and unreflecting manner. A book, moreover, which deserves the praise of being good, has cost its author efforts which cannot be appreciated at a single reading."—*Dr. Porter: Advantages of Science*, p. 20.

10. Reading connected with Writing.

"For want of retiring and writing, many a learned man has lost several useful meditations of his own, and could never recall them. . . . If a book has no index nor good table of contents, it is very useful to make one as you are reading it. . . . It is sufficient in your index, to take notice only of those parts of the book which are new to you, or which you think well written, and well worthy of your remembrance or review. Shall I be so free as to assure my younger friends, from my own experience, that these methods of reading will cost some pains in the first years of your study, and especially in the first authors, which you peruse in any science, or on any particular subject; but the profit will richly compensate the pains. And in the following years of life, after you have read a few valuable books on any special subject in this manner, it will be very easy to read others of the same kind; because you will not usually find very much new matter in them, which you have not already examined. If the writer be remarkable for any peculiar excellencies or defects in his style or manner of writing, make just observations upon this also; and whatever ornaments you find there, or whatever blemishes occur in the language or manner of the writer, you may make just remarks upon them. And remember, that one book, read over in this manner, with all this laborious meditation, will tend more to enrich your understanding, than skimming over the surface of twenty. . . . . It is useful *to note down matters of doubt and inquiry* and take the first opportunity to get them resolved either by persons or books. . . . Lawyers and Divines write down short notes or hints of the principal heads of what they desire to commit to memory, in order to preach or plead. . . . The art of *short hand* is of excellent use for this, as well as other purposes. . . . . Those who scarcely ever take a pen in their hands to write short notes or hints of what they are to learn, need a double degree of power to *retain* or recollect what they read or hear."—*Dr. Watts on the Mind*, pp. 43, 61, 65, 72, 178.

"Nor is it merely to the philosopher, who wishes to distinguish himself by his discoveries, that *writing affords an useful instrument of study*. Important assistance may be derived from it by all those who wish to impress on their minds the investigations which occur to them *in the course of their reading*."—*Dugald Stuart: Philos. of the Mind*, *Vol.* 1. *p.* 32.

"Seek opportunities to *write and converse* on subjects about which you read. '*Reading*,' says Bacon, 'maketh a *full* man, *conference*, a ready man, and *writing*, an *exact* man.'"—*Dr. Potter: Hand Book, &c.*, p. 19.

"I add one more suggestion in the words of another. Young persons especially, will pardon the suggestion, that in no way, perhaps, can their store of applicable knowledge be more certainly, though at first almost imperceptibly, increased, than *by habitually reading with a pen in the hand*. There is much good sense in these doggerel verses, for which we are indebted to no ordinary thinker."

> "In reading authors, when you find
> Bright passages that strike your mind,
> And which, perhaps, you may have reason
> To think on at another season,
> Be not contented with the sight,
> *But take them down in black and white;*
> Such a respect is wisely shown,
> *As makes another's sense one's own.*'"

Dr. Potter: Advantages of Science, p. 30.

11. Method of Reading—General Hints and Directions.

"*Books of importance* of any kind, and especially *complete treatises* on any subject, should be *first* read in a *more general* and cursory manner, to learn a little what the treatise promises, and what you may expect from the writer's manner and skill. And for this end, I would advise always, that *the preface be read*, and a survey taken of the *table of contents*, if there be one, *before* this first survey of the book. By this means, you will not only be better fitted to give the book the first reading, but you will be much assisted in your second perusal, *which should be done with greater attention and deliberation*; and you will learn with more ease and readiness what the author pretends to teach. In your reading, mark what is new or unknown to you before; and review those chapters, pages, or paragraphs. . . . . Other things, also, of the like nature may be usefully practiced with regard to the authors which you read. If *the method of a book be irregular*, reduce it into form by *a little analysis of your own*, or by *hints in the margin*; if those things are *heaped together* which should be separated, you may *wisely distinguish* and divide them. If several things relating to the same subject are *scattered up and down separately* through the treatise, you may bring them all *to one view, by references*; or if the *matter* of a book be really valuable and deserving, you may throw it into a better *method*, reduce it to a more logical scheme, or abridge it into a lesser form. All these practices will have a tendency both to advance your skill in logic and method, to improve your judgment in general, and to give you a fuller survey of that subject in particular. When you have finished the treatise, with all your observations upon it, recollect and determine what real improvements you have made by reading that author. . . . Endeavor to apply every speculative study, as far as possible, to *some practical use, that both yourself and others may be the better for it*."—*Dr. Watts*, pp. 59, 64, 139.

"Always have some useful and pleasant book ready to take up in 'odd ends' of time. A good part of life will otherwise be wasted. 'There is,' says Wyttenbach, 'no business, no avocation whatever, which will not permit a man who has *an inclination* to give a little time every day to the studies of his youth. . . . Be not alarmed because *so many* books are recommended. They are not all to be read at once, nor in a short time. '*Some travelers*,' says Bishop Hall, '*have more shrunk at the map than at the way*; between both, how many stand still with their arms folded.' . . . . Do not attempt to read *much or fast*. 'To call him *well read*, who reads *many authors*,' says Shaftsbury, 'is improper.' 'It does not matter,' says Seneca, '*how many*, but *how good* books you have.' . . . . Endeavor to find opportunities to *use your knowledge*, and apply it in practice. 'They proceed right well in all knowledge,' says Bacon, 'which do couple study with their practice, and do not first study altogether, and then practice altogether."—*Dr. Potter: Hand Book, &c.*, pp. 18, 20.

"How should we Read? First, thoughtfully and critically; secondly, in company with a friend or with our family; thirdly, repeatedly; fourthly, with pen in hand."—*Dr. Potter: Advantages of Science*, p. 31.

12. Effects of Books—Influence of Authors.

"Wherefore should not the literary character be associated in utility or glory with the other professional classes of society? . . . . . The commercial prosperity of a nation inspires no renovation in mankind; nor will its military power with their affection. There is an interchange of opinions, as well as of spices and specie, which induces nations to esteem each other; and there is a glorious succession of authors, as well as of seamen and soldiers, forever standing before the eyes of the universe. It is by our authors that foreigners have been taught to subdue their own prejudices. . . . . . The small cities of Athens and of Florence will perpetually attest the influence of the literary character over other nations; the one received the tributes of the mistress of the universe, when the Romans sent their youth to be educated at Athens; while the other, at the revival of letters, beheld every polished European crowding to its little court. . . . . . Those who govern a nation, cannot at the same time enlighten them;—authors stand between the governors and the governed. . . . . . The single thought of a man of genius has sometimes changed the dispositions of a people, and even of an age. . . . . . When Locke and Montesquieu appeared, the old systems of government were reviewed; the principles of legislation were developed; and many changes have succeeded, and are still to succeed. . . . . . Observe the influence of authors in forming the character of men, where the solitary man of genius stamps his own on a people. The habits, the precepts, &c., of Dr. Franklin imprinted themselves on his Americans; while the elegant tastes of Sir William Jones could inspire the servants of a commercial corporation to open new and vast sources of knowledge. . . . . . While Britain retains her awful situation among the nations of Europe, the 'Sylva' of Evelyn will endure with her triumphant oaks. In the third edition of that work, the heart of the patriot exults at its results. He tells Charles I. 'how many millions of timber trees, besides requisite others, have been propagated and planted at the *instigation, and by the sole direction of this work*.' It was an author in his studious retreat, who, casting a prophetic eye on the age we live in, secured the late victories of our naval sovereignty. Inquire at the Admiralty how the fleets of Nelson have been constructed, and they can tell you that it was with the oaks which the genius of Evelyn planted. . . . . . The same character existed in France, where De Lerres, in 1599, composed a work on the cultivation of mulberry trees, in reference to the art of raising silk-worms. He taught his fellow-citizens to convert a leaf into silk, and silk to become the representative of gold. . . . . . A work in France, under the title of 'L'Ami des Hommes,' first spread there a general passion for agricultural pursuits; and although the national ardor carried all to excess, yet marshes were drained, and waste lands inclosed. . . . The commercial world owes to two retired philosophers, in the solitude of their study, Locke and Smith, those principles which dignify trade into a liberal pursuit, and connect it with the happiness of a people. . . . In the history of genius, there is no chronology, for to us everything it has done is present; and the earliest attempt is connected with the most recent. . . . . . My learned and reflecting friend, (Sharon Turner, Esq.,) whose original researches have enriched our national history, has thus observed on the character of Wickliffe:—'To complete our idea of the importance of Wickliffe, it is only necessary to add, that as his writings made John Huss the Reformer of Bohemia, so the

writings of John Huss led Martin Luther to be the Reformer of Germany; so extensive and so incalculable are the consequences which sometimes follow from human actions.' Our historian has accompanied this, by giving the very feelings of Luther in early life on his first perusal of the works of John Huss; we see the spark of creation caught at the moment; a striking influence of the generation of character! Thus a father-spirit has many sons...... Such are the 'great lights of the world,' by whom the torch of knowledge has been successively seized and transmitted from one to the other..... The torch of genius is perpetually transferred from hand to hand amidst this fleeting scene."
D'Israeli's Literary Character, &c.; Alexandrian edition, pp. 414, 446.

13. Early Reading—First Studies.

The serious caution and conscientious watchfulness to be exercised by parents and friends, in the selection of books for the young, and for those who have not been accustomed to reading, (on the minds of both which classes, vivid and permanent, and therefore most important impressions will necessarily be produced by the authors recommended,) are forcibly suggested by the illustrations which follow. The practical teachings of these examples make it proper that they should have the place of emphasis and chief effect, at the close of our collations.

"The first studies form an epoch in the history of genius, and unquestionably have sensibly influenced its productions. Often have the first impressions stamped a character on the mind adapted to receive one, as often the first step into life has determined its walk...... An early attachment to the works of Sir Thomas Browne produced in Johnson an excessive admiration of that Latinized English, which violated the native graces of the language. The first studies of Rembrandt affected his after labors; that peculiarity of shadow which marks all his pictures, originated in the circumstance of his father's mill receiving light from an aperture at the top, which habituated that artist afterwards to view all objects as if seen in that magical light. When Pope was a child, he found in his mother's closet a small library of mystical devotion; but it was not suspected till the fact was discovered, that the effusions of love and religion poured forth in his Eloisa, were derived from the seraphic raptures of those erotic mystics, who to the last retained a place in his library among the classical bards of antiquity. The accidental perusal of Quintus Curtius first made Boyle 'in love with other than pedantic books, and conjured up in him,' as he expresses it, 'an unsatisfied appetite of knowledge; so that he thought he owed more to Quintus Curtius than did Alexander.' From the perusal of Rycaut's folio of Turkish history in childhood, the noble and impassioned bard of our times, (Lord Byron,) retained those indelible impressions which gave life and motion to the 'Giaour, the Corsair and Alp.' A voyage to the country produced the scenery..... The influence of first studies, in the formation of the character of genius, is a moral phenomenon, which has not sufficiently attracted our notice. Dr. Franklin acquaints us that when young and wanting books, he accidentally found De Foe's 'Essay on Projects,' from which work impressions were derived which afterwards influenced some of the principal events of his life.... Such is the influence through life of those first unobserved impressions on the character of genius, which every author has not recorded." Such, too, in a greater or less degree, is the influence of first impressions on all minds. As the impressions can never be obliterated, the influence is to last forever.—*See D'Israeli's Literary Character, &c.; Alexandrian edition*, p. 412.

14. Hints to Young Ladies as to What to Read and How to Read.

"Think, my dear young friends, of the difference that is made in the character of a human being, simply by reading. Compare an Irish girl who comes to this country at fifteen or sixteen, who has never been taught to read, with one of your own countrywomen in the humblest condition, of the same age, who *loves to read*, and who has read the books within her reach? . . . . . Books are the best property of the rich; think what they are to the poor who *really love them*. Compare the pampered boy, who cares for nothing so much as the indulgence of his sensual appetites, fretting over a table spread luxuriously, to a little fellow who, coming from the district-school, with his empty luncheon basket, snatches his Robinson Crusoe from the shelf; and, while his half frozen toes are warming, devours it, forgetful of every evil in life. . . . . . It was but yesterday that I was at the humble home of a revolutionary soldier—a pensioner. I found his wife reading. Her eight children are dispersed south and west, and the old pair are left alone. They live far away from the village, and hardly put their heads out of doors from November till March. I involuntarily expressed my sympathy in their solitary condition. 'Oh,' replied the old lady most cheerily, 'I have company—*books*, the best of company!' . . . . . Think over your acquaintance, my young friends; I am sure you will find among them some old person, some invalid, some one cut off from social pleasures, to whom life would be a tedious burden, if it were not for books. . . . . If there is a real love of books, there is hardly a limit to be set to the knowledge that may be acquired from them without the aid of instructors, schools, or colleges. . . . A love for reading is with some merely the keen appetite of a superior mind. It would be felt under any circumstances whatever. But these are the few—the gifted. With most persons, the taste for reading must be cultivated. I believe there is no habit easier to form. Intelligent children, who live in reading families, with very few exceptions, are fond of reading as soon as they can read with facility. . . . . But, if you have been so unfortunate as not to acquire this habit of reading early, form it now for yourself. If you are not capable of selecting your own books, take the advice of some friend who knows the wants of your mind. Resolve to devote a portion of every day, for a year to come, to reading; and then, if you forget your resolution, it will not signify. The love of reading will, by that time, surely take the place of the duty, and do your mind vastly more good.

"It is difficult to give any general advice as to the selection of books, because so much depends on the character, opportunities, and leisure of the individual. . . . . It would be too painful for me to believe that there is one among you, to whom it is necessary to say, 'Regard the bible as the first and best of books.' But I fear, my young friends, that you read the bible much less than you should. The multitude of religious books and tracts have, in some measure, superseded it. You are attracted by a story, and, to get a little pure gold you receive a great deal of dross. Many of these books, I know, derive their spirit from the bible; many of them are useful and delightful; but let them take a subordinate place, and not encroach on the time you have to give to the reading of the bible. Do not be satisfied to drink from the stream which is imbued with much earthy material, when you can go to the pure fountain. . . . . You will find your pleasure in reading the bible incalculably increased, if you will read it not only with a spirit submissive to its Divine instruction, but with your mind awakened, and eager to understand it. There are Dictionaries of the Bible that explain what is obscure; there are books that will give you much light upon the history, customs, and modes of life among the Jews. There are others that explain the prophecies, and show you their fulfilment. . . . . If you can read but few books, be sure that the history of your own country is among them. Make yourself acquainted thoroughly with its institutions, its past and present condition, its extent, climate, laws, productions, and commerce. All these subjects come within our own sphere—they may be called domestic matters. Think you, if a woman was well instructed, well *read* on these topics, she would be as incapable of business, and therefore as dependent as she now is? . . . . Next to the history and condition of your own country, it is important that you acquaint yourselves with the history and condition of the countries whence your ancestors came. Then you will be able to compare your country with other countries, your own times with preceding ages. Thus informed, you will not fall into the common national vanity of fancying all knowledge, all virtue, and all progress, concentrated in the United States; nor into a worse error, a culpable ignorance of the advantages of your own country, and insensibility to them. . . . You will find well written and authentic travels a very improving and delightful kind of reading. You may lack money and opportunity to travel twenty miles from home, when for one or two dollars you may buy a book that will take you, with a well-instructed and all-observing companion, half over the world. Or, if you cannot expend the cost of the book, you may get it from a society, or district-library; or, borrow it from some kindly disposed person. . . . . . Good biographies are very improving books. The experience of others will often suggest models, advice, and reproof, that comes in the most inoffensive form. . . . Every well educated young person who has leisure for reading, should be well versed in English literature. . . . . In the wide department of fictitious writing, let your consciences restrain and direct your inclination, and rectify your taste. . . . . When our Saviour employed fiction in the parables of the prodigal son, and of the good Samaritan, it was, no doubt, to give to an important truth, a form that should be universally interesting and touching. Few will object to your reading such fictitious writings as do good to your hearts; and while you have such as Sir Walter Scott's, and Miss Edgeworth's, you have no excuse for reading the profligate and romantic novels of the last century, or the no less profligate and far more insidious romances of the present day.

"Next to 'what to read,' comes the great question 'how to read,' and I am not sure the last is not the weightier of the two. . . . . No book will improve you which does not make you think; which does not make your own mind work. This is as certain as that the mill is not improved by the corn that passes through it, or that the purse is none the richer for the money that has been in it. . . . . When you read, do not *take for granted*, believing, with ignorant credulity, whatever you see stated in a book. Remember an author is but one witness, and often a very fallible one. Pause in your reading, reflect, compare what the writer tells you with what you have learned from other sources on the subject, and, above all, use your own judgment independently, not presumptuously. . . . . . Knowing how short and precious time is, be more careful in the selection of your books than eager to read a great many. When you do read, read thoroughly and understandingly. . . . . It is a good practice to talk about a book you have just read; not to display your knowledge, for this is pedantry or something worse; but to make your reading a social blessing by communicating liberally to those in your family circle, who may have less time and opportunity for reading than you have. You may often, too, by the superior knowledge of a friend, correct the false impressions you have received. Or, your friend may have read the same book, and then it is a delightful point of sympathy. . . . . One word before I close this subject, as to the preservation of your books. If you love them, you will respect them, and unless you are incorrigibly slovenly and careless, you will not break off the covers, soil the leaves, and dog-ear the corners. . . . . There is a common and offensive habit destructive to books, which we should not presume to caution any *educating* little girl against, if we had not seen it practiced by *educated* men. This is wetting the fingers to turn over the leaves. . . . . Surely this should not be. When you borrow a book, put a cover on it before you read it. Use it with clean hands. Never lay it down on the face, nor where it is exposed to be knocked down by the next passer-by. Do not readily yield to any one's request to lend it again, but return it promptly and punctually. Perform the borrower's duty strictly, and Heaven bless you with liberal lenders."—*Miss C. M. Sedgwick: Means and Ends.*

Plan of Reading recommended by Thomas S. Grimke.

1. Before I commenced an author, I made myself thoroughly master *of the whole scheme of his work*, (if a table of contents and chapters enabled me to do so,) of the character of his whole system, of the *principles* on which he had separated and arranged the parts, and of their relation to each other, and to the whole. 2. I then studied the author in the following manner. After reading the first sentence, I meditated on it, developing the author's thought, as well as I was able; and reducing the whole, as nearly as possible, to a single, distinct, concise expression. I then read the second sentence, and did the same: and next compared the two sentences together, meditating on them, and gathering out of them their substance. Thus I went through the paragraph, and then reflected on the whole, until I had reduced it to a single sentence, containing its essence. I then studied the next paragraph in like manner: and having finished it I compared the two together, and gathered out of them their substance. The same plan was followed in the comparison of sections with sections, chapters with chapters, books with books, until the author was finished. This may appear, at first sight, an exceedingly tedious process; but any one, acquainted with the nature of the mind, knows the wonderful facility that would soon be acquired by a faithful, patient adherence to this mode of study, even through a single chapter. 3. A third rule was to pass nothing unexamined, nothing without reflection, whether in poetry or fiction, history or travels, politics, philosophy, or religion. Gratitude will not allow me to pass unnoticed the vast advantages derived from a humble, patient, thankful perusal of Watts' admirable book on the Improvement of the Mind. Nor ought I to omit the three rules of Professor Whitaker, of Cambridge, given to John Boyse, one of the eminent translators of the Bible in the time of James the 1st, to study chiefly standing or walking, never to study at a window, and not to go to bed, on any account, with cold feet.

It is an error to suppose that a course of study is confined to the period of *youth*, and that when a young man has left school or college, he has finished his education, and has nothing to study but his profession. In truth he has done little more than treasure up some of the important materials, and acquire the elementary habits and discipline, which are indispensable to the continued improvement of his mind. If he expects to be a scholar, not in the *literary* sense of the word, but in a far higher and nobler sense, as a Christian, patriot, philanthropist, and public servant, in the state or national councils, in literary, benevolent, and religious institutions; if he means to be distinguished for his sense of duty, and his spirit of usefulness, for just principles, enlarged views, dignified sentiments and liberal feelings, for sound thinking, and clear, close reasoning, let him be assured that he has done little more than lay the foundations, in the school, or even in the college, up to the age of twenty. He must make up his mind to be a devoted student, in spite of his professional engagements, for ten years at least; until he shall have been able to deepen and strengthen, and enlarge, and elevate his mind, so as to fit himself for solid, honorable, permanent usefulness. Let him remember, that the *school* only prepares the *youth* to enter on the course of study, appropriate to the *young man*: and that the *college* only enables the *young man* to enter on the course of study appropriate to the *man*. Manhood has its appropriate course of study, and the difference between men arises very much from their selection and pursuit of a right course of study. Many fine minds, capable of enlarged and durable improvement and usefulness, are lost every year to the community, in which their lot is cast, to the country they are bound to serve, to the cause of religion, humanity, justice and literature: because they have failed in this great duty, they have neglected the course of study, appropriate to manhood. And here let it be remarked, that the *true* student never considers how much he reads, but rather *how little*, and only *what* and *how* he reads.—*Grimke on Science, Education, and Literature*, p p. 54-56.

EDUCATION, STUDIES AND CONDUCT.

FOREIGN TRAVEL AS PART OF EDUCATION.

LETTER OF SIR PHILIP SIDNEY TO HIS BROTHER ROBERT, (EARL OF LEICESTER).

This letter originally appeared in a little volume entitled "Instructions for Travelers, by Robert Earl of Essex, Sir Philip Sidney and Secretary Davison, 1633." It was written in 1578, probably on the application of his brother Robert, about to set out on his travels, who had been urged by his father, Sir Henry Sidney, at that time Lord Deputy to the Queen for Ireland, "to look to the practice of your most loving brother. Imitate his virtues, exercises, studies and actions. Seek the knowledge of the estate of every prince, court, and city you pass through. Address yourself to the company, to learn this of the elder sort, and yet neglect not the younger. By one you shall gather learning, wisdom, and knowledge; by the other, acquaintance, languages and exercise."

Sir Philip Sidney, whose act and words on the fatal field of Zutphen, to the poor wounded soldier who, as he was borne by on a litter, cast a longing look on a bottle of wine which the wounded knight was putting to his own lips—"Poor fellow! thy necessity seems greater than mine," and pushed the bottle towards him—has outlived the memory of his 'Defense of Poesy,' or his 'Arcadia,' and all but the traditions of his many personal and intellectual accomplishments, was born November 29, 1554, at Penshurst, and died, as above intimated, from the wound received at Zutphen, October 16, 1586, in the very prime of his days, "the idol of his times—the soldier's, scholar's, courtier's eye, tongue, and word." His dying words to his brother were: 'Love my memory, cherish my friends. But above all, govern your will and affections by the will and word of your Creator, in me beholding the end of this world with all her vanities.' In his own travels, which occupied three years, he devoted himself to the studies, exercises and society for which each city had special opportunities,—at Vienna, to horsemanship; at Padua, to geometry and astronomy, for which the University was then famous; at Frankfort he cultivated the society of Hubert Languet, and at Venice, of Tasso.

My good brother,

You have thought unkindness in me that I have not written oftener unto you, and have desired I should write unto you something of my opinion touching your travels; you being persuaded my experience thereunto be something, which I must needs confess, but not as you take it; for you think my experience grows from the good things which I have learned; but I know the only experience which I have gotten, is to find how much I might have learned, and how much indeed I have missed, for want of directing my course to the right end, and by the right means. I think you have read Aristotle's Ethics; if you have, you know it is the beginning and foundation of all his works, the end to which every man doth and ought to bend his greatest and smallest actions. I am sure you have imprinted in your mind the scope and mark you mean by your pains to shoot at: for if you should travel but to travel, or to say you had traveled, certainly you should prove a pilgrim to no purpose. But I presume so well of you, that though a great number of us never thought in ourselves why we went, but a certain tickling humor to do as other men had done, you purpose, being a gentleman born, to furnish yourself with the knowledge of such things as may be serviceable for your country and calling; which certainly stands not in the change of air, for the warmest sun makes not a wise man; no, nor in learning languages, although they be of serviceable use, for words are but words in what language soever they be, and much less in that all of us come home full of disguisements, not only of apparel, but of our countenances, as though the credit of a traveler stood all upon his outside; but in the right informing your mind with those things which are most notable in those places which you come unto.

Of which as the one kind is so vain, as I think ere it be long, like the mountebanks in Italy, we travelers shall be made sport of in comedies; so may I justly say, who rightly travels with the eye of Ulysses, doth take one of the most excellent ways of worldly wisdom. For hard sure it is to know England, without you know it by comparing it with some other country, no more than a man can know the swiftness of his horse without seeing him well matched. For you, that are a logician, know, that as greatness of itself is a quantity, so yet the judgment of it, as of mighty riches and all other strengths, stands in the predicament of relation; so that you can not tell what the Queen of England is able to do defensively or offensively, but through knowing what they are able to do with whom she is to be matched. This, therefore, is one notable use of travelers, which stands in the mind and correlative knowledge of things, in which kind comes in the knowledge of all leagues betwixt prince and prince; the topographical description of each country; how the one lies by situation to hurt or help the other; how they are to the sea, well harbored or not; how stored with ships; how with revenue; how with fortification and garrisons; how the people, warlike, trained, or kept under, with many other such considerations, which as they confusedly come into my mind, so I, for want of leisure, hastily set them down; but these things, as I have said, are of the first kind.

The other kind of knowledge is of them which stand in the things which are in themselves either simply good, or simply bad, and so serve for a right instruction or a shunning example. These the poet meant in this verse, "Qui multos hominum mores cognovit et urbes." For he doth not mean by "mores" how to look, or put off one's cap with a new-found grace, although true behavior is not to be despised; marry my heresy is, that the English behavior is best in England, and the Italian's in Italy. But "mores" he takes for that from whence moral philosophy is so called; the certainness of true discerning of men's minds both in virtue, passion and vices. And when he saith, "cognovit urbes," he means not, if I be not deceived, to have seen towns, and marked their buildings; for surely houses are but houses in every place, they do but differ "secundum magis et minus;" but he attends to their religion, politics, laws, bringing up of children, discipline both for war and peace, and such like. These I take to be of the second kind, which are ever worthy to be known for their own sakes. As surely in the great Turk, though we have nothing to do with him, yet his discipline in war matters is worthy to be known and learned.

Nay, even in the kingdom of China, which is almost as far as the Antipodes from us, their good laws and customs are to be learned; but to know their riches and power is of little purpose for us, since that can neither advance nor hinder us. But in our neighbor countries, both these things are to be marked, as well the latter, which contain things for themselves, as the former, which seek to know both those, and how their riches and power may be to us available, or otherwise. The countries fittest for both these, are those you are going into. France is above all other most needful for us to mark, especially in the former kind; next is Spain and the Low Countries; then Germany, which in my opinion excels all others as much in the latter consideration, as the other doth in the former, yet neither are void of neither; for as Germany, methinks, doth excel in good laws, and well administering of justice, so are we likewise to consider in it the many princes with whom we may have league, the places of trade, and means to draw both soldiers and furniture thence in time of need. So on the other side, as in France and Spain, we are principally to mark how they stand towards us both in power and inclination; so are they, not without good and fitting use, even in the generality of wisdom to be known. As in France, the courts of parliament, their subaltern jurisdiction, and their continual keeping of paid soldiers. In Spain, their good and grave proceedings; their keeping so many provinces under them, and by what manner, with the true points of honor; wherein since they have the most open conceit, if they seem over curious, it is an easy matter to cut off when a man sees the bottom. Flanders likewise, besides the neighborhood with us, and the annexed considerations thereunto, hath divers things to be learned, especially their governing their merchants and other trades. Also for Italy, we know not what we have, or can have, to do with them, but to buy their silks and wines; and as for the other point, except Venice, whose good laws and customs we can hardly proportion to ourselves, because they are quite of a contrary government; there is little there but tyrannous oppression, and servile yielding to them that have little or no right over them. And for the men you shall have there, although indeed some be excellently learned, yet are they all given to counterfeit learning, as a man shall learn among them more false grounds of things than in any place else that I know; for, from a tapster upwards, they are all discoursers in certain matters and qualities, as horsemanship, weapons, painting, and such are better there than in other countries; but for other matters, as well, if not better, you shall have them in nearer places.

Now resteth in my memory but this point, which indeed is the chief to you of all others; which is the choice of what men you are to direct yourself to; for it is certain no vessel can leave a worse taste in the liquor it contains, than a wrong teacher infects an unskillful hearer with that which hardly will ever out: I will not tell you some absurdities I have heard travelers tell; taste him well before you drink much of his doctrine. And when you have heard it, try well what you have heard, before you hold it for a principle; for one error is the mother of a thousand. But you may say, how shall I get excellent men to take pains to speak with me? truly in few words, either by much expense or much humbleness.

Your most loving Brother,

PHILIP SIDNEY.

LORD BACON. ESSAY.—OF TRAVEL.

TRAVEL, in the younger sort, is a part of education; in the elder, a part of experience. He that travelleth into a country, before he hath some entrance into the language, goeth to school and not to travel. That young men travel under some tutor, or grave servant, I allow (*approve*) well; so that he be such a one that hath the language, and hath been in the country before; whereby he may be able to tell them what things are worthy to be seen in the country where they go, what acquaintances they are to seek, what exercises or discipline the place yieldeth; for else young men shall go hooded, and look abroad little. It is a strange thing that, in sea voyages, where there is nothing to be seen but sky and sea, men should make diaries; but in land travel, wherein so much is to be observed, for the most part they omit it; as if chance were fitter to be registered than observation: let diaries, therefore, be brought in use. The things to be seen and observed are the courts of princes, especially when they give audience to ambassadors; the courts of justice, while they sit and hear causes; and so of consistories ecclesiastic; the churches and monasteries, with the monuments that are therein extant; the walls and fortifications of cities and towns; and so the havens and harbors, antiquities and ruins, libraries, colleges, disputations, and lectures, where any are; shipping and navies; houses and gardens of state and pleasure, near great cities; armories, arsenals, magazines, exchanges, burses, warehouses, exercises of horsemanship, fencing, training of soldiers, and the like: comedies, such whereunto the better sort of persons do resort; treasuries of jewels and robes; cabinets and rarities; and, to conclude, whatsoever is memorable in the places where they go; after all which the tutors or servants ought to make diligent inquiry. As for triumphs, masks, feasts, weddings, funerals, capital executions, and such shows, men need not to be put in mind of them: yet they are not to be neglected. If you will have a young man to put his travel into a little room, and in short time to gather much, this you must do: first, as was said, he must have some entrance into the language before he goeth; then he must have such a servant, or tutor, as knoweth the country, as was likewise said: let him carry with him also some card, or book, describing the country where he travelleth, which will be a good key to his inquiry; let him keep also a diary; let him not stay long in one city or town, more or less as the place deserveth, but not long; nay, when he stayeth in one city or town, let him change his lodging from one end and part of the town to another, which is a great adamant (*loadstone*) of acquaintance; let him sequester himself from the company of his countrymen, and diet in such places where there is good company of the nation where he traveleth: let him, upon his removes from one place to another, procure recommendation to some person of quality residing in the place whither he removeth, that he may use his favor in those things he desireth to see or know: thus he may abridge his travel with much profit. As for the acquaintance which is to be sought in travel, that which is most of all profitable is acquaintance with the secretaries and employed men of ambassadors: for so in traveling in one country, he shall suck the experience of many: let him also see and visit eminent persons in all kinds, which are of great name abroad, that he may be able to tell how the life agreeth with the fame. For quarrels, they are with care and discretion to be avoided; they are commonly for mistresses, healths, place, and words: and let a man beware how he keepeth company with choleric and quarrelsome persons, for they will engage him in their own quarrels. When a traveler returneth home, let him not leave the countries where he hath traveled altogether behind him; but maintain a correspondence by letters with those of his acquaintance which are of most worth; and let his travel appear rather in his discourse than in his apparel or gesture; and in his discourse let him be rather advised in his answers than forward to tell stories: and let it appear that he doth not change his country manners for those of foreign parts; but only prick in some flowers of that which he hath learned abroad into the customs of his own country.

SHAKSPEARE—POLONIUS TO HIS SON LOTHARIO.

There, my blessing with you:
And these few precepts in thy memory
Look thou character:—
Give thy thoughts no tongue,
Nor any unproportioned thought his act.
Be thou familiar, but by no means vulgar:
The friends thou hast, and their adoption tried,
Grapple them to thy soul with hooks of steel;
But do not dull thy palm with entertainment
Of each new-hatched unfledged comrade. Beware
Of entrance to a quarrel; but, being in,
Bear 't, that th' opposer may beware of thee.
Give every man thine ear, but few thy voice;
Take each man's censure, but reserve thy judgment.
Costly thy habit as thy purse can buy,

But not express'd in fancy; rich, not gaudy:
For the apparel oft proclaims the man;
And they in France, of the best rank and station,
Are most select and generous, chief in that.
Neither a borrower, nor a lender be;
For loan oft loses both itself and friend,
And borrowing dulls the edge of husbandry.
This above all,—to thine ownself be true;
And it must follow, as the night the day,
Thou canst not then be false to any man.—*Hamlet.*

JOHN MILTON.

Milton, having improved every facility of culture at home and school, and tested the value of foreign travel in his own experience, but entering on it only when his own mind was well disciplined, and furnished with a knowledge of the government, history, language and literature of the countries which he proposed to visit, and furnished too with letters from scholars and statesmen which introduced him to men eminent in science and public administration—thus educated and equipped, Milton, in his 'plan of a complete and virtuous education to fit the ingenuous youth of England for the exigencies of private and public life, in peace or war,' thus speaks of the advantages of travel:

Besides these constant exercises at home, there is another opportunity of gaining experience to be won from pleasure itself abroad; in those vernal seasons of the year, when the air is calm and pleasant, it were an injury and sullenness against nature not to go out and see her riches, and partake of her rejoicing with heaven and earth. I should not, therefore, be a persuader to them of studying much then, after two or three years that they have well laid their grounds, but to ride out in companies, with prudent and staid guides, to all quarters of the land, learning and observing all places of strength, all commodities of building, and of soil for towns and tillage, harbors and ports for trade. Sometimes taking sea as far as to our navy, to learn there also what they can in the practical knowledge of sailing and sea-fight. These ways would try all the peculiar gifts of nature, and if there were any secret excellence, would fetch it out and give it fair opportunities to advance itself by, which could not but mightily redound to the good of this nation, and bring into fashion again those old admired virtues and excellences with far more advantage now in this purity of Christian knowledge. If they desire to see other countries at three or four-and-twenty years of age, not to learn principles, but to enlarge experience and make wise observation, they will by that time be such as shall deserve the regard and honor of all men where they pass, and the society and friendship of those, in all places, who are best and most eminent.

LORD LITTLETON.

Me other cares in other climes engage—
In various knowledge to improve my youth,
And conquer prejudice, worst foe to Truth;
By foreign arts, domestic faults to mend,
Enlarge my notions and my views extend;
The useful science of the world to know,
Which books can never teach, or pedants show.

LORD HARDWICKE.

I WISH, sir, you would make people understand that travel is really the last step to be taken in the instruction of youth: and that to set out with it, is to begin where they should end. Certainly the true end of visiting foreign parts is to look into their customs and policies, and observe in what particulars they excel or come short of our own; to unlearn some odd peculiarities in our manners, and wear off such awkward stiffnesses and affectations in our behavior, as may possibly have been contracted from constantly associating with one nation of men, by a more free, general, and mixed conversation. But how can any of these advantages be attained by one who is a mere stranger to the customs and policies of his native country, and has not yet fixed in his mind the first principles of manners and behavior? To endeavor it, is to build a gaudy structure without any foundation; or, if I may be allowed the expression, to work a rich embroidery upon a cobweb.

Another end of traveling, which deserves to be considered, is the improving our taste for the best authors of antiquity, by seeing the places where they lived, and of which they wrote; to compare the natural face of the country with the description they have given us, and observe how well the picture agrees with the original. This must certainly be a most charming exercise to the mind that is rightly turned for it; besides that it may in a good measure be made subservient to morality, if the person is capable of drawing just conclusions concerning the uncertainty of human things, from the ruinous alterations time and barbarity have brought upon so many places, cities, and whole countries, which make the most illustrious figures in history. And this hint may be not a little improved by examining every spot of ground that we find celebrated as the scene of some famous action, or retaining any footsteps of a Cato, Cicero, or Brutus, or some such great virtuous men. A nearer view of any such particular, though really little and trifling in itself, may serve the more powerfully to warm a generous mind to an emulation of their virtues, and a greater ardency of ambition to imitate their bright examples, if it comes duly tempered and prepared for the impression. But this I believe you will hardly think those to be, who are so far from entering into the sense and spirit of the ancients, that they do not yet understand their language with any exactness.

PHILIP YORKE (afterwards Earl of Hardwicke), in Spectator 364.

MACAULAY.—ON DR. JOHNSON'S ESTIMATE OF TRAVEL AND HISTORY.

IT is remarkable that to the last he [Dr. Johnson] entertained a fixed contempt for all those modes of life and those studies which tend to emancipate the mind from the prejudices of a particular age or particular nation. Of foreign travel and of history he spoke with the fierce and boisterous contempt of ignorance. "What does a man learn by traveling? Is Beauclerk the better for traveling? What did Lord Charlemont learn in his travels, except that there was a snake in one of the pyramids of Egypt?" History was, in his opinion, to use the fine expression of Lord Plunket, 'an old almanac.' Historians could, as he conceived, claim no higher dignity than that of almanac-makers; and his favorite historians were those who, like Lord Hailes, aspired to no higher dignity. He always spoke with contempt of Robertson. Hume he would not even read. He affronted one of his friends for talking to him about Cataline's conspiracy, and declared that he never desired to hear of the Punic war again as long as he lived.

Assuredly one fact which does not directly affect our own interest, considered in itself, is no better worth knowing than another fact. The fact that there is a snake in a pyramid, or the fact that Hannibal crossed the Alps, are in themselves as unprofitable to us as the fact that there is a green blind in a particular house in Threadneedle Street, or the fact that a Mr. Smith comes into the city every morning on the top of one of the Blackwall stages. But it is certain that those who will not crack the shell of history, will never get at the kernel. Johnson, with hasty arrogance, pronounced the kernel worthless, because he saw no value in the shell. The real use of traveling to distant countries and of studying the annals of past times, is to preserve men from the contraction of mind which those can hardly escape whose whole communion is with one generation and one neighborhood, who arrive at conclusions by means of an induction not sufficiently copious, and who therefore constantly confound exceptions with rules, and accidents with essential properties. In short, the real use of traveling and of studying history is to keep men from being what Tom Dawson was in fiction, and Samuel Johnson in reality.

DR. AIKIN—HOW TO OBSERVE.

JOHN AIKIN, M. D., was born in Kibworth, in Lancashire, in 1747, educated at Warrington and Edinburgh, and took his medical degree at Leyden in 1784. He was for a time principal of a dissenting academy at Warrington, but pursued his medical practice at Yarmouth and Stoke Newington, London. He commenced his literary career by publishing, in connection with his sister, (Mrs. Anna Letitia Barbauld) Evenings at Home, in which the following illustration of the too common practice of travelers, old and young, first appeared:

EYES AND NOT EYES; OR THE ART OF SEEING.

Conversation between a Tutor and his two pupils, Robert and William.

Tutor. Well, Robert, where have you been walking this afternoon? (said a Tutor to one of his pupils at the close of a holyday.)

Robert. I have been to Broom-heath, and so round by the windmill upon Camp-mount, and home through the meadows by the river side.

T. Well, that is a pleasant round.

R. I thought it very dull, sir; I scarcely met with a single person. I would much rather have gone along the turnpike-road.

T. Why, if seeing men and horses is your object, you would, indeed, be better entertained on the high-road. But did you see William?

R. We set out together, but he lagged behind in the lane, so I walked on and left him.

T. That was a pity. He would have been company for you.

R. O, he is so tedious, always stopping to look at this thing and that! I would rather walk alone. I dare say he is not got home yet.

T. Here he comes. Well, William, where have you been?

William. O, the pleasantest walk! I went all over Broom-heath, and so up to the mill at the top of the hill, and then down among the green meadows by the side of the river.

T. Why, that is just the round Robert has been taking, and he complains of its dullness, and prefers the high-road.

W. I wonder at that. I am sure I hardly took a step that did not delight me; and I have brought home my handkerchief full of curiosities.

T. Suppose, then, you give us an account of what amused you so much. I fancy it will be as new to Robert as to me.

W. I will do it readily. The lane leading to the heath, you know, is close and sandy, so I did not mind it much, but made the best of my way. However, I spied a curious thing enough in the hedge. It was an old crabtree, out of which grew a great bunch of something green, quite different from the tree itself. Here is a branch of it.

T. Ah! this is mistletoe, a plant of great fame for the use made of it by the Druids of old, in their religious rites and incantations. It bears a very slimy white berry, of which birdlime may be made, whence the Latin name *viscus*. It is one of those plants which do not grow in the ground by a root of their own, but fix themselves upon other plants; whence they have been humorously styled *parasitical*, as being hangers on, or dependents. It was the mistletoe of the oak that the Druids particularly honored.

W. A little further on I saw a green woodpecker fly to a tree, and run up the trunk like a cat.

T. That was to seek for insects in the bark, on which they live. They bore holes with their strong bills for that purpose, and do much damage to the trees by it.

W. What beautiful birds they are!

T. Yes; they have been called, from their color and size, the English parrot.

W. When I got upon the open heath, how charming it was! The air seemed so fresh, and the prospect on every side so free and unbounded! Then it was all covered with gay flowers, many of which I had never observed before. There were at least three kinds of heath, (I have got them in my handkerchief here,) and gorse, and broom, and bellflower, and many others of all colors, of which I will beg you presently to tell me the names.

T. That I will, readily.

W. I saw, too, several birds that were new to me. There was a pretty grayish one, of the size of a lark, that was hopping about some great stones; and when he flew, he showed a great deal of white above his tail.

T. That was a wheat-ear. They are reckoned very delicious birds to eat, and frequent the open downs in Sussex, and some other counties, in great numbers.

W. There was a flock of lapwings upon a marshy part of the heath, that amused me much. As I came near them, some of them kept flying round and round just over my head, and crying *pewet* so distinctly, one might almost fancy they spoke. I thought I should have caught one of them, for he flew as if one of his wings was broken, and often tumbled close to the ground; but as I came near, he always contrived to get away.

T. Ha, ha! you were finely taken in, then! This was all an artifice of the bird's, to entice you away from its nest: for they build upon the bare ground, and their nest would easily be observed, did not they draw off the attention of intruders, by their loud cries and counterfeit lameness.

W. I wish I had known that, for he led me a long chase, often over shoes in water. However, it was the cause of my falling in with an old man and a boy, who were cutting and piling up turf for fuel; and I had a good deal of talk with them, about the manner of preparing the turf, and the price it sells at. They gave me, too, a creature I never saw before—a young viper, which they had just killed, together with its dam. I have seen several common snakes, but this is thicker in proportion, and of a darker color than they are.

T. True. Vipers frequent those turfy boggy grounds pretty much, and I have known several turf-cutters bitten by them.

W. They are very venomous, are they not?

T. Enough so to make their wounds painful and dangerous, though they seldom prove fatal.

W. Well—I then took my course up to the windmill on the mount. I climbed up the steps of the mill in order to get a better view of the country round. What an extensive prospect! I counted fifteen church steeples; and I saw several gentlemen's houses peeping out from the midst of green woods and plantations; and I could trace the windings of the river all along the low grounds, till it was lost behind a ridge of hills. But I'll tell you what I mean to do, if you will give me leave.

T. What is that?

W. I will go again, and take with me Carey's county map, by which I shall probably be able to make out most of the places.

T. You shall have it, and I will go with you, and take my pocket spying-glass.

W. I shall be very glad of that. Well—a thought struck me, that as the hill is called *Camp-mount*, there might probably be some remains of ditches and mounds, with which I have read that camps were surrounded. And I really believe I discovered something of that sort running round one side of the mount.

T. Very likely you might. I know antiquaries have described such remains as existing there, which some suppose to be Roman, others Danish. We will examine them further when we go.

W. From the hill I went straight down to the meadows below, and walked on the side of a brook that runs into the river. It was all bordered with reeds, and flags, and tall flowering plants, quite different from those I had seen on the heath. As I was getting down the bank to reach one of them, I heard something plunge into the water near me. It was a large water-rat, and I saw it swim over to the other side, and go into its hole. There were a great many large dragon-flies all about the stream. I caught one of the finest, and have got him here in a leaf. But how I longed to catch a bird that I saw hovering over the water, and every now and then darting down into it! It was all over a mixture of the most beautiful green and blue, with some orange color. It was somewhat less than a thrush, and had a large head and bill, and a short tail.

T. I can tell you what that bird was—a kingfisher, the celebrated halcyon of the ancients, about which so many tales are told. It lives on fish, which it catches in the manner you saw. It builds in holes in the banks; and is a shy, retired bird, never to be seen far from the stream where it inhabits.

W. I must try to get another sight of him, for I never saw a bird that pleased me so much. Well, I followed this little brook till it entered the river, and then took the path that runs along the bank. On the opposite side I observed several little birds running along the shore, and making a piping noise. They were brown and white, and about as big as a snipe.

T. I suppose they were sand-pipers, one of the numerous family of birds that get their living by wading among the shallows, and picking up worms and insects.

W. There were a great many swallows, too, sporting upon the surface of the water, that entertained me with their motions. Sometimes they dashed into the stream; sometimes they pursued one another so quickly, that the eye could scarcely follow them. In one place, where a high steep sand-bank rose directly above the river, I observed many of them go in and out of holes, with which the bank was bored full.

T. Those were sand-martins, the smallest of our four species of swallows. They are of a mouse-color above, and white beneath. They make their nests, and bring up their young in these holes, which run a great depth, and by their situation are secure from all plunderers.

W. A little further I saw a man in a boat, who was catching eels in an odd way. He had a long pole, with broad iron prongs at the end, just like Neptune's trident, only there were five instead of three. This he pushed straight down into the mud, in the deepest parts of the river, and fetched up the eels sticking between the prongs.

T. I have seen this method. It is called, spearing of eels.

W. While I was looking at him, a heron came flying over my head, with his large flagging wings. He alighted at the next turn of the river, and I crept softly behind the bank to watch his motions. He had waded into the water as far as his long legs would carry him, and was standing with his neck drawn in, looking intently on the stream. Presently he darted his long bill as quick as lightning into the water, and drew out a fish, which he swallowed. I saw him catch another in the same manner. He then took alarm at some noise I made, and flew away slowly to a wood at some distance, where he settled.

T. Probably his nest was there, for herons build upon the loftiest tree they can find, and sometimes in society together, like rooks. Formerly, when these birds were valued for the amusement of hawking, many gentlemen had their *heronries*, and a few are still remaining.

W. I think they are the largest wild birds we have.

T. They are of great length and spread of wing, but their bodies are comparatively small.

W. I then turned homewards across the meadows, where I stopped awhile to look at a large flock of starlings, which kept flying about at no great distance. I could not tell at first what to make of them; for they rose altogether from the ground as thick as a swarm of bees, and formed themselves into a kind of black cloud hovering over the field. After taking a short round they settled again, and presently rose again in the same manner. I dare say there were hundreds of them.

T. Perhaps so; for in the fenny countries their flocks are so numerous as to break down whole acres of reeds, by settling on them. This disposition of starlings to fly in close swarms, was remarked even by Homer, who compares the foe flying from one of his heroes, to a *cloud* of starlings retiring dismayed at the approach of the hawk.

W. After I had left the meadows, I crossed the cornfields in the way to our house, and passed close by a deep marl pit. Looking into it, I saw, on one of the sides, a cluster of what I took to be shells; and upon going down, I picked up a clod of marl, which was quite full of them; but how sea shells could get there, I can not imagine.

T. I do not wonder at your surprise, since many philosophers have been much perplexed to account for the same appearance. It is not uncommon to find great quantities of shells and relics of marine animals, even in the bowels of high mountains, very remote from the sea.

W. I got to the high field next to our house just as the sun was setting, and I stood looking at it till it was quite lost. What a glorious sight! The clouds were tinged with purple and crimson, and yellow of all shades and hues, and the clear sky varied from blue to a fine green at the horizon. But how large the sun appears just as it sets! I think it seems twice as big as when it is over head.

T. It does so; and you may probably have observed the same apparent enlargement of the moon at its rising.

W. I have; but pray what is the reason of this?

T. It is an optical deception, depending upon principles which I can not well explain to you, till you know more of that branch of science. But what a number of new ideas this afternoon's walk has afforded you? I do not wonder that you found it amusing; it has been very instructive, too. Did you see nothing of all these sights, *Robert?*

R. I saw some of them, but I did not take particular notice of them.

T. Why not?

R. I do not know. I did not care about them; and I made the best of my way home.

T. That would have been right, if you had been sent on a message; but as you only walked for amusement, it would have been wiser to have sought out as many sources of it as possible. But so it is—one man walks through the world with his eyes open, and another with them shut; and upon this difference depends all the superiority of knowledge the one acquires above the other. I have known sailors who had been in all the quarters of the world, and could tell you nothing but the signs of the tippling-houses they frequented in different ports, and the price and quality of the liquor. On the other hand, a Franklin could not cross the channel without making some observations useful to mankind. While many a vacant, thoughtless youth is whirled throughout Europe without gaining a single idea worth crossing a street for, the observing eye and inquiring mind find matter of improvement and delight in every ramble in town and country. Do you then, *William*, continue to make use of your eyes; and you, *Robert*, learn that eyes were given you to use.

STUDIES AND CONDUCT.

MANNERS, OR GOOD BEHAVIOR.

Manners, Behavior or Good Breeding, holds an important place in every scheme of liberal culture. It has been variously defined or rather described—by Swift 'as the art of making those people easy with whom we converse;' by Chesterfield 'as the result of much good sense, some good nature, and a little self-denial for the sake of others, and with a view to obtain the same indulgence from them,' and again as that 'without which the scholar is a pedant, the philosopher a cynic, the soldier a brute, and every man disagreeable;' by Ralph Waldo Emerson 'as the silent and subtle language of the figure, movement and gesture, and the whole action of the human machine;' by Landor 'as a power, which takes away the weight and galling from any other power we may exercise, and the want of which always leaves room for a suspicion of folly;' by Steele 'as supplying the small change for ordinary traffic, even if the coffers are filled with gold;' by Lord Chatham, as 'benevolence in trifles, or the preference of others to ourselves in the little daily, hourly occurrences in the commerce of life. The habitual attention to the little wants of those we are with, by which we prevent or remove them.' It is in brief the application of the Christian Rule 'of doing unto others as we would have others do unto us,' in the small as well as the great matters of life.

Good sense, a sincere desire to please, quick observation and analysis of the subtle influences which go out from the presence, speech and movements of a well-bred person, and the frequenting the society of men and women, to whom good manners is an unconscious habit—are the best school and teachers of this branch of social training.

We propose to bring together suggestions which have received the stamp of success, for the cultivation of this social virtue and grace of character—not the chief end of man here below, but the Corinthian capital of the solid fabric of a consummate education.

JONATHAN SWIFT, D.D.

The following suggestions constitute "*The treatise on Good Manners and Good Breeding*," which was published soon after the Dean's death, and are substantially the same as printed in No. 20 of the Tatler, issued March 6, 1710–11. They have been very much praised as "containing the substance of all the doctrine on this subject."

GOOD MANNERS.

Good manners is the art of making those people easy with whom we converse.

Whoever makes the fewest persons uneasy is the best bred in the company.

As the best law is founded upon reason, so are the best manners. And as some lawyers have introduced unreasonable things into common law, so likewise many teachers have introduced absurd things into common good manners.

One principal point of this art is, to suit our behavior to the three several degrees of men; our superiors, our equals, and those below us.

For instance, to press either of the two former to eat or drink is a breach of manners; but a tradesman or a farmer must be thus treated, or else it will be difficult to persuade them that they are welcome.

Pride, ill-nature, and want of sense, are the three great sources of ill-manners: without some one of these defects, no man will behave himself ill for want of experience, or of what, in the language of fools, is called knowing the world.

I defy any one to assign an incident wherein reason will not direct us what to say or do in company, if we are not misled by pride or ill-nature.

Therefore I insist that good sense is the principal foundation of good manners; but because the former is a gift which very few among mankind are possessed of, therefore all the civilized nations of the world have agreed upon fixing some rules upon common behavior best suited to their general customs or fancies, as a kind of artificial good sense, to supply the defects of reason. Without which the gentlemanly part of dunces would be perpetually at cuffs, as they seldom fail when they happen to be drunk, or engaged in squabbles about women or play. And, God be thanked, there hardly happens a duel in a year, which may not be imputed to one of these three motives. Upon which account, I should be exceedingly sorry to find the legislature make any new laws against the practice of duelling; because the methods are easy and many for a wise man to avoid a quarrel with honor, or engage in it with innocence. And I can discover no political evil in suffering bullies, sharpers, and rakes, to rid the world of each other by a method of their own, where the law has not been able to find an expedient.

As the common forms of good manners were intended for regulating the conduct of those who have weak understandings; so they have been corrupted by the persons for whose use they were contrived. For these people have fallen into a needless and endless way of multiplying ceremonies, which have been extremely troublesome to those who practice them, and insupportable to everybody else: insomuch that wise men are often more uneasy at the over-civility of these refiners than they could possibly be in the conversation of peasants or mechanics.

The impertinencies of this ceremonial behavior are nowhere better seen than at those tables where the ladies preside, who value themselves upon account of their good-breeding; where a man must reckon upon passing an hour without doing any one thing he has a mind to; unless he will be so hardy as to break through all the settled decorum of the family. She determines what he loves best, and how much he shall eat; and if the master of the house happens to be of the same disposition, he proceeds in the same tyrannical manner to prescribe in the drinking part: at the same time you are under the necessity of answering a thousand apologies for your entertainment. And although a good deal of this humor is pretty well worn off among many people of the best fashion, yet too much of it still remains, especially in the country; where an honest gentleman assured me, that having been kept four days against his will at a friend's house, with all the circumstances of hiding his boots, locking up the stable, and other contrivances of the like nature, he could not remember, from the moment he came into the house to the moment he left it, any one thing wherein his inclination was not directly contradicted; as if the whole family had entered into a combination to torment him.

But, beside all this, it would be endless to recount the many foolish and ridiculous accidents I have observed among these unfortunate proselytes to ceremony. I have seen a duchess fairly knocked down, by the precipitancy of an officious coxcomb running to save her the trouble of opening a door. I remember, upon a birthday at court, a great lady was rendered utterly disconsolate by a dish of sauce let fall by a page directly upon her head-dress and brocade, while she gave a sudden turn to her elbow upon some point of ceremony with the person who sat next to her. Monsieur Buys, the Dutch envoy, whose politics and manners were much of a size, brought a son with him, about thirteen years old, to a great table at court. The boy and his father, whatever they put on their plates, they first offered round in order, to every person in company; so that we could not get a minute's quiet during the whole dinner. At last their two plates happened to encounter, and with so much violence, that, being china, they broke in twenty pieces, and stained half the company with wet sweetmeats and cream.

There is a pedantry in manners, as in all arts and sciences; and sometimes in trades. Pedantry is properly the over-rating of any kind of knowledge we pretend to. And if that kind of knowledge be a trifle in itself, the pedantry is the greater. For which reason I look upon fiddlers, dancing-masters, heralds, masters of the ceremony, &c., to be greater pedants than Lipsius, or the elder Scaliger. With this kind of pedants, the court, while I knew it, was always plentifully stocked; I mean from the gentleman usher (at least) inclusive, downward to the gentleman porter: who are, generally speaking, the most insignificant race of people that this island can afford, and with the smallest tincture of good manners; which is the only trade they profess. For, being wholly illiterate, and conversing chiefly with each other, they reduce the whole system of breeding within the forms and circles of their several offices: and, as they are below the notice of ministers, they live and die in court under all revolutions, with great obsequiousness to those who are in any degree of credit or favor, and with rudeness and insolence to everybody else. Whence I have long concluded, that good manners are not a plant of the court growth: for if they were, those people, who have understandings directly of a level for such acquirements, who have served such long apprenticeships to nothing else, would certainly have picked them up. For, as to the great officers, who attend the prince's person or councils, or preside in his family, they are a transient body, who have no better a title to good manners than their neighbors, nor will probably have recourse to gentlemen ushers for instruction. So that I know little to be learned at court upon this head, except in the material circumstance of dress; wherein the authority of the maids of honor must indeed be allowed to be almost equal to that of a favorite actress.

I make a difference between good manners and good breeding;

although, in order to vary my expression, I am sometimes forced to confound them. By the first, I only understand the art of remembering and applying certain settled forms of general behavior. But good-breeding is of a much larger extent; for, beside an uncommon degree of literature sufficient to qualify a gentleman for reading a play or a political pamphlet, it takes in a great compass of knowledge; no less than that of dancing, fighting, gaming, making the circle of Italy, riding the great horse, and speaking French; not to mention some other secondary or subaltern accomplishments, which are more easily acquired. So that the difference between good breeding and good manners lies in this, that the former can not be attained to by the best understandings without study and labor; whereas a tolerable degree of reason will instruct us in every part of good manners, without other assistance.

I can think of nothing more useful upon this subject than to point out some particulars, wherein the very essentials of good manners are concerned, the neglect or perverting of which does very much disturb the good commerce of the world, by introducing a traffic of mutual uneasiness in most companies.

First, A necessary part of good manners is a punctual observance of time at our own dwellings, or those of others, or at third places; whether upon matter of civility, business, or diversion; which rule, though it be a plain dictate of common reason, yet the greatest minister I ever knew was the greatest trespasser against it; by which all his business doubled upon him, and placed him in a continual arrear. Upon which I often used to rally him, as deficient in point of good manners. I have known more than one ambassador and secretary of state, with a very moderate portion of intellectuals, execute their offices with good success and applause, by the mere force of exactness and regularity. If you duly observe time for the service of another, it doubles the obligation; if upon your own account, it would be manifest folly, as well as ingratitude, to neglect it; if both are concerned, to make your equal or inferior attend on you to his own disadvantage is pride and injustice

Ignorance of forms can not properly be styled ill manners, because forms are subject to frequent changes; and consequently, being not founded upon reason, are beneath a wise man's regard. Besides, they vary in every country; and after a short period of time, very frequently in the same; so that a man who travels must needs be at first a stranger to them in every court through which he passes; and, perhaps, at his return, as much a stranger in his own; and after all, they are easier to be remembered or forgotten than faces or names.

Indeed, among the many impertinencies that superficial young men bring with them from abroad, this bigotry of forms is one of the principal, and more predominant than the rest; who look upon them not only as if they were matters capable of admitting of choice, but even as points of importance; and are therefore zealous on all occasions to introduce and propagate the new forms and fashions they have brought back with them; so that, usually speaking, the worst bred person in company is a young traveler just returned from abroad.

Hints on Good Manners, by Swift.

Good manners is the art of making every reasonable person in the company easy, and to be easy ourselves.

What passes for good manners in the world generally produces quite contrary effects.

Many persons, of both sexes, whom I have known, and who passed for well-bred in their own and the world's opinion, are the most troublesome in company to others and themselves.

Nothing is so great an instance of ill-manners as flattery. If you flatter all the company, you please none: if you flatter only one or two, you affront the rest.

Flattery is the worst and falsest way of showing our esteem.

Argument, as usually managed, is the worst sort of conversation; as it is generally in books the worst sort of reading.

Good conversation is not to be expected in much company, because few listen, and there is continual interruption. But good or ill manners are discovered, let the company be ever so large.

Perpetual aiming at wit a very bad part of conversation. It is done to support a character; it generally fails: it is a sort of insult on the company, and a constraint upon the speaker.

For a man to talk in his own trade, or business, or faculty, is a great breach of good manners. Divines, physicians, lawyers, soldiers, particularly poets, are frequently guilty of this weakness.

Courts are the worst of all schools to teach good manners.

A courtly bow, or gait, or dress, are no part of good manners; and therefore every man of good understanding is capable of being well-bred upon any occasion.

To speak in such a manner as may possibly offend any reasonable person in company, is the highest instance of ill manners. Good manners chiefly consist in action, not in words. Modesty and humility the chief ingredients.

THE WELL ORDERING OF LIFE.

MONEY—ITS ACQUISITION AND MANAGEMENT.

INTRODUCTION.

There is no one subject on which the young—of either sex, and in all conditions and professions, and especially those who aim at high scholarship and culture, and desire to live with character, independence, and power—need to form clear conceptions and practical aims, than on money—its acquisition, utilities, and management. In this country, the art of acquisition is pretty well understood; for which we are indebted, mainly, to the necessities of a poor but intelligent ancestry, and the possession of rich but undeveloped material and facilities, but in no small degree to the maxims of POOR RICHARD, which, by household and school-book repetition, have become inwrought into the texture of every American mind. But with increased prosperity, we have enough of prodigal spending, as well as munificent giving; but there is a sad sacrifice of health, intellect, and conscience in the pursuit of wealth, and still larger waste of happiness, utilities, and power in its management and final disposition. On all of these points, our English literature is rich with APPLES OF GOLD—*the words of the wise.*

DR. FRANKLIN AS POOR RICHARD.

THE WAY TO WEALTH.

The sayings in the following paper were first published by Benjamin Franklin (born at Boston, in 1706, and died at Philadelphia, in 1790) in successive issues of an almanac entitled "Poor Richard," and subsequently printed under the name of The Way to Wealth:

COURTEOUS READER,

I have heard that nothing gives an author so great pleasure as to find his works respectfully quoted by others. Judge, then, how much I must have been gratified by an incident I am going to relate to you. I stopped my horse lately, where a great number of people were collected at an auction of merchants' goods. The hour of the sale not being come, they were conversing on the badness of the times; and one of the company called to a plain, clean old man, with white locks, "Pray, father Abraham, what think you of the times? Will not these heavy taxes quite ruin the country? how shall we be ever able to pay them? What would you advise us to?" Father Abraham stood up, and replied, "If you would have my advice, I will give it you in short; 'for a word to the wise is enough,' as poor Richard says." They joined in desiring him to speak his mind, and, gathering round him, he proceeded as follows:

"Friends," said he, "the taxes are indeed very heavy; and, if those laid on by the government were the only ones we had to pay, we might more easily discharge them; but we have many others, and much more grievous to some of us. We are taxed twice as much by our idleness, three times as much by our pride, and four times as much by our folly; and from these taxes the commissioners cannot ease or deliver us by allowing an abatement. However, let us hearken to good advice, and something may be done for us; 'God helps them that help themselves,' as poor Richard says.

"I. It would be thought a hard government that should tax its people one-tenth part of their time to be employed in its service; but idleness taxes many of us much more: sloth, by bringing on diseases, absolutely shortens life. 'Sloth, like rust, consumes faster than labor wears; while the used key is always bright,' as Poor Richard says. 'But dost thou love life, then do not squander time, for that is the stuff life is made of,' as Poor Richard says. How much more than is necessary do we spend in sleep! forgetting that 'The sleeping fox catches no poultry,' and that 'there will be sleeping enough in the grave,' as Poor Richard says.

"'If time be of all things the most precious, wasting time must be,' as Poor Richard says, 'the greatest prodigality;' since, as he elsewhere tells us, 'Lost time is never found again; and what we call time enough, always proves little enough.' Let us then up and be doing, and doing to the purpose, so by diligence shall we do more with less perplexity. 'Sloth makes all things difficult, but industry all easy;' and 'he that riseth late, must trot all day, and shall scarce overtake his business at night;' while laziness travels so slowly, that poverty soon overtakes him. 'Drive thy business, let not that drive thee;' and 'early to bed, and early to rise, makes a man healthy, wealthy, and wise,' as Poor Richard says.

So what signifies wishing and hoping for better times? We may make these times better, if we bestir ourselves. 'Industry need not wish, and he that lives upon hopes will die fasting.' 'There are no gains without pains; then help hands, for I have no lands;' or if I have, they are smartly taxed. 'He that hath a trade, hath an estate; and he that hath a calling, hath an office of profit and honor,' as Poor Richard says; but then the trade must be worked at, and the calling well followed, or neither the estate nor the office will enable us to pay our taxes. If we are industrious, we shall never starve; for 'at the workingman's house hunger looks in, but dares not enter.' Nor will the bailiff or the constable enter, for 'industry pays debts, while despair increaseth them.' What though you have found no treasure, nor has any rich relation left a legacy. 'Diligence is the mother of good luck, and God gives all things to industry.' 'Then plough deep, while sluggards sleep, and you shall have corn to sell and to keep.' Work while it is called to-day, for you know not how much you may be hindered to-morrow. 'One to-day is worth two to-morrows,' as Poor Richard says; and farther, 'Never leave that till to-morrow, which you can do to-day.' If you were a servant, would you not be ashamed that a good master should catch you idle? Are you then your own master? Be ashamed to catch yourself idle, when there is so much to be done for yourself, your family, your country, and your king. Handle your tools without mittens; remember, that 'The cat in gloves catches no mice,' as Poor Richard says. It is true there is much to be done, and, perhaps, you are weak-handed; but stick to it steadily, and you will see great effects; for 'Constant dropping wears away stones;' and 'by diligence and patience the mouse ate in two the cable;' and 'little strokes fell great oaks.'

"Methinks I hear some of you say, 'Must a man afford himself no leisure?' I will tell thee, my friend, what Poor Richard says: 'Employ thy time well, if thou meanest to gain leisure; and, since thou art not sure of a minute, throw not away an hour.' Leisure is time for doing something useful; this leisure the diligent man will obtain, but the lazy man never; for 'A life of leisure and a life of laziness are two things. Many, without labor, would live by their wits only, but they break for want of stock;' whereas industry gives comfort, and plenty, and respect. 'Fly pleasures and they will follow you.' 'The diligent spinner has a large shift; and now I have a sheep and a cow, everybody bids me good morrow.'

"II. But with our industry we must likewise be steady, settled, and careful, and oversee our own affairs with our own eyes, and not trust too much to others, for, as Poor Richard says,

'I never saw an oft removed tree,
Nor yet an oft removed family,
That throve so well as those that settled be.'

"And again, 'Three removes is as bad as a fire;' and again, 'Keep thy shop, and thy shop will keep thee;' and again, 'If you would have your business done, go; if not, send;' and again,

'He that by the plough would thrive,
Himself must either hold or drive.'

And again, 'The eye of the master will do more work than both his hands;' and again, 'Want of care does us more damage than want of knowledge;' and again, 'Not to oversee workmen, is to leave them your purse open.' Trusting too much to others' care is the ruin of many; for 'In the affairs of this world, men are saved, not by faith, but by the want of it;' but a man's own care is profitable, for, 'If you would have a faithful servant, and one that you like, serve yourself.' 'A little neglect may breed great mischief;' 'for want of a nail the shoe was lost; for want of a shoe the horse was lost; and for want of a horse the rider was lost,' being overtaken and slain by the enemy; all for want of a little care about a horse-shoe nail.

"III. So much for industry, my *friends*, and attention to one's own business; but to these we must add frugality, if we would make our industry more certainly successful. A man may, if he knows not how to save as he gets, keep his nose all his life to the grindstone, and die not worth a groat at last. 'A fat kitchen makes a lean will;' and,

'Many estates are spent in the getting,
Since women for tea forsook spinning and knitting,
And men for punch forsook hewing and splitting.'

'If you would be wealthy, think of saving, as well as of getting.' 'The Indies have not made Spain rich, because her out-goes are greater than her in-comes.'

"Away then with your expensive follies, and you will not then have so much cause to complain of hard times, heavy taxes, and chargeable families; for

'Women and wine, game and deceit,
Make the wealth small, and the want great.'

And farther, 'What maintains one vice would bring up two children.' You may think, perhaps, that a little tea, or a little punch now and then, diet a little more costly, clothes a little finer, and a little entertainment now and then, can be no great matter; but remember, 'Many a little makes a mickle.' Beware of little expenses; 'A small leak will sink a great ship,' as Poor Richard says; and again, 'Who dainties love, shall beggars prove;' and moreover, 'Fools make feasts, and wise men eat them.' Here you are all got together at this sale of fineries and nick-nacks. You call them goods, but, if you do not take care, they will prove evils to some of you. You expect they will be sold cheap, and perhaps they may, for less than the cost; but if you have no occasion for them, they must be dear to you. Remember what Poor Richard says, 'Buy what thou hast no need of, and ere long thou shalt sell thy necessaries.' And again, 'At a great pennyworth pause a while;' he means, that perhaps the cheapness is apparent only, and not real; or the bargain, by straitening thee in thy business, may do thee more harm than good. For in another place he says, 'Many have been ruined by buying good pennyworths.' Again, 'It is foolish to lay out money in a purchase of repentance;' and yet this folly is practised every day at auctions, for want of minding the Almanac. Many a one, for the sake of finery on the back, have gone with a hungry belly, and half starved their families; 'Silks, satins, scarlet, and velvets, put out the kitchen fire,' as Poor Richard says. These are not the necessaries of life; they can scarcely be called the conveniences; and yet, only because they look pretty, how many want to have them? By these and other extravagances, the greatest are reduced to poverty, and forced to borrow of those whom they formerly despised, but who, through industry and frugality, have maintained their standing; in which case it appears plainly, that 'A ploughman on his legs is higher than a gentleman on his knees,' as Poor Richard says. Perhaps they have had a small estate left them, which they knew not the getting of; they think 'It is day, and will never be night;' that a little to be spent out of so much is not worth minding; but 'always taking out of the meal-tub, and never putting in, soon comes to the bottom,' as Poor Richard says; and then, 'When the well is dry, they know the worth of water.' But this they might have known before, if they had taken his advice. 'If you would know the value of money, go and try to borrow some; for he that goes a borrowing, goes a sorrowing,' as Poor Richard says; and, indeed, so does he that lends to such people, when he goes to get it in again. Poor Dick farther advises, and says,

'Fond pride of dress is sure a very curse;
Ere fancy you consult, consult your purse.'

And again, 'Pride is as loud a beggar as want, and a great deal more saucy.' When you have bought one fine thing, you must buy ten more, that your appearance may be all of a piece; but Poor Dick says, 'It is easier to suppress the first desire, than to satisfy all that follow it.' And it is as truly folly for the poor to ape the rich, as for the frog to swell, in order to equal the ox.

'Vessels large may venture more,
But little boats should keep near shore.'

It is, however, a folly soon punished; for, as Poor Richard says, 'Pride that dines on vanity, sups on contempt: Pride breakfasted with Plenty, dined with Poverty, and supped with Infamy.' And, after all, of what use is this pride of appearance, for which so much is risked, so much is suffered? It cannot promote health nor ease pain; it makes no increase of merit in the person, it creates envy, it hastens misfortune.

"But what madness it must be to run in debt for these superfluities! We are offered by the terms of this sale, six months' credit; and that, perhaps, has induced some of us to attend it, because we cannot spare the ready money, and hope now to be fine without it. But, ah! think what you do when you run in debt; you give to another power over your liberty. If you cannot pay at the time, you will be ashamed to see your creditor; you will be in fear when you speak to him; you will make poor pitiful, sneaking excuses, and, by degrees, come to lose your veracity, and sink into base, downright lying; for 'The second vice is lying, the first is running in debt,' as Poor Richard says; and again, to the same purpose, 'Lying rides upon debt's back;' whereas a freeborn Englishman ought not to be ashamed nor afraid to see or speak to any man living. But poverty often deprives a man of all spirit and virtue. 'It is hard for an empty bag to stand upright.' What would you think of that prince, or of that government, who should issue an edict forbidding you to dress like a gentleman or gentlewoman, on pain of imprisonment or servitude? Would you not say that you were free, have a right to dress as you please, and that such an edict would be a breach of your privileges, and such a government tyrannical? And yet you are about to put yourself under that tyranny, when you run in debt for such dress! Your creditor has authority, at his pleasure, to deprive you of your liberty, by confining you in jail for life, or by selling you for a servant, if you should not be able to pay him. When you have got your bargain, you may, perhaps, think little of payment; but, as Poor Richard says, 'Creditors have better memories than debtors; creditors are a superstitious sect, great observers of days and times.' The day comes round before you are aware, and the demand is made before you are prepared to satisfy it; or, if you bear your debt in mind, the term, which at first seemed so long, will, as it lessens, appear extremely short: Time will seem to have added wings to his heels as well as his shoulders. 'Those have a short Lent, who owe money to be paid at Easter.' At present, perhaps, you may think yourselves in thriving circumstances, and that you can bear a little extravagance without injury; but

'For age and want save while you may,
No morning sun lasts a whole day.'

"Gain may be temporary and uncertain; but ever, while you live, expense is constant and certain; and 'It is easier to build two chimneys than to keep one in fuel,' as Poor Richard says: so, 'Rather go to bed supperless than rise in debt.'

'Get what you can, and what you get hold,
'Tis the stone that will turn all your lead into gold.'

And, when you have got the philosopher's stone, sure you will no longer complain of bad times, or the difficulty of paying taxes.

"IV. This doctrine, my friends, is reason and wisdom; but, after all, do not depend too much upon your own industry, and frugality, and prudence, though excellent things; for they may all be blasted without the blessing of Heaven; and, therefore, ask that blessing humbly, and be not uncharitable to those that at present seem to want it, but comfort and help them. Remember, Job suffered, and was afterwards prosperous.

"And now to conclude, 'Experience keeps a dear school, but fools will learn in no other,' as Poor Richard says, and scarce in that; for it is true, 'We may give advice, but we cannot give conduct.' However, remember this, 'They that will not be counselled, cannot be helped;' and farther, that, 'If you will not hear reason, she will surely rap your knuckles,' as Poor Richard says."

Thus the old gentleman ended his harangue. The people heard it, and approved the doctrine, and immediately practised the contrary, just as if it had been a common sermon; for the auction opened, and they began to buy extravagantly. I found the good man had thoroughly studied my Almanac, and digested all I had dropped on those topics during the course of twenty-five years. The frequent mention he made of me must have tired any one else; but my vanity was wonderfully delighted with it, though I was conscious that not a tenth part of the wisdom was my own which he ascribed to me; but rather the gleanings that I had made of the sense of all ages and nations. However, I resolved to be the better for the echo of it; and, though I had at first determined to buy stuff for a new coat, I went away, resolved to wear my old one a little longer. Reader, if thou wilt do the same, thy profit will be as great as mine.—I am, as ever, thine to serve thee,

RICHARD SAUNDERS.

Note.—The maxims of Poor Richard above quoted, were first printed in the vacant spaces between the remarkable days in the calendar in Poor Richard's Almanac, from 1733 to 1757. In 1757 they were collected into the above discourse of Father Abraham, and prefixed to the Almanac of that year. The piece was copied in all the newspapers of the American Continent, reprinted in England on a folio sheet, to be stuck up in houses, and translated into French, and, quite recently, in modern Greek.

LORD BACON.—ESSAY.—OF RICHES.

I cannot call riches better than the baggage of virtue; the Roman word is better—*impedimenta* (*hindrances*); for as the baggage is to an army, so is riches to virtue,—it cannot be spared nor left behind, but it hindereth the march; yea, and the care of it sometimes loseth or disturbeth the victory. Of great riches there is no great use, except it be in the distribution; the rest is but conceit. So saith Solomon, "Where much is, there are many to consume it; and what hath the owner but the sight of it with his eyes?" The personal fruition in any man cannot reach to feel great riches; there is a custody of them, or a power of dole (*distribution*), and a donative of them, or a fame of them, but no solid use to the owner. Do you not see what feigned prices are set upon little stones or rarities, and what works of ostentation are undertaken, because (*in order that*) there might seem to be some use of great riches? But then, you will say, they may be of use to buy men out of dangers or troubles; as Solomon saith, "Riches are a stronghold in the imagination of the rich man;" but this is excellently expressed, that it is an imagination, and not always in fact; for certainly great riches have sold more men than they have bought out. Seek not proud riches, but such as thou mayest get justly, use soberly, distribute cheerfully, and leave contentedly; yet have no abstract or friarly contempt of them, but distinguish, as Cicero saith well of Rabirius Posthumus, "In studio rei amplificandae, apparebat, non avaritiae praedam, sed instrumentum bonitati quaeri (*In his desire of increasing his riches, he sought not, it is evident, the gratification of avarice, but the means of beneficence*). Hearken also to Solomon, and beware of hasty gathering of riches: *Qui festinat ad divitias, non erit insons* (*He that maketh haste to be rich shall not be innocent*). The poets feign that when Plutus (which is riches) is sent from Jupiter, he limps, and goes slowly; but when he is sent from Pluto, he runs, and is swift of foot,—meaning that riches, gotten by good means and just labor, pace slowly, but when they come by the death of others (as by the course of inheritance, testaments, and the like), they come tumbling upon a man; but it might be applied likewise to Pluto taking him for the devil; for when riches come from the devil (as by fraud and oppression and unjust means), they come upon speed. The ways to enrich are many, and most of them foul; parsimony is one of the best, and yet is not innocent, for it withholdeth men from works of liberality and charity. The improvement of the ground is the most natural obtaining of riches, for it is our great mother's blessing, the earth; but it is slow. And yet, where men of great wealth do stoop to husbandry, it multiplyeth riches exceedingly. I knew a nobleman of England, that had the greatest audits of any man in my time—a great grazier, a great sheep-master, a great timber man, a great collier, a great corn-master, a great lead man, and so of iron, and a number of the like points of husbandry; so as the earth seemed a sea to him in respect of the perpetual importations. It was truly observed by one, "that himself came very hardly to little riches;" for when a man's stock has come to that, that he can expect (*wait for*) the prime of markets, and overcome (*come upon*) those bargains which, for their greatness, are for men's money, and the partner in the industries of younger men, he cannot but increase mainly (*greatly*). The gains of ordinary trades and vocations are honest, and further by two things, chiefly, by diligence, and by a good name for good and fair dealing; but the gains of bargains are of a more doubtful nature, when men shall wait upon others' necessity; broke by servants, and instruments to draw them on; put off others cunningly, that would be better chapmen (*purchasers*), and the like practices, which are crafty and naughty (*bad*). As for the chopping of bargains, when a man buys not to hold, but to sell over again, that commonly grindeth double, both upon the seller and upon the buyer. Sharings do greatly enrich, if the hands be well chosen that are trusted. Usury is the certainest means of gain, though one of the worst, as that whereby a man doth eat his bread, "*in sudore vultus alieni*" (*in the sweat of another's brow*), and besides, doth plough upon Sundays; but yet, certain though it be, it hath flaws; for that the scriveners and brokers do value (*represent as trustworthy*) unsound men to serve their own turn. The fortune in being the first in an invention or in a privilege, doth cause sometimes a wonderful overgrowth in riches; so it was with the first sugar man in the Canaries; therefore, if a man can play the true logician, to have as well judgment as invention, he may do great matters, especially if the times be fit. He that resteth upon gains certain, shall hardly grow to great riches; and he that puts all upon adventures, doth oftentimes break and come to poverty; it is good, therefore, to guard adventures with certainties that may uphold losses. Monopolies, and coemption of wares for resale, where they are not restrained, are great means to enrich; especially if the party have intelligence what things are like to come into request, and so store himself beforehand. Riches gotten by service, though it be of the best rise, yet when they are gotten by flattery, feeding humors, and other servile conditions, they may be placed among the worst. As for "fishing for testaments executorships" (as Tacitus saith of Seneca, "*Testamenta et orbos tanquam indagine capi*"), it is yet worse, by how much men submit themselves to meaner persons than in service.

Believe not much them that seem to despise riches, for they despise them that despair of them; and none worse when they come to them. Be not penny-wise; riches have wings, and sometimes they fly away of themselves; sometimes they must be set flying to bring in more. Men leave their riches either to their kindred or to the public; and moderate portions prosper best in both. A great estate left to an heir, is as a lure to all the birds of prey round about to seize on him, if he be not the better stablished (*to establish*) in years and judgment. Likewise glorious (*splendid*) gifts and foundation are like sacrifices without salt, and but the painted sepulchres of alms, which soon will putrefy and corrupt inwardly. Therefore measure not thine advancement (*gifts in money or property*) by quantity, but frame them by measure, and defer not charities till death; for, certainly, if a man weigh it rightly, he that doth so is rather liberal of another man's than his own.

JOHN KYRLE—THE MAN OF ROSS.

From Pope's Moral Essays—Epistle Third,—addressed to Allen, Lord Bathurst, On the *Use of Riches.*

After discussing in his terse way the point, whether the invention of money had been more beneficial or detrimental to mankind, the Poet draws pictures of various characters, but too well known in his day for their abuse of wealth, and for the shameful end to which they came at last, and then passing a deserved compliment on Lord Bathurst and Lord Oxford, asks:

But all our praises why should lords engross?
Rise, honest Muse! and sing the Man of Ross:
Pleas'd Vaga echoes through her winding bounds,
And rapid Severn hoarse applause resounds.
Who hung with woods yon mountain's sultry brow?
From the dry rock who bade the water flow?
Not to the skies in useless columns tost,
Or in proud falls magnificently lost,
But clear and artless, pouring through the plain
Health to the sick and solace to the swain.
Whose causeway parts the vale with shady rows?
Whose seats the weary traveler repose?
Who taught that heaven-directed tower to rise?
"The Man of Ross," each lisping babe replies.
Behold the market-place with poor o'erspread,
The Man of Ross divides the weekly bread:
He feeds yon almshouse, neat, but void of state,
Where age and want sit smiling at the gate:
Him portion'd maids, apprentic'd orphans blest,
The young who labor the old who rest.
Is any sick? the Man of Ross relieves,
Prescribes, attends, the medicine makes and gives.
Is there a variance? enters but his door,
Balk'd are the courts and contest is no more:
Despairing quacks with curses fled the place,
And vile attorneys, now a useless race.
B. Thrice happy man! enabled to pursue
What all so wish, but want the power to do!
Oh say, what sums that generous hand supply?
What mines to swell that boundless charity?
P. Of debts and taxes, wife and children clear,
This man possess'd five hundred pounds a year.
Blush, grandeur, blush! proud courts, withdraw your blaze,
Ye little stars! hide your diminished rays.
B. And what? no monument, inscription, stone,
His race, his form, his name almost unknown?
P. Who builds a church to God and not to fame,
Will never mark the marble with his name:
Go, search it there, where to be born and die,
Of rich and poor makes all the history:
Enough that virtue fill'd all the space between,
Prov'd by the ends of being to have been.

The Man of Ross immortalized in the above lines, was John Kyrle—a native of the parish of Dymock, in Gloucestershire and a descendant of John Hampden. He was born in 1634 and educated at Baliol College, Oxford, and took up his residence soon after in Ross on a small property given him by his father, and which he enlarged by the purchase of an estate on the banks of the Wye—"the Sylvan Wye of Wordsworth" on which Tintern Abbey stands.

The title of "The Man of Ross" was given to him by a country friend, in his lifetime; and Mr. Kyrle was highly pleased with the appellation, because it "conveyed a mixture of plain honest dealing and unaffected hospitality." The principal addition to his landed property was an estate, called the Cleve, consisting of fields that extend along the left bank of the river, but raised considerably above its level. Along the skirts of these fields, Mr. Kyrle made a public walk, which still bears his name; he planted it with elms, and continued the plantation down the steep sides of the bank, which overhang the graceful, ever-winding Wye. It is to this plantation that Pope alludes in the lines,—

Who hung with woods yon mountain's sultry brow?

Mr. Kyrle's income has been pretty accurately stated at £500 a year. His favorite occupations were building and planting, in which his skill and taste were as freely exerted for the benefit of his friends as on his own improvements; he frequently planned and superintended architectural works, for persons who gladly availed themselves of his skill and taste.

While improving his own property, he added to the beauties of his favorite spot, and freely imparted to his townsmen the advantages which he had provided for the enjoyment of the lovely scenery around him. The churchyard was planted with elms by Kyrle, and a gate was erected by him leading to a field called "The Prospect," from its commanding a noble view of the rich scenery of the Wye. In times when the art of conveying water by pipes, for the accommodation of all the dwellers in a town, was yet in its infancy, a great benefit was conferred on the inhabitants of Ross, by the skill and enterprise of Mr. Kyrle, who made, in this field, an oval basin of considerable extent, lined it with brick, and paved it with stone, and caused the water from the river to be forced into it by an engine, and conveyed by under-ground pipes to the public cocks in the streets. When a more effectual mode of supply was introduced, the use of the fountain was abandoned, and the basin was filled up. This public work is recorded by the poet, in the lines,—

From the dry rock, who bade the waters flow?
Not to the skies, in useless columns tost,
Or in proud falls magnificently lost;
But clear and artless, pouring through the plain
Health to the sick, and solace to the swain.

The next work noticed by Pope is a causeway, which was constructed through the exertions of Mr. Kyrle, and paid for by a subscription, to which he largely contributed. It crossed the low ground between the town and the bridge, on the high road to Hereford and Monmouth. This causeway has been since extended, and rendered permanent by the Commissioners of Turnpikes, who have converted it into a spacious driving-way, better adapted to the more frequent and rapid journeyings of modern times.

The walk in the Cleve-fields above alluded to, was not only beautified with elms, his favorite tree, but seats were placed at intervals, where the "weary traveler" might "repose," or the lover of fine scenery contemplate at his ease, the beauties before him.

The passage which relates to the church of Ross is calculated to convey an erroneous notion of what was actually done by Mr. Kyrle. The line

Who taught that heaven-directed spire to rise?

coupled with another,—

Who builds a church to God, and not to fame;

has led many to suppose, that the church was built by Kyrle. The facts are these:

The elegant spire which ornaments the landscape from whatever point it be viewed, was at one time in a dangerous state, which Mr. Kyrle's knowledge of architecture led him to discover. A parish meeting was convened at his special motion, and about forty-seven feet of the spire taken down and rebuilt, himself daily inspecting the work and contributing, over and above the assessment, towards its speedy conclusion. The great bell was given by Kyrle, who attended when it was cast at Gloucester, and threw into the melting pot his large own silver tankard, having first drunk his favorite toast of "Church and King."

Behold the market-house, with poor o'erspread,
The Man of Ross divides the weekly bread.

The distribution of the "weekly bread" at the market-house is a circumstance of peculiar interest in the life of Kyrle. The donation of bread was furnished by a grant, renewed by successive lords of the manor, of certain tolls on all corn brought to market. The man of Ross acted as the lord's almoner. Tradition reports, in homely language, that "it would have done one's heart good to see how cheerful the old gentleman looked, while engaged in the distribution." At length the toll, thus voluntarily transferred to the poor at the will of each succeeding lord, was claimed by the townsmen as their's of right. The question was referred to the Man of Ross by consent of both parties; and he, preferring truth and justice before popularity and self-gratification, determined, as the evidence compelled him to do, that the toll belonged to the lord. So are pride and covetousness found in communities as well as individuals.

The remaining lines refer to various private acts of charity, for which a man of Kyrle's noble disposition would find frequent opportunities in whatever part of the world he might be placed. The town of Ross could tell of many who, before and since his time, and at this day, clothe the naked, feed the hungry, instruct the ignorant, and teach the infant's tongue to praise the name of Creator and Redeemer.

There is, however, one anecdote of Mr. Kyrle, which we are unwilling to omit, as it exhibits that noble confidence, which none but an honest man can feel or express towards his fellow-men. About a year after the death of the Man of Ross, a tradesman of the town came to the executor, and said privately to him, "Sir, I am come to pay you some money that I owed to the late Mr. Kyrle." The executor declared he could find no entry of it in the accounts. "Why, sir," said the tradesman, "that I am aware of. Mr. Kyrle said to me, when he lent me the money, that he did not think I should be able to repay it in his lifetime, and that it was likely you might want it before I could make it up; and so, said he, I wont have any memorandum of it, besides what I write and give you with it; and do you pay my kinsman when you can; and when you show him this paper, he will see that the money is right, and that he is not to take interest."

The Man of Ross died in 1724, at the advanced age of ninety, a bachelor. At the time of his decease, he owed nothing, and there was no money in his house. He was borne to the grave by his workmen and usual attendants, and amidst the whole population of Ross.

Though he disliked large parties, his house was open to the reception of his friends, in the genuine spirit of old-fashioned English hospitality. "He loved a long evening; enjoyed a merry tale, and always appeared discomposed when t'was time to part." His dishes were generally plain; malt liquor and cider were the only beverages introduced; there was no roast beef except on Christmas-day. At his kitchen fire-place was a large block of wood, for poor people to sit on; and a piece of boiled beef and three pecks of flour, in bread, were given to the poor every Sunday. The Man of Ross was a daily attendant at the service of the parish church. When the chiming of the bells began, all business ceased with him; he washed his hands and proceeded to his pew. When the church was newly pewed, about twenty years after his death, the rector and parishioners resolved that Mr. Kyrle's seat should remain, as it does at this day, in its original condition and style. A handsome tablet, with a bust of the Man of Ross, has long since removed the stigma imputed in the concluding lines of Pope's eulogy of Kyrle.

The Man of Ross, then, it has been seen, was a private gentleman of small fortune, with a talent for architecture, and a taste for what is now termed the picturesque, which he employed in the improvement and adorning of his town and neighborhood. Simple in his manners, he lavished no money on gaudy show or equipage. Faithful to his God, and upright in his dealings with man; intelligent, active, and benevolent; he was confided in as a friend, as an umpire, as a receiver and dispenser of the subscriptions of others, whether to be employed in works for the public good, or in relieving the wants of indigence and age.

HENRY TAYLOR.

In his *Notes from Life*, Mr. Taylor devotes an Essay to the management of money, portions of which we here present, especially what relates to getting and spending

OF MONEY.

The philosophy which affects to teach us a contempt of money, does not run very deep; for, indeed, it ought to be still more clear to the philosopher than it is to ordinary men, that there are few things in the world of greater importance. And so manifold are the bearings of money upon the lives and characters of mankind, that an insight which should search out the life of a man in his pecuniary relations, would penetrate into almost every cranny of his nature. He who knows, like St. Paul, both how to spare and how to abound, has a great knowledge; for if we take account of all the virtues with which money is mixed up—honesty, justice, generosity, charity, frugality, forethought, self-sacrifice—and of their correlative vices, it is a knowledge which goes near to cover the length and breadth of humanity; and a right measure and manner in getting, saving, spending, giving, taking, lending, borrowing, and bequeathing, would almost argue a perfect man.

FIRSTLY—As to the *getting* of money. This involves dangers which do not belong to the mere possession of it. "Blessed is the rich that is found without blemish, and hath not gone *after* gold," says the Son of Sirach; and again, "He that loveth gold shall not be justified, and he that followeth corruption shall have enough thereof." Yet industry must take an interest in its own fruits; and God has appointed that the mass of mankind shall be moved by this interest, and have their daily labor sweetened by it. And there may be a blessing even upon the going after gold, if it be not with an inordinate appetite,—if the gold be not loved for its own sake, and if the manner of it be without blemish. But the danger arises out of the tendency of the human mind to forget the end in the means, and the difficulty of going after gold for the love of the benefits which it may confer, without going after it also for the mere love of getting it and keeping it, which is "following corruption." It behooves him who is getting money, therefore, even more than him who has it by inheritance, to bear in mind what are the uses of money, and what are the proportions and proprieties to be observed in saving, giving, and spending; for rectitude in the management of money consists in the symmetry of these three.

Sudden and enormous gains almost always disturb the balance; for a man can scarcely change his state suddenly, and yet hold his proportions; and hence proceeds one of the many evils of highly speculative commerce, with its abrupt vicissitudes of fortune. The man who engages in it can scarcely have any fixed and regulated manner of dealing with his net income; he knows not how much he ought to save, how much he may permit himself to spend, how much he can afford to give; whilst, even if he could know, the extreme excitements of fear and hope to which he lies open, occupy his mind too much for him to give many thoughts to such matters. And if what is called bold commercial enterprise be a thing to be rejoiced in as promoting the physical well-being of mankind, and thereby, perhaps, in the train of consequences, their moral interests, it is only through that Providence by which good is brought out of evil. And the actors in such enterprises, when, as is mostly the case, they are merely "going after gold," and not considering either the physical or moral results, are, in their own minds and hearts, "following corruption," and are likely to "have enough thereof."

A moderated and governed course in the getting of money is the more difficult because this is, of all pursuits, that in which a man meets with the greatest pressure of competition. So many are putting their hearts into this work, that he who keeps his out of it is not unlikely to fare ill in the strife. And for this reason it were well for a man, not perhaps altogether to abate his desire of gain (though this should be done if it be excessive), but more assiduously still to direct his desires beyond, and purify the desire of gain by associating with it the desire to accomplish some scheme of beneficent expenditure. And let no man imagine that the mere investment for reproduction, though economists may justly regard it as beneficial to mankind, will react upon his own heart for good.

SECONDLY—As to the *saving* of money. The saving, like the getting, should be intelligent of a purpose beyond; it should not be saving for saving's sake, but for the sake of some worthy object to be accomplished by the money saved. And especially we are to guard against that accumulative instinct or passion which is ready to take possession of all collectors.

THIRDLY—As to the *spending* of money The art of living easily as to money, is to pitch your scale of living one degree below your means. Comfort and enjoyment are more dependent upon easiness in the detail of expenditure, than upon one degree's difference in the scale.

Guard against false associations of pleasure with expenditure,—the notion that because pleasure can be purchased with money, therefore money cannot be spent without enjoyment. What a thing costs a man is no true measure of what it is worth to him; and yet, how often is his appreciation governed by no other standard, as if there were a pleasure in expenditure *per se*.

Let yourself feel a want before you provide against it. You are more assured that it is a real want; and it is worth while to feel it a little, in order to feel the relief from it.

When you are undecided as to which of two courses you would like best, choose the cheapest. This rule will not only save money, but save also a good deal of trifling indecision.

Too much leisure leads to expense; because when a man is in want of objects, it occurs to him that they are to be had *for* money; and he invents expenditures in order to pass the time.

A thoroughly conscientious mode of regulating expenditure implies much care and trouble in resisting imposition, detecting fraud, preventing waste, and doing what in you lies to guard the honesty of your stewards, servants, and tradesmen, by not leading them into temptation, but delivering them from evil.

Prodigality is indeed the vice of a weak nature, as avarice is of a strong one; it comes of a weak craving for those blandishments of the world which are easily to be had for money, and which, when obtained, are as much worse than worthless as a harlot's love is worse than none.

FOURTHLY—As to *giving and taking*. All giving is not generous; and the gift of a spendthrift is seldom given in generosity; for prodigality is, equally with avarice, a selfish vice. Nor can there be a more spurious view of generosity than that which has been often taken by sentimental comedians and novelists, when they have represented it in combination with recklessness and waste. He who gives only what he would as readily throw away, gives without generosity; for the essence of generosity is in self-sacrifice. Waste, on the contrary, comes always by self-indulgence; and the weakness and softness in which it begins will not prevent the hard-heartedness to which all selfishness tends at last. When you give, therefore, take to yourself no credit for generosity, unless you deny yourself something in order that you may give.

I have known a man who was never rich, and was, indeed, in a fair way to be ruined, make a present of several hundred pounds, under what he probably conceived to be an impulse of generous friendship; but if that man had been called upon to get up an hour earlier in the morning to serve his friend, I do not believe that he would have done it. The fact was that he had no real value for money, no real care for consequences which were not to be immediate. In parting with some hundreds of pounds, he flattered his self-love with a show of self-sacrifice; in parting with an hour's folding of the hands to sleep, the self-sacrifice would have been real, and the show of it not very magnificent.

Again, do not take too much credit even for your self-denial, unless it be cheerfully and genially undergone. Do not dispense your bounties only because you know it to be your duty, and are afraid to leave it undone; for this is one of those duties which should be done more in the spirit of love than in that of fear. I have known persons who have lived frugally, and spent a large income almost entirely in acts of charity and bounty, and yet, with all this, they had not the open hand. When the act did not define itself as a charitable duty, the spirit of the God-beloved giver was wanting, and they failed in all those little genial liberalities towards friends, relatives, and dependents, which tend to cultivate the sympathies and kindnesses of our nature quite as much as charity to the poor, or munificence in the contribution to public objects. The kindness from which a gift proceeds will appear in the choice as well as in the cost of it.

There is often as much generosity in accepting gifts as there can be in bestowing them—the generosity of a nature which stands too strong in its humility to *fear* humiliation, which knows its own independence and is glad to be grateful.

Upon a very different sense of generosity are some of the practices of the present time founded. It is not an uncommon thing amongst some persons, with peculiar notions of doing things delicately, for contributions to be conveyed to some decayed gentlewoman under various pretences which are meant to disguise, more or less transparently, the fact that she receives money in charity. If a gentlewoman be in want, she should say so with openness, dignity, and truth, and accept in the manner that becomes a gentlewoman, in all lowliness, but without the slightest humiliation or shame, whatever money she has occasion for, and others are willing to bestow. The relations between her and them will in that case admit of respect on the one side, and gratitude on the other. But where false and juggling pretences are resorted to, no worthy or honest feeling can have place. Delicacy is a strong thing; and whether in giving or taking, let us always maintain the maxim that what is most sound and true is most delicate.

Lastly, there is a rule in giving which is often overlooked by those whose generosity is not sufficiently thoughtful and severe. Generosity comes to be perverted from its uses when it ministers to selfishness in others; and it should be our care to give all needful support to our neighbor in his self-denial, rather than to bait a trap for his self-indulgence; in short, to give him pleasure only when it will do him good, not when sacrifices on our part are the correlatives of abuses on his; for he who pampers the selfishness of another, does that other a moral injury which cannot be compensated by any amount of gratification imparted to him.

> "Give thou to no man, if thou wish him well,
> What he may not in honor's interest take;
> Else shalt thou but befriend his frailty, allied
> Against his better with his baser self."

FIFTHLY—As to *lending* and *borrowing*. Never lend money to a friend unless you are satisfied that he does wisely and well in borrowing it. Borrowing is one of the most ordinary ways in which weak men sacrifice the future to the present, and thence it is that the gratitude for a loan is so proverbially evanescent. Take to heart therefore, the admonition the ancient courtier:

> "Neither a borrower nor a lender be;
> For loan oft loseth both itself and friend,
> And borrowing dulls the edge of husbandry."

I have never known a debtor or a prodigal who was not, in his own estimation, an injured man; and I have generally found that those who had not suffered by them were disposed to side with them; for it is the weak who make an outcry, and it is by the outcry that the world is wont to judge. They who lend money to spendthrifts should be prepared, therefore, to suffer in their reputation as well as in their purse.

Let us learn from the Son of Sirach: "Many, when a thing was lent them, reckoned it to be found, and put them to trouble that helped them. Till he hath received, he will kiss a man's hand; and for his neighbor's money he will speak submissly; but when he should repay, he will prolong the time, and return words of grief, and complain of the time. If he prevail, he shall hardly receive the half, and he will count as if he had found it; if not, he hath deprived him of his money, and he hath gotten him an enemy without cause: he payeth him with cursing and railings, and for honor he will pay him with disgrace."

SIXTHLY—The subject of *bequeathing*; and some topics which might have fallen under this head have been anticipated in treating of motives for saving.

To make a will in one way or another is of course the duty of every person whose heir-at-law is not the proper inheritor of all he possesses; and unless where there is some just cause for setting them aside, expectations generated by the customs of the world are sufficient to establish a moral right to inherit, and to impose a corresponding obligation to bequeath. For custom may be presumed, in the absence of any reasons to the contrary, to have grown out of some natural fitness; and, at all events, it will have brought about an amount of adaptation which is often sufficient, as regards individual cases, to make a fitness where there was none. Unless in exceptional instances, therefore, in which special circumstances are of an overruling force, the disappointment of expectations growing out of custom is not to be inflicted without some very strong and solid reasons for believing that the custom needs to be reformed.

If it be not well for the natural or customary heirs that they should be disappointed, neither is it good for those to whom an inheritance is diverted, that wealth should come upon them by surprise. Sudden and unexpected accessions of wealth seldom promote the happiness of those to whom they accrue, and they are for the most part morally injurious, especially when they accrue by undue deprivation of another.

In general, the rule of judgment should be to avoid lifting people out of one station into another; and to aim at making such moderate additions to moderate fortunes in careful hands, as may not disturb the proportion of property to station: or, still better, may rectify any disproportion, and enable those who are living with a difficult frugality to live with a free frugality.

This rule is not, I fear, very generally regarded; for mere rectitude, and the observance of measures and proportions, does not much lay hold of the minds of men. On the contrary, there is a general disposition to add to anything which affects the imagination by its magnitude; and there is also in some people a sort of gloating over great wealth, which infects them with a propensity to feed a bloated fortune. Jaques took note of this when he saw the deer that was weeping in "the needless stream:"

> "Thou mak'st a testament
> As worldlings do, giving thy sum of more
> To that which had too much."
>
> —SHAK. *As You Like It*, Act ii. scene 1.

Thus it is that in the most solemn acts which men have to perform in the management of their money—in those, too, from which selfish ends seem most removed—they will often appear to be as little sensible of moral motives and righteous responsibilities as in any other transactions; and even a *testator jamjam moriturus* will dictate his will with a sort of posthumous cupidity, and seem to desire that his worldliness should live after him.

LORD LYTTON ON THE MANAGEMENT OF MONEY.

Lord Edward Bulwer Lytton has issued, in a little volume entitled *Caxtonia*, a series of essays on Life, Literature, and Manners, originally published in successive numbers of Blackwood's Magazine in 1862, the results of wide observation and experience on topics of great practical interest to the young, from one of which, on the management of money, we give copious extracts:

VALUE OF MONEY IN CHARACTER AND POWER.

In the humbler grades of life, certainly character is money. The man who gives me his labor in return for the wages which the labor is worth, pledges to me something more than his labor—he pledges to me certain qualities of his moral being—such as honesty, sobriety, and diligence. If, in these respects, he maintain his character, he will have my money as long as I want his labor; and, when I want his labor no longer, his character is money's worth to him from somebody else. If, in addition to the moral qualities I have named, he establish a character for other attributes which have their own price in the money market—if he exhibit a superior intelligence, skill, energy, zeal—his labor rises in value. Thus, in the humblest class of life, character is money; and, according as the man earns or spends the money, money in turn becomes character.

As money is the most evident power in the world's uses, so the use that he makes of money is often all that the world knows about a man. Is our money gained justly and spent prudently? our character establishes a claim on respect. Is it gained nobly and spent beneficently? our character commands more than respect—it wins a place in that higher sphere of opinion which comprises admiration, gratitude, love. Is money, inherited without merit of ours, lavished recklessly away? our character disperses itself with the spray of the golden shower,—it is not the money alone of which we are spendthrifts. Is money, meanly acquired, selfishly hoarded? it is not the money alone of which we are misers; we are starving our own human hearts—depriving them of their natural aliment in the approval and affection of others. We invest the money which we fancy so safe out at compound interest, in the very worst possession a man can purchase, viz., an odious reputation. In fact, the more we look round, the more we shall come to acknowledge that there is no test of a man's character more generally adopted than the way in which his money is managed. Money is a terrible blab; she will betray the secrets of her owner whatever he do to gag her. His virtues will creep out in her whisper—his vices she will cry aloud at the top of her tongue.

Money is character—money also is power. I have power not in proportion to the money I spend on myself, but in proportion to the money I can, if I please, give away to another. We feel this as we advance in years. How helpless is an old man who has not a farthing to give or to leave! But be moderately amiable, grateful, and kind, and, though you have neither wife nor child, you will never want a wife's tenderness nor a child's obedience if you have something to leave or to give. This reads like satire: it is sober truth.

ART OF MANAGING MONEY.

But the management of money is an art? True; but that which we call an art means an improvement, and not a deterioration of a something existent already in nature; and the artist can only succeed in improving his art in proportion as he improves himself in the qualities which the art demands in the artist. Now, the management of money is, in much, the management of self. If heaven allotted to each man seven guardian angels, five of them, at least, would be found, night and day, hovering over his pockets.

On the first rule of the art of managing money, all preceptors must be agreed. It is told in three words—"Horror of debt."

Horror of Debt.

Nurse, cherish, never cavil away the wholesome horror of DEBT. Personal liberty is the paramount essential to human dignity and human happiness. Man hazards the condition and loses the virtues of freeman, in proportion as he accustoms his thoughts to view, without anguish and shame, his lapse into the bondage of debtor. Debt is to man what the serpent is to the bird; its eye fascinates, its breath poisons, its coil crushes sinew and bone, its jaw is the pitiless grave. If you mock my illustration, if you sneer at the truth it embodies, give yourself no further trouble to learn how to manage your money. Consider yourself doomed; pass on your way with a jaunty step; the path is facile—paths to Avernus always are. But if, while I write, your heart, true to the instinct of manhood, responds to my words—if you say, "Agreed; that which you call the first rule for the management of money, I hold yet more imperative as the necessity to freedom and the life-spring of probity"—then advance on your way, assured that wherever it wind it must ascend. You see but the temple of Honor; close behind it is the temple of Fortune. You will pass through the one to the other.

No Endorsing. Give, but don't Lend.

Now comes the next danger. You will not incur debt for yourself; but you have a friend. Pythias, your friend, your familiar—the man you like best and see most of—says to you, "Damon, be my security—your name to this bill!" Heaven forbid that I should cry out to Damon, "Pythias means to cheat thee—beware!" But I address to Damon this observation, "Pythias asks thee to guarantee that three, six, or twelve months hence he will pay to another man—say to Dionysius—so many pounds sterling." Here your first duty, as an honest man, is not to Pythias, but to Dionysius. Suppose some accident happen—one of those accidents which, however impossible it may seem to your Pythias, constantly happen to the Pythiases of other Damons who draw bills on the bank of Futurity; suppose that the smut or the rain spoil the crops on which Pythias relies—or the cargoes he expects from Marseilles, Califor-

sia, Utopia, go down to the bottomless seas—Dionysius must come upon you! Can you pay to Dionysius what you pledge yourself to pay to him in spite of those accidents? He thinks those accidents not only possible, but probable, or he would not require your surety, nor charge twenty per cent. for his loan; and, therefore, since he clearly doubts Pythias, his real trust is in you. Do you merit the trust? Can you pay the money if Pythias cannot? And, allowing that you can pay the money, are your other obligations in life such as to warrant that sacrifice to friendship? If you cannot pay, or if you owe it to others more sacred than Pythias himself—owe it to your parents, your plighted bride, or wedded wife, or the children to whom what, before their birth, was your fortune, has become the trust-money for their provision—not to hazard for Pythias that for which, if lost, not you alone, but others must suffer,—then, do not common duty and common honesty forbid you to say, "I am surety to Pythias for that which it belongs not to Pythias but to Chance to fulfil?" I am the last man to say, "Do not help your friend," if you honorably can. If we have money, we manage it ill when we cannot help a friend at a pinch. But the plain fact is this, Pythias wants money. Can you give it, at whatever stint to yourself, in justice to others? If you can, and you value Pythias more than the money, give the money, and there is an end of it; but if you cannot give the money, don't sign the bill. Do not become what, in rude truth, you do become—a knave and a liar—if you guarantee to do what you know that you cannot do should the guarantee be exacted. He is generous who gives; he who lends may be generous also; but only on one condition, viz., that he can afford to give what he can afford to lend. Of the two, therefore, it is safer, friendlier, cheaper, in the long run, to give than to lend. Give, and you may keep your friend if you lose your money; lend, and the chances are that you lose your friend if ever you get back your money.

But, if you do lend, let it be with the full conviction that the loan is a gift, and count it among the rarest favors of Providence if you be ever repaid. Lend to Pythias on the understanding,—"This is a loan if you can ever repay me. I shall, however, make this provision against the chance of a quarrel between us, that if you cannot repay me, it stands as a gift."

And whatever you lend, let it be your money and not your name. Money you may get again, and, if not, you may contrive to do without it; name, once lost, you cannot get again, and, if you can contrive to do without it, you had better never have been born.

Having settled these essential preliminaries—1st. Never to borrow where there is a chance, however remote, that you may not be able to repay; 2dly. Never to lend what you are not prepared to give; 3dly. Never to guarantee for another what you cannot fulfil if the other should fail—you start in life with this great advantage—whatever you have, be it little or much, is your own. Rich or poor, you start as a freeman, resolved to preserve, in your freedom, the noblest condition of your being as man.

Independence, not Wealth, the true Aim in getting Money.

Now, fix your eyes steadily on some definite end in the future. Consider well what you chiefly wish to be; then compute at the lowest that which you are by talent, and at the highest that which you can be by labor. Always under-estimate the resources of talent; always put as against you the chances of luck. Then set down on the other side, as against talent defective, against luck adverse, all that which can be placed to the credit of energy, patience, perseverance. These last are infinite. Whatever be placed against them is finite.

The finest epithet for genius is that which was applied to Newton's genius, "patient." He who has patience coupled with energy is sure, sooner or later, to obtain the results of genius; he who has genius without patience, and without energy (if, indeed, such genius be a thing possible), might as well have no genius at all. His works and aims, like the plants of nature before the deluge, have no roots.

The man who succeeds above his fellows is the one who, early in life, clearly discerns his object, and toward that object habitually directs his powers. Thus, indeed, even genius itself is but fine observation strengthened by fixity of purpose. Every man who observes vigilantly and resolves steadfastly, grows unconsciously into genius.

Assuming that fortune be your object, let your first efforts be, not for wealth, but independence. Whatever be your talents, whatever your prospects, never be tempted to speculate away, on the chance of a palace that which you need as a provision against the workhouse.

Let your first care be, then, independence. Without pecuniary independence, you are not even intellectually free; with independence, even though it be gained through some occupation which you endure as a drudgery, still, out of the twenty-four hours, there will be always some hours for the occupation in which you delight.

Spend Less than you Earn.

To attain independence, so apportion your expenditure as to spend less than you have or you earn. Make this rule imperative. I know of none better. Lay by something every year, if it be but a shilling. A shilling laid by, net and clear from a debt, is a receipt in full for all claims in the past, and you go on, with light foot and light heart, to the future. "How am I to save and lay by?" saith the author, or any other man of wants more large than his means. The answer is obvious: "If you cannot increase your means, then you must diminish your wants." Every skilled laborer, of fair repute, can earn enough not to starve, and a surplus beyond that bare sufficiency.

A man of £300 a year, living up to that income, truly complains of poverty; but if he live at the rate of £250 a year, he is comparatively rich. "Oh," says Gentility, "but I must have this or that, which necessitates the yearly £50 you ask me to save; I must be genteel." Why that must? That certain folks may esteem you? Believe me, they esteem you much more for a balance at your banker's, than for that silver tea-pot or that mannikin menial in sugar-loaf buttons. "But," says Perental Affection, "I must educate my boy; that £50 saved from my income is the cost of his education." Is it so? Can all the schoolmasters in Europe teach him a nobler lesson than that of a generous thrift, a cheerful and brave self-denial? If the £50 be really the sum which the boy's schooling needs, and you can spare nothing else from your remaining £250, still save and lay by for a year, and, during that year, let the boy study at home, by seeing how gladly you all are saving for him.

He who has saved for one year, finds the security, pleasure, and pride in it a luxury so great that his invention will be quickened to keep it. Lay by! lay by! What makes the capital of nations? Savings; nothing else. Neither nations nor men are safe against fortune, unless they can hit on a system by which they save more than they spend. When that system is once established, at what a ratio capital accumulates! What resources the system gradually develops! In that one maxim is the secret of England's greatness! Do you think it mean to save more than you spend? You do in that what alone gives your country its rank in the universe. The system so grand for an empire cannot be mean for a citizen.

Earn More than you Spend.

Whatever your means be, so apportion your wants that your means may exceed them. Every man who earns but 10s. a week can do this if he please, whatever he may say to the contrary; for if he can live upon 10s. a week, he can live upon 9s. 11d.

In this rule mark the emphatic distinction between poverty and neediness. Poverty is relative, and, therefore, not ignoble; neediness is a positive degradation. If I have only £100 a year, I am rich as compared with the majority of my countrymen. If I have £3,000 a year, I may be poor compared with a majority of my associates; and very poor compared to my next-door neighbor. With either of these incomes, I am relatively poor or rich; but with either of these incomes I may be positively needy, or positively free from neediness. With the £100 a year, I may need no man's help; I may at least have "my crust of bread and liberty." But with £3,000 a year, I may dread a ring at my bell; I may have my tyrannical masters in servants whose wages I cannot pay; my exile may be at the fiat of the first long-suffering man who enters a judgment against me; for the flesh that lies nearest to my heart, some Shylock may be dusting his scales and whetting his knife. Nor is this an exaggeration. Some of the neediest men I ever knew, have a nominal £3,000 a year. Every man is needy who spends more than he has; no man is needy who spends less. I may so ill manage my money that, with £3,000 a year, I purchase the worst evils of poverty—terror and shame; I may so well manage my money that, with £100 a year, I purchase the best blessings of wealth—safety and respect.

POWER OF MONEY WELL MANAGED.

You have got money—you have it; and with it, the heart and the sense and the taste to extract from the metal its uses. Talk of the power of knowledge! What can knowledge invent that money cannot purchase? Money, it is true, cannot give you the brain of the philosopher, the eye of the painter, the ear of the musician, nor that inner sixth sense of beauty and truth by which the poet unites in himself, philosopher, painter, musician; but money can refine and exalt your existence with all that philosopher, painter, musician, poet, accomplish. That which they are, your wealth cannot make you; but that which they do is at the command of your wealth. You may collect in your libraries all thoughts which all thinkers have confided to books; your galleries may teem with the treasures of art; the air that you breathe may be vocal with music; better than all, when you summon the Graces, they can come to your call in their sweet name of Charities. You can build up asylums for age, and academies for youth. Pining Merit may spring to hope at your voice, and "Poverty grow cheerful in your sight." Money well managed deserves, indeed, the apotheosis to which she was raised by her Latin adorers; she is *Diva Moneta*—a Goddess.

Motives for Acquisition and Economy.

The first object connected with money is the security for individual freedom—pecuniary independence. That once gained, whatever is surplus becomes the fair capital for reproductive adventure. Adhere but to this rule in every speculation, however tempting; preserve free from all hazard that which you require to live on without depending upon others.

1. It is a great motive to economy, a strong safeguard to conduct, and a wonderful stimulant to all mental power, if you can associate your toil for money with some end dear to your affections. I once knew a boy of good parts, but who seemed incorrigibly indolent. His father, a professional man, died suddenly, leaving his widow and son utterly destitute. The widow resolved to continue the education of her boy, however little he had hitherto profited by it, engaged herself as teacher at a school, and devoted her salary to her son. From that moment the boy began to work in good earnest. He saw the value of money in this world; he resolved to requite his mother—to see her once more in a home of her own; he distinguished himself at school; he obtained, at the age of sixteen, an entry in a mercantile house. At the age of twenty, his salary enabled him to place his mother in a modest suburban lodging, to which he came home every night. At the age of thirty he was a rich man, and, visiting him at his villa, I admired his gardens. He said to me, simply, "I have no taste for flowers myself, but my mother is passionately fond of them. I date my first step in life from my resolve to find her a home; and the invention in my business to which I owe my rise from a clerk to a partner, could never have come into my brain, and been patiently worked out, if, night and day, I had not thought of my mother's delight in flowers."

2. A common motive with a young man is an honest love for the girl whom he desires to win as his wife. Nay, if no such girl yet has been met on the earth, surely she lives for him in the cloudland of Fancy. Wedlock, and wedlock for love, is the most exquisite hope in the innermost heart of every young man who labors; it is but the profligate idlers who laugh at that sacred ideal. But it is only the peasant or mechanic who has a right to marry on no other capital than that which he takes

from nature in sinews and thews. The man whose whole condition of being is in his work from day to day must still have his helpmate. He finds his helpmate in one who can work like himself, if his honest industry fail her. I preach to the day laborer no cold homilies from political economy. The happiness and morality of the working class necessitate early marriages; and for prudent provision against the chances of illness and death, there are benefit clubs and societies, which must stand in lieu of jointure and settlement. But to men of a higher grade in this world's social distinctions, Hymen must generally contrive to make some kind of compromise with Plutus. I grant that your fond Amaryllis would take your arm to the altar, though you have not a coat to your back; but Amaryllis may have parents, who not unreasonably ask, "How, young Strephon, can you maintain our daughter? and if your death demolish all those castles in the air, which you are now building without brick and mortar, under what roof will she lay her head?"

And suppose that no parents thus unkindly interpose between Amaryllis and you, still it is a poor return to the disinterested love of Amaryllis, to take her, thoughtless child, at her word. Amaryllis proves her unselfish love; prove yours, my friend Strephon. Wait, hope, strive—her ring is on your finger; her picture, though it be but a villainous photograph, hangs by your bedside; her image is deep in the deepest fold of your heart. Wait till you can joyously say, "Come, Amaryllis; Plutus relaxes his frown; here is a home which, if humble, at least is secure; and, if death suddenly snatch me away, here is no castle in air for my widow. Amaryllis shall never live upon alms!"

How your love will deepen and strengthen in that generous delay; and with your love, how your whole nature, mental and moral, will deepen and strengthen! Here, indeed, is an object for climbing the rough paths on to fortune; and here the first friendly opposition of Plutus only serves to place upon surer foundations the blessings promised by Hymen. Constancy in love necessitates patience and perseverance in all efforts for fortune; and, with patience and perseverance, a man of fair average capacities is the master of fortune.

3. The taste for books, and the desire to collect them, are no mean tests of a school-boy's career as man.

One of the most distinguished personages in Europe, showing me his library—which is remarkable for its extent and its quality (it was formed on the principle of including all works that treat, directly or indirectly, on the human mind, and thus necessarily includes almost every book worth the reading)—said to me: "Not only this collection, but my social successes in life, I trace back to the first franc I saved from the cake-shop to spend on the book-stall. When I was a young man, and received an invitation to a ball, not being then rich, I calculated what it would cost me in kid gloves and coach hire, and, refusing the ball, bought a book with the money. The books I bought, I read; the books I read influenced my career." Perhaps this eminent person might have thought of the balls thus refused in his early youth, when, being still young, he gave his own first ball as prime minister.

4. In the management of money, there are some things we do for show

—wisely, if we can afford it. Money is station, as well as character and power.

For a young man of a gentleman's station and a cadet's income, the only show needed is that which probably pleases himself the most—the effect produced by his own personal appearance. Dress will, therefore, not unreasonably, and by no means frivolously, demand some of his thoughts and much of his money. To the station of a young aspirant of fashion in the polite world, who is known not to be rich, it matters nothing what he pays for his lodging; he can always give his address at a club or hotel. No one cares how much or how little he pays for his dinner. No fine lady inquires if he calls at her house on foot or in a carriage. But society expects him to dress as much like a gentleman as if he were a young duke; and, fortunately, as young dukes nowadays do not wear gold lace and miniver, this is no unreasonable exaction on the part of society. A gentleman's taste in dress is, upon principle, the avoidance of all things extravagant. It consists in the quiet simplicity of exquisite neatness; but, as the neatness must be a neatness in fashion, employ the best tailor; pay him ready money, and, on the whole, you will find him the cheapest.

Mere dandies are but cut flowers in a bouquet,—once faded, they can never reblossom. In the drawing-room, as everywhere else, Mind, in the long run, prevails. And, O well-booted Achaian! for all those substantial good things which money well managed commands, and which, year after year, as you advance in life, you will covet and sigh for,—yon sloven, thick-shod, and with cravat awry,—whose mind, as he hurries by the bow-window at White's, sows each fleeting moment with thoughts which grow not blossoms for bouquets, but corn-sheaves for garners—will, before he is forty, be far more the fashion than you. He is commanding the time out of which you are fading. And time, O my friend, is money! time wasted can never conduce to money well managed.

Note—LORD LYTTON was originally known to fame, in this country, as Edward Lytton Bulwer, and our people had hardly got used to the honorable title which Queen Victoria conferred on him and the astronomer Herschel, as the best representatives of the literature and science of her kingdom at the date of her inauguration (1838), when, in 1844, by royal license, and in pursuance of his mother's will, by which he succeeded to the Lytton estate of Knebworth, the popular author Bulwer was apparently lost in the less familiar designation of Sir Edward Bulwer Lytton, and again as Lord Lytton (since [illegible]), when, on the recommendation of the Premier (Lord Derby), in whose cabinet he had a seat as Secretary for the Colonies, he was elevated to the peerage as Baron Lytton; thenceforth we find his name recorded as the Rt. Hon. Lord Edward George Earle Bulwer Lytton. By whatever name he or the Queen or the Herald's College may choose to designate the author of the 'Caxtons,' his numerous works will be treasured as valuable contributions to the literature of the English language.

STUDIES AND CONDUCT.

KNOWLEDGE.—WISDOM.

THOUGHTS AND OPINIONS OF A STATESMAN.

WILLIAM VON HUMBOLDT, from whose Letters to a Lady, in whose loss of fortune incident to the German war with Napoleon I. he became interested as Envoy of Prussia to the Congress of Vienna, and whose disappointment he afterwards sought to alleviate by delicate pecuniary assistance, and friendly correspondence, was born in 1761, and died in 1835. Although less known out of Germany than his brother Alexander, his reputation, as a wise statesman, in Germany is second to no man of his time. These letters were published after his death, and an English edition appeared in 1850, in the series of *Small Books on Great Subjects*, by Pickering, under the secondary title given above. The English translator says: "Never was religion shown in a more amiable light than in the outpourings of his benevolent, yet firm mind. We see it as his guide and his support under all circumstances, and yet so unostentatiously so, that but for the publication of these Letters, probably none but his intimates would have known Wilhelm Von Humboldt than that he was a profound scholar, and an able statesman: and the moving spring of all his actions would have remained concealed till the day when the secrets of all heart shall be made known. It is well for the world that this has not been so; it is well to see the nobleman and the minister of state gathering from Christianity the rule of his life, and depending on its promises with the child-like confidence so acceptable to God."

BIBLE—OLD AND NEW TESTAMENT—ENGLISH AND GERMAN VERSION.

When the human race was nearer its origin, men seem to have had more greatness, more simplicity, more depth and nature in their thoughts and feelings, as well as in the expression of them. It is true we must arrive at the full and clear sight of this by laborious and often by mechanical acquirements; but in this very labor there is a charm; or even if not, it is at least soon over when we are accustomed to application. Among the strongest, purest, and finest tones in which the voice of antiquity has reached us, may be reckoned the books of the Old Testament; and we can never be enough thankful that in our translation they have lost so little of their reality and strength of expression.* I have often reflected with pleasure on the existence of so much that is exalted, rich, and varied, as is contained in the Bible, in the books of the Old and New Testament; and if this be, as is very frequently the case, the only book in the hands of the people, yet have they in this a compendium of human thought, history, poetry, and philosophy so complete, that it would be difficult to find a feeling or a thought which has not its echo in these books. Neither is there much in them which is incomprehensible to a common simple mind. The learned may penetrate deeper, but no one can go away unsatisfied.

I have always sought so to weave myself into the present, so as to be able to win, as far as possible, an interior victory over outward discomfort; and exactly in this point of view the reading of the Bible is an infinite, and certainly far the surest source of consolation. I know nothing to be compared to it. The consolation of the Bible flows equally, though in different ways, from both the Old and New Testament. In both, the general guidance of God, and the universal government of his Providence is the prevailing idea; and from hence, in religiously disposed minds, springs the deeply fixed, and ineffaceable conviction, that even the order of things under which we ourselves suffer, is the most wisely appointed, and the most beneficial not only for the whole, but, in consequence of that, for the sufferer himself. In the new testament there is such a full predominance of the spiritual and the moral; every thing is so completely rested upon and carried back to purity of mind, that whatever else external or internal may happen to man, if he but strive earnestly and eagerly after this, all the rest falls back into shadow. Hence misfortune and every other sorrow loses a part of its oppressive influence, and at all events none of its bitterness remains. The infinite mildness of the whole New Testament doctrine, which figures God almost entirely on the merciful side, and in which the self-sacrificing love of Christ for the human race, is everywhere brought forward; joined with the example which he himself has set us, alleviates like a healing balsam, every pain both of mind and body. In the Old Testament we do not find this, but there again appear, and always with more of comfort than terror, the omnipotence and omniscience of the Creator and Beholder of all things, raising us above our own individual sorrows by the grandeur of the representation.

LOVE OF NATURE—TREES—SKY.

The sight of the heavens, under whatever aspect, has an unceasing charm for me, by night, whether it be gloomy or starlight; by day, whether the eye loses itself in deep blue, or amid passing clouds, or in an unvaried grey, makes

---

* Luther's translation is among the finest renderings ever made of the Hebrew Scriptures. It has the same simplicity and strength which characterizes the English version. Of this a writer in the Catholic Dublin Review (attributed to Prof. J. H. Newman), remarks on the Protestant English version of the Bible: "It lives on the ear like music that can never be forgotten—like the sound of a church bell which a convert hardly knows he can forego. Its felicities seem to be almost things rather than mere words. It is part of the national mind, and the anchor of national seriousness. The memory of the dead passes into it. The potent traditions of childhood are stereotyped in its verses. The power of all the griefs and trials of a man is hidden beneath its words. It is the representative of his best moments, and all that there has been about him of soft, and gentle, and pure, and penitent, and good, speaks to him forever out of the English Bible. It is his sacred thing, which doubt has never dimmed, and controversy never soiled. In the length and breadth of the land there is not a Protestant with one spark of righteousness about him, whose spiritual biography is not in his Saxon Bible."

no difference: every one of these aspects awakens some especial tone of mind in man; and when we have the happiness not to be dependent on the weather for our mood, we are not obliged to be melancholy because the sky is dark, but can bring forth from our own mind continually fresh thoughts as outward circumstances vary; a colorless sky is no evil. Complaints about the weather are quite foreign to my nature, and I do not like to hear others complain of it. I consider Nature as a combination of forces, which may afford the purest pleasure if we quietly acquiesce in and accommodate ourselves to all its varying developments, and look at it as a whole, of which it matters little whether the smaller details be pleasant, so long as its great cycle of events completes its course. I have an especial delight in living face to face with Nature in the country, so that I may watch the progress of every season in turn.

Even without attaching any thought of religion to the sight of the heavens, there is something inexpressibly exciting to the mind in thus losing one's self in the infinity of space: it at once takes away from life its little cares and desires, and from reality its otherwise oppressive weight. As surely as the knowledge of man is the first and weightiest concern in the affairs of men, so surely, on the other hand, is there nothing more narrowing to the mind than the perpetually keeping our eyes fixed on the small circle of human beings by whom we are hemmed in. We must return often to the contemplation and feeling of a higher power ruling in human affairs, as we see it in nature, ere we can safely come back to the fetters of society. Only thus do we learn to hold the things of real life to be matters of minor importance, to make less account of good or ill fortune, to be careless about wants and vexations, and to fix our attention solely on the changes which take place in it, so as to leave exterior life to a certain degree out of our consideration. The thought of death has then nothing in it which can frighten or sadden us; we rather enjoy the recalling it, and look on the farewell to life which must follow, as a natural step in the development of being.

Natural objects themselves, even when they make no claim to beauty, excite the feelings and occupy the imagination. Nature pleases, attracts, delights, merely because it is nature. We recognise in it an Infinite Power, greater and more effective than that of man, and yet not terrible: for a mild and beneficial influence seems to be extended on every object around us. Indeed the general character of nature is kind and good. When we talk of tremendous cliffs, and terribly sublime scenery, nature herself, nevertheless, is not to be feared. We soon become confident and at home among the wildest rocks, and feel that to the hermit who flies to her for shelter, she readily imparts tranquillity and peace.

Faith only can raise us above our little daily life, and worldly business;—that only can give the soul a direction to higher things, and to objects and ideas which alone have value or importance. It bestows what certainly you have not failed to enjoy, and which you doubtless value far beyond all that is called happiness or good fortune,—I mean the peace of the soul. It is grounded chiefly, no doubt, on an untroubled and clear conscience, but it is not attained by that alone: we must be content with our lot, and be able to say calmly and truly that we have not murmured at it, but on the contrary have received it when prosperous, with humility, when adverse, with resignation and real confidence in God's wise government. As a difficult, perplexing situation enhances the merit of accommodating ourselves to it without complaint, or of freeing ourselves from it by our own exertions, so we thus grow into better accord with our lot, whatever it may be.

We perceive in the immutable course of Nature, always following fixed laws, something infinitely consoling and tranquillizing. There is something here, then, that does not change; "an immovable pole amid the circling course of appearances," as Schiller beautifully expresses it in one of his poems. Man, then, belongs to a great and immutable order of things; and this as certainly leads to something higher, and finally to a point at which all doubts will be explained, and all difficulties made plain; when all the involved and apparently discordant laws will at last unite into one mighty diapason;—so must he, too, proceed with it to this same point. The character, moreover, which is impressed upon nature is always so gentle a one, that the finest feelings can not be wounded by it. The tranquillity, the joy, the splendor which she spreads around; the magnificence and grandeur in which she clothes herself, have nothing in them either of pretension or of haughtiness to repulse us. However deep may be the affliction, the mind nevertheless opens itself willingly to the feelings awakened by the numberless flowers of the renewed year, the joyful twitter of the birds, the splendor of the objects touched by the still brightening and strengthening sun, as he goes forth in his might. Grief then assumes the form of a gentle melancholy, which is not a stranger to a certain peace and sweetness even. If, finally, we regard nature as not really all, merely the bond between the spiritual and corporeal world; if we take it as the operation of matter and its forces, acting in obedience to the Creator, then it is the earthly shell only of man that belongs to it; himself, his higher and proper existence, steps beyond its bounds, and associates itself to another and nobler order of things. You will see from this, nearly, how I am influenced by the slowly approaching, yet beautiful Spring; how I enjoy it; and how it mingles with all my deepest feelings.

All the things which surround us contain in themselves matter for contemplation, for enjoyment, and for delight, both for the mind and feelings, which is wholly different from, and independent of, the peculiar destination and physical uses of any of them. The more we abandon ourselves to the pursuit of it, the more does this deeper sense—this meaning which belongs half to the natural object, and half to us who find it—open upon us. Let us only, for instance, look at the clouds. In themselves they are nothing but shapeless mist, the consequence of moisture and warmth; yet how, when viewed from the earth, do they enliven the sky with their forms and colors, and how many fancies and feelings do they give rise to in the mind.

The leaves of the trees are beginning to take the varied colors which so much ornament the autumn, and to a certain degree make up for the loss of the first fresh green. The little place which I inhabit (Tegel) is admirably made to show all the beauties which large handsome trees of different kinds exhibit through all the changing seasons of the year. All round the house they stand broad and spreading, like a green fan. Over the land alleys extend in various directions; in the garden and the vineyard there are fruit trees; in the park is a thick dark growth of underwood; the lake is surrounded with a forest, and the islands in it are bordered with trees and bushes. I have a particular love for trees, and I do not like to cut them down, nor even to transplant them. There is something melancholy in removing a poor tree from the society in which it has lived so long, to bring it into fresh soil, from which, however much it may disagree with its constitution, it has no chance of escaping any more, but must pine away through a slow exhaustion, awaiting its final death. There is generally an extraordinary character of anxious wish in trees, when they stand so fixed and cramped in the earth, and try to extend their summits and their branches as far as possible beyond the bounds of their roots. I know nothing in nature so formed to be the symbol of desire. Man, too, in fact, with all his apparent freedom of motion, is very much in the same state. He is still confined within a certain space, however widely he may roam; sometimes he can never stir from his small circle, (and this is often the case with women) the same little spot sees his cradle and his grave; or if he removes from it, he is drawn back to it from time to time by his inclination or his duty.

OCCUPATION—SILENT THINKING.

Occupation, in my mind, is as much a need as eating and drinking; even those who do nothing which a sensible man would call work, fancy at least that they are doing something: an idler, if even in his heart he means to remain such, does not tell the world so. There is, however, one employment, though of a different kind, which may be enjoyed while traveling: namely silent thought, which goes on without moving a finger, without reading and without writing. It is not indeed impossible to enjoy it at home, but very often business does not allow of it, and we can hardly attain it excepting in a lonely walk. I set a particular value upon it, and for this reason pass sleepless nights very willingly,—though this seldom happens to me except in illness, for I am a good and sound sleeper. Upon a journey it becomes almost necessary, and thus I can have my enjoyment with a clear conscience. . . . It is certainly true that men in general do not allow themselves time enough for thought: they do any thing rather than think, even when they are quite free from business; or when they have no higher demand on their time and attention, they give themselves up to mere empty nothings. The occupations of men are, unfortunately, for the most part such that they shut out all deep thought whilst they are going on, and yet make no ennobling claim on the mind: yet many have the folly to attach a value to these occupations, and even to pride themselves upon their diligence in them.

It is far better and more beneficial to read and think; that is, to read merely for the sake of matter to think about; because thought must have some object, some thread which may give it connection and sequence; and for this purpose we need only to take up any book that comes to hand, and can lay it aside again for any other. If this be done for some weeks, a person must be quite wanting in intellectual vigor and activity, if ideas do not arise of themselves which he will wish to pursue farther; or things which he desires to know more about; and then he enters upon a study of his own choice, not one imposed upon him by another. This is what I think I have seen done by all the women who lead any thing like an active intellectual life.

HAPPINESS.

God has given life to man in order that he may employ it in a way pleasing to Him, and conformable to duty; and that he may be happy in the consciousness of so doing. It is undoubtedly given us for our happiness. But happiness has always this condition attached to it, that, whether at first, or when longer days have brought their trials with them, we shall find it only in the practice of duty and self-command. I therefore never ask myself what value life has for me: I endeavor to fill it well, and leave the rest to Providence. The diminution which our powers sustain as age advances, I know full well by my own experience; but I can not on that account retract what I lately wrote to you, namely, that the proper aim of life is to increase to the utmost the mental capacity of the individual, according to the circumstances he is placed in, as well as to the length of life and power of knowledge granted him.

Happiness does not depend on those outward circumstances from which vexation and contradiction arise; and heaven has so wisely distributed these last, that he who outwardly appears the most favored, is not on that account the more free, even for a moment, from occasion and causes of interior grief. In a life already tolerably long, and certainly not spent in the easiest of positions, many things have happened to me which, for a longer or shorter time, have thrown me out of my usual course of life, exactly in those parts which touched me the most nearly.

LIFE AND DEATH.

Life and death, unalterably connected together, are but developments of the same being; and it would be inconsiderate and childish to wish to alter or delay the moral and physical maturity appointed to all men. Still less is it from the slightest weariness of life. I had the same feeling in my happiest days, and now that I am no longer susceptible of pleasure from without, but live quietly in myself and my recollections, I can still less have any quarrel with life. But the lapse of time has something in it delightful to me: time does not flow on emptily;—it brings, and takes, and leaves behind; through it we become continually richer, not exactly in enjoyment, but in something higher. I do not mean by this, mere dry experience;—no,—it is an elevation to a greater clearness of perception, and a fuller self-knowledge: what our nature is capable of, we are more thoroughly;—and we more clearly comprehend why it is capable of so much, and will be of yet more. And this being the center point of the present and future being of man, is the highest and the most important to him. . . .

I very early cherished the feeling that we must always be prepared to make our way manfully through whatever lot be appointed to us. Nevertheless, it is impossible not to regard life as an ocean through which we must steer our vessel with better or worse fortune, and then it is a natural feeling to like rather to have a short than a long voyage before us. This view of life,—as a whole, as a work that must be gone through with,—has always appeared to me a powerful aid towards the meeting death with equanimity. If, on the contrary, we look at life piecemeal, if we try only to add one pleasant day to another, as if we thought this could endure to all eternity, there is nothing more comfortless than to stand close upon the boundary where the series will at once be broken off. . . .

Man may make life what he pleases, and give it as much worth, both for himself and others, as he has energy for. Of course this must be understood only in a moral and spiritual sense; for we do not hold outward circumstances in our power; and it is only over our intellectual and moral being that we can rule: but over this our sway is complete. On this account,—if we can but bring ourselves to think calmly,—life has truly an inestimable value, even under the most unpleasant circumstances.

Death, and a new life, can only be for those who are already mature for the change. Man must seek to advance this ripeness in himself; for the ripeness of death, and that for the new life is one and the same. It consists in a separation from what is earthly; in an indifference to earthly enjoyments, and earthly activity; in a life in thoughts far removed from this world; in a casting off of anxious wishes for happiness here; in short, in a state of mind which looks without anxiety to what may be our lot in this world, and only considers the end after which we are striving: which exercises fortitude and self-denial, and maintains a strict self-government. From hence arises the serene, fearless peace of mind, which needs nothing exterior, and which extends over our intellectual existence a heavenly brightness, like the unclouded blue of an earthly sky.

Weariness of life,—insensibility to its enjoyments,—a wish that it were ended,—these have no share in my solitude.

Life is an outward occupation, an actual work, in all ranks and all situations. It is not, however, exactly this occupation or this work itself which is of such great value, but it is the thread by which better things, namely, our thoughts and feelings, are connected, or along which they run. It is the ballast without which the ship would have no steadiness on the waves.

WILLIAM WORDSWORTH.

CHARACTER OF THE HAPPY WARRIOR.

Who is the happy Warrior? Who is he
That every Man in arms should wish to be?
—It is the generous Spirit, who, when brought
Among the tasks of real life, hath wrought
Upon the plan that pleased his childish thought:
Whose high endeavors are an inward light
That makes the path before him always bright:
Who, with a natural instinct to discern
What knowledge can perform, is diligent to learn;
Abides by this resolve, and stops not there,
But makes his moral being his prime care;
Who, doomed to go in company with Pain,
And Fear, and Bloodshed, miserable train!
Turns his necessity to glorious gain;
In face of these doth exercise a power
Which is our human nature's highest dower;
Controls them and subdues, transmutes, bereaves
Of their bad influence, and their good receives:
By objects, which might force the soul to abate
Her feeling, rendered more compassionate;
Is placable—because occasions rise
So often that demand such sacrifice;
More skillful in self-knowledge, even more pure,
As tempted more; more able to endure,
As more exposed to suffering and distress;
Thence, also, more alive to tenderness.
—'Tis he whose law is reason; who depends
Upon that law as on the best of friends;
Whence, in a state where men are tempted still
To evil for a guard against worse ill,
And what in quality or act is best
Doth seldom on a right foundation rest,
He fixes good on good alone, and owes
To virtue every triumph that he knows:
—Who, if he rise to station of command,
Rises by open means; and there will stand
On honorable terms, or else retire,
And in himself possess his own desire;
Who comprehends his trust, and to the same
Keeps faithful with a singleness of aim;
And therefore does not stoop, nor lie in wait
For wealth, or honors, or for worldly state;
Whom they must follow; on whose head must fall,
Like showers of manna, if they come at all:
Whose powers shed round him in the common strife,
Or mild concerns of ordinary life,

A constant influence, a peculiar grace;
But who, if he be called upon to face
Some awful moment to which heaven has joined
Great issues, good or bad for human kind,
Is happy as a Lover; and attired
With sudden brightness, like a Man inspired;
And, through the heat of conflict, keeps the law
In calmness made, and sees what he foresaw;
Or if an unexpected call succeed,
Come when it will, is equal to the need:
—He who though thus endued as with a sense
And faculty for storm and turbulence,
Is yet a Soul whose master-bias leans
To homefelt pleasures and to gentle scenes;
Sweet images! which, wheresoe'er he be,
Are at his heart; and such fidelity
It is his darling passion to approve;
More brave for this, that he hath much to love:—
'Tis, finally, the Man, who, lifted high,
Conspicuous object in a Nation's eye,
Or left unthought of in obscurity,—
Who, with a toward or untoward lot,
Prosperous or adverse, to his wish or not,
Plays, in the many games of life, that one
Where what he most doth value must be won:
Whom neither shape of danger can dismay,
Nor thought of tender happiness betray;
Who, not content that former worth stand fast,
Looks forward, persevering to the last,
From well to better, daily self-surpast:
Who, whether praise of him must walk the earth
For ever, and to noble deeds give birth,
Or he must go to dust without his fame,
And leave a dead unprofitable name,
Finds comfort in himself and in his cause;
And, while the mortal mist is gathering, draws
His breath in confidence of Heaven's applause:
This is the happy Warrior; this is He
Whom every Man in arms should wish to be.

ODE TO DUTY.

Stern Daughter of the Voice of God!
O Duty! if that name thou love
Who art a Light to guide, a Rod
To check the erring, and reprove;
Thou, who art victory and law
When empty terrors overawe;
From vain temptations dost set free;
And calm'st the weary strife of frail humanity.

HENRY TAYLOR—1800.

Henry Taylor has won and holds permanently a high place among English dramatists and essayists, by his "Philip Van Artevelde," "Edwin the Fair," "The Statesman," and "Notes from Life." His maxims and reflections are the results of an attentive observation of life in office or at large, noted down at the time, and digested and shaped by a well balanced mind, enriched by liberal studies. Mr. Taylor, in his "*Notes from Life*," has an Essay on Wisdom, which is the offspring of the same spirit that prompted Southey in the utterance of Doctor Dove on Wisdom and Knowledge, in a chapter of the "Doctor," already given.

WISDOM IN THE CONDUCT OF AFFAIRS AND OF LIFE.

Wisdom is not the same with understanding, talents, capacity, ability, sagacity, sense, or prudence—not the same with any one of these; neither will all these together make it up. It is that exercise of the reason into which the heart enters—a structure of the understanding rising out of the moral and spiritual nature.

Wisdom is corrupted by ambition, even when the quality of the ambition is intellectual. For ambition, even of this quality, is but a form of self-love, which, seeking gratification in the consciousness of intellectual power, is too much delighted with the exercise to have a single and paramount regard to the end; and it is not according to wisdom that the end—that is, the moral and spiritual consequences—should suffer derogation in favor of the intellectual means. God is love, and God is light; whence it results that love is light; and it is only by following the effluence of that light, that intellectual power issues into wisdom. The intellectual power which loses that light and issues into intellectual pride, is out of the way to wisdom, and will not attain even to intellectual greatness. For though many arts, gifts, and attainments may co-exist in much force with intellectual pride, an open greatness can not; and of all the correspondences between the moral and intellectual nature, there is none more direct and immediate than that of humility with capaciousness. If pride of intellect be indulged, it will mark out to a man conscious of great talents the circle of his own intellectual experiences as the only one in which he can keenly recognize and appreciate the intellectual universe; and there is no order of intellectual men which stands in a more strict limitation than that of the man who can not conceive what he does not contain. Men who are accustomed to write or speak for effect, may write or speak what is wise from time to time, because they may be capable of thinking and intellectually adopting what is wise: but they will not be wise men; because the love of God, the love of man, and the love of truth not having the mastery with them, the growth and structure of their minds must needs be perverted if not stunted. Thence it is that so many men are observed to speak wisely and yet act foolishly; they are not deficient in their understandings, but the wisdom of the heart is wanting to their ends and objects, and to those feelings which have the direction of their acts. And if they do speak wisely, it is not because they are wise; for the permanent shape and organization of the mind proceeds from what we feel and do, and not from what we speak, write, or think. There is a great volume of truth in the admonition which teaches us that the spirit of obedience is to prepare the way, action to come next, and that knowledge is not precedent to these, but consequent: "Do the will of my Father which is in heaven, and thou shalt know of the doctrine."

In some discussions, a wise man will be silenced by argumentation, only because he knows that the question should be determined by considerations which lie beyond the reach of argumentative exhibition. And indeed, in all but purely scientific questions, arguments are not to be submitted to by the judgment as first in command; rather they are to be used as auxiliaries and pioneers; the judgment should profit by them to the extent of the services they can render, but after their work is done, it should come to its conclusions upon its own free survey. I have seldom known a man with great powers of argumentation abundantly indulged, who could attain to an habitually just judgment. In our courts of law, where advocacy and debate are most in use, ability, sagacity, and intellectual power flourish and abound, whilst wisdom is said to have been debarred.

Ambition and self-love will commonly derange that proportion between the active and passive understanding which is essential to wisdom, and will lead a man to value thoughts and opinions less according to their worth and truth, than according as they are his own or another's. The objection made by Brutus to Cicero in the play,—that he "would never follow any thing which other men began"—points to one corruption operated by self-love upon a great understanding. Some preference a man may reasonably accord to what is the growth of his own mind apart from its absolute value, on the ground of its specific usefulness to himself; for what is native to the soil will thrive better and bear more fruit than what has been transplanted: but, on the other hand, if a man would enlarge the scope and diversify the kinds of his thoughts and contemplations, he should not think too much to apprehend nor talk too much to listen. He should cherish the thoughts of his own begetting with a loving care and a temperate discipline—they are the *family* of his mind and its chief reliance—but he should give a hospitable reception to guests and to travelers with stories of far countries, and the family should not be suffered to crowd the doors.

Even without the stimulant of self-love, some minds, owing to a natural redundance of activity and excess of velocity and fertility, can not be sufficiently passive to be wise. A capability to take a thousand views of a subject is hard to be reconciled with directness and singleness of judgment; and he who can find a great deal to say for any view, will not often go the straight road to the one view that is right.

The temptation by which a man of genius, with a general capacity of enjoyment, is assailed, consists in imagining that he has within himself and by virtue of his temperament, sources of joy altogether independent of conduct and circumstances. It is true that he has these sources on this unconditional tenure for a time; and it is owing to this very truth that his futurity is in danger,—not in respect of wisdom only, but also in respect of happiness. And if we look to recorded examples, we shall find that a great capacity of enjoyment does ordinarily bring about the destruction of enjoyment in its own ulterior consequences, having uprooted wisdom by the way.

A man of genius, so gifted—or, let us rather say, so tempted—lives, until the consummation approaches, as if he possessed some elixir or phylactery, reckless of consequences, because his happiness, being so inward to his nature, seems to be inherent and indefeasible. Wisdom is not wanted. The intellect, perhaps, amidst the abundance of its joys, rejoices in wise contemplations; but wisdom is not adopted and domesticated in the mind, owing to the fearlessness of the heart. For wisdom will have no hold on the heart in which joy is not tempered by fear. The fear of the Lord, we know, is the beginning of it; and some hallowing and chastening influences of fear will always go along with it. Fear, indeed, is the mother of foresight; spiritual fear, of a foresight that reaches beyond the grave; temporal fear, of a foresight that falls short; but without fear there is neither the one foresight nor the other; and as pain has been truly said to be the deepest thing in our nature, so is it fear that will bring the depths of our nature within our knowledge:—

> "What sees rejoicing genius in the earth?
> A thousand meadows with a thousand herds
> Freshly luxuriant in a May-day dawn;
> A thousand ships that caracole and prance
> With freights of gold upon a sunny sea;
> A thousand gardens gladdened by all flowers,
> That on the air breathe out an odorous beauty."

Genius may see all this and rejoice; but it will not exalt itself into wisdom, unless it see also the meadow in the livid hues of winter, the ship under bare poles, and the flower when the beauty of the fashion of it perishes.

On the other hand, wisdom without genius (a far more precious gift than genius without wisdom) is, by God's blessing upon the humble and loving heart, though not as often met with as "the ordinary of Nature's sale-work," yet not altogether rare; for the desire to be right will go a great way towards wisdom. Intellectual guidance is the less needed where there is little to lead astray—where humility lets the heart loose to the impulses of love. That we can be wise by impulse will seem a paradox to some; but it is a part of that true doctrine which traces wisdom to the moral as well as the intellectual mind, and more surely to the former than to the latter—one of those truths which is recognized when we look into our nature through the clearness of a poetic spirit:—

> "Moments there are in life—alas how few!—
> When casting cold prudential doubts aside,
> We take a generous impulse for our guide,
> And following promptly what the heart thinks best,
> Commit to Providence the rest;
> Sure that no after-reckoning will arise
> Of shame or sorrow, for the heart is wise.
> And happy they who thus in faith obey
> Their better nature: err sometimes they may,
> And some sad thoughts lie heavy in the breast,
> Such as by hope deceived are left behind;
> But like a shadow these will pass away
> From the pure sunshine of the peaceful mind."—Southey.

The doctrine of wisdom by impulse is no doubt liable to be much misused and misapplied. The right to rest upon such a creed accrues only to those who have so trained their nature as to be entitled to trust it. It is the impulse of the *habitual* heart which the judgment may fairly follow upon occasion—of the heart which, being habitually humble and loving, has been framed by love to wisdom. Some such fashioning love will always effect; for love can not exist without solicitude, solicitude brings thoughtfulness, and it is in a thoughtful love that the wisdom of the heart consists. The impulse of such a heart will take its shape and guidance from the very mold in which it is cast, without any application of the reason expressed; and the most inadvertent motion of a wise heart will for the most part be wisely directed; providentially, let us rather say: for Providence has no more eminent seat than in the wisdom of the heart.

Wisdom by impulse, then, is to be trusted in by those only who have habitually used their reason to the full extent of its powers in forming the heart and cultivating the judgment, whilst, owing to its constitutional deficiency, or to its peculiarity (for the reason may be unserviceable from other causes than deficiency), they are conscious that their judgment is likely to be rather perplexed than cleared by much thinking on questions on which they are called upon to act or decide.

An eminent statesman is said to have averred, that when he was conscious of having taken a decision with all due care and consideration, to the best of his judgment and with the best intentions, he never looked back to it with a moment's regret, though the result might prove it to have been wholly erroneous. This is a frame of mind highly conducive to civil courage, and therefore not without its advantages in political life. But it is not easily conducive to wisdom. Nor, perhaps, in this unqualified form, is it to be altogether vindicated in morals. At all events, so much regret might be felt, if no more, as would suffice to awaken some self-questionings, not merely as to the specific moral rectitude accompanying or proximately preceding the particular act, but as to that general and life-long training of the heart to wisdom, which gives the best assurance of specific results, and of which, therefore, specific failures should suggest the deficiency. Some short-comings of this kind there must of course be in all human beings, and they should be at all times aware of it; but it is in the order of Nature that this consciousness should be quickened from time to time by the contemplation of evil consequences arising from specific errors of judgment, however innocent in themselves; which contemplation, accompanied with a natural regret, constitutes what may be called a repentance of the understanding—not easily to be escaped by a plain man, nor properly to be repudiated by a philosopher.

The main scope and design of this disquisition having been to inculcate that wisdom is still more essentially a moral and spiritual than it is an intellectual attribute, that genius can mount to wisdom only by Jacob's ladder, and that knowledge can only be converted into wisdom by an application of the heart, I can not better close it than with that declaration of the nature of wisdom which is delivered in the 28th chapter of the book of Job:—

"Whence then cometh wisdom? and where is the place of understanding?

"Seeing it is hid from the eyes of all living, and kept close from the fowls of the air.

"Destruction and death say, we have heard the fame thereof with our ears.

"God understandeth the way thereof, and he knoweth the place thereof.

"For he looketh to the ends of the earth, and seeth under the whole Heaven;

"To make the weight for the winds; and he weigheth the waters by measure.

"When he made a decree for the rain, and a way for the lightning of the thunder:

"Then did he see it, and declare it; he prepared it, yea, and searched it out.

"And unto man he said, Behold, the fear of the Lord, that is wisdom; and to depart from evil is understanding."

He was one
Of many thousand such that die betimes,
Whose story is a fragment known to few;
Then comes the man who has the luck to live,
And he's a prodigy. Compute the chances,
And deem there ne'er a one in dangerous times
Who wins the race of glory, but than him
A thousand men more gloriously endowed,
Have fallen upon the course; a thousand others
Have had their fortunes foundered by a chance,
Whilst lighter barks pushed past them; to whom add
A smaller tally, of the singular few,
Who, gifted with predominating powers,
Bear yet a temperate will and keep the peace.
The world knows nothing of its greatest men.

H. Taylor.—*Philip Van Artevelde.*

All my life long,
I have beheld with most respect the man
Who knew himself, and knew the ways before him,
And from among them chose considerately,
With a clear foresight, not a blind courage;
And having chosen, with a steadfast mind
Pursued his purposes. I trained myself
To take my place in high or low estate
As one of that scant order of mankind.

H. Taylor.—*Philip Van Artevelde.*

EDUCATION OF GIRLS.

INSTITUTIONS AND SUGGESTIONS.

SUGGESTIONS ON THE EDUCATION OF GIRLS.

BY VARIOUS AUTHORS.

In addition to elaborate articles, new and old, on the subject of *Female Education*, we propose to bring together, in successive numbers, the best suggestions we have taken note of in our reading, by different authors in different ages and countries, as to the instruction and practical training of girls.

St. Jerome.

Jerome—or Eusebius Hieronymus Sophronius—and better known from his canonical title as *St. Jerome*, was born of Christian parents, at Stridon, a town in Pannonia, on the confines of Italy, about the year 331. Gifted with fine natural powers, he enjoyed and improved all the opportunities of learning which the best schools and the most erudite teachers in Rome and Gaul could afford, and to the acquisitions from books and living teachers, he added the fruits of the widest travel, and of profound meditation for years in the solitudes of the East. He wrote on almost every subject—defending the doctrines of the church as held at Rome, preaching religious abstinence and mortification, and obtaining a remarkable influence over the women of his time. Under his eloquent exhortations, many of the wealthy and noble ladies of Rome devoted themselves to perpetual chastity, distributed their possessions among the poor, and spent their time in attendance on the sick. Among these converts was Paula, a descendant of the Scipios and the Gracchi, who, on the death of her husband, having provided for her family, visited the holy places of the East and finally established herself at Bethlehem—building three monasteries for devout women, all under one rule, and a house for St. Jerome and his brethren. Her son, Toxotius, married *Læta*, a daughter of a Pagan priest, who became a convert under Jerome's preaching. For the education of their daughter, St. Jerome wrote a letter, which has been the highest authority in regard to female training with devout Catholics ever since. This daughter resided for a time with her grandmother at Bethlehem, and succeeded her in the government of the monasteries which St. Paula founded. St. Jerome is best known to the general scholar for his translation and edition of the Scriptures, styled the "*Latin Vulgate*," and for his "*Catalogue of Ecclesiastical History*." Incidents in his life and representations of his character are favorite subjects in pictures, prints, and sculpture. The "*Last Communion of St. Jerome*," by Domenichino, in the Vatican at Rome, is one of the most celebrated pictures of the world.

LETTER* OF ST. JEROME TO LÆTA, ON THE EDUCATION OF HER DAUGHTER.

Of this kind must be the education of a soul which is intended for a temple of the Holy Ghost:—Let her not learn to hear or say any thing but what savors of the fear of God. Impure language let her not understand, or know any thing of worldly songs; while her tongue is yet tender, let its acquaintance be only with sweet psalms. Keep her away from the wantonness of youth; nay, let even her maidens and attendants be debarred all secular connections, lest what they have learnt amiss they should teach worse. Let her have letters made of box and ivory, and learn to call them by their proper names; these will amuse her, and thus amusement will become instruction. And let her not only know the letters in their order, so as to repeat their names by rote, but change the order frequently, mixing the middle with the first, and the last with the middle, till she can recognize them by sight as well as sound. But when her trembling hand begins to hold a pen, let its tender joints be guided by the hand of another, placed over hers; or else let the letters be engraved upon a tablet, so that she may trace out their forms without wandering from the lines of the engraving. Induce her to put syllables together by rewards, and encourage her with such little gifts as please the mind of infancy. Give her also companions in her lessons, to excite her emulation, and even sting her by the praises they receive. Do not find fault with her, if she is slow; but call out her powers by commendation, making her feel pleasure in excelling, and pain in being excelled. Above all things, take care that she does not get disgusted with her studies; lest any prejudice against them, contracted in her infancy, should extend beyond it. Let the very names by which she learns to make up letters into words be not taken at random, but selected and brought together with a view to some good purpose; the names, for instance, of prophets and apostles, with the whole line of patriarchs, from Adam downward, according to St. Matthew and St. Luke; thus, while otherwise engaged, her memory will be preparing for its future duties. Then you must look out for a tutor of approved age, and character, and learning; nor will a man of learning blush to do that for a relation, or for any noble virgin, which Aristotle did for the son of Philip, for whose sake that philosopher condescended to the office of a clerk, and instructed him in the first rudiments of knowledge. Small things must not be despised, when great things can not come to pass without them. The letters themselves, and the first rules of education, sound very differently from the mouth of the rustic and the learned. You must take care, therefore, that the silly affectation of women does not give her a habit of pronouncing her words imperfectly; and that she does not idly amuse herself in dress and jewels,—of which things, one is fatal to the morals, the other to the elocution: do not let her learn in infancy what she will have to unlearn afterward. The Gracchi are said to have been not a little indebted for their eloquence to their mother's conversation. The style of Hortensius was formed in his father's bosom. It is a hard thing to get rid of that which the untutored mind has first imbibed. Who can restore the wool of purple dye to its native whiteness? The vessel long retains the taste and smell with which it has been fresh imbued. Greek history tells us that Alexander, the most powerful of kings, the conqueror of the world, never could throw off the defects in manner and gait which he had contracted in his infancy from his instructor, Leonides. For we are all disposed to imitate the bad; and we can soon copy a man's vices, though we can not reach unto his virtues. Take care, therefore, that her nurse is not

* St. Jerome's Works, Vol. I., Ep. [illegible]. Edition of Erasmus, Basil, 1516. We have omitted a few introductory paragraphs of St. Jerome's Letter to Læta as irrelevant to the main subject.

drunken, or wanton, or fond of talking; but let her have a modest woman to carry her, and one of becoming gravity to nurse her. Above all, let the infant soldier know the Captain, and the army, for whose service she is trained. Let her long for them, and threaten to go over to them. Let even her dress and apparel remind her for whom she is intended. Do not pierce her ears for ear-rings, or defile with artificial colors the beauty that is consecrated unto Christ. Load not her neck with gold and pearls, nor burden her head with jewels, nor give her hair a flaming dye,—too true an omen of the flames of hell. Let her pearls be of a different kind from such as she may sell and buy, "the pearl of great price."

Eli, the high-priest, offended God by the vices of his sons. A man can not be a bishop, if he has profligate and disobedient children. On the other hand, we are told that "a woman shall be saved in child-bearing, if they continue in faith, and charity, and holiness, with sobriety." If the virtues of those who are of mature age and independent will are imputed to the parents, how much more of those who are but babes and sucklings, and do not know their right hand from their left,—the difference, that is, between good and evil! If you are so anxious that your daughter should avoid a viper's sting, why are you not equally careful that she be not stricken by "the hammer of the whole earth;" that she drink not of the golden cup of Babylon; that she go not forth with Dinah, or wish to see the daughters of a strange land; that her feet grow not wanton, or her garments trail behind her? Poisons are never given, unless the cup is smeared with honey; and vices can not deceive, except under the shade of virtues. How, then, you will say, are the sins of the fathers not imputed to the children, and of the children to the fathers, but "the soul which sinneth, it shall die?" This is spoken of those whose years admit of wisdom, of whom it is written in the gospel, "He is of age, let him speak for himself." But so long as he is a child, and thinks as a child, till he has arrived at years of discretion, and the point where good and evil, like the Pythagorean letter,* become divergent—up to that time his actions, good or evil, are imputed to his parents. Unless, indeed, you suppose that the sons of Christians, if they continue unbaptized, bear all the guilt of sin themselves, and that none of it falls on the head of those who refuse to bestow that sacrament upon them, especially at a time when its recipients could not reject it; just as, on the other hand, the salvation of the infant is a gain unto the parents. It was in your own power to offer your daughter or not (though here your condition is peculiar, inasmuch as you had vowed her to God's service before she was conceived;) but now she is offered, you can only neglect her at your own peril. He who offers a victim lame or mutilated, or blemished in any other way, is guilty of sacrilege; how much heavier the punishment of him who offers a part of his own body, and the purity of an untainted soul, to the acceptance of his King, if he is careless in preserving that which he has so disposed!

When she is growing up, and beginning, like her Bridegroom, to increase in wisdom, and stature, and favor with God and man, let her go with her parents to the temple of her heavenly Father; but let her not depart from the temple. Let them seek her in the journeys of the world, among her kinsfolk and acquaintance, and find her nowhere but in the sanctuary of the Scriptures, asking questions of prophets and apostles about the spiritual marriage of the soul with Christ. Let her imitate Mary, whom the angel Gabriel found alone in her chamber; and therefore, perhaps, she was alarmed, because she beheld the form of a man to whom she was a stranger. Let her imitate her of whom it is said, "The king's daughter is all glorious within."

---

* The letter Y was made by the Pythagoreans a symbol of the parting road of human life, one of its branches representing virtue, the other vice.

Let her, moreover, not eat in public, that is, be present at her parents' meals; lest she should see dainties to excite her longing. For though some persons think it a higher virtue to despise present pleasure, to my mind there is greater security for temperance in not knowing the object of desire. I remember reading in a book at school, "that you will hardly find fault with that which has become habitual." Let her learn, even now, not to drink wine, "wherein is excess." However, abstinence is irksome and dangerous to the young, before the body has attained its full strength and proportions. Up to that time, therefore, let her use the bath, if necessity requires; and take a little wine, for her stomach's sake; and have animal food, lest her limbs fail her before they begin to do their duty. I say this as a matter of indulgence unto her, not of command to you—to prevent weakness, not to inculcate luxury. Otherwise, why should not a Christian virgin do that altogether which Jewish superstition does in part, by the rejection of certain animals and meats; not to mention the Indian Bramins and Egyptian Gymnosophists, who live entirely upon barley flour, and rice, and fruits? If glass is of such a value, are not pearls of greater price? Let the daughter of promise live as those lived who were the children of promise. Where the grace is equal, let the labor be equal also. Let her be deaf to instruments of music, and be a stranger to the very use of the pipe, and harp, and lyre.

Let her every day repeat a lesson culled from the flowers of Scripture, learning a number of verses in Greek, and immediately afterward being instructed in Latin; for, if the tender mouth is not properly molded from the very commencement, the pronunciation will acquire a foreign accent, the faults of which will pass into her native tongue. You must be her governess, and the model of her untutored infancy; take care that she sees nothing in you, or in her father, which she would be wrong in doing. Remember that you are her parents, and that she learns more from your example than your voice. Flowers are soon dead; the violet, and the lily, and the crocus, soon fade in an unwholesome air. Never let her go into public, unless accompanied by you; nor enter the sanctuaries built over martyrs' tombs, or churches, without her mother. Beware of the nods and smiles of the young and gay; let the solemn vigils and nocturns be spent without departing from her mother's side. Do not let her attach herself too closely to any one of her maidens, or make her ear the depositary of her secrets. All should hear what is said to one. Let the companion she chooses be not well dressed or beautiful, or with a voice of liquid harmony; but grave, and pale, and meanly clad, and of solemn countenance. Set over her an aged virgin, of approved faith, and modesty, and conduct, to teach and habituate her, by her own example, to rise up by night for prayer and psalms, to sing her morning hymns, and to take her place in the ranks, like a Christian warrior, at the third, and sixth, and ninth hours; and, again, to light her lamp and offer up her evening sacrifice. Let the day pass, and the night find her at this employment. Prayer and reading, reading and prayer, must be the order of her life; nor will the time travel slowly when it is filled by such engagements.

Teach her also the working of wool, to hold the distaff, to place the basket in her lap, to ply the spindle, and draw out the threads. But let her have nothing to do with silk, or golden thread. Let the clothes she makes be such as to keep out the cold, and not a mere compromise with nakedness. Her food should be a few herbs, and so forth, with sometimes a few small fishes. But not to go into details on this subject, of which I have elsewhere spoken more at length,—let her always leave off eating with an appetite, so that she may be able to read and sing immediately. I do not approve of protracted and inordinate fastings, especially for those of tender years, where week is added unto week, and the use of oil and fruit prohibited. I have experienced the truth of the proverb, "A tired ass will not go straight." But the rule to be constantly observed in fasting is this: take care that your strength is equal to your journey, lest, after running the first stage, you break down in the middle of it.

But to return to the subject: when you go into the country, do not leave you daughter at home; she must neither be able or know how to do without you, and be afraid of being left alone. She must not converse with people of the world, or be in the same house with ill-conducted virgins. She must not be present at the marriages of her servants, or have any thing to do with the games of noisy domestics.

Let her delight not in silk and jewels, but in the holy writings, where there is no gold or mosaic painting, like that on Babylonian leather, to arrest the eye; but sound learning, corrected by sound faith, to inform the mind. Let her first learn the Psalter, and give her hours of leisure to these holy songs. From the proverbs of Solomon she will gather practical instruction; Ecclesiastes will teach her to despise the world; in Job she will find examples of virtue and endurance. Then let her go to the Gospels, and never lay them down. The Acts of the Apostles, with the Epistles, must be imbibed with all the ardor of her heart. When her mind is thoroughly stored with these treasures, she may commit the prophets to her memory, together with the Heptateuch, and the books of Kings and Chronicles, with those of Esdras and Esther. The Song of Solomon she may read last without danger; if she reads it earlier, she may not discern that a spiritual union is celebrated under carnal words. All the Apocryphal books should be avoided; but if she ever wishes to read them, not to establish the truth of doctrines, but with a reverential feeling for the truths they signify, she should be told that they are not the works of the authors by whose names they are distinguished, that they contain much that is faulty, and that it is a task requiring great prudence to find gold in the midst of clay. The works of Cyprian should be ever in her hands. She may run over the Epistles of Athanasius, and the books of Hilary, without any danger of stumbling. Let her pleasures be in such treatises and writers of such character as most evince the piety of an unwavering faith. All other authors she should read to judge of what they say, not simply to follow their instructions.

You will answer here, "How can a woman living in the world, in the midst of so vast a population as that of Rome, look after all these things?" Do not, therefore, undertake a burden which you are unable to bear; but as soon as you have weaned her with Isaac, and clothed her with Samuel, send her to her grandmother and aunt. Restore its most precious jewel to the chamber of Mary, and place her in the cradle of the infant Jesus. Let her be brought up in the convent, in the company of virgins; let her never learn to swear; to think falsehood a sacrilege; be ignorant of the world; live the life of an angel; be in the flesh, but not of it; believe every human being to be of the like nature with herself. Thus, to say nothing more, you will be released from the difficulty of keeping her, and the risk of watching over her. Better to regret her absence than to be in perpetual anxiety, what she is saying, with whom she is conversing, whom she is recognizing, whom she is glad to see. Resign to the care of Eustochium the infant whose very cries are even now a prayer for thine own good. Make her the companion of her holiness, hereafter to be its heiress. From her earliest years let her look to her, love her, admire her, whose very words, and gait, and dress, are a lesson of the virtues. Let her dwell in the bosom of her grandmother, who may reproduce in her grandchild what she before experienced in her daughter, and who knows by experience how to bring up, and keep and instruct virgins, whose glory it is, in the virgins she has nurtured, to be daily bringing forth fruit a hundred fold. O happy Paula! happy virgin! happy child of Toxotius, more ennobled by the virtues of her aunt and grandmother than by her high descent! O Læta, that you could see your mother-in-law and sister-in-law, and the mighty souls that animate their feeble bodies! I doubt not your natural modesty would then set the example to your daughter, and change the first command of God for the second law of the Gospel. You would then care little for the longing after other children, but would rather offer up yourself to God. But as there is a time for indulging, and a time for abstaining from it; as a wife has no power over her body; as unto what calling soever a man is called, in that let him remain in the Lord; as he, who is under the yoke, ought to run so as not to leave his fellow in the mire,—restore that whole in thy daughter which thou hast divided in thyself. Hannah never received again the son whom she had vowed to God, after he had been once presented in the temple, thinking it unbecoming that a future prophet should be brought up in the house with one who was yet looking to have children. When she conceived and brought forth, she dared not enter the temple and appear empty before God, till she had first payed what she owed; but after this sacrifice she returned home, and brought forth five children, because she had brought forth her first-born unto God. Admirest thou the happiness of that holy woman? Imitate her faith. If you only send Paula, I will undertake the office of her nurse and teacher; I will carry her on my shoulders, old as I am; I will mold into form her lisping words, much prouder of my office than any worldly philosopher,—training up not a Macedonian king to die by Babylonian poison, but a hand-maiden and bride of Christ, a fit offering to an everlasting kingdom.

XII. EDUCATION OF GIRLS.

[Translated from the German of Karl von Raumer, for the American Journal of Education.]

I. FAMILY LIFE.

We have seen how important Luther considered the influence of home life; and that he considered good family management the basis of a good government of the people and of their true happiness. "Family government," he says, "is the first thing; from which all other governments and authorities take their origin. If this root is not good, neither can the stem be good nor can good fruit follow. Kingdoms are composed of single families. Where father and mother govern ill, and let the children have their own way, there can neither city, market, village, country, principality, kingdom nor empire, be well and peacefully governed. For out of sons are made fathers of families, judges, burgomasters, princes, kings, emperors, preachers, schoolmasters, &c.; and where these are ill trained, there the subjects become as their lord; the members as their head.

"Therefore has God ordained it to be first, as most important, that the family should be well governed. For where the house *is* well and properly governed, all else is well provided for."

These observations are, after Luther's fashion, extremely simple; and refer us to family life as the source both of the happiness and misery of nations. Is our own father-land to receive a blessing or a curse from this source?

II. USUAL MANAGEMENT OF FAMILY LIFE AND FEMALE EDUCATION.

Pestalozzi has given us, in his "*Leonard and Gertrude*," a very beautiful and attractive picture of life in a pious family, without losing sight of reality in exaggeration and romance, or setting up an impossible ideal. Upon comparing his representation, however, with ordinary family life, especially that of our so-called "educated dames," the latter does not commonly in the remotest degree correspond with Pestalozzi's ideal. I speak of "ordinary" family life, for I am far from referring to the frightfully disorderly situation of too many entirely immoral, corrupted and abandoned families. But how many families are considered quite irreproachable, which are governed by an entirely vulgar spirit, destitute of reverence for goodness and truth, of any aspiration after true culture, of love for the father-land, of earnest religious feeling; utterly superficial, short-sighted and narrow-souled! For such persons, the highest moral authority is that most useless and corrupting rule, the prevailing fashion; which they unquestioningly obey without examining it conscientiously or decidedly withstanding it if necessary. Their highest appeal is, What will people say? and the broadest path always seems to them the most certain.

There are many indications of the profoundly corrupting influence of such vulgar and low modes of thought, upon family life and upon instruction. I shall suggest a few instances.

Suppose a father so debased in mind as not to feel any care for his country; to be contented if he is enabled to go on peacefully and prosperously in his own daily labor or business, and in his wretched amusements; must not the example of such a father both destroy every germ of patriotism, and quicken every germ of selfishness?

Nor can such a father maintain a truly and permanently Christian life within his family. He will forever be asking, "What will people say?" He will be ashamed to ask a blessing at table, and will not even think of family prayers; nor will he even consider whether either the one or the other is pleasing to God. But he will be as frightened at the idea that such devotions are exceedingly disagreeable to some of his friends and acquaintances, and that they will call him a pietist for practicing them, as if such fault-finding were the worst misfortune that could befall him. He is a Laodicean, neither cold nor hot; incapable equally of a hearty love and practice of what is good, or of hearty hatred of evil. This regard for consequences continually deceives him.

In thus describing what is at present the condition of too many German families, I do not by any means lose sight of my subject, the education of girls. For there are many homes in which there is no such thing as family life; no such thing as a close union, knit together by the sincere and earnest love of father, mother and children, and thus profoundly happy. On the other hand, a chilly *ennui* prevails at home, and to escape it they resort elsewhere to seek diversion and occupation. The father only enjoys himself when he passes every evening at the casino, or, as it is called, "in society," in card-playing; the mother, and the elder children, attend feminine coffee or tea circles, &c.; and as for the younger children, they are given over to the tender mercies of the servants.

"Nothing can put my heart at rest," says a mother in Jean Paul's

"*Levana*,"* who considers herself very affectionate, "except to take all possible pains to select for my dear little children a conscientious nurse-maid who will swear to treat them like their own mother, and will pray heaven to punish her if she shall neglect her duty to the poor little things, or shall for a single minute trust them out of her sight or in strange hands. Great God, only to think of such a thing! But ah, what do such persons know of the solicitudes of an affectionate mother's heart? And therefore I also am in the habit—which is a great encouragement to me—of having all my children come to see me twice a day, after breakfast and after dinner."

How true to life is this! We may see the nurse-maids with the poor neglected children every day on all the city promenades. How often do these servant-girls form improper acquaintances, which they follow up even in an abandoned manner, without any reference to the children. In the Berlin Zoölogical Garden, a lady was once begged of by a woman who had a child in her arms. On looking at the child, the lady was terrified to recognize it as her own. A wicked nurse-maid had been for sometime in the habit of renting the child for money to the beggar, who had misused it in order to excite the sympathies of the public. "Thus," as Fenelon had already complained, "are such little children surrendered to improper and sometimes disreputable women, and that at a time of life when the deepest impressions are made!" And if such young children are given up in such a manner, how will they be afterwards educated?

Now, can the girls of such a family as has been—and truly—described, be educated piously and in a manner pleasing to God? Must not such a result be impossible, since parents of degraded or perverted ways of thinking must necessarily direct the education of their daughters toward a degraded and perverted purpose? This purpose is nothing except to educate their girls in such a way that they will soon get married, no matter to whom, provided he only has a good income.

Accordingly, how shall girls be educated so as to please men? This question states the pedagogical problem of parents, especially of mothers.†

If girls are devoted merely to become pleasing to men, every opportunity must first of all be taken to extend their acquaintance. As soon as they are old enough, therefore, they must go into society, and especially must attend every ball. Even the most avari-

* Vol. I., p. 41.

† Madame Necker says, (Vol. I., p. 68.) "Those mothers who have no aim in educating their daughters except marrying them, and to this end are slavishly obedient to the demands of the public, devote their children, in our opinion, to an unavoidable mediocrity."

cious mother thinks it her duty to purchase a costly ball-dress for her daughter. Dancing gives opportunities for making acquaintances on both sides; and how often has a ball-night, and even a single waltz, given time enough to agree upon an unhappy marriage? In Berlin there is even a term for such marriges; they are called "ball-marriages." Their first enchantment scarcely outlives the honeymoon; and many young couples might be separated again, under the Prussian law, on the ground of mutual "insuperable aversion," in a fortnight after their wedding. But the object of vulgar parents is attained, as has been observed, when their daughter has obtained a husband, no matter if she drags out the remainder of her life in the most comfortless wretchedness.

We shall find no occasion to wonder at the subjects and methods of female education, when we have ascertained its object; for this object is pursued with the utmost consistency. "Since every thing is directed," says Madame Necker, Vol. I., p. 32, "to enabling the young woman to become the choice of a young man, all care is bestowed upon the cultivation of outward appearances, no matter how other things turn out. In this pursuit, the mother takes a passionate interest in her daughter's success, and all possible means are used to secure it." The girls must put themselves on exhibition; must make a brilliant appearance in society. For this purpose, dancing is a better means than any thing else which can be taught. No art is more zealously pursued, or with such unheard-of self-sacrifice. During the winter series of balls, it is often remarked, they undermine their health, and are thus obliged to go to the baths in the summer, in order to re-establish their health for the next winter. Thus they alternate, until health is entirely gone.

The next most important pursuit is singing and playing, which girls learn for exhibition in society. The piano is peculiarly adapted for this purpose; for even persons destitute of all musical feeling or talent can be drilled to a wonderful degree of skill in piano-playing, especially upon the lately introduced "dumb pianos," without strings. They are tormented every day with hours of finger-exercises. Where it was formerly usual to play sonatas, &c., it is now the custom to play only finger-exercises, the teacher causing them to play, in specified places, *pianissimo*, *piano*, *forte*, *fortissimo*, and with various other degrees of strength, indicated by their appropriate words. They are taught, in particular to go at once from the softest *piano* to the loudest *forte*, because this produces the greatest "effect;" and what do they play for except "effect?" "In such hands, the fine arts cease to be fine arts; the idea of the effect to be produced upon others quite drives out any attention to the effect to be produced on the mind of the player."*

Piano players thus trained can not fail to gain the approval of most persons, even of those quite without musical capacity, as most persons are; for even such can judge by the eye of the player's skill of hand: it is of no consequence that the player plays utterly without feeling or pleasure, and has tormented herself with laboring in the sweat of her face to acquire her dexterity; the attainment is sufficient, and all else is of subordinate importance. "The principal thing is no longer to love and to admire; it is to be admired. The young woman does not trouble herself about what she herself feels, but about what feelings she awakes in others."† Good manners at present forbid the hearers from permitting it to be seen how much the performance wearies them. They are expected to praise every thing, and so are even those who have talked incessantly during the playing. If such musical exhibitions were made in Madame de Genlis' "Palace of Truth," the expressions of the real feelings and thoughts of the hearers would be well worth listening to.

The pieces of music which pianists prefer are simply such as are the fashion, even if the worst possible; provided only that they are composed for "effect," and will thus serve the desired end.

I have scarcely patience to speak of the mode of singing now usual in society. How disgusting is it to one accustomed to a correct and simple method of singing secular and sacred music, when he hears for the first time this unnatural, vulgar, affected singing, with its jumping from a scarcely audible *piano* to a shrieking ear-piercing *fortissimo*; its insufferable long-winded howling instead of a pure and precise tone! He feels himself suddenly fallen from the cheerful region of a beautiful fine art, amongst musical caricatures. If the singing were visible, as in Tieck's Garden of Poesy, he would think himself another St. Anthony, all beset with swarms of horrible phantoms.

Parents take especial interest in the study of French by their children. What is the object of this study? To enable a girl to read the masterpieces of French literature, or to extend their sphere of mental vision from the province of one language to another foreign one, and thus to acquaint them with other words, idioms and syntax? Are they to institute a comparison between French and German?

If we should put such questions as these to ordinary parents, they would not understand them at all. Our daughters learn French, they would say, for a reason that all the world knows. It is to be a means

* Madame Necker, Vol. I., p. 73. † Madame Necker, Vol. I., 72; and comp. II., p. 164.

of showing themselves cultivated, when they are in cultivated society; especially in the higher circles where French is spoken.

The importance of the objects aimed at in the study of French, best appears from the mode in which instruction is given in it. Yet it is misusing the term "instruction" to apply it here, for this is not instruction, but mere drilling, such as is used to teach starlings and parrots to speak: and this is sought, not only by wealthy parents, but even by those of small means, who often pay high rates to masters, or more frequently, mistresses, French governesses especially, for the sake of this drill. And extraordinary indeed are the creatures who are often sent from Paris to Germany as governesses, and to whom foolish parents confide the care of their children. Mothers who do not understand French, must listen to the chattering of these governesses with their children, without the means of knowing whether they are not talking the most harmful things to them; and even if there were no danger to the morals of the children, still this talk is the most empty stuff; nonsensical conversational phrases, usually such as are current among the lower ranks in France. But governesses of this class are not capable of any thing beyond this unintelligent drill; they know nothing of instruction; having usually never studied at all, and understanding French only because they are French women. I have known these women, to have no ideas whatever of the French declensions and conjugations, and unable, if they read, for instance, *pourriez-vous*, to find the meaning of *pourriez* in the dictionary. But aside from this, their whole stock of knowledge is so entirely made up of the most ordinary conversational phrases, that they were unable to translate the easiest French book, unless it consisted altogether of such phrases.

What has been said is sufficient to show that in this sort of studying French, nothing is thought of except mere drilling: not culture at all, at least in any proper sense; for nothing is more different from it than such French talking. "Shall I learn to speak French," says Goethe, "a foreign language, in which I must appear silly, do what I will, because I can only express common and coarse shades of meaning? For what distinguishes the blockhead from the man of sense, except that the latter comprehends quickly, clearly and accurately, and expresses forcibly the delicate shades of peculiarity in what is around him, while the former, just as every one must do in a foreign language, must get along by the aid of stereotyped memorized phrases?"

Thus Goethe, the representative of German culture, comes into the most diametrical opposition to the so-called "educated classes," who think that ability to speak French constitutes culture. He tells them plainly that they must always appear foolish in their French conversation, and have to get along with stereotyped and memorized phrases. But no such mere babble in French as that, can be admitted to be even a bad substitute for real culture.

And again; it is necessary in order to avoid a waste of labor, that girls should practice talking French from a very early age, if they are to talk it with even a moderate degree of correctness. The wretched influence of this practice on the native language will be understood by any one who comprehends how great a gift of God is that of the mother-tongue, and how wonderfully, by means of it, he is able to express and communicate his deepest thoughts and feelings. But this living speech, welling forth from the inmost being, is exactly the opposite of the entirely mechanical French which children learn, and which includes nothing whatever either of thought or feeling. And if they obtain by practice some facility in French conversational flourishes, they forthwith transfer their lifeless mannerism to their own language, and talk German without feeling or thought. Girls, too, who are sent to female schools, frequently fall into the hands of such French women as have already been described. Some parents, who think no attainment valuable in comparison with facility in speaking French, send their daughters to French or Swiss schools, where they can hear and speak nothing but French. In such a foreign atmosphere, they too often become quite estranged from their native home and country.

This unnatural over-valuation of the French has, unfortunately, nothing whatever in the nature of an antidote, in the methods employed in teaching German. This observation applies, however, not to the rudiments of instruction in reading and writing, but to the more advanced course in German, instruction in which is almost as perverted as that in French, though in quite an opposite manner. While girls are trained to practice French modes of speech without feeling or intelligence, the teacher in German, on the other hand, requires them to understand fully every thing that they read; nay, they must do more than understand it; they must be conscious of their own understanding of it. To this end, all that they read is explained to them at great length, and with great fullness; they are made to write out whatever they have felt and thought while reading; and to torment themselves most pitifully, to waken in themselves some feelings or thoughts which they may write down.

Such instruction is fit enough to train blue-stockings; it is nothing except a school of the most heartless and false hypocrisy. The mode of training used to make them read "with expression," is one quite similar to that used to teach to play the piano "with expression." As in the latter case, so in reading, the *forte* and *piano* tones are in part brought out by numberless oral rules, and partly by showing how the various grades of expression are to be secured by using more or less force in the touch or voice. Thus, in a poem of Gellert's, I find various sizes of type used, as follows:—

"How GREAT is the *almighty* GOODNESS!
Is there one MAN who does not *feel* it—
Who with *hardened* susceptibilities
SMOTHERS the gratitude which he ought to *feel*?
NO! To appreciate God's *love*
Shall ever be my SUPREME duty.
The Lord has *never* forgotten me;
And neither shall my heart forget *him!*"*

Wooden teachers think that to read with stress of voice is to read with expression. It is most repulsive to a natural-minded person to hear girls declaim with such pretentious affectation, especially when, as is often the case, they blunder and throw the accent into the wrong place, thus betraying the whole mindlessness of their art.

Buffon's maxim is often repeated, that "Style is the Man;" but our ordinary method of cultivating the style can certainly not be recognized as a true method of mental culture. How absurdly selected are the themes given to girls for composition! They are, for instance, set to write letters describing the death of a father or brother, or the birth of a sister, and by this means to put themselves into the appropriate state of mind!† Or they are put to write essays upon the usefulness of the sciences, the excellence of virtue, &c., &c. Nothing can be more tiresome than to read the letters written by girls who have been taught in this way; first painfully thought out, and then copied off clean. Such letters contain nothing at all, except a quantity of formal phrases, in which they excuse themselves to their correspondent with hypocritical modesty, as not possessing that faculty for writing letters which the other has; that they have no time to acquire it, and the like; and the whole letter is filled with such matter. If after reading it all, we inquire, What in brief is the substance of that! there is no answer. How different is the case, when an unaffected girl who has escaped such a perverting training, narrates without any painful forethought to her friend, whom she has seen, what journeys she has made, what books she has read, and whatever other things have happened. It is a pleasure

* Rhenish Gazette (*Rheinische Blätter*), 1835, (January to June). p. 354.

† "Waste none of your time in putting yourself into states of mind," says Claudius.

to read such letters, often characterised by poetical feeling and native humor, and free from the encumbering constraint of school discipline.

But this does not by any means complete the list of the constituent parts of the school instruction of our girls. Read, for instance, the first invitation programme that comes to hand, of a girl's school examination: what an excessive number of studies is there! Many of them, rightly taught, would be exceedingly beneficial; and if ill-taught, exceedingly harmful. Such for instance, is natural history. Who does not take pleasure in seeing a girl who loves flowers, carefully watering them every day, placing them in the sun, and taking care of them with as much love and skill as the most industrious and intelligent gardener! But some children nine or ten years old, instead of amusing themselves in a childlike manner with the colors and smell of a flower, are forced by the teacher to pull them apart and determine the correct names of all the parts; as root, stem, leaf-sheath, leaf, upper surface, under surface, circumference, base, apices, veins, &c., &c., or the teacher spins out a lecture on the ordinary violet which would occupy eight or ten printed pages. Just as if God had let the flowers grow, only so that teachers might make use of them for their idle foolish pedagogical experiments. Even what is most alive and beautiful, fades and dies if touched by the hand of a foolish pedant.

This instruction of girls in so many departments, usually with a pedantic discursiveness and pretense of thoroughness, leaves but very little time, as may easily be imagined, for active occupation in housekeeping. I have known girls who labored at their school lessons, even into the night. Young housekeepers find themselves in no very pleasant situation, when they find that the time which they have thus spent leaves them in entire ignorance of what they need to know and do in their new vocation. Their kitchen, for instance, must be entirely under the control of their cook, no matter how ignorant she is; and the young mistress, instead of being able to instruct her servant, is on the contrary forced to take the utmost pains to learn her art from her, and not to make any blunders herself.

It has been attempted to remedy this difficulty by placing girls for a time with a cook or boarding-house keeper. But besides that such an arrangement brings a young girl into a situation not the most desirable, she does not in such a place learn the sort of cooking that she will need to practice at her own house, and much that she does learn will be useless there.

I have already alluded to the manner in which the daughters of families of the class which I have been describing, use their leisure time. Parties, balls, the theater, occupy much of it; and they endeavor to kill time at home, by reading novels. It would be difficult to decide whether the parties, the balls, the theater, or the romances, exert the worst influence on a girl. I have already mentioned balls. Theatrical exhibitions are attended without any discrimination by parents between what is good and bad in morals or artistic value. One of the most corrupting of Kotzebue's plays, in which all the five acts consist of one sustained *double entendre*, is now the favorite performance at Breslau, and is attended by young and old. An improving school indeed is afforded for girls, by an equivocal play, performed by actors of equivocal character, and with professional skill; and where vices are made to appear desirable and virtue wearisome and stupid!

But perhaps the most destructive habit of all is the indiscriminate reading of all romances that girls can find. A morbid voracity possesses them; they read and read, without becoming at all satisfied or nourished by what they devour. It operates, on the contrary, as a poison. If a standard work happens to stray amongst the trash of their circulating library, they pay no attention to it. One of these romance readers, when asked if she had read Goethe's "*Iphigenia*," replied "I believe so!"

This sort of reading destroys the most agreeable and active mental faculties of a girl's mind, and substitutes a fixed character of frivolity which makes them entirely unfit to fulfill their household duties with modesty and efficiency, and to lead a quiet and godly life. Serious and holy thoughts find no place in the minds of such perverted young women; for how could such thoughts dwell in the same mind with frivolous love stories and erroneous, vulgar and fantastic ideals of love?

But it is time to turn away from this too common, godless and hopeless method of educating girls, with all its accompanying errors, and to inquire after the right method.

III. MARRIAGE.—DUTIES OF PARENTS AS TO EDUCATING THEIR CHILDREN.

Luther has referred us to the family, as the source of the happiness or misery of nations; let us proceed to examine what are the sources of the happiness or misery of families.

These states are inaugurated through marriage; and they have as many sources therefore, as there are different marriages. While a consecrated love has caused the marriage, if it was, to use a common expression made in heaven, there are others an infinite distance below these, which have been brought about by the most impure lust or the coldest and most calculating avarice.

A consecrated beginning promises a holy and blessed married life, in truth and love, even to old age; but if the source of the marriage was impure, the subsequent married life will commonly be also impure and unblessed. We have already seen what degraded views are only too common, on the subject of marriage, even amongst those of the higher ranks; and this may indicate the corruption that prevails in such marriages.

Let us now consider what are the duties of the father and mother, whose marriage is such as God approves, in relation to the education of their children.

I have already referred to the beautiful delineation of a sanctified family life which is presented in Pestalozzi's "*Leonard and Gertrude.*" We necessarily love and respect Gertrude, when we see her so full of faithful love to her husband, her children, the neglected poor of the parish, and at the same time so intelligent and active in her comprehensive benevolence.

I find but one fault found, even by women, who well understand what is agreeable to them. Leonard, they say, is a good-hearted man, and industrious at his work; but weak, and often wanting in tact, and easily led astray. Such a person is not fit to be a father of a family; a wife could find no support from him; she would on the contrary have to take him under her protection and guidance, and make up for his deficiencies. But they exclaim, if he were only as a father what Gertrude is as a mother, especially with reference to the education of the children!

These very correct observations lead us very naturally to the consideration of the respective duties of father and mother in teaching their daughters.

Many persons believe that this department of education belongs to the mother alone; that the father should scarcely have any thing to do with it. This may appear correct, but it is appearance only. The man who marries with a sense of the sacredness of the step, must to some extent know what he is doing; must have some sort of idea and conception of marriage. He will reflect upon the duties which he assumes to his wife and to his children—in case he should have children. Love and conscientiousness will oblige him to consider the subject of children's education; its objects, and the road toward them. With every year and with every child who is sent him by God, his pedagogical problem becomes clearer to him, and his skill in solving it increases. An intelligent and modest wife will find herself sup-

20

ported by such a man, and will willingly learn from him; and on the other hand an intelligent husband, who knows his abilities and duties, can with confidence entrust to his wife all the details of the education of her daughters. For however great his good will, he will not be in circumstances to undertake the management of this detail. Such a labor would usually require more time than his duties as a citizen will permit; and what is more, would require gifts which he has not, but with which women are richly endowed.

But what is the proper duty of the father in educating his daughters, is a question not answered in Pestalozzi's character of Leonard. He has made the wife conduct the whole of it, without advising on the subject with her husband at all. In this department, in fact, she performs the double duty of both father and mother.

At the same time it is not to be denied that the importance of the labors of the wife, even in the education of boys, can not be too highly estimated. The most skillful educators are agreed on this point.

Thus Fenelon says, in his valuable book on the education of girls, "Are not the duties of wives the basis of all of life? Is it not they who destroy or uphold the family? They exert the most important influence upon the good or bad morals of almost all the world. An intelligent, industrious, profoundly religious wife, is the soul of the whole household; she governs it in things both temporal and spiritual."

Fenelon then proceeds to show more at length, how the wife's influence may tend either to the salvation or the destruction of her husband and her children; so that her labors for the good of society are scarcely less important than those of her husband.

Luther says that pious families establish the happiness of nations; and Fenelon and Pestalozzi add to this, that pious wives are the chief basis of the happiness of families. Even though they have no direct influence upon church and state, they still have an indirect one which is important, by reason of its influence upon the education not only of girls, but also of boys.

Every one knows how great have been the obligations of eminent men, such as the Gracchi, St. Augustine, &c., to their mothers. And how many obscure and unknown labors of mothers, in the education of their sons, are known only to God! Innumerable are the men who have all their lives blessed the memory of the dear mothers who brought them up to goodness from their youth, with unfailing faithfulness.

And if the influence of mothers upon the education of boys is so great, notwithstanding that fathers, teachers, fellow-pupils, and so many others, exert a coincident influence in this education, how much greater must it be upon that of girls, who are intrusted almost exclusively to their mother's care.

The consideration of the importance of this influence has of late years led to the establishment of institutions expressly to train girls as teachers; it has even been suggested that teachers' seminaries for girls should be established. In such institutions, the inspector and his wife and children are intended to form a normal family, in and by whose influence the pupils are to be trained; and in particular, especial care is taken to teach them, as much as is possible, in accurately fixed hours.

A sensible man will feel at once the unnatural character of this plan. Girls belong to their own families; family life is their school; their own father is the normal father, their own mother the normal mother; such is the ordinance of God. The older girls, in assisting their mothers in housekeeping, in teaching the younger children, &c., learn in the simplest and most natural way what they will subsequently need to know, as housewives; without being pedantically and coarsely instructed about their future duties as mothers, and being only made into governesses after all. For nothing but governesses can be formed by such a seminary as we have made mention of; stiff governesses, who will bring their husbands no dowry except a system of education; and who will believe that only they understand this subject, having studied it *secundum artem*, whereas the husband not having graduated at such a school, can know nothing of it, and has no business to say any thing about it.

IV. REMEDIES FOR DEFECTS IN HOME LIFE AND FEMALE EDUCATION.—INTRODUCTION.

Fenelon's work on "*Female Education*," begins with these words:—"Nothing is so much neglected as the education of girls." At present, perhaps he would write, instead of "neglected," something like "bescribbled and perverted." So much we have already seen. But what is the remedy? It is easy to find fault, but difficult to effect improvement, and doubly so when we scarcely know how or where to begin. Yet it will not suffice to fall into inactive despair.

Let us above all things retain our belief that God has planted maternal love in the heart of every mother; and that every mother, at least generally speaking, will gladly fulfill her duties to her children, if she knows what they are. But if they pursue the most mistaken measures, as we have seen they do, if they even do this at a cost of self-sacrifice, it is usually for the reason that they think these mistaken measures are the right ones, and such as will promote the good of their daughters. If, for instance, a mother fancies that the greatest misfortune to her daughter would be to remain unmarried, she would resort even to the silliest means to prevent such a misfortune. But if they could be convinced that it is by no means always a misfortune to remain unmarried, or at any rate a much smaller one than that of an unhappy marriage, such as we have referred to—if they could be convinced that good men are not commonly to be found where they look for them, in balls and parties of pleasure—surely they would not remain in their wrong ways; surely maternal love would then bring them back to the right path.

But sensible mothers will reply: "We are no better off for this delineation of the common perversions of education, even though we are forced with sorrow to acknowledge its truth. What we need is, to know how to rescue ourselves from the current of evil customs, and how to educate our children in an intelligent and Christian manner."

"Nor is it of any use to us to acquaint us with general principles of education. We may be convinced of their truth, but if we attempt to put them in practice, we shall quickly see how great a gulf there is between counsel and action. "To act according to our own reflections brings us inconveniences," says Goethe; but the case is worse than this. Inconveniences we were accustomed to; these would be no obstacle to our good will. But abstract pedagogical rules are of no use whatever; no more than a couple of algebraical formulas would be, to enable us to teach our girls all the practical arithmetic of housekeeping."

"What our children need is little details of training; the smallest details; we need advice upon points which men contemptuously term minutiae, and trifles. But things of great importance are hidden within these trifles, as in seeds, whose germ only develops in after years."

From my own conviction of the truth of such claims as these, I shall in the sequel discuss as much of these details as I have been able to master from my own observation of the pedagogical labors of women within the circle of their own family.

I have already devoted a chapter each to "Early Infancy" and "Religious Instruction."* Although in these chapters I have considered details, yet it has been with too little reference to their management in daily life. I should therefore expose myself to the blame

* "In addition to what I shall say in the following chapters, especially the last, on religious and moral education and instruction, I would refer to these two chapters, and also to the subsequent section, headed 'Christianity in Education.'" See Barnard's "*American Journal of Education*," Vol. VII., 381—412.

of which I have been speaking, if I did not endeavor in the following pages to make up for such deficiencies.

V. RELIGIOUS AND MORAL CULTURE.

1. *Before the preparation for confirmation.*

The parents are bound to the sacred duty of cultivating the seeds of the new birth. The mother should pray for the child, and should teach it to pray for itself as early as possible; so that prayer shall become a second nature to it. Our ancient morning and evening hymns contain stanzas very proper to be used as prayers by children. Such a short prayer in verse should be taught the child by the mother as soon as it can speak; and it should repeat it after her, with its hands folded, syllable by syllable. It should afterwards learn to pray without having the words repeated to it; still with folded hands.

The mother should relate to the child Bible stories, particularly about the child Christ. After the third year, Luther's smaller catechism may be taught it by heart, but only in very small portions and without the explanations, which Luther himself directs to be taught to children of from seven to ten. The child may during this period also learn short verses of the Bible, and stanzas from hymns, particularly Christmas hymns. The children will often come to their mother at times when she can hear them repeat their texts and verses; and she can often find other occasions to remind them of what they have learned, and to make brief and forcible applications; which must not however be extended into long sermons. A good picture Bible will strikingly illustrate these maternal instructions; and an older sister will find much pleasure in showing the pictures to the younger ones, and telling them the appropriate stories.

The shorter and more simple the prayer which the mother hears her child repeat at evening and morning, the greater will be its tendency to cause the child to add petitions relating to its own little affairs. It will at night thank God for all His favors given during the day, will pray for parents, brothers and sisters, and if it has done any thing wrong, will sincerely ask God's forgiveness.

However insignificant such little beginnings of Christian instruction may seem, they still contain the living germs of the subsequent Christian life. They are the seeds of profound love and undoubting confidence toward God, of humble confession of sin and hearty gratitude to him who died that we might obtain forgiveness; seeds of love toward all mankind. Thus, Christianity will become a second nature to the child, so firmly rooted within its nature that it can never be uprooted, even by the most violent tempest.

It is evident of course that Christian education can exist only in Christian families; but even Christian parents must exercise great watchfulness to see that their lives harmonize with their teachings to their children. Otherwise the little ones will be altogether perplexed and doubtful. Even earnest Christians easily fall into many errors, such especially as tend toward a false pietism. Such errors are, too frequent and verbose admonitions to the children; too long devotional exercises; obliging them to express pious feelings; and continual, wearisome, pietistic sermonizing. I might add, the too early carrying the children to church. Ordinary sermons are too long and too hard of understanding for children, which indeed is a reason why a special divine service, shorter and adapted to children's minds, is needed. But such a service will be found very liable to degenerate into an insipid, affectedly childish, and entirely useless pietistic style of sermonizing. Various errors are practiced in the mode of conducting religious exercises. They weary by their length, and still more by their frequent abstract dogmatizing. Teachers frequently give out to female pupils themes, for composition, on religious subjects, far beyond their powers, and leading them into a class of discussions where they are not at home, and ought not to be. At a period like the present, when so many of the clergy believe so profoundly in the reflective theology, in the so-called "Christian consciousness," at such a time as this, the poor school-girls fare but ill. What they need is, to grow up in Christian simplicity, in an undoubting, deep-rooted, common-sense faith; and to remain all their lives children, in the sense in which Christ requires it, of such as are to constitute the kingdom of heaven. Dogmatical discussions, which they are usually unable to follow, only confuse them, and render them liable to errors in doctrine.

While instruction of this sort strains and over-exerts the understanding very foolishly, there is an over-exertion of a still more harmful but opposite kind. I refer to the mode pursued by some sentimental religious teachers; who, instead of earnestly and seriously pointing out to their pupils the way of salvation, devote all their attention to the purpose of influencing the feelings of the girls, for merely the moment. For the moment, I say, because this sort of overstrained feeling is usually followed by a reaction into entire indifference. Too often, also, the teacher, in his joy at having produced the desired state of feeling, adds a further complimentary notice of the pupil, for her possession of feelings so susceptible, pure, &c. The excitement of the girl's feelings soon passes away; but not so the unblessed vanity which the poor child thus contracts from her instruction in religion.

Girls educated at home in the Bible, the smaller catechism, and the old religious hymns, to a knowledge of the elements of Christianity, are thus properly prepared for the instructions which precede confirmation.

2. *Fear of death.*

One blessing of early Christian instruction is, that it leaves no room in children's hearts for the fear of death. This good result is, however, sometimes hindered by foolish parents, who speak of death in the hearing of their children as a terrible thing, of which every one must be afraid; or who say on one occasion and another, "Don't do so; it will kill you."

If children are taught, even when those die who are most beloved, that the dead are with God, and happy; and are taught the texts of the Bible on this subject, and the beautiful encouraging verses of our ancient hymns, then all the tears which they would shed would be only for the absence of the beloved dead. They would weep no doubt, being only feeble children. But if they should not, it should not be considered a mark of hard-heartedness; and still less should they be blamed as for indifference; for such treatment will be very likely to make them hypocritical.

Children who have from early youth been taught from the Holy Scriptures that through death we pass to heaven, and to the Saviour, will by means of their encouraging and profound faith be found most efficient comforters to their parents, if afflicted by the death of those they love.

3. *Awakening of envy and covetousness in children.*

I have already referred to Hufeland's book, "*Good Counsel to Mothers on the Physical Management of Infants;*"* a book which every mother should become familiar with; which Jean Paul even says she should learn by heart, before the birth of her first child. Hufeland says, "Few persons will ever believe that it can be of any importance to secure for children, in the very earliest portion of their lives, the enjoyment of open air, and various other things herein prescribed; and yet this is exactly the time in which the foundation of sound bodily health for the child must necessarily be laid." Precisely as important and fundamental as physical management in this early period of life, is for the body, is its moral training for the soul. A child often receives impressions which last its whole lifetime, before we have any idea that it can receive any impressions at all. "If the disfigurements of the soul," remarks Jean Paul, "which wrong management during the first years of life entails upon children, were

* *Guter Rath an Mütter über die physische Behandlung kleiner Kinder.*"

as visible as broken bones, deformed limbs, and other corporeal defects what a terrible sight would the rising generation present!"

I will instance a few cases of such wrong management:—

We often hear it said to little children, "Eat quickly, or else your sister will get it;" or, "If you don't eat it right up, I will." If a child has a new garment or toy, it is told, "This is yours all alone; your little brother can't have it. See; the other children have nothing so pretty; nobody but you." I have often observed mothers look on quite indifferently at such things, and even do the like themselves; a most painful sight. Such things implant and cultivate ill-will and vanity in children, before they are old enough to feel the pleasure of giving or of sympathy. It would be better to let other children be about when a child is eating, even when it is very young; and to let it give them now and then a mouthful. They will be pleased, and will show it. Or if there is no other child to be present the person who feeds it might perhaps take a spoonful of the food, and commend it, as received from the child. Such methods would early accustom it to have some regard for others, and not for itself alone. If a child receives a gift of flowers, or any playthings that can be divided without being spoiled, it should early be accustomed to give away some part of them. Things not divisible, it should be taught to use alternately with other children. Almost every child, thus taught, will even desire to impart of its possessions to others.

It is exceedingly dangerous to excite any sort of rivalry in children; although it is frequently done. I have seen not merely ignorant nurses, but mothers and fathers too, caress the children of others until their own children became angry and cried. The parents would then say, "See how that child loves me!"

4. *Love of brothers and sisters.*

This seems a perfectly natural and inborn disposition; and yet we find many families whose children never agree, but are constantly quarreling with each other.

I am not one of those who with Rousseau would charge all the faults and sins of children upon their parents and teachers; although incompatibility of dispositions in parents often brings much harm upon the children.

Many if not the most of children's quarrels arise from questions of *meum* and *tuum*. We often hear such dialogues as "It is mine!" "No, it is mine." "She has got my doll!" &c. The egoistic tendencies of property result in most harmful envy, quarreling, reviling and blows. Parents or adults in charge must be to blame, in part at least, when the difficulty becomes so serious as this. We have already seen that they sometimes themselves stir up envy and covetousness in their children.

A second cause which interferes with children's affection for one another, is one which is eminently the fault of the parents; namely, the preference of some one child by the latter, and the consequent worse treatment and stricter discipline of the rest. Such conduct excites in the children thus unfairly treated, a profound dislike and envy and grudge against that one who is preferred and favored. It is frequently those who may happen to be less favored with mental or bodily excellencies, who are thus ill-treated by their parents, whereas these are precisely the ones who need a double share of faithfulness. Children of more attractive exterior are, on the other hand, often most foolishly doted on. This kind of conduct has a most evil influence not only in the children who are favored, but on the neglected ones also.

It will not be denied that fraternal love is an innate quality; although it is not so powerful an affection as that between children and parents. Children also, however, unfortunately bring selfishness into the world with them. The problem of education—for mothers especially—is, as much and as early as possible, to extirpate the evil tendency towards disagreement; and to cherish and develop the germs of fraternal affection. We take great pains to root the weeds out of our flower-beds, before they grow strong enough to injure the useful plants. In like manner, should mothers seek to promote love and unity, and to destroy covetousness and envy among their children, and so much the more anxiously, because in this case the planting and the destroying become difficult much more rapidly as time advances.

I shall venture here to call attention to some common failings.

The first child is, until the second is born, the chief object of its mother's cares. If now a second child appears, and, as is natural, receives just as solicitous care, it will easily happen that the first child will seem to itself to be neglected. How can this be prevented? A child must, from the first day of its birth, be the principal object of its mother's care. She must consider of importance even the smallest details which relate to it; and whatever she can not herself do for it, she must carefully see done under her own eyes. But it is exceedingly desirable that the child should not think itself of importance, any more than is absolutely necessary. But however quietly and unobtrusively the necessary care is taken of a child—being at the same time punctual and thorough—and notwithstanding that the little one is as early as possible left part of the time to itself, while lying in the cradle or on the floor, and notwithstanding that the child's necessities are made as few and attended to with as little flourish as possible, still it will be very liable to miss something of the usual attentions when a new-comer must also be attended to.

The birth of a brother or sister should be made an occasion of festivity; and they should frequently be permitted the pleasure of seeing the little one. Nor should the good old custom be omitted, of putting a little case of gilt paper in the cradle of the new-comer, with all sorts of little presents for all the children, who should be permitted to find it there. And the ceremony of baptism should be made one of special enjoyment; so that they may retain a delightful impression of this holy occasion.

If it could be so contrived that the elder children should not feel themselves neglected nor put aside on behalf of the new-comer, they would be certain to greet the increase of the family with unmixed pleasure, and heartily to love this additional brother or sister.

Another error which should be avoided is, to reprove too harshly such little oversights of the elder children as too rough handling of the younger, &c., as if they had intended to inflict pain. We often hear nursery-maids saying, for instance, "Naughty child, you have hurt your little sister;" when perhaps the poor child, out of nothing except pure love for the baby, squeezed it a little too hard, or threw some toy into its cradle, with the idea of amusing it. Such actions should be prevented, no doubt; but should not be treated as if they were intentional ill-conduct. Children should be told, from the beginning, "You must be very tender with your little brother or sister; and you must not cry nor make a noise in the room where your mother is taking care of it." If they cry, they should at once be taken out; and should be made to look upon it as a penalty to be taken away from the cradle, but as a reward, to be allowed to stay there.

It is very bad, for a nurse-maid in charge of an older child, to say to it, "Never mind, you shall be my darling; you are better than the baby." Although such expressions may be used from affection, and with the best intentions, they should not be allowed; for they set the children in a sort of opposition of interests, which every possible means should be used to prevent from coming into their minds at all.

When children have grown old enough to play with each other, if they should quarrel, it will not be best to punish one of them on behalf of the other, but to endeavor with few words to re-establish a good understanding; scarcely to observe at all which was to blame; but to direct the attention of both to the evils of quarreling. For it is very easy, if an investigation is entered into, to do injustice to one of the parties, by failing to take notice of some little occasion of discord.

By thus never punishing one child on account of the other, it will come about that any penalties inflicted on one will grieve the other; that both their joys and sorrows will be common to both.

Many other similar details might be added, each perhaps insignificant in itself, but all together tending powerfully toward the important result of maintaining peace and unity among children.

I have seen children of from three to six years of age, old enough, that is, to begin to learn texts from the Bible, very deeply struck with that passage from the hundred and thirty-third psalm, "Behold how good and how pleasant it is for brethren to dwell together in unity! * * * for there the Lord commanded the blessing, even life for evermore." And a mere reference to these words of holy writ, without any extended admonitions, would frequently make them ashamed of a disagreement.

Boys should learn texts and hymns, along with their sisters, from their mother, and should be kept in the nursery, until they reach the school age. During all this time, all the mother's efforts to preserve unity amongst them should be exerted equally toward both. If she shall be affectionate, firm and intelligent enough to succeed in this, a charmingly affectionate relation will continue to exist among them afterwards. The girls will feel a careful love toward their brothers, and the latter will soon feel themselves the protectors of the former.

These efforts of the mother should be under the influence of the father; which ought to be the soul and the impulse of all her labors for her children. And even if he is not in a situation himself to take charge of all the details, he should control the spirit of them all.

5. *Timidity. Antipathy.*

Parents should be extremely careful not to have their children frightened. A fright, even in jest, perhaps by means of some sudden appearance in the dark, would very probably not only implant a timidity which would last for years, and could only be got rid of with great pains, but might also bring on permanent nervous disorders.

Children should never be threatened with wild beasts, nor told, as they frequently are, "If you do so, the dog will come and bite you," &c. Nor should they be threatened with the chimney-sweep, whose appearance is of itself sufficiently frightful to little children. They should rather be told, "He is a good man, but can not wash himself except on Sundays. Then he is as white as anybody." I have seen a child so well cured in that way of his apprehensions, as to shake hands with the sweep in the friendliest manner.

The fear so common among girls, of spiders, caterpillars, mice, frogs, &c., can very soon be cured by judicious care, without at all interfering with feminine delicacy.* There is a mistaken notion, often found even among servants, that to be frightened, to cry out, and to show great horror at any thing repulsive, indicates great tenderness and delicacy of feeling; and that such sickly nervousness is very elegant. Educated people should be the first to overcome such weaknesses.†

If any one should be inclined to consider this horror at every thing of a disagreeable appearance, as an allowable trifle, he should reflect that it is closely connected with something of much more importance. Girls who declare that they can not see a spider or a mouse without being frightened and trembling, are also in the habit of saying that they can not look at an open wound, or see blood let; in short, that they "can not endure the sight of blood." And it is often the duty of a mother, at home or among her neighbors, to take the part of a Sister of Charity, if needed, and to be helpful and kind, with coolness and skill, without being frightened.

6. *Greeting. Asking. Thanking. Asking pardon.*

Children should be taught as early as possible to salute properly every person who comes into the house, and to return thanks for whatever is given them; and also to ask for what they want. If they are not taught to thank and to ask, they will very soon come to think that every thing and any thing they think of must be given to them; and that they are entitled to command, and must be obeyed by all. Thanking and asking teach them that they depend upon their older friends; and that things are given them and done for them, out of love, and not from obligation. They thus also learn to give thanks to God, and to prefer their requests to him, who gives us all our daily bread, even without our asking, and yet commands us to pray to Him. Children who are not taught by their parents to ask for any thing nor to give thanks for it, will never think of asking a blessing at table.

It will of course be understood that the requests and thanks here spoken of, are not mere feelingless and memorized forms of empty politeness. Children should not salute strangers with any specially

* I speak only of harmless animals. The antipathy to snakes is a correct instinct, although not keen enough to distinguish between the poisonous and harmless varieties. There are many cases where no natural instinct holds children away from dangerous animals, and they must be warned not to play with or tease them; such as ill-tempered dogs, &c.

† See the "*Wandsbeck Messenger* (*Wandsbecker Bothen*)," Vol. II., p. 68.

adjusted formularies, but with the same ease which they use to their parents and neighbors.

Young children should also be accustomed, when, for instance, they cry angrily, or throw any thing away in a pet, or do any other passionate thing, to ask pardon for it, if only by saying "I will not do so any more, if you will be pleasant to me again." If they are not early accustomed to do this, it will be more difficult to bring them to it afterwards; they will be found contrary and obstinate. And children who have thus grown up obstinate, will be found to conceal any fault which they have committed, and to be resolute in refusing to confess it, from a feeling that either confession or asking forgiveness is shameful. Children, on the other hand, who have from an early age been accustomed to ask forgiveness, if they once yield to the temptation to conceal a fault committed, will be made very unhappy by doing so. Like David, though after the measure of their youth, the concealment of the matter will be a pain in their bones, and like him, they will become cheerful again when they have confessed and been forgiven. One who has thus learned to confess to his parents and to be forgiven, will learn to confess and find peace before God; but one who has from his youth been persistently silent, because he has not learned to humble himself by honest confession, can find no such peace.

7. *Truthfulness. Fairness.*

It should never be allowed to set before young children, to make them behave well, either good or bad consequences of their actions, which are not actually to result, and which usually can not happen at all. A thousand small lies are told children, which are thought quite harmless; but they are not so. The more we permit little girls to enjoy the wonders of fairyland, and the less we practice dissecting for them a beautiful poem, so that they shall understand how much of it is true and how much not, so much the more strictly must we adhere to the truth in our daily intercourse with them. A child can not preserve his unlimited and impregnable faith in the words of his elders, if he discovers as he grows older that they have told him falsehoods about one thing and another. There is even danger that such a discovery may weaken his faith in God's own word.

Truthfulness is the firm basis of all moral instruction. If the mother succeeds in cultivating her daughter's disposition to openness and candor, so that she is always uneasy until her mother knows every thing, little or great, which concerns her, then she may hope for success in her general plan of education. I know, of course, that success here, as everywhere, depends upon God's blessing; but parents are co-workers with God in this particular, and must do their part with faithful and unceasing labor.

Of all the means by which a child may be kept from lying, the chief is, that it should always find its elders telling the truth. Nor should children be punished for doing some accidental injury, or for an omission which does not imply positive disobedience, provided they confess what has happened with entire truthfulness and a proper regret. Many mothers think it the greatest fault their children can commit, to break by accident, a cup, or a pane of glass; and such an offence they punish most severely. If an unlucky child, accordingly, meets with such a misfortune, he tells lies about it from fear of being punished; committing a fault for which his unjust mother is really to blame.

But if a careful and judicious mother finds her child concealing or denying what it has done, it should be emphatically punished for the lie. If a child, otherwise honest, should for once tell a lie, and be punished, then when it confesses its fault, at the next occurrence of one, it should not be treated angrily, but with increased love. It should be made to see that its lying had caused grief, and that now there is joy at its returning to the truth.

Children should early be taught that "Lying is a shame to men." And severe punishment should be inflicted for lying, and for direct intentional disobedience.

8. *Obedience.*

In order to give as few occasions as possible for punishment, it will be well for the mother to give as few commands as possible; only when they are absolutely necessary. Fathers do not so often fail in this particular; but I have known good mothers who all day long were constantly crying out, "Don't do that," and "Always do so," and who consequently quite failed to make these innumerable commands impressive. Nothing should be forbidden except what it is decided not to permit any longer; and nothing should be commanded except what can and will be carried through. This will soon bring about the pleasant result of making obedient and happy children; for there is no more unhappy and uneasy creature than a disobedient and ill-trained child.

Mothers often commit the error of refusing to a child's request, and often without reason, the same thing which they afterwards yield to its crying. It does not help the matter for the mother to say, "First be still, and then you may have it." The child should not have at all what it cries for. If it thus never gets any thing by crying, and above all, nothing by crying for the thing which has once been refused, it will very soon leave off trying to get its own way by that means, and will quietly acquiesce in its mother's negative. But this rule should be very early observed; even before the child can walk or speak; for it is incredible how soon children observe when they can count upon this mistaken complaisance, and will endeavor always to accomplish what they have succeeded in once.

9. *Crying.*

Much complaint is made of children's whining and crying; although, as has already been shown, an intelligent mother can do much to prevent it. It is very common, for instance, for a child to cry out, as often as it falls, or runs against any thing. This habit, however, is usually a result of mistaken tenderness on the part of those about the child. It can not be expected that a mother shall not be frightened at seeing her child fall down, but even the most timid mother must govern her feelings, and treat the accident as quite unimportant. She might exclaim in a cheerful manner "Hurra," or "Jump right up again!" and ought not to help the child up or lament over it, however much she may desire to do so; and least of all should she give it sugar or any thing else to comfort it. When she sees that the child is going to cry, she should promptly direct its attention to something to look at, or say, "Come, we'll go quick and get this or that," pointing out something at the other end of the room, or something out of the door. In this way the child may be made to forget its fright, for it is this, and not pain, which is commonly the matter when it falls; and if it felt pain, it would thus learn to bear it without making a noise.

There are other cases where the mother can prevent the child's crying, without its being noticed by the latter. Thus, if she sees that the child is getting tired of playing by itself, and is therefore losing its interest in its amusement, or that it has run about until it begins to feel tired, she may, before any outbreak of unhappiness occurs, take it upon her lap for a little while, and tell it a story, or sing it a song. Or she may herself join in its play, and invent some new variations of it. If the trouble comes from hunger, and it is nearly the time for eating, the hour may be anticipated a little, without the child's noticing it, for the sake of keeping it quiet.

Very small children should not be permitted to see the preparations for meals, much before the time of eating; it would be a daily incentive to crying, instead, as many suppose, of teaching them patience, and would teach them still more effectually, greediness in eating and drinking. The child's food should also be made all ready before being brought to it, and should be brought in with all the apparatus, and not too hot, so that it can be given at once. This will secure the satisfaction of feeding a good-humored child, without having to bear its crying.

The mother should prescribe the limit of the quantity which the child may eat. If it stops before eating it all, it should not be made to eat more. But if all is eaten and the child sets up a crying, be careful not to give it more; for the child would notice this, and very soon there would be raised after every meal, a shrieking for more. If the mother is convinced that the crying was from an absolute need, she must merely be careful to give rather more next time.

These are perfectly simple and harmless means, and may be used by every intelligent mother to prevent her child from crying, without any danger of flattering or accommodating its whims and fancies. Such management will render the nursery pleasant to her husband; whereas no one can find fault with him if he avoids it when filled with constant crying.

10. *Watching children. Plays.*

It is one of the first rules for a mother, to watch her young children closely, but to do it so quietly and unobtrusively that they will not observe it. However important they are among the objects of her attention, it is equally important that they should not know this. When the child is playing by itself, it should suppose itself entirely unnoticed. Nothing is more delightful to see than a child entirely absorbed in its play, without any thought of any persons who may happen to be near; and nothing is more disagreeable than a child who at every motion looks round to see if it is observed how prettily it plays, or asks "Am I not playing prettily?"

Children should be permitted to play by themselves as much as possible; and should be supplied not with too many toys, but with such as can be made some sort of use of. The simpler the toy, the more room is there for the imagination, and the greater the child's enjoyment of it. It is not, however, by any means intended that the mother should not sometimes amuse both herself and her child by joining in its plays, but only that the child must not be permitted to suppose that it must always have some one to play with.

11. *Amusements of girls.*

For little girls there is no better amusement than playing with dolls. In their earlier infancy they will find pleasure in nursing their dolls, putting them to sleep, and imitating all the management of their mother with the babies; and at a later period they will enjoy making dresses for them. This should be encouraged by the mother; for although the little girls will not think of it, this will be an excellent preparation for their future duties. But I would not recommend too many dolls; it will be found best for each girl to have one, whom she will love about as well as if it were a little sister. In like manner, cooking for the dolls in little cooking utensils is a good occupation for little girls; and they will find a special pleasure in entertaining their brothers with the results of their culinary labors. The excessive luxury and superfluity which I at present observe exhibited in the dolls and other playthings of children, I consider very harmful.

All games of chance with dice or cards are decidedly to be rejected; as is the game of loto. There are an abundance of harmless games in summer, ball, battledore, graces; and in winter, when the children sit round the table on long evenings, there are many others, in which all the children may join, and the parents too. Such are games with songs and with words of more than one meaning; riddles, charades, telling stories, &c. Such games are not merely modes of passing away the time, but they are useful in many ways. It is a good sign in a child to take a lively interest in them; and their enjoyment of them should be marred as little as possible by any prohibitions, especially by any austere ones. Games of forfeits often lead to foolish tricks; and are not to be recommended.

12. *Greediness. Love of dainties.*

Two faults often noticed in children are, a desire to eat whenever they see another person eating, which renders them infinitely troublesome to those about them; and a love of dainties. These two faults may be prevented before they become fixed, by accustoming the child, as soon as it is weaned, to set times for eating. For the nature of its food, I refer to Hufeland. At no other time should the child receive any thing, nor should even the most honored guest be permitted to give him any thing. If the mother strictly observes this rule, and the nurse also, and the father, the child will learn to see other grown-up persons or children eating, without the least desire to partake.

A child brought up under this rule, and with simple and regular diet, and also so that unconditional obedience to parental commands has become a second nature to it, will not readily learn the habit of greediness. I have known children so trained, from three to six years old, who could be left alone for hours together amongst fruit and confectionery, without any desire to obtain them.

These rules are not meant to prevent children from the innocent enjoyment of their fruit and cake on feast-days. On the contrary, a child plainly brought up, with a healthy appetite, and hungry, will enjoy such things much more than those who suffer, from constant devouring of dainties, under a morbid craving for eatables, and a disordered stomach.

13. *Cleanliness and order.*

For the bodily treatment of children I refer to Hufeland; and also for rules for cleanliness in particular; a point upon which he is very strenuous. Cleanliness should be made a habit for children. It should be an invariable rule, especially for girls, to keep their bodies, as well as their clothes, clean; and not only this, but they should also be accustomed to observe and set right even the least dirt about them, and any disorder or disarrangement. It is scarcely calculable how much time may be saved by strict and punctual order. Little girls should early be accustomed not to go to sleep until their play-things are all in their places; for every thing, even the minutest, should have its own place. And older girls should be taught to consider it their duty, not only to clean up every piece of work which they are doing before beginning another, but always to put in the right place whatever they see out of it. This trouble will be saved however, if all the rest of the household are in the habit, which we have advised, of always putting every thing in the right place, and never any thing in the wrong one. They should also be taught always, before they leave a room, to observe whether there is any thing which ought to be carried out; and when they are going into one, whether any thing needs to be carried in; so as not to be going about with empty hands.

A young girl thus brought up to order and punctuality, so that they have become to her a second nature, will never be one of those order-crazy housewives, whose incessant restlessness and furious stirring up of the inmates of the family are almost more uncomfortable than any possible degree of disorder. The object of these good people seems to be not so much a quiet and well-arranged household, as constantly moving things about, and cleaning up. A girl brought up from youth in a household of the proper habits of quiet good order, will understand how to maintain the same without restlessness or a pedantic stiffness of management. She would not value little things above great ones, nor, like those inordinately orderly women just spoken of, consider the days and hours of house-cleaning absolutely invariable, even if a change was demanded by the sickness of a child, or to accommodate some important business of the master of the house.

14. *Good manners; modesty.*

Girls must from the earliest period be trained with special care to polished and elegant manners; which can be done without the pedantry of some governesses, or the help of a dancing-master. The movements of healthy and well-managed little children are naturally graceful, and those of girls have often a special elegance. As the last grow somewhat older, there arises in them a certain tendency to wildness, and a degree of coarseness along with it. To prevent any evil results from these tendencies in girls, is the task of an intelligent mother. But it is wrong to say, as is often said, "Don't do this; what will people say?" or "Don't; what if any one were looking at you!" and the like. It will be quite enough for the mother to say, "Do not do that; it is disagreeable;" or, "I wish you not to do so;" or, "Your father has forbidden you to do it." To violate such an indication of parental wishes, should be always considered and treated as a thing totally out of the question.

Wild and boyish plays should never be permitted to girls, either in company with boys or when alone.* However great our pleasure in seeing them heartily enjoy running, jumping, and similar hilarious sports, it is still necessary that these sports should be restrained within moderate limits; so as not to become inelegant or vulgar. A vulgar habit once learned, is unlearned only with difficulty; and there is much more reason to expect polished and agreeable ease of manner from a young lady who has from infancy been brought up in habits of elegance and modesty, than from one whose attention is only directed to the importance of their cultivation after she has grown up. One thus neglected must always be thinking, "How am I acting? How do I stand! How do I step!" whereas the most attractive of all qualities in a young girl is unconsciousness; entire freedom from self-observation and self-examination. And if elegant manners have become a second nature to her, she will show it, whether at home or in the largest circles of society.

16. *Clothes.*

Girls may perhaps have an innate tendency towards vanity and love of ornament; which, like all other innate faults, may be counteracted by early good management. Thus, girls should be accustomed from childhood to be always neat and orderly in their dress, but not to be conspicuously ornamented. It will do no harm to cultivate their taste for elegant and appropriate dress, and a distaste for that which is inelegant and unappropriate. Little girls should be simply dressed in clothes proper for their age. There should be no day in the week in which they may go in a disorderly dress, but they should be dressed every day nearly alike, without very frequent changes. It

* "In choosing amusements, all company liable to suspicion must be avoided. No boys and girls together." So says Fenelon. The application to mixed schools is easy.

is of course proper to wear their Sunday dress on Sundays; for it is the Lord's day.

The great importance attributed by very many women and girls to dress, ornament, and such externals, is often and very truly spoken of as ridiculous, and as showing that heads which have so much room for entirely idle unimportant things, must be pretty empty of every thing else. But this is not often so felt that it is made a subject of grave admonition to girls.

16. *Amusements.*

In like manner, I am inclined to consider the usual amusements indulged in by grown-up girls, as matters in which a well-trained and domestic young woman should be brought up to find no pleasure. If her susceptibilities to such higher pleasures as really strengthen and stimulate the mind through the eye and the ear have early been cultivated, she will not easily be brought to find pleasure in the ordinary foolish kinds of diversion. And if a young girl who reflects, as one brought up in a Christian manner would be most likely to do, that time so idly spent can do the mind no good, and will very easily do it harm, she will refrain without constraint or argument from occupations so dangerous to the purity of the soul.

But it will not be fair to charge these amusements upon girls as sins, because it will be found that most of those persons whom they are bound to respect and love, think otherwise on the subject. But there is no respect in which a mother needs to exercise more care, than in watching lest her daughters should take credit to themselves for not partaking in one or another class of amusements; and that they do not for any such reason despise other people, or set themselves above them. For spiritual pride is far more destructive to the soul than vanity, or love of adornments.

To direct their daughters between these two rocks, must be the endeavor of all Christian parents.

17. *Relations of the sexes.*

There are many mothers who think it necessary—in my opinion very erroneously indeed—to initiate their daughters in all the mysteries of the family relation, even in those of the sexes to each other; and upon points which they think they may profitably find themselves informed in case they should get married. We have seen to what a point of coarseness and caricature these views were carried in the Philanthropinum, after the teaching of Rousseau.

Other parents err in the opposite direction, by telling little girls many things which as soon as they grow up they will find quite untrue. This practice has already been mentioned as always hurtful;

and it is so in this case. Such matters should not be discussed at all in the presence of children; and least of all in a mysterious manner, which stimulates curiosity. Let the children believe, as long as they will, that an angel brings their mother the babies; a common explanation in many places, and preferable to the messenger which some substitute, namely, the stork. If children grow up under the immediate eye of their mother, they will very seldom ask unseasonable questions on the subject, even when her confinement keeps her away from them; and such a belief as that suggested will be found not to clash unpleasantly with the pious instructions which she has given them.

If girls ask, subsequently, how do little children come? they may be told, that the good God gives the little child to the mother, and that its guardian angel is in heaven, where it was undoubtedly an invisible agent in procuring so desirable a gift; but that they, the inquirers, need not know, and can not understand, how God gives the children. Girls have to receive a similar answer to a hundred such questions; and the mother's duty in this particular is, to keep her daughter's thoughts so fully occupied with what is good and beautiful, that she will have no leisure for curiosity about such matters.

A mother whose mental authority over her child is what it ought to be, will only need to say once, seriously, "It would not be well for you to know about it; you must avoid hearing it spoken of." A daughter brought up with the proper moral feelings, would from that time feel an entire distaste to listen to any references to things of the kind.

That girl is fortunate whose mind remains a genuinely childlike mind until she becomes married. Afterwards, as her understanding becomes enlightened, she will be profoundly grateful to the mother who has watched over the purity of her life, and the purity of her thoughts also.

18. *Nursery-maids.*

There can be no greater pleasure nor more delightful employment for a young mother, than herself to take care of her child, and to have it always about her. This does not, however, imply that she is to have constantly and exclusively the duty of holding it and waiting on it, which would very likely lead to the neglect of the older children. It would be her best plan to secure the services of a female attendant, young, and if inexperienced, then at any rate uncontaminated; and this attendant she should teach, under her own eyes, how to take care of the child in the proper manner. If the mother likes the maid, and is willing that she should have a part in the affections of the child, the child will soon like her, and she it. Such treatment will in a measure render the maid acquainted with the wishes and ideals of the mother for her child's training. A well-disposed young woman will very soon acquire a feeling that it is a high honor to be employed in preserving the child from any harm, whether of body or soul.

Where the family is not in circumstances to keep more than one maid, the mother should so arrange that the maid may do most of the domestic labor, while she herself takes charge of the child. A careful and ingenious manager will always be able to find some hours, from time to time, in which the maid can take care of the child, or take it to walk, but in the mother's presence. I add this condition because even the very best young girl ought not easily to be permitted to take children out to walk by herself; as so doing would expose them to many risks consequent upon her own youth, even if only those are reckoned which consist in the opportunity for idle chat.

The case is, however, altered when any thing happens which renders it absolutely necessary for the children to be intrusted for some one occasion, to the maid. The servant, having seen that her mistress is always faithful in attending to her children, and never neglects them for any idle amusement, will be very much more careful in watching over the children and seeing that they receive no harm, than a maid would be to whom the children should be often and entirely intrusted, while the mother is pursuing her own pleasure.

It may be asked, if there are so many disadvantages connected with the employment of young nursery-maids, why it would not be better for the mother to employ some old and experienced nurse, to whom she can confidently commit the whole charge of the children? The answer is, that greater reliance can not be felt upon an older woman, because there is no security that she will love the children better, or be more prudent in taking care of them; and thus even such older women as are well qualified for the physical management of children, might thus exert a most harmful intellectual influence upon them. Such an experienced nurse-maid will not be disposed to receive instructions from a young wife, how the child is to be managed, because she will feel that she understands the subject much better herself. And as she will commonly have served in other families before, she will be always critically comparing her previous service with her present one, and will remain a stranger in the house.

But the feelings of a young girl who grows up to become, as it were, a member of the family, will be very different. The nursery, the garden where she has lived, frolicked, sung, and played with the children, where she has entertained herself and them with fairy tales, histories and hymns, the chamber where she has prayed with them, and with their mother for them;—all these things will, as will the mother and the children themselves, remain during after years, a most happy recollection in her mind.

I have myself known such cases; and if they are few, the reason is, doubtless, that mothers do not exercise conscientious faithfulness toward their children, nor pass their pleasantest hours in their company.

Toward other servants, with whom their relations are not so close as with their nurse-maids, children should be taught never to be guilty of using an unkind manner, nor insulting language; and still less to give them orders. They may only request what they want. Parents are often to blame for the improper conduct of their children to servants. They find fault with them in a passionate manner in the presence of the children, who are only too quick to observe it and to imitate it. If a parent is satisfied that a nurse-maid is a worthless person, her duty toward her daughters, with whom such a servant must often come in contact, will require that she be dismissed at once.

19. *Holidays for children.*

People entirely worldly-minded are often found to be of the opinion that in families which live in a religious and retired manner, there prevails gloom, and a contempt and avoidance of all enjoyment. "These pious folks" they say, "think every pleasure a sin, and forcibly restrain their children from all worldly enjoyments; a proceeding which for that very reason makes them doubly eager for them." Those who say this do not remember what the apostle said, "Rejoice in the Lord, and again I say, rejoice;" an expression utterly at variance with their theories of Christian family life. And even if they were cognizant of it, they would necessarily misunderstand the expression "in the Lord," until they should themselves have escaped out of the restless tumult of the pleasures of this world, and themselves experienced what it is to rejoice in the Lord.

But I am now to speak not of the seducing pleasures of adult persons, but the innocent and beautiful holidays, and the little festivals of children. The mother will naturally bestow much more attention than the father upon the management of these, and the modes of securing to the children a real enjoyment of them.

Although I quite agree with Claudius, that children should have many holidays in a year, yet the three great church feasts of Christmas, Easter and Whitsuntide, should be distinctly marked by superior magnificence, so as to be quite different in the children's minds from the other holidays.

Of these three festivals, Christmas is that usually most elaborately celebrated as a children's festival. From the latter part of autumn up to Christmas day, the children, small as well as great, should devote their labor, however awkward, to preparations for furnishing little Christmas gifts for their parents, grand-parents, &c., and for poor children. While at work, an advent or Christmas hymn should from time to time be sung. The more nearly the festival approaches for which there has been so much preparation and anticipation, the more will the joyous anticipations of the children increase, and the easier it will be to teach them appropriate verses and texts, and thus to secure the spiritual blessing of the birth of Christ.*

It is very important that in family devotions, during the period of Advent, there should be read, not a book of the Bible without any special reference to the time; but that there should rather be read portions from the prophets, Isaiah especially, and toward the latter part, the first chapter of Luke, which includes the birth of John, the Annunciation, and the visit to Elizabeth. And the hymns sung on the same occasions should be in like manner selected as appropriate.

The giving of the presents is better on Christmas eve, than on the morning of Christmas day. To postpone the presents until New Year's takes out the very heart of the festival, the rejoicing over Christ's birth. And besides, New Year's is usually devoted to the business of contemplating the mutability of human things, and to the melancholy recollection of departed friends.

When the children are assembled round the Christmas tree, three or four verses of the hymn "From heaven high" should be sung, then the father should read the gospel for the day (Luke, chap. 2, 1–14), then two or three verses of the hymn "Praised be thou, O Jesus Christ" may be sung, and then old and young may joyously turn to the distribution of the presents.

These should be appropriately varied, as the giver and receiver are old or young, rich or poor, or prefer one thing or another. Nothing superfluous should be given, and nothing too expensive for the giver's means. Nor should the other extreme be practiced, and nothing be given the children except mere absolute necessaries, such as shoes,

* Such are, Isaiah, chap. 60, 1–3; John, chap. 3, 16; 1 Epistle John, chap. 4, 19; John, chap. 15, 13; Ephesians, chap. 5, 1–2; the first two stanzas of the Advent Hymn, "How then shall I receive thee," and of Luther's two Christmas hymns, "Praised be thou," and "From Heaven high;" of these last, as many stanzas as can easily be learned.

stockings, and other ordinary garments. These must be had at any rate, if there were no Christmas; or the family were heathens or Mohammedans. Books or pictures may be given, however—such as the children like; those for instance of Spekter, Pocci, Richter; Grimm's stories for children, Wackernagel's reading book; or a box of tools, &c. The Christmas tree should not be turned into a confectioner's shop, but should be made fantastically beautiful with gilded apples and nuts, stars and lilies. At its foot should be a meadow with a pond, in which should be swans and gold-fish; and close to the trunk, a little hut with Joseph, Mary, and the Christ-child, adored by the shepherds or the wise men of the east; and over the hut should be seen the star.

To the children, the whole occasion should be made to appear like a beautiful dream, quite separated from their daily life. With this dream upon them they should go to sleep, and should wake up in the morning to a renewed enjoyment of the festive occasion.

The cheerful Christmas time is followed by the very different passion week. During this time should be read at family prayers the account of Christ's passion; on Good Friday, the account of the crucifixion, and also Isaiah, chap. 53; and then should be sung the hymns, "O Lamb of God, &c.," "O head with blood, &c.," "We thank thee now, Lord Jesus Christ, that thou for us wast sacrificed," and the like. And the children should learn the following texts relating to Christ's passion; Isaiah, chap. 53, 4, 5; John, chap. 1, 29.

But it would perhaps be better, instead of so very directly instructing the children in the history of the Passion, to omit indoctrinating them, and to leave them to the impressions which they will derive from family worship, reading the accounts of the passion, singing the hymns which relate to it, and the general effect of the whole atmosphere of their home and their life during the passion-week.

This gloomy and dark period is followed by the brilliant day of Easter: the festival of Christ's resurrection. On this occasion may be sung "Jesus my trust;" and the gospel for the day may be read.

On Easter day should be read also the fifteenth chapter of 1 Corinthians, on victory and triumph over death, and on the joyful and assured hope of eternal life, with a reference to Christ risen, "the first fruits of them that slept." "If he had not arisen, then the world had been lost."

At Easter, also, it is well to give the little ones a lamb out of the toy-shop, which their vivid childish fancy will regard as alive, and they will take as much care of it as if it were a real lamb. When the children are older, playing with Easter-eggs is a game that will amuse them for a good while before the day comes.

If the quiet period which precedes Easter is really passed in a peaceful and retired manner, the children will from an early age receive an indelible impression of the alternations of rejoicing and grief in the course of the ecclesiastical year, without the necessity of any extended verbal explanation of the difference. The gospel for Easter-day, and the sparkling Easter hymns, will fill their childish hearts with joy; and if as at Christmas, innocent childish pleasures are provided in connection with the day, the Easter festival will become a time of the greatest rejoicing, whose profounder significance will become every year more clear to them, as will in like manner the more serious meaning of the preceding passion-week.

Our ancestors were accustomed to apply to the spring festival of Whitsuntide, some expressions of the psalmist relating to adornments for feasts. At this time, mothers fasten green boughs over the children's heads on the bed, before they wake, and hang on them flowers and little things, that will please them. Old persons whose parents observed this custom, always remember the delightful feeling with which they went to sleep the night before, and looked up amongst the green boughs in the morning.

In after life, these three chief festivals will remain in our memories of childhood, as far back as they reach, days of blessing, mystery, and holiness.

There are other Christian festivals which have descended to us from the earliest period, which might well continue to be celebrated in the family, even though they are not by the church. On the day of the Three Kings, the gospel of the Adoration of the Wise Men of the East might be read, and the Christmas tree lighted up again with the hut at its root with Joseph, Mary and the Christ-child, and the wise men adoring; and the shining star over-head.* St. John's day is celebrated in many parts of Germany, by hanging over the door garlands of flowers gathered for the purpose the day before. Little children have also a wreath bound to the arm, which they wear to church. In other places, St. John's fire is lighted on some elevated place.

In like manner, St. Michael's day should remind us of the angels, especially of the guardian angels of our children; and on St. Martin's day, we should tell the children the story of the charitable bishop, and should remind them also of the baptism of Martin Luther on that day.

But I can not go into details of all the numerous festivals which are

* The sport of making a bean-king on the eve of this festival is well known.

celebrated in so many parts of Germany for the children or by all the community. Such are May-day, when the children sing over the departure of winter; the spring procession, when old and young, the clergyman at their head, go all round the fields, praying for the blessings for which they are to return thanks in the autumn; the harvest-home, when harvest crowns are worn, and all sing joyously, "Now let us all thank God." Those who were brought up in the country will remember this festival with pleasure.

The celebration of the national anniversaries is, and should continue to be sacredly observed. Above all should every German family continue to commemorate the battle of Leipzig. On the 18th of October, the account of that glorious day should be read over, patriotic hymns sung, and children and children's children thank God for their escape from a severe servitude; for the preservation of the national life of our people. Even if all the fires on the mountain tops should go out, and if sinful ingratitude toward God and the heroes who have fallen in a sacred strife, and a stupid indifference to freedom and the independence of the father-land should dishonor thousands, let us remain faithful.

> "No! howsoe'er may alter
> The chance and change of time,
> My memory ne'er shall falter
> From thee, thou dream sublime!"

Children take great delight in celebrating their birthdays. We may allow to their natural egoism, the pre-eminence which each in turn enjoys on his own birthday; to be the king of the feast, to receive the presents, to enjoy his favorite delicacies, and to invite his young friends to visit him. But still, the day should not fail to be distinctly made a day of thanksgiving for the blessings of the past year, and of asking a further blessing upon that which is to come.

I thus make some allowance for the egoism of children. But it is delightful to see children as much delighted at the birthdays of their parents as at their own, and contriving for weeks beforehand what they can do to make the occasion pleasant, and to provide presents.

But I must quit the subject. Holidays for the children, if interest is felt in them, are cheerful and joyous occasions in family life. Yes: "Rejoice in the Lord; and again I say, rejoice." Pleasures such as these here alluded to leave no bitter taste behind; are followed by no painful and sickly feeling. On the contrary, they vivify both soul and body, and refresh and strengthen both young and old.

And if children have been early trained to partake and enjoy such pure and innocent pleasures as these, they will, when grown up, be tormented with no lust after destroying and impure ones.

VI. HOUSEHOLD OCCUPATIONS, HIGHER CULTURE.

It is a main point in the education of girls, so to cultivate their minds that they may always have an inclination towards what is noble, good and beautiful, and that the many useless thoughts so ready to creep into empty heads, may be kept out by better ones.

Jean Paul says in "*Levana*," after making bitter complaints of the prevalence of the evil just alluded to, "But what help is there for it? I answer, the help actually in existence among the poorer classes. Let girls practice, instead of the common useless and vision-cherishing kinds of ornamental work, the various kinds of household labor; by the help of which, dreams and reveries will be driven off, by the new tasks and requirements which every minute will bring."

In another place the same author says, "Let no woman, however etherial—or rather windy-brained—say that housekeeping is too mechanical for the dignity of her intellect; and that she prefers pursuits as purely intellectual as those of men. Was there ever any intellectual pursuit without a mechanical one with it?"

It is my own opinion also, that every young woman, no matter what her rank or circumstances, should without fail be instructed in the details of practical housekeeping; and even that her education can not be termed complete if this part of it has been neglected; although at the same time, I do not consider a training to such domestic duties exclusively, to be sufficient to occupy the minds of young women. There are many whose daughters are taught, besides the usual elementary studies and those of a religious kind, nothing except housekeeping duties and manual labor; the purpose thus sought being to keep them in simplicity of mind, and occupied, aside from their work, with none except religious thoughts. This is, however, a mistaken course; for in default of an appropriate higher culture, the minds of girls will become interested in a very useless and indeed dangerous way, in things of the idlest and foolishest kind.

Fenelon says, "Ignorance is often a cause of *ennui* to a young girl, and prevents her from finding an innocent employment for her leisure. When a girl has grown up to a certain age without the habit of serious occupations, she can neither after that acquire a taste for them nor learn to estimate them fairly. Every thing serious is disagreable to her; every thing that requires continued attention, wearies her. The love of pleasure which is so strong in the young, the example of her companions, occupied in their diversions, all serve to give her a distaste for regular and industrious occupation."

And in another place he says, of the occupations of such ignorant and empty-minded girls, "They burn with eagerness to have experimental knowledge of all that they hear of, and that people are doing. They love to hear news, to write letters, to receive them. They want to be talked to about every thing, and to talk about every thing; they are vain, and vanity makes them talkative; light-minded, and their light-mindedness prevents them from having any of those serious thoughts which would predispose them to silence."

I now turn to the consideration of the means of preventing young girls from occupying their thoughts with foolishness, and of turning them toward useful things. I shall first discuss the mode of making them familiar and skillful in the duties of housekeeping.

I have already mentioned how at a very early age a girl may begin to be of some use to her mother in domestic duties; but she should by no means be permitted, until well past her childhood, to have any knowledge of the solicitudes of housekeeping. The mother should be careful not to say before her children that such a thing is expensive; that it had to be bought once, and must now be bought over again, because it is broken or spoiled. The children should be careful not to injure or break any thing, not because it costs money, but because their mother has told them to be careful, and because it makes her feel sorry to have any thing spoiled, and still more so, to have her children careless, awkward, and most of all, disobedient. Little girls should never hear it remarked that a thing costs much or little. Boys are less inclined to trouble themselves about such matters; but girls notice them very early; and nothing sounds more disagreeably than for a little thing to be saying "Mother gave a good deal for that," or, when a thing is broken, "They can buy another."

Girls should not have what is called pocket money. As long as they are children, they should receive whatever they have from their parents, and with gratitude, but without adverting to the large or small expense of it. Thus they will receive any little thing with as much pleasure, and will be as thankful for it, as if it were something far more costly. It is much more affecting and more beautiful to see children on a birthday presenting flowers which they have gathered or cultivated themselves, or to see them, with the innocent notion that what they like best, must be most agreeable to others also, making a present of one of their playthings, than to see them presenting things that they have bought with money which was given them before.

In like manner, any thing produced by the labor of older girls is more valuable than any purchased gift. This mode of managing will also early teach girls the better way of assisting the poor, by giving them some article of property, or something to eat.

At a subsequent period comes the time when it is the duty of the grown-up daughter to aid her mother in all the cares of the latter; and to exercise independently all the various accomplishments in which she has gradually been trained by her industrious assistance in housekeeping. If she is a good scholar in arithmetic, she will easily keep the housekeeping accounts; and will feel herself honored to be allowed to take part in the household cares of her mother, in return for the untroubled careless happiness in which her childhood was passed. All the assistance in housekeeping and cooking, which children according to their capacity can give their mothers, will be made pleasant to them by the very fact that they are not obliged to exercise the foresight which is necessary.

An older daughter, by helping her mother consult and manage for the necessities and enjoyments of the younger ones, will learn better how to manage money than by having an allowance with which to supply her own clothing, &c. Nor will she need any pocket money. To a grown-up, modest, intelligent and well trained daughter, her mother can safely say, "Whatever is mine is yours also."

My reason for claiming that girls of every rank and condition should learn to be skillful and efficient housekeepers is, that when they become mistresses of a household, no matter how splendid their situation in life, they will need to exercise a keen supervision and a reliable judgment over their household mangement; and will need to know what they may properly require from their servants; from whom we find sometimes that too much is demanded, and sometimes too little. But she can not use such a supervision and judgment, without having before become acquainted with the details of housekeeping by actual practice in managing them herself.

Still less can the mistress of a family afford to be without this previous preparation, where her pecuniary resources are limited. Early training will enable her to manage a household even in difficult and narrow circumstances, and still to preserve enough ease of mind and leisure for intellectual pursuits. It is true that a shrewd woman may even without such previous experience in housekeeping, by means of a resolute will and steady industry, learn to fulfill her housewifely duties; but she can never avoid a preoccupation with them, and a certain anxiety, the necessary consequences of her want of experience. This will prevent her from feeling that freedom and ease of mind which are indispensable for the further cultivation of some talents very important in the family, which she has probably somewhat developed before. A sense of pressure and solicitude about household matters will also operate to prevent her ear and her mind from being open to the interests of her husband; in whose vocation, and intellectual life, she ought to take a lively interest.

A Christian and educated housewife, whose judicious and patiently efficient industry proclaims itself in but few words, and still less in incessant restless hurry and scolding and unquiet; whose virtues and talents render her home a more pleasant and peaceful spot to her husband than any other; who trains up her children in Christian simplicity and piety, without any of the narrow and mistaken pietism which contemns and neglects any of the talents which God gives us;—such a housewife should be the ideal result sought for by female education. Such a one will unite the highest attainments in housekeeping and in elegant culture.

The Christian ideal of higher mental culture is something which so intimately permeates and inspires to the whole being, that it must be extremely difficult to set it forth; to do thus I shall however endeavor.

Culture is something not confined to any single points; and should begin in the earliest childhood. It is a great mistake to suppose that it can be given by any the greatest number of hours of instruction, although instruction is as indispensable to culture as are strings or keys to a good musical instrument. The instrument will produce no music, unless it has both the vibrating body and the whole structure for acting upon it.

A young girl may be instructed, even thoroughly instructed, to use a favorite mode of expression, on all possible subjects, without possessing a single trace of the higher grade of culture. This consists, not merely in development of understanding or memory, but of the feelings also; in fact, of the whole being; of all the sacred gifts of heart and head. It is evidenced by the whole life; by the atmosphere of the family; by the tone of conversation; by a certain faculty of observing every thing quietly, but of retaining and considering only what is good, what is proper. It moderates the passions, watches over enthusiasm, preserves the power of loving deeply and purely, and keeps alive the power of feeling true and pious enjoyment in nature and art. Culture, in young women, should never develop into learning; for then it ceases to be delicate feminine cul ture. A young woman can not and ought not to plunge with the obstinate and persevering strength of a man into scientific pursuits, so as to become forgetful of every thing else. Only an entirely unwomanly young woman could try to become thoroughly learned, in a man's sense of the term; and she would try in vain, for she has not the mental faculties of man.

In opposition to these sentiments I may be directed to learned ladies; a second-rate article, which, thank God, is extremely rare. Of the well-known Madame Dacier, Jöcher remarks, "She had acquired uncommon skill in Latin, Greek, and criticism." She edited many classical authors; translated, amongst others, Plautus, the "*Clouds*" and the "*Plutus*" of Aristophanes; and "then applied herself to Terence with so much zeal that she got up every morning at four o'clock, and labored at the work all the forenoon." According to this account, Madame Dacier was certainly a very "thoroughly instructed" lady. But she was just as deficient in delicate womanly culture as she was thoroughly learned; for otherwise how could she have translated those most indecent works?

Compare with her the princess in Goethe's "*Torquato Tasso*," who says, "I rejoice in being able to understand what intelligent men say. If an opinion is given about a character of antiquity, or his deeds, or if mention is made of any department of learning, which wide experience shows to be useful to mankind, because elevating in tendency, I follow with pleasure such discourses of noble souls, because it is easy for me to follow it."

Only compare such a princess with that other caricature of a female pedant, coarse, amidst all her learning. The princess was called a scholar of Plato; but so far was she from measuring herself with men, that she only rejoiced in being able easily to understand and follow the discourse of intelligent men.

High culture shows itself in the whole demeanor of a young woman, before she utters a single word about any thing which she has learned; while girls too often display the most utter want of culture, by the tactless manner in which they try to lug in their little bits of school knowledge. The studies of girls should be intended not to make them know much, and still less to make them as it were hang about themselves their scraps of knowledge, like lifeless and tasteless ornaments, trying to look splendid in them; but that they should thoroughly assimilate whatever they do learn with their whole being, and make it a well-chosen and valuable ornament of their minds. Such a mode of studying will secure them the permanent possession of what they learn, to their own pleasure and the pleasure of all around them; and as mothers, they will be able to communicate their knowledge to their daughters in the best way; not merely to instruct them, but to cultivate them.*

VII. READING.

The entire opposite of an elevated Christian culture is that vulgar, frivolous perversion of it too often found in German families. I have already referred to the elements of this perverted culture, and have cited as one of the most pernicious of them, the wretched habit of reading romances of all sorts, just as they may come to hand. This habit produces a sickly voracity; they read and read without being either satisfied or nourished by what they swallow down so greedily. On the contrary, it is a poison to them. If a classical work happens to stray by mistake into their circulating library, they take no notice of it. I have quoted the young lady who replied, when asked if she had read Goethe's "*Iphigenia*," "I believe so."

All readiness and activity of mind are, by such a course of reading, destroyed in girls; and they fall into habits of constant absent-mindedness, which render them totally unfit to fulfill their household duties skillfully and prudently; to live in simplicity and godliness. Serious and holy thoughts find no place in the mind of such a silly ill-read girl; and indeed, how could they abide in the same mind with frivolous love stories and perverted, vulgar, fantastic notions about love?

The miserable results of such wretched habits of reading should admonish us to watch carefully over the reading of our daughters, and to select for them, ourselves, and with conscientious care, books which shall promote our object of giving them a pure and noble culture, and one pleasing to God. On the subject of this selection, however, we find the most various and conflicting opinions. One eminent authority goes so far as to say that it is prudery to prevent girls from reading Boccacio's "*Decameron*;" while others pass to the opposite extreme of rejecting books which are entirely harmless. Among the latter are most conspicuous the fanatical and narrow-minded pietists, who, in order to be certain to avoid all offense, take offense at all and sundry books, scarcely excepting books of religious edification.

It is between these extremes that the proper rule of proceeding will be found.

But I shall hear it suggested that it would be well, if instead of this admonition, I should set forth a list of books which might safely

* On the relations between these views of culture and the Christian ideal of the image of God, see under the head of "Christianity in Education," in "*American Journal of Education*," Vol. VIII., p. [illegible]—[illegible].

be put into children's hands, I answer, that I have endeavored to draw up such a list, both by myself and with the aid of friends interested in the subject, and have failed. I very soon perceived, moreover, the reasons why it must of necessity fail; which I can easily explain by a comparison. Let it be attempted to prepare a list of selected articles of food, which shall be adapted to and healthful for the most various human constitutions. How many faults would be found with the choice made? One can not bear this, another that; one likes this, another that; many will miss their favorite dishes; and the doctor will prohibit many of them to the ill or sickly.

Quite similar would be the result of making out a list of books selected for reading. One and the same volume would be sound and nutritious food for one girl, and quite unsuitable to another; would be very pleasant to one, not at all to another. In short, I became convinced that so great are the differences between girls, in respect to age, character, talent, taste, and cultivation, that it would be totally impossible to make out a list which would be suitable for all. It must instead be a duty of intelligent parents and teachers to select books suitable for each individual child; and for this purpose to become thoroughly acquainted both with the children and the books.

In thus selecting, the following principles must be borne in mind:—

1. To consider, whether in the case of many books, they shall be put into the hand of the girl, to be read through by herself without any omissions, or whether they should first be read over by a competent person, and any unsuitable portions left out. This course would be beneficial, especially with many poetical masterpieces.

2. That in the family library there are frequently books suitable enough for men, but not at all for girls. They should therefore not be permitted to pick and choose for themselves from the whole collection, and still less should they be permitted to take out whatever books they may fancy from a circulating library.

3. That fashions prevail also in the reading world. Romances of chivalry had their day, and so did family romances, bandit romances, ghost romances, the "*Mysteries of Paris*," "*Amaranth*," and so on, *ad infinitum*. While these were the fashion, each was in turn eagerly devoured, and talked of in all circles; but how soon were they forgotten! And it was best that they should be forgotten. It would be well if girls could avoid ever occupying themselves with such mere transient, fashionable stuff, but should rather read over and over again the best standard works.

VIII. INSTRUCTION.

We have seen that a young woman may possess a great store of knowledge and skill, and yet not be "cultivated." The mental acquirement of girls are too often mere memorized stuff. Like Locke, their teachers have taken their minds to be originally nothing but a *tabula rasa*, a piece of blank paper, a canvass, on which the painter may represent many different things, the canvass remaining canvass, however, all the while.

Instruction should be of such a kind as to produce an actual vital assimilation of what is taught; so that all which is learned may be as it were mental food, be turned into flesh and blood, may serve to increase, strengthen and improve the whole being; in short, may promote the process of culture.

The culture of girls commonly requires a process of instruction entirely different from that of boys. The latter, with their tendency to unruliness, must early be subjected to discipline, reproved, accustomed to steady and persevering mental labor, to obedient subjection to a regular order of things. Such a training is required by the destined life and labors of a man.

But such a course of discipline would not be the best preparation for the duties of girls. I have known girls for whom their fathers had prescribed strict plans of study, with time-tables, &c., like those for a school, to which they were holden so closely that I believe they would scarcely have given themselves time during one of the prescribed exercises, to carry a sick brother a glass of water. No one could approve such a scheme as that.

But should there be no regular school-like plan for the studies of girls? Certainly; there must be order; but quite different from that of a school. Real order requires that every thing be done at the moment when that thing especially is needed. For example: if a pastor, profoundly engaged in reflecting upon his sermon, were summoned to a death-bed, he ought to leave his work on the spot and hasten to the sick man. The more sacred duties of his office must take precedence of all study.

This example may be applied to the whole life of a girl. A regular order for the daily occupations should be prescribed for them; but they must also be accustomed from early childhood to leave books or piano at any moment when necessary, to assist a smaller child, or to be of use to their parents. Such cases can not of course be provided for in the order of the day: they are the exceptions to the rule. But girls should also be trained, as soon as the exceptional service is over, to return at once to books or instrument, and go quietly on with their studies as if nothing had interrupted.

School instruction is inferior, for girls, to home instruction, because it affords no interval for these services of love. And if the studying for several hours, one after another, is the one chief thing sought, then the school is unsuitable for girls.

Any one who disagrees with these views, and so highly estimates the importance of continuous study, uninterrupted by any thing whatever, as to consider such domestic services of comparatively little importance, may perhaps learn a better way of thinking from Goethe:—

"Early let woman learn to serve, for that is her calling:
For by serving alone she attains to ruling;
To the well-deserved power which is hers in the household.
The sister serves her brother while young; and serves her parents;
And all her life is still a continual going and coming,
A carrying ever and bringing, a making and shaping for others.
Well for her if she learns to think no road a foul one,
To make the hours of the night the same as the hours of the day;
To think no labor too trifling, and never too fine the needle;
To forget herself altogether, and live in others alone.
And lastly, as mother, in truth, she will need every one of the virtues."

These golden words describe the most important object in the education of girls. They ought to learn to serve, in order that they may learn to love, not merely with the tongue and with words, but in deed and in truth. And the poet adds, by such serving they become able to rule; at least within the department where the authority belongs to them, if they are capable of exercising it.

Fenelon strongly objects to the plan of insisting upon strictly observed hours of instruction, like a school, and that for other reasons than those already quoted from him. "A too pedantic regularity," he observes, "which insists upon continuous study without any intermission, is very injurious to girls. Teachers often affect to prefer such a regularity, because it is much more easy for them to do so than to exercise that incessant attention which takes advantage of any favorable moment."

And in another place he thus describes the too regular kind of instruction: "There is no freedom nor cheerfulness in it; it is study and nothing but study; silence, stiffness, constant prohibition and threatening."*

* Madame Necker expresses herself strongly opposed to an excessive number of study hours, and to too long lessons (I. 67). She says, "A quarter of an hour is the shortest time which I have allowed for one lesson; but Miss Edgeworth has limited many to five minutes and with good results."

Fenelon requires an attention which shall seize upon every favorable opportunity. But such opportunities will occur far more often to a mother who teaches at home, than to a teacher who works in school; and the teacher, tied fast to his fixed hours, can not make the best use of such favorable opportunities. I shall further state other weighty reasons against educating girls at schools; after having first explained why it is so very desirable that mothers should as far as possible instruct their daughters at home.

It may be supposed that in our day, when girls are more than ever obliged to learn every thing school-wise, they would, on becoming mothers, find themselves able to teach all that they have learned, more especially as the very power, the art of teaching, is made one of the objects of their studies.

But I am grieved to say that I know more than one woman who has been instructed for years at a girl's school, and distinguished herself there, and yet has not been able to do any thing at all for the instruction of her children.

May it not be the fact that the very practice of learning in school is the reason why, when grown up, they find themselves quite incapable of teaching? Thus educated, they know of no mode of instruction except the so-called "methodical" one; and if they have themselves remained natural and simple, they will find that their whole nature revolts at the attempt to teach in the manner in which they were taught. That which in their teachers was so frequently a stiff pedantic manner, must, when imitated by a woman, appear the most ridiculous caricature. And what mother would desire to appear unnatural and ridiculous to her own children?

If a mother who was educated at school is desirous of herself instructing her daughters, she will commonly find it necessary to neglect and forget the methods which were pursued with her, and to seek to adopt for her own purposes a simple and artistic one.

There are but few studies in which a mother can not direct her daughters sufficiently. Some however require the aid of a teacher who possesses both capacity and experience, and whose long practical labors have made him acquainted with many means of lightening and abridging the work of study. This is especially the case in the first beginnings of some studies; such as reading, writing, and playing the piano.

But such considerations are by no means the only ones which mothers urge against undertaking to instruct their daughters. They repeat, "We have not the time; we have not the knowledge; we have no skill in teaching;" there is almost nothing which they have not, except one thing whose deficiency they do not willingly admit—steady, persevering, conscientious good-will.

Many a mother says she has no time to teach her daughters, who nevertheless has abundance of time for useless and idle society, for the theater, for all manner of similar purposes. If they would only reckon up the hours which they thus waste in one week! But they lack the requisite knowledge. How easily might they acquire it, if they would only make use of a small part of the time they spend so uselessly; if more especially they would learn by the very work of teaching.* Do they lack skill in teaching? A sensible mother, who sincerely loves her children, who makes it a conscientious duty to educate them well, will, by God's help, soon discover the best method, a simple mode of teaching, not encumbered with artistic rules; and for which she can consult to good advantage with her husband, and with intelligent friends.†

If she is fully in earnest in her task, and still finds that her attainments are unequal to it, it will then be time enough to look for help.

The best auxiliary plan will be, where several families are like-minded and in sufficiently close social relations, for one of the mothers, say one who knows French best, to admit the daughters of the rest to the instruction which she gives her daughters in French; for another in like manner to take charge of singing; and so on.

If circumstances do not admit of this arrangement, a number of associated families might employ a private teacher, who might instruct their daughters either in one of their houses, or in turn at each, at fixed hours‡.

In addition to the reasons already adduced against instructing girls of the higher classes in the so-called "Institutes,"§ may be mentioned the following:—

When children from families of the same general character, standing and modes of thinking are taught together, none of them hears from the other any thing inconsistent with what he hears at home, or with his home impressions. But the case is quite different at the Institutes, even at the best of them. At these are found a collection

* "*Docendo discimus.*" "We learn by teaching."

† There is a great difference between modest mothers who distrust their own powers, and those mis-educated, over-educated, conceited women, who think the work of instructing their children far below their dignity; a business proper enough for mediocre, subordinated drudges, but not for etherial and elevated minds. Such mistaken mothers are sounding brass and tinkling cymbals; they are destitute of maternal love. But they have their reward.

‡ I have not mentioned, because it seemed to me too self-evident, that every father ought to instruct his own daughters, so far as his knowledge, faculty for teaching, and leisure will admit; and that he ought to have a general charge of their instruction and education, and is more or less responsible for it.

§ Female boarding-schools.

of girls from families of the most various and even diametrically opposite views on religious and national subjects, and especially on matters connected with social life and amusements. Girls who at home hear little of frivolous worldly matters, such as balls, theaters, &c., here come in contact with others who describe these things to them as most delightful. It is no wonder that this arouses in them the most lively desires to attend theaters and balls, so that from that time forward they plague their parents incessantly with requests to go there, even to such a degree that the latter are often weak enough to let them go, to get rid of the annoyance.

Having thus spoken generally of the instruction of girls, let us proceed to the separate departments of it.

1. *Reading.*

The study of reading should never be commenced before the sixth or seventh year. The more determinate and surer methods which an intelligent and experienced schoolmaster will use will enable him to teach reading very quickly. A mother, however, will proceed very uncertainly in the business; will for that reason make the study very disgusting to the children, and by means of the consciousness that she is to blame for this, will herself become disgusted and impatient.

When this happens, the child will imbibe not only a distaste for learning to read, but against every thing that she may try to teach him.

But I do not deny to all mothers the ability to instruct in reading, for I myself learned to read from a most loving and patient mother.

When the children have learned to read, they no longer need a teacher; an intelligent, educated, pious mother will herself be very competent to conduct their further studies.

The question will now arise, What shall the children read? Shall it be the "*Children's Friends*," of which so many hundreds of thousands of copies have been issued, with their tiresome stories of good children and bad children, of good William and naughty Louis, &c.? Shall they at the same time commit to memory the verses in these books, such for instance as that most remarkable one composed in the name of one of these good Williams, by some foolish pedant well grounded in vanity, but thoroughly ignorant of his catechism, which begins thus:—

"When I do what's right
And with all my might,
Nor ever dawdle,
How happily I play!
Praise from my papa,
Love from my mamma—
Every thing I see
Loves and praises me."

But I will devote no more time to these flat and tiresome books; most of which originated in the equally flat and wearisome period of "Nationalism."

At a later period, other writers, especially Wackernagel, compiled books based on the right principle, namely, that children should read only good matter and such as has a permanent value. This principle is the more important, because what children read at an early age impresses itself so much more deeply upon the memory; being almost indelible by the course of subsequent years.* We merely would not desire to fix in their minds any bad materials, or indifferent ones, which will grow there all their lives like ill weeds; which will be ever re-echoing there, like miserable street music which we happen to hear, and which afterwards continues to haunt us in spite of ourselves.

A second point to be borne in mind in selecting books for young girls is, that they should not only be good in themselves, but adapted to the age and character of these particular girls for whom they are chosen. I would not insist that they must understand all of the books. At the present day, as Goethe observes, the word "understand" is not understood. It is most commonly misused by schoolteachers; and it can not be applied to most of the books which children particularly like. Ought they not to read Grimm's fairy stories until they understand them! They should not be put to read what they are able to understand, but what they like. And it is the duty of the mother to watch conscientiously that they shall learn only to like what is good and beautiful, and that they shall read only such materials; and that no bad books shall get into their hands.

If a child is interested in a book, the mother will be under no necessity to constrain her to read it. She will not, for instance, be obliged to take pains to confine her little scholar's attention while reading the story of Aschenbrödel; or the Little Brothers and Sisters. And it will be a great delight to the child to be able to read the stories which it has learned to like by hearing them often told; and it will be no more satisfied with reading them over and over, than it was before with hearing them told.

Besides Grimm's stories, much good matter for children has been written by Pocci. Such are also Speckter's fables, and many portions of Hebel, Schubert, Claudius and Uhland. I have already spoken of reading the Bible.

If we desire to make the children thoroughly dislike reading, we

---

* Fenelon's observation on this point is, "It must be remembered, that at this age nothing should be put into the mind which we do not desire to have remain there during the whole life."

can find no better mode than by overloading the simplest matter for reading with remarks, expositions, applications, &c.; by making them rewrite it in other words; and performing other insufferable pedantic school exercises. Natural good sense will protect a mother against such absurdities.

It may be inexpedient even to cause the children to repeat stories which they have heard or read. Fenelon says, on this point, with great good judgment, "Stories should not be told them as if they were lemons; the children should not be made to repeat them. Such repetitions, unless quite spontaneous, are irksome to the children, and deprive them of all enjoyment of the stories. If the child has a facility in talking, he will of his own accord tell over such stories as he likes best, to persons whom he loves. But such an exception should not be made the rule." The same principle might well be applied to the subsequent exercise of written repetition.

I have already spoken of the insufferable affected style of reading which is so unnaturally taught to girls. Against this style Fenelon appeared, as an advocate of a natural style of reading; and in an age and country where unnatural fashions were culminating, in vast periwigs, and in hoop-petticoats. We Germans ought to be ashamed of ourselves! Fenelon's observations are as follows: "All the advantage of instruction in reading is nullified by the practice of teaching children to use an artificial mode of emphasizing. It should not be attempted to make them read without any faults. The proper object is, to make them read naturally; as they speak. If they read in any other tone, their practice is worthless; it is mere school declamation."

2. *Writing.*

As soon as girls have learned to read, they may be taught writing; which should be done by a skillful teacher. When they have learned to write, they may begin spelling, which the mother can teach.

I agree with Bormann, that writing is really learned by reading; because it is mainly the eye which acts, by furnishing us the knowledge of the form in which the words must be written.

The mother may proceed by dictating to her daughters something which they have already read, in some good book; what is written may then be corrected by comparison with the book, and then written out clean by the pupils. The faults may be entered in a book by themselves. If the matter was at first written without errors, the transcription may be omitted. I know by experience that under this system, girls will make a progress that is daily perceptible; only continued patience is necessary in the mother. If the mother be not herself entirely perfect in her spelling, she can still correct the writing, by a careful comparison with the print; which will improve her own spelling at the same time.

(*Later additional paragraphs.*) Since writing thus far on the subject of writing and reading, I have, for the first time, become acquainted with that method which begins with teaching writing, and proceeds from that to reading. By this method, the pupils at first learn to write all the single letters, from copies furnished them; then combinations of two letters, say of one consonant and one vowel, such as ba, be, bi, and so on, through the whole alphabet. Then follow combinations of three or more letters; and words. Thus writing and reading of what is written go on hand in hand. After thorough practice in such writing and reading, the written letters may then be compared with the corresponding printed ones, and then syllables, words and sentences; by which they will learn to read print without much trouble. This method seems to possess many advantages.

The first is, that it is adapted to the nature of girls, who like to be employed in something that occupies their hands, and are even too fond of drawing on the slate. Accordingly, they learn to write down and read off letters, words and sentences, by this method with much greater interest than if they were required in a more passive manner merely to recognize and read them from printed pages.

There are also some advantages in respect to spelling; especially in that this method makes it necessary to pay close and particular attention to each single letter. This is a point of great importance for the attainment of a correct habit in orthography; and the method itself brings up the correct spelling of many words.

It is an additional and not insignificant consideration, that this method of teaching reading will supply the place of others frequently used, which are unnatural and disagreeable.

8. *French. English.*

I have already mentioned the common mode of teaching French, and the purpose of it. Although I expressed disapprobation of both of them, still I did not mean that as society is at present constituted, it would be expedient not to learn French at all.

The mother might begin her daughter's instruction in French in an exceedingly quiet way, by saying two or three French words every day to them, while they are knitting or engaged in other employments, and by repeating them until they are well impressed on their minds. In this manner, the children would in the course of a year gather quite a valuable collection of words, which might afterwards be shown to them in print, and then copied by them; a process which will acquaint them with the great difference between the German and French orthography. They may then learn the declensions and regular conjugations; then, by rote, the irregular verbs, and then they may begin to read French, and to translate it orally and in writing. For this latter purpose some good reading-book should be used, arranged upon the principle of proceeding from easier to harder lessons.

Oral translation should at first be as literal as possible, without reference to the German idiom. For instance, "Il me semble que je pourrais aisément répondre à cela," should be first translated:* "It me seems that I could easily answer to that;" and afterwards into the more idiomatic form, "It seems to me that I can easily answer that." If entire periods are translated together, and *freely*, without this direct attention to the sense of each word, the pupils will misunderstand many words, and substitute them for each other.†

The mother may read to the girls the beginning of some interesting story from the German translation; and may then give them the whole in the French, without any translation. Curiosity to know the sequel of the story will impel them to master the whole of it.

The question is frequently asked, What is the best method of instructing in German composition? I reply, careful translation from the French, and afterwards from the English, into good German, is the best exercise in composition. If the mother doubts her capacity to correct such translations, let her give lessons from some French book of which a good translation is at hand, which she can consult in correcting. Madame Necker recommends careful written translation as "practice in good style," and also as "practice in patience; a quality very likely to fail women in intellectual labor."

Besides translations from German into French, may be used also translations from French into German; which may serve to correct the translations of the class, by comparison.

When the girls have got so far in French that they can read an easy book without especial effort and constant use of the dictionary, they may begin English, in the same way in which they began French.

But what will be the result of this course in relation to speaking French? In my opinion, girls who have committed to memory French words, phrases, declensions, and conjugations, have secured a store of French words and idioms by reading and translating from French

* In place of the German translation, English is here given, of course, but the point will be sufficiently clear.—*Trans.*

† What I have said in another place respecting the absurd system of Hamilton, will sufficiently show that I am not here *recommending* it.—"*American Journal of Education*," Vol VI., p. 667.

books, and whose mothers have made them practice speaking French to a moderate extent, will necessarily speak it better than those who have only been practiced in talking over a narrow selection of phrases which embody no thought, but are merely the current conventionalisms of governesses.

In point of literature, England confessedly offers a much greater choice generally, and specially for girls, of valuable, morally pure and interesting books, than France. Among other advantages, it contains many books for children which are so natural and simple as quite to put to shame many of the childish and affected German books for children. For this reason, and for many others, I think that in case it were necessary to select but one of the two languages, French or English, for a girl to study, it should be English.

4. *Arithmetic.*

I have but little additional* to say on the subject of instruction in arithmetic. It will be easy for the mother to teach her little ones to count with beans, nuts, &c., and to instruct them in the rudiments of adding, subtracting and dividing. It would be my advice that they should avail themselves of the counters already described, in order to give the children correct ideas and readiness in writing numbers; and at the same time a thorough understanding of and readiness in managing the decimal system—a very important point. After this period however, it will be best to employ a teacher; not a pedantically methodical one, but a simply practical one, to give the little girls skill in those parts of arithmetic which they will need to use in after-life; especially in mental arithmetic. The degree to which a mother can be of use in this matter depends upon her attainments in arithmetic. She might in any event now and then give the girls a problem in mental arithmetic while they are sewing and knitting.

5. *Singing.*

There are now-a-days but few mothers who have not learned to sing while young, either at school or of a singing-master; but usually, as I have mentioned, only for the sake of making a good appearance in society. But the gift of song ought to accompany women all through their lives. Thus, Madame Necker says,† "If our love of art were perfectly pure, we should not lay aside music as soon as we find ourselves too old to make a show with it in society. It would continue to delight our children, to adorn our domestic life, to sanctify and cheer us, and to encourage and support us even if left to solitude."

I have often heard young mothers say, "I sung much when I was

* "*American Journal of Education*," Vol. VIII., pp. 170—182. † Part I., p. 160.

a young girl, but not such songs as I can sing with my daughters." And it is very true that opera airs, and the artificial affected songs now taught to young ladies, are quite unadapted to children, and that it would be altogether unfortunate to have them introduced into the nursery. If such music is the only kind that the mother knows, she should first buy a good book of church chorals, arranged rhythmically, because children will learn and retain such more easily than unrhythmic ones. Out of this book she should herself learn such hymns as are best for family worship, and should practice them with her children, so that she and they can sing them at morning and evening along with the whole household. Then let her procure a good collection of songs; say the "*German songs for Young and Old*,"* and make use of that. But she should in any case beware of being betrayed into the use of any of the foolish and feeble songs about youth and virtue, which are got up expressly for the young.

The only singing practice proper for little girls, is simply the natural singing together of easy pious or joyous songs,† without any methodical instruction at any prescribed time. They should not be made to sing any longer than is pleasant to them. If any one of them happens to be destitute of a musical ear, and to take no pleasure in singing with the rest, she should be allowed to be silent, so as not to interrupt the rest. She should, however, commit to memory the words that are sung; which the singers will remember without that by repeating them in singing; and it is probable that after a longer or shorter time, she will join in with the rest. If the children fail in singing the first time, they should by no means be laughed at; for practice will remedy the defects. Nor should even very little children be prevented from joining in with the others; and they will be found surprisingly soon to master the melody. It is "out of the mouths of babes and sucklings," that, we are told, God "hath perfected praise."

If the mother is quite incapable of teaching her children singing, *i. e.*, unable to sing a melody, the father, or some other member of the household, or some female friend, should be induced to sing frequently with the children; for if they are to develop into highly cultivated adults, they must not be allowed to grow up without singing.

Scientific instruction in singing should never be given to girls until they are grown up and well developed physically. If it is done

* "*Deutsche Lieder für Jung und Alt.*" Berlin: Reimer, publisher, 1818.

† "*Old and new songs for children, with cuts and melodies, (Alte und neue, Kinder-Lieder. Mit Bildern und Singweisen).*" Edited by F. Focel and R. von Raumer. Press of Gustav Mayer, Leipzig. I would recommend this little book, were I not one of its editors.

before, there is danger of important injury to their health, and also of permanently destroying their voices. There may be some exceptions to this rule, but they do not vitiate it. Grown-up girls, if their health is sound and their lungs strong, may now receive instruction in singing, of an artistic character, but it should be according to the rules of the old school. Unless the mother is entirely capable of superintending this part of their instruction, a skillful teacher, male or female, should have charge of it. It is to be hoped that in every town there may be found at least one such teacher who instructs in the old style, without being infected by the vicious modern method. For the really good training of her voice, a girl should first for a long time sing scales, learn to hold notes, to make runs and trills, to take intervals accurately, &c., until thoroughly able to execute them; all before being taught any difficult song or *aria*. It is only by such practice that the singer gains entire control of her own voice, and learns to manage her breath and voice both, so as to avoid any risk to her health through too much singing. Nor can a truly scientific method of vocalizing be attained without such a symmetrical course of training as this; nor that entire certainty and freedom in execution, without which it is impossible to give herself up to the singing so as to fully apprehend and give the expression.

Many directions for vocalizing may be given by the teacher; for instance, on the mode of increasing or diminishing the volume of the voice; and of always beginning with a soft low tone. This was the practice of the old school; while the present practice is, often to begin with a mere scream, and of delivering the upper notes in an actual yell. But the most essential quality of good vocalization is, that the heart shall be really in the music, and that the singer shall herself really feel what she sings, or if her song be descriptive or narrative, shall entirely sympathize with it. This principle also makes it evident how necessary it is that the text and music of songs should be noble and good in character; for no one would wish his daughters to be singing frivolous meaningless songs with all their hearts, or to put themselves into full sympathy with such. The poor girls, whose practice, commonly, only teaches them to produce an entirely false "effect" in a purely mechanical manner, are fortunate that it is so; that they merely utter the sounds, without feeling or intelligence; without being in the least moved by the matter of what they sing. I once heard a young lady, in a large assembly, sing a new song with so much feeling as to produce in me much sympathy for her, that she should so young be able to enter so fully into the feeling of so passionate a poem. But as I had not understood a single word of it, I afterwards asked her the substance of the text. She replied that it had only been given her to sing in company, and that she had not had time to trouble herself about the meaning of the words. But is it then right to train human beings as one would train a bull-finch, whose nature it is to learn to whistle tunes without inquiring into the words?

A sharp distinction should be made between the scientific instruction in singing, which girls should only receive after they are grown up, and their previous merely natural practice, during which they only sing songs without any methodical training at all, and learn to sing correctly by listening to and following with the correct singing of others.

But however desirable it may be that all whose voices are even moderately good, should pass through the good old-fashioned course of instruction in singing, it is still far better that they should sing by rote all their lives, than that they should be given over to a perverted method. But if confined to such mere natural singing, the pupil should from the beginning take every opportunity to hear good singing, with a view to her own improvement.

A really good method of teaching singing ought no more to destroy, by its study and practice of great masterpieces, the power of enjoying the simplest good music—even popular songs—than the reading of Faust ought to destroy the capacity for enjoying Goethe's minor poems. The greatest singers—Catalani for instance—have produced their most powerful effects by singing "God save the King;" as has Jenny Lind by her national melodies.

6. *Learning the piano-forte.*

Much of what was said of singing, applies to instruction upon the piano-forte; although in one respect they differ essentially. Singing is innate in a well-organized person, as much as in the birds; thousands of people sing merely by instinct; the proportion of really trained singers is very small. But playing the piano is born in nobody. Each person must learn it separately, as if it were a foreign language; while singing is a classified mother tongue.

Playing the piano is therefore an art, in every sense; and should not be studied at too late a period. This instruction the mother should not give unless she is not only a thoroughly trained and skillful player, but also very patient. Otherwise, it will be much better to employ as capable a teacher as can be found.

There quickly appears a difference amongst scholars on the piano. Some are not satisfied with moderate acquirements, but must proceed to studies of a higher grade; while far the most girls, as well as their parents, contemplate a grade of attainment much lower, though still very desirable. Indeed, the circumstances of the case usually confine them within these limits, as will be perceived on a moment's consideration of the sort of instruction on the piano which can be had in the country, and in small towns. In such places it is exceedingly rare to find an instructor skillful enough to teach his pupils to execute the more difficult class of compositions; and the piano is taught mostly by the school-teachers. It is much to be desired that these should be instructed in a good style of piano-playing, that their taste for good music should be developed, so that they shall afterwards be able to teach to play good music, and no other. The kind of music to which I here refer is only the simplest; especially chorals, popular melodies, accompaniments to songs, &c. Ability to execute such music upon the piano, will enable a young girl to give pleasure to her parents and brothers and sisters, and in after-life to her husband and children; and to cheer, adorn, ennoble and sanctify her home.

Opportunities for a higher musical culture are commonly to be found only in cities. But what is learned even there, no matter with how much application and expenditure of time, is unfortunately too often only that mere heartless skill in execution of which I have already spoken. The most important point therefore is, to find the right sort of a music teacher. The model of such a teacher, among those known to me, was music-director Forkel, of Gottingen, an enthusiastic member of the school of the great Sebastian Bach, and who had enjoyed the personal instructions of his son Emanuel Bach at Hamburg.

Forkel's biography of Sebastian Bach contains a chapter on the proper mode of teaching to play the piano-forte. "Bach's method," says Forkel, "was the most instructive, efficient and certain, that ever existed. First he taught the touch. For this purpose he made beginners during several months play nothing except separate exercises for each finger of each hand, with special reference to a clear and definite touch; and for this kind of practice he wrote six little preludes, and six duetts."* "After this, he gave his pupils more important pieces by himself, such as would best exercise their powers. To help them at difficult points, he used the judicious plan of playing the whole piece over to them; saying, 'It should sound so.' It can scarcely be imagined how many are the advantages of this plan." The pupil, "whose business it is to reproduce the whole piece together, in its true character," thus acquired an ideal which he applied

* Published by Peters' of Leipzig.

all his industry to endeavor to equal. The method was exactly the opposite of that used by so many teachers, who merely show the pupils how they ought to execute some single passage before they comprehend the whole character of the piece, and thus the style and execution appropriate to it; although it is this understanding of the whole which is indispensable before the proper mode of playing each part can be understood.

These remarks, it is true, do not apply to those very common pieces of music which consist of nothing but a patchwork of musical scraps and phrases; but only to those which have a symmetrical character, and distinct musical physiognomy. This is the character of Bach's compositions; which we like better the oftener we play them; just as one whom we love, becomes more and more beloved by longer intercourse. When we like a piece of music in that way, when we come, so to speak, into a personal relation with it, we shall execute it with a sort of pious feeling, which will scrupulously avoid whatever may injure its beauty or turn it into caricature.

It would be fortunate if music teachers could be found, capable of instructing in Bach's manner. Could this happen, the compositions of that great master might again come into vogue; compositions profound and full of feeling, but still pure and holy, and without a trace of ungoverned fleshly passion.* Such music is most appropriate for girls; whereas precisely the reverse is true of that very common mawkishly sentimental kind of music which is either full of an impure fire, or quite burned out.

I need not observe that I do not mean that girls ought to play nothing at all except Sebastian Bach's compositions. The especially important point is, that they should not only be thoroughly instructed from the beginning, but that they should never at any time be allowed to play mere musical nonsense of a low grade. Bach's preludes and "inventions" for beginners have however a permanent artistic value.

The rule that children shall never read any thing of a bad or vulgar character is entirely applicable to music. If they are always brought up to hear, sing, and play only good music, as they grow up and their sphere of knowledge increases, it will become a second nature to them to avoid promptly whatever is disagreeable and bad, and to love what is beautiful and good; no matter in what form. They will find pleasure in the works of the great masters however diverse; in Palestrina and Lasso, as well as in Händel and Gluck; and so they will in

* That able musician, Mendelssohn Bartholdy, had the greatest admiration for Bach; and it was by his means that Bach's Easter music was performed in Berlin in 1829, after remaining in silence for a hundred years since 1728.

the simplest popular songs. The case is far otherwise with those very numerous persons who have been so unfortunate as to hear and practice and get accustomed only to bad music. It is very uncommon and very difficult for such to purify their habits, to acquire new ones, and to turn back to what is pure and beautiful. Such an exception was a student who came to Forkel to take music lessons. Forkel, learning that he had already played a good deal, required him to execute some piece on the spot. The young man did so, evidently thinking that he succeeded excellently. When he concluded, Forkel said, "See here, my dear friend, you will have to begin by forgetting every thing that you have learned so far." Without being discouraged, the young man set to work and studied diligently under Forkel, with good success. This story I have from his own mouth.

Most of what I have said of singing and piano-playing is the result of my own experience. If there are any points which seem objectionable, I refer to the most excellent and never sufficiently to be recommended work of Thibaut, "*On Purity in Music* (*Ueber Reinheit in Tonkunst*);" a book which has had an incredible influence towards a renewal of the recognition and practice of good music, and the disuse of bad.* The editor of the last edition, Ministerial-councillor Bähr, takes special notice of the fact that Thibaut, by the term "Purity in music," meant by no means merely technical purity of touch or expression. "What he meant," says Bähr, "was something quite different, much loftier, I might even say a moral quality." For this reason he was "the irreconcilable enemy of every thing shallow, vulgar, unhealthy or flippant." I can not deny myself the satisfaction of quoting the following paragraphs from Thibaut:—

"Music has one particularly dangerous quality. In a painting, if there is a limb wrongly drawn, or an immoral character, the correct eye finds at once a reason for criticism, or modesty turns aside the gaze, at least in the presence of others. But into music can creep every thing impure, spasmodic, immoral; and thus the whole attention may be unreservedly bestowed upon what, if represented by words or the pencil, would for decency's sake be at once repelled. Therefore it is that the work of our composers and musical virtuosos is easy. Tendencies to nervous weakness, to wildness, extravagance, vulgar pleasure, afford only too many strings which easily respond to

* In 1851, eleven years after the author's death, the third edition of this work was published. When it first appeared, in 1825, its interest and value were much increased to me by the fact that ever since 1804, I had been in the habit of hearing sung, with pure minds and pure voices, in the house of my late father-in-law, Chapel-master Reichardt, the very masterpieces so much praised by Thibaut, of Palestrina, Leo, Durante, Handel, &c.

the touch, and even the connoisseur often has to listen in silence to the exclamation of "Oh how beautiful!" for very shame, because the correct explanation of the reason of the phrase could not decently be fully stated. And if the public is played well into such habits of vulgar and evil preferences, this bad taste, once confirmed, will despotically govern artists."

"Plato has spoken against the corrupting tendency of music. But what would he say, if he should hear the musical torments that we have now-a-days to endure; the compositions botched together in so many unnatural ways, so extravagant in softness, in wildness, in amatory expression, and yet so seldom possessing the real musical fire!"

"In music, as at present usually employed as a department of culture, we find everywhere ornament, a mass of wonderful difficulties, overloaded decoration instead of feeling and clearness; but very little material for encouragement or pleasure, except in the way of gratifying vanity or artistic self-conceit. Thus it happens that our young women, as soon as they are mistresses of a home where they can command their time, joyfully throw all the so-called 'scientific compositions,' which they have learned, to the winds."

"Music only shows itself divine to us, when it carries us out of ourselves into an idealized state of susceptibility. A musician who can not accomplish this object is nothing except a mere mechanic, or hod-carrier."

"The favorite 'effects' are for the most part only evidences of ignorance, or of a cowardly desire to serve and please every body. Nature does not proceed by leaps; and healthy feeling does not stray about at random, nor proceed to extravagance. The favorite symphonies, fantasias, pot-pourris, and so forth, are therefore often the most ridiculous things in the world. There is a mysterious introduction; then a sudden volley of explosions; then an equally sudden silence; then an unexpected waltz movement; then, under the natural excitement of such a passage, an equally appropriate transition to a profound and melancholy movement; then, all at once, a furious storm; out of the very hight of the storm, after a brief pause of expectation, a passage of light and fanciful character; and finally, a sort of hurra, which brings the whole piece to an end, with a great shriek of exulting love. It is true that such stuff pleases, but after what manner?"

"But the worst evil of all is, that under this favorite name of 'effect,' the most destructive poison is inculcated; namely, this very same convulsive, perverted, extravagant, delusive, crazy folly, which stirs up every thing evil in the mind, and tends to the ultimate utter destruction of all true musical sense."

"If many of our virtuoso maidens knew what it is that they so often hear, or sing and play, and for what purpose one of our most favorite performers has directly and most cunningly contrived many of his compositions, they would be sickened with shame and mortification."

"It is not enough to astonish with agility of finger, nor with executing in a wonderful manner what amounts to nothing at all. What should be done is, to make our sense of hearing a medium of enrapturing us, without regard to the existence of mechanical difficulties in the music which gives the delight. It may perhaps be pardoned in traveling exhibitors of musical skill, that in order, in their rapid transit to choose what shall be most certain to produce an effect on their audience, they execute their most extravagant music, and almost nothing else; for in like manner the public would much rather see a rope-dancer stand on his head, than to see him represent the most ideally beautiful attitudes by easy and graceful movements. But it is a bitterly provoking thing that everywhere time, money, and health, are squandered in learning what is empty and without significance; and that in the struggle to execute capriccios, the art of executing simple music in a spirited, tender, and song-like manner, has almost entirely disappeared. There is but one encouraging circumstance, namely: that at the end of the period of childishness and caprice, these tormenting studies are usually given up; and that those who have been fortunate enough to learn in their youth affecting, pleasing, elevating melodies, continue to take the greatest pleasure in them even to the extremest age."

I sincerely hope that these extracts may induce some who may not have read Thibaut's book, to peruse it.

After Thibaut, one of the most useful authors in this department, is Winterfeld, who devoted fifty years of persevering labor to the attainment of the most distinguished musical culture and of the most comprehensive historical knowledge; and whose valuable historical writings have thrown new light upon ancient masters and masterpieces, some of them entirely forgotten; such for instance, as the talented Eckard. It is to be hoped that the nineteenth century, which with a few exceptions is so poor in productive musical composers, may apply all its powers to the reproduction of those ancient masterpieces, and to their adequate execution.

7. *Pictorial Art. Drawing.*

We have already laid it down, that girls ought, as much as possible, to be kept from hearing, reading, singing, or playing any thing ugly or bad. To these we add, that they should not see any such thing. It is no doubt impossible to preserve them entirely from it; but we should not fail to do all that is possible to this end.

Thus, we should never have in the house any ill-favored or ambiguous or licentious pictures; but should adorn them, so far as our circumstances will admit, with pure and beautiful ones; such as will by their daily presence exert a quiet, ennobling influence to an incalculable extent. Parents who care for such a purpose, should spend much of the money which they lay out for costly furniture to adorn their rooms, for those much nobler decorations, good engravings and lithographs.

Children are very early given picture-books, in examining and illuminating which, they find an absorbing amusement. In former times, the pictures in these have usually been extremely ugly, even so that it could scarcely be perceived what they represented; although the vivid fancy of the children seemed to find no difficulty in deciphering them. But at the present time, we owe heartfelt thanks to the artists of Munich, who have not disdained to publish beautiful picture-books. These contain correct and vivid representations of beasts, Alpine scenery, hunting, trades, heroic scenes, &c.; and the most laughable illustrations of stories, like Münchhausen's "*Travels*," "*The Father, Son and Ass*," &c. The pictures of Richter and Pocci are exceedingly well adapted to children; their delightful, innocent little boys and girls; Prince Eugene storming Belgrade, drinking Reutlinger wine, &c.

If there are any remarkable works of art at their places of residence, such as churches, palaces, galleries of paintings, &c., girls should be from an early age accustomed to find pleasure in them. I know from my own experience how deep and permanent are the impressions which works of art make upon children's minds. Born in Wörlitz, where the beautiful gardens of the Duke of Dessau are situated, I was, while a boy, there in the habit of seeing in the castle and other buildings, fine pictures, engravings and statues; and now in my age, they all yet remain vividly before my mind. And this habitude of my juvenile years was in the nature of a preparation for my subsequent studies of the more important galleries of pictures and antiques.

When seeing works of art for the first time in the company of girls, it is best to avoid most carefully giving a too hasty opinion upon them. A silent and unaffected examination of the objects,

* "Forgetting itself and the world, and living in the works only."

is the only proper mode of observing them; and this admits of no interruption. All have heard that affected admiration and that most pompous and foolish assumption of criticism, which are so frequent in picture galleries. Ladies look at Raphael's great masterpiece without either love or devotion, and only long enough to think out some opinion upon it, which shall be diametrically opposed to that of all intelligent judges, and thus more piquant; though it is in fact, both stupid and stupidly bold. They observe, for instance, "That foot is quite mis-drawn. Is that meant for St. John? For my part I never could see why they make such a disturbance about Raphael. I think Van der Werf is much superior?" I am not exaggerating; such opinions are really heard.

I do not of course mean that old and young should all be silent about the works of art which they see. It would be well to express without restraint the first impression which they make upon the mind. But to give a critical judgment upon them is quite another thing. The sonnets of A. W. Schlegel, describing works of great masters, are much better adapted to the minds of girls, than critical judgments upon the same paintings. The lives of such painters as they like will also have the greatest interest for them.

In discussing music, I spoke not only of hearing, but of singing and playing. To this active participation in music, drawing corresponds in art. Drawing, as practiced by girls and women, commonly consists in nothing except copying pictures. I knew a young lady to occupy a whole half year in copying one landscape, the original of which, which her own work did not equal in value, she could have bought for a thaler.* An English proverb says, "Time is money." This lady—to hazard a criticism of a somewhat unchivalric nature—had earned, by six months' labor of the most drudging kind, almost one thaler. But this time, wasted in useless mechanical copying, she could certainly have expended to better advantage upon her housekeeping, her children, and their education.

But what is the object of the study of drawing by girls?

First of all, one which will probably be little valued by the over-educated, they should learn to draw for domestic purposes. They should be able to sketch the chair which she wishes the cabinet-maker to make; to draw for the mason a sufficient plan and sketch of a cooking-apparatus of which he knows nothing, but which has been proved successful elsewhere; and so on. She should be able to draws birds, dogs, riders, horses, &c., for the children; who will take the greatest pleasure in observing how it is done, and in trying to

* About seventy-five cents.

draw the same thing, or others. Girls need to know how to draw flowers and embroidery patterns; and, if they have a talent for it, to sketch beautiful landscapes, or buildings, when traveling.

Instruction in drawing ought, according to these views, to aim at securing to the pupil the habit of clearly and correctly seeing, and truly and elegantly representing what she sees; it must train both eye and hand. The teacher should use special pains with drawing after nature; and should treat copying rather as a mere technical practice. Such instruction, and above all the serious and careful study of the works of great masters, will train girls to a love of what is beautiful and good, and to a dislike of what is ugly and bad. This love and dislike will have a great influence even upon their daily domestic life. Their eye, well trained, will instantly detect everything inappropriate or tasteless, and every wrong arrangement about them; and will not permit them to rest until the faults are corrected.

8. *Natural sciences.*

I have already discussed the modes in which these should not be taught, which, however, are unfortunately those most commonly practiced.*

Botany—if the term does not too strongly imply the methods of the schools, and the masculine mode of study—is peculiarly adapted to girls. Science, I have already observed, seeks principally truth; but art, beauty. While the botanist endeavors to establish as correctly and completely as possible the idea of the species Rose, the painter tries to present his ideal of a *Rosa centifolia;* and the poet leads us, through the gardens of poetry, to roses of unimaginable beauty.

It will be evident to every one, that girls should be trained much more in the artist's direction than in that of the botanist. This is indicated by their own tendency to paint and embroider flowers. It seems quite unnatural to every man of plain sense, to see teachers of girls, with a pedantic and wooden stiffness which makes them look as if they thought nobody but themselves had a thorough knowledge of the subject, pulling roses and lilies to pieces, even to their most minute parts, and making their pupils describe them in the technical terms of the botanist. Girls ought not to look at flowers with the destroying eyes of the botanist, armed with his microscope, but with the eyes of a sensitive flower-painter. It is that love of flowers which makes girls cultivate them carefully, and watch their growth from germination to seed-gathering, which is delightful.

Similar to this love of flowers, is a girl's kindly cherishing of domestic animals; lambs, fowls, doves. And here, in like manner,

* "*American Journal of Education*," Vol. VIII., p. 122.

they should not be confined to descriptions of genera and species, but should acquire a detailed personal knowledge of all these animals, their peculiarities and family habits. Caged birds in towns, however carefully cherished, are but a poor substitute for the domestic animals of the country, and the free nightingales and finches and larks of the woods and fields.

The sober, strict, and mathematically governed realm of the mineral kingdom may at first seem quite unadapted to girls. But we forget that the wonderful beauty of the precious stones are the delight of their eyes; and that work in metal also pleases them, not only by beauty of form, but by the attractive brilliancy of the substance of the metal itself.

9. *Instruction in history.**

History is taught, as we have seen, even in educational institutions for men, on very different principles; and it will be even more difficult to come to a general agreement upon the mode most proper for teaching it to girls. Care must be taken not to lower the dignity of history, by making it the subject of a mere leisure conversation; and also, to avoid all that pedantic character so repulsive to the feminine character. A course of historical instruction which treats with equal indifference of all people's and all periods, carries the pupil straight on through thick and thin, and then at the end requires that all this waste stuff shall be preserved in the memory, is out of the question for girls, and indeed for boys either. But further: while every man who pursues any of the more elevated callings, must possess just such a thoroughly impressed knowledge of the career of the most important nations, it would be a great error to require the same of a woman. To represent the different characters of the three chief periods of the Peloponnesian war, may be a very proper subject for an examination for a doctor's degree, and might not be too difficult for the graduating examination of a gymnasium, but as a theme for a composition by a girl, it is an absurdity. And this is not a mere imaginary example; it is a case which actually occurred in a German institution for girls, not long ago.

Such preposterous conduct would rather tend to make an intelligent man inclined to exclude the study of history altogether from the education of girls. At least, he would be quite ready to subscribe to the general views of Immanuel Kant, one of the closest German thinkers on female education, who says: "Never a cold and speculative instruction; always cultivation of the susceptibilities; and this

* On instruction in geography I refer to the previous chapter under that title; which applies both to boys and girls, with a few easily distinguished exceptions. Vol. VIII., p. 111.

as far as possible in a mode adapted to the characteristics of the sex. Such a kind of instruction is rare, because it requires talent, experience, and a heart full of feeling; but women may well dispense with every other kind."

Whatever differences of opinion may prevail respecting what education is appropriate for the female sex, it will certainly be admitted that the cultivation of the susceptibilities, of the feelings, of the sense of what is great and noble, should be the end proposed in the education of girls; and not cramming the memory. They receive no advantage from mere forced impressions on the memory. It would be much better to restrict the matters to be learned by rote, to some twelve or twenty names and dates, between which all the remaining historical knowledge acquired might arrange itself as if between boundary stones. An error in chronology would make a much better appearance in a modest and retiring girl, than would the least appearance of an assumption of historical learning.

With regard to the mode of communicating the historical knowledge which, according to the foregoing views, is proper for female education, it would be very easy to decide what it should be, if the talent for judicious, true and vivid narration were actually so general as it would seem to be, by the tenor of many school programmes and similar writings. But as a thorough investigation will show that the case is quite otherwise, it will be well to fix upon a few books to be used as a basis of instruction. What has already been said will sufficiently indicate that universal histories and compends should not be of this number. However excellent they may be—and we have some excellent ones—the method which they follow is not adapted to girls.

Biblical history, and its collateral studies, pertain to religious instruction. Of the other departments of history, the German history should occupy the first rank, and Greek and Roman the second. As for a German history in all respects satisfactory, it is perfectly well known that no such exists either for men or women. The larger work of Kohlrausch gives a lively and vivid general view of it. For Greece and Rome, I would recommend the appropriate portions of K. L. Roth's "*Compendious View*."* And in connection with both, appropriate portions from our most eminent historians should be read. For the most ancient nations, the Egyptians, Hindoos, Persians, very little time will suffice. And in like manner the subject of Greek and Roman mythology should be restricted to the most indispensable portions. The Greek legends may be learned from Gustav Schwab's

* "*Gedrängte Darstellung*."

well-known work. After this, they would listen with interest to Homer, so far as he is suitable for them. And they might somewhat in the same way be made acquainted with our own *Nibelungen Lied*.

It is of course of the greatest service to young girls, to be familiar with the lives and characters of the chief models of female excellence. But if they should be so unfortunate as to become influenced by the excessive compliments which many well-meant books on these subjects are accustomed to heap upon the female sex, the benefit derived will be less.

10. *Manual labor.*

A child should never be entirely unemployed, even during the first five or six years of its life. As long as a little girl keeps herself busy in her various plays, with her dolls, in looking at pictures, in running about, &c., so that she is never without occupation, and does not say "I don't know what to do," so long she should be allowed to play just as she pleases, except that she should be prevented from playing such games as may be dangerous either to body or mind. But as soon as the mother observes that continual play is no longer satisfactory to the little girl, that she is sometimes at a loss for occupation, she must contrive all manner of little occupations for her, to prevent any such vacant moments. She might give her a horse-hair and some beads, not too small, and of various colors, and show her how to string them; or she may draw on a card a star or a cross in pencil, then pierce the pattern with holes with an embroidering needle, and show the child how to sew through them with different colored threads. Such easy kinds of work, of which there are many, and which permit the children to see clearly what they are doing, afford them far more pleasure from their industry than mere knitting, which is commonly the first thing taught, and which soon wears out children's patience, and hurts their little fingers. It will be better to let the knitting wait a little longer, until such other occupations as those just mentioned have somewhat developed the habit of industry. These occupations, it is true, do not produce any valuable result; they only keep the little ones employed.

All girls, of whatever condition, should learn knitting and sewing. When a little older, they should be taught to sew all sorts of linen with entire neatness, and to knit their own stockings well. If girls gain skill in these sorts of work, they will by that means become capable of artistic and ornamental kinds of work, which they should however be only permitted to practice in the intervals of their ordinary domestic labor, and as a reward for industry. It will be found that girls will take much more interest in learning how to do ornamental work, when it is allowed them as a recreation from their regular sewing, than when it is required of them.

No general rule can be laid down for the time of beginning to teach handiwork to little girls; because they develop so differently. But to go without learning to sew and knit should be as much out of the question as to omit learning to read.

If a girl should appear to be destitute of any natural liking for female handiwork, the attempt should be made to teach her to like it by showing her how to make clothes for her dolls, and afterwards by employing her in making them for the poor. Poor children might be brought to her, or she might be told of such who need clothes, and she might be made to understand that by making the necessary effort, she might help them. Then her mother might cut up old shirts and other garments, and let her daughter help make them up into others for the poor children. She might also teach her to knit stockings for the little feet which she sees naked.

As another means of giving a little girl a taste for sewing and knitting, she might be influenced by a wish to prepare something pretty for a birthday present to her father. If the plan succeeds, pains must be taken to keep up her satisfaction in work of the kind, especially by taking advantage of any further occasions. In such management, each child must be influenced as its peculiarities may require.

It would be desirable that girls should acquire enough skill in work of an artistic kind, to be able to do whatever pertains to the tasteful adornment of a room or a dress; but such work should not consume too much time or money; and must not be pushed to too high a degree of artistic accomplishment. It has often grieved me to see a poor child straining its eyes and sitting bent over its embroidering, to work with her needle a little landscape or a picture of the Madonna, of which a much better copperplate could be bought for less money than the silk cost for the embroidering. And my feelings have been the same to see girls working long and hard with a crochet or netting needle, to make a few yards of lace which could be bought much cheaper and prettier at the shop.

It is very useful to have girls learn to make their own clothes, if only that they may afterwards be able to teach others to do so.

I have already stated how a more intellectual employment may very well be combined with such mechanical work.

IX. EDUCATION OF GIRLS IN THE COUNTRY.—EDUCATIONAL INSTITUTIONS FOR GIRLS.

What has been said thus far, has had reference principally to families living in a city. The condition of families in the country is very different. A teacher competent to instruct little girls in their elementary studies can be found in almost every village; but there is more than one reason against sending girls to a village school.

If a mother is at the head of a very large country household, without servants enough to enable her to find time to instruct her daughters, or if she is actually not competent to the task, I would advise her to take into her house some educated German young woman, as her assistant in the education of her daughters. But even then she is, as a mother, bound to take as large a part in the work as is possible. In a very respectable family known to me, such a German governess was at the same time trained by the mother to the duties of a mistress of a household; and was, indeed, on the footing rather of an oldest daughter than of a governess.

It is always better, unless there is some absolute necessity in the case, to employ such a female assistant at home, than to send daughters to girls' schools; which takes them away from the domestic circle where God meant them to live, and out of the sight of their parents. I may repeat here what I said in regard to infant schools: "The bond of affection which connects the members of a family is at the present time continually slackening. Father, mother, children, each have their own views, and follow their own paths. Every thing which aids in this unfortunate dissolution and scattering of families should be carefully avoided."

I shall be asked, Do you then reject all schools for girls? No; it is unfortunately true in too many cases that a substitute for home education must be had; and that it is therefore absolutely necessary to intrust a daughter to such an institution. And any one having a moderate acquaintance with such a necessity will be ready to thank God for the existence of those noble women who are willing to devote their whole lives to the laborious task of, as far as possible, filling the place of their mothers to orphaned daughters. There is a like necessity where the mother is very ill and suffering, or disordered in mind, and the daughters not grown up. In such cases, Christian institutions for the poor lost children are of infinite advantage. By this I mean, institutions so penetrated and sanctified by Christianity as every household ought to be; without misusing their religion merely as a signboard, or teaching their pupils a gloomy seriousness of demeanor and pietistic habits of speech, as if these were the signs of true faith.*

While therefore I gratefully acknowledge the necessity and the

*Such an institution is the well-known and excellent one of my dear friend, Auguste Tambner, at Waldenburg, in Silesia.

blessing of good schools for girls, as a substitute for home education, I must still repeat—

"Only so far would we adhere strictly to principles and rules, especially the fundamental laws of divine and human order, as to avoid the danger of becoming so estranged from them and accustomed to our substitutes as at last to think these absolutely right. We would rather use all possible means to aid in re-establishing those ancient and obsolete laws, and a pious and honorable family life.".

V. RECREATIONS.

When I wished that every mother might devote as much of her time as possible to occupations with her daughters, I could not of course include those ladies who are accustomed to spend their mornings in making and receiving visits, and several times a week to attend tea-parties and other such assemblies; so that regard must be had not only to the time consumed in these employments, but to that expended in the toilette (I designedly use the French term).

Such a mother wastes the hours which would be pleasantest and most valuable for her children; and her evening amusements even prevent the conclusion of the whole day by the whole family together, parents, children and servants, by a short and simple family prayer. While their mother is away at her evening parties, the little children have to be put to bed by strangers' hands; although it is eminently the mother's duty to hear them say their prayers and to give them a last blessing before they go to sleep. And the older children lose their pleasantest evening hours; which their mother could spend more quietly and uninterruptedly among them, than any others of the day.

Accordingly, the plan of bringing up children, which we are suggesting, would require the sacrifice of such amusements as these; but not that of the best kind of social enjoyment, which is certainly to be found in a happy family life. The little children should, at least in the winter, go to bed at six o'clock; and the other girls should, until they have grown up, go to bed at eight, and get up early. Then the parents and their grown-up children will have the whole evening for that relaxation from their day's labors, which is quite necessary; and they may either spend it at home with any friends who come to see them, or in visiting the families of other friends. This is the time for conversation, music and reading. The father may read aloud the greatest masterpieces of Goethe, Schiller, Shakspeare, &c.; and particularly such as the girls ought not to read for themselves, because they contain passages which should be omitted.

For a mother who spends the whole day in her sacred and often fatiguing duty, such an interval of relaxation is not only permissible, but necessary. If she works and cares and labors straight on until she goes to sleep, she can not wake up next morning refreshed and cheerful and ready to return to her work. This can only be possible by means of such an interruption in her hours of labor. A housewife who labors without any interval, who has no free hours for intellectual pleasure or friendly intercourse, becomes a mere drudge, and will soon be incapable of any vivid mental influence upon her daughters.

Every winter's day should also have its evening relaxation; which may in spring and summer include walks, in which the whole family should take part.

Besides these modes of enjoyment and intercourse, the mother may, as soon as she is no longer kept at home by little children, visit with her family pleasant localities and cities rich in works of art. They will return, rich in mental pictures and pleasant experiences, mentally strengthened and stimulated; and will afterwards often and with pleasure look back to these delightful days.

Such a family life as I have depicted, is so beautiful and so rich in true and innocent pleasure—pleasure which so many seek in vain by means of diversions incessant and restless, unsatisfactory and often at variance with pure morality—that it most bountifully rewards the care and pains of a conscientious mother.

XI. CONCLUSION.

The subject thus far discussed has forced me to go into the examination of many details. But it is out of the question to discuss all of them. If twice as many had been mentioned, any experienced mother could suggest many points which still required explanation. But it has been seen that these details had not always been classified by any system, and their single cases brought together under general rules; and indeed, that mothers, for whom the discussion is designed, do not find satisfaction in general rules and universal principles, but want advice for particular cases.

I shall add a few words on a subject with which I began, namely, family life.

In these present sorrowful times, we look about on all sides for help and salvation from our condition of moral and political corruption. Many are seeking such help, especially in reforms and renovations of church and state; and are hoping that the regeneration of these two, may bring new life, blessing, and health, to all the lesser spheres of life which they include. But my own belief, on the contrary, is, that it is from the smallest of all these spheres, the family, that new life, blessing and health, must come, to church and state; that both state and church, no matter how perfect the forms of their organization, must be mere forms, quite empty, or at most imperfectly filled out, as long as the families which constitute them remain corrupt.

Nor can such families themselves, such unhealthy and corrupt members of state and church, reach a condition of real prosperity, until they rid themselves of the same corruption; and least of all, can good results be hoped for, if that corruption still remains, from the education of girls, which is a matter so entirely included in and depending upon the family.

It is therefore incumbent upon me, as upon every one who undertakes to write upon female education, to state openly and truthfully the darker side of our family life; and to give the best advice in my power, for its improvement.

I know well, and feel deeply how great a responsibility rests upon him who dares to give counsel about education. A woe is denounced upon him who offends even one of the little ones. May such offense be far from this book, and may it contribute to the happiness of the young.

And finally; it is my most heartfelt desire that God may grant that Christian purity and piety, the training of children "in the nurture and admonition of the Lord," and with these the peace of God and the hope of eternal life, may return to the homes of both high and low.

Sir James Mackintosh thus writes in his Journal, after devoting a fortnight (at intervals) to Madame de Sevigné's Letters:

POLITE CONVERSATION AND FAMILIAR LETTERS.

When a woman of feeling, fancy, and accomplishment has learned to converse with ease and grace, from long intercourse with the most polished society, and when she writes as she speaks, she must write letters as they ought to be written: if she has acquired just as much habitual correctness as is reconcilable with the air of negligence. A moment of enthusiasm, a burst of feeling, a flash of eloquence may be allowed; but the intercourse of society, either in conversation or in letters, allows no more. Though interdicted from the long-continued use of elevated language, they are not without a resource. There is a part of language which is disdained by the pedant or the declaimer, and which both, if they knew its difficulty, would dread; it is formed of the most familiar phrases and turns, in daily use by the generality of men, and is full of energy and vivacity, bearing upon it the mark of those keen feelings and strong passions from which it springs. It is the employment of such phrases which produces what may be called colloquial eloquence. Conversation and letters may be thus raised to any degree of animation, without departing from their character. Any thing may be said, if it be spoken in the tone of society; the highest guests are welcome, if they come in the easy undress of the club; the strongest metaphor appears without violence, if it is familiarly expressed; and we the more easily catch the warmest feeling, if we perceive that it is intentionally lowered in expression, out of condescension to our calmer temper. It is thus that harangue and declamation, the last proof of bad taste and bad manners in conversation, are avoided, while the fancy and the heart find the means of pouring forth all their stores. To meet this despised part of language in a polished dress, and producing all the effects of wit and eloquence, is a constant source of agreeable surprise. This is increased when a few bolder and higher words are happily wrought into the texture of this familiar eloquence. To find what seems so unlike author-craft in a book, raises the pleasing astonishment to its highest degree.

Letters must not be on a subject. Lady Mary Wortley's letters on her Journey to Constantinople, are an admirable book of travels; but they are not letters. A meeting to discuss a question of science is not conversation; nor are papers written to another, to inform or discuss letters. Conversation is relaxation, not business, and must never appear to be occupation; nor must letters. Judging from my own mind, I am satisfied of the falsehood of the common notion, that these letters owe their principal interest to the anecdotes of the court of Louis XIV. A very small part of the letters consist of such anecdotes. Those who read them with this idea, must complain of too much Grignan. I may now own that I was a little tired during the two first volumes: I was not quite charmed and bewitched till the middle of the collection, where there are fewer anecdotes of the great and famous. I felt that the fascination grew as I became a member of the Sevigné family: it arose from the history of the immortal mother and the adored daughter, and it increased as I knew them in more minute detail; just as my tears in the dying chamber of Clarissa depend on my having so often drank tea with her in those early volumes, which are so audaciously called dull by the profane vulgar. I do not pretend to say that they do not owe some secondary interest to the illustrious age in which they were written; but this depends merely on its tendency to heighten the dignity of the heroine, and to make us take a warmer concern in persons who were the friends of those celebrated men and women, who are familiar to us from our childhood.

I once thought of illustrating my notions by numerous examples from 'La Sevigné.' The style of Madame de Sevigné is evidently copied, not only by her worshipper, Walpole, but even by Gray; who, notwithstanding the extraordinary merits of his matter, has the double stiffness of an imitator, and of a college recluse.

SIR THOMAS MORE.

LETTERS ON THE EDUCATION OF HIS CHILDREN.

SIR THOMAS MORE—who, as member and speaker of the House of Commons, and Chancellor of England, and in other positions of trust and magistracy, proved himself eminently fit, incorruptible, and efficient; and as son, husband, father, neighbor, and friend, was never surpassed in the exercise of those homely, graceful, and Christian qualities which make up the happiness of home and social life—was born in London in 1480, and to the everlasting discredit of all concerned in his trial and condemnation, was beheaded July 5, 1535,—the victim of the brutal lust and high-handed tyranny of Henry VIII.

The following description of the school, and the views of Sir Thomas More on the education of his children, and especially of his daughters, are taken from *The Life of Sir Thomas More, by his grandson, Cresacre More:*

The Home School of Sir Thomas More.

The school of Sir Thomas More's children was famous over the whole world: for that their wits were rare, their diligence extraordinary, and their masters most excellent men, as above the rest Doctor Clement, an excellent Grecian and physician, who was after reader of the physic-lecture in Oxford, and set out many books of learning. After him one William Gunnell, who read after with great praise in Cambridge; and besides these, one Drue, one Nicholas, and after all, one Richard Hart, of whose rare learning and industry in this behalf, let us see what may be gathered out of Sir Thomas's letters unto them, and, first, to Mr. Gunnell, thus:

SIR THOMAS MORE TO MR. GUNNELL.

I have received, my dear Gunnell, your letters, such as they are wont to be, most elegant, and full of affection. Your love towards my children I gather by your letter; their diligence by their own; for every one of their letters pleaseth me very much, yet most especially I take joy to hear that my daughter Elizabeth hath showed as great modesty in her mother's absence, as any one could do, if she had been in presence; let her know that that thing liked me better than all the epistles besides; for as I esteem learning which is joined with virtue, more than all the treasures of kings; so what doth the fame of being a great scholar bring us, if it be severed from virtue, other than a notorious and famous infamy, especially in a woman, whom men will be ready the more willingly to assail for their learning, because it is a hard matter, and argueth a reproach to the sluggishness of a man, who will not stick to lay the fault of their natural malice upon the quality of learning, supposing that their own unskilfulness by comparing it with the vices of those that are learned, shall be accounted for virtue; but if any woman, on the contrary part (as I hope and wish by your own instruction and teaching all mine will do), shall join many virtues of the mind with a little skill of learning, I shall account this more happiness than if they were able to attain to Crœsus' wealth, joined with the beauty of fair Helen; not because they were to get fame thereby, although that inseparably followeth all virtue, as shadow doth the body, but for that they should obtain by this the true reward of wisdom, which can never be taken away, as wealth may, nor will fade as beauty doth, because it dependeth of truth and justice, and not of the blasts of men's mouths, than which nothing is more foolish, nothing more pernicious; for as it is the duty of a good man to eschew infamy, so it is not only the property of a proud man, but also of a wretched and ridiculous man to frame their actions only for praise; for that man's mind must needs be full of unquietness, that always wavers for fear of other men's judgments between joy and sadness. But amongst other the notable benefits which learning bestoweth upon men, I account this one of the most profitable, that in getting of learning, we look not for praise, to be accounted learned men, but only to use it on all occasions, which the best of all other learned men, I mean the philosophers, those true moderators of men's actions, have delivered unto us from hand to hand, although some of them have abused their sciences, aiming only to be accounted excellent men by the people. Thus have I spoken, my Gunnell, somewhat the more of the not coveting of vain glory, in regard of those words in your letter, whereby you judge that the high spirit of my daughter Margaret's wit is not to be dejected, wherein I am of the same opinion that you are, but I think (as I doubt not but you are of the same mind) that he doth deject his generous wit, whosoever accustometh himself to admire vain and base objects, and he raiseth well his spirits, that embraceth virtue and true good. They are base-minded, indeed, that esteem the shadow of good things (which most men greedily snatch at, for want of discretion to judge true good from apparent), rather than the truth itself. And, therefore, seeing I hold this the best way for them to walk in, I have not only requested you, my dear Gunnell, whom of yourself I know would have done it out of the entire affection you bear unto them; neither have I desired my wife alone, whom her motherly piety by me often and many ways tried, doth stir them up thereto, but also all other my friends I have entreated many times to persuade all my children to this, that avoiding all the gulfs and downfalls of pride, they walk through the pleasant meadows of modesty, that they never be enamored of the glistening hue of gold and silver, nor lament for the want of those things which, by error, they admire in others; that they think no better of themselves for all their costly trimmings, nor any meaner for the want of them; not to lessen their beauty by neglecting it, which they have by nature, nor to make it any more by unseemly art; to think virtue their chief happiness, learning and good qualities the next, of which those are especially to be learned which will avail them most; that is to say, piety towards God, charity towards all men, modesty and Christian humility in themselves, by which they shall reap from God the reward of an innocent life, by certain confidence thereof they shall not need to fear death, and in the meanwhile enjoying true alacrity, they shall neither be puffed up with the vain praises of men, nor dejected by any slander of disgrace; these I esteem the true and solid fruits of learning; which, as they happen not, I confess to all that are learned, so those may easily attain them who begin to study with this intent; neither is there any difference in harvest time, whether he was man or woman that sowed first the corn; for both of them bear name of a reasonable creature equally, whose nature reason only doth distinguish from brute beasts, and, therefore, I do not see why learning, in like manner, may not equally agree with both sexes; for by it, reason is cultivated, and (as a field) sowed with the wholesome seed of good precepts, it bringeth forth an excellent fruit. But if the soil of woman's brain be of its own nature bad, and apter to bear fern than corn (by which saying many do terrify women from learning), I am of opinion, therefore, that a woman's wit is the more diligently by good instructions and learning to be manured, to the end, the defect of nature may be redressed by industry. Of which mind were also many wise and holy ancient fathers, as, to omit others, S. Hierome and S. Augustine, who not only exhorted many noble matrons and honorable virgins to the getting of learning, but also to further them therein, they diligently expounded unto them many hard places of Scriptures; yea, wrote many letters unto tender maids, full of so great learning, that scarcely our old and greatest professors of divinity can well read them, much less be able to understand them perfectly; which Holy Saints' work you will endeavor, my learned Gunnell, of your courtesy, that my daughters may learn, whereby they may chiefly know what end they ought to have in their learning to place the fruits of their labors in God, and a true conscience, by which it will be easily brought to pass, that being at peace within themselves, they shall neither be moved with praise of flatterers, nor the nipping follies of unlearned scoffers. But methinks I hear you reply, that though these, my precepts, be true, yet are they too strong and hard for the tender age of my young wenches to hearken to; for what man, be he never so aged or expert in any science, is so constant or staid, that he is not a little stirred up with the tickling vanity of glory? And for my part, I esteem that the harder it is to shake from us this plague of pride, so much the more ought every one to endeavor to do it from his very infancy. And I think there is no other cause why this almost inevitable mischief doth stick so fast in our breasts, but for that it is ingrafted in our tender minds, even by our nurses, as soon as we are crept out of our shells; it is fostered by our masters, it is nourished and perfected by our parents, whilst that nobody propoundeth any good thing to children, but they presently bid them expect praise as the whole reward of virtue; and hence it is that they are so much accustomed to esteem much of honor and praise, that by seeking to please the worst, who are always the worst, they are still ashamed to be good with the fewest. That this plague may the farther be banished from my children, I earnestly desire that you, my dear Gunnell, their mother and all their friends, would still sing this song unto them: hammer it always in their heads, and inculcate it unto them upon all occasions, that vain glory is abject, and to be despised; neither anything to be more worthy or excellent than that humble modesty, which is so much praised by Christ; the which prudent charity will so guide and direct, that it will teach us to desire virtue rather than to upbraid others for their vices, and will procure rather to love them who admonish us of our faults, than to hate them for their wholesome counsel. To the obtaining whereof nothing is more available than to read unto them the wholesome precepts of the fathers, whom they know not to be angry with them, and they must needs be vehemently moved with their authorities, because they are venerable for their sanctity. If, therefore, you read any such thing unto Margaret and Elizabeth besides their lessons in Sallust, for they are of riper judgment, by reason of their age, than John and Cecily, you shall make both me and them every day more bound unto you; moreover, you shall hereby procure my children being dear by nature, after this more dear for learning, but by their increase of good manners, most dear unto me. Farewell. *From the Court this Whitsun-Eve.*

SIR THOMAS MORE TO HIS CHILDREN.

THOMAS MORE, *to his whole School, sendeth Greeting:*—Behold how I have found out a compendious way to salute you all, and make spare of time and paper, which I must needs have wasted in saluting every one of you, particularly by your names, which would be very superfluous, because you are all so dear unto me, some in one respect, some in another, that I can omit none of you unsaluted. Yet I know not whether there can be any better motive why I should love you than because you are scholars, learning seeming to bind me more straitly unto you than the nearness of blood. I rejoice, therefore, that Mr. Drue is returned safe, of whose safety you know I was careful. If I loved you not so much, I should envy this, your so great happiness to have had so many great scholars for your masters. For I think Mr. Nicholas is with you also, and that you have learned of him much astronomy; so that I hear you have proceeded so far in this science that you now know not only the pole-star or dog, and such like of the common constellations, but also (which argueth an absolute and cunning astronomer) in the chief planets themselves, you are able to discern the sun from the moon. Go forward, therefore, with this, your new and admirable skill, by which you do thus climb up to the stars, which, whilst you daily admire, in the meanwhile I admonish you also to think of this Holy Fast of Lent, and let that excellent and pious song of Boethius sound in your ears, whereby you are taught also with your minds to penetrate heaven, lest when the body is lifted up on high, the soul be driven down to the earth with the brute beasts. Farewell. *From the Court this 23d of March.*

THOMAS MORE *to his best beloved children, and to Margaret Gigs, whom he numbereth amongst his own, sendeth Greeting:*

The merchant of Bristow brought unto me your letters the next day after he had received them of you, with the which I was exceedingly delighted; for there can come nothing, yea, though it were never so rude, never so meanly polished, from this your shop, but it procureth me more delight than any other's works, be they never so eloquent; your writing doth so stir up my affection towards you; but excluding this, your letters may also very well please me for their own worth, being full of fine wit, and of a pure Latin phrase. Therefore, none of them all but joyed me exceedingly; yet to tell you ingenuously what I think, my son John's letter pleased me best, both because it was longer than the other, as also for that he seemeth to have taken more pains than the rest; for he not only painteth out the matter decently, and speaketh elegantly, but he playeth also pleasantly with me, and returneth my jests upon me again very wittily; and this he doth not only pleasantly, but temperately withal, showing that he is mindful with whom he jesteth, to wit, his father, whom he endeavoureth so to delight, that he is also afeared to offend. Hereafter I expect every day letters from every one of you; neither will I accept such excuses as you complain of, that you had no leisure, or that the carrier went away suddenly, or that you have no matter to write; John is not wont to allege any such things; nothing can hinder you from writing, but many things may exhort you thereto; why should you lay any fault upon the carrier, seeing you may prevent his coming, and have them ready made up and sealed two days before any offer themselves to carry them? And how can you want matter of writing unto me, who am delighted to hear either of your studies or of your play; whom you may even then please exceedingly, when, having nothing to write of, you write as largely as you can of that nothing, than which nothing is more easy for you to do, especially being women, and, therefore, prattlers by nature, and amongst whom, daily, a great story riseth of nothing? But this I admonish you to do, that whether you write of serious matters or of trifles, you write with diligence and consideration, premeditating of it before; neither will it be amiss if you first indite it in English, for then it may more easily be translated into Latin, whilst the mind, free from inventing, is attentive to find apt and eloquent words. And although I put this to your choice, whether you will do so or no, yet I enjoin you by all means, that you diligently examine what you have written, before you write it over fair again, first considering attentively the whole sentence; and after examine every part thereof, by which means you may easily find out if any solecisms have escaped you; which being put out, and your letter written fair, yet then let it not also trouble you to examine it over again; for sometimes the same faults creep in at the second writing, which you before had blotted out. By this your diligence you will procure, that those your trifles will seem serious matters. For as nothing is so pleasing but may be made unsavory by prating garrulity, so nothing is by nature so unpleasant that, by industry, may not be made full of grace and pleasantness. Farewell, my sweetest children. *From the Court, this 3d of September.*

SIR THOMAS MORE TO HIS DAUGHTER MARGARET.

Thy letters (dearest Margaret) were grateful unto me, which certified me of the state of Shaw; yet would they have been more grateful unto me if they had told me what your and your brother's studies were, what is read amongst you every day, how pleasantly you confer together, what themes you make, and how you pass the day away amongst you in the sweet fruits of learning. And although nothing is written from you but it is most pleasing unto me, yet those things are most engrafed sweet which I cannot learn of but by you or your brother. [And in the end:] I pray thee, Meg, see that I understand by you what your studies are; for rather than I would suffer you, my children, to live idly, I would myself look unto you, with the loss of my temporal estate, bidding all other cares and business farewell, amongst which there is nothing more sweet unto me than thyself, my dearest daughter. Farewell.

SIR THOMAS MORE TO HIS DAUGHTERS.

Thomas More sendeth greeting to his most dear daughters, Margaret, Elizabeth, and Cecily; and to Margaret Giggs, as dear to him as if she were his own. I cannot sufficiently express, my best beloved wenches, how your eloquent letters have exceedingly pleased me; and this is not the least cause that, I understand by them, you have not in your journeys, though you change places often, omitted anything of your custom of exercising yourselves, either in making of declamations, composing of verses, or in your logic exercises; by this I persuade myself that you dearly love me, because I see you have so great a care to please me by your diligence in my absence as to perform these things, which you know how grateful they are unto me in my presence. And as I find this your mind and affection so much to delight me, so will I procure that my return shall be profitable unto you. And persuade yourselves that there is nothing amongst these my troublesome and careful affairs, that recreateth me so much as when I read somewhat of your labors, by which I understand those things to be true which your most loving master writeth so lovingly of you, that unless your own epistles did show evidently unto me how earnest your desire is towards learning, I should have judged that he had rather written of affection than according to the truth; but now by these that you write, you make him to be believed, and me to imagine those things to be true of your witty and acute disputations, which he boasteth of you almost above all belief. I am, therefore, marvellous desirous to come home, that we may hear them, and set our scholar to dispute with you, who is slow to believe, yea, out of all hope or conceit, to find you able to be answerable to your master's praises. But I hope, knowing how steadfast you are in your affections, that you will shortly overcome your master, if not in disputing, at least in not leaving of your strife. Farewell, dear wenches.

And thus you may conjecture how learned his daughters were; to whom, for this respect, Erasmus dedicated his commentary upon Ovid's "De Nuce." Lewis Vives also writeth great commendations of this school of Sir Thomas More's, in his book to Queen Catherine of England. And both Erasmus dedicated Aristotle in Greek, and Simon Grineus, who, although an heretic, yet, in respect of his learning, had been kindly used by Sir Thomas More, as he writeth himself, did dedicate Plato and other books in Greek, unto my grandfather, John More, as to one that was also very skilful in that tongue. See what Grinaeus speaketh unto him: "There was a great necessity why I should dedicate these books of Proclus (full of marvellous learning, by my pains set out, but not without the singular benefit of your father effected), unto you, to whom, by reason of your father-like virtues, all the fruit is to redound, both because you may be an ornament unto them, and they also may do great good unto you, whom I know to be learned, and for these grave disputations sufficiently provided and made fit by the continual conversation of so worthy a father, and by the company of your sisters, who are most expert in all kinds of sciences. For what author can be more grateful to those desirous minds of most goodly things, such as you and the muses your sisters are, whom a divine heat of spirit to the admiration and a new example of this our age, hath driven into the sea of learning so far, and so happily, that they see no learning to be above their reach, no disputations of philosophy above their capacity. And none can better explicate entangled questions, none sift them more profoundly, nor conceive them more easily, than this author."

SIR THOMAS MORE TO HIS DAUGHTER MARGARET.

You ask money, dear Meg, too shamefully (*modestly*) and fearfully of your father, who is both desirous to give it you, and your letter hath deserved it, which I could find in my heart to recompense, not as Alexander did by Cherilus, giving him for every verse a Philippine of gold, but if my ability were answerable to my will, I would bestow two crowns of pure gold for every syllable thereof. Here I send you as much as you requested, being willing to have sent you more, but that as I am glad to give, so I am desirous to be asked and fawned on by my daughters, thee especially, whom virtue and learning hath made most dear unto me. Wherefore, the sooner you have spent this money well, as you are wont to do, and the sooner you ask me for more, the sooner know you will do your father a singular pleasure. Farewell, my most beloved daughter.

This daughter was likest her father as well in favor as wit, and proved a most rare woman for learning, sanctity, and secrecy, and therefore he trusted her with all his secrets. She wrote two declamations in English, which her father and she turned into Latin so elegantly as one could hardly judge which was the best. She made also a treatise of the *Four Last Things*; which her father sincerely protested that it was better than his, and therefore, it may be, never finished his. She corrected, by her wit, a place in Saint Cyprian, corrupted, as Pamelius and John Coster testify, instead of "*Nisi vos sinceritatis*," restoring "*nervos sinceritatis*." To her Erasmus wrote an epistle, as to a woman not only famous for manners and virtue, but most of all for learning. We have heretofore made mention of her letter that Cardinal Pole so liked, that when he read it, he would not believe it could be any woman's; in answer whereof, Sir Thomas did send her the letter, some part whereof we have seen before; the rest is this, which, though there were no other testimony of her extraordinary learning, might suffice:

In the meantime I thought with myself how true I found that now, which once I remember I spoke unto you in jest, when I pitied your hard hap, that men that read your writings would suspect you to have had help of some other man therein, which would derogate somewhat from the praises due to your works; seeing that you, of all others, deserve least to have such a suspicion had of you, or that you never could abide to be decked with the plumes of other birds. But you, sweet Meg, are rather to be praised for this, that seeing you cannot hope for condign praise of your labors; yet for all this, you go forward with this your invincible courage, to join with your virtue the knowledge of most excellent sciences, and contenting yourself with your own pleasure in learning, you never hunt after vulgar praises, nor receive them willingly, though they be offered you. And for your singular piety and love towards me, you esteem me and your husband a sufficient and ample theatre for you to content you with; who, in requital of this your affection, beseech

God and our Lady, with as hearty prayers as possible we can pour out, to give you an easy and happy childbirth, to increase your family with a child most like yourself, except only in sex; yet if it be a wench, that it may be such a one as would, in time, recompense by imitation of her mother's learning and virtues, what, by the condition of her sex, may be wanting; such a wench I should prefer before three boys. Farewell, dearest daughter.

But see, I pray you, how a most learned Bishop in England was ravished with her learning and wit; as it appeareth by a letter which her father wrote unto her to certify her thereof:

Thomas More sendeth hearty greeting to his dearest daughter Margaret: I will let pass to tell you, my sweetest daughter, how much your letter delighted me; you may imagine how exceedingly it pleased your father, when you understand what affection the reading of it raised in a stranger. It happened me this evening to sit with John, Lord Bishop of Exeter, a learned man, and, by all men's judgment, a most sincere man. As we were talking together, and I, taking out of my pocket a paper which was to the purpose we were talking of, I pulled out, by chance, therewith your letter. The handwriting pleasing him, he took it from me and looked on it; when he perceived it, by the salutation, to be a woman's, he began more greedily to read it, novelty inviting him thereunto; but when he had read it, and understood that it was your writing, which he never could have believed if I had not seriously affirmed it. "Such a letter"—I say no more; yet why should not I report that which he said unto me?—"So pure a style, so good Latin, so eloquent, so full of sweet affections!"—he was marvellously ravished with it. When I perceived that, I brought forth also an oration of yours, which he reading, and also many of your verses, he was so moved with the matter so unlooked for, that the very countenance and gesture of the man, free from all flattery and deceit, betrayed that his mind was more than his words could utter, although he uttered many to your great praise; and forthwith he drew out of his pocket a portegue which you shall receive inclosed herein. I could not possibly shun the taking of it, but he would needs send it unto you, as a sign of his dear affection towards you, although by all means I endeavored to give it him again; which was the cause I showed him none of your other sister's works, for I was afraid lest I should have been thought to have showed them of purpose, because he should bestow the like courtesy upon them; for it troubled me sore, that I must needs take this of him; but he is so worthy a man, as I have said, that it is a happiness to please him thus. Write carefully unto him, and as eloquently as you are able, to give him thanks therefore. Farewell. *From the Court, this 11th of September, even almost at midnight.*

She made an oration to answer Quintilian, defending that rich man which he accused for having poisoned a poor man's bees with certain venomous flowers in his garden, so eloquent and witty that it may strive with his. She translated Eusebius out of Greek, but it was never printed, because Christopherson at that time had done it exactly before. Yet one other letter will I set down of Sir Thomas to this his daughter, which is thus:

Thomas More sendeth greeting to his dearest daughter Margaret: There was no reason, my dearest daughter, why thou shouldst have deferred thy writing unto me one day longer, for fear that thy letters, being so barren, should not be read of me without loathing. For though they had not been most curious, yet in respect of thy sex, thou mightest have been pardoned by any man; yea, even a blemish in the child's face seemeth often to a father beautiful. But these your letters, Meg, were so eloquently polished, that they had nothing in them, not only why they should fear the most indulgent affection of your father More, but also they needed not to have regarded even Momus's censure, though never so testy. I greatly thank Mr. Nicholas, our dear friend (a most expert man in astronomy), and do congratulate your happiness whom it may fortune within the space of one month, with a small labor of your own, to learn so many and such high wonders of that mighty and eternal workman, which were not found but in many ages, by watching, in so many cold nights, under the open skies, with much labor and pains, by such excellent, and above all other men's understanding wits. This which you write pleaseth me exceedingly, that you had determined with yourself to study philosophy so diligently, that you will hereafter recompense by your diligence what your negligence hath heretofore lost you. I love you for this, dear Meg, that whereas I never have found you to be a loiterer (your learning, which is not ordinary, but in all kind of sciences most excellent, evidently showing how painfully you have proceeded therein), yet such is your modesty, that you had rather still accuse yourself of negligence than vainly boast of diligence; except you mean by this your speech that you will be hereafter so diligent that your former endeavors, though indeed they were great and praiseworthy, yet in respect of your future diligence, may be called negligence. If it be so that you mean (as I do verily think you do), I imagine nothing can happen to me more fortunate, nothing to you, my dearest daughter, more happy; for, as I have earnestly wished that you might spend the remainder of your life in studying physic and holy Scriptures, by the which there shall never be helps wanting unto you, for the end of man's life; which is to endeavor that a sound mind be in a healthful body, of which studies you have already laid some foundations, and you shall never want matter to build thereupon; so now I think that some of the first years of your youth, yet flourishing, may be very well bestowed in human learning and the liberal arts, both because your age may best struggle with those difficulties, and for that it is uncertain whether, at any time else, we shall have the commodity of so careful, so loving, and so learned a master; to let pass, that by this kind of learning, our judgments are either gotten, or certainly much helped thereby. I could wish, dear Meg, that I might talk with you a long while about these matters, but behold, they which bring on supper interrupt me, and call me away. My supper cannot be so sweet unto me as this my speech with you is, if I were not to respect others more than myself. Farewell, dearest daughter, and commend me kindly to your husband, my loving son, who maketh me rejoice for that he studieth the same things you do; and whereas I am wont always to counsel you to give place to your husband, now, on the other side, I give you license to strive to master him in the knowledge of the sphere. Farewell again and again. Commend me to all your schoolfellows, but to your master especially.

Early Rising and Morning Occupation in Utopia.

Sir Thomas More, in his *Utopia* (Scheme of a Happy Republic), pictures his ideal people disposing of their time and occupations so as to secure the sufficient use of all their faculties of mind and body. While they gave only six hours to labor, they devoted a portion of their evenings to recreation,—in summer, the early hour after supper in their gardens; and in both summer and winter, to music and discourse; and after eight hours devoted to sleep, "a great many, both men and women, of all ranks, go to hear lectures of one sort or another, according to the variety of their inclinations," which lectures are "every morning before daybreak." In this suggestion he embodies his own daily habit of early rising, and his devotion of those hours to reading, writing, and contemplation.

ROGER ASCHAM AND THE LADY JANE GREY.

(From Walter Savage Landor's "Imaginary Conversations of Literary Men and Statesmen." Volume II., p. 78-84.)

ASCHAM.—Thou art going, my dear young lady, into a most awful state; thou art passing into matrimony and great wealth. God hath willed it so: submit in thankfulness.

Thy affections are rightly placed and well distributed. Love is a secondary passion in those who love most, a primary in those who love least. He who is inspired by it in a great degree, is inspired by honor in a greater: it never reaches its plenitude of growth and perfection, but in the most exalted minds. . . . Alas! alas!

JANE.—What aileth my virtuous Ascham? what is amiss? why do I tremble?

ASCHAM.—I remember a sort of prophecy, made three years ago: it is a prophecy of thy condition and of my feelings on it. Recollectest thou who wrote, sitting upon the seabeach, the evening after an excursion to the Isle of Wight, these verses?

> Invisibly bright water! so like air,
> On looking down I feared thou couldst not bear
> My little bark, of all light barks most light,
> And looked again . . . and drew me from the sight,
> And, hanging back, breathed each fresh gale aghast,
> And held the breath, not to go on so fast.

JANE.—I was very childish when I composed them; and, if I had thought any more about the matter, I should have hoped you had been too generous to keep them in your memory, as witnesses against me.

ASCHAM.—Nay, they are not much amiss for so young a girl, and there being so few of them, I did not reprove thee. Half an hour, I then thought, might have been spent more unprofitably; and I now shall believe it firmly, and if thou wilt but be led by them to meditate a little, on the similarity of situation in which thou then wert to what thou art now in.

JANE.—I will do it, and whatever else you command me; for I am too weak by nature and very timorous, unless where a strong sense of duty holdeth me and supporteth me: there God acteth, and not his creature.

Those were with me at sea who would have been attentive to me, if I had seemed to be afraid, even the worshipful men and women were in the company; so that something more powerful threw my fear overboard: but I never will go again upon the water.

ASCHAM.—Exercise that beauteous couple, that mind and body, much and variously, but at home, at home, Jane! indoors, and about things indoors; for God is there too. We have rocks and quicksands on the banks of our Thames, O lady, such as ocean never heard of; and many, (who knows how soon!) may be engulphed in the smooth current under their garden walls.

JANE.—Thoroughly do I now understand you. Yes indeed, I have read evil things of courts; but I think nobody can go out bad thence who entereth good, if timely and true warning shall have been kindly and freely given.

ASCHAM.—I see perils on perils which thou dost not see, although thou art wiser than thy poor old master. And it is not because love hath blinded thee, for that surpasseth his supposed omnipotence; but it is because thy tender heart, having always leant affectionately upon good, hath felt and known nothing of evil.

I once persuaded thee to reflect much: let me now persuade thee to avoid the habitude of reflection, to lay aside books, and to gaze carefully and stedfastly on what is under and before thee.

JANE.—I have well bethought me of all my duties: O how extensive they are! what a goodly and fair inheritance! But tell me, wouldst thou command me never more to read Cicero and Epictetus and Polybius? the others I do resign unto thee: they are good for the arbor and for the gravel walk: but leave unto me, I beseech thee, my friend and father, leave unto me, for my fireside and for my pillow, truth, eloquence, courage and constancy.

ASCHAM.—Read them on thy marriagebed, on thy childbed, on thy deathbed! Thou spotless undrooping lily, they have fenced thee right well! These are the men for men: these are to fashion the bright and blessed creatures, O Jane, whom God one day shall smile upon in thy chaste bosom . . . Mind thou thy husband.

JANE.—I sincerely love the youth who hath espoused me; I love him with the fondest, the most solicitous affection. I pray to the Almighty for his goodness and happiness, and do forget at times, unworthy supplicant! the prayers I should have offered for myself. O never fear that I will disparage my kind religious teacher, by disobedience to my husband, in the most trying duties.

ASCHAM.—Gentle is he, gentle and virtuous: but time will harden him: time must harden even thee, sweet Jane! Do thou, complacently and indirectly, lead him from ambition.

JANE.—He is contented with me and with home.

ASCHAM.—Ah Jane, Jane! men of high estate grow tired of contentedness.

JANE.—He told me he never liked books unless I read them to him. I will read them to him every evening; I will open new worlds to him, richer than those discovered by the Spaniard; I will conduct him to treasures . . . O what treasures! . . . on which he may sleep in innocence and peace.

ASCHAM.—Rather do thou walk with him, ride with him, play with him, be his faery, his page, his everything that love and poetry have invented: but watch him well, sport with his fancies; turn them about like the ringlets round his cheeks; and if ever he meditate on power, go, toss up thy baby to his brow, and bring back his thoughts into his heart by the music of thy discourse.

Teach him to live unto God and unto thee: and he will discover that women, like the plants in woods, derive their softness and tenderness from the shade.

ADMIRAL LORD COLLINGWOOD, ON THE EDUCATION OF HIS DAUGHTERS.

To his Daughter.

OCEAN, AT MALTA, *Feb.* 5, 1809.

I received your letter, my dearest child; and it made me very happy to find that you and dear Mary were well, and taking pains with your education. The greatest pleasure I have amidst my toils and troubles is, in the expectation which I entertain of finding you improved in knowledge, and that the understanding which it hath pleased God to give you both, has been cultivated with care and assiduity. Your future happiness and respectability in the world depend on the diligence with which you apply to the attainment of knowledge at this period of your life; and I hope that no negligence of your own will be a bar to your progress. When I write to you, my beloved child, so much interested am I that you should be amiable, and worthy of the friendship and esteem of good and wise people, that I cannot forbear to second and enforce the instruction which you receive, by admonition of my own, pointing out to you the great advantages that will result from a temperate conduct and sweetness of manner, to all people, on all occasions. It does not follow that you are to coincide and agree in opinion with every ill-judging person; but, after showing them your reason for dissenting from their opinion, your argument and opposition to it should not be tinctured with anything offensive. Never forget for one moment that you are a gentlewoman,—and all your words and all your actions should mark you gentle. I never knew your mother—your dear, your good mother—say a harsh or a hasty thing to any person in my life. Endeavor to imitate her. I am quick and hasty in my temper; my sensibility is touched sometimes with a trifle, and my expression of it sudden as gunpowder; but, my darling, it is a misfortune which, not having been sufficiently restrained in my youth, has caused me much pain. It has, indeed, given me more pain to subdue this natural impetuosity than anything I ever undertook. I believe that you are both mild; but if ever you feel in your little breasts that you inherit a particle of your father's infirmity, restrain it, and quit the subject that has caused it, until your serenity be recovered. So much for mind and manners; next for accomplishments.

No sportsman ever hits a partridge without aiming at it; and skill is acquired by repeated attempts. It is the same thing in every art; unless you aim at perfection, you will never attain it; but frequent attempts will make it easy. Never, therefore, do anything with indifference; whether it be to mend a rent in your garment, or to finish the most delicate piece of art, endeavor to do it as perfectly as it is possible. When you write a letter, give it your greatest care, that it may be as perfect in all its parts as you can make it. Let the subject be sense, expressed in the most plain, intelligible, and elegant manner that you are capable of. If, in a familiar epistle, you should be playful and jocular, guard carefully that your wit be not sharp, so as to give pain to any person; and before you write a sentence, examine it, even the words of which it is composed, that there be nothing vulgar or inelegant in them. Remember, my dear, that your letter is the picture of your brains; and those whose brains are a compound of folly, nonsense, and impertinence, are to blame to exhibit them to the contempt of the world, or the pity of their friends. To write a letter with negligence, without proper stops, with crooked lines, and great, flourishing dashes, is inelegant; it argues either great ignorance of what is proper, or great ignorance towards the person to whom it is addressed, and is, consequently, disrespectful. It makes no amends to add an apology, for having scrawled a sheet of paper, of bad pens, for you should mend them; or want of time, for nothing is more important to you, or to which your time can be more properly devoted. I think I can know the character of a lady pretty nearly by her handwriting. The dashers are all impudent, however they may conceal it from themselves or others; and the scribblers flatter themselves with a vain hope, that, as their letter cannot be read, it may be mistaken for sense. I am very anxious to come to England, for I have lately been unwell. The greatest happiness which I expect there, is to find that my dear girls have been assiduous in their learning. May God Almighty bless you, my beloved little Sarah, and sweet Mary too.

Extracts from Letters to Lady Collingwood.

This day, my love, is the anniversary of our marriage; and I wish you many happy returns of it. If ever we have peace, I hope to spend my latter days amid my family, which is the only sort of happiness which I can enjoy. After this life of labor to retire to peace and quietness, is all I look for in the world. Should we decide to change the place of our dwelling, our route would, of course, be to the southward of Morpeth; but, then, I should be forever regretting those beautiful views, which are nowhere to be exceeded, and even the rattling of that old wagon that used to pass our door at six o'clock in a winter's morning, had its charms. The fact is, whenever I think how I am to be happy again, my thoughts carry me back to Morpeth, where, out of the fuss and parade of the world, surrounded by those I loved most and who loved me, I enjoyed as much happiness as my nature is capable of. Many things that I see in the world give me a distaste for its finery.

How do the dear girls go on? I would have them taught geometry, which is, of all sciences in the world, the most entertaining: it expands the mind more to the knowledge of all things in nature, and better teaches to distinguish between truths, and such things as have the appearance of being truths, yet are not, than any other. Their education, and the proper cultivation of the sense which God has given them, are the objects on which my happiness most depends. To inspire them with a love of everything that is honorable and virtuous, though in rags, and with contempt for vanity in embroidery, is the way to make them the darlings of my heart. They should not only read, but it requires a careful selection of books; nor should they ever have access to two at the same time; but, when a subject is begun, it should be finished before anything else is undertaken. How would it enlarge their minds if they could acquire a sufficient knowledge of mathematics and astronomy, to give them an idea of the beauty and wonders of the creation! I am persuaded that the generality of people, and, particularly, fine ladies, only adore God because they are told it is proper, and the fashion to go to church; but I would have my girls gain such knowledge of the works of the creation, that they may have a fixed idea of the nature of that Being who could be the author of such a world. Whenever they have that, nothing on this side the moon will give them much uneasiness of mind. I do not mean that they should be stoics, or want the common feelings for the sufferings that flesh is heir to; but they would then have a source of consolation for the worst that could happen. . . .

Do not let our girls be made fine ladies; but give them a knowledge of the world which they have to live in, that they may take care of themselves when you and I are in heaven. They must do everything for themselves, and never read novels, but history, travels, essays, and Shakspeare's plays, as often as they please. What they call books for young persons are nonsense. The memory should be strengthened by getting by heart such speeches and noble sentiments from Shakspeare or Roman history, as deserve to be imprinted on the mind. Give them my blessing, and charge them to be diligent.

II. THOUGHTS ON FEMALE EDUCATION AND EMPLOYMENTS.

(Selected from the French of Monseigneur Dupanloup.)*

The following paragraphs are selected from a little volume of the Bishop of Orleans, translated by R. M. Phillimore—originally written in answer to opinions expressed by M. de Maistre in letters to his daughters, against any thing serious or ennobling in the education and employment of women which is not directly connected with the amusement and well-ordering of the household.

THE AIM AND MERIT OF WOMAN.

The Bishop does not attempt to controvert M. de Maistre's opinion that "the great merit, the most honorable aim of a woman, is to make her home and husband happy, and to bring up her children well, and to make men of her sons—brave lads, who believe in God, and who do not fear cannon"—but he maintains that to do this "she must have a strong intelligence, judgment and character; she must be persevering, industrious, and reflecting; as the Scriptures say, her beauty and her amiability, which are the strength and embellishment of a house must be illuminated from on high. "As the sun rising over the world, so does a good woman shine over her household." The hand which holds the spindle and looks after the details of her house, must be the instrument of a head which is capable of planning and directing. And Solomon's description is not that of a woman only occupied about material life; it is that of the wise woman, and if "her children rise up and call her blessed," it is because she has the elevated sense of the things of life; the care of souls, and the foresight of the future, because she is ready for the noblest duties and disposed for the most serious thoughts; she is the worthy and intelligent companion of a husband, "who is known in the gates, when he sitteth among the elders of the land." What I should wish to see above all things is, not a race of learned women, but—what is necessary to their husbands, their children, and their households—intelligent, judicious women, capable of sustained attention, well versed in every thing that it is useful for them to know, as mothers, mistresses of households, and women of the world; never despising any labor of the hands, and at the same time not only knowing how to occupy their fingers, but their minds also, and to cultivate their souls and their whole being. And I must add, that what is to be dreaded as the very worst of scourges is the frivolous, fickle, effeminate,

---

* Studious Women—translated from the French of Monseigneur Dupanloup, Bishop of Orleans. London: 1868.

idle, ignorant, pleasure-loving women, devoted to dissipation and amusement, and consequently opposed to all exertion, to almost all duty; incapable of all studious pursuits, of all consecutive attention, and therefore not in a condition to take any real share in the education of her children, or the affairs of her husband and her household.

EXAMPLES OF STUDIOUS CHRISTIAN WOMEN IN THE EARLY AGES.

The biographer of the illustrious St. Boniface declares plainly, that St. Boniface loved St. Lioba on account of her solid learning—*eruditionis aspiratio*. This admirable virgin, in whom the light of the Holy Spirit was added to an enlightenment laboriously obtained by study, combined a purity and a humility—virtues that are such universal preservatives—with a learning in theology and the canon law which was of the greatest service to the early Germanic Church. And, indeed, St. Boniface was so far from despising the efforts of his spiritual daughter to raise herself intellectually, that sometimes he took from his apostolic occupations hours, which he did not consider as lost, in order to devote them to the correction of her literary compositions, her Latin verses, which he answered in the same style—poetical messages, carried across the seas by martyrs and confessors.

And if, going still farther back, we examine more closely some facts in history, we shall find that, since the establishment of Christianity, women's names are often seen on those literary monuments that have been most respected by time; for instance, the celebrated Hypatia, the teacher of Clement of Alexandria; the illustrious St. Catherine, who taught Christian philosophy, and confuted the pagan philosophers in the schools of Alexandria; and, again, St. Perpetua, who wrote the account of her martyrdom and the glorious fate of her companions.

When peace was restored to the Church, and the age of the Doctors succeeded the age of the martyrs, who is there more celebrated for the seriousness of their minds and the extent of their learning, than Paula and Marcella, Melania and Eustochium, and so many other holy and illustrious Christian women:—St. Marcella, in whom St. Jerome found so powerful an auxiliary against the heretics; St. Paula, who inspired St. Jerome to undertake his noblest and most important works, the Latin translation of the Bible from the Hebrew original, and a complete commentary on all the prophets.

Nothing is more beautiful than St. Paula's letter to St. Marcella; it shows us all that the latter did to raise the soul and the intellect of the holy women and the young virgins who called her their mother, and it shows us what was the extent of St. Paula's eloquence and intellect. And, in the following century, what an aid Paulinus—who, besides being a great Saint, was the brilliant disciple of Ausonius—found in Therasia; and who ought not to know that Elpicia (the wife of Boethius) composed hymns which are adopted in the Roman Liturgy? In the middle of the barbarous ages one of the first obligations imposed on Christian virgins was to learn letters. As soon as any of them showed an aptitude for literature, they were excused from manual labor, according to St. Cæsarius's precept, in order that they might give themselves up entirely to intellectual pursuits. In the greater part of the monasteries we hear of them devoted to study. They write, translate, copy, and decipher continually. St. Radegunda does not content herself with receiving, at Poitiers, one of the last of the Roman poets, but she intrusts the literary education of her nuns to him, and as writers they soon excel their master. The writings of Baudonovia show a revival of classical purity and elegance.

All the charm of Christian inspiration is shown in a hymn improvised by a nun of Poitiers at the moment of Radegunda's death, and one of the first flowers of Christian poetry blossoms on the tomb of the holy Queen who had always been so devoted to literature. The monasteries of England, Ireland, and France teem with learned and pious women.

"It is certain, from numerous and trustworthy testimonies," writes M. de Montalembert, "that literary studies were cultivated in the seventh and eighth centuries in the women's monasteries in England, with no less care and perseverance than in those of men, and perhaps with still greater enthusiasm. The Anglo-Saxon nuns did not neglect the occupations peculiar to their sex. But manual labor was far from satisfying them. They voluntarily left the needle and the distaff, not only to transcribe manuscripts, and to illuminate them to suit the taste of the age, but above all to read and to study holy books, the Fathers of the Church, and even classical works."* St. Gertrude, in Dagobert's reign, knew all the Scriptures by heart, and translated them into Greek. She sent over the sea for Irish masters to teach music, poetry, and Greek to the cloistered virgins of Nivelle. From all these centres brilliant torches issued forth, such as Lioba, who founded the Abbey of Bischofsheim, Roswitha, and St. Bridget. It was by a holy woman that the study of Greek was inaugurated in the monastery of St. Gall. And the knowledge of the learned Hilda was so highly considered in the Anglo-Saxon church, that more than once the holy abbess assisted at the deliberation of the bishops assembled in council or in synod, who wished to take the advice of her whom they considered as especially enlightened by the Holy Spirit. But were we to enumerate all the examples of women in whom holiness has been accompanied by the gifts of the most luminous learning, the list would be too long, and we should have to go through all the first ages of Christianity.

STUDY—A DUTY.

I assert plainly that it is a duty in women to study and to instruct themselves; and that intellectual labor ought to have its separate part assigned to it, amongst their own special occupations, and their most important obligations. The primordial reasons for this obligation are important, they are of divine origin, and absolutely incapable of being rejected; they are these:—In the first place, God never makes useless gifts; in every thing that God does, there is a reason, an aim; and if man's companion is a reasonable creature; if, like man, she has been created in the image and resemblance of God; if she also has received from the Creator the gift of intelligence, the sublimest of all his gifts, it is in order to make use of it.

Besides, all the gifts received from God, in order to be of some use, ought to be cultivated. The Scriptures tell us that the soul, like the earth when it is

---

* *The Monks of the West*, vol. 5. This fifth volume and the two which precede it, written in the middle of a severe and inveterate disease, are prodigies of powerful inspiration, of tenderness and of elevation, and show the unflinching nature of a Christian, and a courageous soul, in the most grievous physical and moral trials. These are the books that I should like to see in the hands of every body—above all, at the present time, when we are inundated by such a wretched literature, and by so many writings of the most unwholesome description.

allowed to lie fallow, only brings forth wild fruits, "thorns and thistles." And God has not made the souls of women, any more than he has those of men, to be like a shallow, sterile, and unwholesome soil.

Again, every reasonable creature will have to give an account to God of his or her gifts; every one, according to the judgment of God, will be treated in accordance with the gifts received, and in accordance with the profitableness and the works of each.

God has given us all hands, which, according to the commentators, represent vigorous and intelligent action, but on condition that we do not return to him empty-handed. In short, He has explained Himself categorically in the parable of the talents, in which He declares that a strict account will be required of the use of every talent. And I do not know of any Father of the Church, or of any moralist, who has thought hitherto that this parable did not concern women as well as men. There is no distinction made here, each will have to give an account of that which has been intrusted to him or her; and human as well as divine good sense shows plainly enough that women, not more nor less than men, have the right to bury or to squander the gifts conferred upon them by God for the purpose of making a right use of them.

I will then say with St. Augustine, that no creature to whom God has intrusted the lamp of intelligence ought to permit herself to behave like one of the foolish virgins, in imprudently letting her lamp go out for want of trimming it; thus allowing the light to be spent, which is first intended for herself, and next, for others beside herself; and, since the question is about wives and mothers, for her husband and her children.

I say it without any hesitation, Christian morality alone teaches woman, with a decisive and absolute authority, her real rights and duties in their necessary reciprocal relation. Yes; until you have persuaded woman that she is created first of all for God, next for herself and for her own soul, and lastly for her husband and her children, but after God, with God, and always for God, you will have done nothing either for the happiness or the honor of your families.

The contrary system rests on a *Pagan view of their destiny*, and also, as has been truly said, *on the idleness of men who wish to retain their superiority without effort.* The Pagan view is, that women are only charming creatures,—passive, subordinate, and only made for the pleasure and the amusement of man. But, as I have said, Christianity has far other ideas. In Christianity the virtue of a woman, like that of a man, ought to be voluntary, noble, active, and intelligent. She ought to know the whole extent of her duties, and all the divine knowledge which can be derived from them, for the benefit of her husband and her children.

DANGER OF IGNORANCE AND FRIVOLITY.

Human nature requires to be instructed, enlarged, enlightened, and elevated in all its powers; and I must say, for my own part, that I have never found any thing more dangerous than repressed capabilities, unsatisfied desires, and a thirst unquenched. Thence arises that longing for knowledge which, for want of the good and the true, fixes on the bad and the false; thence arise those passions, naturally generous and commendable, which turn against truth and virtue; thence arise those crooked, bad, and perverse notions adopted by an ignorance which knows neither how to exercise choice, judgment, or restraint

—"[illegible]"—as saith the Scripture! Thence, in short, arise so many falls, so many shameless deeds, or, at least, such numerous and wretched frivolities amongst women! If these fine and ardent natures had been better directed, we should not have had to deplore their ruin; we should not have to groan over that sad lowness of level and mental tone—that feeble-mindedness of so many women naturally above par, who are intended to be the ornament of the world and the honor of their families, and whose education, stopped short in its development, has made perhaps elegant and accomplished women, up to thirty years of age, but has rendered them forever frivolous, ordinary, and useless beings.

I have sometimes heard mothers say that they would dread to see in their girls powers of mind rather beyond the usual run, and that they would try to repress them. "What would one do with them?" they say. "How find a vent for those great powers in the midst of that real life, which is so contracted, so paltry, and which is woman's lot at the end of the first years of her youth."

This opinion has always secretly disgusted me. What! You wish to prevent the development of the Divine flame in a soul which God has gifted with a spark of ideal life! You respect this gift in men, on condition however of its being employed in practical life, that is to say, of its being used to gain money and to add to a social position; but as the utility of great things is less lucrative among women, it is deemed more advisable to suppress them. Cut off, then, the branches of this plant, which would want too much air, space, and sun. Do away with this useless sap. But this plant ought to have become a large tree, and you are going to make a stunted shrub of it!

Ah! beware by your mutilation of making it first suffer cruelly, and finally depriving it of all life. To extinguish a soul that God has created to be a shining light, is to inflict an inward suffering that you will never be able to cure, and which will perhaps cause that soul to go astray, and exhaust its powers in vague and exaggerated aspirations. There is no torment to be compared to this sentiment of the beautiful which is quenched at its birth, to that poignant grief of a soul which, perhaps unconsciously, has missed its real *vocation*; and this word, which seems to express a call from on high, that most serious and irresistible call, is as applicable to women as to men—to the ideal as well as to the actual condition of life. "Our soul," it has been said, "is a thought of God;" that is to say, that there is a Divine plan for it, the realization of which is either furthered by our efforts or checked by our want of energy, but which does not exist the less in the Divine goodness and wisdom. And to realize it, all the development of our soul, our heart, and our intelligence is necessary. It is difficult to foresee beforehand the destination God has attached to his gifts, but it is true that He intends them for some object, and that this providential vocation, supposing that we are rigidly faithful to it, will by obeying its behests avert any dangers that we had feared from its consequences.

Above all we must consult the different natures we have to deal with, and only attempt to develop them according to their capabilities. I would not certainly create factitious talents, by means of a cultivation which is not demanded by Nature; but neither would I leave fallow a soil that she has enriched with her gifts. An incomplete development, a smattering of science and accomplishments, are most dangerous for a woman; they show her a higher horizon, without giving her the strength to reach it; they make her believe she knows:

what she is really ignorant of, and they thus entail a disturbance, a disorder, and an ostentation which often produce lamentable aberrations.

A woman of the world, whose position obliges her to see a great deal of it, but who understands her duties and fulfils them well, wrote to me as follows: "In general, women know nothing, *absolutely nothing*. They can only talk about dress, fashions, steeple-chases, the absurdities of each other. If you turn the conversation to a subject of history or geography, or if you talk about the middle ages, the crusades, the institutions of Charlemagne or St. Louis; if you compare Bossuet to Corneille, or Racine to Fénélon; if you pronounce the names of Camoens, or of Dante, of Royer-Collard, or of Frederick Ozanam, of Montalembert, or of Père Gratry, the poor woman will be struck dumb. She can only entertain young women and frivolous young men. Equally incapable of talking on business, art, politics, agriculture, or the sciences, she can neither converse with her father-in-law, her clergyman, or with any man of a serious mind. And yet, *the first talent of a woman is to be able to converse with every body*. If her mother-in-law visits the poor and the schools, and wishes to enlist her in her pious undertakings, she neither understands their aim nor their bearing, for a good and compassionate heart is not sufficient in a certain class for works of charity. In order to acquire influence, to give any benefit its full value and moral bearing, a degree of intelligence is required, which is only attained by attentive study and reflection."

And now I must go still further, and show the fatal consequences of such a state of things for religion, for society, and for families. I will say the whole truth. I know, and I have blessed God for the sight, all that a woman, a Christian mother, is able to do in her family; how many things may be introduced by her influence, how many ideas at first decidedly rejected, are adopted by her means; religious ideas, charitable ideas, ideas of devotion, resignation, pardon, and daily work. But it must be confessed that these ideas of daily work are those which are the most rarely embraced.

The painful truth which I wish to state here is, that education, even a religious education, does not always give, and indeed gives too rarely to young girls and young women, a serious taste for mental labor. Deputies from God to the domestic hearth, guardians of the holy traditions of faith, honor, and fidelity, even Christian and pious women seem too often the enemies of mental labor, whether for their husbands or their children, and especially for their boys. I have seen some who had great difficulty in not considering as a personal theft the time which is given up to it. Was it the fault of their intelligence and their aptitude? I have never thought so—quite the contrary: and I attribute this distaste for mental labor, in the first place, to the flimsy, frivolous, and superficial, not to say, false education that is given to women; and, in the second place, to the part which is allotted to them in the world, and to that assigned to them in their families—even in certain Christian families. Women are not to study; there is to be no studying about them; they are to do nothing. They themselves do not wish to see any body really occupied around them, or at least they encourage neither their husbands nor their children to do any thing that is of a serious kind, and which requires trouble and devoted attention—and sometimes they go so far as to oppose it, when their pleasure or their liberty may suffer by it. And it is a very great misfortune; for here they have the most fatal influence! In vain we say to men: "Work; accept the offer of employment; at least occupy your time." As long as women are there to destroy the effect of our advice, our words will be in vain. As long as mothers advise their daughters not to marry a man who has a settled occupation, as long as a young woman makes use of all her arts to dissuade her husband from working, as long as the young mother does not impress upon her son the necessity of instructing himself, of cultivating his mind and his faculties as he would a precious plant, the law of labor will be despised. Yes, in the actual state of our habits, and family life being what it is, women alone can really promote mental labor, prepare minds for it at an early age, render it possible and easy; yes, even insist upon it, and bestow their esteem, their encouragement, and their admiration on its adoption.

ADVANTAGES OF INTELLECTUAL LABOR.

It is a mother's duty to attend to the soul as well as the body of her child; she can even be more easily replaced in his physical than in his intellectual and moral education. For the former so many people can help her; for the latter, unless she is surrounded by obstacles, she reigns alone. To follow the development of mind and the studies of a young man, to watch over him, to guide him with that influence that is given by a sound and authoritative judgment, by a capacity joined to kindness, and thus inspire confidence and admiration—all this implies a combination of intellectual qualities which are far from ordinary.

How many mothers have lost all power over the souls of their sons, because they have been unable to nourish and to develop their intellectual, as they had done their physical being! To be a mother, a mother in all the elevation, the extent, and the depth of the word—that alone justifies all the noble efforts of a woman to acquire the greatest superiority of mind.

No unity can last in married life, unless the fellowship of hearts is accompanied by the fellowship of minds. As a woman loses the charms of youth, her husband must perceive that her mind is developing, and love must be perpetuated by esteem. The husband, if he has capacity, is then entering into the most active period of life, he is occupied with the most varied pursuits, whilst too often his wife, having only received from her education severe principles, with the habit of futile occupations, bores him with her mechanical devotion, her music, and her canvas-work.

There are numerous serious occupations and interests which prevail more and more in a man's intellect, and with which an idle woman can not sympathize, and then that chasm arises between them which may be called *the separation of minds.* A woman, on the contrary, who has studied, shares her husband's serious occupations, she supports him in his labors, in his struggles. She follows her husband, and precedes her sons; she adopts in her home that high position which renders her the supporter and the counselor of man. She feels that her husband is proud of her, and that he requires her. She does not make a boast of it, but she rests securely on her happiness, for she is confident that nothing can disturb a union which has for its basis the perfect fellowship of two souls and two minds, and that the love of both will last as long as the souls whom it unites.

It ought to be well understood, that a woman, in becoming a Christian, has become the companion of man, "*Socia;*" and what is more, an assistance, a helpmate, a support, and a counselor: "*Adjutorium*"—Religion, which has raised her soul and her heart, has also rendered her mind capable of understanding, sometimes of equaling, and above all of helping the mind of man. In making her weak in body, God has given her the germ of all that is great and morally strong. There are no noble works in which women have not been mixed up; at first the teachers, then the inspiring geniuses of men, and often the sharers of their labors. There are women who have devoted their minds at the same time as their lives, to a man it was their duty to love, and who have continued to share in the tone of the thoughts of which they were made the first confidants, those thoughts that unfold with greater brilliancy and vigor from the double light that shines upon them.

DANGERS OF INTELLECTUAL CULTIVATION.

Doubtless this intellectual cultivation may be accompanied by three dangers, but the remedy is an easy one.

1. *The neglect of practical duties.*—This danger must be averted by strengthening practical education; in growing girls the habits of order and regularity, which double time, and fix a place in life for each thing that is to be done; and above all, a true and real piety, which is nothing else but the courageous accomplishment of every duty.

2. *The undue indulgence of the fancy*, which causes a craving for intellectual enjoyments, that can not always be satisfied. But here, again, all may be balanced. The important point is, that education should be made to correspond with the gifts of God, without either going beyond them or stifling them. Usually they bring with them the counterpoise of their dangers. An excessive cultivation is dangerous, an insufficient cultivation is not less so. Piety is here also a great aid.

3. *Pride and vanity.*—Good sense cultivated in a Christian point of view can alone prevent it. We must, however, observe that if the cultivation of the mind, like the attractions of the body, can excite pride and vanity, study has at least a counterpoise; it puts something serious and luminous into the mind, whilst the success produced by beauty and dress is always accompanied by frivolous or bad sentiments.

Give a woman all the knowledge, all the talents, all the development of which she is capable; and give her at the same time Christian humility—she will be endowed with a much truer and more amiable simplicity and modesty than a poor Hindoo, who thinks herself an animal of a species rather superior to the monkeys in her yard, but very inferior to the nature of her husband. This enlightened humility is a real virtue, and will become the mother of many other virtues, and the inspiration of the highest desire of perfection. For humility does not prevent us from recognizing the progress we have made, nor does it close our eyes to the merit of others; it makes us see our own deficiencies, and even if we had reached the summit of knowledge and human cleverness, it would still show us in every department a superior ideal to excite our efforts without producing pride or discouragement. Let us be well persuaded that a cultivated mind understands its duties better than any other. It is intelligent humility, that is to say, real modesty, which preserves us from pedantry. In learned women, it is not their knowledge which displeases, it is their pretension.

If I press this point, it is because my adversaries insist upon it the most of all. They still repeat, "*that* is the great danger." But, in my turn, I also repeat, the brilliant notoriety that a literary or artistic talent can give a woman, is not the greatest cause of vanity that can be apprehended for her. As I have already said, an empty beauty and worldly triumphs fill a woman with herself in a very different way, and danger is not likely to be corrected by the cause which produces it. Study and the arts, in raising the mind, serve as a counterpoise to any vain feelings they may excite; and I see no similar guarantee in the successes obtained by advantages of another kind. The whole question is contained in these words: that great gifts are accompanied by dangers, against which education must have strengthened the possessors beforehand.

Education must adapt itself to diverse natures; in developing the germs God has placed in those natures, it must direct this development with a firm hand, and prevent its wanderings and its caprices. It must also produce a moral development, in harmony with the intellectual one; it must balance justly ideal and practical life, which are less contrary to each other than is generally supposed, and the harmony of which alone constitutes the dignity of existence. "The example of Germany," says somewhere Alfred Tonnelé, "proves that family and household life, and the fostering of true and simple affections do not exclude cultivation and elevation of mind among women; that, on the contrary, they develop and purify them. Are not those who have most emancipated themselves from household cares, the most frivolous, the emptiest and the vainest, and do we find that this independence has contributed to make them more studious or more accomplished?" I am fain to confess, however, that education is more important and more difficult in a richly endowed nature; but the task is a nobler and a more gratifying one.

THE HOME OF A STUDIOUS WOMAN.

It is in the homes of the artist, the physician, the lawyer, the judge, the professor, the learned man, that are most often seen those studious able women, who understand the arts, who themselves possess true talents, who are very well informed, without the possibility of any body calling them *blue stockings*, because their intelligence is a part of the honor and the treasure of their families, and it is by the help of this intelligence they procure ease and comfort to their homes, and even that delicate luxury with which riches have nothing to do, and which is all owing to a woman's taste. The shape of the furniture is good, and the arrangement is graceful, the engravings recall those works of art which are most preferred, and show what is liked in the house.

Flowers, pictures, books, a small but well-chosen library,* music, pleasant

* There are some women who have no books, because they must have fine editions and expensive bindings. They do not look upon books as helps to study, but as ornaments which add another elegance to the many elegancies of their abode. It is a strange thing to say, but the price of one ball-dress would suffice to purchase a good library. A person once said to me:—"I have given up reading, for only very rich people can afford to have books." I answered: "It is, usually, very rich people who do not possess them." In fact, it is an exception to find the taste for occupation and the earnest love of intellectual pursuits in certain opulent families, with whom the world absorbs every thing, and whose time and money scarcely suffice for the exigencies which are made necessary. In many unpretending and well-regulated houses, on the contrary, intellectual life has its assigned share in daily life, and the sacrifices that are voluntarily made for its cultivation, are precisely what tend to encourage it.

literature, every thing shows a house that is much lived in, seldom left, and where happiness is to be found. It is not one of those empty and magnificent abodes, whose possessors are always absent, pursuing pleasure with a feverish activity, and flying from the weariness of a house which has no charm except during the time spent in furnishing it, and which becomes a bore as soon as the gilded chairs are put in their places. In the little apartments of the third story, the mother is surrounded by her children. She brings them up herself! God be thanked, she is obliged to do so; and how she is rewarded for her trouble! She reigns over her children, who understand the merits and the sacrifices of their mother, and who love her dearly. They soon know the happiness of being born in a condition in which a mother has not fortune enough for servants, tutors, and governesses who would occupy her place. Also, what a difference between the two educations! The sons take the first places at school and at college; the girls receive that superior education which I should like to give as a model to the girls of the fashionable world. They wish to be equal to their mothers, who work with them, who direct them, follow them, and both interest themselves and take an active part in their studies. The law of labor is more incumbent on a mother than on any other creature; the soul of her child is the field that she ought to cultivate by the "*sweat of her brow*," nobody ought to take her place, and if the most complete educations are the products of the humble abodes I have mentioned, all the honor is due to those laborious mothers.

How many young men owe their coarse tastes for horses and dogs to the mercenaries that have brought them up! A mother implants other tastes and ambitions in the heart of her children when she brings them up herself. Sometimes she is a prey to the anxious thought, whether she can give enough honor and faith to the conscience of her children, in order to inspire them with the courage of bearing in their turn this humble existence, without ever consenting to increase their fortune by a base action. In her anxiety, she redoubles her efforts in educating them, for she knows their education is their dowry, and she becomes more painstaking, more virtuous, more courageous, in order to transmit to her children this admirable pride of her soul, and in order that they may obtain this grace from Heaven.

And the children who witness the exertions of their mother, have a secret desire to relieve and to reward her. The wish to do right is much stronger in these homes of humble happiness, and the satisfaction of performed duties makes every member of the family contented with his fate and cheerfully submissive to his God. The whole day is one of active exertion. The father at his work, the mother manages the house, takes the children to their classes and catechetical instructions, and in the evening each member of the family is tired with the labor of the day and wishes to remain at home. It is the hour of rest, of the children's games, the hour of talk, of reading, of music, of intimacy, and of gaiety. The day ends quietly, without that worldly whirl, which is so great a trial, even to the most virtuous and Christian-like women. A mother thus occupied can never think of giving herself up to a purely personal pursuit. She has studied whilst she was a young girl and a young woman. Now she is always at the service of others. But this disinterested labor, which is both labor and sacrifice, raises her soul and her intellect better than any other employment of her faculties. There is no fear that she will be either vain or pedantic. And yet what an immense labor is hers, in giving her children all their lessons! One is astonished at the extraordinary efforts produced by maternal love that a mother makes to fulfill her duties. Do not marvel, then, to find her so full of capacity, so elevated, so active, so intelligent, so indifferent to the empty gossip and the frivolous coquetries of the world.

BAD EDUCATION.

What is wanting the most in the education of young girls, and in the life of young women, is consecutive study and attentive reflection. This is a serious and almost always an irreparable evil, and as it is the fault of education, I will say in a few words what I think of the education of girls, and of its deficiencies.

The greater number of girls spend seven or eight years of their education in practicing the piano, two and often three and four hours a day. But this accomplishment, to which so much time is given up, and which might enlarge the mind and the soul to so great an extent, usually only ends in those "soulless talents" of which Töpffer speaks, which derive their existence from vanity alone; talents which are both useless in practical life and "unconnected with the mind," and which are almost always given up after marriage.

This charming writer, who breaks out with so much energy against the use that is made of the arts, in the education of young people, and on what are usually called "ornamental talents," or accomplishments, exclaims:—"How many of these ornamental talents I have seen and heard, and how few pleasant ones! Girls take interest in nothing, understand but little, and do not feel at all. . . . . I think, on the contrary, that they might seek in the arts, together with an amusing pastime, a refreshment for their hearts, minds, and imaginations; and derive from so many faculties, that the usual occupations of women either destroy or leave uncultivated, a result which would lend an inexpressible charm to their souls." Instead of this, music is made a sort of material study, which scarcely ever reaches the soul, and not even the most ordinary comprehension of the art! Most girls only aspire to mechanical perfection, they do not attempt to penetrate into the sanctuary of the art, and find nothing in it to raise and exercise the nobler faculties. How many spend four hours a day at the piano, and yet have no knowledge of the masters, the schools, or the styles—no æsthetic sentiment, and neither the sense nor the perception of what they are doing! "Music," says the Père Gratry, "has been transformed into a brilliant noise, which does not even soothe the nerves."

The music-masters only care about giving a rapid execution; very few endeavor to form a good style, to make the composers understood and appreciated, and to explain the connection of the ideas of harmony and melody. The result is, that these poor girls, after they have spent a good part of their lives at the piano, execute skilfully with their fingers what their minds do not at all apprehend. It is about the same as if they incessantly recited passages in an unknown tongue. No! Literature and musical æsthetics must be attended to quite as much as mechanical dexterity; otherwise the pursuit is a species of barbarism. In Germany, where music has a great share in the education of girls, it is made a more serious pursuit. They learn harmony, they ascend from mechanism to art.

Drawing is often treated in the same manner. I have seen people who drew with accuracy, and even facility, not able to distinguish between a good and a bad picture, and who do not know whether Raphael was the master or the pupil of Perugino. Even their talent for drawing did not develop the sense of the beautiful in their minds.

The world gives up to girls the province of music, on condition that their souls shall not be raised by it, and that they will make it a means of wasting their time; and as to the plastic arts, the taste for painting is already beginning to awaken criticism, and M. de Maistre was frightened at seeing his daughter paint in oils. In one word, the arts are to be reduced to ornamental accomplishments, and the sumptuary laws are still more severe about literary studies.

At a certain age, with the exception of music and drawing, the education of a girl is considered to be finished. "Since my eighteenth year," a young lady to whom I recommended study thus writes to me, "whenever I begin to study, I am always asked if I have not finished my education." Finish one's education; that means, to write nothing but letters, to embroider, and to cultivate accomplishments, if one happens to have any!

"But," say my objectors, "young girls are taught a vast quantity of things during their education."

Doubtless they are, and this is exactly what I complain of: girls have not to take a degree, and all their education tends to give very extensive and very superficial general notions. Nothing serious, grave, or deep, but a smattering of every thing; and, as was said by an intelligent minister, "who does not know, that what is gained in point of surface, is lost in point of depth?"

General notions, and no real knowledge, ornamental accomplishments, and no serious talents, nothing which raises the soul and matures the mind; this is exactly what is wanted, to shine for a moment, and to fall short of being "*something*" and "*somebody*." This is exactly what is wanted, to leave off doing any thing, as soon as the education of the convent is over. Now, it is precisely an opposite course that ought to be adopted, if the object is to produce serious and persevering women, who may be one day useful to their husbands and their children.

CONTINUOUS STUDY AND WORK.

Work is a faithful friend at every age and to every disposition, for those who have adopted it as a companion in the journey of life, and it gives cheerfulness to the outward, and serenity to the inward man. In order to give women the habit of work, they must be impressed as girls with the fact that their education is not finished at eighteen, and that their first ball-dress does not possess, any more than a bachelor's degree for young men, the power of giving the finishing touch to their attainments. At that age they scarcely know even the primary notions that would enable them to study by themselves. They no longer want any leading-strings in their education, and that is all. They are only ready to go on and to enjoy the pleasure of working by themselves. If a girl could be made to believe this, a wise future would be her sure portion.

RIGHT BRINGING UP.

What does it mean to be well brought up? It means, to develop her intelligence, her heart, her conscience, her character, at the same time as her practical faculties, without neglecting her health, her physical strength, nor even, within due limits, her outward charms; in one word, to render her capable of forming not only an element in the life of man, but of sympathizing with his thoughts, and to realize in marriage that intellectual union which is the perfection of a moral bond and a fellowship of interests.

There is sometimes a distinction made, in classing women, between *the useful woman, the agreeable woman, and the clever woman.* The useful woman understands business and the management of her house; the agreeable woman makes herself pleasant in society; the clever woman can both read and talk.

Well, I should say that a woman, to be what she ought, and to fulfill her mission, should combine these three things. United, they would make a harmonious being, that I should call *the distinguished* woman, that is to say, a woman capable of managing, understanding, and doing every thing in her family; a woman who can be pleasant without being flighty, careful of her dress without being frivolous; a woman who rules her life by submitting to its exigencies; who accepts the material part of it without neglecting it, but without allowing it to absorb her existence; and if I may be allowed the expression, makes it the pedestal of a higher state of being. Her soul gathers from noble sentiments and solid principles, courage enough for every form of devotedness; her intellect finds in the sense of the beautiful, in the intercourse of great minds, and the habit of serious thought, that elevated good sense which Joubert called *the exquisite form of good sense*, and which he wished to infuse into common sense, in order to render it more than ever the *primum mobile* of human life; the wise common sense which would be as solicitous about material as well as all other interests, and which, in that science of life which is above all other sciences, would know how to regulate all its elements, and give to every want of the mind and body, to every mental aspiration and every social relation, the part conformable to the order, the duty, and the dignity of the soul of man.

The best stimulant for women is the taste for the beautiful, which finds its own reward in the noble enjoyments it affords, in the dignity it imparts, and the assistance that it renders to its votaries. But, however this may be, the principle which, in our opinion, ought to predominate in the education of women is incontestable. If the qualities which ought to be combined in a woman are separated, what is the consequence? A useful managing woman, that is, a woman who is a pedant in her own way, tiresome, graceless, incapable of coping with any thing but material life: or a woman of outward show, a frivolous woman, reigning over dress, or rather allowing herself to be ruled by it; or, finally, a variety of the clever woman or of the woman of letters who, in order to mimic man, forgets the charms, the gifts, as well as the duties of her sex.

PURSUITS ALLOWABLE TO WOMEN.

The pursuits, even according to M. de Maistre, which are allowed to women are:

1. *The best Literature.* Serious and agreeable literature, which is a very wide field, and possesses both a substantial and a superficial charm. To speak only of *History*, the field is indeed an extensive one. It even comprehends a philosophy which their minds are perfectly capable of understanding, and the ideas of which—partaking at the very least of the nature of essential ideas—are necessary in order to fix their "mobile" minds, and to give them accuracy.

To teach a woman to reason aright, and consequently to put duty before every thing else, this is essentially educating her, in a way that is necessary for all classes and all conditions.

2. *The Arts;* which suit so well their imagination and the grace and delicacy of their natures. And here I can not help remarking, before I proceed, that the most dangerous of the arts is freely conceded to women, an art which is really the most incompatible of all with their duties and their vocation, while the pure and elevated regions of intelligence are considered not to be their province. Several men who depreciate women's esthetic writings and performances in art, would not on any account do away with female singers and tragic actresses. But the answer to this will be, that it is precisely because women artists degrade themselves more or less, that virtuous women can not be artists. Certainly, I quite agree, and even go farther than merely agreeing, but I can not help adding, that at least the fact is recognized, that women are capable of taking a high position in art, and that some among them have received the Divine gift. If they have received it, then it must be in order to make use of it, honestly and nobly, without doubt; but *to make use of it*. This very fact refutes the restriction.

3. *The Beautiful.* If a woman is able to express this, she is able to express it in all its diverse languages. Art is identical to itself in its principle, whatever mode of expression it adopts. Painting, music, poetry, eloquence; the beautiful expressed in language, the beautiful expressed in style, or by an inspired voice, is always the same beautiful which has taken a perceptible form to reveal itself to our souls through the medium of the senses. Every one can invest it with a form, which is, however, not a matter of choice. If you allow one form to women, and that form the most frivolous and the most dangerous of all forms, why forbid them the others? It is not because they lower themselves with the art which caters to *your* pleasures, that they are therefore unable to raise themselves with noble, honest, and serious art. If a woman can be a singer, she can also be a musician in the elevated sense of the word; she can also be a writer and a painter.

4. I have elsewhere said, how far, in my opinion, a woman can take up the sciences, and, indeed, study agriculture. This last operation has created some astonishment. I will only answer this by quoting some fragments of a letter that a very remarkable and a very sensible woman, who speaks of what she herself practices, wrote to me on this subject.

"How right you are, my Lord, to advise women to take their part in business, to learn to be serious, and even to study agriculture. I am an instance in point; for now that my sons are in the army, that I am separated from all my family, almost constantly alone with my husband, and always in the country, what would become of me, if my mother, from my infancy upward, had not given me the habit of interesting myself in every thing I saw and heard? Agriculture, with its hindrances and its progress, forms an inexhaustible source of conversation with my husband, with the priests, the village attorneys, the farmers, the country neighbors, the small town's people; a less exciting subject than politics, and which can be discussed with all of them according to their several capacities. My husband does not disdain to talk to me about manure, or alternation of crops; I have my theories about draining, beetroot, and colza, and he thinks me very advanced, perhaps too much so; nevertheless he never builds a ahead without consulting me; and before a lease is signed he always reads it over to me, two or three times over. I think it is very important for women and for their children that they should be initiated into business, and that they should know something about the employment of capital in the management of money; they ought not *to decide*, but *to listen and advise*. Most husbands like to talk over these matters openly, this subject being more interesting to them than any other. But in a general way they are not listened to, they are yawned at and not understood; so the husband becomes silent on the subject, takes the habit of managing alone, and following his own inclination, and there's an end. At the beginning of marriage, a young husband says every thing that a wife will condescend to listen to; later, he will think that she wishes to exercise some control over his affairs, and the more necessary her interference might be, the more wounded he would feel by it. Capacity, and some serious occupation, are necessary for women."

5. In one word, I wish women to be able to cultivate such and such an art or science, and even endeavor to attain rather an eminent proficiency in it, undisturbed in this very honorable pleasure without incurring the terrible anathema—and for the last time we will use this current and coarse expression —hurled against "blue-stockings." For, if there are women who, at the same time that they attend both seriously and thoroughly to the management of their house, raise themselves above purely material life by the love and the comprehension of the beautiful, endeavor to derive from it a refined enjoyment and pure emotions; who, in short, like to cultivate their mind, and are engrossed by all the interests of the good and the true, it is really odious to make this a matter of reproach.

6. I have also spoken elsewhere of the great use a woman would find in noting down from time to time and consecutively, as in a sort of private diary, her impressions and her reflections, at least on the important events of her life. But there is also another diary to be kept, besides this one, of the inner life of the soul, and the usually limited events of family life. A woman might keep a second journal, in which she might note down, not every day, (this would be too much,) but from time to time, some serious reflections or graver thoughts, a sort of journal in which she might write an analysis, or even a phrase of a discourse or of a conversation that had happened to strike her, an observation made on some journey or excursion, on some building, or in some gallery; and these are valuable recollections to fix, because they soon evaporate, and when they are thus fixed, they remain as a sort of triumphant acquisition for the mind. The habit is thus taken of intelligently seeing and listening, and of incorporating what one has seen and heard. As for "*the diary*," properly so-called, not written at all in a serious and Christian-like spirit, I own that this sort of diary would *rather* frighten me!

7. Above all, there is the study of religion. I have dilated very much on this subject in a former work: "*Letters to Men and Women of the World*," and I will only add one thing: It is above all in the higher classes, in which fortune authorizes what may be called the luxury of education, that religious instruction ought to be carried as far as the capabilities of a young man and woman will allow—doctrines, morality, the proofs of religion, the explanation of ceremonies, ecclesiastical history, works chosen from the early Fathers, great pulpit eloquence, lives of the saints, &c. &c. I have entered into detail about all this.

But above all, I should wish, that in the course of education, there should be an historical and progressive study on all that concerns religion. And besides, religious facts are intimately connected with the facts of modern history; a true idea of the latter can not be gained without a knowledge of the former.

A PLAN OF LIFE AND A METHODICAL ORDER.

Life is a serious thing, and it must not be given up to caprice or chance. Life is long, and during the succession of its years, and its diverse phases, it entails many duties; and together with these duties, heavy responsibilities. Life is sometimes hard to lead; we are not always young and smiling; trials, struggles, laborious exertions, crosses of all kinds, soon fall to our share, and they are the real essence of human existence, for amusement and pleasure are only its brilliant and deceiving surface.

Human life is complex, and it really includes three lives, each of which has its necessities, its labors, and its duties. There is the material life: it is lowest, but it must be thought of; then, in a higher region, there is intellectual life—woe to those who despise it; and finally, rising and towering above the two others, there is the spiritual life, for "man is not made for bread alone," but for eternity. There is the life of the body, the life of the mind, and the religious life of the soul.

The guidance and responsibilities of life assume gigantic proportions, when one begins to enter personally into existence, and assume control both of self, and of one other existence, and possibly of many other existences which are to arise from this God-ordained union. Have you thought of these duties and responsibilities? There are the conventional duties of society. There are the duties of your position—your special work. There is a house to be kept up, a fortune to be acquired, or to be attended to, and the current expenses to be balanced by your income. There is, if you wish to be somebody, and something, your individual life, your pursuits, your particular studies. There are also the claims of charity and of good works. And finally, as you have a soul, an immortal and a celestial destiny, there is, supposing you are Christians, the care of the soul, and your duties toward God. In short, duties and obligations of all kinds surround you. And no one has the right to tear asunder these united existences or to disregard their diverse and associated responsibilities, and they can not be regulated and discharged without reflection, forethought and plan.

It is beforehand, and from the beginning of their marriage, that the husband and wife ought to consult together about the plan of their future life, and this plan ought to be a wide and a serious one, which embraces the whole of existence. The duties of each, the profession and the position of the head of the family in his country; the children, their future and social relations; individual life; middle age, old age, and death; in one word, real existence, with its great features and its great phases: and it is to these great features, that all their actions, at the very first and from the earliest beginning, must be attuned in perfect harmony. In this way only, can a man show himself worthy of the authority and the dignity he has received from God. In this way only, can a woman make sure of the goodness and the unity of her life, and avoid the sad want of harmony that must arise in an existence which has never been subject to rule, between her youth and her old age.

Whilst, on the contrary, if life is well regulated, there can be a wonderful agreement between the different ages that God has decreed that she shall pass through, and that she ought to be prepared to meet one after the other; shedding a charm and a general atmosphere of goodness around her.

It has even been observed among women whose lives have thus been spent in regularity and virtue, that when the fugitive beauty of youth is past, there remains a certain pure and superior beauty, which arises from the serenity and peace engendered in the mind by the happy harmony of their lives, and the constant and intelligent devotion to their duties. Then, as it happens to a well-built edifice, years pass over it; but far from their weight overwhelming it, they only add to its firmness and its beauty. And, if its rude breath sometimes carries away a delicate tracery, the building is not shaken, it is but touched by the storm, and the noble and beautiful harmony of its great features remains unscathed.

I do not pretend to say, that in the plan of life, however well it may have been laid out, one is able to foresee and to master all possible events; I only say, that a plan, and a plan alone, can introduce unity, harmony, and real beauty—which is the beauty of the whole—into a human existence.

The plan of life shows the aim to be attained, the methodical order gives the means of attaining it. The plan of life is the conception, the ideal, the theory: the methodical order is the daily and incessant practice of it. The first is the attainment of that supreme art which I should like to call the secret of life, that is to say, *the secret of conciliation*. In fact, do not duties, affections, and tastes often seem to contradict each other?

I know that a great deal of firmness, gentleness, and perseverance is necessary in order to gain one's liberty, to make one's hours of occupation respected, without neglecting at the same time any duty; in short, to give oneself up, and to keep oneself back at the right moment. It is a question of method and of order, like most questions of daily conduct. In order to have courage enough for this contest, women must be well convinced of its justice. But they are too much afraid of only consulting a taste, when, on the contrary, it is a *duty*, not to leave the powers of their mind uncultivated; yes, both a pleasant task *and a duty*.

Study makes women like their homes, where they are always called back by the love of some pursuit they have in hand. How little they then want the excitement of visiting and the whirl of the world! What a pleasure they find in getting back to their room, their books, and their drawing! How quickly and lightly they walk, in order to get home! And how a love for study occupies all the place in the heart and life, usually taken up by the unbridled and ruinous taste for dress and luxury! Another great art, that will be shown by a good method, is what I shall call, the *art of utilizing lost moments*.

They will get up,* but health will interfere; the husband will come in, and

---

* Let those who like to sleep longer than they ought, and have not the courage to accustom themselves to the easy effort necessary to make early rising so little an exertion, allow me to quote those beautiful verses of Dante. Dante had just sat down, being quite exhausted, and Virgil reanimates his failing courage by this vigorous exhortation:

"You must arise at once. Fame is not to be attained on a feathery couch;

"And he who does not spend his life in the pursuit of Fame, will leave no more trace upon earth than the smoke in the air or the foam on the wave;

"Then arise; conquer yourself by that force of mind which can conquer in every contest, if it does not allow itself to be overcome by the weighty body."

DANTE, *Inferno*, Canto 24.

talk over business, plans, &c.; the workmen, the children, small and great, will invade the room; a mother of a family has no hour to shut herself up, and to prevent any access to her.

How many women, and even girls, spend their lives under the yoke of these really tyrannical habits. And it is so much the more difficult to break through them, as they are called by the name of devotedness and family virtues. If you say to these girls, "crushed, flattened," according to M. de Maistre's expression, "by the enormous weight of nothing:" "Make an individual life for yourselves, withdraw for a few moments;" they answer—"But I can not. I haven't a minute I can call my own. If I leave the drawing-room, my room is invaded, there is 'just one word' to be said, and one has to stand for a quarter of an hour; and after that one sits down, another person comes in, and time is thus swallowed up; so that, notwithstanding all my patient efforts, I am unable to hide my annoyance sufficiently not to be considered as a rigid person and as a woman *who is full of occupations*"—a term synonymous with a blue-stocking!

Well, my answer to this is, that in the absence of regular hours, if there are really none at her disposal, let a woman devote her lost moments to study; there are always some in the best employed lives. One has at least, almost every day, disengaged moments several times in the course of the twenty-four hours; and a woman thus placed must accustom herself to study at odd times. When one knows how to profit by the least portions of time, one works wonders. The Chancellor d'Aguesseau used to say, "These are the volumes I have written during the five minutes of each day for the last twenty years, that Madame d'Aguesseau has been too late for dinner."

The women who are the most cheerful, the most even-tempered, the most ready to do a service, and I will add, the most healthy, are intelligent and industrious women, who have found in a methodical activity the secret of never losing a moment, and of thus conciliating their duties towards God, towards their families, towards the world, and towards themselves.

It is impossible for a woman—no less than for a man—to do any thing really serious, if she *goes into the world every day*, and keeps late hours at night and gets up late in the morning. It is the death of intellectual life; too many hours are given to the world in the evening, and to visits paid or received in the day-time. And what is most favorable to intellectual pursuits is a methodical arrangement of the day, is to devote *the morning hours* to them. I can quote here a great example, that of the illustrious Madame Swetchine, and I find in her life the following passage: "Madame Swetchine had strongly exhorted me to reserve myself, at all times, some hours of entire liberty every morning. 'Time is different,' she used to say, 'in the morning, to what it is at any other hour of the day.' And it was not only in order to consecrate to God the first hours of the day, that she began it so early, but also to have a considerable time to devote to study. She told me, that the pleasure she derived from study only increased with her years. 'It has reached such a point,' she added, 'that when I approach my table, in order to set to my beloved occupations, my heart beats with joy.'"

I will just add the following advice to that given by Madame Swetchine: "Examine, set in order, and resolve upon your morrow's work; the evening before, arrange the matters in hand relatively to their importance, and act accordingly. You will thus learn the secret quickly of finding time for study and for every thing else."

The success of Pastor Fliedner's "*Diaconissen Anstalt*," at Kaiserswerth, has led to the establishment of fifteen similar institutions for training of Protestant nurses and teachers, on the continent; and in England, the popular acknowledgment for the services of Miss Nightingale and her associates, has been expended in founding a hospital which is to become a Training Institution for similar purposes. In furtherance of the general object of widening the sphere of woman's benevolent activity, Mrs. Jameson has published two lectures, delivered by her privately in London, the first entitled, "*Sisters of Charity, Catholic and Protestant, Abroad and At Home*," on the 14th of February, 1855, and the other, "*Communion in Labor, or the Social Employment of Women*," on the 28th of June, 1856. These lectures are valuable contributions to the educational literature of the English language, and, in the absence of any American edition, we give copious extracts.

SOCIAL POSITION AND EMPLOYMENT OF WOMEN.

There are many different theories concerning the moral purposes of this world in which we dwell, considered, I mean, in reference to us, its human inhabitants; for some regard it merely as a state of transition between two conditions of existence, a past and a future; others as being worthless in itself, except as a probation or preparation for a better and a higher life; while others, absorbed or saddened by the monstrous evils and sorrows around them, have really come to regard it as a place of punishment or penance for sins committed in a former state of existence. But I think that the best definition — the best, at least, for our present purpose — is that of Shakspeare: he calls it, with his usual felicity of expression, "*this working-day world;*" and it is truly this; it is a place in which work is to be done — work which *must* be done — work which it is *good* to do; — a place in which labor of one kind or another is at once the condition of existence, and the condition of happiness.

Well, then, in this working-day world of ours we must all work. The only question is, what shall we do? To few is it granted to choose their work. Indeed, all work worth the doing seems to leave us no choice. We are called to it. Sometimes the voice so calling is from within, sometimes from without; but in any case it is what we term expressively our *vocation*, and in either case the harmony and happiness of life in man or woman consists in finding in our vocation the employment of our highest faculties, and of as many of them as can be brought into action.

And work is of various kinds; there are works of necessity, and works of mercy; — *head* work, *hand* work; — man's work, woman's work; — and, upon the distribution of this work in accordance with the divine law, and what Milton calls the faultless proprieties of nature, depends the well-being of the whole community, not less than that of each individual.

Domestic life, the acknowledged foundation of all social life, has settled by a natural law the work of the man, and the work of the woman. The man governs, sustains, and defends the family; the woman cherishes, regulates, and purifies it; but, though distinct, the relative work is inseparable, — sometimes exchanged, sometimes shared; so that, from the beginning, we have, even in the primitive household, not the *division*, but the *communion* of labor.

If domestic life be then the foundation and the bond of all social communities, does it not seem clear that there must exist between man and woman, even from the beginning, the communion of love, and the communion of labor? By the first I understand all the benevolent affections and their results, and all the binding charities of life, extended from the home into the more ample social relations; and in the latter I comprehend all the active duties, all intellectual exercise of the faculties, also extended from the central home into the larger social circle. When from the cross those memorable words were uttered by our Lord, "*Behold thy Mother! Behold thy Son!*" do you think they were addressed only to the two desolate mourners who then and there wept at his feet? No — they were spoken, like all his words, to the wide universe, to all humanity, to all time!

I rest, therefore, all I have to say hereafter upon what I conceive to be a great vital truth, — an unchangeable, indisputable, natural law. And it is this: that men and women are, by nature, mutually dependent, mutually helpful; that this communion exists not merely in one or two relations, which custom may define and authorize, and to which opinion may restrict them in this or that class, in this or that position; but must extend to every possible relation in existence in which the two sexes can be socially approximated. Thus, for instance, a man, in the first place, merely sustains and defends his home; then he works to sustain and defend the community or the nation he belongs to: and so of woman. She begins by being the nurse, the teacher, the cherisher of her home through her greater tenderness and purer moral sentiments; then she uses these qualities and sympathies on a larger scale, to cherish and purify society. But still the man and the woman must continue to share the work; there must be the communion of labor in the large human family just as there was within the narrower precincts of home.

The great mistake seems to have been that in all our legislation it *is* taken for granted that the woman is always protected, always under tutelage, always within the precincts of a home; finding there her work, her interests, her duties, and her happiness; but is this true? We know that it is altogether false. There are thousands and thousands of women who have no protection, no guide, no help, no home; — who are absolutely driven by circumstance and necessity, if not by impulse and inclination, to carry out into the larger community the sympathies, the domestic instincts, the active administrative capabilities, with which God has endowed them; but these instincts, sympathies, capabilities, require, first, to be properly developed, then properly trained, and then directed into large and useful channels, according to the individual tendencies.

As to the want, what I insist on particularly is, that the means do not exist for the training of those powers; that the sphere of duties which should occupy them is not acknowledged; and I must express my deep conviction that society is suffering in its depths through this great mistake, and this great want.

We require in our country the recognition, — the public recognition, — by law as well as by opinion, of the woman's privilege to share in the communion of labor at her own free choice, and the foundation of institutions which shall train her to do her work well.

Mrs. Jameson proceeds to illustrate her position by certain facts drawn from her observation and study of the administration of various public institutions at home and abroad.

HOSPITALS.

What is the purpose of a great hospital? Ask a physician or a surgeon, zealous in his profession: he will probably answer that a great hospital is a great medical school, in which the art of healing is scientifically and experimentally taught; where the human sufferers who crowd those long vistas of beds are not men and women, but "cases" to be studied: and so under one aspect it ought to be, and must be. A great, well-ordered medical school is absolutely necessary; and to be able to regard the various aspects of disease with calm discrimination, the too sensitive human sympathies must be set aside. Therefore much need is there here of all the masculine firmness of nerve and strength of understanding. But surely a great hospital has another purpose, that for which it was originally founded and endowed, namely, as a refuge and solace for disease and suffering. Here are congregated in terrible reality all the ills enumerated in Milton's visionary lazar-house:

> "All maladies
> Of ghastly spasm or racking torture, qualms
> Of heart-sick agony, wide-wasting pestilence"—

I spare you the rest of the horrible catalogue. He goes on:

> "Dire was the tossing, deep the groans; despair
> Tended the sick, busiest from couch to couch."

But why must despair tend the sick? We can imagine a far different influence "busiest from couch to couch"!

There is a passage in Tennyson's poems, written long before the days of Florence Nightingale, which proves that poets have been rightly called prophets, and see "the thing that shall be as the thing that is." I will repeat the passage. He is describing the wounded warriors nursed and tended by the learned ladies:

> "A kindlier influence reigned, and everywhere
> Low voices with the ministering hand
> Hung round the sick. The maidens came, they talked,
> They sang, they read, till she, not fair, began
> To gather light, and she that was, became
> Her former beauty treble; to and fro,
> Like creatures native unto gracious act,
> And in their own clear element they moved."

This you will say is the poetical aspect of the scene: was it not poetical, too, when the poor soldier said that the very shadow of Florence Nightingale passing over his bed seemed to do him good?

Paula, a noble Roman lady, a lineal descendant of the Scipios and the Gracchi, is mentioned among the first Christian women remarkable for their active benevolence. In the year 385 she quitted Rome, then still a Pagan city; with the remains of a large fortune, which had been expended in aiding and instructing a wretched and demoralized people, and, accompanied by her daughter, she sailed for Palestine, and took up her residence in Bethlehem of Judea. There, as the story relates, she assembled round her a community of women "as well of noble estate as of middle and low lineage." They took no vows, they made no profession, but spent their days in prayer and good works, having especially a well-ordered hospital for the sick.

In the old English translation of her life there is a picture of this charitable lady which I cannot refrain from quoting: "She was marvellous debonair, and piteous to them that were sick, and comforted them, and served them right humbly; and gave them largely to eat such as they asked; but to herself she was hard in her sickness and scarce, for she refused to eat flesh how well she gave it to others, and also to drink wine. She was oft by them that were sick, and she laid the pillows aright and in point; and she rubbed their feet, and boiled water to wash them; and it seemed to her that the less she did to the sick in service, so much the less service did she to God, and deserved the less mercy; therefore she was to them piteous and nothing to herself."

It is in the seventh century that we find these communities of charitable women first mentioned under a particular appellation. We read in history that when Landry, Bishop of Paris, about the year 660, founded an hospital, since known as the Hotel-Dieu, as a general refuge for disease and misery, he placed it under the direction of the *Hospitalières*, or nursing-sisters of that time, — women whose services are understood to have been voluntary, and undertaken from motives of piety. Innocent IV., who would not allow of any outlying religious societies, collected and united these hospital-sisters under the rule of the Augustine Order, making them amenable to the government and discipline of the church. The noviciate or training of a *Sœur Hospitalière* was of twelve years' duration, after which she was allowed to make her profession. At that time, and even earlier, we find many hospitals expressly founded for the reception of the sick pilgrims and wounded soldiers returning from the East, and bringing with them strange and hitherto unknown forms of disease and suffering. Some of the largest hospitals in France and the Netherlands originated in this purpose, and were all served by the Hospitalières; and to this day the Hotel Dieu, with its one thousand beds, the hospital of St. Louis, with its seven hundred beds, and that of *La Pitié*, with its six hundred beds, are served by the same sisterhood, under whose care they were originally placed centuries ago.

For about five hundred years the institution of the *Dames* or *Sœurs Hospitalières* remained the only one of its kind. During this period it had greatly increased its numbers, and extended all through western Christendom; still it did not suffice for the wants of the age; and the thirteenth century, fruitful in all those results which a combination of wide-spread suffering and religious ferment naturally produces, saw the rise of another community of compassionate women destined to exercise a far wider influence. These were the *Sœurs Grises*, or Grey Sisters, so called at first, from the original color of their dress. Their origin was this: The Franciscans (and other regular orders) admitted into their community a third or secular class, who did not seclude themselves in cloisters, who took no vows of celibacy, but were simply bound to submit to certain rules and regulations, and united together in works of charity, devoting themselves to visiting the sick in the hospitals, or at their own homes, and doing good wherever and whenever called upon. Women of all classes were enrolled in this sisterhood. Queens, princesses, ladies of rank, wives of burghers, as well as poor widows and maidens. The higher class and the married women occasionally served; the widows and unmarried devoted themselves almost entirely to the duties of nursing the sick in the hospitals. Gradually it became a vocation apart, and a novitiate or training of from one to three years was required to fit them for their profession.

The origin of the Béguines, so well known in Flanders, is uncertain; but they seem to have existed as hospital sisters in the seventh century, and to have been settled in communities at Liege and elsewhere in 1173. They wear a particular dress (the black gown, and white hood), but take no vows, and may leave the community at any time, — a thing which rarely happens.

No one who has travelled in Flanders, visited Ghent, Bruges, Brussels, or indeed any of the Netherlandish towns, will forget the singular appearance of these, sometimes young and handsome, but always staid, respectable-looking women, walking about, protected by the universal reverence of the people, and busied in their compassionate vocation. In their few moments of leisure the Béguines are allowed to make lace and cultivate flowers, and they act under a strict self-constituted government, maintained by strict traditional forms. All the hospitals in Flanders are served by these Béguines. They have besides, attached to their houses, hospitals of their own, with a medical staff of physicians and surgeons, under whose direction, in all cases of difficulty, the sisters administer relief; and, of the humility, skill, and tenderness, with which they do administer it, I have never heard but one opinion;* nor did I ever meet with any one who had travelled in those countries who did not wish that some system of the kind could be transferred to England.

In the fifteenth century (about 1443), when Flanders was under the dominion of the Dukes of Burgundy, a few of the Béguines were summoned from Bruges to Beaune to take charge of the great hospital founded there by Rollin, the Chancellor of Philip the Good. They were soon joined by others from the neighboring districts, and this community of nurses obtained the name *Sœurs de Ste. Marthe*, Sisters of St. Martha. It is worth notice that Martha, who is represented in Scripture as troubled about household cares, while her sister Mary "sat at the feet of Jesus, and heard his words," was early chosen as the patroness of those who, instead of devoting themselves to a cloistered life of prayer and contemplation, were bound by a religious obligation to active secular duties. The hospital of Beaune, one of the most extensive and best managed in France, is still served by these sisters. Many hospitals in the South of France, and three at Paris, are served by the same community.

In Germany, the Sisters of Charity are styled "Sisters of St. Elizabeth," in honor of that benevolent enthusiast, Elizabeth of Hungary, whose pathetic story and beautiful legend has been rendered familiar to us by Mr. Kingsley's drama. When Joseph II. suppressed the nunneries throughout Austria and Flanders, the Elizabethan Sisters, as well as the Béguines, were excepted by an especial

* Howard mentions them with due praise, as serving in their hospital at Bruges: "There are twenty of them; they look very healthy; they rise at four, and are constantly employed about their numerous patients." "They prepare as well as administer the medicines. The Directress of the Pharmacy last year celebrated her jubilee or fiftieth year of her residence in the hospital." (P. 149.)

A recent traveller mentions their hospital of St. John at Bruges as one of the best conducted he had ever met with: "Its attendants, in their religious costume, and with their snow-white head-dresses, moving about with a quiet tenderness and solicitude, worthy their name as 'Sisters of Charity;' and the lofty wards, with the white linen of the beds, present in every particular an example of the most accurate neatness and cleanliness."

denres, "because of the usefulness of their vocation." At Vienna, a few years ago, I had the opportunity, through the kindness of a distinguished physician, of visiting one of the houses of these Elizabethan Sisters. There was an hospital attached to it of fifty beds, which had received about four hundred and fifty patients during the year. Nothing could exceed the propriety, order, and cleanliness, of the whole establishment. On the ground-floor was an extensive "Pharmacie," a sort of Apothecaries' Hall; part of this was divided off by a long table or counter, and surrounded by shelves filled with drugs, much like an apothecary's shop; behind the counter two Sisters, with their sleeves tucked up, were busy weighing and compounding medicines, with such a delicacy, neatness, and exactitude, as women use in these matters. On the outside of this counter, seated on benches, or standing, were a number of sick and infirm, pale, dirty, ragged patients; and among them moved two other Sisters, speaking to each individually in a low, gentle voice, and with a quiet authority of manner, that in itself had something tranquillizing. A physician and surgeon, appointed by the government, visited this hospital, and were resorted to in cases of difficulty, or where operations were necessary. Here was another instance in which men and women worked together harmoniously and efficiently. Howard, in describing the principal hospital at Lyons, which he praises for its excellent and kindly management, as being "so clean and so quiet," tells us that at that time (1776), he found it attended by nine physicians and surgeons, and managed by twelve Sisters of Charity. "There were Sisters who made up, as well as administered, all the medicines prescribed; for which purpose there was a laboratory and apothecary's shop, the neatest and most elegantly fitted up that can be conceived."*

It can easily be imagined that institutions like these, composed of such various ingredients, spread over such various countries, and over several centuries of time, should have been subject to the influences of time; though from a deep-seated principle of vitality and necessity they seem to have escaped its vicissitudes, for they did not change in character or purpose, far less perish. That in ages of superstition they should have been superstitious, that in ages of ignorance they should have been ignorant, — debased in evil selfish times, by some alloy of selfishness and cupidity, — in all this there is nothing to surprise us; but one thing does seem remarkable. While the men who professed the healing art were generally astrologers and alchymists, dealing in charms and nativities, — lost in dreams of the Elixir Vitæ and the Philosopher's Stone, and in such mummeries and quackeries as made them favorite subjects for comedy and satire, — these simple Sisters, in their hospitals, were accumulating a vast fund of practical and traditional knowledge in the treatment of disease, and the uses of various remedies; — knowledge which was turned to account and condensed into rational theory and sound method, when in the sixteenth century Surgery and Medicine first rose to the rank of experimental sciences, and were studied as such. The poor Hospitalières knew nothing of Galen and Hippocrates, but they could observe, if they could not describe, and prescribe, if they could not demonstrate. Still, in the course of time great abuses had certainly crept into these religious societies, — not so bad or so flagrant, perhaps, as those which

* Howard also mentions the hospitals belonging to the order of Charity, in all countries, as the best regulated, the cleanest, the most tenderly served and managed, of all he had met with. (In 1778.)

disgraced within a recent period many of our own incorporated charities, — but bad enough, and vitiating, if not destroying their power to do good. The funds were sometimes misappropriated, the novices ill-trained for their work, the superiors careless, the sisters mutinous, the treatment of the sick remained rude and empirical. Women of sense and feeling, who wished to enrol themselves in these communities, were shocked and discouraged by such a state of things. A reform became absolutely necessary.

This was brought about, and very effectually, about the middle of the seventeenth century.

Louise de Marillac — better known as Madame Legras, when left a widow in the prime of life, could find, like Angela da Brescia, no better refuge from sorrow than in active duties, undertaken "for the love of God." She desired to join the Hospitalières, and was met at the outset by difficulties, and even horrors, which would have extinguished a less ardent vocation, a less determined will. She set herself to remedy the evils, instead of shrinking from them. She was assisted and encouraged in her good work by a man endued with great ability and piety, enthusiasm equal, and moral influence even superior, to her own. This was the famous Vincent de Paul, who had been occupied for years with a scheme to reform thoroughly the prisons and the hospitals of France. In Madame Legras he found a most efficient coadjutor. With her charitable impulses and religious enthusiasm, she united qualities not always, not often, found in union with them: a calm and patient temperament, and that administrative faculty, indispensable in those who are called to such privileged work. She was particularly distinguished by a power of selecting and preparing the instruments, and combining the means, through which she was to carry out her admirable purpose. With Vincent de Paul and Madame Legras was associated another person, Madame Goussaut, who besieged the Archbishop of Paris till what was refused to reason was granted to importunity, and they were permitted to introduce various improvements into the administration of the hospitals. Vincent de Paul and Louise Legras succeeded at last in constituting, not on a new, but on a renovated basis, the order of Hospitalières, since known as the Sisterhood of Charity. A lower class of sisters were trained to act under the direction of the more intelligent and educated women. Within twenty years this new community had two hundred houses and hospitals; in a few years more it had spread over all Europe. Madame Legras died in 1660. Already before her death the women prepared and trained under her instructions, and under the direction of Vincent de Paul (and here we have another instance of the successful communion of labor), had proved their efficiency on some extraordinary occasions. In the campaigns of 1652 and 1658 they were sent to the field of battle, in groups of two and four together, to assist the wounded. They were invited into the besieged towns to take charge of the military hospitals. They were particularly conspicuous at the siege of Dunkirk, and in the military hospitals established by Anne of Austria at Fontainebleau. When the plague broke out in Poland in 1672, they were sent to direct the hospitals at Warsaw, and to take charge of the orphans, and were thus introduced into Eastern Europe; and, stranger than all, they were even sent to the prison-infirmaries where the branded *forçats* and condemned felons lay cursing and writhing in their fetters. This was a mission for Sisters of Charity which may startle the refined, or confined, notions of Englishwomen in the nineteenth century. It is not, I believe, generally known in this country that the same experiment has been lately tried, and with success, in the prisons of Piedmont, where the Sisters were first employed to nurse the wretched criminals perishing with disease and despair; afterwards, and during convalescence, to read to them, to teach them to read and to knit, and in some cases to sing. The hardest of these wretches had probably some remembrance of a mother's voice and look thus recalled, or he could at least feel gratitude for sympathy from a purer, higher nature. As an element of reformation, I might almost say of regeneration, this use of the feminine influence has been found efficient where all other means had failed.

At the commencement of the French Revolution the Sisterhood of Charity had four hundred and twenty-six houses in France, and many more in other countries; the whole number of women then actively employed was about six thousand. During the Reign of Terror, the superior (Mdlle. Duleau), who had become a Sister of Charity at the age of nineteen, and was now sixty, endeavored to keep the society together, although suppressed by the government; and, in the midst of the horrors of that time — when so many nuns and ecclesiastics perished miserably — it appears that the feeling of the people protected these women, and I do not learn that any of them suffered public or personal outrage. As soon as the Consular government was established, the indispensable Sisterhood was recalled by a decree of the Minister of the Interior.

I cannot resist giving you a few passages from the preamble to this edict, — certainly very striking and significant, — as I find it quoted in a little book on "Hospitals and Sisterhoods" now before me. It begins thus:

"Seeing that the services rendered to the sick can only be properly administered by those whose vocation it is, and who do it in the spirit of love; —

"Seeing, further, that, among the hospitals of the Republic, those are in all ways best served wherein the female attendants have adhered to the noble example of their predecessors, whose only object was to practise a boundless love and charity; —

"Seeing that the members still existing of this society are now growing old, so that there is reason to fear that an order which is a glory to the country may shortly become extinct; —

"It is decreed that the Citoyenne Duleau, formerly Superior of the Sisters of Charity, is authorized to educate girls for the care of the hospitals," &c.

Previous to the Revolution, the chief military hospitals, and the naval hospitals at Brest, Saint-Malo, and Cherbourg, had been placed under the management of the Sisters of Charity. During the Reign of Terror, those Sisters who refused to quit their habit and religious bond were expelled; but, as soon as order was restored, they were recalled by the naval and military authorities, and returned to their respective hospitals, where their reäppearance was hailed with rejoicing, and even with tears. At present the naval hospitals at Toulon and Marseilles, in addition to those I have mentioned, are served by these women, acting *with*, as well as *under*, authority.

The whole number of women included in these charitable orders was, in the year 1848, at least twelve thousand. They seem to have a quite marvellous ubiquity. I have myself met with them not only at Paris, Vienna, Milan, Turin, Genoa, but at Montreal, Quebec, and Detroit; on the confines of civilization; in Ireland, where cholera and famine were raging. Everywhere, from the uniform dress, and a certain similarity in the placid expression, and quiet deportment, looking so like each other, that they seemed, wherever I met them, to be but a multiplication of one and the same person. In all the well-trained Sisters of Charity I have known, whether Protestant or Roman Catholic, I have found a mingled bravery and tenderness, if not by nature, by habit; and a certain tranquil self-complacency, arising, not from self-applause, but out of that very abnegation of self which had been adopted as the rule of life.

The Paris hospitals are so admirably organized by the religious women, who, in almost every instance, share in the administration so far as regards the care of the sick, that I have often been surprised that hitherto the numbers of our medical men who have studied at Paris have not made any attempts to introduce a better system of female nursing into the hospitals at home. But they appear to have regarded everything of the kind with despair or indifference.

In my former lecture, I mentioned several of the most famous of these hospitals. During my last visit to Paris, I visited an hospital which I had not before seen, — the hospital Lariboisière, — which appeared to me a model of all that a civil hospital ought to be, — clean, airy, light, and lofty; above all, cheerful. I should observe that generally, in the hospitals served by Sisters of Charity, there is ever an air of cheerfulness caused by their own sweetness of temper and voluntary devotion to their work. At the time that I visited this hospital, it contained six hundred and twelve patients, three hundred men and three hundred and twelve women, in two ranges of building divided by a very pretty garden. The whole interior management is entrusted to twenty-five trained Sisters of the same Order as those who serve the Hôtel-Dieu. There are besides about forty servants, men and women, — men to do the rough work, and male nurses to assist in the men's wards under the superintendence of the Sisters. There are three physicians and two surgeons in constant attendance, a steward or comptroller of accounts, and other officers. To complete this picture, I must add that the hospital Lariboisière was founded by a lady, a rich heiress, a married lady, too, whose husband, after her death, carried out her intentions to the utmost with zeal and fidelity. She had the assistance of the best architects in France to plan her building; medical and scientific men had aided her with their counsels. What the feminine instinct of compassion had conceived, was by the manly intellect planned and ordered, and again by female aid administered. In all its arrangements this hospital appeared to me a perfect example of the combined working of men and women.

In contrast with this splendid foundation, I will mention another not less admirable in its way.

When I was at Vienna, I saw a small hospital, belonging to the Sisters of Charity there. The beginning had been very modest, two of the Sisters having settled in a small old house. Several of the adjoining buildings were added one after the other, connected by wooden corridors: the only new part which had any appearance of being adapted to its purpose, was the infirmary, in which were fifty-two patients, — twenty-six men and twenty-six women, — besides nine beds for cholera. There were fifty Sisters, of whom one half were employed in the house, and the other half were going their rounds amongst the poor, or nursing the sick in private houses. There was a nursery for infants, whose mothers were at work; a day-school for one hundred and fifty girls, in which only knitting and sewing were taught; all clean, orderly, and, above all, cheerful. There was a dispensary, where two of the Sisters were employed in making up prescriptions, homœopathic and allopathic. There was a large, airy kitchen, where three of the Sisters, with two assistants, were cooking. There were two priests and two physicians. So that, in fact, under this roof we had the elements, on a small scale, of an English workhouse; but very different was the spirit which animated it.

I saw at Vienna another excellent hospital, for women alone, of which the whole administration and support rested with the ladies of the Order of St. Elizabeth. These are *cloistered*, that is, not allowed to go out of their house to nurse the sick and poor; nor have they any schools; but all sick women who apply for admission are taken in without any questions asked, so long as there is room for them — cases of childbirth excepted. At the time I visited this hospital, it contained ninety-two patients; about twenty were cases of cholera. There were sixteen beds in each ward, over which two Sisters presided. The dispensary, which was excellently arranged, was entirely managed by two of the ladies. The Superior told me that they have always three or more Sisters preparing for their profession under the best apothecaries; and there was a large garden, principally of medicinal and kitchen herbs. Nothing could exceed the purity of the air, and the cleanliness, order, and quiet, everywhere apparent.

In the great civil hospital at Vienna, one of the largest I have ever seen, — larger, even, than the *Hôtel-Dieu*, at Paris, — I found that the Sisters of Charity were about to be introduced. One of my friends there, a distinguished naturalist and philosopher, as well as physician, told me that the disorderly habits and the want of intelligence in the paid female nurses, had induced him to join with his colleagues in inviting the coöperation of the religious Sisters, though it was at first rather against their will. In the hospital of St. John, at Salzburg, the same change had been found necessary.

The hospital of St. John, at Vercelli, which I had the opportunity of inspecting minutely, left a strong impression on my mind. At the time I visited it, it contained nearly four hundred patients. There was, besides, in an adjacent building, a school and hospital for poor children. The whole interior economy of these two hospitals was under the management of eighteen women, with a staff of assistants both male and female. The Superior, a very handsome, intelligent woman, had been trained at Paris, and had presided over this provincial hospital for eleven years. There was the same cheerfulness which I have had occasion to remark in all institutions where the religious and feminine elements were allowed to influence the material administration; and everything was exquisitely clean, airy, and comfortable. In this instance, the dispensary (*Pharmacie*) was managed by apothecaries, and not by the women.

Now, in contrast with this hospital, I will describe a famous hospital at Turin. It is a recent building, with all the latest improvements, and considered, in respect to fitness for its purpose, as a *chef-d'œuvre* of architecture. The contrivances and material appliances for the sick and convalescent were exhibited to me as the wonder and boast of the city; certainly they were most ingenious. The management was in the hands of a committee of gentlemen; under them a numerous staff of priests and physicians. Two or three female servants of the lowest class were sweeping and cleaning. In the convalescent wards I saw a great deal of card-playing. All was formal, cold, clean, and silent; no cheerful kindly faces, no soft low voices, no light active figures, were hovering round. I left the place with a melancholy feeling, shared, as I found, by those who were with me. One of them, an accomplished physician, felt and candidly acknowledged the want of female influence here.

One of the directors of the great military hospital at Turin told me that he regarded it as one of the best deeds of his life, that he had recommended and carried through the employment of the Sisters of Charity in this institution. Before the introduction of these ladies, the sick soldiers had been nursed by orderlies sent from the neighboring barracks — men chosen because they were unfit for other work. The most rigid discipline was necessary to keep them in order; and the dirt, neglect, and general immorality, were frightful. Any change was, however, resisted by the military and medical authorities, till the invasion of the cholera; then the orderlies became, most of them, useless, distracted, and almost paralyzed with terror. Some devoted Sisters of Charity were introduced in a moment of perplexity and panic; then all went well — propriety, cleanliness, and comfort prevailed. "No day passes," said my informant, "that I do not bless God for the change which I was the humble instrument of accomplishing in this place!"

Very similar was the information I received relative to the naval hospital at Genoa; but I had not the opportunity of visiting it.

Another excellent hospital at Turin, that of St. John, contained, when I visited it, four hundred patients, a nearly equal number of men and women. There were, besides, a separate ward for sick children, and two wards containing about sixty "incurables" — the bedridden and helpless poor, of the same class which find refuge in our workhouses. The whole of this large establishment was under the management of twenty-two religious women, with a staff of about forty-five assistants, men and women, and a large number of medical men and students. All was clean, and neat, and cheerful. I was particularly struck by the neatness with which the food was served; men brought it up in large trays, but the ladies themselves distributed it. Some friends of the poor sick were near the beds. I remember being touched by the sight of a little dog, which, with its fore paws resting on the bed, and a pathetic, wistful expression in its drooping face, kept its eyes steadfastly fixed on the sick man; a girl was kneeling beside him, to whom one of the Sisters was speaking words of comfort.

In this hospital and others I found an excellent arrangement for the night-watch. It was a large sentry-box, of an octagon-shape, looking each way, the upper part all of glass, but furnished with curtains; and on a kind of dresser or table were arranged writing materials, all kinds of medicine and restoratives which might be required in haste, and a supply of linen, napkins, etc. Here two sisters watched all night long; here the accounts were kept and the private business of the wards carried on in the daytime. A certain degree of privacy was thus secured for the ladies on duty when necessary. The Superior, whom we should call the matron, was an elderly woman, wearing the same simple, convenient religious dress as the others, and only recognized by the large bunch of keys at her girdle.

The Marchese A——, one of the governors of the *Hospice de la Maternité*, described to me in terms of horror the state in which he had found the establishment when under the management of a board of governors who employed hired matrons and nurses. At last, in despair, he sent for some trained Sisters, ten of whom, with a Superior, now directed the whole in that spirit of order, cheerfulness, and unremitting attention, which belongs to them. The Marchese particularly dwelt on their economy. "We cannot," said he, "give them unlimited means (*des fonds à discrétion*), for these good ladies think that all should go to the poor; but if we allow them a fixed sum, we find that they can do more with that sum than we could have believed possible, and they never go beyond it; they are admirable accountants and economists."

LUNATIC ASYLUMS.

With regard to the employment of women in the lunatic asylums, I can only say that I have the testimony of men of large experience that feminine aid, influence, presence, would in many cases be most beneficial in the male wards.* Of course there are certain cases in which it would be dangerous, inadmissible; but it is their opinion that in most cases it would have a soothing, sanitary, harmonizing effect. In reference to this subject let me mention a lady with whom I had the honor to be personally acquainted. She is a native of the United States, and has given her attention for many years to the management of the insane, and the improvement of mad-houses. She has travelled alone through every part of the United States — from New York to Chicago, from New Orleans to Quebec. She has been the means of founding nineteen new asylums, and improving and enlarging a greater number. She has won those in power to listen to her, and is considered in her own country a first-rate authority on such subjects, just as Mrs. Fry was here in regard to prisons, Mrs. Chisholm in regard to emigration, and Miss Carpenter in regard to juvenile criminals. As to the use of trained women in lunatic asylums, I will say no more at present, but throw it out as a suggestion to be dealt with by physiologists, and entrusted to *time*.

"Gentle as angels' ministry,
The guiding hand of love should be,
Which seeks again those chords to bind
Which human woe hath rent apart, —
To heal again the wounded mind,
And bind anew the broken heart.
The hand which tunes to harmony
The cunning harp whose strings are riven,
Must move as light and quietly
As that meek breath of summer heaven
Which woke of old its melody; —
And kindness to the dim of soul,
Whilst aught of rude and stern control
The clouded heart can deeply feel,
Is welcome as the odors fanned
From some unseen and flowering land
Around the weary seaman's keel!"

* Of the Salpêtrière, Howard says that, at the time of his visit (1776), the whole house "was kept clean and quiet by the great attention of the religious women who served it; but it was terribly crowded, containing more than five thousand poor, sick, and insane persons."

Again: "Here (at Ghent) is a foundation belonging to the Béguines for the reception of twelve men who are insane, and for sick and aged women. The insane have, when requisite, assistance from their own sex; and the tenderness with which both these and the poor women are treated by the Sisters, gave me no little pleasure." — *Howard on Prisons*, p. 148.

PRISONS AND REFORMATORY SCHOOLS.

Howard, — well named the Good, — when inquiring into the state of prisons, about the middle of the last century, found many of those in France, bad as they generally were, far superior to those in our own country; and he attributes it to the employment and intervention of women "in a manner," he says, "which had no parallel in England." In Paris, he tells us, there were religious women "authorized to take care that the sick prisoners were properly attended to; and who furnished the felons in the dungeons with clean linen and medicine, and performed kind offices to the prisoners in general." This, you will observe, was at a period when in England felons, debtors, and untried prisoners, were dying by inches of filth, and disease, and despair.

Forty years after the publication of Howard's "State of Prisons," what was the state of the greatest prison in England? When Elizabeth Fry ventured into that "den of wild beasts," as it was called, the female ward in Newgate, about three hundred women were found crammed together, begging, swearing, drinking, fighting, gambling, dancing, and dressing up in men's clothes, and two jailers set to watch them, who stood jeering at the door, literally afraid to enter. Elizabeth Fry would have been as safe in the men's wards as among her own sex; she would certainly have exercised there an influence as healing, as benign, as reforming; but she did well in the first instance, and in the *then* state of public feeling, to confine her efforts to the miserable women.*

In the General Report to the Minister of the Interior on the state of the prisons in Piedmont, it is said:

"It is an indisputable fact that the prisons which are served by the *Sisters* are the best-ordered, the most cleanly, and in all respects the best-regulated, in the country; hence it is to be desired that the number should be increased; and this is the more desirable because, where the Sisters are not established, the criminal women are under the charge of jailers of the other sex, which ought not to be tolerated."

To this I add the testimony of the minister himself, from a private communication. "Not only have we experienced the advantage of employing the Sisters of Charity in the prisons, in the supervision of the details, in distributing food, preparing medicines, and nursing the sick in the infirmaries; but we find that the influence of these ladies on the minds of the prisoners, when recovering from sickness, has been productive of the greatest benefit, as leading to permanent reform in many cases, and a better frame of mind always; for this reason, among others, we have given them every encouragement."

In the Reformatory prison at Neudorf is an experiment which, as yet, has only had a three years' trial, but it has so completely succeeded up to this time, that they are preparing to organise eleven other prisons on the same plan. From a conversation I had with one of the government officers, I could under-

* The act of parliament, procured through Mrs. Fry's influence, ordered the appointment of matrons and female officers in all our prisons; but no provision has been made for their proper training, nor are the qualifications at all defined.

My idea is, that besides a superior order of female superintendents, we should have lady visitors also, as it is like an infusion of fresh life and energy; but I do not think that such visiting should be confined to the female wards.

stand that the economy of the administration is a strong recommendation, as well as the moral success. Its origin is worth mentioning. It began by the efforts made by two humane ladies to find a refuge for those wretched creatures of their own sex who, after undergoing their term of punishment, were cast out of the prisons. These ladies, not finding at hand any persons prepared to carry out their views, sent to France for two women of a religious order which was founded for the reformation of lost and depraved women; and two of the Sisters were sent from Angers accordingly. After a while this small institution attracted the notice of the government. It was taken in hand officially, enlarged, and organised as a prison as well as a penitentiary; the original plan being strictly adhered to, and the same management retained.

At the time that I visited it, this prison consisted of several different buildings, and a large garden enclosed by high walls. The inmates were divided into three classes completely separated. The first were the criminals, the most desperate characters, brought there from the prisons at Vienna, and the very refuse of those prisons. They had been brought there six or eight at a time, fettered hand and foot, and guarded by soldiers and policemen.

The second class, drafted from the first, were called the penitents; they were allowed to assist in the house, to cook, and to wash, and to work in the garden, which last was a great boon. There were more than fifty of this class.

The third class were the voluntaries, those who, when their term of punishment and penitence had expired, preferred remaining in the house, and were allowed to do so. They were employed in work of which a part of the profit was retained for their benefit. There were about twelve or fourteen of this class. The whole number of criminals then in the prison exceeded two hundred, and they expected more the next day.

To manage these unhappy, disordered, perverted creatures, there were twelve women, assisted by three chaplains, a surgeon, and a physician; none of the men resided in the house, but visited it every day. The soldiers and police officers, who had been sent in the first instance as guards and jailers, had been dismissed. The dignity, good sense, patience, and tenderness, of this female board of management were extraordinary. The ventilation and the cleanliness were perfect, while the food, beds, and furniture, were of the very coarsest kind. The medical supervision was important, where there was as much disease — of frightful physical disease — as there was of moral disease, crime and misery. There was a surgeon and physician, who visited daily. There was a dispensary under the care of two Sisters, who acted as chief nurses and apothecaries. One of these was busy with the sick, the other went round with me. She was a little, active woman, not more than two or three and thirty, with a most cheerful face, and bright, kind, dark eyes. She had been two years in the prison, and had previously received a careful training of five years — three years in the general duties of her vocation, and two years of medical training. She spoke with great intelligence of the differences of individual temperament, requiring a different medical and moral treatment.

The Sister who superintended the care of the criminals was the oldest I saw, and she was bright-looking also. The Superior, who presided over the whole establishment, had a serious look, and a pale, careworn, but perfectly mild and dignified, face.

The difference between the countenances of those criminals who had lately arrival, and those who had been admitted into the class of penitents, was extraordinary. The first were either stupid, gross, and vacant, or absolutely frightful from the predominance of evil propensities. The latter were at least humanised.

When I expressed my astonishment that so small a number of women could manage such a set of wild and wicked creatures, the answer was, "If we want assistance, we shall have it; but it is as easy, with our system to manage two hundred or three hundred as one hundred or fifty." She then added, devoutly, "The power is not in ourselves; it is granted from above." It was plain that she had the most perfect faith in that power, and in the text which declared all things possible to faith.

We must bear in mind that here men and women were acting together; that in all the regulations, religious and sanitary, there was mutual aid, mutual respect, an interchange of experience; but the women were subordinate only to the chief civil and ecclesiastical authority; the internal administration rested with them.*

The extreme difficulty of finding masters at the best of all our reformatory schools, that at Redhill, was the subject discussed in a recent meeting of benevolent and intelligent men, interested in this institution. I happened to be present. I heard the qualifications for a master to be set over these unhappy little delinquents thus described: He must have great tenderness and kindness of heart, great power of calling forth and sympathising with the least manifestations of goodness or hopefulness; quick perception of character; great firmness, and judgment, and command of temper; skill in some handicraft, as carpentering and gardening; a dignified or at least attractive presence, and good manners, — the personal qualities and appearance being found of consequence to impress the boys with respect. Now it is just possible that all these rare and admirable qualities, some of which God has given in a larger degree to the woman and others to the man, might be found combined in one man; but such a man has not yet been met with, and many such would hardly be found for a stipend of thirty pounds or forty pounds a year. Then, in this dilemma, instead of insisting on a combination of the *paternal* and the *maternal* qualifications in one person, might it not be possible, by associating some well-educated and well-trained women in the administration of these schools, to produce the required influences — the tenderness, the sympathy, the superior manners, and refined deportment, on one hand, and the firmness and energy, the manly government, and skill in handicrafts and gardening, on the other? This solution was not proposed by any of the gentlemen who spoke; it did not seem to occur to any one present; and yet, is it not worth consideration? At all events, I must express my conviction that, going on as they are now doing, without the combination of those influences which ought to represent in such a community the maternal and sisterly, as well as the paternal and fraternal, relations of the home, their efforts will be in vain; their admirable institution will fail to

* I hope it will be remembered here, and in other parts of this essay, that I am not arguing for any particular system of administration, or discipline, or kind or degree of punishment; but merely for this principle, that, whatever the system selected as the best, it should be carried out by a due admixture of female influence and management combined with the man's government.

plaints sooner or later, and people will attribute such a result to every possible cause except the real one.

When I was at Turin, I visited an institution for the redemption of "unfortunate girls" (as they call themselves,* poor creatures!) which appeared to me peculiarly successful. I did not consider it perfect, nor could all its details be imitated here. Yet some of the *natural* principles, recognized and carried out, appeared to me most important. It seemed to have achieved for female victims and delinquents what Mettrai has done for those of the other sex.

This institution (called at Turin *il Refugio*, the Refuge) was founded nearly thirty years ago by a "good Christian," whose name was not given to me, but who still lives, a very old man. When his means were exhausted, he had recourse to the Marquise de Barol, who has from that time devoted her life, and the greater part of her possessions, to the objects of this institution.

In the Memoirs of Mrs. Fry† there may be found a letter which Madame de Barol addressed to her on the subject of this institution and its objects, when it had existed for three or four years only. The letter is dated 1829, and is very interesting. Madame de Barol told me candidly, in 1855, that in the commencement she had made mistakes; she had been too severe. It had required twenty years of reflection, experience, and the most able assistance, to work out her purposes.

The institution began on a small scale, with few inmates. It now covers a large space of ground, and several ranges of buildings for various departments, all connected, and yet most carefully separated. There are several distinct gardens enclosed by these buildings, and the green trees and flowers give an appearance of cheerfulness to the whole.

There is, first, a refuge for casual and extreme wretchedness. A certificate from a priest or a physician is required, but often dispensed with. I saw a child brought into this place by its weeping and despairing mother — a child about ten years old, and in a fearful state. There was no certificate in this case, but the wretched little creature was taken in at once. There is an infirmary, admirably managed by a good physician and two medical Sisters of a religious order. There are also convalescent wards. These parts of the building are kept separate, and the inmates carefully classed, all the younger patients being in a separate ward.

In the penitentiary and schools, forming the second department, the young girls and children are kept distinct from the elder ones, and those who had lately entered from the others. I saw about twenty girls under the age of fifteen, but only a few together in one room. Only a few were tolerably handsome; many looked intelligent and kindly. In one of these rooms I found a tame thrush hopping about, and I remember a girl with a soft face crumbling some bread for it, saved from her dinner. Reading, writing, plain work, and embroidery, are taught; also cooking and other domestic work. A certain number assisted by rotation in the large, lightsome kitchens and the general service of the house, but not till they had been there some months, and had received badges for good conduct. There are three gradations of these badges of merit, earned by various terms

* If you ask a good-looking girl in an hospital, or the infirmary of a workhouse, what is her condition of life, she will perhaps answer, "If you please, ma'am, I'm an unfortunate girl," in a tone of languid indifference, as if it were a profession like any other.

† Vol. II., p. 83.

of probation. It was quite clear to me that these badges were worn with pleasure. Whenever I fixed my eyes upon the little bits of red or blue ribbon attached to the dress, and smiled approbation, I was met by a responsive smile, sometimes by a deep, modest blush. The third and highest order of merit, which was a certificate of good conduct and steady industry during three years at least, conferred the privilege of entering an order destined to nurse the sick in the infirmary, or entrusted to keep order in the small classes. They had also a still higher privilege. And now I came to a part of the institution which excited my strongest sympathy and admiration. Appended to it is an infant hospital for the children of the very lowest orders — children born diseased or deformed, or maimed by accidents, — epileptic, or crippled. In this hospital were thirty-two poor, suffering infants, carefully tended by such of the penitents as had earned this privilege. On a rainy day I found these poor little things taking their daily exercise in a long airy corridor. Over the clean shining floor was spread temporarily a piece of coarse gray drugget, that their feet might not slip; and so they were led along, creeping, crawling, or trying to walk or run, with bandaged heads and limbs, carefully and tenderly helped and watched by the nurses, who were themselves under the supervision of one of the religious Sisters already mentioned.

There is a good dispensary, well supplied with common medicines, and served by a well-instructed Sister of Charity, with the help of one of the inmates whom she had trained.

Any inmate is free to leave the Refuge whenever she pleases, and may be received a second time, but not a third time.

I was told that when these girls leave the institution, after a probation of three or four years, there is no difficulty in finding them good places as servants, cooks, washerwomen, and even nurses; but all do not leave it. Those who, after a residence of six years, preferred to remain, might do so. They were devoted to a religious and laborious life, and lived in a part of the building which had a sort of conventual sanctity and seclusion. They are styled "*les Madeleines*" (Magdalens). I saw sixteen of such, and I had the opportunity of observing them. They were all superior in countenance and organization, and belonged apparently to a better class. They were averse to re-entering the world, had been disgusted and humiliated by their bitter experience of vice, and disliked or were unfitted for servile occupations. They had a manufactory of artificial flowers, were skilful embroiderers and needlewomen, and supported themselves by the produce of their work. They were no longer objects of pity or dependent on charity; they had become objects of respect, and more than respect, of reverence. One of them, who had a talent for music, Madame de Barol had caused to be properly instructed; she was the organist of the chapel and the music-mistress; she had taught several of her companions to sing. A piano stood in the centre of the room, and they executed a little concert for us: everything was done easily and quietly, without effort or display. When I looked in the faces of these young women, — the eldest was not more than thirty, — so serene, so healthful, and in some instances so dignified, I found it difficult to recall the depth of misery, degradation, and disease, out of which they had risen.

The whole number of inmates was about one hundred and forty, without reckoning the thirty-two sick children. Madame de Barol said that this infant

•

hospital was a most efficient means of thorough reform: it called out what was best in the disposition of the penitents, and was indeed a test of the character and temper.*

If this institution had been more in the country, and if some of the penitents (or patients), whose robust *physique* seemed to require it, could have been provided with plenty of work in the open air, such as gardening, keeping cows or poultry, etc., I should have considered the arrangements, for a Catholic country, perfect. They are calculated to fulfil all the conditions of moral and physical convalescence; early rising; regular, active, *useful* employment; thorough cleanliness; the strictest order; an even, rather cool, temperature; abundance of light and fresh air; and, more than these, religious hope wisely and kindly cultivated; companionship, cheerfulness, and the opportunity of exercising the sympathetic and benevolent affections.

If these conditions could be adopted in some of the female penitentiaries at home, I think failure would be less common; but, since the difficulty of redemption is found to be so great, should we not take the more thought for prevention? Among the causes of the evil are some which I should not like to touch upon here; but there are others, and not the least important, which may be discussed without offence. The small payment and the limited sphere of employment allotted to the women of the working-classes are mentioned by a competent witness as one of the causes of vice leading to crime. "Much I believe would be done towards securing the virtue of the female sex, and therefore towards the general diminution of profligacy, if the practical injustice were put an end to by which women are excluded from many kinds of employment for which they are naturally qualified. The general monopoly which the members of the stronger sex have established for themselves, is surely most unjust, and, like all other kinds of injustice, recoils on its perpetrators."† The same writer observes, in another place: "The payment for the labor of females in this country is often so small as to demand, for obtaining an honest living, a greater power of endurance and self-control than can reasonably be expected."

* The above account of the Penitentiary at Turin is from memoranda made on the spot, and from verbal information in November, 1855.

I have since received (while this sheet is going through the press) a letter from a very accomplished and benevolent ecclesiastic, containing some further particulars relative to Madame de Barol's Institution. It appears that the number of inmates is at present two hundred.

The Refuge itself, and the ground on which it stands, were purchased by the government, after Madame de Barol had expended a large sum of money in the original arrangements. The government granted 10,000fr. a year to the necessary expenses, and have since made over the Penitentiary to the Community of Turin; but the hospital for the children, and the convent with the gardens adjoining, have been erected on land belonging to Madame de Barol, and at her sole expense. The infant hospital contains eighty beds. The whole institution is managed by Madame de Barol, and she has the entire control of the funds which the city has placed at her disposal, in addition to those contributed by herself.

† On Crime, its Amount, Causes, and Remedies, by F. Hill, p. 55.

ENGLISH PEDAGOGY IN THE NINETEENTH CENTURY.

FREDERICK WILLIAM TEMPLE.

FREDERICK W. TEMPLE, D. D., was born Nov. 30, 1821, and educated at the Grammar School at Tiverton, and Oxford (Balliol College), where he took his degree in 1842 as a double first class. He was elected Fellow and Tutor, and after his ordination in 1846, became Principal of the Training College for masters of Pauper Schools at Kneller Hall in 1848. This post he resigned in 1855, to become Inspector of Schools, in which he continued till 1858, when he was made Head Master of Rugby School, from which high position he was promoted to the See of Exeter, to succeed Bishop Philpotts. His evidence and opinions on the studies of secondary schools had great weight with the Public Schools Commission, which reported to Parliament in 1864. He was the author of the first of the seven "*Essays and Reviews*" which caused some controversy as to his orthodoxy at the time (1860), and of a volume of *Sermons Preached in Rugby Chapel* in 1858–60.

*Greek and Roman Language and Literature.**

I can not suggest any change in our system of education. By degrees the present system may be much improved. But I understand the Commissioners to ask whether I wish to suggest, not such alterations as we can make for ourselves, and I trust are endeavoring to make, but such as would require superior authority to introduce: the total or partial surrender, for instance, of the classics as the staple of instruction. Such alterations I can not advise.

The studies of boys at school fall under three heads,—literature, mathematics, and physical science. For every branch of each of these studies very strong arguments may be adduced. A boy ought not to be ignorant of this earth on which God has placed him, and ought therefore to be well acquainted with geography. He ought not to walk in the fields in total ignorance of what is growing under his very eyes, and he ought therefore to learn botany. There is hardly an occupation in which he can be employed where he will not find chemistry of service to him. Mathematics rule all other sciences, and contain in themselves the one perfect example of strict logic. It is absurd that an English youth should be ignorant of the history of England; equally absurd

* Extract from communication to the Public Schools Commission, 1864.

that he should not be well acquainted with its noble literature. So each study in its turn can give reasons why it should be cultivated to the utmost. But all these arguments are met by an unanswerable fact—that our time is limited. It is not possible to teach boys every thing. If it is attempted, the result is generally a superficial knowledge of exceedingly little value, and liable to the great moral objection that it encourages conceit and discourages hard work. A boy who knows the general principles of a study, without knowing its details, easily gets the credit of knowing much, while the test of putting his knowledge to use will quickly prove that he knows very little. Meanwhile he acquires a distaste for the drudgery of details, without which drudgery nothing worth doing ever yet was done.

It is therefore necessary to make a choice among these studies, to take one as the chief and to subordinate all others to that. It is an accident, but I think a most fortunate accident, that in England the study thus chosen to take the lead in our highest education has been that of the classics. I should not be prepared to maintain that the only possible system of education for all ranks in this country is one based on the classics. But I assume that the schools commonly called public schools are to aim at the highest kind of education; and to give that education, I think the classics decidedly the best instrument. When we have to choose between literature, mathematics and physical science, the plea advanced on behalf of the latter is utility. They supply a man with tools for future work. Man's chief business, it is said, is to subdue nature to his purposes, and these two studies show him how. Those who use this plea seem to forget that the world in which we live consists quite as much of the men and women on its surface, as of the casts of its constituent materials. If any man were to analyze his own life he would find that he would have far more to do with his fellow-men than with any thing else. And if, therefore, we are to choose a study which shall preëminently fit a man for life, it will be that which shall best enable him to enter into the thoughts, the feelings, the motives of his fellows.

The real defect of mathematics and physical science as instruments of education is that they have not any tendency to humanize. Such studies do not make a man more human, but simply more intelligent. Physical science, besides giving knowledge, cultivates to some degree the love of order and beauty. Mathematics give a very admirable discipline in precision of thought. But neither of them can touch the strictly human part of our nature. The fact is that all education really comes from intercourse with other minds. The desire to supply bodily needs and to get bodily comforts would prompt even a solitary human being—if he lived long enough—to acquire some rude knowledge of nature. But this would not make him more of a man. That which supplies the perpetual spur to the whole human race to continue incessantly adding to our stores of knowledge that which refines and elevates and does not merely educate the moral nor merely the intellectual faculties, but the whole man, is our communication with each other, and the highest study is that which most promotes this communion, by enlarging its sphere, by correcting and purifying its influences, by giving perfect and pure models of what ordinary experience can for the most part only show in adulterated and imperfect forms.

The same thing is said in another way when we assert that that study is the chief instrument of education which makes a man in the fullest sense a Christian gentleman. Taking this word in its highest and best meaning, it certainly represents the aim of the highest education. Now of course it is quite certain that more than half of all education in any given instance, comes not from the studies but from the teacher. If teachers at school and parents at home are gentlemen, they will do more to make the boys the same than any study can do. But this perhaps would remain the same whatever study we make the chief; meanwhile so far as the study selected can influence the result,—and it would be absurd to deny that its influence must be great—that study will do so most which most familiarizes a boy's mind with noble thoughts, with beautiful images, with the deeds and the words which great men have done and said, and all others have admired and loved. So again all studies up to a certain point help each other. I have no doubt at all that a boy of eight, who has been well instructed in arithmetic, will find it easier to learn Latin than one who has not. And so physical science will prepare the way in some degree for mathematics. Every study has a considerable power of helping every other study. But among all the possible studies this power appears to me preëminently to belong to those which I have classed under the general name of literature. I believe the kind of education given in a public school is preëminently that which fits a youth to take up any study whatever. When I had to deal with a very different class of minds, the students of Kneller Hall, I found that studies of the sort included under the name of literature did more to fit them for all other studies than any thing else that I could teach them. My experience here is still the same. I once asked a tradesman who had himself been at Rugby School, and was intending to send his son, whether he had learnt any thing here that was of use to him afterwards. He answered: "I was at school several years, and I have never regretted it. I learnt there what I don't think I could have learnt as well any where else, how to learn any thing I wanted." The Principal of Wellington College, who has peculiar facilities for deciding this question, has come, I believe, to the same conclusion. The studies pursued at a public school, and the method of study, do not always give a boy the precise thing that he wants for immediate use in after life, but they give a training which enables him to study almost any thing afterwards with ease. I must repeat what I said above, that I am not now considering whether other systems of education may not be needed in this country; but whether it would be wise to change the system in use in our public schools. If the staple of education is to be found in the different branches of literature, the classics in a perfect system must be the substratum. In the first place, modern literature is not fully intelligible, except to those who have studied the classics. A student of mathematics does not find it any help to him to study the early writers on the science. No one is aided in learning the differential calculus by going back to fluxions. Nor will the study of physical science gain much by beginning with the writings of earlier discoverers. But literature can only be studied thoroughly by going to its source. Modern theology, modern philosophy, modern law, modern history, modern poetry, are never quite understood, unless we begin with their ancient counterparts.

In the next place, the perfect and peculiar beauty of the classical literature will always put it at the head of all other. Thirdly, the classic life contains, as Mr. J. S. Mill has remarked, "precisely the true corrective for the chief defects of modern life. The classic writers exhibit precisely that order of virtues in which we are apt to be deficient. They altogether show human nature on a grander scale, with less benevolence, but more patriotism,—less sentiment, but more self-control; if a lower average of virtue, more striking individual examples of it; fewer small goodnesses but more greatness, and appreciation of greatness; more which tends to exalt the imagination and inspire high conceptions of the capabilities of human nature." If, as every one must see, the want of affinity of these studies to the modern mind is gradually lowering them in popular estimation, this is but a confirmation of the need of them, and renders it more incumbent on those who have the power, to do their utmost to aid in preventing their decline. Lastly—and this is a practical consideration of the greatest weight—the classical system of education has been in possession of our great schools for two centuries; and in consequence, the best method of using classical learning for purposes of education is so far understood, that it is comparatively easy to find thoroughly efficient masters. How far from easy it is to find thoroughly efficient masters of the modern languages, every one knows. Men who can teach French or German can be found; but it is exceedingly difficult to find any man who can so teach French and German as at the same time to form the minds and characters of the learners.

One obvious reply may be made to all this: that many boys need something more than the cultivation of their faculties. The necessities of their life require them to be furnished, over and above this, with knowledge which can be immediately applied to the business of life. Even if they have learned how to learn, others, who have already got the peculiar learning required, will have the start of them, which, in this age of competition, can never be made up. This is to some extent true, and I think it clear that in this country there is room for other systems of education besides the classical. I should be glad to see great schools established in which Greek was left optional, or nearly so, and Latin, French and German made the staple of instruction, while a little more time was allowed to mathematics and physical science. The education would not be so good, but would be more ready for use; and though not equal to the classical, need not fall short of it. Such a school, or very nearly such a school, is Wellington College; and the modern departments of Cheltenham and Marlborough Colleges approach the same idea. But I think it would be most unwise, because such schools are needed, to attempt to convert the public schools to the purpose; nor should I consider it wise to follow the Cheltenham and Marlborough example, by attaching modern departments to the public schools. The classical work would lose; the other work would not gain.

ROBERT LOWE.

Robert Lowe was born in Bingham in 1811, and educated at Winchester, and at University College, Oxford, where he graduated in high honors in 1833; was elected Fellow of the Magdalen in 1835, and became tutor at Oxford. After being called to the Bar, by the Society of Lincoln's Inn in 1842, he practiced law in Australia, where he sat in the council of that colony from 1843 till 1850, when he returned to England. In 1852 he became joint Secretary of the Board of Control from 1852 to 1855; Vice-President of the Board of Trade and Paymaster General in 1855, and Vice-President of the Education Board from 1859 to 1864. He was elected member from Kidderminster in 1852 and for Calme in 1859. He was made Chancellor of the Exchequer under Gladstone in 1868. He was the author, or at least the main advocate, of the policy of paying out the appropriations for primary education according to results in teaching the elementary branches, ascertained by the examination of the schools by authorized inspectors. In Parliament, and with his pen, he ranks with the advocates of a modern curriculum.

CLASSICAL EDUCATION.*

It seems to me, if one can form an abstract idea of what ought to be taught, that it is to teach a person every thing important to know, and, at the same time, to discipline his mind. But as the period during which education can be communicated is very short, we must qualify that view, I think, by saying that the business of education is to teach persons as much of that which it is important they should know as can be taught within a limited time, and with reference to the ordinary faculties of mankind, and that also in so doing care should be taken to discipline the mind of the pupil as far as possible. That is what I conceive to be the object of education. Well, that being so, you see a question arises of very great difficulty—What is it most important that persons should know?—and till we can answer that question, we can not satisfactorily solve the question which I am now proposing to consider—What is the education that ought to be given to the middle and upper classes of this country? We must invent for ourselves a sort of new science—a science of weights and measures; of ponderation, if I may coin a word—in which we shall put into the scales all the different objects of human knowledge, and decide upon their relative importance. All knowledge is valuable, and there is nothing that it is not worth while to know; but it is a question of relative importance—not of decrying this branch of knowledge, and praising and puffing that—but of taking as far as possible the whole scale of human knowledge, and deciding what should have priority, which should be taught first, and to which our attention should be most urgently directed. That is a problem, you will allow, of most enormous difficulty. I can only suggest one or two considerations

* *Primary and Classical Education; An Address at Edinburgh, November 1, 1867.* By Rt. Hon. Robert Lowe, M. P.

which may assist us in solving it. I think it will be admitted by all who hear me that as we live in a universe of things, and not of words, the knowledge of things is more important to us than the knowledge of words. The first few months and the first few years of a child's existence are employed in learning both, but a great deal more in making itself acquainted with the world than with the knowledge of language. What is the order of Nature? Nature begins with the knowledge of things—then with their names. It is more important to know what a thing is, than what it is called. To take an easy illustration, it is more important to know where the liver is situated, and what are the principles which affect its healthy action, than to know that it is called *jecur* in Latin or *ἧπαρ* in Greek. I go a little farther. Where there is a question between true and false, it is more important to know what is true than what is false. It is more important to know the history of England than the mythologies of Greece and Rome. I think it more important that we should know those transactions out of which the present state of our political and social relations have arisen, than that we should know all the lives and loves of all the gods and goddesses that are contained in Lempriere's dictionary. And yet, according to my experience—I hope things are better managed now—we used to learn a great deal more about the Pagan than the Christian religion in the schools. The one was put by to Sunday, and dismissed in a very short time; the other was every day's work, and the manner in which it was followed out was by no means agreeable. The slightest slip in the name or history of any of the innumerable children of the genealogy of Jupiter or Mars was followed by a form and degree of punishment which I never remember being bestowed upon any one for any slip in divinity. Then, gentlemen, I venture to think, as we can not teach people every thing, it is more important that we should teach them practical things than speculative things. There must be speculation, and there must be practice, but I think if we can not do both, we should rather lean to the practical side. For instance, I think it more important that a man should be able to work out a sum in arithmetic, than that he should be acquainted with all the abstract principles of Aristotle's logic, and that the moods of a syllogism are not so important as the rule of three, practice, and keeping accounts. If we must choose in the matter, we should lean to the practical side. One more rule I will venture to submit—they are four in all—if we must choose in these matters, the present is more important to us than the past. Institutions, communities, kingdoms, countries, with which we are daily brought into contact, are more important than institutions, kingdoms, and countries that have ceased to exist for upwards of 2,000 years. I will pursue this topic no farther.

Having made these general observations as my little contribution towards the new science of ponderation or measurement which I am anxious to found, to enable us to compare one branch of knowledge with another, I will proceed, with your permission, to inquire how far the education of the middle and upper classes corresponds with this idea. Without going into detail, I may say the principal subjects of education—I don't say in Scotch Universities, for you are more liberal than we are in England, though even in your universities not quite sufficiently so—in Oxford and Cambridge are analytical mathematics, and what are called the learned languages—viz., Latin and Greek.

Now I admit that mathematics are a most admirable study, and are calculated to train the mind to strict habits of reasoning, and habits of close and sustained attention. But these are the synthetical, not the analytical mathematics. Consider to what this form of study trains a man. It educates him to approach a subject analytically. He takes his conclusion for granted, and then investigates the conditions upon which it rests. Well, that is not a good way of reasoning. The best way of reasoning is to fix upon principles and facts and see what conclusion they give you, and not to begin with a conclusion and see what principles or facts you may be able to pick up in order to support it. Then any one who has gone through this training knows that you go by steps. One understands step by step, but the whole very often eludes our grasp, and we find ourselves landed in a conclusion without knowing how. We see each step we have taken, but we see not how we arrived at the conclusion. This is a system in one sense too easy, because each step is easy; and in the other it is too difficult, because it is an immense strain on the mind to grasp the whole effect of what is done. Then you are aware of this also, that perhaps the most useful lesson a man can learn is the estimation of probabilities and sifting of evidence. But this is wholly excluded from mathematics, which deal purely with necessary truth. Therefore, it has often been observed, and by no one more forcibly than your own Sir William Hamilton, that a mind formed upon this kind of study is apt to oscillate between the extreme of credulity and scepticism, and is little trained to take those sensible and practical views of the probabilities and the possibilities affecting our daily life, upon which, far more than upon abstract reasoning, the happiness of mankind depends. I may here mention in illustration what was said by a great judge of men and ability—Napoleon Buonaparte. He took for one of his ministers La Place—one of the greatest, perhaps the greatest of mathematicians, and he said of him—"He was a geometer of the first rank; but whose only idea of transacting the business of his department was with reference to the differential and integral calculus."

Now, I pass on to the other study that is the principal occupation of our youth, and that is the study of the Latin and Greek languages, and the history, science, geography, and mythology connected with them—the principal study being language, and the rest only accessories to it. Now, it strikes one, in the first instance, it is rather a narrow view of education that it should be devoted mainly—I had almost said exclusively—to the acquisition of any language whatever. Language is the vehicle of thought, and when thought and knowledge are present, it is desirable as the means of conveying it. It is not a thing to be substituted for it—it is not its equivalent. It pre-supposes knowledge of things, and is only useful where that knowledge is attained for the purpose, namely, of communicating it. I will venture to read a few lines from Pope in illustration of what I say; I should only weaken the thought if I attempted to state the effect of them. They are 140 or 150 years old, and that only shows you how abuses and mistakes may be pointed out in the most vigorous language, and with the most conclusive reasoning, and yet they may remain utterly uncared for:—

> Since man from beasts by words is known,
> Words are man's province; words we teach alone,
> When reason doubtful, like the Samian letter,
> Points him two ways, the narrower is the better.
> Placed at the door of learning youth to guide,
> We never suffer it to stand too wide,

To ask, to guess, to know, as they commence,
As fancy opens the quick springs of sense,
We ply the memory, we load the brain,
Bind rebel wit, and double chain on chain,
Confine the thought, to exercise the breath,
And keep them in the pale of words till death.

I think it is a poor and imperfect conception of education that should limit it to the learning of any languages whatever; but surely if we are to make language the whole or a part of education, it should be the language which we are most concerned with; and I must be permitted to say that, in my scheme of ponderation I think English has a prior claim over Latin and Greek. I do not disparage Latin or Greek; but I am speaking of what is most important to be taken first; and I think it is melancholy to consider the ignorance of our own language in which the best educated of our young men are brought up. Latin is, of course, of great use. It is the only means of opening up a great store of information which is locked up in it, and which is not to be found elsewhere. It has a noble literature of its own, and it is the key to most of the modern languages, and therefore it is a study of very great importance. But we must remember that those persons who spoke a language which was the most marked by felicity of expression, and which is the model of all literature—the inhabitants of Greece, I mean—knew no language but their own. The Romans knew just enough Greek to make them neglect their Latin, and the consequence is their literature is inferior to that of the race that came before them who knew one language. And only see how you set about learning three languages. Learning the language is a joke compared with learning the grammar. The grammar is one thing, and the language another. I agree with the German wit, Heine, who said—"How fortunate the Romans were that they had not to learn the Latin grammar, because if they had done so they never would have had time to conquer the world." Montaigne, 300 years ago, saw this, and pointed it out most forcibly, and by learning the language colloquially, "without a lash, without a tear," he became able to speak it by being talked to in Latin. But that would not answer the purpose. Because it is said "you must discipline the mind," therefore a boy is put through torture of elaborate grammars, which he is forced to learn by heart, and every syllable of which he forgets before he is twenty years of age. There seems something like a worship of inutility in this matter; it seems to be considered very fine to learn something that can not by possibility do any body any thing of good—

The languages, especially the dead,
The sciences, especially the abstruse—
The arts, at least all such as could be said
To be the most remote from common use.

It is an idea that a thing can not be good discipline for the mind unless it be something that is utterly useless in future life. Now, I do not think so. There is no doubt that Greek is a language of wonderful felicity of expression; but what is more beautiful, more refined, or will exercise taste better than to study the best modern French prose to be found in M. Prevost Paradol, Sainte Beuve, and other French writers? There is nothing that can approach it in the English language. If a man wishes to exercise himself in these things he can not possibly have a better subject than French prose. The discipline of the mind is quite as good, and it has this advantage, that when he goes to Paris he will be able to go to a hotel and make known his wants without becoming a laughing-stock to everybody; but this would be too useful, and therefore this must be put aside for some discipline in the Greek language, which he is sure to forget before he is thirty. It depends upon what you mean to make men. If you want to make them a race of sophists, poetasters, and schoolmasters, we are going about it in the right way; but for the business of life we have a little too much Latin and Greek, and if we are to have them taught, they ought to be taught on a very different system. There is nothing more absurd than to attempt to untie knots that have never been tied. If language had been made on a set of general principles—if it had been laid down by the wise men of all nations that the nominative should always agree with the verb, and a verb should always govern the accusative—and language had been made like Euclid—every one of these rules which had been tied we could untie, and a language having been put together in that way we could analyze it into rules. But, gentlemen, language was not so made. Language grew we know not how—like a tree or a plant; it was not made under general rules, and therefore, when you are trying to form general rules for it, you are sowing the sand—you will never attain to what you want; and the result is that when you come to reflect, you will find that you have wasted much time, and the best years of your life have been made miserable by studying rules, whose exceptions are often as numerous as their illustrations, and of which you never know whether they apply or not.

Latin Versification.

There is another thing I enter my protest against, and that is Latin verses. I do not think the history of poets is so prosperous that the end and object of mankind should be to make as many young people as possible poetasters. One of the least profitable of the little talents that a man can have is that of scribbling verses, and yet years of our lives are taken up in the attempt to teach us to write Latin verses, which, after all, are a mere cento of expressions stolen from different authors, the meaning of which we may not ourselves know. I know that I have been highly commended for verses I could not construe myself. This of course gives a most unfair predominance to boys who have been early taught how to use a gradus. The knack is so absurd and repulsive that no one ever acquired it late in life. It must be taught early if at all. I have known men of high classical attainments who have not got honors because they have not had the knack of stringing words together, called doing Latin verses. There is a movement going on against the system, and I hope we shall get rid of it. Another absurd thing is this—I think that a man knows a language when he can read with fluency and ease a good, plain, straightforward author, who writes grammatically and sensibly. This may very soon be done in Latin and Greek; but that is not half enough. There is no torture in that—that is very simple. But what you must do is to take a place that is hopelessly corrupt, where the amanuensis has gone to sleep, or has been tipsy, or has dropped a line, or something or other; you must read two or three pages of notes by everybody who has read at these places, written in bad Latin, stating their idea of how they ought to be reformed and translated. If Æschylus came to life again he would be easily plucked in one of his own choruses; and as for Homer, I am quite certain he did not know the difference between the nominative and accusative case; and yet the best hours of our lives are spent in this profitless analysis of works produced by men utterly unconscious of the rules we are endeavoring to draw from them.

Ancient History.

Ancient history is a very important matter, and a very beautiful study; but it is not so important as modern history, and it does not bear nearly so much upon our transactions. Consider what it is. Ancient history has but two phases—the one is a monarchy, the other is a municipality. The notion of a large community existing by virtue of the principle of representation—of a popular government extended beyond the limits of a single town—is a thing that never entered into the minds of the ancients, so that the best years of our lives are spent in studying history in which that which makes the difference between modern history and ancient—the leading characteristic of our society—that principle of representation which has made it possible in some degree to reconcile the existence of a large country with the existence of a certain amount of freedom—was utterly unknown. The Roman Empire was established, from the necessity of the case, because when Rome became too large to be a municipality, the ancients knew of no other means than to place a Cæsar—a tyrant—over the whole of it, and the idea of sending, as we should do, representatives of the different provinces to meet in Rome, and consult upon the general welfare of the Empire, never occurred to them. That was not known at that time. That was a discovery of many hundred years later. And yet to study all this history, which wants the one thing that is the leading characteristic of modern history, the best time of our life is devoted. I do not say that the time is thrown away, but it is melancholy to reflect that this history is taught, not as an adjunct but as a substitute for modern history. If a man has a knowledge of modern and mediæval history, it is important that he should have this knowledge of ancient history with which he has to compare it; but if he has no modern history he has not the means of comparison. It is useless then by itself. That state of things has utterly passed away. It perished, never to return, with the fall of the Roman Empire, and on its ruins sprung up a new state of things—the feudal system and the polity of the Middle Ages, which ripened into the present state of things. Of all that our youth are taught nothing—they know nothing of it. The subject is never brought before them, and their study is limited and confined to the wars and intrigues of petty republics, the whole mass of which would hardly, perhaps, amount to as many people as are in this great city. There is a well-known passage in a letter by Servius Sulpicius, one of Cicero's friends, in which he endeavors to console him for the death of his daughter Tullia. This is a translation of it:—"Behind me lay Ægina, before me Megara, on my right Piræus, on my left Corinth; these cities, once so flourishing, now lie prostrate and demolished before my eyes. I thought, 'Are we little mortals afflicted when one of us perishes, whose life must at any rate be brief, when in one place lie the corpses of so many towns?'" Well, that is one way of looking at the question. I have been in the same place, and also had my thoughts, and I thought how many irretrievable years of my life have I spent in reading and learning the wars, and the intrigues, and the revolutions of these little towns, the whole of which may be taken in at a single glance from the Acropolis of Athens, and would not make a decently-sized English county. I think that reflection must force itself on the mind of any one who has gone to Greece, and has seen the wonderfully small scale on which these republics are laid out, to which the earlier years of his life were almost exclusively devoted.

Idea of Progress Wanting.

There is another great fault in this exclusive direction of the mind of youth to antiquity, and that is, that their conception of knowledge wants entirely that which is our leading conception in the present day. I do not think that you will find any where in the study of antiquity that which is now in everybody's mouth—the idea of progress. The notion of the ancients was that knowledge was a sort of permanent fixed quantity—that it could not be increased—that it was to be sought for; and if a man wanted to seek for knowledge he did not sit down and interrogate Nature, and study her phenomena, and also analyze and inquire, but he put on his seven-leagued boots and traveled to Egypt or Persia, or as far as he possibly could, in the expectation of finding some wise man there who could tell him all about it. That was the case with Plato, and almost all the great men of antiquity. Now it is no small fault of the modern system of education that it withholds that conception, the key of modern society—that is, not to look at things as stationary, but to look at the human race as, like a glacier, always advancing, always going on from good to better, from better to worse, as the case may be—an endless change and development that never ceases, although we may not be able to mark it every day. That conception is entirely wanting in the antique world; and therefore it is not too much to ask that that idea should be imparted to youth before we give so much time to study the state of society in which it is wholly wanting. I won't detain you with any discussion in this place on the morals and metaphysics of the ancients. I suspect that they knew as much of the mental sciences as we do now—neither much more nor much less; and, without speaking disrespectfully of them, we may say this, that no two of them had the same opinion on the same subject. Then we are dosed with the antiquities of the ancients. Every man is expected to know how many Archons there were at Athens, though he does not know how many Lords of the Treasury there are in London; he must know all the forms of their courts, though he knows hardly the names of our own. He must be dosed with their laws and institutions—things excessively repulsive to the young mind—things only valuable for comparing with our own institutions, of which he is kept profoundly ignorant.

Ancient Geography.

A large portion of time is spent in studying divisions of countries that have long ceased to exist, or have any practical bearing on the world. Of course, if you are to study the language of the ancients, these things must be learned; but is it not melancholy to think how much modern geography is sacrificed to this knowledge? There is nothing in which young men are more deficient than in geography. I shall just mention a few things within my own knowledge. Take, for instance, Australia. It is very rare to find a person who knows where the colonies of Australia are. The island of Java is said to have been given up by Lord Castlereagh at the Treaty of Vienna to the Dutch because he could not find it in the map, and was ashamed to confess his ignorance. I remember a very eminent member of the House of Commons indeed —I will not mention his name—who made a speech in which it was quite manifest to me that he thought that Upper Canada was nearest the mouth of the St. Lawrence, and Lower Canada was higher up the river. If I were to tell you his name you would be astonished. Well, we are going to make an expedition to Abyssinia. The whole thing depends upon the nature of the country. Now, what do we know about it? There is a great deal to be known about it. A great many men have traveled there, and a great deal has been written about it. It is as much as most men can do to find it on the map, and very few know a single town in it. I have amused myself trying to see how few men know where Gondar, the capital of this country, is situated on the map; and as the prisoners we are going to attempt to rescue can probably only be reached by going there, and so to Magdala, it is nearly as important to know where it is as to know that Halicarnassus was the capital city of Caria, or that there were twenty-three cities of the Volscians in the Campagna of Rome. There is another illustration I may give. The name of the place is in the Bible, and we might have hoped better things. You will remember that Mr. Bright in last session of Parliament denominated certain gentlemen by a name derived from a cave. Well, I assure you, gentlemen, there was not one person in twenty whom I met who knew any thing about the Cave of Adullam, and I was under the melancholy and cruel necessity of explaining it to them, and of pointing the arrow that was aimed against my own breast. After all, gentlemen, education is a preparation for actual life, and I ask you—though no doubt the memory is exercised and the faculties are sharpened by these studies in some degree—whether they really in any degree fulfill that condition. I say there is nothing so valuable for a man as to avoid credulity. If he discounts a man's bill, he should inquire before he does it. But what we are taught by this kind of study, our attention being so much placed upon words, is to take every thing for granted. We find a statement in Thucydides, or Cornelius Nepos, who wrote 400 years afterwards, and we never are instructed that the statement of the latter is not quite as good as the former. And so with other things. The study of the dead languages precludes the inquiring habit of mind which measures probability, which is one of the most important that a man can acquire.

Deficiencies in the Education of a Public School or University Man.

I will now give you a catalogue of things which a highly-educated man—one who may have received the best education at the highest public schools, or at Oxford—may be in total ignorance of. He probably will know nothing of the anatomy of his own body. He will not have the slightest idea of the difference between the arteries and the veins, and he may not know whether the spleen is placed on the right or the left side of his spine. He may have no knowledge of the simplest truths of physics, and would not be able to explain the barometer or thermometer. He knows nothing of the simplest laws of animal or vegetable life. He need not know, he very often does not know, any thing about arithmetic, and that ignorance sticks to him through life; he knows nothing of accounts, he does not know the meaning of double entry, or even a common debtor and creditor account. He may write an execrable hand; good clear writing—perhaps the most important qualification a gentleman or man of business can possess—is totally neglected. He may be perfectly deficient in spelling. I knew an eminent person who got a first-class honor, and in his essay—a most excellent English essay—there were forty-six mis-spellings. He may know nothing of the modern geography of his own country; he may know nothing of the history of England. I knew an instance not long ago of a gentleman who had attained high honors at the University, and who became a contributor to a periodical, in which it was suggested he should illustrate some fact by reference to Lord Melbourne's Ministry. He said he had never heard of Lord Melbourne. He need know nothing whatever of modern history—how the present polity of Europe came into effect. He need know nothing of mediæval history, and that is a matter of serious importance, because important results have flowed from ignorance of that history. Great schisms have arisen in the Church of England from absurdly-exaggerated ideas of the perfection of every thing in that dreadful period; and the state of gross ignorance in which people are left as to these times seems almost to lead them to suppose that the best thing that modern society could aim at would be to return to the state of things which existed when the first crusade was projected. He may be in a state of utter ignorance of the antiquities or the law of England; he knows the laws and antiquities of Greece and Rome. The English laws and antiquities are bound up with our freedom and history, and are important to every day's business; but he knows about them nothing whatever. We have, I here say boldly, a literature unparalleled in the world. Which of our great classical authors is a young man required to read in order to attain the highest honors our educational institutions can give him? He studies in the most minute manner the ancient writings of Rome or Greece. But as for Chaucer and Spenser, or the earlier classics, the old dramatists, or the writers of the reigns of Queen Elizabeth and Charles I, he knows nothing of them; and the consequence is that our style is impoverished, and the noble old language of our forefathers drops out of use, while the minds of our young men are employed instead in stringing together scraps of Latin poets learned by heart, and making them into execrable hexameters. Then as for modern languages:—There is some feeble sort of attempt to teach them, but nothing effective; and yet surely, if English is to have a preference over modern languages, as it ought to have, modern languages ought to have a preference, as far as the practical affairs of life are concerned, over ancient languages. I have been with a party of half-a-dozen first-class Oxford gentlemen on the Continent, and not one spoke a word of French or German; and if the waiter had not been better educated than we, and known some other language than his own, we might all have starved. That is not nearly all, but that is enough. I think you will agree with me that, as Dr. Johnson said of the provisions of the Highland inn, the negative catalogue is very copious, and I therefore sum up what I have to say on this point by making this remark, that our education does not communicate to us knowledge, that it does not communicate to us the means of obtaining knowledge, and that it does not communicate to us the means of communicating knowledge.

These three capital deficiencies are undoubted; and what makes these so painful is the thought of the enormous quantities of things eminently worth knowing in this world. I have spoken only of modern history, of modern languages; but what are modern history and languages compared with the boundless field that nature opens out—with the new world which chemistry is expanding before us—with the old world that geology has called again into existence—with the wonderful generalisation with regard to plants and animals, and all those noble studies and speculations which are the glory and distinction and life-blood of the time in which we live, and of which our youth remain, almost without exception, totally ignorant? It is not too much to say, that the man who becomes really well educated must begin his education after it has closed. After all had been done for him that the present miserable, contracted, and poor system can do, he has to begin and educate himself over again, with a feeling that he has wasted the best and most precious years of his life on things neither useless nor unprofitable in themselves, but which were the mere by-paths or appanages to the knowledge which constitutes the mental stock of a man of erudition.

Influence of Educational Endowments.

How are we to account for this phenomenon—how, with physical science in the state that it is, with such a history as ours, with such a literature as ours, with such a literature as that of modern Europe before us, we should turn aside from this rich banquet, and content ourselves with gnawing at mouldy crusts of speculations which have passed away upwards of two thousand years? How are we to account for this? It is easily accounted for. It is mainly the fault of educational endowments. When the educational endowments of Universities were made, there really existed no English literature. Modern history had not begun; mediæval history was only to be found in meagre annals of monkish chroniclers. Physical science was not in existence at all; and there really was nothing to direct the mind except Latin and Greek, and Aristotelian logic. No blame, therefore, attaches to those noble and philanthropic persons who made these foundations. The blame is in those who, after the immense expansion of knowledge, have not found means to expand the objects to which these endowments may apply in a similar proportion. Nor does any blame attach to our Universities, considered strictly as such—meaning by a University a body that ought to examine and test the advancement of its pupils; because our Universities do give examinations, and are willing, I am sure, to give them on any subject on which pupils can be found. But the blame lies with the Government of this country, because these endowments which are now exclusively given to Latin, Greek, and mathematics, are really, in my opinion, public property, for the use of which the State, as representing the public, is responsible. So long as they answer the end that endowments should answer, they should be let alone. When they do not, it is our business to reform them. Now what end do they answer? The end that they answer is this—they give an enormous bounty, an enormous premium, on the study of the dead languages, and of pure mathematics. Well, the studies of the dead languages, and of pure mathematics, are noble and valuable studies, and if that was all I would not object. But you know very well you can not give a premium to one study without discouraging another, and though their first effect is to give a premium to these studies, their collateral and far more important effect is to discourage, and, I would say, prevent, all those other studies which appear to me infinitely more worthy of a place in education. If a young man has talent, and is in want of money, as any young man is apt to be, and wants to turn his talent to advantage, suppose he devotes himself to physical science in Oxford, he can gain a first-class, whatever good that will do him. But there is hardly an endowment open to him; whereas, if he gave the same trouble to Latin and

Greek, he might be a Fellow of half a dozen different colleges with the most perfect ease. How can you expect these studies to get fair play, when they are so handicapped, when the whole weight of these endowments, amounting to about half a million annually, is thrown into the scale of the dead languages, and the study of pure mathematics? The fault lies, therefore, with the Government, which has not reformed these endowments; and the remedy, as it appears to me, is that these endowments should be emancipated from this narrow application, so that the emoluments that are to be obtained for learning, may be impartially distributed among all the branches of human knowledge—not proscribing the subjects to which I have alluded, but not giving them these invidious preferences over all the rest.

The same thing applies to our public schools. They are really adventure schools, kept by masters for their own profit. There is a foundation which forms the nucleus, and that foundation is generally for the purpose of teaching Latin and Greek, and that overrules and dominates the schools. The remedy is in the hands of parents; but these schools have got a good-will such as no other institution in the country has got. A man that has been at a school, however badly taught he has been, however much he has been flogged, always goes away with an affection for it. He forgets his troubles. It is a time that appears to us all very pleasant in the retrospect; and as these troubles are to be undergone not again by himself, but by his son, he always sends him there. No doubt, if we could only secure a fair stage and no favor for all the different branches of instruction, the thing would remedy itself. Do not misunderstand me. I do not think it is any part of the duty of Government to prescribe what people should learn, except in the case of the poor, where time is so limited that we must fix upon a few elementary subjects to get any thing done at all. I think it is the duty of the parents to fix what their children should learn. But then the State should stand impartial, and not by endowments necessarily force education into these channels, and leave those others dry. And, therefore, what I would press is, that somehow or other the endowments should be so recast as to give all subjects—physical science, modern history, English history, English law, ancient languages, ancient literature, ancient history, ancient philosophy, all a fair and equal start.

You will say, How is it possible for this to be done? I don't presume to say what is the best way of doing it, but I can tell you one way it can be done, because I have done it myself. I was Secretary to the India Board at the time when the writerships were thrown open to public competition. We had of course the problem to solve then, because if we had restricted them to Latin and Greek, of course we should have excluded a great number of very meritorious candidates—gentlemen, for instance, coming from the Scotch Universities, who, though very well versed in the philosophy of mind, and many other valuable studies, would not have been able to compete perhaps successfully in classics with boys trained in the English public schools. And therefore we had to attempt to do something of the kind that I have endeavored to point out to you as being necessary to do. In order to solve the problem of education, I, with the assistance of Lord Macaulay and other eminent men, prepared a scale which has since, with very little change, been the scale upon which these offices have been distributed; that is, we took every thing that we could think of that a well-educated man could learn. We took all the languages: we took

Latin and Greek, we took French and English, and all the modern languages of Europe; we took the principal branches of physical science, we took history, English literature, philosophy of mind as taught in Scotland, and at Oxford, and at other places; we took every thing, and we gave marks to each according to their relative importance, as near as we could arrive to it; and under that system all persons have been admitted equally and fairly to the benefits of those offices, whatever their line of study may have been. Instead of loading the dice in favor of the dead languages, we gave them all a fair start, and the thing, so far as I know, has worked perfectly smoothly and with perfect success. Now, I say something of that kind should be done if we are to reform endowments so as to place all studies on a level, and then let the best study win. I won't pretend to influence the decision of parents, but I should give to them no bribe, no inducement, to choose one study more than another, but allow them to take whatever they like best. And I think you would find that the public appetite for Latin verses, the difficult parts of Greek choruses, and the abstrusest rules of grammar, such as are given in the Latin Primer recently issued for the use of public schools, would begin to abate; and the people would think it is better to know something of the world around them, something about the history of their own country, something about their own bodies and their own souls, than it is to devote themselves entirely to the study of the literature of the republics of Greece and Rome.

The time has gone past evidently when the higher classes can hope by any indirect influence, either of property or coercion of any kind, to direct the course of public affairs. Power has passed out of their hands, and what they do must be done by the influence of superior education and superior cultivation; by the influence of mind over mind—"the sign and signet of the Almighty to command," which never fails being recognized wherever it is truly tested. Well, then, gentlemen, how is this likely to be done? Is it by confining the attention of the sons of the wealthier classes of the country to the history of those old languages and those Pagan republics, of which working men never heard, with which they are never brought in contact in any of their affairs, and of which, from the necessity of the case, they know nothing? Is it not better that gentlemen should know the things which the working men know, only know them infinitely better in their principles and in their details, so that they may be able, in their intercourse and their commerce with them, to assert the superiority over them which greater intelligence and leisure is sure to give, and to conquer back by means of a wider and more enlightened cultivation some of the influence which they have lost by political change? I confess, for myself, that whenever I talk with an intelligent workman, so far from being able to assert any such superiority, I am always tormented with the conception, "What a fool a man must think me when he finds me, upon whose education thousands of pounds have been spent, utterly ignorant of the matters which experience teaches him, and which he naturally thinks every educated man ought to know." I think this ought easily to be managed. The lower classes ought to be educated to discharge the duties cast upon them. They should also be educated that they may appreciate and defer to a higher cultivation when they meet it; and the higher classes ought to be educated in a very different manner, in order that they may exhibit to the lower classes that higher education to which, if it were shown to them, they would bow down and defer.

WILLIAM EWART GLADSTONE.

William Ewart Gladstone was born in Liverpool Dec. 29, 1809, educated at Eton, and Christ Church, Oxford, where he graduated in 1829, taking a double class in 1831. After traveling on the continent, he was returned to Parliament in 1832, and was in 1834 made a junior Lord of the Treasury, and in 1835 under Secretary for Colonial Affairs, by Sir Robert Peel. In the same year he retired from office with his leader, and returned with him in 1841 as Vice-President of the Board of Trade, and Master of the Mint. In this capacity he gave the explanation required of the commercial policy of the government and of the revived tariff in 1842. In 1843 he was made President of the Board of Trade, and in 1846, succeeded Lord Stanley as Secretary of State for the Colonies. In the following year he resigned, and in a few months he was elected member of the House for the University of Oxford, and in 1853 became Chancellor of the Exchequer. In 1855 he was in Parliament but out of office, until 1859, when he resumed office as Chancellor of the Exchequer, assisted in negotiating the commercial treaty with France, and aided the Oxford University Commissioners. He was rejected as member from Oxford in 1865, but was immediately returned for South Lancashire, and after the death of Lord Palmerston became leader in the House of Commons and Chancellor of the Exchequer under Lord Russell's administration. In 1866 he brought in a Reform Bill, and again in 1868, when he was successful. As Premier after 1868 he signalized his ministry by disestablishing the Irish Church, and inaugurating a new system of land tenure in Ireland.

Mr. Gladstone has kept up his classical studies, for which he was eminent at Eton and Oxford, and published an elaborate work on Homer. He maintains the classical side of the question of a modern curriculum for secondary and superior schools.

Classical Training, the Basis of a Liberal Education.

The relation of pure science, natural science, modern languages, modern history, and the rest, to the old classical training, ought to be founded on a principle, and that these competing branches of instruction ought not to be treated simply as importunate creditors that take one shilling in the pound to-day because they hope to get another shilling to-morrow, and in the meantime have a recognition of their title. This recognition of title is just what I would refuse; I deny their right to a parallel or equal position; their true position is ancillary; and as ancillary it ought to be limited and restrained without scruple as much as a regard to the paramount matter of education may dictate. But why, after all, is the classical training paramount? Is it because we find it established?

because it improves memory, or taste, or gives precision, or develops the faculty of speech? All these are but partial and fragmentary statements, so many narrow glimpses of a great and comprehensive truth. That truth I take to be, that the modern European civilization from the middle age downwards is the compound of two great factors, the Christian religion for the spirit of man, and the Greek (and in a secondary degree the Roman) discipline for his mind and intellect. St. Paul is the Apostle of the Gentiles, and is in his own person a symbol of this great wedding. The place, for example, of Aristotle and Plato in Christian education is not arbitrary, nor in principle mutable. The materials of what we call classical training were prepared, and we have a right to say were advisedly and providentially prepared, in order that it might become, not a mere adjunct, but (in mathematical phrase) the complement of Christianity in its application to the culture of the human being, as a being formed both for this world and the world to come.

If this principle be true, it is broad, and high, and clear enough; and it supplies a key to all questions connected with the relation between the classical training of our youth, and all other branches of their secular education. It must of course be kept within its proper place, and duly limited as to things and persons. It can only apply in full to that small proportion of the youth of any country who are to become in the fullest sense educated. It involves no extravagant or inconvenient assumptions concerning those who are to be educated for trades and professions, in which the necessities of specific training must more or less limit general culture. It leaves open every question turning upon individual aptitudes and inaptitudes; and by no means requires that boys without a capacity for imbibing any of the spirit of classical culture are still to be mechanically plied with the instruments of it after their unfitness in the particular subject matter has become manifest. But it lays down the rule of education for those who have no internal and no external disqualification; and that rule becoming a fixed and central point in the system, becomes also the point around which all others may be grouped.

CLASSICAL SCHOLARSHIP.

DR. DONALDSON,* in an Essay on Liberal Education in 1856, entitled *Classical Scholarship and Classical Learning, considered with especial reference to Competitive Tests and University Teaching*, takes strong ground in favor of maintaining the supremacy of classical studies in the public schools and universities, to the still further subordination of mathematical study, and to the assignment of instruction in the natural sciences to special schools.

If we confine ourselves to the province of the intellect, *Education* is properly a cultivation and development of those faculties, which all men have in common, though not all in the same degree of activity. *Information*, when it is nothing more, merely denotes an accumulation of stray particulars by means of the memory. On the other hand, *Knowledge* is information appropriated and thoroughly matured. We speak of knowledge of the world, knowledge of our profession or business, knowledge of ourselves, knowledge of our duties—all of which employ a completeness and maturity of habit and experience. And when knowledge extends to a methodical comprehension of general laws and principles, it is called *Science*. It is the natural and proper tendency of information to ripen into knowledge, just as knowledge itself is not complete until it is systematized into science. And as intellectual education necessarily presumes a certain increase in the information or acquired knowledge of the person under training, it is clear that, while the main object of education, namely, the gradual development of the faculties, should never be neglected, the information conveyed and the method of imparting it should be such as to lay the foundation and pave the way, for the super-structure of knowledge and science, in the case of those persons whose capacity and tastes render such an enlargement of the future field of study either probable or desirable. From this it follows, that the great object of education is utterly ignored by those teachers, who, when the mind is unformed and undisciplined, force upon the memory a crowd of unconnected and unprolific recollections, which can neither be digested nor retained, and which, if retained, produce no results on the healthy action of the understanding.

Even in cases, when this process is postponed beyond the period of earliest boyhood, even when it is adopted after a certain course of real mental discipline, its effects are prejudicial to the ripening mind, and unfavorable to the confirmation of those accurate habits without which information seldom settles into knowledge or rises into science. And it is always desirable that the process of liberal education should be carried on as long as possible, and that the acquirement of special knowledge, whether tending to science or applicable immediately to professional practice, should be postponed until the youth has accomplished more than half of the third septennium of his life. That periods of seven years constitute a real element in the life of man is acknowledged by the tacit consent or familiar language of all nations. At any rate, our own experience teaches us that at seven years old the child passes into the boy, by a change of dentition; that at 14, the age of puberty is attained; at 21 the age of manhood; at 42 the age of maturity; and at 63—the grand climacteric as it is called—the period of senility. Such a subdivision presumes that while growth of body is completed at 20, strength of body must be reached, if at all, at 30, and strength of mind, when we have well passed 35, which Dante calls

---

* JOHN WILLIAM DONALDSON, D. D., was born in London, June 10, 1811—was educated first at the University of London, then at Trinity College, Cambridge, where he stood second in the first class of the [illegible] Tripos, in [illegible], and the year following was elected fellow. His first publication, *The Theater of the Greeks*, was issued in [illegible], which was followed by *New Cratylus* in [illegible], of which a new and enlarged edition was issued in [illegible], and which, with his *Varronianus* issued in [illegible], ranked him with the great scholars of Germany. In [illegible] he married the daughter of Sir Thomas Mortlock, and became head master of Bury St. [illegible] Grammar School. His editions of *Antigone* of Sophocles, of the *Book of Jasher*, of the *Odes* of Pindar, his *Greek and Latin School Grammars* and *Greek Lexicon*, all show fine and accurate scholarship. He died February 10, 1861.

'the midway of our life.' And taking this view of the matter we might maintain with great confidence, that the education of the reasoning powers can not really terminate before the body has attained to maturity; that no man can be set free from the duty of forming and invigorating his mind before the period at which he reaches a full development of his material growth; that while his frame is still unformed his understanding can not have reached its completion, and that his intellect can not be perfect as an instrument of thought until nature has set the stamp of manly beauty on the young man's brow.

This necessity for a commensurate progress in mental and bodily growth, this presumption that accomplishment of the mind and beauty of person are attained at the same period, namely, when the boy has grown into a man, is involved in the language of that nation which understood better than any other wherein beauty consists, and by what means the graces and refinements of body and mind can best be imparted and secured. The Greeks had only one word to express personal beauty and mental accomplishment. The adjective *καλός*, in its primary sense, 'furnished with outward adornments' in general; that of which the outward form or the outward effects are pleasing and grateful. 'But,' as I have said elsewhere (*New Cratylus*, § 321), 'to the Greek idea of *κάλλος* something beyond mere outward garnishing of the person was required; it was not a languishing beauty, a listless though correct set of features, an enervated voluptuousness of figure, to which the homage of their admiration was paid. It was the grace and activity of motion, which the practice of gymnastic exercises was calculated to promote—the free step, the erect mien, the healthy glow, combined with the elegances of conversation and the possession of musical accomplishments; it was in fact the result of an union of the *γυμναστική* and *μουσική* of which their education was made up.' The name, which the Greeks gave to the process of making the mind and body both elegant or handsome or clever, implied that the business was not complete till a fullness of stature and a maturity of understanding had been attained. They called it *παιδεία*, or 'boy-training,' and the word also noted the period of life during which this bringing up or education was to be carried on.

With the Greeks, then, I believe that a liberal or general education—that which the Romans called *humanitas*, because the pursuit and discipline of science is given to man only of all the animals—ought to be carried on as long as the mind and body are still immature, that is, nearly till the twentieth year if possible; and while I believe with Plato that the boy-training, which alone is worthy of the name, is that which is pursued for its own sake without reference to extrinsic objects (*Legg.* I. p. 643 E), I think also that we import into the legitimate province of the teacher that which does not belong to it, when we crowd a mass of multifarious acquirements into the period allotted to the growth and improvement of our reasoning powers and our physical energies.

The true object of a liberal education is thus described by Döderlein:

'Even at the present day, one hears voices which tell us that the school forms a more appropriate preparation for the business of life when it encourages such employments as are most subservient to this, and most connected with it. For example, the medical man will be best trained by the earliest possible study of the physical sciences. But reason has prophesied, and experience has fulfilled the prediction, that this sort of education (the infallibility of which has always found the quickest acceptance with the most narrow-minded, and which appears to the most superficial the only road to an adequate training) is calculated only to debase every one of the more intellectual occupations to the rank of a better sort of trade. Accordingly, all public schools, unless they mistake their destination, hold this as an unassailable principle: that although a classical education presumes that all its pupils are designed for some intellectual employment, it does not trouble itself to inquire what particular sort of employment this is to be. The future physician and lawyer, as well as the future clergyman and teacher, essentially different as their contemplated employments may be, are trained precisely in the same manner, having regard only to that which they have in common, namely, that their ulterior occupation, whatever it may be, will demand the most practised exercise of the intellectual faculties.

'It is the primary object of the education of classical schools to impart to the mind of every pupil a capacity for learning that business of which the Universities and other higher institutions profess to convey the definite teaching. The schoolmaster, therefore, is not deterred by the thought, that so much of the learning which he has, with great pains and infinite labor, conveyed to his scholars, and which they have acquired with no little exertion of their own, has been learned by many of them only to be forgotten sooner or later. As the sculptor, when he has finished his statue, does not hesitate to break up the model (the most troublesome part of his work), so the grown-up man does not forget or lay aside, what he was taught at school, until he has derived the full advantage from these studies. He may fail to recognize their unseen fruits, but he can not eradicate them: for his lessons have strengthened his mind in learning and thinking, just as his exercise in the playground braced and invigorated his body.'—*Heiden and Aufsätze.*

And Frederic Jacobs has protested in language equally forcible.

'It has been repeatedly said, that it is of less consequence in youth what a man learns, than how he learns it, and that the saying of Hesiod, 'The half is often better than the whole,' admits of an application here. The heaping up of knowledge for the sake of knowledge brings no blessing; and all education, in which vanity bears the sceptre, misses its object. The young are not called upon to learn all that may by possibility be useful at some future period; for if so, as Aristotle facetiously remarks, we should have to descend to learning cookery; but only such particulars as excite a general activity of mind, sharpen the understanding, enliven the imagination, and produce a beneficial effect on the heart. Not only on grounds of science, but also, and especially, on moral grounds, it is more important to be master of one subject than to be superficially acquainted with many. Knowledge strengthens; superficial acquaintance with many branches of knowledge puffs up and produces a pedantic arrogance; and this is perhaps the most unhappy endowment which a youth can carry with him from school into the world. It is hated because it is illiberal. Illiberality, however, with regard to knowledge, always prevails in those who know neither its root nor its summit.'

To attempt to support by arguments a view of liberal education, which has been held by enlightened men from the days of Plato and Aristotle down to our time, would be only to waste words. And I shall consider myself entitled to start from the postulates, that, wherever it is possible, that is, in all cases which fall within the scope of University teaching, the discipline of the mind should be carried on to the end of the period of adolescence; that this discipline should be general and not professional; and that it should not consist in sciolism or a smattering of miscellaneous acquirements.

ENGLISH AND GERMAN SCHOLARSHIP COMPARED.

Having introduced into the exposition of the present drift of English opinion, on the relative value of studies in the curriculum for a modern liberal education—much that is relatively disparaging to English scholarship, we cite the following passages from an elaborate defense of English Classical Training by Dr. Donaldson.

In order, however, that I may confute the educational objectors on their own ground, and meet the invidious comparison with the Scholarship of Germany, to which they provoke us, I must inquire into the system of classical education pursued in that country, and I must examine the means which they possess of producing scholars, and the causes which create so large a number of writers on learned subjects. In such an inquiry it would not be fair to take as our text-books the biographical sketches of two scholars recently deceased—Godfrey Hermann, of Leipsig, the greatest Greek scholar among the modern Germans, who died on the last day of 1848, and Charles Lachmann, of Berlin, their greatest Latin scholar and general philologer, who died soon after, though at a much earlier age, on March 13, 1849. By selecting these two specimens of German scholarship we should indeed adduce the most favorable instances which could be found, but we should not exemplify the general character of the German philologer. For, in their activity of mind and body, Hermann and Lachmann came nearer to Englishmen than 99 out of 100 Germans; and both of them made more progress in classical composition than any *Gelehrten* of their time. In a word, Hermann and Lachmann deserved to be called scholars, and wanted nothing to give a perfect finish to those accomplishments for which nature had so well qualified them, except the advantages of an English education, and the competition of an English University. . . .

Let me, however, leave these exceptional cases of extraordinary men, and trace the ordinary career of one of the best class of German philologers. My imaginary *Bursch* shall have every advantage at starting. He shall not, like Heyne and Lobeck, be obliged to struggle with the inconveniences which result from the *res angusta domi*. His father shall be, if you please, a learned man and *Garnison-Prediger* in some great city, which contains a first-rate *Gymnasium*. His mother shall be the intelligent and accomplished daughter of a field-officer in the Prussian army. With such parents his education will commence at home, and he will not need the *Progymnasium* or preparatory school. I will suppose that he shows at an early age great docility and a considerable power of acquiring knowledge, and that in fact he promises from the first to be a *Philolog*. In due course of time he is sent to the *Gymnasium* or grammar-school of the place. If he enters at the age of eight or nine, he passes through all six classes of a school of some 150 boys. Here he not only learns Latin and Greek with some Hebrew, but is also instructed in his own language and French, and receives regular lessons in geography, history, mathematics, and natural philosophy. I am only concerned with his classical training, which will be best inferred from an account of his studies during his last year in the first class. He has read 450 lines of Homer's *Iliad*, half the *Œdipus Tyrannus* of Sophocles, and the *Euthyphro* of Plato; he has also been worked in Rost's Greek Grammar. In Latin he has read some odes of Horace and some Orations of Cicero, and has been exercised in the theory of Latin style both out of Zumpt's Grammar, and out of one of the numerous exercise-books which they have in Germany. He has done some of Vömel's Greek exercises; and has written Latin themes. But we hear nothing of his verse composition, except perhaps that he has volunteered some Latin Alcaics as the fruit of his private studies. Under the same head we find it recorded that he has read a good deal of Cicero and Livy, Horace's *Satires*, a little Plautus, some Homer, Xenophon, and Plato. And so, at the age of 18 or 19, he is sent to the University with some such character as this: "Egregie institutus, post examen publicum cum laude dimissus, Academiam Bonnensem petiit, philologorum studiis deditus." As this is the only real training, *as a scholar*, which our young philologer will have, it is worth while to inquire what it amounts to. He has acquired the faculty of writing tolerable Latin prose, and it must be admitted that the Germans generally surpass us in this; nor is the fact surprising, when we recollect that the Universities keep up, as we shall see, a practical demand for the accomplishment. In Latin verse, however, he has had no experience, and has probably never written a line of metrical Greek. Indeed his knowledge of quantity is very uncertain, and as in some *Gymnasiums* they are taught to pronounce Greek by the accent, the longs and shorts are as often wrong as right. The manner in which our student has read the few classical authors with which he is acquainted, depends on the abilities and scholarship of his Rector, and it is to be remarked that in Germany nearly all the really good scholars remain settled as Professors at the Universities, and are not, as with us, as frequently found at the head of the public schools. If our young philologer has not received a scholarlike training at school, he will hardly make good his deficiencies at the University. He will there have the option of attending a great number of lectures, *publice*, *privatim*, and *privatissime*, when his occupation will be writing down for an hour at a time the dictations of the Professor. There will probably be a *Seminarium Philologicum*, in which some Professor will exercise a class in Latin writing and disputation, or preside at discussions on the text and interpretation of the classical writers. The whole curriculum is calculated to stimulate and assist private study, to give systematic information on the pet subjects of the leading Professors, and to prepare a young man for the profession or trade of learned book-making. After some years spent in this way, and perhaps diversified by occasional employment as a private tutor, he takes his degree as "Doctor in Philosophy" by a public disputation on certain theses appended to a Latin dissertation on some philological subject, which, if he is really an original man, may contain the germ of his future literary labors. If his first effort is favorably received, he is at once launched as a teacher and writer of books. He must print something to obtain his *Habilitation*, and he must go on writing if he wishes to rise from the *Privat-docent* to the *Professor Extra Ordinem*, and so to ascend to the ordinary or regular Professorship. Nor can his pen be allowed to rest even when he has obtained this ultimate object of his ambition. He must publish books to keep his name before the world and attract pupils to his lecture-room. And so from first to last he is a book-maker *ex rei necessitate*. He acquires knowledge, not as a labor of love from the improvement of his own mind, but as fuel for his reputation and ammunition for his literary artillery. .

While then the system of education pursued in Germany is less calculated than our own to produce finished scholars, the mode prescribed for the attainment of Professorships and the other educational positions, which abound in that country, furnishes a demand for literary production, which must lead to a vast amount of needless book-making. The cases of Dr. Parr and Professor Dobree, with others that might be named, show that in England a reputation for scholarship may exist independently of literary production, and even without reference to the test of University distinctions. This results from the diffusion of scholarlike acquirements in general society, and from the voice of general opinion, which connects the separate links of private circles. In Germany, this social influence of scholarship is non-existent. It is only as a *Gelehrte*, or writer on learned subjects, that a philological student can become distinguished; and thus in the two countries the amount of scholarship and the number of learned books stand in a reciprocal ratio. Though there can be no doubt that the German habit of book-making leads many men to write who have no real vocation for authorship, and thus deteriorates the learned literature of the country, it can not be denied on the other hand that the facilities afforded for literary production have also their advantages. In this way, we are less likely to be deprived of the services of the few men in every age who are competent to instruct the world on these subjects. . . .

There can be no doubt that nearly all our best writers on classical literature for the last 20 years have been familiar with the philology of the Germans, and have derived great benefit from this widening of the field of contemporary knowledge, a benefit from which the Germans too often exclude themselves. And even those of our scholars, who are unacquainted with the German language, have been enabled, by means of translations, to read and appropriate the best books on learned subjects which the Germans have produced. There has been in fact a reaction since the termination of the last European war. We paid too little attention to German learning before that time; we now run into the opposite extreme, and seem to think that there is no learning out of Germany. We forget in point of fact that classical education has been so long established in England, and has produced such influence on the tastes, habits and character of Englishmen, that even when eminent writers on learned subjects, like Colonel Mure and Mr. Kenrick, are indebted to the Germans, not only for a good deal of the materials of their learning, but also for a part of their education, they remain to the end distinguished by that knowledge of the world, acquaintance with political science, practical good sense, and facility of expression, which seem to be the essential property of our countrymen, and are too generally wanting in German writers. It would have been eminently absurd, if we had not placed our mathematical studies on the advanced basis of the improved calculus, and had neglected the works of Lagrange and Laplace: but no one imagines that the countrymen of Herschel, Babbage, Adams, Rowan Hamilton, Hinds, Stokes, Hopkins, and Airy are inferior in mathematical knowledge to the teachers of the *École Polytechnique*. Why is this the case in regard to German philology? Why may we not take cognizance of Niebuhr, Böckh and Müller, without seeming to relinquish our own claim to rank as their equals? If this were the rule for our guidance in estimating the literary merits of a particular nation at a particular time, we must, on the same principle, consider the Germans, whose works have been most immediately suggestive to us of late years, as mere offshoots of an English school of philology, previously existing. For Niebuhr himself has pronounced F. A. Wolf 'the hero and eponymus of the race of German philologers,' and it is universally admitted that Wolf was a literary representative of Bentley. Indeed, a German writer, who claims all that he can for his countrymen, has not hesitated to avow, that historical philology, though it is the heritage and the glory of German scholars, was the discovery of Richard Bentley, and the dissertation on Phalaris must take rank before all the constructive or reconstructive efforts of continental criticism. Our greatest obligation to modern German scholarship is the revival among us of the spirit of Bentley; in this, no doubt, we have been stimulated by the example of the great German scholars—Wolf, Böckh, Niebuhr, C. O. Müller, Hermann, Lachmann, and others—who have declared themselves his disciples. And the general tone of German literature, which, revived by Lessing, reached its culminating point in Göthe, has produced a marked influence on Englishmen of the largest minds and clearest discernment. But if we try to trace backwards the mutual obligations of the two countries, we shall always find the first entry to the credit of England.

COMPETITIVE EXAMINATION FOR CIVIL SERVICE APPOINTMENTS.

The Report of the Commission of which T. B. Macaulay was chairman, and the author, on the East India Civil Service, in December, 1854, constitutes an epoch in the educational history of England. It maintains the principle, that the education which is to prepare young men for the higher business of life, must begin with a general discipline of the intellect, and that a special or professional training ought to be reserved until the process has been brought to some satisfactory stage, or landing-place. Dr. Donaldson cites the following passages as in harmony with his own views:

'We believe that men who have been engaged, up to 21 or 22, in studies which have no immediate connection with the business of any profession, and of which the effect is merely to open, to invigorate, and to enrich the mind, will generally be found, in the business of every profession, superior to men who have, at 18 or 19, devoted themselves to the special studies of their calling. The most illustrious English jurists have been men, who have never opened a law-book till after the close of a distinguished academical career; nor is there any reason to believe that they would have been greater lawyers, if they had passed in drawing pleas and conveyances the time which they gave to *Thucydides*, to *Cicero*, and to *Newton*.'

Of the Mathematical portion of the examination they say:—

'We think it important that not only the acquirements, but also the mental powers and resources of the competitors should be brought to the test.'

Speaking of the Moral Sciences, as included in the scheme, they remark:—

'Whether this study shall have to do with mere words or things, whether it shall degenerate into a formal and scholastic pedantry, or shall train the mind for the highest purposes of active life, will depend, to a great extent, on the way in which the examination is conducted. . . . The object of the examiners should be rather to put to the test the candidate's powers of mind than to ascertain the extent of his metaphysical reading.'

With the same reference to the immediate objects of a competitive test, they recommend that eminence in classical composition should have a considerable place in determining the issue of the competition:—

'Skill in Greek and Latin versification has, indeed, no direct tendency to form a judge, a financier, or a diplomatist. But the youth who does best what all the ablest and most ambitious youths about him are trying to do well, will generally prove a superior man; nor can we doubt that an accomplishment, by which Fox and Canning, Grenville and Wellesley, Mansfield and Tenterden first distinguished themselves above their fellows, indicates powers of mind which, properly trained and directed, may do great service to the state.'

And with regard to the Examination in general they observe with truth:—

'Experience justifies us in pronouncing with entire confidence that, if the examiners be well chosen, it is utterly impossible that the delusive show of knowledge, which is the effect of the process popularly called cramming, can ever be successful against real learning and ability.'

It is clear, from these explicit statements of their views, that the able and eminent persons, who framed the scheme for the civil service examination, had no wish to send out to India clever smatterers, feeble bookworms, scholastic pedants, and one-sided mathematicians; but to select the most energetic and vigorous young men from the crowds who were likely to offer themselves as candidates for a share in the administration of our most important Satrapies. The particular kind of knowledge, which would be most serviceable to them in the presidencies, was to be prescribed to those selected by the first test, and this subsequent course of study was to be stimulated by a second examination. But, for the preparatory selection, it was only necessary to test existing methods of education, and to discover the best men they could produce. The reasonableness of this procedure was manifest. On the one hand, as the candidates would come from schools and colleges, which had long pursued fixed systems of instruction, differing in different parts of the country, it was necessary that the touchstone should be applied fairly to them all. On the other hand, as only a limited number of the candidates could be successful, it was essential that the whole body of applicants should not be drawn away from their general studies by specialities, which might be of little or no use to those who would not ultimately proceed to India. But, independently of these considerations, suggested by the distinctive peculiarities of the appointments themselves and the means of filling them, the framers of the scheme of examination could not but foresee that such an object of competition would soon produce an effect on the educational system of the whole country, and that teachers would address themselves to the immediate preparation of candidates. They, therefore, wisely laid down some general principles, applicable to the future no less than to the present. They have declared unreservedly that they want the fruits of real mental discipline, that they desire habits of exact thought, and not a wide range of diversified information; and thus they give their adhesion to the old rather than to the new form of education, and would prefer the solid groundwork of the old school of arts rather than the showy stucco-work of modern sciolism. They indicate that, up to a certain time of life, it is of much less consequence what we read than how we read it; and that the young man, who would prepare himself for future distinction, must be frequently less anxious to advance than to know the route which he has already traversed. The student, who is worthy of the name, must be willing to acquiesce in those teachers, who, in the older universities, were called *repetentes* —a sort of intellectual drill-sergeants; he must often remind himself of the words of the Platonic Socrates: 'Perhaps it would not be amiss to go over this ground again; for it is better to accomplish a little thoroughly, than a great deal insufficiently.' In the words of a modern philosopher (Hamilton), he will thus learn that 'as the end of study is not merely to compass the knowledge of facts, but, in and from that knowledge, to lay up the materials of speculation; so it is not the quantity read, but the degree of reading which affords a profitable exercise to the student. Thus it is far more improving to read one good book ten times, than to read ten good books once; and *non multa sed multum*, 'not much, perhaps, but accurate,' has, from ancient times, obtained the authority of an axiom in education, from all who had any title to express an opinion on the subject.'

Adopting these principles and thus confining the competitive test to the results of a liberal or general education, these exponents of the newest demands upon intellectual culture have not only given the most important place to the old basis of instruction, namely, classics and mathematics, but have even declared their preference for the more old fashioned of these two departments of study. For while mathematics have only 1,000 marks assigned as the maximum of credit, 1,500 marks are allotted to Greek and Latin. And thus in our newest educational stimulus we have, as in our oldest academical institutions, a premium for the cultivation of classical scholarship even as compared with mathematical science.

CLASSICAL INSTRUCTION:—ITS USE AND ABUSE.

Under the above title Dr. Hodgson issued, in 1854, a pamphlet of 70 pages, an essay, originally published in the Westminster Review for October, 1853, which attracted much attention at the time, and contains in its reasonings and citations food for thought, until the abuse of what Sidney Smith calls *Too much Latin and Greek* for all pupils of liberal culture, is utterly eradicated from the enforced curriculum of a majority of children who have useful work of any kind to do in this world. It is as true now in England, as it was when first uttered by Sidney Smith in the Edinburgh Review in 1809, and again by Lord Ashburton in 1853.

The complaints we have to make are, at least, as old as the time of Locke and Dr. Samuel Clarke; and the evil which is the subject of these complaints, has certainly rather increased than diminished since the period of those two great men. A hundred years, to be sure, is a very little time for the duration of a national error; and it is so far from being reasonable to look for its decay at so short a date, that it can hardly be expected, within such limits, to have displayed the full bloom of its imbecility.

Sydney Smith.

In this *progressive* country, we neglect all that knowledge in which there is progress, to devote ourselves to those branches in which we are scarcely, if at all, superior to our ancestors. In this *practical* country, the knowledge of all that gives power over nature, is left to be picked up by chance on a man's way through life. In this *religious* country, the knowledge of God's works forms no part of the education of the people,—no part even of the accomplishments of a gentleman.

Lord Ashburton.

Prof. Blackie of Edinburgh is cited thus:

'I claim for the ancients no faultless excellence, no immeasurable superiority. The raptures which some people seem to feel in perusing Homer and Virgil, Livy and Tacitus, while they turn over the pages of Shakspeare and Milton, Hume and Robertson, with coldness and indifference, I hold to be either pure affectation, or gross self-delusion; being fully satisfied that we are in no want of models in our own English tongue, which, for depth of thought, soundness of reasoning, for truth of narrative, and what has been called the philosophy of history, nay, *even for poetical beauty, tenderness, and sublimity*, may fairly challenge comparison with the most renowned productions of antiquity.'

In truth, it is not merely in general literary beauty, or in the 'romantic' graces, that modern literature may court the severest comparison with the ancient. Even in the charmed circle of 'classic' inspiration itself, more of the divine aura is to be caught from such poems as the 'Laodamia' of Wordsworth, the 'Endymion' of Keats, the 'Orion' of Horne, the 'Œnone' and 'Lotos Eaters' of Tennyson, the 'Dead Pan' of Mrs. Browning, than is ever dreamed of by many a laborious searcher of lexicons and collator of various readings in 'classic' texts. If the 'Andromache' of Racine, and the 'Cinna' of Corneille, be thought by any to be more French than Greek or Roman; of Göthe it has been said that he was more Hellenic than Teutonic, less Christian than pagan. There is much truth, as well as beauty, in the words of Professor Blackie: 'Milton, who learned from Homer, has become a Homer to us; and not to us only, but to the right-minded of the whole Christian world, he stands where Virgil stood in reference to Dante, and much more fitly. Many persons there are, in these days, who assert that the famous chorus of Aristophanes descriptive of the clouds (*aénaoi nephelai*, &c.), is a poor specimen of the poetic art compared with Shelley's Ode on the same subject; that John Keats, in his 'Hyperion,' sees deeper—certainly with a more tender clearness and a severer purity—into the soul of Greek mythology, than Bœotian Hesiod did in his 'Theogony;' and that Roman Horace is but a dull singer in presence of the sparkling Moore, and the combination of nice artistic touch with the most subtle and delicate sentiment in Tennyson.'

ASSOCIATIONS OF SCHOOL-DRUDGERY WITH TEACHERS AND AUTHORS.

Dr. Hodgson cites high authorities in confirmation of the assertion of Prof. Blackie: "Persons are often sent to study the classical languages, and to read the works of the highest classics, at an age when it is impossible even for clever boys to read them with intelligence and sympathy." Southey, Scott, Byron, Coleridge, and other men of poetic genius, have recorded their inability in after-life to divest the ancient classics of the associations of ennui, satiety, and disgust, caused by their premature study. To the schoolboy it is the sting, and not the honey, that proclaims the attic bee.

If the dead have any cognizance of posthumous fame, one would think it must abate somewhat of the pleasure with which Virgil and Ovid regard their earthly immortality, when they see to what base purposes their productions are applied. That their verses should be administered to boys in regular doses, as lessons or impositions, and some dim conception of their meaning whipt into the tail when it has failed to penetrate the head, can not be just the sort of homage to their genius which they anticipated, or desired.

SOUTHEY.—*The Doctor.*

These boys have been dragged through grammar as through a cactus bush. They know all about verse; Delectus they were taught to find a choice of evils, and the Anabasis a going down into some lower deep. They had learned to wish that Homer's works were in a single copy, and so fell into their claws; they knew what they would do, though they got flogged for it. They are now translating Philoctetes, wondering when Ulysses will be done with, for they are reading about him also with the French usher in 'Télémaque.' As for the son of Pœas the Melian, all they can make out is a connection between his sore foot and their sore hands. To this extent, perhaps, they recognise his claim to sympathy on their part, and also they can understand his hatred of Ulysses. Philoctetes agrees with the boys thoroughly about that, for Ulysses is the man,

'Whom of all other Greeks he would desire
To lay his fist upon.'

The Greeks fight a hard battle, and retire to suck their wounds.

A Defence of Ignorance.

The flowers of classic genius with which the teacher's solitary fancy is most gratified, have been rendered degraded in his imagination by their connection with tears, with errors, and with punishments; so that the Eclogues of Virgil and Odes of Horace are each inseparably allied in association with the sullen figure and monotonous recitation of some blubbering schoolboy.

SIR WALTER SCOTT.—*Old Mortality.*

I abhorr'd
Too much, to conquer for the poet's sake,
The drill'd dull lesson, forced down word by word
In my repugnant youth, with pleasure to record
Aught that recalls the daily drug which turned
My sickening memory; and though Time hath taught
My mind to meditate what then it learned,

Yet such the fixed inveteracy wrought
By the impatience of my early thought,
That, with the freshness wearing out before
My mind could relish what it might have sought,
If free to choose, I can not now restore
Its health; but what it then detested still abhor.

Byron's Childe Harold.

Byron adds, in a note—'I wish to express, that we become tired of the task before we can comprehend the beauty; that we learn by rote before we can get by heart; that the freshness is worn away, and the future pleasure and advantage deadened and destroyed, by the didactic anticipation, at an age when we can neither feel nor understand the power of compositions which it requires an acquaintance with life, as well as Latin and Greek, to relish, or to reason upon.'

Dr. Hodgson solves the problem—how to introduce more of modern languages and physical sciences into the school, which is at once disciplinary, and preparatory in knowledge for the old universities, and for the new higher institutions which are rising to meet the demands of modern life; (1,) by beginning the classical course later in life, and thus allowing time for a good groundwork in English reading, spelling, and writing, the geography and history of the country, the principal practical points in mathematics and grammar, and an appreciation of music, drawing, and poetry; (2,) by beginning the study of either French or German before Latin, inasmuch as their utility in the intercourse of life, the wealth (large and still growing) of literature which they contain, their etymological relationship to the mother tongue entitle them to this precedence. The experience and opinion of Dr. Franklin is cited in favor of this course, as well of Dr. Jerrard, formerly classical lecturer at Cambridge, and later, principal of Bristol College, and classical examiner at the London University. "My experience in Bristol college has convinced me, that twelve or even fourteen would be better than eight or ten, to commence Latin. The technical grammar, required now of very young pupils, is too burdensome and repulsive. Unless the pronunciation of a modern language is fixed early, it is always defective, and discourages the practice of speaking—the want of which is now universally felt." To exclude either the ancient or modern tongues with their literatures, will leave the curriculum of liberal study incomplete; still each must take its place according to its relative importance in this age. If comparison must be instituted, we maintain that there is no advantage, intellectual, moral or æsthetic, that the study of the ancient languages can confer, which may not be derived to an almost equal degree, from the modern, while the modern yield peculiar advantages, to which the ancient can make no claim.

STUDY OF LANGUAGE IN MENTAL DISCIPLINE.

Rev. James Martineau, in his Inaugural Lecture in University Hall, London, indicates the place which language holds in a system of liberal studies.

"And among these central studies," (*i. e.*, the literary, which hold the middle ground between the outward and the inward, between the physical sciences and metaphysics) "it is easy to see why *language* occupies the very focal place, and has been justly recognized as supplying the faculties with their most effective discipline. For here the equipoise between external attention and internal reflection is maintained more perfectly than is possible elsewhere. Who can say whether language is an outer or an inner fact? It is evidently both. As a realized object of sense, transmitted from point to point of space, and recorded from age to age of time, it is manifestly external, and spreads its relations visibly before the eye, and lies open, like any material product of physical nature, to the simultaneous notice of innumerable observers. On the other hand, as the mere passage of thought and feeling out of silence, the direct out-come of our intellectual and spiritual life, it is a primary function of the inner mind, the mere incarnation (so to speak) of our highest energy. Accordingly, it has no significance, it is not an object of study at all, except on the condition of self knowledge; its distinctions, its classifications, its shades of relations, its forms of structure, are the very distinctions, and classifications, and relations, and architecture of thought itself; and whoever engages himself with them does but see his own intelligence externalized. Dealing with a fact of physical nature, you have to collect or guess its place and meaning in the system of things from its grouping or its look; but in handling the phenomena of language, you invert the proceeding, and carry into it from your own consciousness the idea that gives it shape; having the essence at home, you interpret by it the foreign form. I believe it is this necessary action and re-action of acute observation and thoughtful reflection, to which a philological discipline owes its peculiar advantage for training the faculties with less distortion than any other single pursuit."

PHYSICAL SCIENCES AND CLASSICAL STUDIES.

Prof. H. H. Vaughan, Regius Professor of Modern History in the University of Oxford, in the discussions which grew out of the Examination and Report of Royal Commissioners on the Studies of Oxford and Cambridge, published a pamphlet entitled "*Oxford Reform*," from which we make brief extracts.

"Dr. Pusey insinuates or states of these subjects (the physical sciences, which require the aid of the eye) that they only convey information of facts to the general student, and therefore that they have not been made a subject of general study. The main proposition and the historical inference drawn from it, are both, I conceive, incorrect. The thoughtless and superficial learner will make any instruction whatsoever mere matter of information at the best: and certainly, for such as these, the physical sciences do offer this peculiar advantage, that the information given is, in some sense, real; whereas, in more abstract sciences—Grammar and Logic, or History—the careless or dull receive little but words. When the eye dwells upon an object, it catches some of the properties of the object, at least; when, on the other hand, the word, which is the mere symbol of an object, falls upon the ear, the mind may be vacant of every thing whatsoever, beyond the sounds of the syllables. True it is, therefore, that physical sciences give information more easily, naturally, and therefore more efficiently to the languid student than any other can. But not on that account does such knowledge impart nothing but information. The vital appropriation and application of it involve acts of memory, comprehension, comparison, imagination, deduction; they involve the use of many and admirable faculties, the exercise of which is a discipline truly noble. The intelligent comprehension of a single compound substance, and the laws under which it is combined; the intelligent comprehension of the action of one compound on another, under the various given conditions of light, temperature, and electric forces, are quite elementary acts of mind to the earnest student, but may enforce the use of many admirable and useful mental powers. I do not presume to measure how old or how general is the doctrine, that natural science is mere information. But such a view is in itself a proof that opinions may be both trite and incorrect; and it should appear nowhere any longer save in some historical museum which shall preserve the history of prejudice or pretext. Nor do I believe that the absence or neglect of physical science as a subject of general study is practically owing to this impression, so much as to the joint operation of two other causes. The first of these is, that our general education is traditional, and has been handed down (subject to some slight modification by new ideas and convictions) from times in which physical sciences had no definite and acknowledged existence. At such a period they could not possibly form a part of general education; and when we reflect that men commonly learn but what they have been taught, and teach what they have learned, we can fully understand how it is that changes have not been made in the common subjects or method of instruction, and how it is, therefore, that classical language once established as the instruments and matter of education, have thus long remained so. A second reason is, perhaps, to be found in the fact, that the sciences spoken of are disliked by the jealous teachers of other branches of knowledge, and feared by many, either anxious to preserve the whole body of accepted traditions on all subjects, or fearful lest knowledge, unknown to ancient times, should shake the absolute authority or the traditional interpretation of ancient writings." * * *

"I cannot assign that very great practical effect to the actual study of languages, as a means of giving a discipline to the mind, which many claim for them. I conceive that such advocates have before them some ideal, possible, and occasional method of study, not the actual and general cultivation of language as it is realized. Most men begin to learn grammar through the dead languages (and surely they are the finest instruments for the purpose) before the powers of reflection are nearly strong enough to master and appropriate its principles, which are of a nature highly abstract. Rules, therefore, are learned by the ear and by rote, without any digestion of the understanding; a habit is generated of accepting and using words without an insight into their meaning, and of applying principles in practice without a thought of their real nature. This applies to the industrious. Meanwhile sixty out of a hundred boys learn carelessly or not at all; and I believe there is no study which could prove more successful in producing often through idleness and vacancy of mind, parrot repetition, and sing-song knowledge,—to the abeyance and destruction of the intellectual powers,—as well as to the loss and paralysis of the outward senses,—than our traditional study and idolatry of language. Thinking as highly as a rational being can of the discipline which may be given to good natural faculties, well ripened, by linguistic studies, I protest against the one assumption—not uncommon—that no other studies could administer a discipline to the reason; or the other assumption, hardly less general, that all the mental gifts have, in most cases, been cultivated and fully developed through this."

THOROUGH KNOWLEDGE OF THE SUBJECT, AND HABITS OF MIND.

PROFESSOR A. DE MORGAN, in a Lecture at University College, London, remarks:—

There is in every branch of knowledge a beginning, a middle, and an end; a beginning, in which the student is striving with new and difficult principles, and in which he is relying in a great measure on the authority of his instructor; a middle, in which he has gained some confidence in his own knowledge, and some power of applying his first principles. He is now in a state of danger, so far as the estimate which he is likely to form of himself is concerned. He has as yet no reason to suppose that his career can be checked—nothing to humble the high notion which he will entertain of himself, his teachers, and his subject. Let him only proceed, and he will come to what I have called the end of the subject, and will begin to see that there is, if not a boundary, yet the commencement of a region which has not been tracked and surveyed, and in which not all the skill which he has acquired in voyaging by the chart will save him from losing his way. It is at this period of his career that he will begin to form a true opinion of his own mind, which, I fully believe, is not done by many persons, simply because they have never been allowed to pursue any branch of inquiry to the extent which is necessary to show them where their power ends.

The powers which we expect to give by liberal education, or at least a very considerable portion of the whole, may be comprised under two heads, which I will take separately.

Firstly, it is one of the most important points of education that the subject of it should be made a *good learner*. What is it that can be done before the age of twenty-one, either at school or college? Is the education then finished? Is the pupil to pursue no branch of study further? Nay, does not a professional career open upon him immediately? He is thrown upon the world to learn, with the resources of his education to rely on, and little other help; for it is well known that, throughout our different plans of professional education, there is found but a small amount of teaching, with free permission for the aspirant to teach himself. Now, in this new career there is no stopping half way, in accordance with a previous system of education, in which many subjects were only half taught. The lawyer or physician must be a finished lawyer or physician, able to investigate his subjects at the boundaries of knowledge, and to carry his previous studies successfully up to that point. So soon as either has arrived at the height where his education left him, as to the species of mental effort requisite to carry on his subject, from that moment his future professional study becomes, in point of fact, an awkward substitute for the education which his former teachers professed to supply. He must apply himself with pain to an isolated subject, under great difficulties and with small helps, to gain that power which might so much more easily have been gained when the mind was more supple, and formation of habits more easy.

Secondly, among the educated classes we find those who can readily combine the ideas which they possess, and can turn their previous acquirements to the original consideration of such questions as arise; and we also find those who are slow at such exercise, or almost altogether incapable of it.

That the faculty of thinking easily, and originating thought, should be carefully cultivated, needs not to be maintained; and it cannot be effectively done without a considerable degree of attention paid to the method of thinking which is chosen.

He must go through the elements, during which he will find neither the materials for his original investigations, nor power to pursue them. He must first patiently collect knowledge, and the power of application will come by very slow degrees, and will not be in that state of activity which will answer the purpose, until something more than mere elements is effectively learnt. Considerations of the same character apply to every department of knowledge: there is a lower stage in which the pupil can do little more than collect; there is a higher state of knowledge in which he can begin effectively to apply thought to his collected stores, and thus make them help him to useful habits of mind.

Generally speaking, correctness in any branch of knowledge is a result only of much study. However simple the subject may be, however absurd the only possible mistake may be, I believe it may be taken as an axiom that the beginner is always inaccurate, and remains subject to this defect until he has acquired something more than elements. It has always appeared to me that the value of accuracy does not begin to be soon felt, and that it is only when the student has something of considerable extent to look back upon, that he begins to understand how much depends upon correctness. The same may be said as to lucid arrangement, of which it is clear that the learner will never see the value, until he has a considerable quantity of matter on which to employ himself.

A small quantity of learning quickly evaporates from a mind which never held any learning except in small quantities; and the intellectual philosopher can perhaps explain the following phenomenon,—that men who have given deep attention to one or more liberal studies, can learn to the end of their lives, and are able to retain and apply very small quantities of other kinds of knowledge; while those who have never learnt much of any one thing, seldom acquire new knowledge after they attain to years of maturity, and frequently lose the greater part of that which they once possessed.

SCIENTIFIC EDUCATION, MATHEMATICS, PHYSICAL SCIENCES.

GEORGE BEDELL AIRY, Astronomer Royal, and Fellow of the Royal Society, in his evidence before the Public Schools Commission in 1862, in answer to questions, replied as follows:

The effect of the scientific education at the universities depends in a great measure on the character of the examiners. At the University of Cambridge, which is the only one with which I can profess to be acquainted, the great scientific subject is mathematics in its various applications, and the examiners are for the most part Masters of Arts who have just taken their degrees, and who are put forward at their own wish and through the interest of their respective colleges, as proper persons to be mathematical examiners.

I should like very well that freshmen should have a good deal of what may be called the mechanism of mathematics, and in that I would include algebra generally; but with regard to the demonstrative mathematics I should require the most moderate amount, because I do not think it could be taken up with great advantage till a later period of time; but the study of algebra opens the mind, and the mechanical part could be learned by a boy very well.

I am in the habit of receiving at the Observatory supernumerary computors. They are for the most part the sons of tradesmen in the neighborhood; boys whom I engage at a low rate of payment, and whose parents are very glad to send them to the Observatory for the acquirement of habits of order and so on. I have instituted an examination for these boys,—not a competitive examination, which I tried once or twice, and of which I am effectually sickened, but an examination of efficiency, and I found only two or three days ago, when I examined one of the boys of the age of fifteen, that he mastered algebra very well indeed to the extent of which I have spoken.

There are things with which boys might acquire some familiarity, and which do not involve a strain on the mind, but which would be valuable to them in after life. I remember when I was a school boy learning several things which I did not trouble myself much about at the time, but from which I got ideas which have been extremely useful to me ever since. I remember when I was under a writing master in our school that he would make me go through a course of book-keeping by double entry. I did not care about it, but still I got enough instruction to remember it and to acquire the logic of it, and it has been of infinite value to me since. Now I never cared for that at the time I was at school, and I may say the same in respect to chemistry and electricity, as to their being extremely useful to me. I learned a little in reference to electricity. I cannot say how, but that little has been of great value to me. I mention this to show that knowledge acquired at that age, although not the subject of intense or well ordered study, does prove advantageous afterwards.

In public schools the general tone should undoubtedly be classical; but with the elements of mathematical education, I think there might be added a considerable knowledge of the less severe kind of physical sciences. And with advancing years, as during the years spent at the Universities, I think it very important that sound demonstrative mathematics, with a strong tendency to applied science, should constitute a large part of the education. I think it most desirable that the college course should not be a mere continuation of the school course.

MICHAEL FARADAY.

MICHAEL FARADAY, the son of a blacksmith in Newington Butts, was born September 24, 1791. At the age of 13, after such rudimentary instruction as the father's limited means could secure, he was apprenticed to a bookbinder and stationer, when in looking through the volumes sent to be bound, the boy's attention was attracted, among other subjects, to Electricity, and to apply his knowledge he converted a medicine phial to the purposes of a Leyden jar, and thus began his experiments in a field of science in which he afterwards won his brightest laurels. His bias to science gave him an aversion to trade, when being presented with a ticket by Mr. Dance to the four closing lectures of Prof. Davy (not then Sir Humphrey), in his course for 1812, in the Royal Institution. These lectures decided his career. Writing out his notes, he forwarded them with a letter to the lecturer, setting forth his desire to continue his studies in that direction. An encouraging answer was returned, which was followed soon after by the tender of the position of assistant in his laboratory. In the year following he accompanied the professor to Paris, Montpellier, Genoa, Rome, and Naples, at all of which places he met men of science, and saw new experiments made in the best laboratories of Europe. On his return, in 1815, he applied himself diligently to the work of the laboratory, where he continued as a subordinate and assistant till 1826, when he became Lecturer on Chemistry in the Chair established by Mr. Fuller. In 1821 he obtained new views of electro-magnetism and electro-chemistry, which he followed out for a series of years, and on the results of these researches his fame principally rests. In 1823 he was elected corresponding member of the *Académie des Sciences* of Paris, and in 1844 one of the eight foreign associates; in 1846 he received the Rumford Medal and the Royal Medal; in 1832 Oxford conferred the degree of Civil Law (D.C.L.), and in 1830 he was made Fellow of the Royal Society (F.R.S.). In 1835 he received from Lord Melbourne's government a pension of £300; in 1836 he was appointed Scientific Advisor to the Trinity House, and subsequently, to the Board of Trade; and from 1829 to 1842, he was chemical lecturer at the Royal Military Academy at Woolwich. With opportunities to become rich by the commercial value of this scientific work, Faraday deliberately declined them, and stuck to his laboratory and study, with an average income of £1,000 to £2,000 a year, instead of an accumulating fortune of £150,000—as a compensation he hints to Prof. Tyndal, "Our subjects are so glorious, that to work at them rejoices and encourages the feeblest; delights and enchants the strongest."

OBSERVATIONS ON MENTAL EDUCATION.

If the term education may be understood in so large a sense as to include all that belongs to the improvement of the mind, either by the acquisition of the knowledge of others, or by increase of it through its own exertions, then I may hope to be justified for bringing forward a few desultory observations respecting the exercise of the mental powers in a particular direction, which otherwise might seem out of place.

Deficiency of Judgment in every Direction.

I know that in physical matters multitudes are ready to draw conclusions who have little or no power of judgment in the cases; that the same is true of other departments of knowledge; and that, generally, mankind is willing to leave the faculties which relate to judgment almost entirely uneducated, and their decisions at the mercy of ignorance, prepossessions, the passions, or even accident. * * *

There are multitudes who think themselves competent to decide, after the most cursory observation, upon the cause of this or that event (and they may be really very acute and correct in things familiar to them):—a not unusual phrase with them is, that "it stands to reason," that the effect they expect should result from the cause they assign to it, and *yet it is very difficult*, in numerous cases that appear plain, to show this reason, or to deduce the true and only rational relation of cause and effect. In matters connected with natural philosophy, we have wonderful aid in the progress and assurance in the character, of our final judgment, afforded us by the facts which supply our data, and the experience which multiplies their number and varies their testimony. A fundamental fact, like an elementary principle, never fails us, its evidence is always true; but, on the other hand, we frequently have to ask what is the *fact*?—often fail in distinguishing it,—often fail in the very statement of it,—and mostly overpass or come short of its true recognition.

The *laws of nature*, as we understand them, are the foundation of our knowledge in natural things. So much as we know of them has been developed by the successive energies of the highest intellects, exerted through many ages. After a most rigid and scrutinizing examination upon principle and trial, a definite expression has been given to them; they have become, as it were, our belief or trust. From day to day we still examine and test our expressions of them. We have no interest in their retention if erroneous; on the contrary, the greatest discovery a man could make would be to prove that one of these accepted laws was erroneous, and his greatest honor would be the discovery. Neither would there be any desire to retain the former expression:—for we know that the new or the amended law would be far more productive in results, would greatly increase our intellectual acquisitions, and would prove an abundant source of fresh delight to the mind.

These laws are numerous, and are more or less comprehensive. They are also precise; for a law may present an apparent exception, and yet not be less a law to us, when the exception is included in the expression. Thus, that elevation of temperature expands all bodies is a well defined law, though there be an exception in water for a limited temperature; because we are careful, whilst stating the law, to state the exception and its limits. Pre-eminent among these laws, because of its simplicity, its universality, and its undeviating truth, stands that enunciated by Newton (commonly called the *law of gravitation*), that matter attracts matter with a force inversely as the square of the distance. Newton showed that, by this law, the general condition of things on the surface of the earth is governed; and the globe itself, with all upon it, kept together as a whole. He demonstrated that the motions of the planets round the sun, and of the satellites about the planets, were subject to it. During and since his time, certain variations in the movements of the planets, which were called irregularities, and might, for aught that was then known, be due to some cause other than the attraction of gravitation, were found to be its necessary consequences. By the close and scrutinizing attention of minds the most persevering and careful, it was ascertained that even the distant stars were subject to this law; and, at last, to place as it were the seal of assurance to its never-failing truth, it became, in the minds of Leverrier and Addams (1845), the foreteller and the discoverer of an orb rolling in the depths of space, so large as to equal nearly sixty earths, yet so far away as to be invisible to the unassisted eye. What truth, beyond that of revelation, can have an assurance stronger than this!

Yet this law is often cast aside as of no value or authority, because of the unconscious ignorance amidst which we dwell. You hear at the present day, that some persons can place their fingers on a table, and then elevating their hands, the table will rise up and follow them; that the piece of furniture, though heavy, will ascend, and that their hands bear no weight, or are not drawn down to the wood; you do not hear of this as a conjuring manœuvre, to be shown for your amusement, but are expected seriously to believe it; and are told that it is an important fact, a great discovery amongst the truths of nature. Your neighbor, a well-meaning, conscientious person, believes it; and the assertion finds acceptance in every rank of society, and amongst classes which are esteemed to be educated. Now, what can this imply but that society, speaking generally, is not only ignorant as respects education of the judgment, but is also ignorant of its ignorance. The parties who are thus persuaded, and those who are inclined to think and to hope that they are right, throw up Newton's law at once, and that in a case which of all others is fitted to be tested by it; or if the law be erroneous, to test the law.

Why should not one who can thus lift a table, proceed to verify and simplify his fact, and bring it into relation with the law of Newton? Why should he not take the top of his table (it may be a small one), and placing it in a balance, or on a lever, proceed to ascertain how much weight he can raise by the draught of his fingers upwards; and of this weight, so ascertained, how much is unrepresented by any pull upon the fingers downward? He will then be able to investigate the further question, whether electricity, or any new force of matter, is made manifest in his operations; or whether, action and reaction being unequal, he has at his command the source of a perpetual motion. Such a man, furnished with a nicely constructed carriage on a railway, ought to travel by the mere draught of his own fingers. A far less prize than this would gain him the attention of the whole scientific and commercial world; and he may rest assured, that if he can make the most delicate balance incline or decline by attraction, though it be only with the force of an ounce, or even a grain, he will not fail to gain universal respect and most honorable reward.

When we think of the laws of nature (which by continued observation have become known to us), as the proper tests to which any new fact or our theoretical representation of it should, in the first place, be subjected, let us contemplate their assured and large character. Let us go out into the field and look at the heavens with their solar, starry, and planetary glories; the sky with its clouds; the waters descending from above or wandering at our feet; the animals, the trees, the plants; and consider the permanency of their actions and conditions under the government of these laws. The most delicate flower, the tenderest insect, continues in its species through countless years, always varying, yet ever the same.

I do not object to table-moving, for *itself*: for being once stated it becomes a fit, though a very unpromising subject for experiment; but I am opposed to the unwillingness of its advocates to investigate; their boldness to assert; the credulity of the lookers-on; their desire that the reserved and cautious objector should be in error; and I wish, by calling attention to these things, to make the general want of mental discipline and education manifest.

Education of the Judgment in the Study of Nature.

I am persuaded that all persons may find in natural things an admirable school for self-instruction, and a field for the necessary mental exercise; that they may easily apply their habits of thought, thus formed, to a social use; and that they ought to do this, as a duty to themselves and their generation.

Let me first try to illustrate the former part of the case, and at the same time state what I think a man may and ought to do for himself.

The *self-education* to which he should be stimulated by the desire to improve his judgment, requires no blind dependence upon the dogmas of others, but is commended to him by the suggestions and dictates of his own common sense. The first part of it is founded in mental discipline: happily it requires no unpleasant avowals; appearances are preserved, and vanity remains unhurt; but it is necessary that a man *examine himself*, and *that* not carelessly. On the contrary, as he advances, he should become more and more strict, till he ultimately prove a sharper critic to himself than any one else can be; and he ought to intend this, for, so far as he consciously falls short of it, he acknowledges that others may have reason on their side when they criticise him. A first result of this habit of mind will be an internal conviction of *ignorance in many things respecting which his neighbours are taught*, and, that his opinions and conclusions on such matters ought to be advanced with reservation. A mind so disciplined will be *open to correction upon good grounds in all things*, even in those it is best acquainted with; and should familiarize itself with the idea of such being the case; for though it sees no reason to suppose itself in error, yet the possibility exists. The mind is not enfeebled by this internal admission, but strengthened; for, if it cannot distinguish proportionately between the probable right and wrong of things known imperfectly, it will tend either to be rash or to hesitate; while that which admits the due amount of probability is likely to be justified in the end. It is right that we should stand by and act on our principles; but not right to hold them in obstinate blindness, or retain them when proved to be erroneous. I remember the time when I believed a spark was produced between voltaic metals as they approached to contact (and the reasons why it might be possible yet remain); but others doubted the fact and denied the proofs, and on re-examination I found reason to admit their corrections were well founded. Years ago I believed that electrolytes could conduct electricity by a conduction proper; that has also been denied by many through long time: though I believed myself right, yet circumstances have induced me to pay that respect to criticism as to reinvestigate the subject, and I have the pleasure of thinking that nature confirms my original conclusions.

Among those points of self-education which take up the form of *mental discipline*, there is one of great importance, and, moreover, difficult to deal with, because it involves an internal conflict, and equally touches our vanity and our ease. It consists in the *tendency to deceive ourselves* regarding all we wish for, and the necessity of *resistance to these desires*. It is impossible for any one who has not been constrained, by the course of his occupation and thoughts, to a habit of continual self-correction, to be aware of the amount of error in relation to judgment arising from this tendency. The force of the temptation which urges us to seek for such evidence and appearances as are in favor of our desires, and to disregard those which oppose them, is wonderfully great. In this respect we are all, more or less, active promoters of error. In place of practising wholesome self-abnegation, we ever make the wish the father to the thought: we receive as friendly that which agrees with, we resist with dislike that which opposes us; whereas the very reverse is required by every dictate of common sense. Let me illustrate my meaning by a case where the proof being easy, the rejection of it under the temptation is the more striking. In old times, a ring or a button would be tied by a boy to one end of a long piece of thread, which he would then hold at the other end, letting the button hang within a glass, or over a piece of slate-pencil, or sealing-wax, or a nail; he would wait and observe whether the button swung, and whether in swinging it tapped the glass as many times as the clock struck last, or moved along or across the slate-pencil, or in a circle or oval. In late times, parties in all ranks of life have renewed and repeated the boy's experiment. They have sought to ascertain a very simple fact—namely, whether the effect was as reported; but how many were unable to do this? They were sure they could keep their hands immovable,—were sure they could do so whilst watching the result,—were sure that accordance of swing with an expected direction was not the result of their desires or involuntary motions. How easily all these points could be put to the proof by *not looking at the objects*, yet how difficult for the experimenter to deny himself that privilege. I have rarely found one who would freely permit the substance experimented with to be screened from his sight, and then its position changed.

The *inclination* we exhibit in respect of any report or opinion that harmonizes with our preconceived notions, can only be compared in degree with the *incredulity* we entertain towards everything that opposes them; and these opposite and apparently incompatible, or at least inconsistent, conditions are accepted simultaneously in the most extraordinary manner. At one moment a departure from the laws of nature is admitted without the pretence of a careful examination of the proof; and at the next, the whole force of these laws, acting undeviatingly through all time, is denied, because the testimony they give is disliked.

It is my firm persuasion, that no man can examine himself in the most common things, having any reference to him personally, or to any person, thought, or matter related to him, without being soon made aware *of the temptation* and the difficulty of opposing it. I could give you many illustrations personal to myself, about atmospheric magnetism, lines of force, attraction, repulsion, unity of power, nature of matter, &c.; or in things more general to our common nature, about likes and dislikes, wishes, hopes, and fears; but it would be unsuitable and also unnecessary, for each must be conscious of a large field sadly uncultivated in this respect. I will simply express my strong belief, that that point of self-education which consists in teaching the mind to resist its desires and inclinations, until they are proved to be right, is the most important of all, not only in things of natural philosophy, but in every department of daily life.

One exercise of the mind which largely influences the power and character of the judgment, is the habit of forming *clear and precise ideas.* If, after considering a subject in our ordinary manner, we return upon it with the special purpose of noticing the condition of our thoughts, we shall be astonished to find how little precise they remain. On recalling the phenomena relating to a matter of fact, the circumstances modifying them, the kind and amount of action presented, the real or probable result, we shall find that the first impressions are scarcely fit for the foundation of a judgment, and that the second thoughts will be best. For the acquirement of a good condition of mind in this respect, the thoughts should be trained to a habit of clear and precise formation, so that vivid and distinct impressions of the matter in hand, its circumstances and consequences, may remain.

I am persuaded that natural things offer an admirable school for self-instruction, a most varied field for the necessary mental practice, and that those who exercise themselves therein may easily apply the habits of thought thus formed to a social use. As a first step in such practice, clear ideas should be obtained of what is possible and what is impossible. Thus, it is impossible to *create* force. We may employ it; we may evoke it in one form by its consumption in another; we may hide it for a period; but we can neither *create* nor *destroy* it. We may cast it away; but where we dismiss it, there it will do its work. If, therefore, we desire to consider a proposition respecting the employment or evolution of power, let us carry our judgment, educated on this point, with us. If the proposal include the double use of a force with only one excitement, it implies a creation of power, and that *cannot be.* If we could by the fingers draw a heavy piece of wood or stone upward without effort, and then, letting it sink, could produce by its gravity an effort equal to its weight, that would be a creation of power, and *cannot be.*

So again we cannot *annihilate* matter, nor can we *create* it. But if we are satisfied to rest upon that dogma, what are we to think of table-lifting? If we could make the table to cease from acting by the gravity upon the earth beneath it, or by reaction upon the hand supposed to draw it upwards, we *should annihilate it,* in respect of that very property which characterises it as matter.

Considerations of this nature are very important aids to the judgment; and when a statement is made claiming our assent, we should endeavor to reduce it to some consequence which can be immediately compared with, and tried by, these or like compact and never failing truths. If incompatibility appears, then we have reason to suspend our conclusion, however attractive to the imagination the proposition may be, and pursue the inquiry further, until accordance is obtained; it must be a most uneducated and presumptuous mind that can at once consent to cast off the tried truth and accept in its place the mere loud assertion. We should endeavor to separate the points before us, and concentrate each, so as to evolve a clear type idea of the ruling fact and its consequences; looking at the matter on every side, with the great purpose of distinguishing the constituent reality, and recognising it under every variety of aspect.

In like manner we should accustom ourselves to clear and definite language, especially in physical matters, giving to a word its true and full, but measured meaning, that we may be able to convey our ideas clearly to the minds of others. Two persons cannot mutually impart their knowledge, or compare and rectify their conclusions, unless both attend to the true intent and force of language. If by such words as attraction, electricity, polarity, or atom, they imply different things, they may discuss facts, deny results, and doubt consequences for an indefinite time without any advantageous progress. I hold it as a great point in self-education that the student should be continually engaged in forming exact ideas, and in expressing them clearly by language. Such practice insensibly opposes any tendency to exaggeration or mistake, and increases the sense and love of truth in every part of life.

I should be sorry, however, if what I have said were understood as meaning that education for the improvement and strengthening of the judgment is to be altogether repressive of the imagination, or confine the exercise of the mind to processes of a mathematical or mechanical character. I believe that, in the pursuit of physical science, the imagination should be taught to present the subject investigated in all possible, and even in impossible views; to search for analogies of likeness and (if I may say so) of opposition—inverse or contrasted analogies; to present the fundamental idea in every form, proportion, and condition; to clothe it with suppositions and probabilities, that all cases may pass in review, and be touched, if needful, by the Ithuriel spear of experiment. But all this must be *under government*, and the result must not be given to society until the judgment, educated by the process itself, has been exercised upon it.

When the different data required are in our possession, and we have succeeded in forming a clear idea of each, the mind should be instructed to *balance them* one against another, and not suffered carelessly to hasten to a conclusion. This reserve is most essential; and it is especially needful that the reasons which are adverse to our expectations or our desires should be carefully attended to.

As a result of this wholesome mental condition, we should be able to form a *proportionate judgment*. The mind naturally desires to settle upon one thing or another; to rest upon an affirmative or a negative; and that with a degree of absolutism which is irrational and improper. In drawing a conclusion it is very difficult, but not the less necessary, to make it *proportionate* to the evidence: except where certainty exists (a case of rare occurrence), we should consider our decisions probable only. The probability may appear very great, so that in affairs of the world we often accept such as certainty, and trust our welfare or our lives upon it. Still, only an uneducated mind will confound probability with certainty, especially when it encounters a contrary conclusion drawn by another from like data. Occasionally and frequently the exercise of the judgment ought to end in *absolute reservation*. It may be very distasteful, and, great fatigue, to suspend a conclusion, but as we are not infallible, so we ought to be cautious; we shall eventually find our advantage, for the man who rests in his position is not so far from right as he who, proceeding in a wrong direction, is ever increasing his distance.

The education which I advocate will require *patience* and *labor of thought* in every exercise tending to improve the judgment. It matters not on what subject a person's mind is occupied, he should engage in it with the conviction that it will require mental labor. A powerful mind will be able to draw a conclusion more readily and more correctly than one of moderate character, but both will surpass themselves if they make an earnest, careful investigation, instead of a careless or prejudiced one; and education for this purpose is the more necessary for the latter, because the man of less ability may, through it, raise his rank and amend his position.

This education has for its first and its last step *humility*. It can commence only because of a conviction of deficiency; and if we are not disheartened under the growing revelations which it will make, that conviction will become stronger unto the end. But the humility will be founded, not on comparison of ourselves with the imperfect standards around us, but on the increase of that internal knowledge which alone can make us aware of our internal wants. The first step in correction is to learn our deficiencies, and having learned them, the next step is almost complete: for no man who has discovered that his judgment is hasty, or illogical, or imperfect, would go on with the same degree of haste, or irrationality, or presumption, as before. * *

I know that I fail frequently in that very exercise of judgment to which I call others, and have abundant reason to believe that much more frequently I stand manifest to those around me, as one who errs, without being corrected by knowing it.

In his evidence before the Public Schools Commission, Prof. Faraday expressed very decided opinions on several of the mooted questions of the school curriculum.

NEGLECT OF PHYSICAL SCIENCES AND NATURAL HISTORY.

That the natural knowledge which has been given to the world during the last fifty years should remain untouched, is to me a matter so strange that I find it difficult to understand it. This knowledge is required by men of ordinary intelligence in our lighthouse arrangements, and yet we do not find it here, although when we go over to France we find it in the class of men doing the same duty there—men who can give a reason, supply a correction, and act for themselves, if they see action is wanted. In just such service here we are obliged to displace man after man because they could not attend to the electric light intelligently. The French workman was not superior in natural intelligence, but the English keeper had not been in the way of having that instruction. My experience and observations among witnesses in courts of law, and among men of even good school education, have satisfied me of the too general want of judgment as well as of actual ignorance of natural things—little or no power to give a reason why for what they say or do.

The sciences, of which I notice a great and general ignorance even among our best public school educated men—that of the air, the earth, the water—touch us at all points, every day, every hour, every where—they make up life. And it is difficult to make such adult minds comprehend simple explanations, which if addressed to young people in school or in the shop, will be both intelligible, interesting, and profitable. I never yet found a boy so young as not to be able to understand by simple explanation and to enjoy the point of an experiment. I find the grown up minds coming back to me with the same questions over and over again. They are not prepared to receive these notions. They need the a b c of the subjects.

I could teach a little boy of eleven years old, of ordinary intelligence, all those things in mechanics, hydrostatics, hydraulics, optics, which are usually taught at a much later period. These subjects, and chemistry and botany, should receive attention in apposite ways and times at school.

In matters of natural science, and all the uses and applications of the same, I should turn to a man untaught in other respects, but acquainted with these subjects, rather than to a classical scholar, to find that mode or habit of mind to enable him to judge aptly in this department.

MATHEMATICS IN PUBLIC SCHOOL EDUCATION.

SIR J. F. W. HERSCHEL, who was knighted by Queen Victoria in 1838, as the best representative of the science of her kingdom at the time of her inauguration, thus speaks of Mathematics in the school curriculum:

Regarding as a "public school" any considerable permanent educational establishment in which a large number of youths go through a fixed and uniform course of school instruction, from the earliest age at which boys are usually sent to schools to that in which they either enter the universities or pass in some other mode into manly life, and in which it is understood that the education is what is called a liberal one, with no special professional bias or other avowed object than to form a youth for general life and civilized society, I should consider any system radically faulty which should confine itself to the study of the classical languages, and to so much of Greek and Roman History as is necessary to understand the classical authors, as its main and primary feature, and should admit, and that reluctantly, a mere minimum of extra classical teaching. Such a system must necessarily, I conceive, suffer to languish and become stunted and dwarfed for want of timely exercise, the reasoning faculty, in those years, between fourteen and twenty, when the mind has become capable of consecutive thought and of following out a train of logical argument to a legitimate conclusion. In those years it is quite as important that youths should have placed in their hands and be obliged to study books which may best initiate them in this domain of human thought as in that of classical literature. To be able to express ourselves fluently in Latin or Greek prose or verse, to have attained an extensive familiarity with ancient literature, and a perfect knowledge of the niceties of its grammar, prosody, and idiom—all, in short, which is included in the idea of classical scholarship,—is no doubt very desirable, and I should be one of the last to depreciate it. But it is bought too dear if attained at the sacrifice of any reasonable prospect of improving the general intellectual character by acquiring habits of concentrated thought, by familiarizing the mind with the contemplation of abstract truth, and by accustoming it to the attitude of investigation, induction, and generalization, while it is yet plastic and impressible.

It is these, and not mere utilitarian considerations as to the more favorable start which previous mathematical reading may afford a young man on entering a university, or the advantage in life which a certain amount of knowledge acquired on a variety of other subjects may carry with it—or even as to the general expectation which society has begun to entertain that a young man calling himself educated shall not be wholly ignorant of at least the elements of mathematical and physical science (though these considerations are not without their weight), which incline me to advocate the accordance of a very decided place in public instruction in the upper forms to an elementary course of mathematics, carried in geometry as far as plane and spherical trigonometry, the most ordinary propositions in conic sections, and the doctrine of curves; in symbolic analysis as far as the general nature of equations and the development of functions in infinite series, and including, in the region of applied mathematics, at least the primary elements of statics and dynamics. Such a course might, I think, commence with the average of boys about their 14th year, before which, however, I should expect the four rules of arithmetic, simple and compound, and decimal fractions to have been insisted on.

I know that it is a common idea that classical and mathematical proficiency are incompatible and simply fundamentally different constitutions of mind. This, however, (except as regards the higher degrees of proficiency which go to render a man distinguished, either as a scholar or a mathematician, and the proposition might then be extended to every other form of excellence) I disbelieve; if anything further be intended by such an assertion than that tastes differ, and that most men prefer to give their attention to subjects which fill the imagination and interest the feelings rather than to those which appeal to the unimpassioned reason, and call for a prolonged and steady exercise of the thinking powers. As to the common remark that a very large proportion of young men entering the universities with a high degree of classical training evince a repugnance to the mathematical studies there followed, and not unfrequently rather ostentatiously declare, and proceed to illustrate in practice, their inaptitude for such studies, it proves nothing but that the one-sidedness of their previous education has produced its natural effect; and the consequence I believe to be that a great mass of good mental power, which might have become available to human progress if duly fostered and developed, has thus hitherto been lost to the community. All that I intend, however, in thus protesting against this prevalent notion, is to deprecate its being drawn into an argument for not insisting on attendance on the mathematical classes in the case of boys who really do make little progress, and throwing back into an unmitigated classical routine. In every school there are boys of all degrees of capacity and industry, and therefore of progress. But the absence of these qualities is never admitted as a reason for their being excused attendance at school hours, whatever be the lessons in hand, though it may, and must, retard their advance to higher classes. Besides mathematical and physical subjects there are to be considered the modern languages, history, geography, music, drawing, and a variety of other matters of a similar nature.

Dr. WHEWELL, Master of Trinity College, and Vice President of the University of Cambridge, in which he was also at different times, tutor, professor of mineralogy, moral philosophy, &c., in a treatise on *Liberal Education*, published first in 1835, and with additions in 1850, and commended to the Public School Commission in 1862, has the following remarks:

Any one who has thought at all on the subject of the education of the middle and higher classes in England, must be aware that the great classical schools exercise a very powerful influence upon such educations. The flower of our English youth spend at these schools the years during which the greater part is acquired of all that youths do acquire in the way of learning. It is there that their mental habits in a great measure receive the form which they retain in after life. The tastes there generated, the estimates of different kinds of knowledge there communicated by the contagion of society, are not easily afterwards changed. Even if at the university they are introduced to new subjects of thought, new methods of study, new associates, new motives, still the influence of the school continues to be extremely powerful, and though it may be modified, is never obliterated by subsequent agencies. But the views which have been presented in the preceding pages show us this influence operating still more powerfully in another way. If the scholars who come from the great schools to the university are not in a great degree afterwards moulded by the university system; if they are not engaged upon new subjects and modes of study; if they obtain university honors, and college emoluments, merely by continuing the pursuit of their school-boy labors; if, having done this, they become so numerous in the governing body of the university as to be able to control and direct its measures; if they exercise this power so as to perfect the next generation of school boys from being constrained to any studies except those of the schools; then the university is no longer a place of higher education, supplying the deficiencies of the schools, balancing their partial system, liberalizing their necessarily narrow plan, converting the education of the grammar school into a university education; the university then is merely an appendage to the great schools, rewarding their best scholars, but teaching them nothing; giving prizes, but giving these to proficiency acquired at school, exercising little influence to modify or correct, but much to confirm the impressions made by the mere classical education of boyhood.

After what I have already said, my readers will not be surprised at my again saying that the mathematics ought to be taught at school, so far as to be a preparation for the mathematics which are to be studied at the university; nor at my adding that the present mathematical teaching at several of our great schools fails of satisfying this condition with regard to a great number of their scholars, many of them very well instructed in the classics. Nor shall I here attempt further to illustrate these propositions. That mathematics is a necessary portion of a liberal education, I have endeavored to show in this first part. But mathematics cannot be studied to any purpose at the university, except an effectual beginning is made at school. This is true, even of speculative portions of mathematics, such as geometry, in which the main point is to be able to understand and to state the proofs of the propositions which belong to the science. It is still more true of practical sciences, such as arithmetic, algebra, and practical trigonometry, in which the learner has to apply rules and to perform operations which it requires considerable time and application to learn to apply and to perform correctly, and still more, to perform both correctly and rapidly. If this is not learnt during the period of boyhood, at least with regard to arithmetic, it is never learnt; and when this is the case, all real progress in mathematics is impossible. Yet how imperfectly arithmetic is generally learnt at our great schools, is remarkable to the extent of being curious, besides being, as I conceive it is, a great misfortune to the boys. The sons of great merchants, bankers, and fund-holders, when they leave school, are very generally incapable of calculating the discount upon a bill, and often not able to add up the sums of an account. And few indeed of the sons of our great landowners can calculate the area of a field of irregular, or even of regular form, and given dimensions. This appears to be a lamentable state of things on every account; in its first and lowest bearings, because such ignorance is a great impediment in the practical business of life; in the next place, because arithmetic is in itself a good discipline of attention and application of mind, and when pursued into its applications, an admirable exercise of clearness of head and ingenuity; in the next place, because, as the boys of the middle classes at commercial schools are commonly taught arithmetic (and generally mensuration also) effectively and well, the boys from the great schools have, in this respect, an education inferior to that which prevails in a lower stage of society; and in the next place, again, because the want of arithmetic makes it impossible that such young men should receive a good education at the university. On all these accounts, it appears to me in the highest degree desirable, that arithmetic, at least, should hold a fixed and prominent place in the system of our great schools.

Arithmetic, and when that has been mastered, geometry, mensuration, algebra, and trigonometry in succession, should form a part of the daily business of every school which is intended to prepare students for the university. I am aware that it has been said that any substantial attention to such subjects interferes with the classical teaching; because the classes of boys framed according to their knowledge of Greek and Latin will differ from the classes according to their knowledge of mathematics. Of course this is a difficulty; but one which should be overcome. It has hitherto in a great measure been overcome in the university and in our colleges. It is a difficulty which, if we yield to it, and allow it to deter us from the attempt to improve our education, will make it impossible for us to have a liberal education; because it will exclude all but one element. At this rate, we shall teach our boys Greek and Latin, and not teach them anything else, for fear it should interfere with Greek and Latin; and this, during the first eighteen or nineteen years of life, when they might learn the elements of all human knowledge and acquire habits which would lead them into any part of literature or science, according to their intellectual tendencies.

Arithmetic has usually been a portion of education on somewhat different grounds, namely, not so much on account of its being an example of reasoning, as on account of its practical use in the business of life. To know and to be able familiarly to apply the rules of arithmetic is requisite on innumerable occasions of private and public business; and since this ability can never be so easily and completely acquired as in early youth, it ought to be a part of the business of a boy at school. For the like reasons mensuration ought to be learnt at an early period; that is, the rules for determining the magnitude in numbers of lines, spaces, and solids, under given conditions; a branch of knowledge which differs from geometry as the practical from the speculative, and which, like other practical habits, may be most easily learnt in boyhood, leaving the theoretical aspect of the subject for the business of the higher education which comes at a later period. There is another reason for making arithmetic a part of the school learning of all who are to have a liberal education, namely, that without a very complete familiarity with actual arithmetical processes, none of the branches of algebra can be at all understood. Algebra was, at first, a generalization and abstraction of arithmetic; and whatever other shape it may take by successive steps in the minds of mathematicians, it will never be really understood by those students who do not go through this step. And, as we have already said, there is, in a general education, little or nothing gained by going beyond this. The successive generalizations of one or another new calculus may form subjects of progressive study for those whose education is completed, but cannot enter into a general education without destroying the proportion of its parts.

It is not quite so necessary that geometry should be well studied at school as it is that arithmetic should be well taught there; because in geometry the learner has only to understand and to remember, whereas in arithmetic he has to work in virtue of acquired habit. A student at the university, if he had very good mental talents, might perhaps go forward and acquire a good knowledge of mathematics, even if he had his geometry to begin after his arrival. Still it is not very likely that he would do so. The habits of mental attention and coherence of thought should be cultivated before the age of eighteen, or they will hardly be cultivated to much purpose. It appears to be, in the present state of things, quite necessary that youths who are to come to the university should become masters of some considerable portion of Euclid before they come. Indeed this appears to be the more necessary now, because, so far as I can judge, boys in general are more slow in understanding any portion of mathematics than they were thirty years ago. It may be that I am mistaken, but so it appears to me; and I do not conceive it to be at all improbable that a long continuance of mere classical learning, of the kind which I have already attempted to characterize, should have led to that which not I alone think likely to result from such an education; namely, an incapacity for all continuous thought and all intellectual labor. I do not think it at all incredible that a long course of indulgence in the pleasures of taste and imagination, without any corresponding exercise of the reason, may have emasculated the intellects of the rising generation, so that they prove feeble in comparison with their fathers, when they are called to any task requiring continuous and systematic thought.

In the treatise (Part I. and II.), from which the foregoing extracts are taken, Dr. Whewell maintains the supremacy of mathematical study in the cultivation of the reasoning faculty over the classics or natural science, and as a useful gymnastic of the mind, far superior to logic itself. In this field he encountered an antagonist at least worthy of his steel.

SIR WILLIAM HAMILTON.

In an elaborate essay in the Edinburgh Review for January, 1836, Sir William Hamilton examines the claims set forth by Dr. Whewell, and summons a cloud of witnesses to the soundness of his own views in contradiction of those claims.

How opposite are the habitudes of mind which the study of the Mathematical and the study of the Philosophical sciences* require and cultivate, has attracted the attention of observers from the most ancient times. The principle of this contrast lies in their different objects, in their different ends, and in the different modes of considering their objects;—differences in the sciences themselves, which calling forth, in their cultivators, different faculties, or the same faculty in different ways and degrees, determine developments of thought so dissimilar, that in the same individual a capacity for the one class of sciences has, not without reason, been considered as detracting from his qualification for the other.

* It may be proper here to remark upon the vague universality which is given to the terms philosopher and philosophical in common English; an indefinitude limited specially to this country. Mathematics and Physics may here be called philosophical sciences; whereas, on the Continent, they are excluded from philosophy, philosophical being there applied emphatically to those sciences which are immediately or mediately mental. Hegel, in one of his works, mentions that in looking over what in England are published under the title of "Philosophical Transactions," he had been unable to find any philosophy at all. This abusive employment of the words is favored, I believe, principally, at Cambridge; for if Mathematics and Physics are not philosophical, then that university must confess that it now encourages no philosophy whatever. The history of this insular peculiarity might easily be traced.

As to their *objects*.—In the first place:—The Mathematical sciences are limited to the relations of quantity alone, or, to speak more correctly, to the one relation of quantities—equality and inequality; the Philosophical sciences, on the contrary, are astricted to none of the categories, are coëxtensive with existence and its modes, and circumscribed only by the capacity of the human intellect itself. In the second place:—Mathematics take no account of things, but are conversant solely about certain images; and their whole science is contained in the separation, conjunction, and comparison of them. Philosophy, on the other hand, is mainly occupied with realities; it is the science of a real existence, not merely of an imaginal existence.

As to their *ends*, and their procedure to these ends.—Truth or knowledge is, indeed, the scope of both; but the kind of knowledge proposed by the one is very different from those proposed by the other.—In Mathematics, the whole principles are given; in Philosophy, the greater number are to be sought out and established.—In Mathematics, the given principles are both material and formal, that is, they afford at once the conditions of the construction of the science, and of our knowledge of that construction (*principia essendi et cognoscendi*). In Philosophy, the given principles are only formal—only the logical conditions of the abstract possibility of knowledge. In Mathematics, the whole science is virtually contained in its data; it is only the evolution of a potential knowledge into an actual, and its procedure is thus merely explicative. In Philosophy, the science is not contained in data; its principles are merely the rules for our conduct in the quest, in the proof, in the arrangement of knowledge; it is a transition from absolute ignorance to science, and its procedure is therefore ampliative. In Mathematics we always depart from the definition; in Philosophy, with the definition we usually end.—Mathematics know nothing of causes; the research of causes is Philosophy; the former display only the *that* (τὸ ὅτι); the latter mainly investigates the *why* (τὸ διότι).—The truth of Mathematics is the harmony of thought and thought; the truth of Philosophy is the harmony of thought and existence. Hence the absurdity of all applications of the mathematical method to philosophy.

It is, however, proximately in the different modes of considering their objects that Mathematics and Philosophy so differently cultivate the mind.

In the *first* place:—Without entering on the metaphysical nature of Space and Time, as the basis of concrete and discrete quantities, of geometry and arithmetic, it is sufficient to say that Space and Time, as the necessary conditions of thought, are, severally, to us absolutely one; and each of their modifications, though apprehended as singular in the act of consciousness, is, at the same time, recognized as virtually, and in effect, universal. Mathematical science, therefore, whose notions (as number, figure, motion) are exclusively modifications of these fundamental forms, separately or in combination, does not establish their universality on any *a posteriori* process of abstraction and generalization; but at once contemplates the general in the individual. The universal notions of philosophy, on the contrary, are, with a few great exceptions, generalizations from experience; and as the universal constitutes the rule under which the philosopher *thinks* the individual, philosophy consequently, the reverse of mathematics, views the individual in the general.

In the *second* place:—In Mathematics, quantity, when not divorced from form, is itself really presented to the intellect in a lucid image of phantasy, or in a sensible diagram; and the quantities which can not thus be distinctly construed to imagination and sense, are, as only syntheses of unity, repetitions of identity, adequately, though conventionally, denoted in the vicarious combination of a few simple symbols. Thus both in geometry, by an extensive construction, and in arithmetic and algebra, by a symbolical, the intellect is relieved of all effort in the support and presentation of its objects; and is therefore left to operate upon these in all the ease and security with which it considers the concrete realities of nature. Philosophy, on the contrary, is principally occupied with those general notions which are *thought* by the intellect but are not to be *pictured* in the imagination; and yet, though thus destitute of the light and definitude of mathematical representations, philosophy is allowed no adequate language of its own; and the common language, in its vagueness and insufficiency, does not afford to its unimaginable abstractions that guarantee and support, which, though less wanted, is fully obtained by its rival science, in the absolute equivalence of mathematical thought and mathematical expression.

In the *third* place:—Mathematics, departing from certain original hypotheses and these hypotheses exclusively determining every movement of their procedure, and the images or the vicarious symbols about which they are conversant being clear and simple, the deductions of the sciences are apodictic or demonstrative; that is, the possibility of the contrary is, at every step, seen to be excluded in the very comprehension of the terms. On the other hand, in Philosophy (with the exception of the Theory of Logic), and in our reasonings in general, such demonstrative certainty is rarely to be attained; *probable* certainty, that is, where we are never conscious of the impossibility of the contrary, is all that can be compassed; and this also, not being internally evolved from any fundamental data, must be sought for, collected, and applied from without.

From this general contrast it will easily be seen, how an excessive study of mathematical sciences not only does not prepare, but absolutely incapacitates the mind, for those intellectual energies which philosophy and life require. We are thus disqualified for observation, either internal or external—for abstraction and generalization—and for common reasoning; nay disposed to the alternative of blind credulity or of irrational skepticism. * * *

But the study of mathematical demonstration is mainly recommended as a practice of reasoning in general, and it is precisely, as such a practice, that its inutility is perhaps the greatest. General reasoning is almost exclusively occupied on contingent matter; if mathematical demonstration therefore supplies, as is contended, the best exercise of practical logic, it must do this by best enabling us to counteract the besetting tendencies to error, and to overcome the principal obstacles in the way of our probable reasonings. Now, the dangers and difficulties of such reasoning lie wholly—1, in its *form*—2, in its *vehicle*—3, in its *object-matter*. Of these severally.

1. As to the *form*:—The study of mathematics educates to no sagacity in detecting and avoiding the fallacies which originate in the thought itself of the reasoner.—Demonstration is only demonstration, if the necessity of the one contrary and the impossibility of the other be, from the nature of the object-matter itself, absolutely clear to consciousness at every step of its deduction. Mathematical reasoning, therefore, as demonstrative, allows no room for any sophistry of thought; the necessity of its matter necessitates the correctness of its form, and, consequently, it cannot forewarn and arm the student against this formidable principle of error. * * *

2. In regard to the *vehicle*:—Mathematical language, precise and adequate, nay, absolutely convertible with mathematical thought, can afford us no example of those fallacies which so easily arise from the ambiguities of ordinary language;

its study can not, therefore, it is evident, supply us with any means of obviating those illusions from which it is itself exempt. The contrast of mathematics and philosophy, in this respect, is an interesting object of speculation; but, as imitation is impossible, one of no practical result.

3. In respect of the *matter*:—Mathematics afford us no assistance, either in conquering the difficulties, or in avoiding the dangers which we encounter in the great field of probabilities wherein we live and move.

As to the *difficulties*:—Mathematical demonstration is solely occupied in deducing conclusions; probable reasoning, principally concerned in looking out for premises.—All mathematical reasoning flows from, and—admitting no tributary streams—can be traced back to its original source: principle and conclusion are convertible. The most eccentric deduction of the science is only the last ring in a long chain of reasoning, which descends, with adamantine necessity, link by link, in one simple series, from its original dependence.—In contingent matter, on the contrary, the reasoning is comparatively short; and as the conclusion can seldom be securely established on a single antecedent, it is necessary, in order to realise the adequate amount of evidence, to accumulate probabilities by multiplying the media of inference; and thus to make the same conclusion, as it were, the apex of many convergent arguments. In general reasoning, therefore, the capacities mainly requisite, and mainly cultivated, are the prompt acuteness which discovers what materials are wanted for our premises, and the activity, knowledge, sagacity, and research able competently to supply them.—In demonstration, on the contrary, the one capacity cultivated is that patient habit of suspending all intrusive thought, and of continuing an attention to the unvaried evolution of that perspicuous evidence which it passively recognises, but does not actively discover. Of Observation, Experiment, Induction, Analogy, the mathematician knows nothing. What Mr. Whewell, therefore, alleges in praise of demonstration—"that the mixture of various grounds of conviction, which is so common in other men's minds, is rigorously excluded from the mathematical student's," is precisely what mainly contributes to render it useless as an exercise of reasoning. In the practical business of life the geometer is proverbially but a child: and for the theory of science!—the subtlety of mind, the multiformity of matter, lie far beyond calculus and demonstration; mathematics are not the net in which *Psyche* may be caught, nor the chain by which *Proteus* can be fettered.

As to the *dangers*:—How important soever may be the study of general logic, in providing us against the fallacies which originate both in the form and in the vehicle of reasoning, the error of our conclusions is, in practice, far less frequently occasioned by any vice in our logical inference from premises, than by the sin of a rash assumption of premises materially false. Now if mathematics, as is maintained, do constitute the true logical *catharticon*, the one practical *propædeutic* of all reasoning, it must of course enable us to correct this the most dangerous and prevalent of our intellectual failings. But, among all our rational pursuits, mathematics stand distinguished, not merely as affording us no aid toward alleviating the evil, but as actually inflaming the disease. The mathematician, as already noticed, is exclusively engrossed with the deduction of inevitable conclusions, from data passively received; while the cultivators of the other departments of knowledge, mental and physical, are for the most part, actively occupied in the quest and scrutiny, in the collection and balancing of probabilities, in order to obtain and purify the facts on which their premises are to be established.

HISTORICAL DEVELOPMENT OF CLASSICAL STUDIES.*

The Greek and Latin tongues, with the literature to which these tongues are the keys, obtained their foothold in the schools of Christian nations, not because the study of a dead language was the best mental discipline for young students, or the only means of their acquiring a masterly freedom in the use of their own tongue, but because at the time they were introduced into schools, as branches of study, they were the languages of educated men, and were employed for public business, literature, philosophy, science and religion. Once introduced, they have retained their position partly for the same reasons, and partly by the influence of endowments and the force of habit.

Greek Language.

It arose from the relations in which the Greek and Latin languages have stood in the past, to the whole higher life, intellectual and moral, literary and scientific, civil and religious, of Western Europe. Greeks and Romans, as well as Jews, are our spiritual ancestors. They left treasures of recorded thought, word, and deed, by the timely and judicious use of which their heirs have become the leaders of mankind. But they left them in custody of their native tongues.

After Alexander, the Greek tongue spread widely through the East, and became the means of blending Oriental with Western modes of thought. Commerce prepared the way for liberal intercourse. Ideas were exchanged freely with reciprocal advantage. But the Greek, offering new philosophy for old religion, obtained for Europe the more precious gift—

Χρύσεα χαλκείων, ἑκατόμβοι' ἐννεαβοίων.

No faith attracted more attention than that of the Jews. Their sacred books were carefully translated into the Greek language, and afterwards, by fanciful adaptation, and by real insight, expressed in terms of Greek thought. Greek philosophy, meanwhile, embracing with reverence the long-sought wisdom of the East, went beyond the measure of Pythagoras, Socrates, or Plato, and often beyond the guidance of sober reason, in ascetic abstraction from the things of sense, and ardent longing after spiritual truth.

Christianity itself had Greek for its mother-tongue. St. Paul, a Roman citizen, writes in Greek to the Christians of Rome. The Epistle to the Hebrews is Greek, and so is that of St. James "to the twelve tribes scattered abroad."

For great part of three centuries, the churches of the West were mainly "Greek religious colonies." † Their language, their organization, their liturgy,‡ their Scriptures, were Greek. The Apostolic Fathers, the apologists and historians of the early church, the great theologians, orthodox and heretic, wrote and spoke Greek. The proceedings of the first seven Councils were carried on, and the speculative form of the Christian faith defined, in that language. It

---

* This article is mainly from an "*Essay on the History of Classical Education*," in McMillan's Essays on Liberal Studies. 1867, by Charles Stuart Parker. The author refers to Von Raumer, and Schmidt, for his material.

† Milman's Latin Christianity, i. 27.

‡ It is significant that the word *liturgy* is Greek, as are *hymn, psalm, homily, and catechism, baptism and eucharist, priest, bishop, and pope.*

was hardly possible to handle the profounder questions in any other. Augustine is at a loss for words to speak of them in Latin. Seven centuries later Anselm undertakes the task with diffidence; nor is it clear whether in his own judgment he succeeds or fails.

Thus, when Christianity became the State religion, and the emperor, in such broken language as he could command, took a modest part in the discussions of Nicæa, it was a last and signal spiritual triumph of captive Greece over Rome.

The ancient Church encouraged the study of heathen literature, but with a paramount regard to morality and Christian truth. Plato, Cicero, and Quintilian had pointed out the danger of using the poets indiscriminately as school-books; and the Father who slept with Aristophanes under his pillow would not have placed him in the hands of boys. But even Tertullian allowed Christian boys to attend the public schools under pagan masters.

Origen made the study of heathen poets and moralists preparatory to that of higher Christian truth. His master, Clement, taught that philosophy was the testament or dispensation given to the Greeks, the schoolmaster to bring them, as the Mosaic law brought the Jews, to Christ. And his teaching was generally accepted. To this day "along the porticoes of Eastern churches, both in Greece and Russia, are to be seen portrayed on the walls the figures of Homer, Thucydides, Pythagoras, and Plato, as pioneers preparing the way for Christianity." When Julian forbade the Christians to institute public schools of rhetoric and literature, in which pagan authors might be read, the bishops protested.

During this first Christian age, Greek was the common language of literature, while Latin, after Tacitus and Pliny, rapidly declined. The "Meditations" of the Emperor Marcus Aurelius are composed in the vernacular of the freedman Epictetus. No Latin names can be placed beside those of Lucian and Plutarch, Arrian and Dion Cassius, Ptolemy and Galen. At Athens and Alexandria, the great conservative and liberal universities, studies in grammar and criticism were conducted side by side with philosophy and science. In both alike the Greek tongue was employed. Of all the considerable intellectual production which went on throughout the Roman world, jurisprudence alone was Latin.

Latin Language.

If Greek was the chosen language which carried literature, science, and wisdom, Christian, as well as heathen, to the highest pitch in the ancient world, Latin also was an appointed means of transferring them to Western Europe.

The imperial art of Rome laid the solid foundations on which, when the flood of barbarism began to subside, much of the old fabric was laboriously reconstructed, before the thoughts of man took a wider range. In Spain and Gaul Latin became the mother tongue. But in uneducated mouths it resumed that process of decay and regeneration, the natural life of a language spoken and not written, which only literature can arrest. Hence in time, Italians, as well as Spaniards and French, had to learn book-Latin as a foreign language. It was to them what the writings of our forefathers would be to us, if "English" literature excelled English as Roman did "Romance." But other than literary interests maintained the old Latin as a common language beside the provincial dialects of the new.

The laws of the Western Empire, the last and greatest product of the ancient Roman mind, were adopted by the Gothic, Lombard, and Carlovingian dynasties, and in the twelfth century the first great European school at Bologna was thronged by students of Roman law. At one time there were twenty thousand, from different countries, dividing their attention between civil and canon law, the Pandects and the Decretals. Both were studied with a view to advancement in life, but especially to Church preferment.

Indeed it may be said, with as much truth as is required in metaphor, that the ark which carried through the darkest age, together with its own sacred treasures, the living use of ancient Latin, and some tradition of ancient learning, was the Christian Church.

What at first had been everywhere a Greek became in Western Europe a Latin religion. The discipline of Rome maintained the body of doctrine which the thought of Greece had defined. A new Latin version, superseding alike the venerable Greek translation of the Old Testament and the original words of Evangelists and Apostles, became the received text of Holy Scripture. The Latin Fathers acquired an authority scarcely less binding. The ritual, lessons, and hymns of the Church were Latin. Ecclesiastics transacted the business of civil departments requiring education. Libraries were armories of the Church: grammar was part of her drill. The humblest scholar was enlisted in her service; she recruited her ranks by founding Latin schools. "Education in the rudiments of Latin," says Hallam, "was imparted to a greater number of individuals than at present;" and, as they had more use for it than at present, it was longer retained. If a boy of humble birth had a taste for letters, or if a boy of high birth had a distaste for arms, the first step was to learn Latin. His foot was then on the ladder. He might rise by the good offices of his family to a bishopric, or to the papacy itself by merit and the grace of God. Latin enabled a Greek from Tarsus (Theodore) to become the founder of learning in the English church; and a Yorkshireman (Alcuin) to organize the schools of Charlemagne. Without Latin, our English Winfrid (St. Boniface) could not have been apostle of Germany and reformer of the Frankish Church; or the German Albert, master at Paris of Thomas Aquinas; or Nicholas Breakspeare, Pope of Rome. With it, Western Christendom was one vast field of labor: calls for self-sacrifice, or offers of promotion, might come from north or south, from east or west.

Thus in the Middle Ages Latin was made the groundwork of education; not for the beauty of its classical literature, nor because the study of a dead language was the best mental gymnastic, or the only means of acquiring a masterly freedom in the use of living tongues, but because it was the language of educated men throughout Western Europe, employed for public business, literature, philosophy, and science; above all, in God's providence, essential to the unity, and therefore enforced by the authority, of the Western Church.

But the Latin of the Middle Ages was not classical, and in the West Greek became an unknown tongue. Cicero did less to form style than Jerome; Plato was forgotten in favor of Augustine; Aristotle alone, translated out of Greek into Syriac, out of Syriac into Arabic, out of Arabic into Latin, and in Latin purged of every thing offensive to the mediæval mind, had become in the folios of Thomas Aquinas a buttress, if not a pillar, of the Christian Church.

PROF. MAX MÜLLER, Taylorian Professor of Modern Languages at Oxford, remarks on the study of these languages:

The experience of German schools, as well as of English, as generally constituted, is this: fluency in speaking is never acquired. The time spared from other studies is only sufficient to give the pupil a good grounding in grammar, and the mastery of a sufficient number of words to enable him to read a newspaper or an historical author.

Some boys have no ear for accents at all, just as some have no ear for music, and, although they may hear a word pronounced by a Frenchman, they cannot imitate it.

Much more might be saved in the teaching French at public schools if it was grafted on the knowledge of Latin which most of the boys possess. There is no feature of French grammar which does not find its explanation in Latin, and if the connecting links were clearly put before the pupil, he would find that his knowledge of Latin enables him at once to understand the apparently new parts of French grammar that come before him. The experiment was made in France in 1852, under the recommendation of the Minister, and in a text-book prepared by M. Egger, a member of the Institute.

In a public school, French should be taught by an Englishman properly instructed in the language, assisted by a French teacher, who should have charge of the pronunciation and idiomatic part of the language.

The study of French and German has increased in Oxford—nearly all its good scholars try to learn German, because it opens a vast literature.

Socially and educationally, I think the study of Latin and Greek is of the highest importance. Frederick the Great said to his teachers: "Whatever you do, do not let a boy grow up without knowing Latin."

PROF. GOLDWIN SMITH distinguishes between the earlier and the later motives for the excessive devotion to classical studies thus:

Then (in the period of the Tudors and earlier Stuarts) education was classical, but classical learning was then, not a gymnastic exercise of the mind in philology, but a deep draught from what was the great and almost the only spring of philosophy, science, history, and poetry at that time. It introduced the student to a great treasure of wisdom and knowledge, and not to philological niceties and beauties. Latin was then the language of literary, ecclesiastic, diplomatic, loyal, academic Europe; and familiarity with it was the first and most indispensable accomplishment, not only of the gentlemen, but of the high born ladies of the time.

In choosing the subjects of boys studies, you may use your own discretion; in choosing the subjects of a man's studies, if you desire any worthy and fruitful effect, you must choose such as the world values, and such as may receive the allegiance of a manly mind. It has been said that six months study of the language of Schiller and Goethe, will now open to the student more enjoyment than six years study of the language of Greece and Rome. It is certain that six months study of French will now open to the student more of Europe, than six years of that which was once the European tongue.

BARON HOUGHTON (Richard Monckton Milnes, raised to the peerage in 1863), in an Essay on the Social Results of Classical Education (published in 1867), advocates "the more frank recognition of the worth and use of translations into modern languages, which represent, as truly as may be, the graces of form, and the essential merits of the original writers: versions, not merely accurate, but sympathetic with the matter and style they are handling—of poetry, by poets, of oratory, by orators, of history and philosophy, by affectionate students of the emotions and reflections of mankind. These should, by right, be the most effective material of school training, instead of being prohibited, and regarded as substitutes for severe study and inducements to juvenile indolence. But the true encouragement to a more general and unpedantic cultivation of what is universal and enduring in classic literature and life, beyond the mechanism of language, would result from such an alteration of the habitual methods of instruction as would strive, first and foremost, to fill the mind of each pupil with the realities of the past, and to make the thoughts and deeds of their old excellencies as intelligible to him as the events of his own time in the working of his own observation."

BOTANICAL SCIENCE.

ARTHUR HENFREY, in a Lecture before the London Society of Arts, advocates the claims of Botanical science for public schools:

The most remarkable of the classifications of the sciences which have been given to the world, may be briefly characterized by arrangement under three heads, indicating the really distinct points of view from which they set out:

1. Those based upon the sources of knowledge.
2. Those based upon the purpose for which the knowledge is sought; and
3. Those based upon the nature of the objects studied.

1. The classifications of the first kind,—those which arrange the various branches of knowledge according to the character of the intellectual methods and processes by means of which they are cultivated, are termed subjective, as regarding alone the nature of the recipient mind, or subject.

If we disregard the technicalities of metaphysics, or rather psychology, we may conveniently restrict our analysis of this, to the distinction of two qualities, those of *perception* and *reflection*.

By perception, by the aid of the senses, we observe facts: these facts may be either independent of our influence, when we call the *observation* proper; or they may be the result of special contrivance on our parts, when the mode of observation is called *experimentation*; and, again, we may receive information of observed facts by *testimony* of others. All these processes involve the acquisition of *experience*, direct or indirect, of phenomena; the sciences pursued especially by their means are called *experimental*, and the truths of experience are *facts*.

Reflection is the action of the reasoning faculty, according to its own laws, upon the simple ideas furnished by perception, dealing with certain *properties* of these, which it abstracts from the facts of perception, and, by the comparison and classification of them, arriving at generalizations, principles, laws, and the like, known by the collective name of *theory*. Those sciences which depend almost entirely upon the reason, are called *rational*, *abstract*, or *theoretical*.

Now, when we consider that there exists no science purely abstract from its origin, and that the measure of advancement of every science in the degree to which it has co-ordinated the ideas with which it deals under general propositions and laws, it becomes obvious that the division into *experimental* and abstract is totally inapplicable to the existing state of science.

2. The classifications according to purpose, the division into *speculative* and *applied or practical* sciences, fall almost in the same way, since the progression of every science is marked step by step, by the removal of certain truths from the position of abstract theories, interesting only to the learned, into the rank of axioms from which practical results of the greatest value are derived.

3. The third point of view is that from which we regard only the objects of our study, without considering either the faculties or processes by which we obtain our knowledge, or the advantages we may derive from its acquisition.

When we reflect upon the ordinary operations of our reasoning faculties, upon the common rules of logic, it becomes evident that this last mode of classification is the only one that can be called *rational*, since it is the only one which proceeds, according to the indispensable rule, of advancing from the most simple to the more complex of the ideas, which we wish to co-ordinate in our minds. The other two modes, the division into experimental and rational, abstract and applied sciences, must not only, from their nature, continually shift their ground as knowledge progresses, but they both set out from considerations of a highly complex character, which it would be vain to attempt to analyze, until a very large portion of the whole field of human inquiry has been cleared.

The principle is laid down by Descartes in his "Method," in the following terms:—"To conduct my thoughts in order, commencing with the objects which are simplest and easiest to know, so as to rise gradually to the knowledge of the more compound;" and in a subsequent chapter he traces the course of his inquiries through mathematics, general physics, botany, zoology, and the sciences relative to man, according to the progressive complexity of the subjects.

In the chain or series thus formed, there not only exists a logical sequence, a relation of progression of the number of *kinds of ideas* with which we have to deal, but there is a relation of dependence, inasmuch that each science rests upon that preceding it for a certain proportion of its data, and in turn constitains the necessary basis for that which follows,—added to which we find the history of the development of the individual sciences bringing a striking confirmation of the validity of the principle, by showing that, although the first steps were made almost simultaneously in all the great divisions of science here laid down, the most simple have, from their nature, outstripped, in exact proportion to their relative simplicity, those which involve more complicated classes of generalities; so that, as it has been well expressed, the *logical antecedents* have always been the *historical antecedents*.

The objective classification of the sciences may be briefly explained here.

The primary divisions depend upon the groups or classes of truths, which must be arranged according to their simplicity, or, what amounts to the same, their generality: in other words, the small number of qualities attached to the notions with which they deal.

The mathematical sciences deal with ideas which may be abstracted entirely from all material existence, retaining only the conceptions of space and number.

The physical sciences require, in addition, the actual recognition of matter, or force, or both, in addition to relations in space and time, but they are still confined to *universal* properties of matter.

The biological sciences are distinguished, in a most marked manner, by their dependence; the laws of life relate to objects having relations in space and time, and having material existence; they display, moreover, in their existence, a dependence upon physical laws, which form their medium; but they are distinguished by the presence of organization and life, characterized by a peculiar mobility and power of resistance to the physical forces, and an individuality of a different kind from that found in inorganic matter.

The sciences relating to man, to human society, are removed another step, by the interference, among all the preceding laws, of those relating to the human mind in its fullest sense.

We thus obtain four groups. The following table illustrates these remarks.—

Truths,	Abstract or absolute,	. . . .	Mathematical Sciences.
	Relative . . .	to Matter, .	Physical Sciences.
		to Life, . .	Biological Sciences.
		to Man, . .	Social Sciences.

These four groups include respectively a number of secondary sciences derived from, dependent on, or forming essential constituents of the groups. With these we shall only so far engage ourselves here as relates to the subdivisions of biological science. Certain common characters run through these, life and organization being attributes of all the objects with which they are conversant. Physiology and morphology traverse the whole field of organic nature, animal as well as vegetable. But as animals and vegetables exhibit, in mass, a manifest difference in the degree of complexity of the vital powers and the organization,—since the animal kingdom exhibits qualities which are superadded to, and conjoined with those which it shares with the vegetable kingdom,—it becomes necessary to distinguish the branches of biology relating to these, and to divide these sciences under two heads, Botany and Zoology.

The greater simplicity of the physiological processes of vegetables, is alone sufficient to indicate their inferiority, or antecedent position in the scale of natural objects; and this is further confirmed, in accordance with the principle of objective classification, by their greater generality, since they extend through the succeeding group, in the vegetative or organic life of animals, while the animal life proper is restricted to the latter. And this physiological distinction is in agreement with a morphological or anatomical difference; for not only is the apparatus of organic life more complicated in animals, but these possess a system of organs, the nervous system, which is not represented in any way in vegetables, and constitutes the especial instrument or seat of that kind of spontaneity which is the most striking characteristic of animal life.

We will now direct our attention to some further considerations regarding the relations of botany, as one of the biological sciences, to those preceding it in the classification we have adopted. That branch of physics which immediately precedes it is chemistry, the most special of the physical sciences, and its relations with this it will be sufficient for us to examine among the antecedents.

Chemistry, like the biological sciences, penetrates into the intimate constitution of natural bodies, and moreover, the bodies subject to its domain exhibit a kind of individuality not dependent upon ideas of number, density, color, &c.,

alone, but upon this said intimate constitution. We arrive here at the formation of certain abstract notions, for the purpose of classification, which include in the particulars from which they are derived, both statical and dynamical characters. These abstractions refer to the idea of a *species*, which, however, is far more general here than in botany or zoölogy. A species in chemistry is a definite compound of two or more elements, in obedience to certain general laws, possessing certain definite characters, by which it may be known from all other species; the relation between the objects represented in this conception is one of identity in all respects but that of simple material continuity; the individuality of separate natural objects belonging to the given species depends solely upon their being mechanically separated from each other. There do indeed exist *varieties* in chemical species analogous to the varieties of species in living nature, but these partake of the same unstable individuality, and depend upon physical causes of great generality. Thus the allotropic conditions of some chemical substances, and even perhaps the crystalline or amorphous states of many, may be regarded as varieties of this kind. These species are remarkable, not only from the generality of their nature but from their immobility. The only possible change in a chemical species is its conversion into other species, or transformation, in which the relations become entirely changed, and the name altered. There is nothing like development here,—the gradual unfolding by assimilation and transformation of material received from without.

In the organic kingdoms the idea of the species is an abstraction from very different facts. The objects to which it refers have a separate individuality, dependant upon characters non-existent in inorganic bodies. They are incapable of transformation, but susceptible of change according to certain laws; and while the chemical individual is homogeneous, and can only be divided into parts, of which each equally well represents the species, the biological individual is divisible in parts of different kinds, which have relations of harmony and continuity, but by no means of homogeneity, these parts making up together what constitutes the organism. Thus we see a distinct gradation between chemistry and biology, in reference to the generality of the notion which forms the basis of all classification in each.

In biology itself we find that the notion of the individual is modified in an analogous manner, when we carry it up from the vegetable into the animal kingdom; at all events, in those subjects of the latter, in which animality is most clearly manifest. In regard to taxonomy, then, or classification, botany stands between chemistry and zoölogy. * * *

As the taxonomy, or the classification of plants, is that department of botany which gives it a special utility as a means of mental training; as it is on this ground, above all, that it founds a claim to form a part of general education, it may be permitted me to enter into some technical details here, to illustrate and enforce the propositions just laid down. In the first place, the terminology of botany demands attention. It is a fundamental condition of the existence of organography, that the botanist should possess a rigidly defined technical language, a store of descriptive terms, sufficiently copious, to denote every part and every quality of the parts of plants by a distinct name, fixed, and unalterable in the sense in which it is employed. The technical language of botany, as elaborated by Linnæus and his school, has long been the admiration of logical and philosophical writers and has indeed been carried to great perfection. Every word has its definition, and can convey but one notion to those who have once mastered the language. The technicalities, therefore, of botanical language, which are vulgarly regarded as imperfections, and as repulsive to the inquirer, are in reality the very marks of its completeness, and far from offering a reason for withholding the science from ordinary education, constitute its great recommendation, as a method of training in accuracy of expression and habits of describing definitely and unequivocally the observations made by the use of the senses. The acquisition of the terms applied to the different parts of plants exercises the memory, while the mastery of the use of the adjectives of terminology cultivates, in a most beneficial manner, a habit of accuracy and perspicuity in the use of language. What is called the nomenclature of botany refers to the names given to the abstract notions of the kinds of beings dealt with in classification—to the species, genera, families, and so on. These refer not merely to the possession of particular attributes, but carry with them the idea of those attributes being distinctive of a *kind* of things; that is, they carry with them not only their definition founded upon qualities, but the idea, superadded to their definition, that these qualities are characteristic of an abstraction.

In the first place, it must be evident to every one that the general physiology of plants (which presupposes a knowledge of the physical and chemical laws influencing them), together with the concrete natural history of the species dealt with, must form the only secure basis of scientific agriculture; that it has not been fully recognized as such hitherto, depends upon its inevitable imperfections, which, however, will be the sooner removed, in proportion as agriculturists devote themselves to the study of physiological laws.

Secondly, botany finds a place in the two cosmological sciences studying the past and present conditions of the globe—Geology and Geography.

The perishable nature of vegetable structures does, indeed, render fossil remains of plants less valuable as objects for palaeontological reasonings, than the better-preserved hard parts of animals, especially as the latter afford safer grounds for estimating how much has been lost, how much preserved, of ancient forms of organization. But botanical reasonings form an essential link in geological inductions, although it is requisite to be very careful in applying the analogical method, derived from classification, to the history of the development of the organic creation.

In geography, that is, physical geography, the concrete natural history of plants becomes a portion of the concrete natural history of the globe; the physiological laws are involved with physical laws of climate, soil, &c., in the explanations of possible distributions, either in an abstract point of view, or for the purpose of practical application; while the systematic classifications, and the natural history of particular species, become the only guide by which we can attempt to trace back the existing conditions of distribution towards their origin, and thus perform the share due from botany; in the historical connection of physical geography with geology, of which it is properly only the statical part.

PROF. J. HOOKER, Director of the Botanical Gardens at Kew:

From my experience, I should judge that any study systematically pursued and mastered must necessarily expand the mental powers; but I think I should put classics at the bottom and mathematics next, and I should put natural history first, not because it is better than mathematics, but because it can be taught at an age when mathematics would injure the mind, and, further, it is applicable to minds which have no capacity for mathematics. A child can begin natural history at eight or nine years old, and it could be made an amusement and a pleasure if properly taught. A child, after having examined one buttercup, is enabled thereby to recognize another, though dissimilar, kind of buttercup, and the process affords pleasure.

I know that in conducting the examination of medical men for the army, which I have now conducted for several years, and those for the East India Company's service, which I have conducted for, I think, seven years, the questions which I am in the habit of putting, and which are not answered by the majority of the candidates, are what would have been answered by the children in Professor Henslow's village school. I believe the chief reason to be, that their observing faculties as children have never been trained, such faculties having lain dormant with those who naturally possessed them in a high degree, and having never been developed by training in those who possessed them in a low degree. Furthermore, in most medical schools the whole sum and substance of botanical science is crammed into a four weeks of lectures, and the men leave the class without an accurate knowledge of the merest elements of the science.

The advantage of botany is that you can teach it anywhere and everywhere. The child as he walks along can make use of his botanical knowledge, can preserve his specimen, and, having put his information into writing, can preserve this alongside of the specimen itself. This cannot be done to such advantage by a child in the case of geology, nor any branch of science except natural history ones, of which the most facile for the purpose is botany.

This science cannot be taught properly, or at least exclusively, by lectures. The learner must be accustomed to pull plants to pieces with skill and judgment. Now plants are always accessible, every child has the skill, and judgment comes by experience and teaching. This is why I so strongly advocate botany as the readiest, simplest, and most practical means for training the observing and reasoning faculties. Such training cannot be given by lectures.

NATURAL HISTORY.—STUDY OF ZOOLOGY.

PROF. T. H. HUXLEY, in a Lecture before the Science Classes at the South Kensington Museum, remarks:

Natural History is the name familiarly applied to the study of the properties of such natural bodies as minerals, plants, and animals; the sciences which embody the knowledge man has acquired upon these subjects are commonly termed Natural Sciences, in contradistinction to other, so called "physical," sciences; and those who devote themselves especially to the pursuit of such sciences have been, and are, commonly termed "Naturalists."

Linnæus was a naturalist in this wide sense, and his "Systema Naturæ" was a work upon natural history, in the broadest acceptation of the term; in it, that great methodising spirit embodied all that was known in his time of the distinctive characters of minerals, animals, and plants. But the enormous stimulus which Linnæus gave to the investigation of nature soon rendered it impossible that any one man should write another "Systema Naturæ," and extremely difficult for any one to become a naturalist such as Linnæus was.

Great as have been the advances made by all the three branches of science, of old included under the title of natural history, there can be no doubt that zoölogy and botany have grown in an enormously greater ratio than mineralogy; and hence, as I suppose, the name of "natural history" has gradually become more and more definitely attached to these prominent divisions of the subject, and by "naturalist" people have meant more and more distinctly to imply a student of the structure and functions of living beings.

However this may be, it is certain that the advance of knowledge has gradually widened the distance between mineralogy and its old associates, while it has drawn zoölogy and botany closer together; so that of late years it has been found convenient (and indeed necessary) to associate the sciences which deal with vitality and all its phenomena under the common head of "biology;" and the biologists have come to repudiate any blood-relationship with their foster-brothers, the mineralogists.

Certain broad laws have a general application throughout both the animal and the vegetable worlds, but the ground common to these kingdoms of nature is not of very wide extent, and the multiplicity of details is so great, that the student of living beings finds himself obliged to devote his attention exclusively either to the one or the other. If he elects to study plants, under any aspect, we know at once what to call him; he is a botanist, and his science is botany. But if the investigation of animal life be his choice, the name generally applied to him will vary, according to the kind of animals he studies, or the particular phenomena of animal life to which he confines his attention. If the study of man is his object he is called an anatomist, or a physiologist, or an ethnologist; but if he dissects animals, or examines into the mode in which their functions are performed, he is a comparative anatomist or comparative physiologist. If he turns his attention to fossil animals, he is a palæontologist. If his mind is more particularly directed to the description, specific discrimination, classification, and distribution of animals, he is termed a zoölogist.

For the purposes of the present discourse, however, I shall recognise none of these titles save the last, which I shall employ as the equivalent of botanist, and I shall use the term zoölogy as denoting the whole doctrine of animal life, in contradistinction from botany, which signifies the whole doctrine of vegetable life.

Employed in this sense, zoölogy, like botany, is divisible into three great but subordinate sciences, morphology, physiology, and distribution, each of which may, to a very great extent, be studied independently of the other.

Zoölogical morphology is the doctrine of animal form or structure. Anatomy is one of its branches, development is another; while classification is the expression of the relations which different animals bear to one another, in respect of their anatomy and their development.

Zoölogical distribution is the study of animals in relation to the terrestrial conditions which obtain now, or have obtained at any previous epoch of the earth's history.

Zoölogical physiology, lastly, is the doctrine of the functions or actions of animals. It regards animal bodies as machines impelled by certain forces, and performing an amount of work, which can be expressed in terms of the ordinary forces of nature. The final object of physiology is to deduce the facts of morphology on the one hand, and those of distribution on the other, from the laws of the molecular forces of matter.

My own impression is, that the best model for all kinds of training in physical science is that afforded by the method of teaching anatomy, in use in the medical schools. This method consists of lectures, demonstrations, and examinations.

The object of lectures is, in the first place, to awaken the attention and excite the enthusiasm of the student; and this, I am sure, may be effected to a far greater extent by the oral discourse and by the personal influence of a respected teacher, than in any other way. Secondly, lectures have the double use of guiding the student to the salient points of a subject, and at the same time forcing him to attend to the whole of it, and not merely to that part which takes his fancy. And lastly, lectures afford the student the opportunity of seeking explanations of those difficulties which will arise in the course of his studies. * *

But for a student to derive the utmost possible value from lectures, several precautions are needful.

I have a strong impression that the better a discourse is, as an oration, the worse it is as a lecture. The flow of the discourse carries you on without proper attention to its sense; you drop a word or a phrase, you lose the exact meaning for a moment, and while you strive to recover yourself, the speaker has passed on.

The practice I have adopted of late years, in lecturing to students, is to condense the substance of the hour's discourse into a few dry propositions, which are read slowly and taken down from dictation; the reading of each being followed by a free commentary, expanding and illustrating the proposition, explaining terms, and removing any difficulties that may be attackable in that way, by diagrams made roughly, and seen to grow under the lecturer's hand. In this manner you, at any rate, insure the co-operation of the student to a certain extent. He cannot leave the lecture-room entirely empty if the taking of notes is enforced; and a student must be preternaturally dull and mechanical, if he can take notes and hear them properly explained, and yet learn nothing.

What books shall I read? is a question constantly put by the student to the teacher. My reply usually is, "None: write your notes out carefully and fully; strive to understand them thoroughly; come to me for the explanation of anything you cannot understand; and I would rather you did not distract your mind by reading."

But, however good lectures may be, and however extensive the course of reading by which they are followed up, they are but accessories to the great instrument of scientific teaching—demonstration. If I insist unweariedly, nay fanatically, upon the importance of physical science as an educational agent, it is because the study of any branch of science, if properly conducted, appears to me to fill up a void left by all other means of education.

All that literature has to bestow may be obtained by reading and by practical exercise in writing and in speaking; but I do not exaggerate when I say, that none of the best gifts of science are to be won by these means. On the contrary, the great benefit which a scientific education bestows, whether as training or as knowledge, is dependent upon the extent to which the mind of the student is brought into immediate contact with facts—upon the degree to which he learns the habit of appealing directly to Nature, and of acquiring through his senses concrete images of those properties of things, which are, and always will be, but approximatively expressed in human language.

The great business of the scientific teacher is, to imprint the fundamental, irrefragable facts of his science, not only by words upon the mind, but by sensible impressions upon the eye, and ear, and touch of the student, in so complete a manner that every term used, or law enunciated, should afterwards call up vivid images of the particular structural, or other facts which furnished the demonstration of the law, or the illustration of the term. * *

What is the purpose of primary intellectual education? I apprehend that its first object is to train the young in the use of those tools wherewith men extract knowledge from the ever-shifting succession of phenomena which pass before their eyes; and that its second object is to inform them of the fundamental laws which have been found by experience to govern the course of things, so that they may not be turned out into the world naked, defenceless, and a prey to the events they might control.

A boy is taught to read his own and other languages, in order that he may have access to infinitely wider stores of knowledge than could ever be opened to him by oral intercourse with his fellow men; he learns to write that his means of communication with the rest of mankind may be indefinitely enlarged, and that he may record and store up the knowledge he acquires. He is taught elementary mathematics, that he may understand all those relations of number and form, upon which the transactions of men, associated in complicated societies, are built, and that he may have some practice in deductive reasoning.

But, in addition, primary education endeavors to fit a boy out with a certain equipment of positive knowledge. He is taught the great laws of morality; the religion of his sect; so much history and geography as will tell him where the great countries of the world are, what they are, and how they have become thus.

The system is excellent, so far as it goes. But if I regard it closely, a curious reflection arises. I suppose that, fifteen hundred years ago, the child of any well-to-do Roman citizen was taught just these same things; reading and writing in his own, and, perhaps, the Greek tongue; the elements of mathematics; and the religion, morality, history, and geography current in his time. Furthermore, I do not think I err in affirming, that, if such a Christian Roman boy, who had finished his education, could be transplanted into one of our public schools, and pass through its course of instruction, he would not meet with a single unfamiliar line of thought; amidst all the new facts he would have to learn, not one would suggest a different mode of regarding the universe from that current in his own time. And yet surely there is some great difference between the civilization of the fourth century and that of the nineteenth, and still more between the intellectual habits and tone of thought of that day and of this.

Modern civilization rests upon physical science; take away her gifts to our own country, and our position among the leading nations of the world is gone to-morrow; for it is physical science only, that makes intelligence and moral energy stronger than brute force.

Physical science, its methods, its problems, and its difficulties, will meet the poorest boy at every turn, and yet we educate him in such a manner that he shall enter the world as ignorant of the existence of the methods and facts of science as the day he was born. The modern world is full of artillery; and we turn out our children to do battle in it, equipped with the shield and sword of a gladiator.

It is my firm conviction that the only way to remedy it is, to make the elements of physical science an integral part of primary education. I have endeavored to show you how that may be done for that branch of science which it is my business to pursue; and I can but add, that I should look upon the day when every school-master throughout this land was a centre of genuine, however rudimentary, scientific knowledge, as an epoch in the history of the country.

Sir Charles Lyell, the eminent geologist, in his evidence, remarks substantially respecting physical science and natural history:

These branches of knowledge have been ignored in our educational system. Their neglect in the schools is owing to the fact that the chief rewards, prizes, and honors of the universities are given for proficiency in other studies, where preparatory work must be done in the schools, and all the instruction in these institutions is based on the idea that these pupils are all to go to the universities, whereas a majority of these pupils do not, but pass at once into business without any special preparation therefor. The teachers, too, of the public schools, have all been trained in the universities, and are themselves ignorant of the sciences which touch all the mechanical and mercantile interests of the state, and do not appreciate even their educational worth.

The universities do not, relatively, give as much attention to these subjects now as they did two hundred years ago, and this grew out of the revolution in the academical system at the time of the Reformation, when the separate colleges, each with an inadequate teaching force, were forced each to undertake the whole work of the university, and they have not since been able to keep up with the progress of the new sciences.

If these subjects are ever to go into the universities with advantage, the grammar of each must be mastered in the schools. The amount may be moderate, but the elements must be mastered, and the taste for one or more developed, if it is afterward to be pursued with a strong option.

The time can be gained by diminishing the quantity of Latin and Greek, except with those to whom these branches are to be specialties.

NATURAL HISTORY.

RICHARD OWEN, F. R. S., and Superintendent of the Natural History Department of the British Museum, and author of works of high reputation in comparative anatomy, paleontology, and kindred subjects, in his evidence before the Public School Commission, says:

I have long felt a great desire to see the time arrive when our larger educational establishments for youths, particularly the great public schools, to which the sons of the wealthy and territorial families in England are sent, should possess the means of imparting to them the elements and methods of natural history, either in botany or zoology, or both.

I am not aware of any arrangement or organization for a systematic instruction of the youths in those elements and methods at our great public schools, nor that they receive the smallest amount of natural history instruction. If I were to select a particular group it would be the governing and legislative class, which, from the opportunities I have had of hearing remarks in conversation or debate, appears to be least aware of the extent of many departments of natural history science, of the import of its generalizations, and especially of its use in disciplining the mind, irrespective of its immediate object of making known the different kinds of animals, plants, or minerals. Grammar and classics, arithmetic and geometry, may be the most important disciplinary studies; we know the faculties of the mind they are chiefly calculated to educe; but they fail in bringing out those which natural history science more especially tends to improve. I allude now to the faculty of accurate observation, of the classification of facts, of the coordination of classes or groups; the arrangement of topics, for example, in their various orders of importance in the mind, giving to a writer or public speaker improved powers of classifying all kinds of subjects. Natural history is essentially a classificatory science. Order and method are the faculties which the elements and principles of the science are best adapted to improve and to educe.

Natural history would represent, zoology, relating to animals; botany, to plants; mineralogy, to minerals. Of course it branches off into collateral subjects, as anatomy; some knowledge of that, indeed, would be necessarily acquired, because boys could not learn the classification of animals without getting some idea of the general principles of their construction. And so with regard to the classification of plants. Zoology and botany are both based on anatomy, or that which relates to the construction of animals and plants. With respect to geology, that would be too complex, and not necessary, I apprehend, for the main aim in view. All the disciplinary effect would be got by the lectures on natural history, which might be limited to one of the three classes, but I would recommend the branch relating to vegetables or animals.

Chemistry is a good subject to be taught. It induces, in the first instance, dexterity and nicety in the use of the fingers, besides caution in making a comparison of experimental results. No doubt there are useful faculties of the mind brought out well by chemistry. At the same time, there are the practical difficulties of the apparatus for experiments, and if I were to refer to age in regard to the teaching of natural science, I should be induced to raise the age in reference to the applicability of chemistry as a disciplinary science. The elder boys would be more careful and less mischievous, and therefore more likely to obtain a benefit from the laboratory in chemical teaching, without being so subject to its accompanying evils.

The modern languages I should be disposed to place first in importance, natural history next, chemistry last. With regard to astronomy and mechanics, these, I think, are already in part provided for in the illustrations of geometrical and algebraic teaching.

I think the uniform practice in the continental schools where natural sciences are taught is, to begin with natural history. The students learn the elements of zoology or botany first before going to chemistry and higher sciences.

I should be sorry to advocate natural history to the entire exclusion of chemistry or natural philosophy; but I do not think it would be wise to omit natural history in any great school and consider chemistry as its substitute chiefly on the grounds before stated; and partly for this reason, that in every community of two hundred or more youths, there must be some few, the constitution of whose minds is specially adapted to the study of natural history, to the work of observation and classification, who, consequently, are impelled by innate aptitude to that kind of study, but who are not at present afforded the slightest opportunity of working their minds in that way; so that it may happen that the faculty or gift for natural history, if it be not actually destroyed by exclusive exercise in uncongenial studies, is never educed. What is the result? In all our great natural history movements, we have looked in vain, since the death of Sir Joseph Banks, for any man having a sufficient standing in the country to fraternise with us, to understand us, to help us in debate or council on questions most vital to the interests of natural history. It has often occurred to me to ask how such should be the case, and my answer has been, that in the education of the noblemen and gentlemen, the great landed proprietors of England, of those destined to take part in the legislation and government of the country, there has been complete absence of systematic imparting of the elements of natural history, no demonstration of the nature and properties of plants and animals, no indication of the aims and importance of natural history, no training of the faculties for which it affords the healthiest exercise; consequently they have not been educed. I cannot doubt that this must have been the effect of the present restricted system. There must have been, by nature, many Sir Joseph Banks since he died, but they have been born, have grown up, and passed away without working out their destined purpose; their peculiar talent has never been educed, their attention has never been turned to those studies, but they have been wholly devoted to classics. It must be remembered that minds of this class are usually very averse to classical studies and mere exercises of memory and composition; they never take to them; they get through them as well or ill as they can, doing little or nothing to the purpose, and they fail to achieve that for which they are naturally fitted from the want of having their special faculties educed. I consider it a loss to the nation that, in our great educational establishments for youths, there should be no arrangements for giving them the chance of knowing something of the laws of the living world and how they are to be studied.

Prof. Jukes, in opening the business of the Geological Section of the British Association, over which he presided at Cambridge, remarks:

"The natural sciences are now considered as worthy of study by those who have a taste for them, both in themselves and as a means of mental training and discipline. In my time, however, no other branches of learning were recognised than classics and mathematics, and I have with shame to confess that I displayed but a truant disposition with respect to them, and too often hurried from the tutor's lecture room to the river or field to enable me to add much to the scanty store of knowledge I had brought up with me. Had it not been, then, for the teaching of Professor Sedgwick in geology, my time would have been wasted."

So that it was just the accident, so to speak, of one short course on a branch of natural history, grafted through an old bequest upon the main studies of his university, that led Professor Jukes to his appreciation of the method of study and value of the science which owes so much to his labours. I could also, with your permission, adduce a higher authority on the main point, and that is Baron Cuvier's, who, in the preface to the first edition of his elementary book on Natural History, expresses himself as follows:

"The habit necessarily acquired in the study of natural history, of mentally classifying a great number of ideas, is one of the advantages of this science, which is seldom spoken of, and which, when it shall have been generally introduced into the system of common education, will perhaps become the principal one; it exercises the student in that part of logic which is termed method, as the study of geometry does in that which is called syllogism, because natural history is the science which requires the most precise methods, as geometry is that which demands the most rigorous reasoning. Now, this art of method, when once well acquired, may be applied with infinite advantage to studies the most foreign to natural history. Every discussion which supposes a classification of facts, every research which requires a distribution of matters, is performed after the same manner, and he who has cultivated this science merely for amusement is surprised at the facility it affords for disentangling all kinds of affairs. It is not less useful in solitude; sufficiently extensive to satisfy the most powerful mind, sufficiently various and interesting to calm the most agitated soul; it consoles the unhappy, and tends to allay enmity and hatred. Once elevated to the contemplation of the harmony of nature, invariably regulated by Providence, how weak and trivial appear those causes which it has been pleased to leave dependent upon the will of man! How astonishing to behold so many fine minds consuming themselves so anxiously for their own happiness and that of others in the pursuit of vain combinations, the very traces of which a few years suffice to obliterate! I avow it proudly, these ideas have always been present to my mind, the companions of my labors, and, if I have endeavored by every means in my power to advance this peaceful study, it is because, in my opinion, it is more capable than any other of supplying the want of occupation which has so largely contributed to the troubles of our age."

ON THE STUDY OF PHYSIOLOGY.

PROF. GEORGE E. PAGET, in a Lecture before the British Medical Association at Cambridge in 1864, advocates this study as follows:

THE advantages to be expected from the general teaching of Physiology may be grouped in two classes: the first, including such as would tend to the promotion of the science; the second, such as would belong to the students.

By a wider diffusion of the knowledge of physiology its progress would be accelerated, as that of any other science would, by the increased number of the competent observers of its facts. * * * But a large advantage, and one which, I think, physiology needs more than any other science does, would arise in this,—that the communication would be easier, which is now so difficult, between those who are engaged in it, and those who especially devote themselves to other sciences that might assist it. Almost every process in the living body involves the exercise of mechanical and chemical—perhaps, also, of electrical—forces, whose effects are mingled with those of the more proper vital force; and although this special force may modify, and in some sort veil, the effects of those others, yet must their effects be reckoned and allowed for, in nearly every case we have to study. Therefore, the complete solution of any new physiological problem must require such a master of all these sciences of dead and living matter as cannot now, I believe, be found, or else it must have the coöperation of many workers, each skilled in some simple science, and able to communicate with all the rest. * * *

I believe that a moderate acquaintance with the principles of physiology, acquired in early life, would benefit a man, with regard to both his body and his mind; and that it would do this by guiding him in the maintenance and improvement of health, by teaching him the true economy of his powers, whether mental or corporal, by providing worthy materials for thought, and by cultivating peculiar modes, and suggesting peculiar ends, of thinking. * * *

I would not have its teaching limited to a bare declaration of the use and exact fitness of each part or organ of the body. This, indeed, should not be omitted; for there are noble truths in the simplest demonstrations of the fitness of parts for their simplest purposes, and no study has been made more attractive than this by the ingenuity, the acuteness, and eloquence of its teachers. But I would go beyond this, and, striving, as I said before, to teach general truths as well as the details of science, I would try to lead the mind to the contemplation of those general designs, from which it might gather the best lessons for its own guidance. * * *

It must be an object of all education to supply, in early life, those studies from which, in later years, may arise reflections that may mingle happily with the business-thoughts of common days; that may suggest to the reason, or even to the imagination, some hidden meaning, some future purpose, some noble end, in the things about us. Reflections such as these, being interwoven with our common thoughts, may often bring to our life a tone of joy which its general aspect will not wear; like brilliant threads shot through the texture of some sombre fabric, giving lustre to its darkness.

PHYSICS, CHEMISTRY, PHYSIOLOGY, GERMAN.

H. W. ACKLAND, Regius Professor of Medicine at Oxford, and teacher of Anatomy and Physiology in Christ Church College, said:

We are living in a period of transition with reference to the educational question; and if I look back to the time when I became Reader in Anatomy at Oxford, which was in the year 1845, I should say that it was a very rare thing for any person to come with his mind previously directed to scientific pursuit. In the seventeen years which have elapsed, that state of things has somewhat changed. We find that boys come to the University from several schools quite able to appreciate the opportunities of scientific study which they have now in Oxford; and I can see that the younger men who have left the universities with enlarged tastes in these directions, who are not destined to follow scientific pursuits, are beginning to carry away with them into the country, into different situations to which they may go, and, among others, to private schools, scientific knowledge, sometimes of a very precise kind; and so in that way necessarily these tastes will be gradually disseminated, and react on the universities.

About fifteen or sixteen years ago, Professor Jewett and Dr. Stanley, who were then young tutors, and engaged in some extensive inquiries with regard to the promotion of a wider sphere of education in Oxford, asked my opinion what scientific studies should be introduced. The opinion which I gave them after much reflection was this, that there were three fundamental subjects, which unquestionably ought to be required before young men were allowed to pursue any other; and that they might not take honours or pass except they showed proficiency in these three. These were, Physics, so-called, Chemistry, and Physiology, to use the word physiology in a very general sense. These three subjects were so fundamental to all other organic sciences, and so necessary to the study of most branches of scientific knowledge, that all pass men ought to be required to pass in these subjects, before they were allowed to take other more detailed ones, such as geology, mineralogy, or zoology, or many other "ologies," which might be mentioned. Accordingly, wisely or unwisely, that became the law at Oxford, and at Oxford now no person can pass in a scientific subject, except he passes in two at least of these which we held to be educationally fundamental.

Just as I said fifteen years ago, Physiology, Physics, and Chemistry should be the fundamental subjects at the universities, so I think that those who come to the universities, if they really are to progress, and if their education is to be carried on systematically, had much better come trained, as far as boys should be trained in such subjects at all, in Physics, in Chemistry, or in both, before they come to the university, and then they would either carry on those subjects to a higher pitch at the university where the greatest opportunities ought to be found, or they might pass on to the biological or other sciences as they pleased.

I may add, generally, that I should value all knowledge of these physical sciences very little indeed unless it was otherwise than bookwork. If it is merely a question of getting up certain books, and being able to answer certain book questions, that is merely an exercise of the memory of a very useless kind. The great object, though not the sole object of this training, should be to get the boys to observe and understand the action of matter in some department or another; and although I am perfectly aware that what is called practical knowledge, if merely manipulatory, in any subject whatever, is a humble thing enough; yet, on the other hand, I must say that the utmost amount of knowledge on these subjects without that practical and experimental knowledge is to most persons nearly as useless. You want the combination of the two; and for youths, I value very little the mere acquisition of a quantity of book facts on these subjects. I want them to see and know the things, and in that way they will evoke many qualities of the mind which the study of these subjects is intended to develop, and which are not evoked by the study of the classics; but I am not at all prepared to say that those same qualities or any similar qualities may not be evoked by other means, although not by the classics. I mean to put this reservation in stating my opinion, that I cannot think that the study of the physical sciences is, as I sometimes hear it stated, absolutely necessary for everybody. There may be good men, as good as anybody else, without it. It is perhaps unnecessary to make that reservation, but I am in the habit of hearing the subject spoken of sometimes as though a man must be an inferior man because he is unacquainted with any branch of physical science. I do not hold that at all, because observation, practical habits, manual dexterity, and many such things are acquired in a high degree by persons who have no scientific knowledge.

I thought it so necessary to the general national education, that the power of studying Physiology in its highest departments, and in the best possible manner, should exist in Oxford, that I labored with other persons to enable the University to possess the means of that study, which it had not to a similar extent before, and which should be pursued with the greatest advantage at the universities; but the study of precise Physics, and a knowledge of Chemistry are becoming more necessary to understand Physiological works, so that the older Physiologists, unless they are able to bring up their knowledge of those subjects to the present level, will be left entirely behind. Therefore, it would further the cause of education if they were first learnt at schools, so that those who came up to the universities should have the opportunity of studying Physiology as an advanced subject if they came up with the necessary preliminary knowledge.

I must say as a physician, that being my main business now, that I really view with alarm the way in which boys are pressed at school. I must ask your forgiveness for introducing an extraneous subject, but I say truly that I view with alarm the pressure which is put on good boys. I am afraid it remains to be seen fifty years hence what the effect of this system on the *physique* of the country will be. Children are surrounded by every means of cramming things into their brains, and a number of us are seeing how we can force in something more in their very earliest years. I confess I think this a matter of much anxiety.

I feel confident that a great deal of the learning by heart is useless; the physical sciences exercise the memory in a higher degree than anything else; at least anything with which I am acquainted. If you go over a book of human descriptive anatomy, the quantity of facts which have to be mastered are astonishing. I do not believe that boys' tastes are refined or their higher intellectual qualities called out by learning to gallop over so many lines of Virgil or Homer. It is an effort of memory, and has no corresponding effect on the character; I believe by the other study they would acquire a certain quantity of useful knowledge, and the faculties of attention and memory are quite as much exercised. They are taught to think; which no amount of learning by heart can teach.

It is a great advantage to a scientific man now-a-days to know German, and a great disadvantage not to know it. I know it imperfectly, so I know the disadvantage. I think that the possession of an additional language in early life is so invaluable to a youth, that I would take the chance of his obtaining his science at a later period, when he would have the further aid of German in acquiring it.

PHYSICS AS A MEANS IN MENTAL DEVELOPMENT.

PROFESSOR JOHN TYNDALL, in a Lecture at the Royal Institution of Great Britain, on the study of Physics, remarks:—

The term Physics, as made use of in the present Lecture, refers to that portion of natural science which lies midway between astronomy and chemistry. The former, indeed, is Physics applied to masses of enormous weight, while the latter is Physics applied to atoms and molecules. The subjects of Physics proper are, therefore, those which lie nearest to human perception:—the light and heat of the sun, color, sound, motion, the loadstone, electrical attractions and repulsions, thunder and lightning, rain, snow, dew, and so forth. The senses of Man stand between these phenomena, between the external world, and the world of thought. He takes his facts from Nature and transfers them to the domain of mind; he looks at them, compares them, observes their mutual relations and connexions, and thus brings them clearer and clearer before his mental eye, until, finally, by a kind of inspiration, he alights upon the cause which unites them. This is the last act of the mind, in this centripetal direction, in its progress from the multiplicity of facts to the central cause on which they depend. But, having guessed the cause, he is not yet contented: he now sets out from his centre and travels in the other direction: he sees that if his guess be true, certain consequences must follow from it, and he appeals to the law and testimony of experiment whether the thing is so. Thus he completes the circuit of thought,—from without inward, from multiplicity to unity, and from within outward, from unity to multiplicity. He traverses the line between cause and effect both ways, and, in so doing, calls all his reasoning powers into play. The mental effort involved in these processes may be justly compared to those exercises of the body which invoke the co-operation of every muscle, and thus confer upon the whole frame the benefits of healthy action.

A few days ago a Master of Arts, who is still a young man, and therefore the recipient of a modern education, stated to me that for the first twenty years of his life he had been taught nothing regarding Light, Heat, Magnetism, or Electricity: twelve of these years had been spent among the ancients, all connexion being thus severed between him and natural phenomena. Now, we cannot, without prejudice to humanity, separate the present from the past. The nineteenth century strikes its roots into the centuries gone by, and draws nutriment from them. The world cannot afford to lose the record of any great deed or utterance; for such deeds and such utterances are prolific throughout all time. We cannot yield the companionship of our loftier brothers of antiquity,—of our Socrates and Cato,—whose lives provoke us to sympathetic greatness across the interval of two thousand years. As long as the ancient languages are the means of access to the ancient mind, they must ever be of priceless value to humanity; but it is as the avenues of ancient thought, and not as the instruments of modern culture, that they are chiefly valuable to Man. Surely these avenues might be kept open without demanding such sacrifices as that above referred to. We have conquered and possessed ourselves of continents of land, concerning which antiquity knew nothing; and if new continents of thought reveal themselves to the exploring human spirit, shall we not possess them also? In these latter days, the study of Physics has given us glimpses of the methods of Nature which were quite hidden from the ancients, and it would be treason to the trust committed to us, if we were to sacrifice the hopes and aspirations of the Present out of deference to the Past.

The study of Physics, as already intimated, consists of two processes, which are complementary to each other—the tracing of facts to their causes, and the logical advance from the cause to the fact. In the former process, called *induction*, certain moral qualities come into play. It requires patient industry, and an humble and conscientious acceptance of what Nature reveals. The first condition of success is an honest receptivity and a willingness to abandon all preconceived notions, however cherished, if they be found to contradict the truth.

The second process in physical investigation is *deduction*, or the advance of the mind from fixed principles to the conclusions which flow from them. The rules of logic are the formal statement of this process, which, however, was practised by every healthy mind before ever such rules were written. In the study of Physics, induction and deduction are perpetually married to each other. The man observes,—he strips facts of their peculiarities of form, and tries to unite them by their essences; having effected this, he at once deduces, and thus checks his induction. Here the grand difference between the methods at present followed, and those of the ancients, becomes manifest. They were one-sided in these matters: they omitted the process of induction, and substituted conjecture for observation. They do not seem to have possessed sufficient patience to watch the slow processes of Nature, and to make themselves acquainted with the conditions under which she operates. Ignorant of these conditions, they could never penetrate her secrets nor master her laws. This mastery not only enables us to turn her forces against each other, so as to protect ourselves from their hostile action, but makes them our slaves. By the study of Physics we have opened to us treasuries of power of which antiquity never dreamed: we lord it over Matter, but in so doing we have become better acquainted with the laws of Mind; for to the mental philosopher material Nature furnishes a screen against which the human spirit projects its own image, and thus becomes capable of self inspection.

Thus, then, as a means of intellectual culture, the study of Physics exercises and sharpens observation: it brings the most exhaustive logic into play: it compares, abstracts, and generalizes, and provides a mental imagery admirably suited to these processes. The strictest precision of thought is everywhere enforced, and prudence, foresight, and sagacity are demanded. By its appeals to experiment, it continually checks itself, and builds upon a sure foundation.

Thus far we have regarded the study of Physics as an agent of intellectual culture; but like other things in Nature, it subserves more than a single end. The colors of the clouds delight the eye, and, no doubt, accomplish moral purposes also; but the self-same clouds hold within their fleeces the moisture by which our fields are rendered fruitful. The sunbeams excite our interest and invite our investigation; but they also extend their beneficent influences to our fruits and corn, and thus accomplish, not only intellectual ends, but minister, at the same time, to our material necessities. And so it is with scientific research. While the love of science is a sufficient incentive to the pursuit of science, and the investigator, in the prosecution of his inquiries, is raised above all material considerations, the results of his labors may exercise a potent influence upon the physical condition of Man.

As an instrument of intellectual culture, the study of Physics is profitable to all: as bearing upon special functions, its value, though not so great, is still more tangible. Why, for example, should Members of Parliament be ignorant of the subjects concerning which they are called upon to legislate? In this land of practical physics, why should they be unable to form an independent opinion upon a physical question? Why should the senator be left at the mercy of interested disputants when a scientific question is discussed, until he deems the nap a blessing which rescues him from the bewilderments of the committee-room? The education which does not supply the want here referred to, fails in its duty to England. With regard to our working people, in the ordinary sense of the term working, the study of Physics would, I imagine, be profitable, not only as a means of mental culture, but also as a moral influence to woo these people from pursuits which now degrade them. * * *

The world was built in order: it is the visual record of its Maker's logic, and to us have been trusted the will and power to grapple with the mighty argument. Descending for a moment from this high ground to considerations which lie closer to us as a nation—as a land of gas and furnaces, of steam and electricity: as a land which science, practically applied, has made great in peace and mighty in war;—I ask you whether this "land of old and just renown," has not a right to expect from her institutions a culture which shall embrace something more than declension and conjugation? They can place physical science upon its proper basis; they can check the habit, now too common, of regarding science solely as an instrument of material prosperity; they can dwell with effect upon its nobler use, and raise the national mind to the contemplation of it as the last development of that "increasing purpose" which runs through the ages and widens the thoughts of men.

J. M. WILSON ON TEACHING NATURAL SCIENCE.

PROF. WILSON, Assistant Master in Mathematics and Natural Science in Rugby School, who has been eminently successful in introducing Natural Science into this great public school, has published an admirable Essay (McMillan's Liberal Studies) on teaching this subject in schools.

FAILURE OF THE LATIN AND GREEK DISCIPLINE.

The astonishing ignorance of Latin and Greek, or at least of all the finer part of this knowledge on which so much stress is laid; and the ignorance—which is less surprising, if not less lamentable—of everything else, with which so many boys leave most schools, has been dwelt on again and again. Is it remediable or is it not? Is it due to the carelessness and inability of masters; to the inherent unsuitability of the subjects taught; to neglected early education and bad preparatory schools; or to the illiterate tone of the society in which boys are brought up; to excessive novel reading and devotion to games; or to the great fact that the majority of the species are incapable of learning much? Partly perhaps to them all; certainly to an ill-advised course of study. For at present, literature, or the studies which are subordinate to it, has almost a monopoly: and on language the great majority of boys fail in getting much hold. The exclusive study of language at schools weakens the fibre of those who have genius for it, fails to educate to the best advantage the mass who have fairly good sense but no genius for anything, but obscures and depresses the few who have special abilities in other lines; and it precludes the possibility of learning much besides. So that even at a school where classics are well taught, where the masters are able and skillful, and the boys industrious, not very much is learnt. It was said of a Scotchman who enjoyed a cheap reputation for hospitality, "that he kept an excellent table, but put verra leetle upon it." This epitomizes the report of the Public School Commission: the schools are excellent, but they teach "verra leetle." And this is the less excusable because the experience of the best foreign schools is showing the advantage of introducing greater variety into the course of study. A wider net is cast; fewer minds repose in undisturbed apathy; more varied abilities are recognized; there is less over-estimation of special branches of knowledge; and, what is more important, the variety is itself a stimulus.

DIGNITY AND GRANDEUR OF SCIENTIFIC KNOWLEDGE.

We count a man educated in proportion to the exactness, width, and nobleness of his ideas. What is needed to elevate a man's intellectual nature is not that he should be an encyclopædia, but that he should have great ideas. And these must be based on knowledge. They do not, indeed, always accompany knowledge. Great ideas may be got by various studies, and all studies may be pursued by men who fail to gain great ideas. I know men with a wide and microscopic knowledge of history who know nothing of the love of freedom, of national justice, of the progress of the world, of the power of genius and will;—men who are theologians by profession, whose thoughts still revolve in the narrowest circle of earthly prejudices;—scholars indifferent alike to literature and learning. And so there are scientific men who combine poverty of intellect with width of knowledge. A botanist may be as foolish as a crest collector; a geologist, and even an astronomer, may, perhaps, be a pedant not more ennobled by the sphere of his thoughts than a cathedral spider is affected by the majesty of his abode; but I will venture to assert, that the great thoughts and principles which are to be gained only by scientific knowledge are not only of a quality that increases the dignity of a man's mind, are not only intrinsically glorious and elevating, but are not inferior, whether we regard their effect on the intellect or on the imagination, to those which may be reached by other studies. And I am not speaking only of the discoverers in science. There is a special charm, indeed, and stimulating power in original research, in exploring new regions; but there are splendid ideas, magnificent points of view, which, though others have reached them before, yet to attain is a lifelong pleasure. The ordinary tourist may climb to some well-worn spot in the Alps, he may ascend by the beaten track, he may even be carried there, and yet he will be richly rewarded by the view that unfolds itself before his eyes. He may not feel the glow of health, the buoyant soul of the first mountaineer that stood there; but he will see what he will remember for ever; he will get more than a new sensation, he will have enlarged his soul. So to be the first to climb, as Newton did, with solitary steps, to the untrodden heights from which he gazed on the solar system spread out at his feet, can never again be given to mortal man; but to attain the knowledge, to see the magnificent orderliness and progress, to be profoundly impressed with the infinities of space and time which it silently suggests, is to have gained a treasure that lasts as long as life will last. So also geology has a sublimity of its own, slowly reached by many steps and much toil. And, above all, the great ideas of natural law and harmonious adjustment can only be obtained by patient study in the fields of science; and are they not priceless to those who have in any degree won them? Who can contemplate our globe in this orderly system of the universe, with all the delicate adjustments that astronomy reveals, and all the splendid mechanism of the heavens—contemplate our atmosphere, with all its mechanical, chemical, and physical properties—the distant sun darting its light and heat and power on the globe, and fostering all the varied beautiful animal and vegetable life, giving rise to winds and showers and fruitful seasons, and beauties of form and richness of color, filling our hearts with food and gladness; who can know something of the inexorable sequences, see something of the felicitous combination of all the varied forces of nature that are employed,—and not feel impressed and awed by the view; not feel that he is in the presence of a Power and Wisdom that as far transcends the power and wisdom of man as the universe surpasses a watch in magnitude?

'To see in part
That all, as in some piece of art,
Is toil, coöperant to an end,'

is to see that which he who sees it not is as incapable of estimating as the deaf man is of judging of music, or the blind of enjoying the glories of a sunset. Such are some of the ideas which crown science, and it is not granted to us to attain them except by slow degrees. Step by step must the growing mind approach them; and to exclude from our schools the preliminary steps is to debar from the attainment of such ideas all whose leisure in after-life is so curtailed that they can never break ground in any fresh subject for thought or labor.

EXACTNESS AND POWER OF SCIENCE.

Science is not only knowledge, but it is also power. The mind is not only an instrument for advancing science, but, what is more to our present point, science is an instrument for advancing the mind. All that can be said on this point has been said over and over again, and I can contribute nothing except my daily experience that what is said is true. Mill speaks of "the indispensable necessity of scientific instruction, for it is recommended by every consideration which pleads for any high order of intellectual education at all." Science is the best teacher of accurate, acute, and exhaustive observation of what is; it encourages the habit of mind which will rest on nothing but what is true; truth is the ultimate and only object, and there is the ever-recurring appeal to facts as the test of truth. And it is an excellent exercise of memory; not the verbal, formal memory, but the orderly, intelligent, connected, accurate storing up of knowledge. And of all processes of reasoning it stands alone as the exhaustive illustration. It is pre-eminently the study that illustrates the art of thinking. "The processes by which truth is attained," to quote again from Mill, "reasoning and observation have been carried to their greatest known perfection in the physical sciences." In fact the investigations and reasoning of science, advancing as it does from the study of simple phenomena to the analysis of complicated actions, form a model of precisely the kind of mental work which is the business of every man, from his cradle to his grave; and reasoning, like other arts, is best learnt by practice and familiarity with the highest models. Science teaches what the power and what the weakness of the senses is; what evidence is, and what proof is. There is no characteristic of an educated man so marked as his power of judging of evidence and proof. The precautions that are taken against misinterpretation of what is called the evidence of the senses, and against wrong reasoning, and tracing the thoughts backward down to the ground of belief; the constant verification of theories; the candid suspension of judgment where evidence is still wanting; that wedding of induction and deduction into a happy unity and completeness of proof, the mixture of observation and ratiocination—are precisely the mental processes which all men have to go through somehow or other in their daily business, and which every human being who is capable of forming an intelligent opinion on the subject sees would be better done if men had familiarized themselves with the models of these processes which are furnished by science. I do not mean that a boy knows he is doing all these things; but he is doing them visibly. And when he applies the analysis of logic to the processes of his mind, he will find that he has been thinking logically, though unconsciously so.

Thinking is learnt by thinking; and it is my strongest conviction, as it is my daily experience, that boys can and do learn to think,—learn all the varied operations of the mind we sum up in that word,—by the study of science. A more vigorous school of thought, and a habit of mind less inclined to the faults of dogmatism on the one side, and deference to authority on the other, with more reverence for truth, and more confidence in knowledge, is the natural product of scientific instruction. * * *

Moreover, taking education in its broad sense as the training of all the powers that go to make up the man, I would point out how much science contributes towards increasing the powers of the senses. All science is based, some one has said, on the fact that we have great curiosity, and very weak eyes; and science gives man a marvelous extension of the power and range of the acuteness of those eyes. "Eyes and no eyes" is the title of an old story; and it scarcely seems too strong a way of marking the difference between the powers of perception of a cultivated naturalist, and those of the ordinary gentleman ignorant of everything in nature. To the one the stars of heaven, and the stones on earth, the forms of the hills, and the flowers in the hedges, are a constant source of that great and peculiar pleasure derived from intelligence. And day by day do I see how boys increase their range of sight, and that not only of the things we teach them to see, but they outrun us, and discover for themselves. And the power, once gained, can never be lost. I know many instances of boys whose eyes were opened at school by the ordinary natural science lectures, who have since found great pleasure and constant occupation in some branch of scientific study.

And I would add that whatever may be the defects of a purely literary education, which I obviously do not intend to discuss, they cannot be remedied by mathematics alone. Mathematics are so often thought, by those who are ignorant of them, to be the key to all reasoning, and to be the perfection of training, and so often spoken of by proficients in them as mysteries that it is worth the labor of half a lifetime to understand, that it is worth while to remember that after all they are only compendious and very limited methods of applying deductive reasoning, assisted by symbols, to questions of which the data are, or are supposed to be, extremely precise. They no more teach reasoning in the ordinary sense of the word than traveling by railway fits a man for exploring in Central Africa. And hence, while I set a very high value on arithmetic and geometry in all education, it is not because they supply the place of science in any sense, but on entirely different grounds. They form the language of science, however, and are indispensable to its study.*

DEFICIENCY OF A MERELY SCIENTIFIC CURRICULUM.

The vague impression that reverence, faith, belief in the unseen and the spiritual, and in truths derived from individual consciousness, are diminished, as superstitions are diminished, by the school of science, must not be met by an off-hand denial that there is any foundation for it; for constant dealing with nature and exercise of the intellect alone, as contrasted with humanity and the exercise of the moral feelings, unquestionably tend to exclude men from the highest thoughts. All that may be said about the dignity of the study of created things—and this is a truth that often needs to be enforced—must not make its advocates lose sight of the relation of this study to others. The wish of many men of science that it should form the staple of liberal education, if gratified, would probably lead to a loss of gracefulness and unconscious art in style, which characterizes nations which study the classics, and moreover would produce a peculiar and dangerous one-sidedness, which may be distinctly seen in many individual cases. In such cases, their constant study of one kind of evidence raises a secret disinclination and real inaptitude, for the time being, to accept

* It is singular that the Mathematical Tripos at Cambridge is so unscientific, and the Natural Science Tripos at Oxford so unmathematical. At Cambridge a man may get the highest honors in mathematics and natural philosophy and have never seen a crystal, a lens, an air pump, or a thermometer; and at Oxford a man may get his First in natural science without knowing the Binomial Theorem or the solution of a triangle. Surely these are mistakes.

evidence of a different kind, and induces them openly or tacitly, to depreciate and distrust it. They are constantly tempted to consider the finer mental and religious sensibilities as useless, and as if they proved nothing. They are facts, of course, but facts which verge on fancies; and they have acquired a distaste for this kind of reflection, and something of contempt for its value in others. They seem to have raised a wall between themselves and certain truths; to have dazzled their eyes by a study of the glaring truths of external nature, and to be for the time incapable of discerning the dimmer but nobler truths of the soul and its relations. They distrust what may not be referred to the mechanism of organization, and disbelieve that the reason alone can be the source of real truths. Yet all this does not tend to prove that science should be excluded from schools, but that it should not form the staple of our education.

TIME—SUBJECTS AND METHODS OF SCIENTIFIC STUDY.

Two hours a week, with the same time for preparation out of school, is the time given at Rugby, and is as much as I would wish to see the subject started with. I do not doubt however that ultimately it will be thought better to increase this, in the upper part of the school, to three or four hours a week. This seems too little to ask, and the advocates of science outside schools will disallow so petty a claim. But there is very little experience of the working of scientific teaching in great schools; there is at present so slight a recognition of science in schools on the part of the Universities, that any public school which gave up much time to science, would be hopelessly out of the race at the Universities. And this would be suicidal. If the reform is on sound principles, let science gain a footing only, and a friendly struggle for existence will point out whether the foreigner can be naturalised, and flourish.

Next as to the parts of science to be taught, and the methods of teaching; and the discussion of these must be given at some length.

It is important to distinguish at once, and clearly, between *scientific information* and *training in science*. 'In other words,' to quote from the Report of the Committee appointed by the Council of the British Association to consider the best means for promoting Scientific Education in Schools, 'between general literary acquaintance with scientific facts, and the more minute and accurate knowledge that may be gained by studying the facts and methods at first hand, under the guidance of a competent teacher. Both of these are valuable; it is very desirable, *for example*, that boys should have some general information about the ordinary phenomena of nature, such as the simple facts of Astronomy, of Geology, of Physical Geography, and of elementary Physiology. On the other hand, the scientific habit of mind, which is the principal benefit resulting from scientific training, and which is of incalculable value, whatever be the pursuits of after life, can better be attained by a thorough knowledge of the facts and principles of one science, than by a general acquaintance with what has been said or written about many. Both of these should co-exist, we think, at any school which professes to offer the highest liberal education.'

There may be used in the lower part of the school, some work on Physical Geography, embracing the elements of the subjects above-named; and it will be found extremely convenient to introduce short courses of lectures on such subjects as these, even in the higher parts of the school. For since new boys are perpetually coming, and it is impossible that a new course of lectures on Botany, or on Mechanics, should be started in every division of the school at the beginning of every term, without requiring the number of natural science masters to be almost indefinitely increased, there must be some collecting place, a class in which the new boys shall accumulate until they are numerous enough to form a body to enter on the regular course. This must be a class in which Physical Geography, including if the master likes, the elements of Geology and Astronomy, is taught. In such classes as these the ideas of boys are expanded, fresh books are opened to them; and some will avail themselves of the opening, and learn a good deal about the subjects spoken of, but the value is more literary than scientific; and even after the most careful teaching will be found disappointing. In lecturing on such subjects as Geology, Astronomy, or Physical Geography, the master never can be sure that the ideas he has so clearly in his own mind are seized by all his boys. There seems to be a deficiency in powers of conception on the part of very many boys. Theorists may say what they please, but it is true that the act of the mind in forming a conception is difficult to excite. There is a marvelous, truly marvelous, want of imagination in many minds, want of power to form and keep in view a distinct image of the thing reasoned or spoken about. It is not only want of attention, but there seems to be a total separation in some minds between words and things, perhaps the result, in part, of early teaching; so that the knowledge apparently gained is sometimes wholly unsound.

Meaning of Mental Training.

The mental training to be got from the study of science is the main reason for its introduction into schools. It is with reference to this that the subjects of instruction, and the methods of instruction, must be chosen. It is important therefore, that what is meant by *mental training* should be distinctly understood. Training is the cultivation bestowed on any set of faculties with the object of developing them. It is possible to train the body, and to train the mind, for a great variety of purposes, some very foolish ones. But in all cases the training consists in *doing*. If you wish to swim, you must go into the water and swim as best you can: if you wish to box, there is no way of learning but by boxing: if you wish to study music or drawing, you must play and sing or draw: and thus in educating others you must make them *do* whatever you intend them to learn to do, and select subjects and circumstances in which *doing* is most facilitated. Now, laying aside out of consideration the accumulation of statistical information, and all kinds of education except intellectual, it is clear that this ultimately divides itself into the training of the artistic and logical faculties. And the logical faculties are of two kinds. It is by a logical faculty that we are able to understand other men's thoughts and apprehend new ideas. The cultivated, intelligent, imaginative mind is one in which this receptive faculty is strong. Nothing so marks the uneducated man as his dullness, his incapacity, in understanding what you say to him, if you depart in the slightest degree from the range of his daily thoughts. For the ordinary intercourse of men of education, for the spread and fertility of active thought, this faculty of intelligence is invaluable. Again, it is by a logical faculty that the mind deals with things and the relations of things. The mind which is thoughtful rather than receptive or imaginative, which studies phenomena, be they in mental philosophy, in politics, or in natural science, with a view to elicit and establish the true relations that exist among these phenomena, is the type of the mind in which the logical faculty of investigation is well trained. Nothing so marks the imperfectly educated man as his helplessness when dealing with facts instead of men, and his insecurity both in arriving at truth from them, and in judging of the validity of the conclusions of others. For the advance of thought, on all subjects which require thought, this faculty of investigation is indispensable. Probably no study will cultivate one of these faculties and wholly neglect the others, but all studies aim principally at one or the other of these. A study of the classical languages, for example, is an artistic exercise, and moreover it educates the receptive faculties in a manner in which no other study educates them. The study of a language and literature not our own is the best preparation for entering into the thoughts of others; but even when best taught and best learned it can only be a very imperfect exercise in logic, for it omits nearly the whole of the logic of induction. The study of science, on the other hand, while not without its influence on even the artistic powers, and exercising in a remarkable degree the powers of intelligence of a certain kind, deals mainly with the faculty of investigation, and trains the mind to ponder and reflect on the significance of facts. And the methods of these studies are in many respects precisely the same. Models and exercises are given by the one; models and exercises by the other. Thucydides must be read, and Latin prose must be written, by the student of form and style; and the man who would cultivate his powers of thought must read his Newton, and study Experimental Physics. And as the student of Thucydides and Plato is likely to gain in clearness and brilliancy of expression, and an insight into history and humanity, in intelligent and ready apprehension of the thoughts of others, in versatility and in polish; so the student of natural science is likely to bring with him to the study of philosophy, or politics, or business, or his profession, whatever it may be, a more active and original mind, a sounder judgment, and a clearer head, in consequence of his study. A good style perhaps may be got by reading and writing; thinking is learnt by thinking. And therefore that method of giving scientific instruction is best which most stimulates *thought*; and those subjects which afford the best illustrations of the best method ought to be selected for instruction in schools.

Different Methods of Teaching Science.

Now there are two methods of teaching science: one, the method of investigation; the other, the method of authority. The first starts with the concrete and works up to the abstract; starts with facts and ends with laws: begins with the known, and proceeds to the unknown; the second starts with what we call the principles of the science; announces laws and includes the facts under them: declares the unknown and applies it to the known. The first demands faith, the second criticism. Of the two, the latter is the easier, and the former by far the better. But the latter is seen in most text-books, and is the method on which many unscientific people ground their disapproval of science. What this former method is, and why it is the better, will be seen by the following remarks.

In the first place, then, *knowledge must precede science*: for science is nothing else but systematized experience and knowledge. In its extreme applications this principle is obvious enough: it would be absurd to teach boys classification from minerals, or the power of experimental science by an investigation into the organic bases. A certain broad array of facts must pre-exist before scientific methods can be applied.* This order cannot be reversed. And this is illustrated by the profound analogy that exists between the growth of scientific knowledge in an individual and in the world. Generation after generation of men passed away, and the world patiently accumulated experience and observation of facts; and then there sprang up in the world the uncontrollable desire to ascertain the sequences in nature, and to penetrate to the deep-lying principles of natural philosophy. And the same desire is based in the individual on the same kind of experience. Where there is wide knowledge of facts, science of some kind is sure to spring up. After centuries of experience the *Philosophiæ naturalis principia* were published.

And, secondly, this knowledge must be homogeneous with pre-existing knowledge. It is of no use to supply purely foreign facts; they must be such as the learner already knows something of, or be so similar in kind that his knowledge of them is equally secure: such that he can piece them in with his own fragmentary but widening experience. It is to his existing knowledge, and to that alone, that you must dig down to get a sure foundation. And the facts of your science must reach continuously down, and rest securely thereon. Otherwise you will be building a castle in the air. Hence the master's business is to take up the knowledge that already exists; to systematise and arrange it; to give it extension here, and accuracy there; to connect scraps of knowledge that seemed isolated; to point out where progress is stopped by ignorance of facts; and to show how to remedy the ignorance. Rapidly knowledge crystallises round a solid nucleus; and anything the master gives that is suited to the existing knowledge is absorbed and assimilated into the growing mass: and if he is unwise and impatient enough (as I have been scores of times) to say something which is to him perhaps a truth most vivid and suggestive, but for which his boys are unripe, he will see them, if they are really well trained, reject it as the cock despised the diamond among the barley (and the cock was quite right), or still worse, less wise than the cock, swallow it whole as a dead and choking formula.

On these grounds then, in addition to other obvious ones, Botany and Experimental Physics claim to be the standard subjects for the scientific teaching at schools. In both there pre-exists some solid and familiar knowledge. Both can so be taught as to make the learner advance from the known to the unknown—from his observations and experiments to his generalisations and laws, and ascend by continuous steps from induction to induction, and never once feel that he is carried away by a stream of words, and is reasoning about words rather than things. The logical processes they involve are admirable and complete illustrations of universal logic, and yet are not too difficult. These considerations mark the inferiority in this respect, of Geology and Physiology, in which the doctrines must far outrun the facts at a boy's command, and which require so much knowledge before the doctrines can be seen to be well founded. And these considerations exclude Chemistry, as an elementary subject at least, since there is so little pre-existing knowledge in the learner's mind on which the foun-

* This truth has been entirely lost sight of in teaching elementary geometry. The extreme repulsiveness of Euclid to almost every boy is a complete proof, if indeed other proofs were wanting, that the ordinary methods of studying geometry in use at preparatory and public schools are wholly erroneous. To this I can do no more than allude here, as being my conviction after considerable experience,—a conviction which has overcome every possible prejudice to the contrary. It is much to be hoped that before long the teaching of practical geometry will precede the teaching of the science of geometry.

dations can be laid. On all grounds the teaching of Chemistry should follow that of Experimental Physics.

Unless this method of investigation is followed, the teaching of science may degenerate, with an amazing rapidity, into cramming. To be crammed is to have words and formulæ given before the ideas and laws are realised. Geology and Chemistry are frightfully crammable. But Botany and Experimental Physics are by no means so easy to cram. What they might become with bad text-books and a bad teacher, I cannot, indeed, say; but it is a very important consideration. For it is possible to teach even Botany and Experimental Physics with exquisite perverseness, so as to deprive them of all their singular advantages as subjects for elementary training in science. It is possible to compel the learning the names of the parts of a flower before the condition of existence of a name, viz. that it is seen to be wanted, is fulfilled; to encumber the learner with a terminology that is unspeakably repulsive when given too soon; given before the induction which justifies the name has been gone through; to give the principles of classification before a sufficient acquaintance with species has called out the ideas of resemblance and difference, and has shown the necessity of classification; to give theories of typical form when it seems a wild and grotesque romance; to teach, in fact, by the method of authority. And this may be done by truly scientific men, fully believing that this is the true and only method. Witness Adrien Jussieu's "Botanique."

The true method is assuredly to begin by widening for your boys the basis of facts, and instantly to note uniformities of a low order, and let them hazard a few generalisations.

Specimen Lesson in Botany.

Suppose then your class of thirty or forty boys before you, of ages from thirteen to sixteen, as they sit at their first botanical lesson; some curious to know what is going to happen, some resigned to anything; some convinced that it is all a folly. You hand round to each boy several specimens, say of the Herb Robert, and taking one of the flowers, you ask one of them to describe the parts of it. "Some pink leaves" is the reply. "How many?" "Five." "Any other parts?" "Some little things inside." "Anything outside?" "Some green leaves." "How many?" "Five." "Very good. Now pull off the five green leaves outside, and lay them side by side; next pull off the five pink leaves, and lay them side by side: and now examine the little things inside. What do you find?" "A lot of little stalks or things." "Pull them off and count them:" they find ten. Then show them the little dust-bags at the top, and finally the curiously constructed central column, and the carefully concealed seeds. By this time all are on the alert. Then we resume: the parts in that flower are, outer green envelope, inner colored envelope, the little stalks with dust bags, and the central column with the seeds. Then you give them all wall flowers: and they are to write down what they find: and you go round and see what they write down. Probably some one has found six "*stalks*" inside his wall flower, and you make him write on the black-board for the benefit of the class the curious discovery, charging them all to note any such accidental varieties in future; and you make them very minutely notice all the structure of the central column. Then you give them all the common pelargonium and treat it similarly; and by the end of the hour they have learnt one great lesson, the existence of the four floral whorls, though they have yet not heard the name.

Next lesson-time they come in looking more in earnest, and you give them single stocks and white alyssum, which they discover to be wonderfully like the wall flower; and you have a lot of flowers of vegetable marrow, some of which are being passed round while you draw two of them on the board. The difference is soon discovered; and you let them guess about the uses of the parts of the flower. The green outer leaves protect it in the bud; the central organ is for the seeds; but what is the use of the others. Then you relate stories of how it was found out what the use of the dust-bags is: how patient Germans lay in the sun all day to wait for the insects coming: and how the existence of a second rare specimen of some foreign tree was found out in Paris, by its long-widowed spouse in the Jardin des Plantes at last producing perfect seeds. A little talk about bees, and moths, and midges, and such creatures, finding out what they have seen, and your second lecture is over.

In the third lecture you take the garden geranium, and beg them to examine it very closely to see if it is symmetrical. Several will discover the unsymmetrical outer green leaves; one or two will discover the hollow back of the stem: then the pelargonium, and its more visible unsymmetry; then the common tropæolum: in each of which they find also the same parts, and count and describe them: and lastly the tropæolum Canariense, with its grotesque irregularity: and they are startled to find that the curious-looking flower they knew so well is constructed on the same type, and is called by the same name; and by the end of the lesson they have learned something of irregular flowers, as referred to regular types,—something of continuity in nature.

So in succession, for I cannot give more detail, you lead them through flowers where the parts cohere, as in the campanula, through plants deficient or odd, through roses, and mignonette, and honeysuckle, and all the simple flowers you can find; till they thoroughly know the scheme on which a simple flower is made. Then you challenge them to a dandelion or daisy: and each has to write down his ideas. Your one or two geniuses will hit it: some will be all wrong, without a shadow of doubt; the majority fairly puzzled. You give them no hint of the solution, tell them to lay it aside; and you give them the little thrift and challenge them to find its seeds, and how they are attached. This many will do, and pick out the little seed with its long thread of attachment, and then they will go back to their dandelions with the key to the structure; and find its seeds too, and be charmed to discover the remains of its poor outer green envelope, and even its little dust-bags. How proud they are of the discovery! they think they have the key of knowledge now. And then you begin a little terminology,—calyx and sepals, corolla and petals, stamens and pollen, pistil and stigma, and so on; and test their recollection of the forms of all the flowers they have examined. Then you notice the spiral arrangement of leaves on a twig of oak, or thorn, or willow, and the internodes; and the over-lapping of the sepals of the rose and Herb Robert; the alternance of the parts; and finally they work out the idea, that the floral whorls grow on the stem, and are a sort of depressed spiral of leaves with the internodes suppressed. A few monstrosities and pictures are shewn, and the grand generalisation is made; the pistils are re-examined with fresh interest to test the theory; and all their old knowledge is raked up once more. Then, too, the value of the theory is criticised; and a lesson of caution is learnt.

Then a step forward is made towards classification, by cohesion and adhesion of parts; and the floral schedule is worked; and so step by step to fruits, and leaves, and stems, and roots, and the wondrous modification of parts for special uses, as in climbing plants; and the orchids, which are a grand puzzle till a series of pictures from Darwin step in to explain the use of the parts and plan of the flower. Then some chemistry of the plant is introduced with some experiments, and the functions of all the organs are discussed. And lastly, strict descriptive terms are given, and the rest of the course is occupied by the history and the systems of classification, with constant reference however to the other conceptions that the class has gained.

Such a method as this has many advantages. It is thoroughly scientific, however irregular it may seem, and a professor of Botany may smile or shed tears over it for anything I care; and the knowledge is gained on a sound basis of original observation. Whatever flower a boy sees after a few lessons, he looks at with interest, as modifying the view of flowers he has attained to. He is tempted by his discoveries: he is on the verge of the unknown, and perpetually transferring to the known: all that he sees finds a place in his theories, and in turn reacts upon them, for his theories are growing. He is fairly committed to the struggle in the vast field of observation, and he learns that the test of a theory is its power of including facts. He learns that he must use his eyes, and his reason, and that then he is equipped with all that is necessary for discovering truth. He learns that he is capable of judging of other people's views, and of forming an opinion of his own. He learns that nothing in the plant, however minute, is unimportant; that he must observe truthfully and carefully; that he owes only temporary allegiance to the doctrines of his master, and not a perpetual faith. No wonder that Botany, so taught, is interesting: no wonder that M. Demogeot, who visited some English schools last year at the request of the French Emperor, expressed himself to me as charmed with the vivacity and intelligence of the botanical class of one of my colleagues.*

Very possibly a master might make his boys get up a book on Botany, and learn it in the order in which it stands in the book,—cellules and parenchyma, protoplasm and chlorophyll, stems and medullary rays, petioles and phyllodes, rhizomes and bulbs, hairs and glands, endosmose and exosmose, secretions and excretions, and so on, and so on; and ultimately come to the flower and fruit; and possibly a boy of good digestion might survive it and pass a respectable examination in a year's time. But this is not the aim. And if in this way a greater number of facts could be learned, it would be far inferior to the method of investigation. A master must never forget that his power of teaching facts and principles is far inferior to a willing pupil's power of learning and mastering them. He must inspire his boys, and rely on them: nor will he be disappointed. Those who have in them anything of the naturalist will collect and become acquainted with a large number of species, and follow out the study with care and accuracy; and the mass, to whom an extensive knowledge of species is a very unimportant matter, but who can appreciate a sound method of investigation and proof, will have gained all that they can gain from botanical teaching. And it must be remembered by those who speak of teaching science, and yet have never tried it, that a method which would succeed with a few naturalists, might utterly fail with the mass.

* The spirit of this method is admirably illustrated in Le Maout's "Leçons Élémentaires de Botanique, fondées sur l'Analyse de 50 Plantes Vulgaires."

EXPERIMENTAL PHYSICS.]

Relative Value of Chemistry, Geology, and Physiology.

The next training subject is unquestionably Experimental Physics. This term is used commonly to denote the sciences which can be studied experimentally, without an extensive knowledge of mathematics, and excludes Chemistry. Mechanics and Mechanism, Heat and Light, Electricity and Magnetism, Hydrostatics, Hydrodynamics, Pneumatics, and Acoustics, are the principal branches of the subject. In selecting from them the subjects most fit for use in schools, and in choosing the order in which they should be taught, we must be guided by the principles already enunciated. We must proceed from the concrete to the abstract, from the familiar to the strange, from the science of masses to the science of molecules. Hence Mechanics and Mechanism must come first. In a year most boys are able to learn the great principles of Statics and Dynamics, and the elements of Mechanism, such as the ordinary methods of converting one kind of motion into another. They become tolerably familiar with the ideas of motion and space, and time, and form, in their exact numerical relations. Ignorance of arithmetic and the want of ideas in practical geometry are the main hindrances in their way; but even they are improved by the many illustrations of arithmetic and geometry that are afforded by Mechanics, and by the growth of exactness in all ideas of quantity and form as expressed by numbers. Arithmetic is too often the science of pounds, shillings, and pence alone; and by being so limited it loses in dignity and in interest, and in clearness. In Mechanics, also, the notion of force is constantly present in its commonest and simplest forms; and in this respect also this branch of science serves as the best introduction to the later branches.

Hydrostatics and Pneumatics, I do not doubt, are the best subjects to take next. the range of these subjects that could be taught at school is not great; and they may be learnt very thoroughly and exactly, and provide very good illustrations of the principles of the subjects that precede them. Hydrodynamics, Acoustics, and Geometrical Optics will be only studied profitably beyond the bare elements by those who have special talent for mathematical or experimental investigation, and should, I think, be in general reserved for University teaching. Physical Optics unquestionably should be excluded from school teaching.

The next year's course should be Heat and the elements of Electricity. By the time boys have reached this stage they are far more able to acquire new subjects than in the previous stages, and are fit to enter on these branches of physics, if they have studied the earlier subjects intelligently. And of all subjects of experimental investigation, Heat seems to me the best for work at schools. Three times I have taken classes in Heat, and with more satisfactory results than in any other subject. The phenomena of Heat are so universal and so familiar; it has so central a position among the physical sciences; its experimental methods are so perfect; it affords such a variety of illustrations of logical processes; that it seems unrivaled as a subject for training in science. And allowing for seventy lectures in the year, it is clear that this year's course will allow of some time being given to Electricity. This may be made an enormous subject, but I apprehend that it will not be worth while to attempt its more difficult branches, but to reserve them for the University and for private study.

I will repeat that a boy can learn, when he knows how to learn, far more than a master can teach; and it is at increasing the boy's power that the master must aim unweariedly. And by combining a voluntary and a compulsory system, giving opportunities for learning something of the higher branches, and insisting on a sound knowledge of the more elementary parts of Physics in which the teaching can be most stimulative and suggestive, all requirements will be met.

The methods of teaching Physics will be different in different hands; they will vary with the knowledge, the enthusiasm, the good sense, the good temper, the practical skill, and the object of the teacher. If the thing to be aimed at is to make them pass a good examination as soon as the subject is read, the best means will be to put a text-book into the hands of every one, and require certain parts of it to be learnt, and to illustrate them in an experimental lecture with explanations. The lecture may be made very clear and good; and this will be an attractive and not difficult method of teaching, and will meet most of the requirements. It fails, however, in one. The boy is helped over all the difficulties; he is never brought face to face with nature and her problems; what cost the world centuries of thought is told him in a minute; his attention, clearness of understanding, and memory are all exercised; but the one power which the study of physical science ought pre-eminently to exercise, and almost to create, the power of bringing the mind into contact with facts, of seizing their relations, of eliminating the irrelevant by experiment and comparison, of groping after ideas and testing them by their adequacy—in a word, of exercising all the active faculties which are required for an investigation in any matter—these may lie dormant in the class while the most learned lecturer experiments with facility and explains with clearness.

Theory and experience alike convince me that the master who is teaching a class quite unfamiliar with scientific method, ought to make his class teach themselves, by thinking out the subject of the lecture with them, taking up their suggestions and illustrations, criticizing them, hunting them down, and proving a suggestion barren or an illustration inapt; starting them on a fresh scent when they are at fault, reminding them of some familiar fact they had overlooked, and so eliciting out of the chaos of vague notions that are afloat on the matter in hand, be it the laws of motion, the evaporation of water, or the origin of the drift, something of order, and concentration, and interest, before the key to the mystery is given, even if after all it has to be given. Training to think, not to be a mechanic or surveyor, must be first and foremost as his object.

For all classes, except those which are beginning, the union of the two methods is best. If they have once thoroughly learnt that the truths of science are to be got from what they see, and not from the assertions of a master or a text-book, they can never quite forget it, and allow their science to exist in a cloud-world apart from the earth. And undoubtedly the rigid and exact teaching from a book, insuring a complete and formularized and producible knowledge, is very valuable, especially with older classes.

The work out of school for a natural science lecture consists chiefly at first in writing notes on the previous lecture. When the lecture has been discursive, and the method hard to follow, some help may be given by a recapitulation; but in general it may be left to the boys. It is an admirable exercise in composition. To reduce to order the preliminary facts, to bring out the unity in them, to illustrate, to describe, to argue, and that about things in which they are interested, and for which they feel a match, are the very best exercises that can be put before boys. They begin with a helplessness and inanity almost incredible, improve constantly, and end generally by writing these notes very well. And in the higher classes the working of examples and problems may well be thrown in part on the out-of-school hours.

I am fully convinced, and could support my conviction by that of others, that Chemistry is not a good subject for lecture instruction to beginners in science. Laboratory work must precede, in order that a certain degree of familiarity with facts may be acquired before they are analyzed and methodized scientifically. It can be taught, even to young boys, and so can anything else; and it has the advantage of being rather amusing; but as an exercise in reasoning it is very deficient. The notions of force, cause, composition of causes, are too abstruse in this subject for boys to get any hold of. Hence it is, as a matter of fact, accepted as a mass of authoritative dogmas. It is not the conclusiveness but the ingenuity of the proofs that is appreciated. It is of all subjects the most liable to cram, and the most useless, as a branch of training, when crammed. Most of it requires memory, and memory alone. As laboratory work is not likely to form an integral part of school education, Chemistry ought not, I think, to take an early place in the scientific course. It is most desirable, however, that schools should possess laboratories, into which boys of some talent may be drafted, and there prepared for the profitable attendance on good chemical lectures in the higher part of the school.

Geology is a popular and attractive subject with boys, but it lies outside the subjects which best illustrate scientific method. The largeness of the ideas in it; the great inferences from little facts, as they seem to boys; the wide experience of scenery, and rocks, and fossils, and natural history, which it seems to require; the very unfinished condition of it; are all reasons which make its advocates enthusiastic, but unfit it for the staple of school teaching. Nevertheless, the value of it on other grounds, such as its interest, its bearing on all kinds of thought, its position as typical of Palætiological sciences, and the opportunities it offers for original investigations in most places, seems to me so high, that I think it ought to be introduced parenthetically into the course of instruction in whatever way or place may seem most convenient.

Physiology cannot be taught to classes at school. Nor ought it to be learnt before Physics and Chemistry. A most enthusiastic advocate of Physiology at school talked over the subject with me at Rugby. Practical work, he admitted, was necessary; and that it was impossible. I cannot give my class forty rats on Tuesday, at 9.15, to dissect for an hour, and then put them away till Saturday at the same hour. And the other subjects, if well taught, will have given boys a method and a knowledge which will fit them for acquiring, by reading alone, even if they cannot have practical work, some intelligent acquaintance with the doctrines and facts of Physiology.

SCIENCE WILL NOT RID SCHOOLS OF DUNCES.

The truth is, there is no place like school for having notions of equality driven, by dire experience, out of one's head. There are scores and scores of boys, whom you may educate how you will, and they will know very little when you have done, and know that little ill. There are boys of slipshod, unretentive, inactive minds, whom neither Greek grammar nor natural science, neither schoolmasters nor angels, could convert into active and cultivated men.

STUDIES AND CONDUCT.

EDUCATION IN ITS HIGHER ASPECTS AND RELATIONS.

ADDRESS DELIVERED TO THE UNIVERSITY OF ST. ANDREWS, BY JOHN STUART MILL, ON HIS INAUGURATION AS RECTOR. *Extracts.*

John Stuart Mill was born in London, May 1806, and received his entire education at home, under the direction of his father, James Mill, the author of the History of the British Empire in India. He obtained a clerkship in the East India House in 1823, and succeeded his father as examiner of Indian Correspondence in 1856, from which post he retired in 1858, when the affairs of the East India Company were transferred to Her Majesty's government. He was first known as a writer by his contributions to the Westminster Review, of which he became joint and afterwards sole proprietor. His 'System of Logic,' published in 1843; 'Essays on Unsettled Questions in Political Economy,' 1844, and 'System of Political Economy, with some of their Applications to Social Science,' 'Essay on Liberty,' 'Parliamentary Reform,' 'Representative Government,' 'Utilitarianism,' 'Comte and Positivism,' 'Sir William Hamilton's Philosophy,' 'The Subjection of Woman,'—place him among the profoundest thinkers and ablest writers of the age. He was elected to parliament in 1865, but was defeated in the general election of 1868. Mr. Carlyle in an invitation to the writer of this note to meet Mr. Mill at his house to tea in 1835, remarked—"You will meet the best educated man in this town, and no thanks to our Universities for this production."

EDUCATION IN ITS LARGER AND NARROWER SENSE.

Education, in its largest sense, is one of the most inexhaustible of all topics; and of all many-sided subjects, it is the one which has the greatest number of sides. Not only does it include whatever we do for ourselves, and whatever is done for us by others, for the express purpose of bringing us somewhat nearer to the perfection of our nature; it does more: in its largest acceptation, it comprehends even the indirect effects produced on character and on the human faculties, by things of which the direct purposes are quite different: by laws, by forms of government, by the industrial arts, by modes of social life; nay, even by physical facts not dependent on human will; by climate, soil, and local position. Whatever helps to shape the human being; to make the individual what he is, or hinder him from being what he is not—is part of his education. And a very bad education it often is; requiring all that can be done by cultivated intelligence and will, to counteract its tendencies.

I shall confine myself, however, to education in the narrower sense; the culture which each generation purposely gives to those who are to be its successors, in order to qualify them for at least keeping up, and if possible for raising, the level of improvement which has been attained. Nearly all here present are daily occupied either in receiving or in giving this sort of education: and the part of it which most concerns you at present is that in which you are yourselves engaged—the stage of education which is the appointed business of a national University.

THE PROPER FUNCTION OF AN UNIVERSITY.

Universities are not intended to teach the knowledge required to fit men for some special mode of gaining their livelihood. Their object is not to make skillful lawyers, or physicians, or engineers, but capable and cultivated human beings. It is very right that there should be public facilities for the study of professions. It is well that there should be Schools of Law, and of Medicine, and it would be well if there were schools of engineering, and the industrial arts. The countries which have such institutions are greatly the better for them; and there is something to be said for having them in the same localities, and under the same general superintendence, as the establishments devoted to education properly so called. But these things are no part of what every generation owes to the next, as that on which its civilization and worth will principally depend. They are needed only by a comparatively few, who are under the strongest private inducements to acquire them by their own efforts; and even those few do not require them until after their education, in the ordinary sense, has been completed. What professional men should carry away with them from an University, is not professional knowledge, but that which should direct the use of their professional knowledge, and bring the light of general culture to illuminate the technicalities of a special pursuit. Men may be competent lawyers without general education, but it depends on general education to make them philosophic lawyers—who demand, and are capable of apprehending, principles, instead of merely cramming their memory with details. And so of all other useful pursuits, mechanical included. Education makes a man a more intelligent shoemaker, if that be his occupation, but not by teaching him how to make shoes; it does so by the mental exercise it gives, and the habits it impresses.

This, then, is what a mathematician would call the higher limit of University education: its province ends where education, ceasing to be general, branches off into departments adapted to the individual's destination in life. The lower limit is more difficult to define. An University is not concerned with elementary instruction: the pupil is supposed to have acquired that before coming here. But where does elementary instruction end, and the higher studies begin? Some have given a very wide extension to the idea of elementary instruction. According to them, it is not the office of an University to give instruction in single branches of knowledge from the commencement.

What the pupil should be taught here (they think), is to methodize his knowledge: to look at every separate part of it in its relation to the other parts, and to the whole; combining the partial glimpses which he has obtained of the field of human knowledge at different points, into a general map, if I may so speak, of the entire region; observing how all knowledge is connected, how we ascend to one branch by means of another, how the higher modifies the lower, and the lower helps us to understand the higher; how every existing reality is a compound of many properties, of which each science or distinct mode of study reveals but a small part, but the whole of which must be included to enable us to know it truly as a fact in Nature, and not as a mere abstraction.

And doubtless this is the crown and consummation of a liberal education: but before we restrict an University to this highest department of instruction—before we confine it to teaching, not knowledge, but the philosophy of knowledge—we must be assured that the knowledge itself has been acquired elsewhere. Those who take this view of the function of an University are not wrong in thinking that the schools, as distinguished from the universities, ought to be adequate to teaching every branch of general instruction required by youth, so far as it can be studied apart from the rest. But where are such schools to be found? Since science assumed its modern character, nowhere: and in these islands less even than elsewhere.

THE SCOTTISH UNIVERSITY AND ENGLISH UNIVERSITY COMPARED.

This ancient kingdom, thanks to its great religious reformers, had the inestimable advantage, denied to its southern sister, of excellent parish schools, which gave, really and not in pretence, a considerable amount of valuable literary instruction to the bulk of the population, two centuries earlier than in any other country. But schools of a still higher description have been, even in Scotland, so few and inadequate, that the Universities have had to perform largely the functions which ought to be performed by schools; receiving students at an early age, and undertaking not only the work for which the schools should have prepared them, but much of the preparation itself. Every Scottish University is not an University only, but a High School, to supply the deficiency of other schools. And if the English Universities do not do the same, it is not because the same need does not exist, but because it is disregarded. Youths come to the Scottish Universities ignorant, and are there taught. The majority of those who come to the English Universities come still more ignorant, and ignorant they go away.

In point of fact, therefore, the office of a Scottish University comprises the whole of a liberal education, from the foundations upwards. And the scheme of your Universities has, almost from the beginning, really aimed at including the whole, both in depth and in breadth. You have not, as the English Universities so long did, confined all the stress of your teaching, all your real effort to teach, within the limits of two subjects, the classical languages and mathematics. You did not wait till the last few years to establish a Natural Science and a Moral Science Tripos. Instruction in both those departments was organized long ago; and your teachers of those subjects have not been nominal professors, who did not lecture: some of the greatest names in physical and in moral science have taught in your Universities and by their teaching contributed to form some of the most distinguished intellects of the last and present centuries. . . .

GENERAL EDUCATION SHOULD BE BOTH SCIENTIFIC AND LITERARY.

Can any thing deserve the name of a good education which does not include literature and science too? If there were no more to be said than that scientific education teaches us to think, and literary education to express our thoughts, do we not require both? and is not any one a poor, maimed, lop-sided fragment of humanity who is deficient in either? We are not obliged to ask ourselves whether it is more important to know the languages or the sciences. Short as life is, and shorter still as we make it by the time we waste on things which are neither business nor meditation, nor pleasure, we are not so badly off that our scholars need be ignorant of the laws and properties of the world they live in, or our scientific men destitute of poetic feeling and artistic cultivation. I am amazed at the limited conception which many educational reformers have formed to themselves of a human being's power of acquisition. The study of science, they truly say, is indispensable: our present education neglects it: there is truth in this too, though it is not all truth: and they think it impossible to find room for the studies which they desire to encourage, but by turning out, at least from general education, those which are now chiefly cultivated. How absurd, they say, that the whole of boyhood should be taken up in acquiring an imperfect knowledge of two dead languages. Absurd indeed: but is the human mind's capacity to learn, measured by that of Eton and Westminster to teach? I should prefer to see these reformers pointing their attacks against the shameful inefficiency of the schools, public and private, which pretend to teach these two languages and do not. I should like to hear them denounce the wretched methods of teaching, and the criminal idleness and supineness, which waste the entire boyhood of the pupils without really giving to most of them more than a smattering, if even that, of the only kind of knowledge which is even pretended, to be cared for. Let us try what conscientious and intelligent teaching can do, before we presume to decide what can not be done.

MODERN LANGUAGES, HISTORY, GEOGRAPHY, SUBORDINATE.

No one can in our age be esteemed a well-instructed person who is not familiar with at least the French language, so as to read French books with ease; and there is great use in cultivating a familiarity with German. But living languages are so much more easily acquired by intercourse with those who use them in daily life; a few months in the country itself, if properly employed, go so much farther than as many years of school lessons; that it is really waste of time for those to whom that easier mode is attainable, to labor at them with no help but that of books and master; and it will in time be made attainable through international schools and colleges, to many more than at present. Universities do enough to facilitate the study of modern languages, if they give a mastery over that ancient language which is the foundation of most of them, and the possession of which makes it easier to learn four or five of the continental languages than it is to learn one of them without it. Again, it has always seemed to me a great absurdity that history and geography should be taught in schools; except in elementary schools for the children of the laboring classes, whose subsequent access to books is limited. Who ever really learnt history and geography except by private reading? and what an utter failure a system of education must be, if it has not given the pupil a sufficient taste for reading to seek for himself those most attractive and easily intelligible of all kinds of knowledge? Besides, such history and geography as can be taught in schools exercise none of the faculties of the intelligence except the memory. An university is indeed the place where the student should be introduced to the philosophy of History; where Professors who not merely know the facts but have exercised their minds on them, should initiate him into the causes and explanation, so far as within our reach, of the past life of mankind in its principal features. Historical criticism also—the tests of historical truth—are a subject to which his attention may well be drawn in this stage of his education. But of the mere facts of history, as commonly accepted, what educated youth of any mental activity does not learn as much as is necessary, if he is simply turned loose into an historical library? What he needs on this, and on most other matters of common information, is not that he should be taught it in boyhood, but that abundance of books should be accessible to him.

GREEK AND LATIN LANGUAGES TO BE STUDIED THOROUGHLY.

The only languages, then, and the only literature, to which I would allow a place in the regular curriculum, are those of the Greeks and Romans; and to these I would preserve the position in it which they at present occupy. That position is justified, by the great value, in education, of knowing well some other cultivated language and literature than one's own, and by the peculiar value of those particular languages and literatures.

There is one purely intellectual benefit from a knowledge of languages, which I am specially desirous to dwell on. Those who have seriously reflected on the causes of human error, have been deeply impressed with the tendency of mankind to mistake words for things. Without entering into the metaphysics of the subject, we know how common it is to use words glibly and with apparent propriety, and to accept them confidently when used by others, without ever having had any distinct conception of the things denoted by them. To quote again from Archbishop Whately, it is the habit of mankind to mistake familiarity for accurate knowledge. As we seldom think of asking the meaning of what we see every day, so when our ears are used to the sound of a word or a phrase, we do not suspect that it conveys no clear idea to our minds, and that we should have the utmost difficulty in defining it, or expressing, in any other words, what we think we understand by it. Now it is obvious in what manner this bad habit tends to be corrected by the practice of translating with accuracy from one language to another, and hunting out the meanings expressed in a vocabulary with which we have not grown familiar by early and constant youth.

But besides the advantage of possessing another cultivated language, there is a further consideration equally important. Without knowing the language of a people, we never really know their thoughts, their feelings, and their type of character; and unless we do possess this knowledge, of some other people than ourselves, we remain, to the hour of our death, with our intellects only half expanded. Look at a youth who has never been out of his family circle: he never dreams of any other opinions or ways of thinking than those he has been bred up in; or, if he has heard of any such, attributes them to some moral defect, or inferiority of nature or education. If his family are Tory, he can not conceive the possibility of being a Liberal; if Liberal, of being a Tory. What the notions and habits of a single family are to a boy who has had no intercourse beyond it, the notions and habits of his own country are to him who is ignorant of every other. Those notions and habits are to him human nature itself; whatever varies from them is an unaccountable aberration which he can not mentally realise: the idea that any other ways can be right, or as near an approach to right as some of his own, is inconceivable to him. This does not merely close his eyes to the many things which every country still has to learn from others; it hinders every country from reaching the improvement which it could otherwise attain by itself. . . .

Even as mere languages, no modern European language is so valuable a discipline to the intellect as those of Greece and Rome, on account of their regular and complicated structure. Consider for a moment what grammar is. It is the most elementary part of logic. It is the beginning of the analysis of the thinking process. The principles and rules of grammar are the means by which the forms of language are made to correspond with the universal forms of thought. The distinctions between the various parts of speech, between the cases of nouns, the moods and tenses of verbs, the functions of particles, are distinctions in thought, not merely in words. Single nouns and verbs express objects and events, many of which can be cognized by the senses; but the modes of putting nouns and verbs together, express the relations of objects and events, which can be cognized only by the intellect; and each different mode corresponds to a different relation. The structure of every sentence is a lesson in logic. The various rules of syntax oblige us to distinguish between the subject and predicate of a proposition, between the agent, the action, and the thing acted upon; to mark when an idea is intended to modify or qualify, or merely to unite with, some other idea; what assertions are categorical, what only conditional; whether the intention is to express similarity or contrast, to make a plurality of assertions conjunctively or disjunctively; what portions of a sentence, though grammatically complete within themselves, are mere members or subordinate parts of the assertion made by the entire sentence. Such things form the subject matter of universal grammar; and the languages which teach it best are those which have the most definite rules, and which provide distinct forms for the greatest number of distinctions in thought, so that if we fail to attend precisely and accurately to any of these, we can not avoid committing a solecism in language. In these qualities the classical languages have an incomparable superiority over every modern language, and over all languages, dead or living, which have a literature worth being generally studied. . . .

Human invention has never produced any thing so valuable, in the way both of stimulation and of discipline to the inquiring intellect, as the dialectics of the ancients, of which many of the works of Aristotle illustrate the theory, and those of Plato exhibit the practice. No modern writing comes near to these, in teaching, both by precept and example, the way to investigate truth, on those subjects, so vastly important to us, which remain matters of controversy, from the difficulty or impossibility of bringing them to a directly experimental test. To question all things; never to turn away from any difficulty;

to accept no doctrine either from ourselves or from other people without a rigid scrutiny by negative criticism, letting no fallacy, or incoherence, or confusion of thought, slip by unperceived; above all, to insist upon having the meaning of a word clearly understood before using it, and the meaning of a proposition before assenting to it: these are the lessons we learn from the ancient dialecticians. With all this vigorous management of the negative element, they inspire no scepticism about the reality of truth, or indifference to its pursuit. The noblest enthusiasm, both for the search after truth and for applying it to its highest uses, pervades these writers, Aristotle no less than Plato, though Plato has incomparably the greater power of imparting those feelings to others. In cultivating, therefore, the ancient languages as our best literary education, we are all the while laying an admirable foundation for ethical and philosophical culture. In purely literary excellence—in perfection of form—the preëminence of the ancients is not disputed. In every department which they attempted, and they attempted almost all, their composition, like their sculpture, has been to the greatest modern artists an example, to be looked up to with hopeless admiration, but of inappreciable value as a light on high, guiding their own endeavor. . . . The secret of the style of the great Greek and Roman authors, is that it is the perfection of good sense. In the first place, they never use a word without a meaning, or a word which adds nothing to the meaning. They always (to begin with) had a meaning; they knew what they wanted to say; and their whole purpose was to say it with the highest degree of exactness and completeness, and bring it home to the mind with the greatest possible clearness and vividness. It never entered into their thoughts to conceive of a piece of writing as beautiful in itself, abstractedly from what it had to express: its beauty must all be subservient to the most perfect expression of the sense. The *curiosa felicitas* which their critics ascribed in a preëminent degree to Horace, expresses the standard at which they all aimed. Their style is exactly described by Swift's definition, "the right words in the right places." Look at an oration of Demosthenes; there is nothing in it which calls attention to itself as style at all; it is only after a close examination we perceive that every word is what it should be, and where it should be, to lead the hearer smoothly and imperceptibly into the state of mind which the orator wishes to produce. The perfection of the workmanship is only visible in the total absence of any blemish or fault, and of any thing which checks the flow of thought and feeling, any thing which even momentarily distracts the mind from the main purpose. But then (as has been well said) it was not the object of Demosthenes to make the Athenians cry out "What a splendid speaker!" but to make them say "Let us march against Philip!" . . .

LIMITATIONS TO CLASSICAL STUDIES.

They should be carried as far as is sufficient to enable the pupil, in after life, to read the great works of ancient literature with ease. Those who have leisure and inclination to make scholarship, or ancient history, or general philology, their pursuit, of course, require much more, but there is no room for more in general education. The laborious idleness in which the school-time is wasted away in the English classical schools deserves the severest reprehension. To what purpose should the most precious years of early life be irreparably squandered in learning to write bad Latin and Greek verses? I do not see that we are much the better even for those who end by writing good ones. The exercise in composition, most suitable to the requirements of learners, is that most valuable one, of retranslating from translated passages of a good author; and to this might be added, what still exists in many Continental places of education, occasional practice in talking Latin. There would be something to be said for the time spent in the manufacture of verses, if such practice were necessary for the enjoyment of ancient poetry; though it would be better to lose that enjoyment than to purchase it at so extravagant a price. But the beauties of a great poet would be a far poorer thing than they are, if they only impressed us through a knowledge of the technicalities of his art. The poet needed those technicalities: they are not necessary to us. They are essential for criticising a poem, but not for enjoying it. All that is wanted is sufficient familiarity with the language, for its meaning to reach us without any sense of effort, and clothed with the associations on which the poet counted for producing his effect. Whoever has this familiarity, and a practised ear, can have as keen a relish of the music of Virgil and Horace, as of Gray, or Burns, or Shelley, though he know not the metrical rules of a common Sapphic or Alcaic. I do not say that these rules ought not to be taught, but I would have a class apart for them, and would make the appropriate exercises an optional, not a compulsory part of the school teaching.

SCIENTIFIC INSTRUCTION IN THE ASCERTAINMENT OF TRUTH.

The most obvious part of the value of scientific instruction, the mere information that it gives, speaks for itself. We are born into a world which we have not made; a world whose phenomena take place according to fixed laws, of which we do not bring any knowledge into the world with us. In such a world we are appointed to live, and in it all our work is to be done. Our whole working power depends on knowing the laws of the world—in other words, the properties of the things which we have to work with, and to work among, and to work upon. We may and do rely, for the greater part of this knowledge, on the few who in each department make its acquisition their main business in life. But unless an elementary knowledge of scientific truths is diffused among the public, they never know what is certain and what is not, or who are entitled to speak with authority and who are not: and they either have no faith at all in the testimony of science, or are the ready dupes of charlatans and impostors. They alternate between ignorant distrust, and blind, often misplaced confidence. Besides, who is there who would not wish to understand the meaning of the common physical facts that take place under his eye? Who would not wish to know why a pump raises water, why a lever moves heavy weights, why it is hot at the tropics and cold at the poles, why the moon is sometimes dark and sometimes bright, what is the cause of the tides? Do we not feel that he who is totally ignorant of these things, let him be ever so skilled in a special profession, is not an educated man but an ignoramus? It is surely no small part of education to put us in intelligent possession of the most important and most universally interesting facts of the universe, so that the world which surrounds us may not be a sealed book to us, uninteresting because unintelligible. This, however, is but the simplest and most obvious part of the utility of science, and the part which, if neglected in youth, may be the most easily made up for afterwards. It is more important to understand the value of scientific instruction as a training and disciplining process, to fit the intellect for the proper work of a human being. Facts are the materials of our knowledge, but the mind itself is the instrument; and it is easier to acquire facts, than to judge what they prove, and how, through the facts which we know, to get to those which we want to know.

The most incessant occupation of the human intellect throughout life is the ascertainment of truth. We are always needing to know what is actually true about something or other. It is not given to us all to discover great general truths that are a light to all men and to future generations; though with a better general education the number of those who could do so would be far greater than it is. But we all require the ability to judge between the conflicting opinions which are offered to us as vital truths; to choose what doctrines we will receive in the matter of religion, for example; to judge whether we ought to be Tories, Whigs, or Radicals, or to what length it is our duty to go with each; to form a rational conviction on great questions of legislation and internal policy, and on the manner in which our country should behave to dependencies and to foreign nations. And the need we have of knowing how to discriminate truth, is not confined to the larger truths. All through life it is our most pressing interest to find out the truth about all the matters we are concerned with. If we are farmers we want to find what will truly improve our soil; if merchants, what will truly influence the markets of our commodities; if judges, or jurymen, or advocates, who it was that truly did an unlawful act, or to whom a disputed right truly belongs. Every time we have to make a new resolution or alter an old one, in any situation in life, we shall go wrong unless we know the truth about the facts on which our resolution depends. Now, however different these searches for truth may look, and however unlike they really are in their subject matter, the methods of getting at truth, and the tests of truth, are in all cases much the same. There are but two roads by which truth can be discovered: observation and reasoning: observation, of course, including experiment. We all observe, and we all reason, and therefore more or less successfully, we all ascertain truths: but most of us do it very ill, and could not get on at all were we not able to fall back on others who do it better. If we could not do it in any degree, we should be mere instruments in the hands of those who could: they would be able to reduce us to slavery. Then how shall we best learn to do this? By being shown the way in which it has already been successfully done.

PROCESSES BY WHICH TRUTH IS ATTAINED.

The processes by which truth is attained, reasoning, and observation, have been carried to their greatest known perfection in the physical sciences. As classical literature furnishes the most perfect types of the art of expression, so do the physical sciences those of the art of thinking. Mathematics, and its application to astronomy and natural philosophy, are the most complete example of the discovery of truths by reasoning; experimental science, of their discovery by direct observation. In all these cases we know that we can trust the operation, because the conclusions to which it has led have been found true by subsequent trial. It is by the study of these, then, that we may hope to qualify ourselves for distinguishing truth, in cases where there do not exist the same ready means of verification.

In what consists the principal and most characteristic difference between one human intellect and another? In their ability to judge correctly of evidence. Our direct perceptions of truth are so limited; we know so few things by immediate intuition, or, as it used to be called, by simple apprehension—that we depend for almost all our valuable knowledge, on evidence external to itself; and most of us are very unsafe hands at estimating evidence, where an appeal can not be made to actual eyesight. The intellectual part of our education has nothing more important to do, than to correct or mitigate this almost universal infirmity—this summary and substance of nearly all purely intellectual weakness. To do this with effect needs all the resources which the most perfect system of intellectual training can command. Those resources, as every teacher knows, are but of three kinds: first, models; secondly, rules; thirdly, appropriate practice. The models of the art of estimating evidence are furnished by science; the rules are suggested by science; and the study of science is the most fundamental portion of the practice.

MATHEMATICS—PURE AND APPLIED.

It is chiefly from mathematics we realise the fact that there actually is a road to truth by means of reasoning; that any thing real, and which will be found true when tried, can be arrived at by a mere operation of the mind. The flagrant abuse of mere reasoning in the days of the schoolmen, when men argued confidently to supposed facts of outward nature without properly establishing their premises, or checking the conclusions by observation, created a prejudice in the modern, and especially in the English mind, against deductive reasoning altogether, as a mode of investigation. The prejudice lasted long, and was upheld by the misunderstood authority of Lord Bacon; until the prodigious applications of mathematics to physical science—to the discovery of the laws of external nature—slowly and tardily restored the reasoning process to the place which belongs to it as a source of real knowledge. Mathematics, pure and applied, are still the great conclusive example of what can be done by reasoning. Mathematics also habituates us to several of the principal precautions for the safety of the process. Our first studies in geometry teach us two invaluable lessons. One is, to lay down at the beginning, in express and clear terms, all the premises from which we intend to reason. The other is, to keep every step in the reasoning distinct and separate from all the other steps, and to make each step safe before proceeding to another; expressly stating to ourselves, at every joint in the reasoning, what new premise we there introduce. It is not necessary that we should do this at all times, in all our reasonings. But we must be always able and ready to do it. If the validity of our argument is denied, or if we doubt it ourselves, that is the way to check it. In this way we are often enabled to detect at once the exact place where paralogism or confusion get in: and after sufficient practice we may be able to keep them out from the beginning. It is to mathematics, again, that we owe our first notion of a connected body of truth; truths which grow out of one another, and hang together so that each implies all the rest; without contradicting another or others, until in the end it appears that no part of the system can be false unless the whole is so. Pure mathematics first gave us this conception; applied mathematics extends to it the realm of physical nature.

Applied mathematics shows us that not only the truths of abstract number and extension, but the external facts of the universe, which we apprehend by our senses, form at least, in a large part of all nature, a web similarly held together. We are able, by reasoning from a few fundamental truths, to explain and predict the phenomena of material objects: and what is still more remarkable, the fundamental truths were themselves found out by reasoning; for they are not such as are obvious to the senses, but had to be inferred by a mathematical process from a mass of minute details, which alone came within the direct reach of human observation. When Newton, in this manner, discovered the laws of the solar system, he created, for all posterity, the true idea of science. He gave the most perfect example we are ever likely to have, of that union of reasoning and observation, which by means of facts that can be directly observed, ascends to laws which govern multitudes of other facts—laws which not only explain and account for what we see, but give us assurance beforehand of much that we do not see, much that we never could have found out by observation, though, having been found out, it is always verified by the result.

DISCIPLINE OF THE EXPERIMENTAL SCIENCES.

While mathematics, and the mathematical sciences, supply us with a typical example of the ascertainment of truth by reasoning; those physical sciences which are not mathematical, such as chemistry, and purely experimental physics, show us in equal perfection the other mode of arriving at certain truth, by observation, in its most accurate form, that of experiment. The value of mathematics in a logical point of view is an old topic with mathematicians, and has even been insisted on so exclusively as to provoke a counter exaggeration, of which a well known essay by Sir William Hamilton is an example: but the logical value of experimental science is comparatively a new subject, yet there is no intellectual discipline more important than that which the experimental sciences afford. Their whole occupation consists in doing well, what all of us, during the whole of life, are engaged in doing, for the most part badly. All men do not affect to be reasoners, but all profess, and really attempt, to draw inferences from experience: yet hardly any one, who has not been a student of the physical sciences, sets out with any just idea of what the process of interpreting experience really is. If a fact has occurred once or oftener, and another fact has followed it, people think they have got an experiment, and are well on the road towards showing that the one fact is the cause of the other. If they did but know the immense amount of precaution necessary to a scientific experiment; with what sedulous care the accompanying circumstances are contrived and varied, so as to exclude every agency but that which is the subject of the experiment—or, when disturbing agencies can not be excluded, the minute accuracy with which their influence is calculated and allowed for, in order that the residue may contain nothing but what is due to the one agency under examination; if these things were attended to, people would be much less easily satisfied that their opinions have the evidence of experience; many popular notions and generalizations which are in all mouths, would be thought a great deal less certain than they are supposed to be; but we should begin to lay the foundation of really experimental knowledge, on things which are now the subjects of mere vague discussion, where one side finds as much to say, and says it as confidently as another, and each person's opinion is less determined by evidence than by his accidental interest or prepossession. . . .

LOGIC.

Logic lays down the general principles and laws of the search after truth; the conditions which, whether recognized or not, must actually have been observed if the mind has done its work rightly. Logic is the intellectual complement of mathematics and physics. Those sciences give the practice, of which logic is the theory. It declares the principles, rules, and precepts, of which they exemplify the observance.

The science of Logic has two parts; ratiocinative and inductive logic. The one helps to keep us right in reasoning from premises, the other in concluding from observation. Ratiocinative logic is much older than inductive, because reasoning in the narrower sense of the word is an easier process than induction, and the science which works by mere reasoning, pure mathematics, had been carried to a considerable height while the sciences of observation were still in the purely empirical period. The principles of ratiocination, therefore, were the earliest understood and systematized, and the logic of ratiocination is even now suitable to an earlier stage in education than that of induction. The principles of induction can not be properly understood without some previous study of the inductive sciences; but the logic of reasoning, which was already carried to a high degree of perfection by Aristotle, does not absolutely require even a knowledge of mathematics, but can be sufficiently exemplified and illustrated from the practice of daily life. . . .

PHYSIOLOGY.

There are other sciences, which are in a more backward state, and tax the whole powers of the mind in its mature years, yet a beginning of which may be beneficially made in university studies, while a tincture of them is valuable even to those who are never likely to proceed further. The first is physiology; the science of the laws of organic and animal life, and especially of the structure and functions of the human body. It would be absurd to pretend that a profound knowledge of this difficult subject can be acquired in youth, or as a part of general education. Yet an acquaintance with its leading truths is one of those acquirements which ought not to be the exclusive property of a particular profession. The value of such knowledge for daily uses has been made familiar to us all by the sanitary discussions of late years. There is hardly one among us who may not, in some position of authority, be required to form an opinion and take part in public action on sanitary subjects. And the importance of understanding the true conditions of health and disease—of knowing how to acquire and preserve that healthy habit of body which the most tedious and costly medical treatment so often fails to restore when once lost, should secure a place in general education for the principal maxims of hygiene, and some of those even of practical medicine.

For those who aim at high intellectual cultivation, the study of physiology has still greater recommendations, and is, in the present state of advancement of the higher studies, a real necessity. The practice which it gives in the study of nature is such as no other physical science affords in the same kind, and is the best introduction to the difficult questions of politics and social life. Scientific education, apart from professional objects, is but a preparation for judging rightly of Man, and of his requirements and interests. But to this final pursuit, which has been called *par excellence* the proper study of mankind, physiology is the most serviceable of the sciences, because it is the nearest. Its subject is already Man; the same complex and manifold being, whose properties are not independent of circumstance, and immovable from age to age, like those of the ellipse and hyperbola, or of sulphur and phosphorus, but are infinitely various, indefinitely modifiable by art or accident, graduating by the closest shades into one another, and reacting upon one another in a thousand ways, so that they are seldom capable of being isolated and observed separately. With the difficulties of the study of a being so constituted, the physiologist, and he alone among scientific inquirers, is already familiar. Take what view we will of man as a spiritual being, one part of his nature is far more like another than either of them is like any thing else. In the organic world we study nature under disadvantages very similar to those which affect the study of moral and political phenomena: our means of making experiments are almost as limited, while the extreme complexity of the facts makes the conclusions of general reasoning unusually precarious, on account of the vast number of circumstances that conspire to determine every result. Yet in spite of these obstacles, it is found possible in physiology to arrive at a considerable number of well ascertained and important truths. This, therefore, is an excellent school in which to study the means of overcoming similar difficulties elsewhere. It is in physiology, too, that we are first introduced to some of the conceptions which play the greatest part in the moral and social sciences, but which do not occur at all in those of inorganic nature. As, for instance, the idea of predisposition, and of predisposing causes, as distinguished from exciting causes. The operation of all moral forces is immensely influenced by predisposition: without that element, it is impossible to explain the commonest facts of history and social life. Physiology is also the first science in which we recognize the influence of habit—the tendency of something to happen again merely because it has happened before. From physiology, too, we get our clearest notion of what is meant by development or evolution. The growth of a plant or animal from the first germ is the typical specimen of a phenomenon which rules through the whole course of the history of man and society—increase of function, through expansion and differentiation of structure by internal forces. . . .

PSYCHOLOGY.

Psychology is simply the laws of the knowledge of human nature. If there is any thing that deserves to be studied by man, it is his own nature and that of his fellow men: and if it is worth studying at all, it is worth studying scientifically, so as to reach the fundamental laws which underlie and govern all the rest. With regard to the suitableness of this subject for general education, a distinction must be made. There are certain observed laws of our thoughts and of our feelings which rest upon experimental evidence, and, once seized, are a clue to the interpretation of much that we are conscious of in ourselves, and observe in one another. Such, for example, are the laws of association. Psychology, so far as it consists of such laws—I speak of the laws themselves, not of their disputed applications—is as positive and certain a science as chemistry, and fit to be taught as such. When, however, we pass beyond the bounds of these admitted truths, to questions which are still in controversy among the different philosophical schools—how far the higher operations of the mind can be explained by association, how far we must admit other primary principles—what faculties of the mind are simple, what complex, and what is the composition of the latter—above all, when we embark upon the sea of metaphysics, properly so called, and inquire, for instance, whether time and space are real existences, as is our spontaneous impression, or forms of our sensitive faculty, as is maintained by Kant, or complex ideas generated by association; whether matter and spirit are conceptions merely relative to our faculties, or facts existing *per se*, and in the latter case, what is the nature and limit of our knowledge of them; whether the will of man is free or determined by causes, and what is the real difference between the two doctrines; matters on which the most thinking men, and those who have given most study to the subjects, are still divided; it is neither to be expected nor desired that those who do not specially devote themselves to the higher departments of speculation should employ much of their time in attempting to get to the bottom of these questions. But it is a part of liberal education to know that such controversies exist, and, in a general way, what has been said on both sides of them.

POLITICS—HISTORY.

Politics can not be learned once for all, from a textbook, or the instructions of a master. Education is not entitled on this subject, to recommend any set of opinions as resting on the authority of established science. But it can supply the student with materials for his own mind, and helps to use them. It can make him acquainted with the best speculations on the subject, taken from different points of view: none of which will be found complete, while each embodies some considerations really relevant, really requiring to be taken into the account. Education may also introduce us to the principal facts which have a direct bearing on the subject, namely the different modes or stages of civilization that have been found among mankind, and the characteristic properties of each. This is the true purpose of historical studies, as prosecuted in an University.

Civil and Political Economy—Jurisprudence—International Law.

Pupils should be taught the outlines of the civil and political institutions of their own country, and in a more general way, of the more advanced of the other civilized nations. Those branches of politics, or of the laws of social life in which there exists a collection of facts or thoughts sufficiently sifted and methodized to form the beginning of a science, should be taught *ex professo*. Among the chief of these is Political Economy; the sources and conditions of wealth and material prosperity for aggregate bodies of human beings. This study approaches nearer to the rank of a science, in the sense in which we apply that name to the physical sciences, than any thing else connected with politics yet does. I need not enlarge on the important lessons which it affords for the guidance of life, and for the estimation of laws and institutions, or on the necessity of knowing all that it can teach in order to have true views of the course of human affairs, or form plans for their improvement which will stand actual trial. The same persons who cry down Logic will generally warn you against Political Economy.

Of no less importance than Political Economy is the study of what is called

Jurisprudence; the general principles of law; the social necessities which laws are required to meet; the features common to all systems of law, and the differences between them; the requisites of good legislation, the proper mode of constructing a legal system, and the best constitution of courts of justice and modes of legal procedure. These things are not only the chief part of the business of government, but the vital concern of every citizen; and their improvement affords a wide scope for the energies of any duly prepared mind, ambitious of contributing towards the better condition of the human race.

To these studies I would add International Law; which I decidedly think should be taught in all universities, and should form part of all liberal education. The need of it is far from being limited to diplomatists and lawyers; it extends to every citizen. What is called the Law of Nations is not properly law, but a part of ethics: a set of moral rules, accepted as authoritative by civilised states. It is true that these rules neither are nor ought to be of eternal obligation, but do and must vary more or less from age to age as the consciences of nations become more enlightened, and the exigencies of political society undergo change. But the rules mostly were at their origin, and still are, an application of the maxims of honesty and humanity to the intercourse of states. They were introduced by the moral sentiments of mankind, or by their sense of the general interest, to mitigate the crimes and sufferings of a state of war, and to restrain governments and nations from unjust or dishonest conduct towards one another in time of peace. Since every country stands in numerous and various relations with the other countries of the world, and many, our own among the number, exercise actual authority over some of them, a knowledge of the established rules of international morality is essential to the duty of every nation, and therefore of every person in it who helps to make up the nation, and whose voice and feeling form a part of what is called public opinion. . .

RELIGION AND ETHICS.

Moral and religious education consist in training the feelings and the daily habits; and these are, in the main, beyond the sphere, and inaccessible to the control of public education. It is the home, the family, which gives us the moral or religious education we really receive; and this is completed, and modified, sometimes for the better, often for the worse, by society, and the opinions and feelings with which we are there surrounded. The moral or religious influence which an university can exercise, consists less in any express teaching, than in the pervading tone of the place. Whatever it teaches, it should teach as penetrated by a sense of duty; it should present all knowledge as chiefly a means to worthiness of life, given for the double purpose of making each of us practically useful to his fellow creatures, and of elevating the character of the species itself; exalting and dignifying our nature. There is nothing which spreads more contagiously from teacher to pupil than elevation of sentiment: often and often have students caught from the living influence of a professor, a contempt for mean and selfish objects, and a noble ambition to leave the world better than they found it, which they have carried with them throughout life. In these respects, teachers of every kind have natural and peculiar means of doing with effect, what every one who mixes with his fellow-beings, or addresses himself to them in any character, should feel bound to do to the extent of his capacity and opportunities. What is special to an university on these subjects belongs chiefly, like the rest of its work, to the intellectual department. An university exists for the purpose of laying open to each succeeding generation, as far as the conditions of the case admit, the accumulated treasure of the thoughts of mankind. As an indispensable part of this, it has to make known to them what mankind at large, their own country, and the best and wisest individual men, have thought on the great subjects of morals and religion. There should be, and there is in most universities, professorial instruction in moral philosophy; but I could wish that this instruction were of a somewhat different type from what is ordinarily met with. I could wish that it were more expository, less polemical, and above all less dogmatic. The learner should be made acquainted with the principal systems of moral philosophy which have existed and been practically operative among mankind, and should hear what there is to be said for each: the Aristotelian, the Epicurean, the Stoic, the Judaic, the Christian in the various modes of its interpretation, which differ almost as much from one another as the teachings of those earlier schools. He should be made familiar with the different standards of right and wrong, which have been taken as the basis of ethics; general utility, natural justice, natural rights, a moral sense, principles of practical reason, and the rest. Among all these, it is not so much the teacher's business to take a side, and fight stoutly for some one against the rest, as it is to direct them all towards the establishment and preservation of the rules of conduct most advantageous to mankind. . . .

ÆSTHETIC CULTURE.

There is a third division of human culture which, if subordinate, and owing allegiance to the two others, is barely inferior to them, and not less needful to the completeness of the human being; I mean the æsthetic branch; the culture which comes through poetry and art, and may be described as the education of the feelings, and the cultivation of the Beautiful. This department of things deserves to be regarded in a far more serious light than is the custom of these countries. It is only of late, and chiefly by a superficial imitation of foreigners, that we have begun to use the word Art by itself, and to speak of Art as we speak of Science, or Government, or Religion: we used to talk of the Arts, and more specifically of the Fine Arts: and even by them were vulgarly meant only two forms of art, Painting and Sculpture, the two which, as a people, we cared least about—which were regarded even by the more cultivated among us as little more than branches of domestic ornamentation, a kind of elegant upholstery. . . .

To find Art ranking on a complete equality, in theory at least, with Philosophy, Learning, and science—as holding an equally important place among the agents of civilization and among the elements of the worth of humanity; to find even painting and sculpture treated as great social powers, and the art of a country as a feature in its character and condition, little inferior in importance to either its religion or its government; all this only did not amaze and puzzle Englishmen, because it was too strange for them to be able to realise it, or, in truth, to believe it possible: and the radical difference of feeling on this matter between the British people and those of France, Germany, and the Continent generally, is one among the causes of that extraordinary inability to understand one another, which exists between England and the rest of Europe, while it does not exist to any thing like the same degree between one nation of Continental Europe and another.

Poetic Cultivation.

It is quite possible to cultivate the conscience and the sentiments too. Nothing hinders us from so training a man that he will not, even for a disinterested purpose, violate the moral law, and also feeding and encouraging those high feelings, on which we mainly rely for lifting men above low and sordid objects, and giving them a higher conception of what constitutes success in life. If we wish men to practice virtue, it is worth while trying to make them love virtue, and feel it an object in itself, and not a tax paid for leave to pursue other objects. It is worth training them to feel, not only actual wrong or actual meanness, but the absence of noble aims and endeavors, as not merely blameable but also degrading: to have a feeling of the miserable smallness of mere self in the face of this great universe, of the collective mass of our fellow creatures, in the face of past history and of the indefinite future—the poorness and insignificance of human life if it is to be all spent in making things comfortable for ourselves and our kin, and raising ourselves and them a step or two on the social ladder. Thus feeling, we learn to respect ourselves only so far as we feel capable of nobler objects: and if unfortunately those by whom we are surrounded do not share our aspirations, perhaps disapprove the conduct to which we are prompted by them—to sustain ourselves by the ideal sympathy of the great characters in history, or even in fiction, and by the contemplation of an idealized posterity: shall I add, of ideal perfection embodied in a Divine Being? Now, of this elevated tone of mind the great source of inspiration is poetry, and all literature so far as it is poetical and artistic. We may imbibe exalted feelings from Plato, or Demosthenes, or Tacitus, but it is in so far as those great men are not solely philosophers or orators or historians, but poets and artists.

Nor is it only loftiness, only the heroic feelings, that are bred by poetic cultivation. Its power is as great in calming the soul as in elevating it—in fostering the milder emotions, as the more exalted. It brings home to us all those aspects of life which take hold of our nature on its unselfish side, and lead us to identify our joy and grief with the good or ill of the system of which we form a part; and all those solemn or pensive feelings, which, without having any direct application to conduct, incline us to take life seriously, and predispose us to the reception of any thing which comes before us in the shape of duty. Who does not feel a better man after a course of Dante, or of Wordsworth, or, I will add, of Lucretius or the Georgics, or after brooding over Gray's Elegy, or Shelley's Hymn to Intellectual Beauty?

I have spoken of poetry, but all the other modes of art produce similar effects in their degree. The races and nations whose senses are naturally finer and their sensuous perceptions more exercised than ours, receive the same kind of impressions from painting and sculpture: and many of the more delicately organized among ourselves do the same. All the arts of expression tend to keep alive and in activity the feelings they express. Do you think that the great Italian painters would have filled the place they did in the European mind, would have been universally ranked among the greatest men of their time, if their productions had done nothing for it but to serve as the decoration of a public hall or a private *salon*? Their Nativities and Crucifixions, their glorious Madonnas and Saints, were to their susceptible Southern countrymen the great school not only of devotional, but of all the elevated and all the imaginative feelings. We colder Northerns may approach to a conception of this function of art when we listen to an oratorio of Handel, or give ourselves up to the emotions excited by a Gothic cathedral. Even apart from any specific emotional expression, the mere contemplation of beauty of a high order produces in no small degree this elevating effect on the character. The power of natural scenery addresses itself to the same region of human nature which corresponds to Art.

To whatever avocations we may be called in life, let us never quash these susceptibilities within us, but carefully seek the opportunities of maintaining them in exercise. The more prosaic our ordinary duties, the more necessary it is to keep up the tone of our minds by frequent visits to that higher region of thought and feeling, in which every work seems dignified in proportion to the ends for which, and the spirit in which, it is done; where we learn, while eagerly seizing every opportunity of exercising higher faculties and performing higher duties, to regard all useful and honest work as a public function, which may be ennobled by the mode of performing it—which has not properly any other nobility than what that gives—and which, if ever so humble, is never mean but when it is *meanly* done, and when the motives from which it is done are mean motives. There is, besides, a natural affinity between goodness and the cultivation of the Beautiful, when it is real cultivation, and not a mere unguided instinct. He who has learnt what beauty is, if he be of a virtuous character, will desire to realise it in his own life—will keep before himself a type of perfect beauty in human character, to light his attempts at self-culture.

DISCIPLINE OF ACTIVE LIFE.

Now, having traveled with you over the whole range of the materials and training which an University supplies as a preparation for the higher uses of life, it is almost needless to add any exhortation to you to profit by the gift. Now is your opportunity for gaining a degree of insight into subjects larger and far more ennobling than the minutiæ of a business or a profession, and for acquiring a facility of using your minds on all that concerns the higher interests of man, which you will carry with you into the occupations of active life, and which will prevent even the short intervals of time which that may leave you, from being altogether lost for noble purposes. Having once conquered the first difficulties, the only ones of which the irksomeness surpasses the interest; having turned the point beyond which what was once a task becomes a pleasure; in even the busiest after-life, the higher powers of your mind will make progress imperceptibly, by the spontaneous exercise of your thoughts, and by the lessons you will know how to learn from daily experience. So, at least, it will be if in your early studies you have fixed your eyes upon the ultimate end from which those studies take their chief value—that of making you more effective combatants in the great fight which never ceases to rage between Good and Evil, and more equal to coping with the ever new problems which the changing course of human nature and human society present to be resolved.

JAMES ANTHONY FROUDE.

James Anthony Froude, youngest son of the venerable R. H. Froude, Archdeacon of Totnes, was born at Dartington, Devonshire, April 23, 1818, and educated at Westminster and at Oriel College, Oxford, where he graduated in classical honors, and obtained the Chancellor's Prize for the English essay (subject, Polititical Economy), and was elected Fellow of Exeter College in 1842. For some time he was connected with the High Church party, under the Rev. J. H. Newman, wrote in "The Lives of the English Saints," and took deacon's orders in 1844. He is the author of "The Shadows of the Clouds," published in 1847, and "The Nemesis of Faith," in 1849; both of which were severely condemned by the University authorities. In 1850 he began to contribute articles to the *Westminster Review*, and to *Fraser's Magazine*, chiefly on English history; and in 1856 published the first two volumes of his "History of England from the fall of Wolsey," which has been continued from time to time; Vols. 9 and 10 having been published in 1866. His "Short Studies on Great Subjects" in 1867, embrace a portion of his contributions to the Reviews, and was followed in 1872 by a second volume, from which we take copious extracts from his address on Education.

THE PLACE AND SUBJECT OF THE ADDRESS.*

Many years ago, when I was first studying the history of the Reformation in Scotland, I read a story of a slave in a French galley, who was one morning bending wearily over his oar. The day was breaking, and, rising out of the gray waters, a line of cliffs was visible, and the white houses of a town and a church tower. The rower was a man unused to such service, worn with toil and watching, and likely, it was thought, to die. A companion touched him, pointed to the shore, and asked him if he knew it.

"Yes," he answered, "I know it well. I see the steeple of that place where God opened my mouth in public to his glory; and I know, how weak soever I now appear, I shall not depart out of this life till my tongue glorify his name in the same place."

Gentlemen, that town was St. Andrew's, that galley slave was John Knox; and we know that he came back and did "glorify God" in this place and others to same purpose.

I am addressing the successors of that remote generation of students whom Knox, at the end of his life, "called round him," in the yard of this very College, "and exhorted them," as James Melville tells us, "to know God and stand by the good cause, and use their time well." It will be happy for me if I, too, can read a few words to you out of the same lesson-book; for to make

* Education: An Address delivered to the Students of St. Andrews, March 19, [illegible].

us know our duty and do it, to make us upright in act and true in thought and word, is the aim of all instruction which deserves the name, the epitome of all purposes for which education exists. Duty changes, truth expands, one age can not teach another either the details of its obligations or the matter of its knowledge, but the principle of obligation is everlasting. The consciousness of duty, whatever its origin, is to the moral nature of man what life is in the seed-cells of all organized creatures: the condition of its coherence, the elementary force in virtue of which it grows.

REVOLUTIONARY MOVEMENT IN EDUCATION.

There is no occasion to tell a Scotchman to value education. Our own great schools and colleges are in the middle of a revolution, which, like most revolutions, means discontent with what we have, and no clear idea of what we would have. The causes are not far to seek. On the one hand there is the immense multiplication of the subjects of knowledge, through the progress of science, and the investigation on all sides into the present and past condition of this planet and its inhabitants; on the other, the equally increased range of occupations, among which the working part of mankind are now distributed, and for one or other of which our education is intended to qualify us. It is admitted by every one that we can not any longer confine ourselves to the learned languages, to the grammar and logic and philosophy which satisfied the seventeenth century. Yet, if we try to pile on the top of these the histories and literatures of our own and other nations, with modern languages and sciences, we accumulate a load of matter which the most ardent and industrious student can not be expected to cope with.

AIM IN ANCIENT ENGLISH AND SCOTCH EDUCATION.

In every thing that we do, or mean to do, the first condition of success is that we understand clearly the result which we desire to produce. The house-builder does not gather together a mass of bricks and timber and mortar, and trust that somehow a house will shape itself out of its materials. Wheels, springs, screws, and dial-plate will not constitute a watch, unless they are shaped and fitted with the proper relations to one another. I have long thought that, to educate successfully, you should first ascertain clearly, with sharp and distinct outline, what you mean by an educated man.

Now our ancestors, whatever their other shortcomings, understood what they meant perfectly well. In their primary education and in their higher education they knew what they wanted to produce, and they suited their means to their ends. They set out with the principle that every child born in the world should be taught his duty to God and man. The majority of people had to live, as they always must, by bodily labor; therefore every boy was, as early as was convenient, set to labor. He was not permitted to idle about the streets or lanes. He was apprenticed to some honest industry. Either he was sent to a farm, or, if his wits were sharper, he was allotted to the village carpenter, bricklayer, tailor, shoemaker, or whatever it might be. He was instructed in some positive calling by which he could earn his bread and become a profitable member of the commonwealth. Besides this, but not, you will observe, independent of it, you had in Scotland, established by Knox, your parish schools where he was taught to read, and, if he showed special talent that way, he was made a scholar of and trained for the ministry. But neither Knox nor any one in those days thought of what we call enlarging the mind. A boy was taught reading that he might read his Bible and learn to fear God, and be ashamed and afraid to do wrong.

An eminent American was once talking to me of the school system in the United States. The boast and glory of it, in his mind, was that every citizen born had a fair and equal start in life. Every one of them knew that he had a chance of becoming President of the Republic, and was spurred to energy by the hope. Here, too, you see, is a distinct object. Young Americans are all educated alike. The aim put before them is to get on. They are like runners in a race, set to push and shoulder for the best places; never to rest contented, but to struggle forward in never ending competition. It has answered its purpose in a new and unsettled country, where the center of gravity has not yet determined into its place; but I can not think that such a system as this can be permanent, or that human society, constituted on such a principle, will ultimately be found tolerable. For one thing, the prizes of life so looked at are at best but few and the competitors many. "For myself," said the great Spinoza, "I am certain that the good of human life can not lie in the possession of things which, for one man to possess, is for the rest to lose, but rather in things which all can possess alike, and where one man's wealth promotes his neighbor's." At any rate, it was not any such notion as this which Knox had before him when he instituted your parish schools. We had no parish schools in England for centuries after he was gone, but the object was answered by the Church catechising and the Sunday-school. Our boys, like yours, were made to understand that they would have to answer for the use that they made of their lives. And, in both countries, they were put in the way of leading useful lives if they would be honest, by industrial training. The essential thing was that every one that was willing to work should be enabled to maintain himself and his family in honor and independence.

Pass to the education of a scholar, and you find the same principle otherwise applied. There are two ways of being independent. If you require much, you must produce much. If you produce little, you must require little. Those whose studies added nothing to the material wealth of the world, were taught to be content to be poor. They were a burden on others, and the burden was made as light as possible. The thirty thousand students who gathered out of Europe to Paris to listen to Abelard, did not travel in carriages, and they brought no portmanteau's with them. They carried their wardrobes on their backs. They walked from Paris to Padua, from Padua to Salamanca, and they begged their way along the roads. The laws against mendicancy in all countries were suspended in favor of scholars wandering in pursuit of knowledge, and formal licenses were issued to them to ask alms. At home, at his college, the scholar's fare was the hardest, his lodging was the barest. If rich in mind, he was expected to be poor in body; and so deeply was this theory grafted into English feeling that earls and dukes, when they began to frequent universities, shared the common simplicity. The furniture of a noble earl's room at an English university at present may cost, including the pictures of opera-dancers and race-horses, and such like, perhaps five hundred pounds. When the magnificent Earl of Essex was sent to Cambridge, in Elizabeth's time, his guardians provided him with a deal table, covered with green baize, a truckle bed, half-a-dozen chairs, and a wash hand-basin. The cost of all, I think, was five pounds.

You see what was meant. The scholar was held in high honor; but his contributions to the commonwealth were not appreciable in money, and were not rewarded with money. He went without what he could not produce, that he might keep his independence and his self-respect unharmed. Neither scholarship nor science starved under this treatment; more noble souls have been smothered in luxury, than were ever killed by hunger. Your Knox was brought up in this way, Buchanan was brought up in this way, Luther was brought up in this way, and Tyndal who translated the Bible, and Milton, and Kepler, and Spinoza, and your Robert Burns. Compare Burns, bred behind the plow, and our English Byron!

This was the old education, which formed the character of the English and Scotch nations. It is dying away at both extremities, as no longer suited to what is called modern civilization. The apprenticeship as a system of instruction is gone. The discipline of poverty—not here as yet, I am happy to think, but in England—is gone also; and we have got instead what are called enlarged minds.

OBJECT OF MODERN SCHOOLS—HIGH AND LOW.

I ask a modern march-of-intellect man what education is for; and he tells me it is to make educated men. I ask what an educated man is; he tells me it is a man whose intelligence has been cultivated, who knows something of the world he lives in—the different races of men, their languages, their histories, and the books that they have written; and again, modern science, astronomy, geology, physiology, political economy, mathematics, mechanics—every thing, in fact, which an educated man ought to know.

Education, according to this, means instruction in every thing which human beings have done, thought, or discovered; all history, all languages, all sciences.

A young man going to Oxford learns the same things which were taught there two centuries ago; but, unlike the old scholars, he learns no lessons of poverty along with it. In his three years' course he will have tasted luxuries unknown to him at home, and contracted habits of self-indulgence which make subsequent hardships unbearable; while his antiquated knowledge, such as it is, has fallen out of the market; there is no demand for him; he is not sustained by the respect of the world, which finds him ignorant of every thing in which it is interested. He is called educated; yet, if circumstances throw him on his own resources, he can not earn a sixpence for himself.

If I go into modern model schools, I find first of all the three R's, about which we are all agreed; I find next the old Latin and Greek, which the schools must keep to while the universities confine their honors to these; and then, by way of keeping up with the times, "abridgments," "text-books," "elements," or whatever they are called, of a mixed multitude of matters, history, natural history, physiology, chronology, geology, political economy, and I know not what besides; general knowledge which, in my experience, means knowledge of nothing; stuff arranged admirably for one purpose, and one purpose only—to make a show in examinations. To cram a lad's mind with infinite names of things which he never handled, places he never saw or will see, statements of facts which he can not possibly understand, and must remain merely words to him,—this, in my opinion, is like loading his stomach with marbles. It is wonderful what a quantity of things of this kind a quick boy will commit to memory, how smartly he will answer questions, how he will show off in school inspections, and delight the heart of his master. But what has been gained for the boy himself, let him carry this kind of thing as far as he will, if, when he leaves school, he has to make his own living? Lord Brougham once said he hoped a time would come when every man in England would read Bacon. William Cobbett, that you may have heard of, said he would be contented if a time came when every man in England would eat bacon. . . .

ALL EDUCATION SHOULD PREPARE FOR OCCUPATIONS.

Before we begin to train a boy's mind, I will try to explain what I, for my part, would desire to see done with it.

I will take the lowest scale first.

I accept without qualification the first principle of our forefathers, that every boy born into the world should be put in the way of maintaining himself in honest independence. No education which does not make this its first aim, is worth any thing at all. There are but three ways of living, as some one has said; by working, by begging, or by stealing. Those who do not work, disguise it in whatever pretty language we please, are doing one of the other two. A poor man's child is brought here with no will of his own. We have no right to condemn him to be a mendicant or a rogue; he may fairly demand, therefore, to be put in the way of earning his bread by labor. The practical necessities must take precedence of the intellectual. A tree must be rooted in the soil before it can bear flowers and fruit. A man must learn to stand upright upon his own feet, to respect himself, to be independent of charity or accident. It is on this basis only that any superstructure of intellectual cultivation worth having can possibly be built. The old apprenticeship, therefore, was, in my opinion, an excellent system, as the world used to be. The Ten Commandments and a handicraft made a good and wholesome equipment to commence life with. Times are changed. The apprentice plan broke down: partly because it was abused for purposes of tyranny; partly because employers did not care to be burdened with boys whose labor was unprofitable; partly because it opened no road for exceptional clever lads to rise into higher positions; they were started in a groove from which they could never afterwards escape.

Yet the original necessities remain unchanged. The Ten Commandments are as obligatory as ever, and practical ability, the being able to do something and not merely to answer questions, must still be the backbone of the education of every boy who has to earn his bread by manual labor.

Add knowledge afterwards as much as you will, but let it be knowledge which will lead to the doing better each particular work which a boy is practicing; every fraction of it will then be useful to him; and if he has it in him to rise, there is no fear but he will find opportunity.

Every occupation, even the meanest—I don't say the scavengers or the chimney-sweeps—but every productive occupation which adds any thing to the capital of mankind, if followed assiduously with a desire to understand every thing connected with it, is an ascending stair whose summit is nowhere, and from the successive steps of which the horizon of knowledge perpetually enlarges. Take the lowest and most unskilled labor of all, that of the peasant in the field. The peasant's business is to make the earth grow food; the elementary rules of his art are the simplest, and the rude practice of it the easiest; yet between the worst agriculture and the best lies agricultural chemistry, the application of machinery, the laws of the economy of force, and the most curious problems of physiology. Each step of knowledge gained in these things can be immediately applied and realized. Each point of the science which the laborer masters will make him not only a wiser man but a better workman; and will either lift him, if he is ambitious, to a higher position, or make him more intelligent and more valuable if he remains where he is.

It sounds like mockery to talk thus of the possible prospects of the toil-worn drudge who drags his limbs at the day's end to his straw pallet, sleeps heavily, and wakes only to renew the weary round. I am but comparing two systems of education, from each of which the expected results may be equally extravagant. I mean only that if there is to be this voice rolling over chaos again, ushering in a millenium, the way of it lies through industrial teaching, where the practical underlies the intellectual. The millions must ever be condemned to toil with their hands, or the race will cease to exist. The beneficent light when it comes, will be a light which will make labor more productive by being more scientific; which will make the humblest drudgery not unworthy of a human being, by making it at the same time an exercise to his mind.

AIM OF HIGHER OR UNIVERSITY EDUCATION.

As the world requires handicrafts, so it requires those whose work is with the brain, or with brain and hand combined—doctors, lawyers, engineers, ministers of religion. Bodies become deranged, affairs become deranged, sick souls require their sores to be attended to; and so arise the learned professions, to one or other of which I presume that most of you whom I am addressing intend to belong. Well, to the education for the professions I would apply the same principle. The student should learn at the university what will enable him to earn his living as soon after he leaves it as possible. I am well aware that a professional education can not be completed at a university; but it is true also that with every profession there is a theoretic or scientific groundwork which can be learnt nowhere so well, and, if those precious years are wasted on what is useless, will never be learnt properly at all. You are going to be a lawyer: you must learn Latin, for you can not understand the laws of Scotland without it; but if you must learn another language, Norman French will be more useful to you than Greek, and the Acts of Parliament of Scotland more important reading than Livy or Thucydides. Are you to be a doctor?—you must learn Latin too; but neither Thucydides nor the Acts of Parliament will be of use to you—you must learn chemistry; and if you intend hereafter to keep on a level with your science, you must learn modern French and German, and learn them thoroughly well, for mistakes in your work are dangerous.

Are you to be an engineer? You must work now, when you have time, at mathematics. You will make no progress without it. You must work at chemistry; it is the grammar of all physical sciences, and there is hardly one of the physical sciences with which you may not require to be acquainted.

History, poetry, logic, moral philosophy, classical literature, are excellent as ornament. If you care for such things, they may be the amusement of your leisure hereafter; but they will not help you to stand on your feet and walk alone; and no one is properly a man till he can do that. You can not learn every thing; the objects of knowledge have multiplied beyond the powers of the strongest mind to keep pace with them all. You must choose among them, and the only reasonable guide to choose in such matters is utility. The old saying, *Non multa sed multum*, becomes every day more pressingly true. If we mean to thrive, we must take one line and rigidly and sternly confine our energies to it. Am I told that it will make men into machines? I answer that no men are machines who are doing good work conscientiously and honestly, with the fear of their Maker before them. And if a doctor or a lawyer has it in him to become a *great* man, he can ascend through his profession to any height to which his talents are equal. All that is open to the handicraftsman is open to him, only that he starts a great many rounds higher up the ladder.

What I deplore in our present higher education is the devotion of so much effort and so many precious years to subjects which have no practical bearing upon life. We had a theory at Oxford that our system, however defective in many ways, yet developed in us some especially precious human qualities. Classics and philosophy are called there *literæ humaniores*. They are supposed to have an effect on character, and to be specially adapted for creating ministers of religion. The training of clergymen is, if any thing, the special object of Oxford teaching. All arrangements are made with a view to it. The heads of colleges, the resident fellows, tutors, professors, are, with rare exceptions, ecclesiastics themselves.

Well, then, if they have hold of the right idea, the effect ought to have been considerable. We have had thirty years of unexampled clerical activity among us: churches have been doubled; theological books, magazines, reviews, newspapers, have been poured out by the hundreds of thousands; while by the side of it there has sprung up an equally astonishing development of moral dishonesty. From the great houses in the city of London to the village grocer, the commercial life of England has been saturated with fraud. So deep has it gone that a strictly honest tradesman can hardly hold his ground against competition. You can no longer trust that any article that you buy is the thing which it pretends to be. We have false weights, false measures, cheating and shoddy every where. Yet the clergy have seen all this grow up in absolute indifference; and the great question which at this moment is agitating the Church of England is the color of the ecclesiastical petticoats.

Many a hundred sermons have I heard in England, many a dissertation on the mysteries of the faith, on the divine mission of the clergy, on apostolic succession, on bishops, and justification, and the theory of good works, and verbal inspiration, and the efficacy of the sacraments; but never, during those thirty wonderful years, never one that I can recollect on common honesty, or those primitive commandments, Thou shalt not lie, and Thou shalt not steal.

Classical philosophy, classical history and literature, taking, as they do, so hold upon the living hearts and imagination of men in this modern age, leave their working intelligence a prey to wild imaginations, and make them incapable of really understanding the world in which they live. If the clergy knew as much of the history of England and Scotland as they know about Greece and Rome, if they had been ever taught to open their eyes and see what is actually round them instead of groping among books to find what men did or thought at Alexandria or Constantinople fifteen hundred years ago, they would grapple more effectively with the moral pestilence which is poisoning all the air. . . .

Education always should contemplate this larger sphere, and cultivate the capacities which will command success there. Britain may have yet a future before it grander than its past; instead of a country standing alone complete in itself, it may become the metropolis of an enormous and coherent empire; but on this condition only, that her children, when they leave her shores, shall look back upon her, not—like the poor Irish when they fly to America—as a stepmother who gave them stones for bread, but as a mother to whose care and nurture they shall owe their after prosperity. Whether this shall be so, whether England has reached its highest point of greatness, and will now descend to a second place among the nations, or whether it has yet before it another era of brighter glory, depends on ourselves, and depends more than any thing on the breeding which we give to our children.

I shall be asked whether, after all, this earning our living, this getting on in the world, are not low objects for human beings to set before themselves. Is not spirit more than matter? Is there no such thing as pure intellectual culture? "Philosophy," says Novalis, "will bake no bread, but it gives us our souls; it gives us heaven; it gives us knowledge of those grand truths which concern us as immortal beings." Was it not said, "Take no thought what ye shall eat, or what ye shall drink, or wherewithal ye shall be clothed. Your Heavenly Father knoweth that ye have need of these things. Behold the lilies of the field, they toil not, neither do they spin. Yet Solomon in all his glory was not arrayed like one of these." This is not entirely a dream! But such high counsels as these are addressed only to few; and perhaps fewer still have heart to follow them. If you choose the counsels of perfection, count the cost, and understand what they mean. I knew a student once from whose tongue dropped the sublimest of sentiments; who was never weary of discoursing on beauty and truth and lofty motives; who seemed to be longing for some gulf to jump into, like the Roman Curtius—some "fine opening for a young man" into which to plunge and devote himself for the benefit of mankind. Yet he was running all the while into debt, squandering the money on idle luxuries which his father was sparing out of a narrow income to give him a college education; dreaming of martyrdom and unable to sacrifice a single pleasure!

The words which I quoted were not spoken to all the disciples, but to the Apostles who were about to wander over the world as barefoot missionaries.

For myself, I admire that ancient rule of the Jews that every man, no matter of what grade or calling, shall learn some handicraft; that the man of intellect, while, like St. Paul, he is teaching the world, yet, like St. Paul, may be burdensome to no one. It hurts no intellect to be able to make a boat or a house, or a pair of shoes or a suit of clothes, or hammer a horseshoe; and if you can do either of these, you have nothing to fear from fortune. "I will work with my hands, and keep my brain for myself," said some one proudly, when it was proposed to him that he should make a profession of literature. Spinoza, the most powerful intellectual worker that Europe had produced during the last two centuries, waving aside the pensions and legacies that were thrust upon him, chose to maintain himself by grinding object-glasses for microscopes and telescopes.

LITERATURE AS A PROFESSION TO LIVE BY.

Literature happens to be the only occupation in which the wages are not in proportion to the goodness of the work done. It is not that they are generally small, but the adjustment of them is awry. It is true that in all callings nothing great will be produced if the first object be what you can make by them. To do what you do well should be the first thing, the wages the second; but except in instances of which I am speaking, the rewards of a man are in proportion to his skill and industry. The best carpenter receives the highest pay. The better he works, the better for his prospects. The best lawyer, the best doctor, commands most practice, and makes the largest fortune. But with literature, a different element is introduced into the problem. The present rule on which authors are paid is by the page and the sheet; the more words the more pay. It ought to be exactly the reverse. Great poetry, great philosophy, great scientific discovery, every intellectual production which has genius, work, and permanence in it, is the fruit of long thought, and patient and painful elaboration. Work of this kind, done hastily, would be better not done at all. When completed, it will be small in bulk; it will address itself for a long time to the few and not to the many. The reward for it will not be measurable, and not obtainable in money except after many generations, when the brain out of which it was spun has long returned to its dust. Only by accident is a work of genius immediately popular, in the sense of being widely bought. No collected edition of Shakspeare's plays was demanded in Shakspeare's life. Milton received five pounds for "Paradise Lost." The distilled essence of the thought of Bishop Butler, the greatest prelate that the English Church ever produced, fills a moderate-sized octavo volume; Spinoza's works, including his surviving letters, fill but three: and though they have revolutionized the philosophy of Europe, have no attractions for the multitude. A really great man has to create the taste with which he is to be enjoyed. There are splendid exceptions of merit eagerly recognized and early rewarded—our honored English Laureate for instance, Alfred Tennyson, or your own countryman Thomas Carlyle. Yet even Tennyson waited through ten years of depreciation before poems which are now on every one's lips passed into a second edition. Carlyle, whose transcendent powers were welcomed in their infancy by Goethe, who long years ago was recognized by statesmen and thinkers in both hemispheres as the most remarkable of living men; yet, if success be measured by what has been paid him for his services, stands far below your Belgravian novelist. A hundred years hence, perhaps, people at large will begin to understand how vast a man has been among them.

Therefore, I say, if any of you choose this mode of spending your existence, choose it deliberately, with a full knowledge of what you are doing. Reconcile yourselves to the condition of the old scholars. Make up your minds to be poor: care only for what is true and right and good. On those conditions you may add something real to the intellectual stock of mankind, and mankind in return may perhaps give you bread enough to live upon, though bread extremely thinly spread with butter. . . .

> This above all. To your own selves be true
> And it must follow as the night the day,
> You can not then be false to any man.

THOMAS CARLYLE.

Thomas Carlyle, essayist, biographer and historian, was born in 1795, at Ecclefechan, a small village in Dumfriesshire. After receiving rudimentary instruction at Annan, he entered the University of Edinburgh at the age of 14, where he remained till he was 21—passing through the regular curriculum, with special attention to mathematics, and later in the course to ethical and theological studies—spending his long vacations among the hills and along the rivers of his native district. For two years he devoted himself to teaching mathematics in Fifeshire, and in 1823 commenced his professional work in literature, by preparing articles for Brewster's *Edinburgh Encyclopædia*, and the *New Edinburgh Review*. In the same year he translated Legendre's *Geometry*, to which he prefixed an *Essay on Proportion*. In the year following, 1824, he published his translation of Göethe's *Wilhelm Meister*, and began a Life of Schiller in the *London Magazine*. In 1827 he married Miss Welch, and located himself at Craigenputtock, engaged in literary work, the outcoming of which, in part, was articles on Göethe and other German writers in the *Foreign Quarterly Review*, *Signs of the Times*, in Edinburgh Review, and *Sartor Resartus* in Fraser's Magazine. In 1834 he removed to Cheyne Row, Chelsea (London), where he still (1872) resides. In 1837 appeared *The French Revolution*; in 1839, his *Chartism*; in 1840, his *Hero Worship*; in 1843, *Past and Present*; in 1845, *Oliver Cromwell's Letters and Speeches*, with *Elucidation*; in 1848, the *Latter Day Pamphlets*; in 1851, *Life of John Sterling*; in 1860–4, the *Life of Frederick the Great*. In 1865 he was elected Rector of Edinburgh University, and delivered his Inaugural Address April 2, 1866, from which we take the following characteristic suggestions:

DILIGENCE AND HONESTY IN STUDY.

There is an advice I must give you—the summary of all advices, and doubtless you have heard it a thousand times; but you must hear it once more, for it is most intensely true, whether you believe it or not. That above all things the interest of your whole life depends on your being diligent and honest, now while it is called to-day, in this place, where you have come to get your education! Diligence! that includes in it all virtues that a student can have: I include in it all those qualities of conduct and attention that lead to the acquirement of real instruction in such a place. This is the seed-time of life—and as you sow, so will you reap; this the fluid condition of your mind, and as it hardens into habits, so will it retain the consistency of rock and of iron to the end. By diligence I mean honesty, not only as to time, but as to your knowledge. Count a thing as known only when it is clearly yours, and is transparent to you, so that you can survey it on all sides with intelligence. Don't flourish about with what you only know the outside, and don't cram with undigested fragments for examinations. Be modest, be humble, or assiduous, and as early as you can find out what kind of work you individually can do in this universe, and qualify yourself for doing it.

UNIVERSITIES SHOULD MAKE BOOKS AVAILABLE.

The old work of Universities has somewhat changed by the invention of printing, and there are some who think 'the true University of our days is a Collection of Books.' Men have not now to go in person to where a Professor is actually speaking; because in most cases you can get his doctrine out of him through a book; and can then read it, and read it again and again, and study it. That is an immense change, that one fact of Printed Books. And I am not sure that I know of any University in which the whole of that fact has yet been completely taken in, and the studies moulded in complete conformity with it. What the Universities can mainly do for you,—what I have found the University did for me, is, That it taught me to read, in various languages, in various sciences; so that I could go into the books which treated of these things, and gradually penetrate into any department I wanted to make myself master of, as I found it suit me.

LEARN TO BE GOOD READERS AND GOOD WORKERS.

Learn to be discriminative in your reading; to read faithfully, and with your best attention, all kinds of things which you have a real interest in, a real not an imaginary, and which you find to be really fit for what you are engaged in. Of course, at the present time, in a great deal of the reading incumbent on you, you must be guided by the books recommended by your Professors for assistance towards the effect of their prelections. And then, when you leave the University, and go into studies of your own, you will find it very important that you have chosen a field, some province specially suited to you, in which you can study and work. The most unhappy of all men is the man who can not tell what he is going to do, who has got no work cut out for him in the world, and does not go into it. For work is the grand cure of all the maladies and miseries that ever beset mankind,—honest work, which you intend doing.

READING IN HISTORY.

As applicable to all of you, I will say that it is highly expedient to go into history; to inquire into what has passed before you on this Earth, and in the Family of Man.

The history of the Romans and Greeks will first of all concern you; and you will find that the classical knowledge you have got will be extremely applicable to elucidate that. There you have two of the most remarkable races of men in the world set before you, calculated to open innumerable reflections and considerations; a mighty advantage, if you can achieve it;—to say nothing of what their two languages will yield you, which your Professors can better explain; model languages, which are universally admitted to be the most perfect forms of speech we have yet found to exist among men. And you will find, if you read well, a pair of extremely remarkable nations, shining in the records left by themselves, as a kind of beacon, or solitary mass of illumination, to light up some noble forms of human life for us, in the otherwise utter darkness of the past ages; and it will be well worth your while if you can get into the understanding of what these people were, and what they did.

I believe, also, you will find one important thing not much noted, That there was a very great deal of deep religion in both nations. This is pointed out by the wiser kind of historians, and particularly by Ferguson, who is particularly well worth reading on Roman history,—and who, I believe, was an alumnus of our own University. His book is a very creditable work. He points out the profoundly religious nature of the Roman people, notwithstanding their ruggedly positive, defiant, and fierce ways. They believed that Jupiter Optimus Maximus was lord of the universe, and that he had appointed the Romans to become the chief of nations, provided they followed his commands,—to brave all danger, all difficulty, and stand up with an invincible front, and be ready to do and die; and also to have the same sacred regard to truth of promise, to thorough veracity, thorough integrity, and all the virtues that accompany that noblest quality of man, valor,—to which latter the Romans gave the name of 'virtue' proper (*virtus*, manhood), as the crown and summary of all that is ennobling for a man. In the literary ages of Rome, this religious feeling had very much decayed away; but it still retains its place among the lower classes of the Roman people. Of the deeply religious nature of the Greeks, along with their beautiful and sunny effulgences of art, you have striking proof, if you look for it. In the tragedies of Sophocles, there is a most deep-toned recognition of the eternal justice of Heaven, and the unfailing punishment of crime against the laws of God. I believe you will find in all histories of nations, that this has been at the origin and foundation of them all; and that no nation which did not contemplate this wonderful universe with an awe-stricken and reverential belief that there was a great unknown, omnipotent, and all-wise and all-just Being, superintending all men in it,—no nation ever came to very much, nor did any man either, who forgot that. If a man did forget that, he forgot the most important part of his mission in this world.

Our own history of England, which you will naturally take a great deal of pains to make yourself acquainted with, you will find beyond all others worthy of your study. For indeed I believe that the British nation,—including in that the Scottish nation,—produced a finer set of men than any you will find it possible to get anywhere else in the world. (*Applause.*) I don't know, in any history of Greece or Rome, where you will get so fine a man as Oliver Cromwell, for example. (*Applause.*) And we, too, have had men worthy of memory, in our little corner of the Island here, as well as others; and our history has had its heroic features all along; and did become great at last in being connected with world-history:—for if you examine well, you will find that John Knox was the author, as it were, of Oliver Cromwell; that the Puritan revolution never would have taken place in England at all, had it not been for that Scotchman. (*Applause.*) This is an authentic fact, and is not prompted by national vanity on my part, but will stand examining. (*Laughter and applause.*) . . .

HOW THE NOTABLE MEN BECOME SO.

I not only found the solution of every thing I expected there (Collins's *Peerage*), but I began gradually to perceive this immense fact, which I really advise every one of you who read history to look out for, if you have not already found it. It was that the Kings of England, all the way from the Norman Conquest down to the times of Charles I., had actually, in a good degree, so far as they knew, been in the habit of appointing as Peers those who deserved to be appointed. In general, I perceived, those Peers of theirs were all royal men of a sort, with minds full of justice, valor and humanity, and all kinds of qualities that men ought to have who rule over others. And then their genealogy, the kind of sons and descendants they had, this also was remarkable:—for there is a great deal more in genealogy than is generally believed at present. I never heard tell of any clever man that came of entirely stupid people. (*Laughter.*) If you look around, among the families of your acquaintance, you will see such cases in all directions;—I know that my own experience is steadily that way; I can trace the father, and the son, and the grandson, and the family stamp is quite distinctly legible upon each of them. So that it goes for a great deal, the hereditary principle,—in Government as in other things; and it must be recognized so soon as there is any fixity in things. You will remark, too, in your Collins, that, if at any time the genealogy of a peerage goes awry, if the man that actually holds the peerage is a fool,—in those earnest practical times, the man soon gets into mischief, gets into treason, probably,—soon gets himself and his peerage extinguished altogether, in short. (*Laughter.*)

From those old documents of Collins, you learn and ascertain that a peer conducts himself in a pious, high-minded, grave, dignified, and manly kind of way, in his course through life, and when he takes leave of life:—his last will is often a remarkable piece, which one lingers over. And then you perceive that there was kindness in him as well as rigor, pity for the poor; that he has fine hospitalities, generosities,—in fine, that he is throughout much of a noble, good and valiant man. And that in general the King, with a beautiful approximation to accuracy, had nominated this kind of man; saying, "Come you to me, sir. Come out of the common level of the people, where you are liable to be trampled upon, jostled about, and can do in a manner nothing with your fine gift; come here and take a district of country, and make it into your own image more or less; be a king under me, and understand that that is your function." I say this is the most divine thing that a human being can do to other human beings, and no kind of thing whatever has so much of the character of God Almighty's Divine Government as that thing, which, we see, went on all over England for about six hundred years. This is the grand soul of England's history. (*Cheers.*) It is historically true that, down to the time of James, or even Charles I., it was not understood that any man was made a Peer without having merit in him to constitute him a proper subject for a peerage. In Charles I.'s time, it grew to be known or said that, if a man was born a gentleman, and cared to lay out £10,000 judiciously up and down among courtiers, he could be made a Peer. Under Charles II. it went on still faster, and has been going on with ever-increasing velocity, until we see the perfectly breakneck pace at which they are going now (*A laugh*), so that now a peerage is a paltry kind of thing to what it was in those old times.

WISDOM, AND NOT PARTICULAR KNOWLEDGE.

And for the rest, in regard to all your studies and readings here, and to whatever you may learn, you are to remember that the object is not particular knowledges,—not that of getting higher and higher in technical perfections, and all that sort of thing. There is a higher aim lying at the rear of all that, especially among those who are intended for literary or speaking pursuits, or the sacred profession. You are ever to bear in mind that there lies behind that the acquisition of what may be called wisdom;—namely, sound appreciation and just decision as to all the objects that come round you, and the habit of behaving with justice, candour, clear insight, and loyal adherence to fact. Great is wisdom; infinite is the value of wisdom. It can not be exaggerated; it is the highest achievement of man: 'Blessed is he that getteth understanding.' And that, I believe, on occasion, may be missed very easily; never more easily than now, I sometimes think. If that is a failure, all is a failure!

ENDOWMENTS—DESIRABLE BUT NOT INDISPENSABLE.

Scotland should not be slow or slack in coming forward in the way of endowments. Money was never so abundant, and nothing that is good to be done with it. (*Hear, hear, and a laugh.*) No man knows,—or very few men know,—what benefit to get out of his money. In fact, it too often is secretly a curse to him. Much better for him never to have had any. But I do not expect that generally to be believed. (*Laughter.*) Nevertheless, I should think it would be a beneficent relief to many a rich man who has an honest purpose struggling in him, to bequeath some house of refuge, so to speak, for the gifted poor man who may hereafter be born into the world, to enable him to get on his way a little. To do, in fact, as those old Norman kings whom I have been describing; to raise some noble poor man out of the dirt and mud where he is getting trampled on unworthily, by the unworthy, into some kind of position where he might acquire the power to do a little good in his generation! I hope that as much as possible will be achieved in this direction; and that efforts will not be relaxed till the thing is in a satisfactory state.

I am bound, however, to say that it does not appear as if, of late times, endowment were the real soul of the matter. The English, for example, are the richest people in the world for endowments in their Universities; and it is an evident fact that, since the time of Bentley, you can not name any body that has gained a European name in Scholarship, or constituted a point of revolution in the pursuits of men in that way. The man who does so is a man worthy of being remembered: and he is poor, and not an Englishman. One man that actually did constitute a revolution was the son of a poor weaver in Saxony; who edited his Tibullus in Dresden, in a poor comrade's garret, with the floor for his bed, and two folios for a pillow; and who, while editing his Tibullus, had to gather pease-shells on the street and boil them for his dinner. That was his endowment. (*Laughter.*) But he was recognized soon to have done a great thing. His name was Heyne. (*Cheers.*) I can remember, it was quite a revolution in my mind when I got hold of that man's edition of Virgil. I found that, for the first time, I understood Virgil; that Heyne had introduced me, for the first time, into an insight of Roman life and ways of thought; had pointed out the circumstances in which these works were written, and given me their interpretation. And the process has gone on in all manner of developments, and has spread out into other countries.

MORE WISDOM AND LESS SPEECH—MODESTY—HEALTH.

There is very great necessity indeed of getting a little more silent than we are. It seems to me as if the finest nations of the world,—the English and the American, in chief,—were going all off into wind and tongue. (*Applause and laughter.*) But it will appear sufficiently tragical by-and-by, long after I am away out of it. There is a time to speak, and a time to be silent. Silence withal is the eternal duty of a man. He won't get to any real understanding of what is complex, and what is more than aught else pertinent to his interests, without keeping silence too. 'Watch the tongue,' is a very old precept, and a most true one.

I don't want to discourage any of you from your Demosthenes, and your studies of the niceties of language, and all that. Believe me, I value that as much as any one of you. I consider it a very graceful thing, and a most proper, for every human creature to know what the implement which he uses in communicating his thoughts is, and how to make the very utmost of it. I want you to study Demosthenes, and to know all his excellences. At the same time, I must say that speech, in the case even of Demosthenes, does not seem, on the whole, to have turned to almost any good account. He advised next to nothing that proved practicable; much of the reverse. Why tell me that a man is a fine speaker, if it is not the truth that he is speaking? Phocion, who mostly did not speak at all, was a great deal nearer hitting the mark than Demosthenes. . . .

I need not hide from you, young gentlemen,—and it is one of the last things I am going to tell you,—that you have got into a very troublous epoch of the world; and I don't think you will find your path in it to be smoother than ours has been, though you have many advantages which we had not. Man is becoming more and more the son, not of Cosmos, but of Chaos. He is a disobedient, discontented, reckless, and altogether waste kind of object (the commonplace man is, in these epochs); and the wiser kind of man,—the select few, of whom I hope you will be part,—has more and more to see to this, to look vigilantly forward; and will require to move with double wisdom. Will find, in short, that the crooked things he has got to pull straight in his own life all round him, wherever he may go, are manifold, and will task all his strength.

On the whole, avoid what is called ambition; that is not a fine principle to go upon,—and it has in it all degrees of *vulgarity*, if that is a consideration. 'Seekest thou great things, seek them not:' I warmly second that advice of the wisest of men. Don't be ambitious; don't too much need success; be loyal and modest. Cut down the proud towering thoughts that get into you, or see that they be pure as well as high. There is a nobler ambition than the gaining of all California would be, or the getting of all the suffrages that are on the Planet just now. (*Loud and prolonged cheers.*)

Finally, gentlemen, I have one advice to give you, which is practically of very great importance, though a very humble one. In the midst of your zeal and ardor,—for such, I foresee, will rise high enough, in spite of all the counsels to moderate it that I can give you,—remember the care of health. I have no doubt you have among you young souls ardently bent to consider life cheap, for the purpose of getting forward in what they are aiming at of high: but you are to consider throughout, much more than is done at present, and what it would have been a very great thing to be attended to continually: that you are to regard that as the very highest of all temporal things for you. (*Applause.*) There is no kind of achievement you could make in the world that is equal to perfect health. What to it are nuggets and millions? The French financier said, "Why, is there no sleep to be sold!" Sleep was not in the market at any quotation. (*Laughter and applause.*)

[MR. CARLYLE in this address, as well as in an article on Goethe in the first volume of his collected Essays, refers to a chapter in *Wilhelm Meister's Travels*, with this emphatic commendation—'that there are some ten pages of that which, if ambition had been my only rule, I would rather have written, been able to write, than all the books that have appeared since I came into the world.' See American Journal of Education, Vol. XXIII.—*Goethe's Pedagogy*.]

THE UNIVERSITY OF BOOKS, AFFAIRS, AND LIVING TEACHERS.

THE UNIVERSITY OF ATHENS.*

WHAT IS A UNIVERSITY?

If I were asked to describe, as briefly and popularly as I could, what a University was, I should draw my answer from its ancient designation of a *Studium Generale*, or "School of Universal Learning." This description implies the assemblage of strangers from all parts in one spot;—*from all parts*; else, how will you find professors and students for every department of knowledge? and *in one spot*; else, how can there be any school at all? Accordingly, in its simple and rudimental form, it is a school of knowledge of every kind, consisting of teachers and learners from every quarter. Many things are requisite to complete and satisfy the idea embodied in this description; but such as this a University seems to be in its essence, a place for the communication and circulation of thought, by means of personal intercourse, through a wide extent of country.

Mutual Education; the Press and Voice.

Mutual education, in a large sense of the word, is one of the great and incessant occupations of human society, carried on partly with set purpose, and partly not. One generation forms another; and the existing generation is ever acting and reacting upon itself in the persons of its individual members. Now, in this process, books, I need scarcely say, that is, the *litera scripta*, are one special instrument. It is true; and emphatically so in this age. Considering the prodigious powers of the press, and how they are developed at this time in the never-intermitting issue of periodicals, tracts, pamphlets, works in series, and light literature, we must allow there never was a time which promised fairer for dispensing with every other means of information and instruction. What can we want more, you will say, for the intellectual education of the whole man, and for every man, than so exuberant and diversified and persistent a promulgation of all kinds of knowledge? Why, you will ask, need we go up to knowledge, when knowledge comes down to us? The Sibyl wrote her prophecies upon the leaves of the forest, and wasted them; but here such careless profusion might be prudently indulged, for it can be afforded without loss, in consequence of the almost fabulous fe-

* From Dr. Newman's *Rise and Progress of Universities*, first published in 1854, in successive numbers of the Dublin "Catholic University Gazette," and collected in a volume, 1856, under the title of *Office and Work of Universities*, and in 1872 issued with other treatises, under the title of *Historical Sketches*. By John Henry Newman, of the Oratory. London: Basil Montagu Pickering, 196 Piccadilly. [illegible] pages.

cundity of the instrument which these latter ages have invented. We have sermons in stones, and books in the running brooks; works larger and more comprehensive than those which have gained for ancients an immortality, issue forth every morning, and are projected onwards to the ends of the earth at the rate of hundreds of miles a day. Our seats are strewed, our pavements are powdered, with swarms of little tracts; and the very bricks of our city walls preach wisdom, by informing us where we can cheaply purchase it.

I allow all this, and much more; such certainly is our popular education, and its effects are remarkable. Nevertheless, after all, even in this age, whenever men are really serious about getting what, in the language of trade, is called "a good article," when they aim at something precise, something refined, something really luminous, something really large, something choice, they go to another market; they avail themselves, in some shape or other, of the rival method, the ancient method, of oral instruction, of present communication between man and man, of teachers instead of learning, of the personal influence of a master, and the humble initiation of a disciple, and, in consequence, of great centers of pilgrimage and throng, which such a method of education necessarily involves. This, I think, will be found to hold good in all those departments or aspects of society which possess an interest sufficient to bind men together, or to constitute what is called "a world." It holds in the political world, and in the high world, and in the religious world; and it holds also in the literary and scientific world.

If the actions of men may be taken as any test of their convictions, then we have reason for saying this, viz.:—that the province and the inestimable benefit of the *litera scripta* is that of being a record of truth and an authority of appeal, and an instrument of teaching in the hands of a teacher; but that, if we wish to become exact and fully furnished in any branch of knowledge which is diversified and complicated, we must consult the living man and listen to his living voice. I am not bound to investigate the cause of this; and anything I may say will, I am conscious, be short of its full analysis; perhaps we may suggest, that no books can get through the number of minute questions which it is possible to ask on any extended subject, or can hit upon the very difficulties which are severally felt by each reader in succession. Or again, that no book can convey the special spirit and delicate peculiarities of its subject with that rapidity and certainty which attend on the sympathy of mind with mind, through the eyes, the look, the accent, and the manner, in casual expressions thrown off at the moment, and the unstudied turns of familiar conversation. But I am already dwelling too long on what is but an incidental portion of my main subject. Whatever be the cause, the fact is undeniable. The general principles of any study you may learn by books at home; but the detail, the color, the tone, the air, the life which makes it live in us, you must catch all these from those in whom it lives already. You must imitate the student in French or German, who is not content with his grammar, but goes to Paris or Dresden: you must take example from the young artist who aspires to visit the great masters in Florence and in Rome. Till we have discovered some intellectual daguerreotype, which takes off the course of thought, and the form, lineaments, and features of truth, as completely and minutely as the optical instrument reproduces the sensible object, we must come to the teachers of wisdom to learn wisdom; we must repair to the fountain and drink there. Portions of it may go from thence to the ends of the earth by means of books; but the fulness is in one place alone. It is in such assemblages and congregations of intellect that books themselves, the master-pieces of human genius, are at least originated.

The School of Manners.

For instance: the polished manners and high-bred bearing which are so difficult of attainment, and so strictly personal when attained, which are so much admired in society, from society are acquired. All that goes to constitute a gentleman,—the carriage, gait, address, gestures, voice; the ease, the self-possession, the courtesy, the power of conversing, the talent of not offending; the lofty principle, the delicacy of thought, the happiness of expression, the taste and propriety, the generosity and forbearance, the candor and consideration, the openness of hand;—these qualities, some of them come by nature, some of them may be found in any rank, some of them are a direct precept of Christianity; but the full assemblage of them, bound up in the unity of an individual character, do we expect they can be learned from books? are they not necessarily acquired, where they are to be found, in high society? The very nature of the case leads us to say so; you cannot fence without an antagonist, nor challenge all comers in disputation before you have supported a thesis; and in like manner, it stands to reason, you cannot learn to converse till you have the world to converse with; you cannot unlearn your natural bashfulness, or awkwardness, or stiffness, or other besetting deformity, till you serve your time in some school of manners. Well, and is it not so in matter of fact? The metropolis, the court, the great houses of the land, are the centers to which at stated times the country comes up, as to shrines of refinement and good taste; and then in due time the country goes back again home, enriched with a portion of the social accomplishments, which those very visits serve to call out and heighten in the gracious dispensers of them.

The School of Statesmanship.

I admit I have not been in Parliament, any more than I have figured in the *beau monde*; yet I cannot but think that statesmanship, as well as high breeding, is learned, not by books, but in certain centers of education. If it be not presumption to say so, Parliament puts a clever man *au courant* with politics and affairs of state in a way surprising to himself. A member of the Legislature, if tolerably observant, begins to see things with new eyes, even though his views undergo no change. Words have a meaning now, and ideas a reality such as they had not before. He hears a vast deal in public speeches and private conversation, which is never put into print. The bearings of measures and events, the action of parties, and the persons of friends and enemies, are brought out to the man who is in the midst of them with a distinctness which the most diligent perusal of newspapers will fail to impart to them. It is access to the fountain-heads of political wisdom and experience, it is daily intercourse, of one kind or another, with the multitude who go up to them, it is familiarity with business, it is access to the contributions of fact and opinion thrown together by many witnesses from many quarters, which does this for him. However, I need not account for a fact, to which it is sufficient to appeal; that the Houses of Parliament and the atmosphere around them are a University of politics.

The School of Science.

As regards the world of science, we find a remarkable instance of the principle which I am illustrating, in the periodical meetings for its advance, which have arisen in the course of the last twenty years, such as the British Association. Such gatherings would to many persons appear at first sight simply preposterous. Above all subjects of study, Science is conveyed, is propagated, by books or by private teaching; experiments and investigations are conducted in silence; discoveries are made in solitude. What have philosophers to do with festive celebrities, and panegyrical solemnities with mathematical and physical truth? Yet on a closer attention to the subject, it is found that not even scientific thought can dispense with the suggestions, the instruction, the stimulus, the sympathy, the intercourse with mankind on a large scale, which such meetings secure. A fine time of year is chosen, when days are long, skies are bright, the earth smiles, and all nature rejoices; a city or town is taken by turns, of ancient name or modern opulence, where buildings are spacious and hospitality hearty. The novelty of place and circumstance, the excitement of strange or the refreshment of well known faces, the majesty of rank or of genius, the amiable charities of men pleased both with themselves and with each other; the elevated spirits, the circulation of thought, the curiosity; the morning sections, the out-door exercise, the well-furnished, well-earned board, the not ungraceful hilarity, the evening circle; the brilliant lecture, the discussions or collisions or guesses of great men, one with another, the narratives of scientific processes, of hopes, disappointments, conflicts, and successes, the splendid eulogistic orations; these and the like constituents of the annual celebration, are considered to do something real and substantial for the advance of knowledge which can be done in no other way. Of course they can but be occasional; they answer to the annual Act, or Commencement, or Commemoration of a University, not to its ordinary condition; but they are of a University nature; and I can well believe in their utility. They issue in the promotion of a certain living and, as it were, bodily communication of knowledge from one to another, of a general interchange of ideas, and a comparison and adjustment of science with science, of an enlargement of mind, intellectual and social, of an ardent love of the particular study, which may be chosen by each individual, and a noble devotion to its interests.

The Great City a University.

In every great country the metropolis itself becomes a sort of necessary University, whether we will or no. As the chief city is the seat of the court, of high society, of politics, and of law, so, as a matter of course, is it the seat of letters also; and at this time, for a long term of years, London and Paris are in fact and in operation Universities, though in Paris its famous University is no more, and in London a University scarcely exists except as a board of administration. The newspapers, magazines, reviews, journals, and periodicals of all kinds, the publishing trade, the libraries, museums, and academies there found, the learned and scientific societies, necessarily invest it with the functions of a University; and that atmosphere of intellect, which in a former age hung over Oxford or Bologna or Salamanca, has, with the change of times, moved away to the centre of civil government. Thither come up youths from all parts of the country, the students of law, medicine, and the fine arts, and the *employés* and *attachés* of literature. There they live, as chance determines, and they are satisfied with their temporary home, for they find in it all that was promised to them there. They have not come in vain, as far as their own object in coming is concerned. They have not learned any particular religion, but they have learned their own particular profession well. They have, moreover, become acquainted with the habits, manners, and opinions of their place of sojourn, and done their part in maintaining the tradition of them. We cannot, then, be without virtual Universities; a metropolis is such; the simple question is, whether the education sought and given should be based on principle, formed upon rule, directed to the highest ends, or left to the random succession of masters and schools.

I end as I began;—a University is a place of concourse, whither students come from every quarter for every kind of knowledge. You cannot have the best of every kind everywhere; you must go to some great city or emporium for it. There you have all the choicest productions of nature and art all together, which you find each in its own separate place elsewhere. All the riches of the land and of the earth are carried up thither; there are the best markets, and there the best workmen. It is the centre of trade, the supreme court of fashion, the umpire of rival talents, and the standard of things rare and precious. It is the place for seeing galleries of first-rate pictures, and for hearing wonderful voices and performers of transcendent skill. It is the place for great preachers, great orators, great nobles, great statesmen. In the nature of things, greatness and unity go together; excellence implies a centre. And such, for the third or fourth time, is a University; I hope I do not weary out the reader by repeating it. It is the place to which a thousand schools make contributions; in which the intellect may safely range and speculate, sure to find its equal in some antagonist activity, and its judge in the tribunal of truth. It is a place where inquiry is pushed forward, and discoveries verified and perfected, and rashness rendered innocuous, and error exposed, by the collision of mind with mind, and knowledge with knowledge. It is the place where the professor becomes eloquent, and is a missionary and a preacher, displaying his science in its most complete and most winning form, pouring it forth with the zeal of enthusiasm, and lighting up his own love of it in the breasts of his hearers. It is the place where the catechist makes good his ground as he goes, treading in the truth day by day into the ready memory, and wedging and tightening it into the expanding reason. It is a place which wins the admiration of the young by its celebrity, kindles the affections of the middle-aged by its beauty, and rivets the fidelity of the old by its associations. It is a seat of wisdom, a light of the world, a minister of the faith, an Alma Mater of the rising generation.

UNIVERSITY LIFE AT ATHENS.

[From Newman's *Rise of Universities*.]

If we would know what a University is, considered in its elementary idea, we must betake ourselves to the first and most celebrated home of European literature and source of European civilization, to the bright and beautiful Athens,—Athens, whose schools drew to her bosom, and then sent back again to the business of life, the youth of the Western World for a long thousand years. Seated on the verge of the continent, the city seemed hardly suited for the duties of a central metropolis of knowledge; yet, what it lost in convenience of approach, it gained in its neighborhood to the traditions of the mysterious East, and in the loveliness of the region in which it lay. Hither, then, as to a sort of ideal land, where all archetypes of the great and the fair were found in substantial being, and all departments of truth explored, and all diversities of intellectual power exhibited, where taste and philosophy were majestically enthroned as in a royal court, where there was no sovereignty but that of mind, and no nobility but that of genius, where professors were rulers, and princes did homage, hither flocked continually from the very corners of the *orbis terrarum*, the many-tongued generation, just rising, or just risen into manhood, in order to gain wisdom.

Pisistratus had in an early age discovered and nursed the infant genius of his people, and Cimon, after the Persian war, had given it a home. That war had established the naval supremacy of Athens; she had become an imperial state; and the Ionians, bound to her by the double chain of kindred and of subjection, were importing into her both their merchandise and their civilization. The arts and philosophy of the Asiatic coast were easily carried across the sea, and there was Cimon, as I have said, with his ample fortune, ready to receive them with due honors. Not content with patronizing their professors, he built the first of those noble porticos, of which we hear so much in Athens, and he formed the groves, which in process of time became the celebrated Academy. Planting is one of the most graceful, as in Athens it was one of the most beneficent, of employments. Cimon took in hand the wild wood, pruned and dressed it, and laid it out with handsome walks and welcome fountains. Nor, while hospitable to the authors of the city's civilization, was he ungrateful to the instruments of her prosperity. His trees extended their cool, umbrageous branches over the merchants, who assembled in the Agora, for many generations.

Those merchants certainly had deserved that act of bounty; for all the while their ships had been carrying forth the intellectual fame of Athens to the western world. Then commenced what may be called her University existence. Pericles, who succeeded Cimon both in the government and in the patronage of art, is said by Plutarch to have entertained the idea of making Athens the capital of federated Greece: in this he failed, but his encouragement of such men as Phidias and Anaxagoras led the way to her acquiring a far more lasting sovereignty over a far wider empire. Little understanding the sources of her own greatness, Athens would go to war: peace is the interest of a seat of commerce and the arts; but to war she went; yet to her, whether peace or war, it mattered not. The political power of Athens waned and disappeared; kingdoms rose and fell; centuries rolled away,—they did but bring fresh triumphs to the city of the poet and the sage. There at length the swarthy Moor and Spaniard were seen to meet the blue-eyed Gaul; and the Cappadocian, late subject of

Mithridates, gazed without alarm at the haughty conquering Roman. Revolution after revolution passed over the face of Europe, as well as of Greece, but still she was there,—Athens, the city of mind,—as radiant, as splendid, as delicate, as young, as ever she had been.

Many a more fruitful coast or isle is washed by the blue Ægean, many a spot is there more beautiful or sublime to see, many a territory more ample; but there was one charm in Attica, which in the same perfection was nowhere else. The deep pastures of Arcadia, the plain of Argos, the Thessalian vale, these had not the gift; Bœotia, which lay to its immediate north, was notorious for its very want of it. The heavy atmosphere of that Bœotia might be good for vegetation, but it was associated in popular belief with the dullness of the Bœotian intellect: on the contrary, the special purity, elasticity, clearness, and salubrity of the air of Attica, fit concomitant and emblem of its genius, did that for it which earth did not;—it brought out every bright hue and tender shade of the landscape over which it was spread, and would have illuminated the face even of a more bare and rugged country.

A confined triangle, perhaps fifty miles its greatest length, and thirty its greatest breadth; two elevated rocky barriers, meeting at an angle; three prominent mountains commanding the plain,—Parnes, Pentelicus, and Hymettus; an unsatisfactory soil; some streams, not always full;—such is about the report which the agent of a London company would have made of Attica. He would report that the climate was mild; the hills were limestone; there was plenty of good marble; more pasture land than at first survey might have been expected, sufficient certainly for sheep and goats; fisheries productive; silver mines once, but long since worked out; figs fair; oil first-rate; olives in profusion. But what he would not think of noting down, was, that that olive tree was so choice in nature and so noble in shape, that it excited a religious veneration; and that it took so kindly to the light soil, as to expand into woods upon the open plain, and to climb up and fringe the hills. He would not think of writing word to his employers, how that clear air, of which I have spoken, brought out, yet blended and subdued, the colors on the marble, till they had a softness and harmony, for all their richness, which in a picture looks exaggerated, yet is after all within the truth. He would not tell, how that same delicate and brilliant atmosphere freshened up the pale olive, till the olive forgot its monotony, and its cheek glowed like the arbutus or beech of the Umbrian hills. He would say nothing of the thyme and thousand fragrant herbs which carpeted Hymettus; he would hear nothing of the hum of its bees; nor take much account of the rare flavor of its honey, since Gozo and Minorca were sufficient for the English demand. He would look over the Ægean from the height he had ascended; he would follow with his eye the chain of islands, which, starting from the Sunian headland, seemed to offer the fabled divinities of Attica, when they would visit their Ionian cousins, a sort of viaduct thereto across the sea: but that fancy would not occur to him, nor any admiration of the dark violet billows with their white edges down below; nor of those graceful, fan-like jets of silver upon the rocks, which slowly rise aloft like water spirits from the deep, then shiver, and break, and spread, and shroud themselves, and disappear, in a soft mist of foam; nor of the gentle, incessant heaving and panting of the whole liquid plain; nor of the long waves, keeping steady time, like a line of soldiery, as they resound upon the hollow shore,—he would not deign to notice that restless living element at all, except to bless his stars that he was not upon it. Nor the distinct detail, nor the refined coloring, nor the graceful outline and roseate golden hue of the jutting crags, nor the bold shadows cast from Otus or Laurium by the declining sun;—our agent of a mercantile firm would not value these matters even at a low figure. Rather we must turn for the sympathy we seek to yon pilgrim student, come from a semi-barbarous land to that small corner of the earth, as to a shrine, where he might take his fill of gazing on those emblems and correlations of invisible unoriginate perfection. It was the stranger from a remote province, from Britain or from Mauritania, who in a scene so different from that of his chilly, woody swamps, or of his fiery choking sands, learned at once what a real University must be, by coming to understand the sort of country, which was its suitable home.

Nor was this all that a University required, and found in Athens. No one, even there, could live on poetry. If the students at that famous place had nothing better than bright hues and soothing sounds, they would not have been able or disposed to turn their residence there to much account. Of course they must have the means of living, nay, in a certain sense, of enjoyment, if Athens was to be an Alma Mater at the time, or to remain afterwards a pleasant thought in their memory. And so they had: be it recollected Athens was a port, and a mart of trade, perhaps the first in Greece; and this was very much to the point, when a number of strangers were ever flocking to it, whose combat was to be with intellectual, not physical difficulties, and who claimed to have their bodily wants supplied, that they might be at leisure to set about furnishing their minds. Now, barren as was the soil of Attica, and bare the face of the country, yet it had only too many resources for an elegant, nay luxurious abode there. So abundant were the imports of the place, that it was a common saying, that the productions, which were found singly elsewhere, were brought all together in Athens. Corn and wine, the staple of subsistence in such a climate, came from the isles of the Ægean; fine wool and carpeting from Asia Minor; slaves, as now, from the Euxine, and timber too; and iron and brass from the coasts of the Mediterranean. The Athenian did not condescend to manufactures himself, but encouraged them in others; and a population of foreigners caught at the lucrative occupation both for home consumption and for exportation. Their cloth, and other textures for dress and furniture, and their hardware—for instance, armor—were in great request. Labor was cheap; stone and marble in plenty; and the taste and skill, which at first were devoted to public buildings, as temples and porticos, were in course of time applied to the mansions of public men. If nature did much for Athens, it is undeniable that art did much more.

Student Life.

So now let us fancy our Scythian, or Armenian, or African, or Italian, or Gallic student, after tossing on the Saronic waves, which would be his more ordinary course to Athens, at last casting anchor at Piræus. He is of any condition or rank of life you please, and may be made to order, from a prince to a peasant. Perhaps he is some Cleanthes, who has been a boxer in the public games. How did it ever cross his brain to betake himself to Athens in search of wisdom? or, if he came thither by accident, how did the love of it ever touch his heart? But so it was, to Athens he came with three drachms in his girdle, and he got his livelihood by drawing water, carrying loads, and the like servile occupations. He attached himself, of all philosophers, to Zeno the Stoic,—to

Zeno, the most high-minded, the most haughty of speculators; and out of his daily earnings the poor scholar brought his master the daily sum of an obolus, in payment for attending his lectures. Such progress did he make, that on Zeno's death he actually was his successor in his school; and, if my memory does not play me false, he is the author of a hymn to the Supreme Being, which is one of the noblest effusions of the kind in classical poetry. Yet, even when he was the head of a school, he continued in his illiberal toil as if he had been a monk; and, it is said, that once, when the wind took his pallium, and blew it aside, he was discovered to have no other garment at all;—something like the German student who came up to Heidelberg with nothing upon him but a great coat and a pair of pistols.

Or it is another disciple of the Porch,—Stoic by nature, earlier than by profession,—who is entering the city; but in what different fashion he comes! It is no other than Marcus, Emperor of Rome and philosopher. Professors long since were summoned from Athens for his service, when he was a youth, and now he comes, after his victories in the battle field, to make his acknowledgments at the end of life, to the city of wisdom, and to submit himself to an initiation into the Eleusinian mysteries.

Or it is a young man of great promise as an orator, were it not for his weakness of chest, which renders it necessary that he should acquire the art of speaking without over-exertion, and should adopt a delivery sufficient for the display of his rhetorical talents on the one hand, yet merciful to his physical resources on the other. He is called Cicero; he will stop but a short time, and will pass over to Asia Minor and its cities, before he returns to continue a career which will render his name immortal: and he will like his short sojourn at Athens so well, that he will take good care to send his son thither at an earlier age than he visited it himself.

But see where comes from Alexandria (for we need not be very solicitous about anachronisms), a young man from twenty to twenty-two, who has narrowly escaped drowning on his voyage, and is to remain at Athens as many as eight or ten years, yet in the course of that time will not learn a line of Latin, thinking it enough to become accomplished in Greek composition, and in that he will succeed. He is a grave person, and difficult to make out; some say he is a Christian, something or other in the Christian line his father is for certain. His name is Gregory, he is by country a Cappadocian, and will in time become preëminently a theologian, and one of the principal Doctors of the Church.

Or it is one Horace, a youth of low stature and black hair, whose father has given him an education at Rome above his rank in life, and now is sending him to finish it at Athens; he is said to have a turn for poetry: a hero he is not, and it were well if he knew it; but he is caught by the enthusiasm of the hour, and goes off campaigning with Brutus and Cassius, and will leave his shield behind him on the field of Philippi.

Or it is a mere boy of fifteen: his name Eunapius; though the voyage was not long, sea-sickness, or confinement, or bad living on board the vessel, threw him into a fever, and, when the passengers landed in the evening at Piræus, he could not stand. His countrymen who accompanied him, took him up among them and carried him to the house of the great teacher of the day, Proæresius, who was a friend of the captain's, and whose fame it was which drew the enthusiastic youth to Athens. His companions understand the sort of place they are in, and, with the license of academic students, they break into the philosopher's house, though he appears to have retired for the night, and proceed to make themselves free of it, with an absence of ceremony, which is only not impudence because Proæresius takes it so easily. Strange introduction for our stranger to a seat of learning, but not out of keeping with Athens; for what could you expect of a place where there was a mob of youths and not even the pretence of control; where the poorer lived any how, and got on as they could, and the teachers themselves had no protection from the humours and caprices of the students who filled their lecture-halls? However, as to this Eunapius, Proæresius took a fancy to the boy, and told him curious stories about Athenian life. He himself had come up to the University with one Hephæstion, and they were even worse off than Cleanthes the Stoic; for they had only one cloak between them, and nothing whatever besides, except some old bedding; so when Proæresius went abroad, Hephæstion lay in bed, and practised himself in oratory; and then Hephæstion put on the cloak, and Proæresius crept under the coverlet. At another time there was so fierce a feud between what would be called "town and gown" in an English University, that the Professors did not dare lecture in public, for fear of ill treatment.

But a freshman like Eunapius soon got experience for himself of the ways and manners prevalent in Athens. Such a one as he had hardly entered the city, when he was caught hold of by a party of the academic youth, who proceeded to practise on his awkwardness and his ignorance. At first sight one wonders at their childishness: but the like conduct obtained in the mediæval Universities; and not many months have passed away since the journals have told us of sober Englishmen, given to matter-of-fact calculations, and to the anxieties of money-making, pelting each other with snow balls on their own sacred territory, and defying the magistracy, when they would interfere with their privilege of becoming boys. So I suppose we must attribute it to something or other in human nature. Meanwhile, there stands the new-comer, surrounded by a circle of his new associates, who forthwith proceed to frighten, and to banter, and to make a fool of him, to the extent of their wit. Some address him with mock politeness, others with fierceness; and so they conduct him in solemn procession across the Agora to the Baths; and as they approach, they dance about him like madmen. But this was to be the end of his trial, for the Bath was a sort of initiation; he thereupon received the pallium, or University gown, and was suffered by his tormentors to depart in peace. One alone is recorded as having been exempted from this persecution; it was a youth graver and loftier than even St. Gregory himself: but it was not from his force of character, but at the instance of Gregory, that he escaped. Gregory was his bosom-friend, and was ready in Athens to shelter him when he came. It was another Saint and another Doctor; the great Basil, then but catechumen of the Church.

But to return to our freshman. His troubles are not at an end, though he has got his gown upon him. Where is he to lodge? whom is he to attend? He finds himself seized, before he well knows where he is, by another party of men, or three or four parties at once, like foreign porters at a landing, who seize on the baggage of the perplexed stranger, and thrust half a dozen cards into his unwilling hands. Our youth is plied by the hangers-on of professor this, or sophist that, each of whom wishes the fame or the profit of having a house full. We will say that he escapes from their hands,—but then he will have to choose for himself where he will put up; and, to tell the truth, with all the praise I have already given, and the praise I shall have to give, to the city of mind, nevertheless, between ourselves, the brick and wood which formed it, the actual tenements, where flesh and blood had to lodge (always excepting the mansions of great men of the place), do not seem to have been much better than those of Greek or Turkish towns, which are at this moment a topic of interest and ridicule in the public prints. A lively picture has lately been set before us of Gallipoli. Take, says Mr. Russell, a multitude of the dilapidated outhouses found in farm-yards in England, of the rickety old wooden tenements, the cracked, shutterless structures of planks and tiles, the sheds and stalls, which our bye lanes, or fish-markets, or river-sides can supply; tumble them down on the declivity of a bare, bald hill; let the spaces between house and house, thus accidentally determined, be understood to form streets, winding of course for no reason, and with no meaning, up and down the town; the roadway always narrow, the breadth never uniform, the separate houses bulging or retiring below, as circumstances may have determined, and leaning forward till they meet overhead;—and you have a good idea of Gallipoli. I question whether this picture would not nearly correspond to the special seat of the Muses in ancient times. Learned writers assure us distinctly that the houses of Athens were for the most part small and mean: that the streets were crooked and narrow; that the upper stories projected over the roadway; and that staircases, balustrades, and doors that opened outwards, obstructed it;—a remarkable coincidence of description. I do not doubt at all, though history is silent, that that roadway was jolting to carriages, and all but impassable; and that it was traversed by drains, as freely as any Turkish town now. Athens seems in these respects to have been below the average cities of its time. "A stranger," says an ancient, "might doubt, on the sudden view, if really he saw Athens."

I grant all this, and much more if you will; but, recollect, Athens was the home of the intellectual and beautiful; not of low mechanical contrivances, and material organization. Why stop within your lodgings, counting the rents in your wall or the holes in your tiling, when nature and art call you away? You must put up with such a chamber, and a table, and a stool, and a sleeping board, any where else in the three continents; one place does not differ from another indoors; your magalia in Africa, or your grottos in Syria are not perfection. I suppose you did not come to Athens to swarm up a ladder, or to grope about a closet: you came to see and to hear, what hear and see you could not elsewhere. What food for the intellect is it possible to procure indoors, that you stay there looking about you? do you think to read there? where are your books? do you expect to purchase books at Athens—you are much out in your calculations. True it is, we at this day, who live in the nineteenth century, have the books of Greece as a perpetual memorial; and copies there have been, since the time that they were written; but you need not go to Athens to procure them, nor would you find them in Athens. Strange to say, strange to the nineteenth century, that in the age of Plato and Thucydides, there was not, it is said, a bookshop in the whole place: nor was the book trade in existence till the very time of Augustus. Libraries, I suspect, were the bright invention of Attalus or the Ptolemies; I doubt whether Athens had a library till the reign of Hadrian. It was what the student gazed on, what he heard, what he caught by the magic of sympathy, not what he read, which was the education furnished.

He leaves his narrow lodging early in the morning; and not till night, if even then, will he return. It is but a crib or kennel,—in which he sleeps when the weather is inclement or the ground damp; in no respect a home. And he goes out of doors, not to read the day's newspaper, or to buy the gay shilling volume, but to imbibe the invisible atmosphere of genius, and to learn by heart the oral traditions of taste. Out he goes; and leaving the tumble-down town behind him, he mounts the Acropolis to the right, or he turns to the Areopagus on the left. He goes to the Parthenon to study the sculptures of Phidias; to the temple of the Dioscuri to see the paintings of Polygnotus. We indeed take our Sophocles or Æschylus out of our coat-pocket; but, if our sojourner at Athens would understand how a tragic poet can write, he must betake himself to the theatre on the south, and see and hear the drama literally in action. Or let him go westward to the Agora, and there he will hear Lysias or Andocides pleading, or Demosthenes haranguing. He goes farther west still, along the shade of those noble planes, which Cimon has planted there; and he looks around him at the statues and porticos and vestibules, each by itself a work of genius and skill, enough to be the making of another city. He passes through the city gate, and then he is at the famous Ceramicus; here are the tombs of the mighty dead; and here, we will suppose, is Pericles himself, the most elevated, the most thrilling of orators, converting a funeral oration over the slain into a philosophical panegyric of the living.

Onwards he proceeds still; and now he has come to that still more celebrated Academe, which has bestowed its own name on Universities down to this day; and there he sees a sight which will be graven on his memory till he dies. Many are the beauties of the place, the groves, and the statues, and the temple, and the stream of the Cephissus flowing by; many are the lessons which will be taught him day after day by teacher or by companion; but his eye is just now arrested by one object; it is the very presence of Plato. He does not hear a word that he says; he does not care to hear; he asks neither for discourse nor disputation; what he sees is a whole, complete in itself, not to be increased by addition, and greater than anything else. It will be a point in the history of his life; a stay for his memory to rest on, a burning thought in his heart, a bond of union with men of like mind, ever afterwards. Such is the spell which the living man exerts on his fellows, for good or for evil. How nature impels us to lean upon others, making virtue, or genius, or name, the qualification for our doing so! A Spaniard is said to have traveled to Italy, simply to see Livy; he had his fill of gazing, and then went back again home. Had our young stranger got nothing by his voyage but the sight of the breathing and moving Plato, had he entered no lecture-room to hear, no gymnasium to converse, he had got some measure of education, and something to tell of to his grandchildren.

But Plato is not the only sage, nor the sight of him the only lesson to be learned in this wonderful suburb. It is the region and the realm of philosophy. Colleges were the inventions of many centuries later; and they imply a sort of cloistered life, or at least a life of rule, scarcely natural to an Athenian. It was the boast of the philosophic statesman of Athens, that his countrymen achieved by the mere force of nature and the love of the noble and the great, what other people aimed at by laborious discipline; and all who came among them were submitted to the same method of education. We have traced our student on his wanderings from the Acropolis to the Sacred Way; and now he is in the region of the schools. No awful arch, no window of many-colored lights marks the seats of learning there or elsewhere; philosophy lives out of doors. No close atmosphere oppresses the brain or inflames the eyelid; no long session stiffens the limbs. Epicurus is reclining in his garden; Zeno looks like a divinity in his porch; the restless Aristotle, on the other side of the city, as if in antagonism to Plato, is walking his pupils off their legs in his Lyceum by the Ilyssus. Our student has determined on entering himself as a disciple of Theophrastus, a teacher of marvelous popularity, who has brought together two thousand pupils from all parts of the world. He himself is of Lesbos; for masters, as well as students, come hither from all regions of the earth,—as befits a University. How could Athens have collected hearers in such numbers, unless she had selected teachers of such power? it was the range of territory, which the notion of a University implies, which furnished both the quantity of the one, and the quality of the other. Anaxagoras was from Ionia, Carneades from Africa, Zeno from Cyprus, Protagoras from Thrace, and Gorgias from Sicily. Andromachus was a Syrian, Proæresius an Armenian, Hilarius a Bithynian, Philiscus a Thessalian, Hadrian a Syrian. Rome is celebrated for her liberality in civil matters; Athens was as liberal in intellectual. There was no narrow jealousy, directed against a Professor, because he was not an Athenian; genius and talent were the qualifications; and to bring them to Athens, was to do homage to it as a University. There was brotherhood and citizenship of mind.

Mind came first, and was the foundation of the academical polity; but it soon brought along with it, and gathered round itself, the gifts of fortune and the prizes of life. As time went on, wisdom was not always sentenced to the bare cloak of Cleanthes; but, beginning in rags, it ended in fine linen. The Professors became honorable and rich; and the students ranged themselves under their names, and were proud of calling themselves their countrymen. The University was divided into four great nations, as the medieval antiquarian would style them; and in the middle of the fourth century, Proæresius was the leader or proctor of the Attic, Hephæstion of the Oriental, Epiphanius of the Arabic, and Diophantus of the Pontic. Thus the Professors were both patrons of clients, and hosts and *proxeni* of strangers and visitors, as well as masters of the schools: and the Cappadocian, Syrian, or Sicilian youth who came to one or other of them, would be encouraged to study by his protection, and to aspire by his example.

Even Plato, when the schools of Athens were not a hundred years old, was in circumstances to enjoy the *otium cum dignitate*. He had a villa out at Heraclea; and he left his patrimony to his school, in whose hands it remained, not only safe, but fructifying, a marvelous phenomenon in tumultuous Greece, for the long space of eight hundred years. Epicurus too had the property of the Gardens where he lectured; and these too became the property of his sect. But in Roman times the chairs of grammar, rhetoric, politics, and the four philosophies, were handsomely endowed by the State; some of the Professors were themselves statesmen or high functionaries, and brought to their favorite study senatorial rank or Asiatic opulence.

Patrons such as these can compensate to the freshman, in whom we have interested ourselves, for the rudeness of his lodging and the turbulence of his companions. In every thing there is a better side and a worse; in every place a disreputable set and a respectable, and the one is hardly known at all to the other. Men come away from the same University at this day, with contradictory impressions and contradictory statements, according to the society they have found there; if you believe the one, nothing goes on there as it should be: if you believe the other, nothing goes on as it should not. Virtue, however, and decency are at least in the minority every where, and under some sort of a cloud or disadvantage; and this being the case, it is so much gain wherever an Herodes Atticus is found, to throw the influence of wealth and station on the side even of a decorous philosophy. A consular man, and the heir of an ample fortune, this Herod was content to devote his life to a professorship, and his fortune to the patronage of literature. He gave the sophist Polemo about eight thousand pounds, as the sum is calculated, for three declamations. He built at Athens a stadium six hundred feet long, entirely of white marble, and capable of admitting the whole population. His theatre, erected to the memory of his wife, was made of cedar wood curiously carved. He had two villas, one at Marathon, the place of his birth, about ten miles from Athens, the other at Cephissia, at the distance of six; and thither he drew to him the *élite*, and at times the whole body of the students. Long arcades, groves of trees, clear pools for the bath, delighted and recruited the summer visitor. Never was so brilliant a lecture-room as his evening banqueting-hall; highly connected students from Rome mixed with the sharp-witted provincial of Greece or Asia Minor; and the flippant sciolist, and the nondescript visitor, half philosopher, half tramp, met with a reception, courteous always, but suitable to his deserts. Herod was noted for his repartees; and we have instances on record of his setting down, according to the emergency, both the one and the other.

A higher line, though a rarer one, was that allotted to the youthful Basil. He was one of those men who seem by a sort of fascination to draw others around them even without wishing it. One might have deemed that his gravity and his reserve would have kept them at a distance; but, almost in spite of himself, he was the center of a knot of youths, who, pagans as most of them were, used Athens honestly for the purpose for which they professed to seek it; and, disappointed and displeased with the place himself, he seems nevertheless to have been the means of their profiting by its advantages. One of these was Sophronius, who afterwards held a high office in the State: Eusebius was another, at that time the bosom-friend of Sophronius, and afterwards a Bishop. Celsus too is named, who afterwards was raised to the government of Cilicia by the Emperor Julian. Julian himself, in the sequel of unhappy memory, was then at Athens, and known at least to St. Gregory. Another Julian is also mentioned, who was afterwards commissioner of the land tax. Here we have a glimpse of the better kind of society among the students of Athens; and it is to the credit of the parties composing it, that such young men as Gregory and Basil, men as intimately connected with Christianity, as they were well known in the world, should hold so high a place in their esteem and love. When the two saints were departing, their companions came around them with the hope of changing their purpose. Basil persevered, but Gregory relented, and turned back to Athens for a season.—*Rise of Universities.*

Macaulay.—University Teaching at Athens.

Dr. Johnson used to assert that Demosthenes spoke to a people of brutes;—to a barbarous people;—that there could be no civilization before the invention of printing. There seems to be, on the contrary, every reason to believe, that in general intelligence, the Athenian populace far surpassed the lower orders of any community that has ever existed. It must be considered, that to be a citizen was to be a legislator, a soldier, a judge,—one upon whose voice might depend the fate of the wealthiest tributary state, of the most eminent public men. The lowest offices, both of agriculture and of trade, were, in common, performed by slaves. The state supplied its meanest members with the support of life, the opportunity of leisure, and the means of amusement. Books were indeed few; but they were excellent; and they were accurately known. It is not by turning over libraries, but by repeatedly perusing and intently contemplating a few great models, that the mind is best disciplined. Demosthenes is said to have transcribed six times the history of Thucydides. * *

Books, however, were the least part of the education of an Athenian citizen. Let us for a moment transport ourselves, in thought, to that glorious city. Let us imagine that we are entering its gates in the time of its power and glory. A crowd is assembled round a portico. All are gazing with delight at the entablature, for Phidias is putting up the frieze. We turn into another street; a rhapsodist is reciting there: men, women, children are thronging round him: the tears are running down their cheeks; their eyes are fixed; their very breath is still, for he is telling how Priam fell at the feet of Achilles, and kissed those hands,—the terrible,—the murderous,—which had slain so many of his sons. We enter the public place; there is a ring of youths, all leaning forward, with sparkling eyes, and gestures of expectation. Socrates is pitted against the famous atheist, from Ionia, and has just brought him to a contradiction in terms. But we are interrupted. The herald is crying—"Room for the Prytanes." The general assembly is to meet. The people are swarming in on every side. Proclamation is made—"Who wishes to speak." There is a shout, and a clapping of hands; Pericles is mounting the stand. Then for a play of Sophocles; and away to sup with Aspasia. I know of no modern university which has so excellent a system of education.

Knowledge thus acquired and opinions thus formed were, indeed, likely to be, in some respects, defective. Propositions which are advanced in discourse generally result from a partial view of the question, and cannot be kept under examination long enough to be corrected. Men of great conversational powers almost universally practise a sort of lively sophistry and exaggeration, which deceives, for the moment, both themselves and their auditors. Thus we see doctrines, which cannot bear a close inspection, triumph perpetually in drawing rooms, in debating societies, and even in legislative and judicial assemblies. To the conversational education of the Athenians I am inclined to attribute the great looseness of reasoning which is remarkable in most of their scientific writings. Even the most illogical of modern writers would stand perfectly aghast at the puerile fallacies which seem to have deluded some of the greatest men of antiquity. Sir Thomas Lethbridge would stare at the political economy of Xenophon; and the author of *Soirées de Pétersbourg* would be ashamed of some of the metaphysical arguments of Plato. But the very circumstances which retarded the growth of science were peculiarly favorable to the cultivation of eloquence: From the early habit of taking a share in animated discussion, the intelligent student would derive that readiness of resource, that copiousness of language, and that knowledge of the temper and understanding of an audience, which are far more valuable to an orator than the greatest logical powers.—*Complete Works of Lord Macaulay, Vol. VII.* Athenian Orators.

True Student Life.

Studies and Conduct: Letters, Essays, and Thoughts, on the relative value of Studies and the right Ordering of Life by Men Eminent in Literature and Affairs: Edited by Henry Barnard, LL. D., 416 pages: *Special Edition*, 344 pages. 1873.

INDEX

TO

SPECIAL EDITION.

DR. HENRY BARNARD'S

STANDARD EDUCATIONAL PUBLICATIONS,

EMBRACING THE

HISTORY, ORGANIZATION, ADMINISTRATION, STUDIES, DISCIPLINE AND STATISTICS OF SCHOOLS OF EVERY GRADE AND FOR ALL CLASSES IN DIFFERENT COUNTRIES

Official Reports.

ANNUAL REPORTS AS SECRETARY OF THE BOARD OF COMMISSIONERS, AND SUPERINTENDENT OF COMMON SCHOOLS IN CONNECTICUT, 1 Vol. $[illegible]

ANNUAL [illegible] AND REPORTS AS COMMISSIONER OF PUBLIC SCHOOLS IN RHODE ISLAND. $[illegible]

REPORTS AND CIRCULARS AS NATIONAL COMMISSIONER OF EDUCATION.

Annual Report for 1867-8, 1 Vol. $[illegible]

Special Report on the Educational Interests of the District of Columbia together with an account of systems and statistics of Public Instruction in American and European Cities, and in Schools for Freedmen and Colored children.

Special Report on National Education. $[illegible]

Special Report on Technical Education. $[illegible]

Educational Periodicals.

CONNECTICUT COMMON SCHOOL JOURNAL, 1838-42, 4 Vols. $[illegible] *Second Series*, 1851-[illegible]

JOURNAL OF R. I. INSTITUTE OF INSTRUCTION, 1845-49, 3 Vols. $[illegible]

AMERICAN JOURNAL OF EDUCATION, 1856-71, [illegible] Vols.

Single Number, as issued, except [illegible], $[illegible]
Single Volume, in cloth, except X, XIII, XIV, $[illegible]
Single Volume, in Half Goat, $[illegible]
Set of [illegible] Volumes, in Cloth, $[illegible]
Set of [illegible] Volumes, in Half Goat, $[illegible]

Biography, History, Organization, &c.

EDUCATIONAL BIOGRAPHY:—

1. AMERICAN TEACHERS AND EDUCATORS, $[illegible] *Second Series*, $[illegible]
2. [illegible] OF AMERICAN [illegible], $[illegible]
3. ENGLISH TEACHERS AND EDUCATORS, $[illegible]
4. FRENCH TEACHERS AND EDUCATORS, $[illegible]
5. SWISS, ITALIAN, AND DUTCH TEACHERS, $[illegible]

TRIBUTE TO GALLAUDET, with an account of the American Asylum for Deaf Mutes, &c., $[illegible]

EDUCATIONAL CONVENTIONS, AND ASSOCIATIONS.

PART I. National Associations.
PART II. State Conventions and Associations.
PART III. European Educational Associations.
PART IV. [illegible]—American and European.

Public Instruction.

NATIONAL EDUCATION IN EUROPE (1854.) $[illegible]

HISTORICAL DEVELOPMENT OF COMMON SCHOOLS, [illegible] GRAMMAR SCHOOLS AND PUBLIC HIGH SCHOOLS IN CONNECTICUT. $[illegible]

ELEMENTARY AND SECONDARY INSTRUCTION:

VOL. I. German States. [illegible] pages $[illegible]
VOL. II. Switzerland, France, Belgium, Holland, Denmark, Norway, Sweden, Russia, Greece, Turkey, Italy, Portugal and Spain. $[illegible]
VOL. III. Great Britain and American States.

UNIVERSITIES, and Superior Instruction:

PART I. German States, with an account of the Universities of the Middle Ages. $[illegible]
PART II. France, Italy, Belgium, Holland, Scandinavia, Russia, Spain and Portugal.
PART III. Great Britain and American States.

PROFESSIONAL AND SPECIAL SCHOOLS:

1. SCIENCE AND NATIONAL INDUSTRIES. $[illegible]
2. [illegible] FOR TEACHERS. $[illegible]
3. MILITARY SCHOOLS, Part I and II. $[illegible]
4. PREVENTIVE AND REFORMATORY SCHOOLS. $[illegible]

Manuals of Organization and Method.

PAPERS FOR THE TEACHER AND SCHOOL OFFICER: or Library of Practical Education, gathered from the experience of different countries. [illegible], in uniform cloth binding. Sold in single volumes, or [illegible].

1. AMERICAN CONTRIBUTIONS TO THE PHILOSOPHY AND PRACTICE OF EDUCATION. *First Series*. $[illegible] Russell, Hall, Thayer, Burgess, Mann, [illegible], Hart, Page.
2. [illegible] TEACHERS AND [illegible] METHODS OF PRIMARY INSTRUCTION in the Model and Training Schools of Great Britain. $[illegible]
3. MODERN GERMAN PEDAGOGY. $[illegible] Ahlwardt, Bruchs, Diesterweg, Fichte, [illegible], Graser, [illegible], Herbart, Raumer.
4. EDUCATIONAL APHORISMS AND SUGGESTIONS—Ancient and Modern. $[illegible]
5. ENGLISH PEDAGOGY: or Treatises and Thoughts on Education, the School and the Teacher in English Literature. First Series. $[illegible] Ascham, Bacon, Wotton, Milton, [illegible], Petty, Fuller, Locke, [illegible], Cowper, Gray, Crabbe, Coleridge, Hood.
6. PESTALOZZI AND PESTALOZZIANISM. $[illegible] [illegible], Leonard and Gertrude, Evening Hours of a Hermit, how Gertrude teaches her children, etc.
7. GERMAN EDUCATIONAL REFORMERS. $[illegible] [illegible], Erasmus, [illegible], Sturm, Luther, Melancthon, Ratich, Comenius, Francke, Basedow, etc.
8. FRENCH SCHOOLS AND PEDAGOGY. $[illegible] Rabelais, La Salle, Fenelon, Montaigne, Rollin, [illegible], [illegible], [illegible], [illegible], [illegible], etc.
9. DUTCH AND SCANDINAVIAN SCHOOLS. $[illegible] Van der Palm, [illegible], Cuvier, Cousin, [illegible], Arnold, [illegible], [illegible] and others.
10. GREEK AND ITALIAN SCHOOLS Ancient and Modern.
11. ENGLISH PEDAGOGY: *Second Series*. $[illegible] Elyot, Colet, [illegible], [illegible], Cowley, Public Schools as they were and as they are, Faraday, Temple, Lowe, Mill and others
12. AMERICAN PUBLIC SCHOOLS AND PEDAGOGY: a Digest of Rules and Regulations, and Courses of Instruction, for graded Schools in American Cities, with an account of Public Schools in the Chief Cities of Europe. $[illegible]
13. SECONDARY INSTRUCTION: Systems, Institutions, Subjects and Methods of Instruction, preparatory to Colleges and Universities, and to Special Schools of Practical Science, $[illegible]
14. DRAWING IN INDUSTRIAL AND [illegible] ART: Programmes and Methods of the best European and American Schools. $[illegible]
15. SCHOOL ARCHITECTURE. *Second Edition*. $[illegible]
16. SCHOOL CODES—Old and New. $[illegible]
17. TRUE STUDENT LIFE: Hints respecting Studies and Conduct by men eminent in letters and affairs. $[illegible]
18. EDUCATIONAL BIBLIOGRAPHY: Catalogue of Books relating to the History, Organization, Administration, Studies, Discipline, and Statistics of Schools and Education in different Countries. $[illegible]

Orders will be received for any of the above Books by E. STEIGER, New York.

AMERICAN PEDAGOGY: Contributions to the Principles and Methods of Education, by Barnard, Burgess, Bushnell, Channing, Cowdery, Dickinson, Doane, Everett, Fairchild, Hart, Hopkins, Huntington, Mann, Page, Philbrick, Pierce, Potter, Sheldon, Wayland, and Wilbur. Selected from Barnard's American Journal of Education. First Series. *Third Ed.* 576 pages. $3.00.

CONTENTS.

SECOND SERIES.

[A Second Volume of Selections from Barnard's American Journal of Education on Topics in the wide field of American Pedagogy, will be issued in 1873, and will contain Reports, Essays, and Thoughts, by Adams, Bache, Barnard, Beecher, Boutwell, Brooks, Bushnell, Choate, Eaton, Emerson, Gregory, Harris, Huntington, Kiddle, Lewis, Lindsley, Mann, Sears, Smith, White, and others.]

PRIMARY SCHOOLS AND ELEMENTARY INSTRUCTION: Object Teaching and Oral Lessons on Social Science and Common Things, with various illustrations of the Principles and Practice of Primary and Elementary Instruction in the Model and Training Schools of Great Britain. *Second Edition.* 544 pp. $3.00.

CONTENTS.

CONTENTS.

CONTENTS.

CONTENTS.

GERMAN PEDAGOGY:—Views of German Educators and Teachers on the Principles of Education, and Methods of Instruction for Schools of different Grades. *Republished from Barnard's American Journal of Education.* 3d Edition, 640 pages.

CONTENTS.

EMINENT TEACHERS AND EDUCATORS OF THE SEVENTEENTH AND EIGHTEENTH CENTURIES: Supplement to Volume II., of Barnard's National Education, with Index. Pages 665–1364. Price, $2.00.

☞ VOLUME II. of Barnard's Comprehensive Survey of "*National Education in different countries*," is devoted to systems of Elementary and Secondary Instruction, with brief notices of Superior and Special Schools, in Switzerland, France, Belgium, Holland, Denmark, Norway, Sweden, Russia, Turkey, Greece, Italy, Spain and Portugal, in continuation of the account of the systems of the several German States as constituted in 1866, in Volume I.

CONTENTS.

INDEX

TO

EDUCATIONAL APHORISMS.

PESTALOZZI AND HIS EDUCATIONAL SYSTEM.

PESTALOZZI AND PESTALOZZIANISM:—Memoir, and Educational Principles, Methods, and Influence of John Henry Pestalozzi, and Biographical Sketches of several of his Assistants and Disciples; together with Selections from his Publications. In Two Parts. By HENRY BARNARD, LL.D. New York: E. STEIGER.

CONTENTS.

PART I.

PART II.

PART III.

ENGLISH PEDAGOGY—OLD AND NEW: or, Treatises and Thoughts on Education, the School, and the Teacher in English Literature. *Second Series.* Republished from Barnard's American Journal of Education. 628 pages. $3.00. 1873.

CONTENTS.

GERMAN EDUCATIONAL REFORMERS; Memoirs of Eminent Teachers and Educators in Germany, from the Fourteenth to the Nineteenth Century, with contributions to the History of Education from the Revival of Classical Learning. From the "*Geschichte der Pädagogik*" of Karl von Raumer. Republished from "*The American Journal of Education*," edited by HENRY BARNARD, LL. D. 636 pages. New York: E. STEIGER.

CONTENTS.

www.ingramcontent.com/pod-product-compliance
Lightning Source LLC
Chambersburg PA
CBHW031939290426
44108CB00011B/610
9783742804860